BURT FRANKLIN: RESEARCH & SOURCE WORKS SERIES 572
Selected Essays in History, Economics, & Social Science 187

THE ANCIENT LOWLY

The Ancient Lowly

A History of the Ancient Working People from the
Earliest Known Period to the Adoption
of Christianity by Constantine

VOLUME I

BY
C. OSBORNE WARD

BURT FRANKLIN
NEW YORK

Published by LENOX HILL Pub. & Dist. Co. (Burt Franklin)
235 East 44th St., New York, N.Y. 10017
Originally Published: 1888
Reprinted: 1970
Printed in the U.S.A.

S.B.N. 8337-3685X
Library of Congress Card Catalog No.: 77-114817
Burt Franklin: Research and Source Works Series 572
Selected Essays in History, Economics, and Social Science 187

Publisher's Note to Fourth Edition

The first editions of Osborne Ward's great work were printed and circulated privately, because no capitalist publishing house would take the responsibility for so revolutionary a book, and no socialist publishing house existed.

Now, nearly twenty years after the first publication of the book, its publication has been taken over by a co-operative publishing house owned by sixteen hundred socialist clubs and individual socialists. A systematic effort will now for the first time be made to give this author's works the wide circulation they deserve.

Osborne Ward's contribution to the history of the working class movement is unique, and its tremendous value is only beginning to be appreciated. In his chosen field, the period of ancient civilization covered by histories and inscriptions, he speaks with an authority based on a minute and comprehensive knowledge of his subject.

The case is different when he comments on another field of investigation, and it is only fair to warn the reader that the author's statements on page 38, which reappear in various forms elsewhere in the book, are now known to be erroneous. The researches of Lewis H. Morgan in "Ancient Society," popularized by Frederick Engels in his "Origin of the Family, Private Property and the State," have stood the test of a generation of criticism, and they show conclusively that a communist form of society existed for ages before the beginning of the era described so graphically in the present work.

CHARLES H. KERR.

January, 1907.

PREFACE.

The author of this volume is aware that a strong opposition may set in and perhaps for a time, object to the thoughts and the facts which it portrays.

Much of its contents is new. The ideas that lay at the bottom of the ancient competitive system, though in their day thoroughly understood, have been so systematically attacked and gnawed away during our nearly 2,000 years' trial of the new institution, that men now, no longer comprehend them. The whole may strike the reader as news. Much of it indeed, reads like a revelation from a sealed book; and we may not at first be able to comprehend it as a natural effect of a cause.

The introduction of Christianity was fought, and for a long time resisted by the laboring element itself; solely on the ground that it seriously interfered with idol, amulet, palladium and temple drapery manufacture. As shown in the chapter on "Image-makers," there were organized trades, whose labor and means of obtaining a living were entirely confined to their skill in producing for the pagan priesthood these innumerable images and paraphernalia of worship. Indeed, the ultimate introduction of certain unmistakable forms of idol worship to be found lingering in the so-called Christianity to-day, must be considered as having been partly motived by the resistance of trades unions against any change which would result in depriving themselves and their babes of bread. This has been a potent hindrance to the ever growing but imperceptible realization of the social revolution.

The great strikes and uprisings of the working people of the ancient world are almost unknown to the living age. It matters little how accounts of five immense strike-wars, involving destruction of property and mutual slaughter of millions of people have been suppressed, or have otherwise failed to reach us;—the fact remains that people are absolutely ignorant of those great events. A meagre sketch of Spartacus may be seen in the encyclopedias, but it is always ruined and its interest pinched and blighted by being classed with crime, its heroes with criminals, its theme with desecration. Yet Spartacus was one of the great generals of history; fully equal to Hannibal and Napoleon, while his cause was much more just and infinitely nobler, his life a model of the beautiful and virtuous, his death an episode of surpassing grandeur.

Still more strange is it, that the great ten-years' war of Eunus should be unknown. He martialed at one time, an army of two hundred thousand soldiers. He manœuvred them and fought for ten full years for liberty, defeating army after army of Rome. Why is the world ignorant of this fierce, epochal rebellion?

Almost the whole matter is passed over in silence by our histories of Rome. In these pages it will be read as news; yet should a similar war rage in our day, against a similar condition of slavery, its cause would not only be considered just, but the combatants would have the sympathy and moral support of the civilized world. The story of this wonderful workman is news.

The great system of labor organization explained in these pages must likewise be regarded as a chapter of news. The portentous fact has lain in abeyance century after century, with the human family in profound ignorance of an organization of trades and other labor unions so powerful that for hundreds of years they undertook and successfully conducted the business of manufacture, of distribution, of purveying provisions to armies, of feeding the inhabitants of the largest cities in the world, of inventing, supplying and working the huge engines of war, and of collecting customs and taxes—tasks confided to their care by the state.

Our civilization has a blushingly poor excuse for its profound ignorance of these facts; for the evidences have existed from much before the beginning of our era—indeed the fragments of the ravaged history were far less broken and the recorded annals much fresher, more numerous and less mutilated than the relics which the author with arduous labor and pains-taking, has had at command in bringing them to the surface. Besides the records that have come to us thus broken and distorted by the wreckers who feared the moral blaze of literature, there were, in all probability, thousands of inscriptions then, where but dozens remain now to be consulted; and they are growing fewer and dimmer as their value rises higher in the estimation of a thinking, appreciative, gradually awakening world.

The author is keenly aware that certain critics will complain of his dragging religion so prominently forward that the work is spoiled. The defense is, that though our charming histories from a point of view of brilliant events, such as daring deeds of heroes, battles and bloodshed, may be found among the ancients without encountering much of a religious nature, yet such is not the case in the lesser affairs of ancient social and political life. The state, city and family were themselves a part of the ancient religion and were a part of its property. Priests were public officers. Home life of the nobles was in constant conformity with the ritual. The organizations of labor were so closely watched by the jealous law that they were obliged to assume a religious attitude they did not feel in order to escape being suppressed. A long list of what we in our time consider honorable, business-like doings, was rated as blasphemy against the gods and punished with death.

Nearly all of the idolatry, with its attendant superstition and nympholepsy, its giants and prodigies, its notions of *elysium* and *tartarus*, its quaking genuflexions, its bloody sacrifices and its gladiatorial wakes, had their real origin in the torture of the menials who delved, and in the rewards of the favored ones who banqueted on the riches which flowed from unpaid labor; and nearly all the iconoclasm of the later sophists may perhaps be traced to an organized resistance of the working people of pre-christian days. These seemingly curious, if not extraordinary truths will, we are confident, be made clear to the intelligent, careful reader of these pages; and in this humble hope, the author has set them forth as an indispensable beginning to those who would logically and correctly understand the great problem of labor as it is to-day.

As rightly mentioned by Bancroft and others occupied in the collection and study of monumental archæology, there is often a readiness among the degenerate natives to ingeniously imitate and palm off for genuine, numbers of fraudulent counterfeit relics upon the unsuspecting and credulous wonder-hunters. This, however, is with us, in our scope of research, placed beyond suspicion. Most of the slabs we mention have already been lying unobserved, on their original sites or in by-nooks of the museums of their own countries, for hundreds of years; but they have long since been recorded, catalogued and even numbered in dingy old books and manuscripts, the importance of their grim inscriptions having been little understood by the capable epigraphists themselves. Besides, no interest having ever been elicited on subjects of which they are so suggestive, there has been no lively demand for them, even as curiosities. They are genuine.

The author may sum up these prefatory remarks with a word on the general lesson taught by this volume; it being one of the first histories yet compiled and written exclusively from a standpoint of social science. That the "still small voice" meant the ever suppressed yet ever living, struggling, co-operating and mutually supporting majorities, is made self-suggestive without forsaking history. The phenomenal fact is moreover brought out, that the present movement whose most radical wing loudly disclaims Christianity, is nevertheless building exactly upon the precepts of that faith, as it was told to us and taught us by Jesus Christ; whatever may or may not have been borrowed by His school from the immense social organization of His own and preceeding ages.

Modern greed with its class hatreds, individualisms, aristocracy, its struggle for personal wealth, dangerous, defiant in our faith and in our political economy, is not Christianity at all; it is the ancient evil still lingering in the roots of the gradually decaying paganism that appears to remain for the labor movement to smother and at last uproot and completely annihilate.

One thing must be solemnly set forth as a very suggestive hint to modern anarchists, however honest their impulses. The historical facts are that the great strikes, rebellions and social wars—if we are permitted to except those of Drimakos and the strike of the 20,000 from the silver mines of Laurium in Attica—all turned out disastrously for the general cause. The punishments meted out to the strikers and insurgents of the working class after their overthrow by the Romans, as in the rebellions of Eunus, of Athenion, of Spartacus, of every one we have treated in this book, with but the above exceptions, was bloody, revengeful and exterminatory to the last degree. An ancient author whom we quote, gives the aggregate number crucified at something more than a million. Crassus and Pompey alone crucified over 6,000 workingmen on the Appian Way as examples of the awful bloodwreaking to be expected from Roman military justice. Twenty thousand were similarly massacred at Enna and Tauromanion. These unscrupulous deeds of retribution that went far toward annihilating the ancient civilization by stimulating a blood-thirsting craze in a long succession of Roman emperors, completely extinguished all hopes of the workingmen for the achievement of liberty by violent means.

PREFACE
TO THE SECOND EDITION.

The author of the Ancient Lowly, on presenting to the public his first and incomplete edition, felt that it was an experiment. It was a mass of facts, withheld for many ages from the human race—some that had been suppressed—and his natural conjecture that there is still a desire to cover and conceal them was verified by a general refusal on the part of publishing firms, to touch it. He published it himself. Large numbers of letters flowing in from kind-hearted readers at every quarter, and a delightful, perhaps overwrought expression of thanks and sympathy in form of sermons, newspaper reviews and lecture themes has been a consolation that cannot be measured by this poor expression of gratitude. Let his loving answer and assurance to them all be, that the book shall not fall into vandal hands for money or for price; but the naked truth shall be unstintedly offered to its generous and appreciative readers who thus announce themselves, after ages of agitation, fully prepared to accept.

Considerable disappointment has been gently hinted, that the author broke off abruptly without writing a chapter of conclusions. The actually written twenty-fourth chapter promised in the table of contents, was prudentially omitted in the first edition. Conclusions are deviations from the historian's compass—this is one explanation. A stronger one is, that the general conviction which overtakes the student, on studying the ancient working people, is of a nature so radical as to be distasteful to many readers.

One curious conclusion is, that the modern and correct doctrine of nationalizing the tools of labor was actually carried out, almost to perfection, especially in the celebrated Spartan state. But alas! the awful incongruity of its system was, that human beings as slaves, were themselves bodily those nationalized tools! though treated with worse contempt of feeling than we have for machines propelled by motors instead of whips; and the demand of the nationalists or socialists to-day is in some points of principle, to return to the nationalization of Lycurgus, only with the chattel-slave tools and wage-slave tools substituted, or supplanted by the inanimate labor-saving implements this much-abused workman has invented, constructed and re duplicated for a higher civilization. When this shall have been accomplished there will be an exact social equality and a status of positive equities—a vast and beneficent rev olution! Surely, under these considerations, the working masses, the "two-thirds majority," can afford to crowd onward until they reach the ambrosial gardens, become themselves masters and re-enjoy the symposium, in a region of equitable distribution and plentitude, the "mansion of the blessed," longed for in those earlier ages.

Another conclusion arrived at from the facts in history, and explained in this terminal chapter is, that the ancient rebellions, although fearfully disastrous, as mentioned by way of warning in our preface to the first edition, were, under the circumstances, just. Workingmen who rebelled and bravely fought and lost, had no other friend to appeal to but their own strong arms; and looking back upon their sufferings and their magnificent resistance, we clearly see that they did not lose after all. They won, though they fell in myriads—a martyrdom, nobler and happier than was their crucial life from which such a death was triumphant relief—for by their fall they taught a lesson to an inexperienced world that is to this day exerting its influence in creating a better era. We may be thankful for their having lived and fought and died; for they were the true forefathers of these struggling wage-slaves, now making themselves felt and feared in these, though still cruel and hateful, yet brighter and more hopeful surroundings.

SOURCES OF INFORMATION.

ÆLIAN (Claudius), *Varia Historia.* Lugduni in Batavis, 1709.
AMERICAN *Cyclopædia*, D. Appleton & Company, N. Y. 1867.
Anonymous, *Seven Essays on Ancient Greece.* Oxford, 1832.
Antoninus (Pius), *Rescript;* Petit, in *Thesaurus Antiquitatum*, Utrecht & Leyden, 1699.
APOCRYPHAL *Gospels of the Infancy. Protevangelion*, Cowper, London, 1881 and Others.
Appian, *Rhomaike Historia*, *Schweighäuser, 3 vols., Leipz. 1785.
Apuleius, *Metamorphosis*, (*Golden Ass*), Ed. *Oudendorp, 1786. German Paraphrase, Sacher-Masoch, Leipzic, 1877.
Aquilius, (M.), *Inscriptio Capuensis*, Orelli, No. 3,308.
Arabic *Gospels of the Infancy.*
Aristotle, *Ethics,*
Aristotle, *Logic,*
Aristotle, *Politics,*
Aristotle, *Metaphysics,* } Immanuel Bekker, Berlin, 1731.
Aristotle, *Œconomics,*
Aristotle, *Physics,*
Aristotle, *Wonders,*
Arnobius, *Disputationes Contra Gentes.* (*Adversus Gentes*), Hildebrand, Œhler, 1845.
Asconius, *De Asconii Commentariis Disputatio*, Madvig, Copenhagen, 1825.
Athenæus, *Deipnosophistæ, sive Cœnœ Sapientium Libri*, "*Banquet of the Learned,*" Natalis, de Comitibus, Veneto, 1556.
AUTHOR of this Work, *Travels on foot through the Papal States*, New York Witness, in autumn of 1870.
Aveling (Edw. B.), *Die Darwin'sche Theorie*, Stuttgart, 1887.
Bancroft, (Hubert Howe), *Native Races*, San Francisco, 1883.
Bellermann, *Nachrichten aus dem Alterthum*, Erfurt, 1789.
BIBLE and *Apocryphal Books.*
Böckh, *Abhandlung der Historisch-Philologischen Classe.*

---

* **Books, Inscriptions etc., consulted by the author personally, in Europe and elsewhere.**

Böckh, *Corpus Inscriptionum Græcarum*, Berlin, 1838-1850.
Böckh, *Die Laurischen Silberbergwerke*, Berlin, 1839.
Böckh, *Staatshaushaltung der Athener*, 1817.
Boissy, *Inscription de Lyon*, 1880.
Bombardini, *De Carcere et Antiquo ejus Usu*, in Supplement of *Thesaurus Antiquitatum;* Grævius et Gronovius, Utrecht, 1694, 6 vols., Folio.
BUREAU of Labor, (United States); First annual Report, 1886.
Bücher (Karl), *Aufstände der unfreien Arbeiter*, Fr'kf't. 1874.
Cæcilius Calactenus, in *Plutarch's Lives of the Ten Orators*, quoted also by other Ancient Authors.
Cardinali (Clemente), *Iscriz. Velletri. Diplomi Imperiali di Privilej accordati a' Militari raccolti e Commentati*, Velletri, 1835. Also *Memorie d' Antichità. Acad. Archaeol.*
Cato (Censorius vel Censorinus), *De Re Rustica*, Paris, 1644.
Cicero, *Ad Atticum*,
Cicero, *De Divinitate*,
Cicero, *Pro Domo Sua*,
Cicero, *Ad Familiares*
Cicero, *Laelius*,
Cicero, *De Legibus*,
Cicero, *Philosophy*, } Orelli (Caspar), Zürich, 1827.
Cicero, *Pro Plancio*,
Cicero, *Pro Quinctio*,
Cicero, *Tusculanarum Disputationum Libri*,
Cicero, *Verres*,
CODEX Justinianus, *Pandectæ, Institutes etc. Corpus Juris Civilis*, Berthelot, Paris, 1809; Genevæ, 1594.
CODEX Theodosii, *Idem.*
Columella, *De Re Rustica, Libri XII.*, Paris, 1543.
Cornelius Nepos, *De Excellentibus Ducibus*, Dietch, Leipzic, in Bibliotheca Teuberiana, 1861; *De Illustribus Viris*, Columbinus, Venice, 1567,
Creuzer, *Symbolik und Mythologie der alten Völker; besonders der Griechen*, Heidelberg, 1810.
Ctesicles per *Athenæus, in Deipnosophistai*, Dindorf, Leipzic 1827
Darwin (Charles), *Descent of Man*, } New York, D. Appleton & Company, 1883.
Darwin (Charles), *Origin of Species*,
Demosthenes, *Orationes*, Recension of Dindorf, Bibliotheca Teubneriana, Leipzic, 1849.
Diodorus Siculus, *Bibliotheca Historica*, Dindorf, Leipzic, 1827.
Diogenes, Lærtius, *Greek Philosophers*, Leipzic, 1829, *Bioi kai Gnomai ton en Philosophia eudokimesanton*, Hühner, Leipzic, 1823.

SOURCES OF INFORMATION. xvii

Dion (Cassius), *Rhomaike Historia,* et *Excerpta Vaticana,* N.
  Lonicenus, Latin Paraphrase, Venice, 1526; *Fragments,*
  Peiresc, Aix, 1629 and Sturz, Leipzic, 1824.
Dionysius (Halicarnassus), *Rhomaike: Archæologia Romana,*
  Hudson and Reiske, *Roman Antiquities.*
Dirksen, *Uebersicht der bisherigen Versuche zur Kritik und Herstellung des Textes der Zwölf-Tafel-Fragmente,* Leipzic, 1824.
Donati (Allessandro), *Roma Vetus et Recens,* Roma, 1632.
D'Oroille, *Sicula,* Paris,
Drumann (W.), *Arbeiter und Kommunisten in Griechenland und Rom,* Königsberg, 1860.
Eckenbrecher, *Die Insel Chios,* Berlin, 1845.
Ely (Richard T.), *French and German Socialisms,* N. Y., 1883.
ENCYCLOPÆDIA, *Britanica,* 8th. and other Editions.
Epiphanius (Pentaglottos, Saint), *Panarion: Essenes, Hemero-Baptists, Ebionites etc.* *Patavinus, 2 v. folio, Paris,1622.
Eratosthenes, *Orations. Eratosthenica,* Berlin, Bernhardy, 1822.
  Hiller, Leipzic. 1872.
Euripides *Iphigenia,*
Euripides, *Troads,*   } W. Dindorf, Leipzic, 4 v., 1863.
Euripides, *Alcestis,*
Eusebius, (Cæsarea,) *Ecclesiastical History,*
Eusebius, (Cæsarea,) *Vita Contemplativa,* Cantabridgæ 1720.
Eusebius (Cæsarea), *Præparatio Evangelica, frag.*
Eutropius (Flavius,) *Epitomies,* or *Breviarium Rerum Romanorum,* Grosse, Halle, 1813.
Fabretti (Raffaello), *Inscriptionum Italicarum, Ævi Antiquioris,* Turin, 1867.
Fabretti (Raffaello). *Inscriptionum Antiquarum Explicatio,* Roma, 1683
Fenestella (Lucius), *Annales.* Quoted by later writers.
Fischer (Johann Friedrich), *Edition of Florus with copious Latin Notes,* Leipzic, 1769.
Fiske (John), *American Political Ideas,* New York, 1885.
Foucart (P.), *Associations Religieuses chez les Grecs: Thiases, Orgéons, Eranes,* Paris, 1883.
Friedländer, *Darstellung aus der Sittengeschichte Roms.*
Frontinus (Sextus Julius), *De Aquis Urbis Romæ,* *Polenus, Pavia, 1722.
Fustel (de Coulanges), *Cité Antique.* Eleventh Edition, Paris, 1885.
Gaius, *Institutes; Digest of Justinian.* Palimpsest of Niebuhr
Gellius (Aulus), *Noctes Atticæ: Attic Nights, Bähr, Geschichte der Römischen Literatur,* Carlsruhe, 1845.
Gibbon (Edward), *Decline and Fall of the Roman Empire,* New York, The Harpers, 1850.

SOURCES OF INFORMATION.

Gorius (Antonius), *Etruscæ Inscriptiones*, Roma, 1726; *Thesaurus Antiquitatum Grævii et Gronovii*, Utrecht, 1699.
Granier (de Cassagnac, Adolphe), *Histoire des Classes Ouvrières, et des Classes Bourgeoises*, Paris, 1838.
Grote (George), *History of Greece*, London, 1846.
Grote (George), *Plato and the other Companions of Socrates*, London, 1865.
Gruter (Jan), *Inscriptiones Antiquæ totius Orbis Romanorum*, Heidelberg, 1604.
Guhl and Koner, *Life of the Greeks and Romans*, Translation of Hüffer, London, n. d.
Hermann [Charles Frederick], *Political Antiquities of Greece*, Oxford, 1836.
Herodotus, *Herodoti Historiæ*, *Schweighäuser, Strasburg, 1816; *Histories*, Cary's Translation, in Bohn's Classical Library, London, 1885.
Hewitt (Abram S.), *Speech in the House of Representatives, on the Emancipation of Labor*, April, 1884.
Homer, *Iliad*, } *Bekker, Berlin, 1843.
Homer, *Odyssey*, }
Horace, *Carmina*, }
Horace, *Epistolae*, } *Orelli, Zürich, 1859.
Horace, *Sermo*, }
Hamilton (William), *Researches in Asia Minor*, London, n. d.
Heer [Oswald], *Urwelt der Schweiz*, Zürich, 1877.
Heeren [A. H.], *Peuple de l' Antiquité*, French Ed., Paris, 1799.
Heinecius, (Johann Michæl), *Works on Antiquities*, Halle, 1722.
Henzen (Guiliemus), *Supplement to Orelliana Inscriptionum Collectio*, Zürich, 1861.
INTERNATIONAL *Cyclopœdia*.
*Isocrates, *Panegyricus*, Baiter and Sauppe. Zürich, 1850.
Ister, *Lost Works*, Aph. Schol., *Aristophanis Byzantii Fragmenta*, Nauck, Leipzic, 1849.
Josephus, (Flavius), *Antiquities and Wars of the Jews*, Whiston's English Translation, London, 1737.
Justin Dial, *Cum Tryphone*. (Certain obscure Passages.)
Kitto, *Cyclopaedia of Biblical Literature*, London, 1850.
Lælius, *In Orelli's Cicero*, Zürich, 1829.
La Rousse, *Dictionnaire Universel*, Paris, Edition of 1870.
Lampridius (Ælius), in *Augusta Historia;—Alexander Severus*, From the *Palatine MS.
Laveleye (Emile de), *Primitive Property*, English Translation of Marriott, London, 1878.
Le Play (F.), *Organization of Labor*, English Translation of Emerson, Philadelphia, 1872.
Livy (Titus), *Annales: Ab Urbe Condita Opera quæ supersunt* Weissenborn, Bibliotheca Teubneriana, Leipzic, 1855.

SOURCES OF INFORMATION.

Lytton–Bulwer, *Last Days of Pompeii*, London, 1835.
Lobeck (Christian August), *Aglaophon*, Königsberg, 1824.
Lucian (Logographos Samosatæ), *Somnium: Vita Luciana*, Jacobitz, in *Bibliotheca Teubneriana*, Leipzic, 1855.
Lucretius (Titus Carus), *De Rerum Natura*, Bernasius, Bibliotheca Teubneriana, Leipzic, 1854.
Lüders, (Otto), *Die Dionysischen Künstler*, Berlin, 1873.
McCullagh (W. Torrens), *Industrial History of Free Nations: The Greeks*, London, 1846.
McCulloch (John Ramsey), *Life of Ricardo*, London, 1876.
Mackenzie (Lord), *Roman Law*, Edinburgh, 1870.
Macrobius (Ambrosius Aurelius Theodosius) *Saturnaliornm et Somnium Scipionis Libri*, Eyssenhardt, Leipzic, 1868.
Maffei (Francisco Scipione), *Museum Veronese*, Verona, 1749.
Mann (Henry), *History of Ancient and Mediæval Republics*, New York, Barnes & Company, n. d.
Mannert (Conrad), *History of the Vandals*, 1785.
Mannert (Conrad), *Geschichte der Vandalen*, Leipzic, 1790.
Marquardt (Becker-Marquardt), *Handbuch des Römischen Alterthums*, Dresden, 1843.
Maurice (Barthélemy), *Histoire Politique et Anecdotique des Prisons de la Seine*, Paris, 1840.
MEMOIRES *Préseniés à l' Académie:* Livre II., 977.
Millar (John), *Origin of Ranks*, Basil, 1793.
Millman (Henry Hart), *History of the Jews*, Oxford, 1829.
Millin (Aubin Louis), *Voyages*, Paris, 1790.
MINOKHIRED, in *Zeitschrift der morgenländischen Gesellschaft.*
Mommsen (Theador), *De Collegiis et Sodaliciis Romanorum*, Killiæ, 1843.
Mommsen (Theador), *Corpus Inscriptionum Latinarum*, with the assistance of the *königl. Akademie der Wissenschaften.*
Morgan, (Lewis H.), *Ancient Societies*, New York, 1878.
Müller (K. O.), *Die Dorier*, Göttengen, 1824.
Muratorius (Ludovicus Antonius,) *Antiquitates Medii Ævi*, Milan, 1742.
Muratorius (Ludovicus Antonius), *Thesaurus Veterum Inscriptionum*, Milan, 1739.
NEW *Testament.*
*Nicolaus (Damascenus), *Fragmenta Historiœ;* also quoted by later ancient Authors, Recensio Orellii, Leipz. 1804.
Nymphodorus, *Nomima Asias*, per Athenæus in *Deipnosophistai*, Dindorf, Leipzic, 1837; also Scholiast Edition, Venice, 1556.
Marini (G.), *Atti Dei Fradelli Arvali*, Roma, 1796.
Oderico (G. L.), *Inscriptions and Numismatics*, Genoa, 1796.

Orellius (Io. Caspar), *Inscriptionum Latinarum Selectarum Amplissima Collectio.* Zürich 1828.
*Orosius (Paulus,), *Libri VII. Historiarum Adversus Paganos,* Editio princeps, Vienna, 1471.
Ovid (Publius Naso), *Fastorum Libri qui supersunt,* Merkel and Riese, 1857.
PANDECTÆ *Justiniani,* Samuel Petit in *Thesaurus Grœvii et Gronovii,* Utrecht, 1699.
Pausanias, *Hellados Periegesis (Descriptio Grœeiœ),* Teubner Series, Leipzic, Schubart, 1850.
Peiresc (Nicholas Claude), *Dionis Cassii Excerpta Vaticana,* Aix, 1635
Petit (Samuel), *Studies of the Arundelian Inscription,* Paris, 1640; also *Several other Criticisms.*
Philo (Judæus), *Quod Omnis Probus Liber,* *Turnebus Paris, 1552; Legarde, *Onomastica Sacra,* Paris, 1870.,
Plato, *Apology of Socrates,*
Plato, *Menexenos,*
Plato, *Minos,*   Bekker, London ed., 1828,
Plato, *Phœdo,*   Stallbaum, Leipzic, 1825,
Plato, *Phœdrus,*   Orell., Winkelmann, Baiter 1840
Plato, *Protagoras,*   Burges, Cary, Davis, trs.
Plato, *De Republica,*
Plato, *Statesman,*
Plato, *Theœtetus,*
Plutarch, *Lives of Illustrious Men,* Teubner *Series,* Leipzic, 1850; English Translation of Langhorne, London, n. d.
Polybius, *Historia Katholike,* Leipzic, 1843.
Pomponius–Mela, *De Orbis Situ,* Tzschucke, Leipzic, 1807.
Porter, (George Richardson), *Progress of the Nation,* Lon. 1836.
Preller (Ludwig), *Mithologie: Demeter und Persephone,* Leipzic, 1854.
Prudentius (Aurelius) *Hymni,* *Arvali, Roma, 1790.
PSEUDO-Plutarch, *De Nobilitate,* in the Teubner *Series,* 1845.
Rangabé–Rhizo, *Antiquités Helléniques,* 2 vols. Paris, 1855.
REAL *Encyclopœdie,* Pauly.
Reinesius (Thomas), *Inscriptionum Antiquarum Syntagma,* Leipzic, 1682, *Oracles: Sibylline Books,* 1704.
Renan (Ernest), *Vie de JÉSUS,* Paris, 1863.
Rinaldo, *Memorie Istoriche della Città di Capua,* Nápoli, 1755.
Ritschl (Friedrich Wilhelm), *Plautus,* Bonn, 1848.
Rodbertus (von Jägetzow), *Der Normal Arbeitstag,* Berlin, 1871.
Roscher (Wilhelm), *Principes d' Economie Politique,* French Edition, Paris, 1872.
Rogers (J. E. Thorold), *Six Centuries of* **Work and Wages,** New York, 1884.

SOURCES OF INFORMATION.

Rohden, *Johannis der Täufer*, Brochure; A Dissertation.
Romanelli (Domenico), *Topografia: Viaggio a Pompej.*
Rose (H. J.), *Inscriptiones Græcæ Vetustissimæ*, Cantabridgiæ,, 1825.
Ross (Ludwig), *Voyages dans les Iles; Les Inscriptions de Scio*, Halle, 1842.
Rossi (Giovanni Bernardo de), *Inscriptiones Christianæ Urbis Romæ*, Roma, 1853.
Saint-Edme (M. B.) *Dictionnaire de la Pénalité*, Paris, 1825.
Sallustius (Caius Crispus), *Historiarum Libri Quinque*, Vatican Fragments; Schambach's *Sklavenaufstand*.
Sanger (William W.), *History of Prostitution*, New York, 1876.
Schambach, *Der Italische Sklavenaufstand*, n. d., n. p., 4to.
Schliemann (Henry), *The Tiryns*, New York, 1885.
Schömann (F. G.), *Assemblies of the Athenians*, English University Translation of Cambridge, 1837.
*Servius, On the *Æneid of Virgil*, Fabricius, Meissen, 1551.
Siefert (Otto), *Sicilische Sklavenkriege*, Altona, 1860.
Smith (William), *Dictionary of the Bible*, Boston, 1886.
Smith (William), *Dictionary of Greek and Roman Biography*, London, 1849.
Solon, *Code*, in Plutarch, Gaius and others.
Stobæus, Quoting *Lost Works of Florilus*, mentioned by Bücher.
Strabo, *Geographica*, Tzschucke, Leipzic, 1812.
Suetonius (Claudius), *Vitæ Duodecim Cæsarum*, Burmann, Amsterdam, 1743.
Syncellus, Quoting *Africanus*, in *Chronica*.
Tarrentenus (Paternus), *De Re Militari*, Quoted by Drumann, Leipzic, 1857.
Terence (Publius Afer), *Heauton-timorumanos*, London, 1857.
Tertulian (Quintus Septimius Florens), *Apologeticus* and *De Idololatria*, Œhler, Leip. 1857; Dr. March, *Douglass Series*, New York, 1876.
Theophrastus, *Ethikoi Karakteres* (*Moral Characters*), Ast, Munich, 1825.
Theopompus, In *Plutarch, *De Iside et Osiride*.
Thiersch (Henry W.) *Christian Commonwealth*, Edinburgh, 1877.
Thucydides, *Polemon ton Peloponnesion* (*De Bello Peloponnesiaco*), Leipzic, *Bibliotheca Teubneriana*, Böhme, 1857.
Tompkins (Henry), *Friendly Societies of Antiquity*, Lon., 1867.
Tompkins (Henry, Acting Secretary to Registry, of Friendly Societies of Great Britain), *Reports*, London, 1867-9.
Ulpian (Domitius), *De Officio Proconsulis;* Vatican *MS.* & *Excerpta Digestorum; De Dominorum Sævitia*, Bonn, 1840.
Uwaroff, *Essai sur les Mystères d' Eleusis*,
Valerius Maximus, *Factorum Dictorumque Memorabilium Libri IX.* Leipzic, 1836.

Varro (Marcus Terentius), *De Re Rustica Libri Tres*, *Schneider, Leipzic, 1796.
Velleius (Paterculus), *Historiæ Romanæ*, Orelli, Leipzic, 1835.
Virgil (Publius Maro), *Æneid*, Teubner *Series*, Leipzic, 1840.
Wallace, (Robert), *Numbers of Mankind*, Edinburgh, 1753.
Weissenborn. *Comments on Livy*, Leipzic, 1871.
Wesseling (Peter) *Veterum Romanorum Itineraria*, Utr't, 1750.
Wescher-Foucart, *Inscriptions recueillies à Delphes*, Paris, 1863.
Wescher (C.), In *Revue Archéologique*, Paris, 1864.
Westermann (Anton), *Nymphodorus*, In *Real-Encyclopædie*.
Wiener-*Jahrbuch*, XX.
Wilkinson (Sir Gardner), *Ancient Egyptians*, Boston, 1883.
Wordsworth (Christopher), *Fragments of Early Latin*, London.
Wright (Carroll D.), *Industrial Depressions*, *Report* of the United States Bureau of Labor, Washington, 1886.
Xenophon, *Conversationes*,
Xenophon, *Memorabilia*,
Xenophon, *Œconomicus*, Leipzic, 1859.
Xenophon, *De Republica*,
Xenophon, *De Vectigali*,

---

* The Asterisks refer to Works that were consulted by the author during his researches abroad.

SYMBOLS OF ANCIENT PERFUMERS' UNIONS.

From an Inscription upon jasper.——See Chapter xix

CONTENTS OF THE VOLUME.

CHAPTER I.

TAINT OF LABOR.

TRAITS AND PECULIARITIES OF RACES.

GRIEVANCES of the Working Classes—The Competitive System among the Ancients—Growing Change of Taste in Readers of History—Inscriptions and suppressed Fragments more recently becoming Incentives to reflecting Readers who seek Them as a means to secure Facts—No true Democracy—No primeval Middle Class known to the Aryan Family—The Taint of Labor an Inheritance through the Pagan Religio-Political Economy. *Page* 37

CHAPTER II.

THE INDO-EUROPEANS.

THEIR COMPETITIVE SYSTEM.

RELIGION AND POLITICS of the Indo-Europeans Identical—Reason for Religion mixing with the Movements of Labor—The Father the Original Slaveholder—His Children the Original Slaves—Both Law and Religion empowered him to kill them—Work of Conscience in the Labor Problem.   47

CONTENTS OF CHAPTERS.

CHAPTER III.

LOST MSS. ARCHÆOLOGY.

TRUE HISTORY OF LABOR FOUND ONLY IN INSCRIPTIONS AND MUTILATED ANNALS.

PROTOTYPES OF Industrial Life to be found in the Aryan and Semitic Branches—Era of Slavery—Dawn of Manumission—Patriarchal Form too advanced a Type of Government possible to primitive Man—Religious Superstition fatal to Independent Labor—Labor, Government and Religion indissolubly mixed—Concupiscence, Acquisitiveness and Irascibility a Consequence of the archaic Bully or Boss, with unlimited Powers—Right of the ancient Father to enslave, sell, torture or kill his Children—Abundant Proofs quoted—Origin of the greater and more humane Impulses—Sympathy beyond mere Self preservation, the Result of Education—Education originated from Discussion—Discussion the Result of Grievances against the Outcast Work-people—Too rapid Increase of their Numbers notwithstanding the Sufferings—Means Organized by Owners for decimating them by Murder—Ample proof—The great Amphyctyonic League—Glimpses of a once sullen Combination of the Desperate Slaves—Incipient Organization of the Nobles. *Page* 67

CHAPTER IV.

ELEUSINIAN MYSTERIES

ANCIENT GRIEVANCES OF THE WORKERS.

WORKING PEOPLE destitute of Souls—Original popular Beliefs—Plato finally gives them half a Soul—Modern Ignorance on the true Causes of certain Developments in History—Sympathy, the Third Great Emotion developed out of growing Reason, through mutual Commiseration of the Outcasts—A new Cult—The Unsolved Problem of the great Eleusinian Mysteries—Their wonderful Story—Grievances of slighted Workingmen—Organization impossible to Slaves except in their Strikes and Rebellions—The Aristocrats' Politics and Religion barred the Doors against Work-people—Extraor-

CONTENTS OF CHAPTERS.

dinary Whims and Antics at the Eleusinian Mysteries—The Causes of Grievances endured by the Castaway Laborers—Their Motives for Secret Organization—The Terrible Cryptia—The horrible Murders of Workingmen for Sport—Dark Deeds Unveiled—Story of the Massacre of 2,000 Workingmen—Evidence—The Grievances in Sparta—In Athens—Free Outcast Builders, Sculptors, Teachers, Priests, Dancers, Musicians, Artisans, Diggers, all more or less Organized—Return to the Eleusinian Mysteries—Conclusion. *Page* 83

CHAPTER V.

STRIKES AND UPRISINGS.

GRIEVANCES CONTINUED. PLANS OF ESCAPE.

First Known and First Tried Plan of Salvation was that of Retaliation—The Slaves test the Ordeal of Armed Force—Irascibility of the Working Classes at length arrayed against their Masters—Typical Strikes of the ancient Workingmen—Their Inhuman Treatment—Famous Strike at the Silver Diggings of Laurium—20,000 Artisans and Laborers quit Work in a Body and go over to the Foes of their own Countrymen—The Great Peloponnesian War Decided for the Spartans, against the Athenians by this Fatal Strike. *Page* 133

CHAPTER VI.

GRIEVANCES.

LABOR TROUBLES AMONG THE ROMANS. MORE BLOODY PLANS OF SALVATION TRIED.

The Irascible Plan in Italy—Epidemic Uprisings—Attempt to Fire the City of Rome and have Things common—Conspiracy of Slaves at the Metropolis—Two Traitors—Betrayal—Deaths on the Roman Gibbet—Another Great Uprising at Setia—Expected Capture of the World—Land of Wine and Delight—Again the Traitor, the Betrayal and Gibbet—The Irascible Plan a Failure—Strike of the Agricultural Laborers in Etruria—Slave Labor—Character of the Etruscans—Expedition of Glabro—Fighting—Slaves Worsted—Punishment on the dreadful Cross, the ancient Block for the Low-born—Enormous Strike in the Land of Labor Organizations—One Glimpse at the Cause and Origin of Italian Brigandage—Laborers, Mechanics and Agriculturers Driven to Despair—The great Uprising in Apulia—Fierce Fighting to the Dagger's Hilt—The Overthrow, the Dungeon and the Cross—Proof Dug from Fragments of Lost History. *Page* 145

CHAPTER VII.

DRIMAKOS.

A QUEER OLD MAN OF THE MOUNTAINS.

STRIKE OF DRIMAKOS, the Chian Slave—Co-operation of the Irascible with the Sympathetic—A Desperate Greek Bondsman at Large—Labor Grievances of the ancient Scio—Temperament and Character of Drimakos—Vast Number of unfortunate Slaves—Revolt and Escape to the Mountains—Old Ruler of the Mountain Crags—Rigid Master and loving Friend—Great Successes—Price offered for his Head—How he lost it—The Reaction—Rich and Poor all mourn his Loss as a Calamity—The Brigands infest the Island afresh since the Demise of Drimakos—The *Heroön* at his Tomb—An Altar of Pagan Worship at which this Labor Hero becomes the God, reversing the Order of the ancient Rights—Ruins of his Temple still extant—Athenæus—Nymphodorus—Archæology—Views of modern Philologists. *Page* 163

CHAPTER VIII.

VIRIATHUS.

A GREAT REBELLION IN SPAIN.

THE Roman Slave System in Spain—Tyranny in Lusitania—Massacre of the People—Condition before the Outbreak—First Appearance of Viriathus—A Shepherd on his Native

Hills—A Giant in Stature and Intellect—He takes Command—Vetillius Outwitted—Captured and Slain—Conflict in Tartessus—Romans again Beaten—Battle of the Hill of Venus—Viriathus Slaughters another army and Humiliates Rome—Segobria Captured—Arrival of Æmilianus—He is Out-generaled and at last Beaten by Viriathus—More Battles and Victories for the Farmers—Arrival of Plautius with Fresh Roman Soldiers—Viriathus made King—More Victories—Treason, Conspiracy and Treachery Lurking in his Camps—Murdered by his own Perfidious Officers—Pomp at His Funeral—Relentless Vengeance of the Romans—Crucifixion and worse Slavery than before—The Cause Lost.

CHAPTER IX

EUNUS.

GRIEVANCES. MORE SALVATION ON THE VINDICTIVE PLAN.

The Irascible Impulse in its Highest Development and most enormous Organization—Greatest of all Strikes found on Record—Gigantic Growth of Slavery—General View of Sicilian Landlordism and Servitude before the Outbreak—Great Increase of Bondsmen and Women—Enna, Home of the Goddess Ceres, becomes the Stronghold of the Great Uprising—Eunus; his Pedigree—He is made King of the Slaves—History of his 10 Years' Reign—Somebody, ashamed to confess it, has mangled the Histories—The Fragments of Diodorus and other Noble Authors Reveal the Facts—Cruelties of Damophilus and Megallis, the immediate Cause of the Grievance—Eunus, Slave, Fire-spitter, Leader, Messiah, King—Vengeance—The innocent Daughter—Sympathy hand-in-hand with Irascibility against Avarice—Wise Selection by Eunus, of Achæus as Lieutenant—Council of War—Mass-meeting—A Plan agreed to—Cruelty of the Slaves—Their Army—The War begun—Prisons broken open and 60,000 Convicts working in the *Ergastula* set free—Quotations—Sweeping Extinction of the Rich—Large Numbers of Free Tramps join—Another prodigious Uprising in Southern Sicily—Cleon—Conjectures regarding this Obscure Military Genius—Union of Eunus, Achæus and Cleon—Harmony—Victories over the Romans—Insurgent Force rises to 200,000 Men—Proof—

Overthrow and Extinction of the Armies of Hypsæus—Manlius—Lentulus—The Victorious Workingmen give no Quarter—Eunus as Mimic, taunts his Enemies by Mock Theatrical, Open-Air Plays in the Sieges—Cities fall into his Hands—His Speeches—Moral Aid through the Social Struggle with Gracchus at Rome—Arrival of a Roman Army under Piso—Beginning of Reverses—Crucifixions—Demoralization—Fall of Messana—Siege of Enna—Inscriptions verifying History—Romans Repulsed—Arrival of Rupilius—Siege of Tauromanion—Wonderful Death of Comanus—Cannibalism—The City falls—Awful Crucifixions—Second Siege of Enna—Its 20,000 People are crucified on the Gibbet—Eunus captured and Devoured by Lice in a Roman Dungeon—Disastrous End of the Rebellion or so-called Servile War. *Page* 191

CHAPTER X.

ARISTONICUS.

A BLOODY STRIKE IN ASIA MINOR.

Freedmen, Bondsmen, Tramps and Illegitimates Rise against Oppression—Contagion of monster Strikes—Again the Irascible Plan of Rescue tried—Aristonicus of Pergamus—Story of the Murder of Titus Gracchus and of 300 Land Reformers by a Mob of Nobles at Rome—Blossius, a Noble, Espouses the Cause of the Workingmen—He goes to Pergamus—The *Heliopolitai*—The Commander of the Labor Army overpowers all Resistance—Battle of Leuca—Overthrow of the Romans—Death of Crassus—Arrival of the Consul Paperna—Defeat of the Insurgents—Their Punishment—Discouragement and Suicide—Aristonicus strangled, Thousands crucified and the Cause Lost—Old Authors Quoted. *Page* 232

CHAPTER XI.

ATHENION.

ENORMOUS STRIKE AND UPRISING IN SICILY.

Second Sicilian Labor-War—Tryphon and Athenion—Greed and Irascibility Again Grapple—The War Plan of Salvation Repeated by Slaves and Tramps—Athenion, another remarkable General Steps Forth—Castle of the Twins in a Hideous Forest—Slaves goaded to Revolt by Treachery and Intrigue of a Politician—Rebellion and the Clangor of War—Battle in the Mountains—A Victory for the Slaves at the Heights of Engyon—Treachery of Gaddæus the Freebooter—Decoy and Crucifixions—Others cast Headlong over a Precipice—The Strike starts up Afresh at Heraclea Minoa—Murder of Clonius a rich Roman Knight—Escape of Slaves from his *Ergastulum*—Sharp Battles under the Generalship of Salvius—Strife rekindles in the West—Battle of Alaba—The Proprætor punished for his bad Administration—Victory Again Wreathes a Laurel for the Lowly—A vast Uprising in Western Sicily—Athenion the Slave Shepherd—Another Fanatical Crank of Deeds—Rushing the Struggle for Existence—Fierce Battles and Blood-spilling—What Ordinary Readers of History have not heard of—Fourth Battle; Triokala—Meek Sacrifices by the Slaves, to the Twins of Jupiter and Thalia—March to Triokala—Jealousy—Great Battle and Carnage—Athenion Wounded—He escapes to Triokala and recovers—Fifth Battle—Lucullus marches to the Workingmen's Fortifications—Battle of Triokala—The Outcasts Victorious—Lucullus is lost from View—Sixth Battle—Servilius, another Roman General Overthrown—The Terrible Athenion Master of Sicily and King over all the Working-People—Seventh and Final Field Conflict—Battle of Macella—Death of Athenion—Victory this Time for the Romans—End of the Rebellion—Satyros, a powerful Greek Slave escapes to the Mountains with a Force of Insurgents—They are finally lured to a Capitulation by Aquillius who treacherously turns upon, and consigns them as Gladiators to Rome—They fight the Eighth and last Battle in the Roman Amphitheatre among wild Beasts—A ghastly mutual Suicide—The Reaction—Treachery of Aquillius Punished—The Gold-Workers pour melted Gold down his Throat.

CHAPTER XII.

SPARTACUS.

THE IRASCIBLE PLAN TESTED ON AN ENORMOUS SCALE.

Rise, Vicissitudes and Fall of a Great General—The Strike of the Gladiators—Grievances that led to the Trouble—Growth of Slavery through Usurpation of the Land by the arrogant Optimates—What is known of Spartacus before being Sold into Slavery—Bolt of the 78 Gladiators from the *Ergastulum* of Lentulus at Capua—Escape of the Runaways—How they seized Weapons—Vesuvius—First Battle—Battle of the Cliffs —Rout of Clodius—Second Battle—Destruction of a Prætorian Army—Battle of the Mineral Baths—Great Increase of the Rebel Force—From a petty Strike it assumes the Proportions of Revolution—Fourth Battle; Hilt to Hilt with Varinius—Destruction of the Main Army of the Romans—Winter Quarters of Spartacus at Metapontem—Honor, Discipline and Temperance of the Workingmen—Proofs by Pliny and Plutarch—Coalision with the Organized Laborers of Italy— Uses of Gold and other Ornaments Forbidden—Wine Banished—Great Numbers Employed in the Armories of Spartacus—Fifth Battle—Battle of Mt. Garganus—Ambuscade of Arrius—Overthrow and Death of Crixus—Sixth Battle— Spartacus Destroys the Consular Army of Poplicola—Seventh Battle—Great Conflict of the River Po—Overthrow of Cassius and Defeat of the 10,000 Romans—Spartacus, now Master, assumes the Offensive—Eighth Battle—Lentulus Defeated; Great Army nearly annihilated—Mortification and Terror of the Romans—Ninth Battle—Mutina—Proconsul Cassius again Routed in a Disastrous Conflict with the wary Gladiator—Spartacus now obliged to contend with the Demon of Insubordination—Crassus elected Consul—**Reverses** Begin—On down to Rhegium—Sedition, Treachery, Betrayals—Workingmen's own Jealousies, Insubordination and Lack of Diplomacy cause their final Ruin—Tenth Battle—Scaling of the Six-Mile Ramparts by Spartacus—Battle of Croton— Destruction of the Seceders, Granicus and Castus—Obstinate Fighting—Spartacus arrives and checks the Carnage—Petelia, the Eleventh Battle—Victory—Twelfth Battle; Silarus —Last and most Bloody Encounter—Spartacus, stabbing his Horse, Rushes sword drawn, in search of Crassus—Heaps of the slain—Dying like a King—End of the War—The great *Supplicium*—Pompey and Crassus, emulous of meagre Honors—Inhuman Cruelties—Awful Wreaking of Vengeance on the Cross—Dangling Bodies of 6,000 Crucified Workingmen along the Appian Way—Thousands of Others crucified—Utter Failure of the Irascible Plan of Deliverance *Page* 275

CHAPTER XII.

ORGANIZATION.

ROME'S ORGANIZED WORKINGMEN AND WOMEN.

Organization of the Freedmen—The *Jus Coeundi*—Roman Unions—The *Collegium*—Its Power and Influence—What the Poor did with their Dead—Cremation—Burial a Divine Right which they were too Lowly to Practice—Worship of borrowed Gods—Incineration or Burial and Trade Unions combined—Proofs—Glance at the Inner social Life of the ancient Brotherhoods—State Ownership and Management—Nationalized Lands—Number and Variety of Trade Unions—Struggles—Numa Pompilius First to Recognize and Uphold Trade Unions—Law of the 12 Tables taken from Solon—Harmony, Peace, Ease, steady Work, Prosperity and Plenty Lasting with little Interruption for 500 Years—Bondmen fared worse. *Page* 333

CHAPTER XIV.

LAWS AGAINST COMMUNES.

THE GREAT ECONOMIC ORGANIZATIONS.

ANCIENT FEDERATIONS of Labor—How they were Employed by the Government—Nomenclature of the Brotherhoods—Categories of King Numa—Varieties and Ramifications—The Masons, Stonecutters and Bricklayers—Federation for Mutual Advantages—List of the 35 Trade Unions, under the *Jus Coeundi*. *Page* 359

CHAPTER XV.

TRADE UNIONS.

ORGANIZED ARMOR-MAKERS OF ANTIQUITY.

TRADE UNIONS TURNED to the Manufacture of Arms and Munitions of War—How it came about—The Iron and Metal Workers—Artists in the Alloys—How Belligerent Rome was Furnished with Weapons, Shoes and Other Necessaries for Her Warriors—The Shieldmakers, Arrowsmiths, Daggermakers, War-Gun and Slingmakers, Battering-Rammakers etc.—Bootmakers who Cobbled for the Roman Troops—Wine Men, Bakers and Sutlers—All Organized—Unions of Oil Grinders; of Pork Butchers; even of Cattle Fodderers—The Haymakers—Organized Fishermen—Ancient Labor brought charmingly near by Inscriptions. *Page* 372

CONTENTS OF CHAPTERS.

CHAPTER XVI.

TRADE UNIONS.

THE GREAT TRADES VICTUALING SYSTEM.

How Rome Was Fed—Unions of Fishermen—Discovery of a Strange Inscription at Pompeii, Proving the Political Power and Organization of the Workingmen and Women's Unions—Female Suffrage in Italy—The Fish Salters—Wine Smokers—Union of Spicemen—The Game-Hunters' Organizations—Unions of Amphitheatre Sweepers—Unions of Wagoners, Ox-Drivers, Muleteers, Cooks, Weighers, Tasters and Milkmen—The Cooking Utensil-Makers—Unions of Stewards—Old Familiar Latin Names, with Familiar English Meanings Reproduced—Gaius and the Twelve Tables—Numerous Notes with References to Archæological Collections and to Histories Giving Pages and many Necessary Renderings, of the Obscure Curiosities Described. *Page* 380

CHAPTER XVII.

INDUSTRIAL COMMUNES

AMUSEMENTS OF OLD. UNIONS OF PLAYERS

The Collegia Scænicorum—Unions of Mimics—Horrible Mimic Performances in Sicily—Bloody Origin of Wakes—Unions of Dancers, Trumpeters, Bagpipers, and Hornblowers—The Flute Players—Roman Games—Unions of Circus Performers—Of Gladiators—Of Actors—Murdering Robust Wrestlers for Holiday Pastimes—Unions of Fortunetellers—Proofs in the Inscriptions—Ferocious Gladiatorial Scenes between the Workingmen and Tigers, Lions, Bears, and Other Wild Beasts made compulsory by Roman Law. *Page* 401

CHAPTER XVIII.

TRADE UNIONS.

THE ANCIENT CLOTHING-CUTTERS.

How the Ancients were Clothed—The Unions of Fullers—Of

CONTENTS OF CHAPTERS xxxiii

Linen Weavers, Wool-carders. Cloth-combers—Inscriptions as Proof—Later Laws of Theodosius and Justinian Revised—Government Cloth Mills—What was Meant by Public Works—Who managed Manufactures—The Dyers—Old-fashioned Shoes of the Forefathers—How made—Origin of the Crispins—The Furriers' Union—Roman Ladies and Fineries of Fur—The great Ragamuffin Trade—Their Innumerable Unions—Ragpickers of Antiquity—Origin of the Cenciajuole—Organization of the Real Tatterdemalions Origin of the Gypsies—Hypothesis. Page 415

CHAPTER XIX.

TRADE UNIONS.

THE PAGAN AND CHRISTIAN IMAGE-MAKERS.

Organizations of People who worked for the Gods—Big and little Godsmiths—Their Unions object to the New Religion of Christianity because this, originally Repudiating Idolatry, Ruined their Business—Compromise which Originated the Idolatry in the Church of to-day—The Cabatores—Unions of Ivory Workers—Of Bisellarii or Deity-Sedan-Makers—Of Imagemakers in Plaster—The Unguentarii or Unions of Perfumemakers—Holy Ointments and the Unions that manufactured them—Etruscan Trinketmakers—Bookbinders—No Proof yet found of their Organization. Page 428

CHAPTER XX.

TRADE UNIONS CONCLUDED.

THE TAX-GATHERERS. FINAL REFLECTIONS.

Unions of Collectors—A Vast Organized System with a Uniform and Harmoniously Working Business—Trade Unions under Government Aid and Security—The Ager Publicus of Rome—True Golden Age of Organized Labor—Government Land—A prodigious Slave System their Enemy—Victims of the Slave System—Premonitions on the Coming of Jesus—Demand by His Teachings for Absolute Equality.
Page 437

CHAPTER XXI.

ROMANS AND GREEKS.

THE COUNTLESS COMMUNES.

UNIONS OF ROMANS AND GREEKS compared—Miscellaneous Societies of Tradesmen—Shipcarpenters—Boatmen—Vesselmakers—Millers—Organization of the *Lupanarii*—Of the Ancient Firemen—Description of the Greek Fraternities—The *Eranoi* and *Thiasoi*—Strange Mixture of Piety and Business—Trade Unions of Syria and North Palestine—Their Officers—Membership and Influence of Women—Large Numbers of Communes in the Islands of the Eastern Mediterranean—Their Organizations Known and Described From their Inscriptions. *Page*

CHAPTER XXII.

THE ANCIENT BANNER.

INCALCULABLY AGED FLAG OF LABOR.

THE OLD, Old Crimson Ensign—An Emblem of Peace and Good Will to Man—Strange Power of Human Habit—Descent of the Red Banner through Primitive Culture—White and Azure the Colors of Mythical Angels, Grandees and Aristocrats—Colors for the Lowly without Family, Souls or other Seraphic Attributes—How the Red Vexillum was Stolen from Labor—Tricks which Compromised Peace Tenets of the Flag—The Flag at the Dawn of Labor's Power—Testimony of Polybius—Of Livy—Of Plutarch—Causes of Working People's Affection for Red—The Emblem of Health and the Fruits of Toil—Ceres and Minerva their Protectresses and Mother-Goddesses Wore the Flaming Red—Emblem of Strength and Vitality—Archæology in Proof—Their Color First Borrowed from Crimson Sun-Beams—More Light and less Darkness—White and Pale Hues for the Priests—Origin of the Word "FLAG"—It is the Word-Root of "Flame" a Red Color—Proofs Quoted—Mediæval Banner in France and England—The Red of All Modern Flags Borrowed from that of the Ancient Unions—Disgraceful Ignorance of Modern Prejudice and Censure.

Evidence showing that the Early Christians were Members—Testimony of Philo—Of Eusebius—Facts Related by One of the Fathers—A Full Rendering—Numbers and Ways of the Secret Orders in and about Canaan at the Time of Christ—The Secret Order of Eranists—Inscriptions deciphered by Böckh and other Masters—Tertulian's Evidence—Community of Goods—The *Eranistes* and *Thiasotes*—Great Numbers of Secret Societies in Asia Minor and Syria. *Page* 276

CHAPTER XXIII.

PALESTINE;

HER PRE-CHRISTIAN COMMUNES.

CRADLE OF A Mighty Reform—Acquisitiveness and Concupiscence in open Conflict with Irascibility and Sympathy—A new Analysis of the Origin of the celebrated Movement in Judæa—Communes of Palestine—Boundaries between the Lowly of Phœnicia, Judæa, Greece and Rome, Unrecognized—Numbers of the Organized About the Cradle of the Saviour—Difficulty of comprehending the true Import of the Judaic Idea in that Movement—Argument and Inscriptions Showing it to have been the Result of a long Line of Culture, Organization and Experiment. *Page* 403

CHAPTER XXIV.

THE FINAL REVIEW.

ANCIENT PLANS OF "BLESSED" GOVERNMENT.

WHY THE FACTS were Suppressed and the Books Mangled—Did our Era rise out of the Great Labor Struggles—An Astonishing Probability Unmasked—Plants and Plans of the Distant Past—Lycurgus—Reverential Criticism—His Fundamental Error—The Citizens were the Nobles—Public Lands, Meals, Schools and Games—The Grotto of Taygetus—"Hell Paved with Infants' Bones"—A Model Young Gentleman—

His Introduction to the Ladies—An Earthquake believed to have been the Spartans' Punishment for Cruelty to the Working People—The Poor and Lowly were called "Slave Souls"—The Great Aristotle's Curse—Lucian's Choice of a Trade—Even Plutarch Lampoons Them—Kings Planting Poisons with which to Destroy Them—Prophets and Messiahs—Eunus the Prophet of Antioch—His Plan of Salvation—No Quarters—Wholesale Extinction of the Wealthy—What Succeeding Ages Learned from the Outcome of this Ordeal of Carnage—Plans of the Anarchists Taught Needful Lessons on Future Political Economy—Drimakos—His Home of Runaway Angels in the Skies—How his Plan Worked—Desperate Plan of Aristonicus in Asia Minor which offers the Toilers the Beatitude of being " Citizens of the Sun '—Sad Outcome—Innocent Plan of Spartacus—His Ideal "Salvation" was his Emancipation Proclamation and Armed Power to Enforce It—He Wanted to Go Home to the Green Hills of His Boyhood—All these Plan-Makers were Messiahs and Prophets—"The Kings Kill the Prophets"—The Great Messiah at Last—Long-Smothered Authors Dragged forth—Their own Utterances Quoted in the Living Tongue—Numerous Excerpts from their Books—Men Growing Wise in Their Understanding—The Vastness of the Revolution from the Pagan Cult which Denied the Majority Both Soul and Liberty, threw the Race into Bewilderment of Two Thousand Years of Trial and Doubt—Plans of the Founders of Government Reviewed—Resemblance of Socrates and Jesus—Paralellisms Drawn—One Agitates by Simile the other, Allegory—Proof that they were Both Great Orators—Their Eloquence—Teaching Precepts that are just Becoming Applicable—The Intellectual Stagnation in after Ages a Natural Consequence upon a Revolution that Overturned the Great Pagan Cult—The Mohammedan Rescue—London's Socialism from Same Old Plant—What two Men Did in Twenty-five Centuries—Pagan Selfishness Exhibited in Prayers—Very Ancient Prayers of Our Germano-Aryan Mothers and Fathers—Specimens Quoted—Prayer of Alcestis—Of Other honest Pagans—All Based upon Self and Family—Prayer of Socrates to Pan for More Wisdom and Humility—Prayer of Juvenal for the Poor Slave's Deliverance—Finally, after many Centuries, the Dying Prayer Begged the Pan of Socrates or Universal Father for Universal Cancellation, to fit the World for a New Era—The Relation of the Jews to the Labor Movement—The Romans, Mad at the Spread of the Christian Doctrines of Universal Equality, Take Vengeance in the Slaughter of the Jews—Progress of Ancient Invention—The Labor-saving Reaper .Conclusion

THE ANCIENT LOWLY.

CHAPTER I.

TAINT OF LABOR

TRAITS AND PECULIARITIES OF RACES.

GRIEVANCE of the Working Classes—The Competitive System among the Ancients—Growing Change of Taste in Readers of History—Inscriptions and Suppressed Fragments more recently becoming Incentives to Reflecting Readers who Seek them as a Means to secure Facts—No true Democracy No primeval Middle Class known to the Aryan Family—The Taint of Labor an Inheritance through the Pagan Religio-Political Economy.

STUDENTS of history appear to be of three distinct classes: first, those who examine it to enjoy the stirring scenes of war and the exhibit that it makes of popular pageant, pomp and military genius; secondly, those who examine it with an object of gleaning facts regarding spiritual, ecclesiastical and other matters of religion; and lastly those who search for recounted deeds as well as clues to tenets of social movements among mankind. In this last, there has been an increasing interest since the beginning of the nineteenth century.

Among the precious obscurities sought by our generation are historical fragments, obscure hints and allusions and queer palæographs on tablets of bronze, stone, earthenware and other objects, containing inscriptions, symbols and emblems, even rules showing the existence of labor societies all through the past civilization. Especially is research quickened in the hearts of a certain class of antiquaries who are interested in the search of history, for its social phases.

It is evident from all clues obtainable that in the open world there has never existed a social government. Efforts have been made to prove that mankind at various intervals and at various points, once enjoyed conditions of life based so radically upon democratic laws as to resemble those now advocated; but such examples do not bear the test of rigid investigation. Although there have existed republics and paternal governments they have been so tinged with patrician leadership on the one hand and patriarchal dictatorship on the other, as to render it impossible to compare them with the socialism now advocated, where the lowly ascend and the lordly descend, to unite on a common level. The deep aim of these great struggles of our age known as the labor movement is to acquire and to enjoy complete and lasting co-operation. This co-operation, or brotherhood of life economies is expected to be not only political but economical, changing both the government and the methods of creating and dispensing the means of life, from the competitive into the purely democratic or co-operative. A practical adoption of this mutualism by any tribe or branch of the human family has probably never yet occurred and never has such a state of things existed except among those secretly organized, of whom we propose to treat.

All the evidences combine to prove that the only method societies have ever yet used, either in political or in economic life, is the competitive one; and as the change from the purely competitive into the purely co-operative involves little less than revolution, or to say the least, introversion, it becomes a study of gravest importance. In the remote past so meagre was the co-operative and so potent the competitive that there existed no intermediary classes and conflicts were common in consequence. Roscher thinks that middlemen are an indispensable element to peace; and it seems evident that his opinions are not without grounds, when applied to every stage of the competitive system in all known ages of the world. [1]

Principes d' Économie politique, Paris, 1857. pp. 175–6. "Tant qu'il existe entre les riches et les pauvres une classe intermédiaire considérable, l'influence morale qu'elle exerce suffit pour empêcher une collision".

Glimpses of evidence reward the researchers into the early history of the laboring masses by establishing the fact that there primarily existed no middle class. But we find great numbers of freedmen or plebeians as early as 700 years before Christ. Men were originally divided into lords and servants. There were masters and there were slaves. The chasm between these two was an empty pit so wide that no leap from one class to the other was considered either practicable or imaginable. As late as the sophists there appears a pronounced aversion to wage taking, especially in all business having for its object educational results. Plato abhorred a sophist who would work for wages. Public servants in the instruction of philosophy and other branches of what was then an ordinary education, were despised when they allowed themselves to belittle their manhood and their calling by this ignoble pay. Plato received gifts from the rich but refused pay. He was a patrician or peer. A statesman of to-day who receives gifts and is not content with his salary is regarded with distrust and aversion, almost as great as that against wages in ancient times. One can account for this metamorphosis of ethics only in the comparative absence in those days of labor among patricians or managers. Although free mercenary soldiers were common who took wages for their recompense, and free hucksters and other petty dealers were known to exist, yet most labor of cultivation, of building, of housekeeping and a considerable amount of the labor of mechanics was performed by slaves.

The law of Moses had partly abolished slavery among the Hebrews as early as B. C. 1400, probably on account of the contempt for that degradation which the Hebrews felt, after the deliverance from their protracted slavery in Egypt. It appears that the Hebrews were the chief originators and conservators of what is now known and advocated in the name of socialism; and their weird life, peculiar language, laws, struggles and inextinguishable nationality scintillate through many of the obcurities of history in a manner to command the wonder if not the awe of all lovers of democratic society. Especially does this remark apply when we consider the intensely and bitterly opposite character of every other community or nationality with which the Hebrew race has ever come in contact.

The Hebrew people were the *Congregation* and the place where they assembled was called the *Tabernacle*. The Pentateuch that records the great Jewish law, quite sufficiently explains that absolute liberty, or relative socialization was the law of Moses.[2] Under no other code of laws have equal rights of man with man been possible among other contemporaneous nations or tribes; because the ethics of the family, the city or state, were grounded upon the competitive rather than the co-operative or mutual principle.[3] Nearly all the ancients were fighters. The Hebrew branch of the great Semitic family seems to have been a partial exception. It is true that they had wars and competed with outsiders; but their peace-loving traits within their own ranks, prevailed over warlike ones, probably somewhat as a result of their long captivity in Egypt, but principally from the peaceful and humane code of laws which they received from Moses. But it appears very certain that Jewish monotheism, together with the social or mutually protective habits of this people and their comparatively mild laws made them the object of hatred among the more competitive and consequently fiercer nations with whom they came in contact.

It is not then, from this Semitic branch of the human family that our struggling, warlike and competitive characteristics are derived. A close observation of the Hebrews discloses that although they were often engaged in strifes it was generally because attacked. The aggressiveness which characterizes mankind springs not from the Semitic so much as from the Aryan germ.[4] Two distinct ideas have been contended for from the dimmest remoteness either of the provable or the conjectural history. One is the co-operative, which means the mutually protective or socialistic, the other the competitive or warlike and aggressive.

[2] Leviticus, xix. Mann's History of Ancient and Mediæval Republics, pp. 3—10.
[3] Fustel de Coulanges. Cité Antique, Chap. i. Croyances sur l'ame et sur la mort.
[4] The Phœnicians are excepted from this remark.

Through thousands of ages men have vigorously contended for these antipodal results, especially in Europe. They have contended for them through religious beliefs, through social inculcation and philosophy, through rigid scholastic training, and through the most implacable hatreds, bloody persecutions and race-wars ever recorded in the annals of mankind. Until we become better acquainted with the history of the poor classes and divest ourselves of clouds that have hitherto obscured the vision of all historians; until we study the past especially the somber life and strange career of the Semitic family, from a standpoint of development or evolution, and analyze their strangely tenacious and persistent views unbiased by the views through which we are still taught to regard others; until we can catch the practical advantages of co-operation, mutually one with another and thoroughly see the savage nature of competitive life, must we remain blind to the true object which inspired the greatest advent of this world;—the visit and labors at Palestine and the movement whose undying germs there planted the world still loves and cultivates.

These words are expressed preliminarily to announcing facts which have perhaps never before been observed and certainly never enough considered:—that the Aryan or Indo-European branch of the human race has always, in private and in public life, in religion, in society conventionalism, in methods of reasoning and in its political economy, been *competitive*, whilst the Semitic branch has ever been *co-operative*. For thousands of years these two great families have lived over against each other, sometimes mixed, sometimes by themselves, have struggled and fought, have built up and torn down, each with its own inexorably fixed notions; and never as we shall prove, did they show anything like a fusion or even a conciliation of the two systems until three hundred years after the death of Christ. They are warring still; and the direct causes of this warfare as well as its direct results are the great labor movements of to-day. We hope in these pages to show that the natural bent of the lowly majority of mankind is toward co-operation; that race hatreds ran so high that it became necessary to have an Intercessor or mediator to act between the two races and their two ideas, in order to bring about a mutually co-operative system under which the large majorities, including working people could better subsist. It became necessary to have this Intercessor not merely to arrange a religion based upon salvation of the soul or immortal principle, but more likely, as our train of evidence goes to prove, to introduce an organizable method for the economic salvation of the downtrodden and realize practically the promised "Heaven on earth."

We mean by this that from the days of Moses, dating something above fourteen hundred years before Christ, there have existed two distinctly opposite sets of ideas or of thought upon which mankind—the arrogant blooded family with its competition on the one hand and the slave with his rebellions, and freedman with his formidable unions on the other—have been struggling to build up civilizations. The transition from a completely competitive to a mutually co-operative system involved complete revolution. The channels in which human thought has run since man has been a mere animal, occupying as the theory of evolution daringly asserts, a hundred thousand or more of years, have, except in the case of the persecuted and sometimes almost exterminated unions, been purely competitive.

The competitive is the oldest system known. It is profoundly aged. It is the system employed by all living beings by which to procure for individuals, each for itself and its species, the means wherewith to subsist. It is, without the least shadow of doubt, the original. It consists in methods of the individual, whether a weed, a tree, fox, reptile, hawk or human being, of subsisting, as an isolated creature or *ego*, independently of others. It has recognized self as uppermost and taken upon its own responsibility for others' sake their care only for gratification of self, as that manifested in preservation of species.

Back in the remote past, as reason began to dawn upon creeping cave-dwellers or troglodytes of our race, when thought was inspired by suspicion and methods of subsistence were based upon cunning, nature, in the vagueness of his understanding was full of terrors. As he began to realize the certainty of death, man established the first religion; but it was purely upon the competitive basis, always with this aristocratical ego uppermost.

Not until uncounted ages had passed, nor until this pagan religion was inconceivably old did another appear, arising from the mutually protective or co-operative idea. This was at so late a period that by groping back into the misty past, we are enabled to know its founder and trace its history. That it was an innovation, intolerably antithetical to this more aged, original competition or brute-force underlying and inspiring both business and religion is proved by the hatreds borne against it, which have so stamped themselves, not so much upon the religion as upon the whole race that kindled its flame, spoke its tongue and cherished its ideas.

The great struggle going on to-day seems best understood by the laborer.[5] Persons brought up under the purely competitive system which governs human affairs, see with difficulty the idea of true socialism; but the Jews even of our day, grasp it with ease. We are at a loss to comprehend this. Why should the two founders of the labor party in Germany have arrived while young, at the same conception of a method which involves a revolution from the prevailing ideas of political economy? Marx and Lasselle had been born and educated under the Mosaic law. Ricardo, a Jewish speculator in stocks, was brought up in strict obedience to the Jewish law by his father; but finding the Hebrew doctrine very adverse to his speculative tendencies, notions of wages and political economy, he withdrew or seceded from his ancestral religion and joined the more numerous ranks of the competitive one.[6]

The Mosaic Law, divested of its idiosyncracies such as

---

[5] See Prof. Ely's French and German Socialisms; Chap. xii. pp. 189-203; Lassalle's Allgemeiner Deutscher Arbeiter Verein. Ferdinand Lassalle and Karl Marx were Jews; and it is conjectured that their ease in comprehending the true theories of the working people eminated from their early training.

[6] McCulloch, Introduction to The Life of Ricardo; London, 1876.

thirty-two hundred years ago, when men were simpler, were suitable enough, condensed into fair English, reads about as follows:

It is compulsory upon every man to stand in awe and obedience before father and mother and to keep the sabbath. Do not turn in favor of idols nor make molten gods for your worship. All sacrifice of a peace offering must be offered of your own free will, and eaten the same day and the next; for if any of it remain until the third, it must be burned as unhallowed and abominable.

When you reap the harvests of your land, leave some in the corners of the field and do not gather the gleanings of the harvest nor glean the vineyards. Leave something for the poor and the stranger.[7] All stealing, false dealing and lying, one to another are forbidden. You must not swear by my name falsely nor profane it. You are forbidden to defraud or rob your neighbor. Pay without delay the wages agreed upon, to those whom you engage to labor for you. Never ill-treat the deaf nor put a stumbling block before the blind. Be careful and discreet in your judgment and your word of honor, treating neighbors with righteous equality. Never go about talebearing among the people, nor stir feuds with neighbors. To hate your brother is forbidden and to prevent him from falling into error you should call his attention to his fault. Abstain from revenges and grudges against the people and love your neighbor as yourself. Cultivate your stock after the natural law of selection. Let the seed of your fields be pure. Let your garments be unmixed; if linen, let them be of pure linen; if wool, let them be all wool.

Then follow many details minutely describing what constitutes crime and what the punishment. Many of the punishments, while probably in very good keeping with an early and semi-barbarous age, appear to us brutal and distasteful in the extreme. The severe punishment of death[8] visited upon all who defiled the peculiar people by mixing their blood with Moloch,[9] has gone far toward preserving the Hebrew stock from admixture with other races of mankind. The purity with which the Jews have

---

[7] *Leviticus.* xxiii. 22.   [8] *Leviticus.* xx. 2. 7.   [9] *Leviticus,* xxi. 14.

thus maintained themselves amid vicissitudes, such as would have swallowed up and annihilated any other family of the human race, is readily pronounced one of the most remarkable phenomena encountered in the study of ethnology. The command is severe against witch, wizzard and spirit-worship.[10] This must be partly accounted for by the fact that the Egyptians, under whose domination the Jews had chafed for 400 years as slaves, were among the most superstitious in their belief in, and worship of all sorts of prestigiation. Charms, incantations, witchcraft and all the sleights of the wand were so popular that the art was for ages interwoven with their religion. However much we may desire to ignore all mention of religion in this history of the ancient lowly, we find this impossible because of the prevalence of priest-power and dictum in political economy. The Hebrews were the only ancients who worshiped one deity;[11] and as that deity is represented to be the very one who dictated the law of Moses, he would naturally be severe against false gods. "I am a jealous God," is an expression often repeated in the bible;[12] and such a one in giving a code of laws for the government of men would scarcely do otherwise than make idolatry a crime. Immodesty also receives a full share of condemnation from the great Hebrew law, which thoroughly defines [13] what constitutes unrefined or immodest actions.

It is thus seen that a lofty spirit of chastity and of moral purity is inculcated into all the Mosaic law. There is nothing in it that binds the Jews to the practice of anything like close community of goods. The law of Moses is not communistical. Competitive methods then as now, were the reigning ones. But the law was mutually protective. The condition of society to-day is toned in a great measure by the practice of the demands of this aged code. Nearly all of the above cited paragraphs are now being obeyed by us; and they act alike, among Jew and

---

[10] *Leviticus*, xx. 6. Witch hanging by our fore-fathers originates here.
[11] By this is meant: one animate, all-powerful being. Ancient *Heliotry* and other Pagan forms, most of which treated the working class with contempt and cruelty as we shall show, paid homage to *inanimate, representative* gods.
[12] *Exodus*, xx. 5. [13] *Leviticus*, xx. 17.

gentile, an effective part in keeping our civilization pure. The command[14] that the people when harvesting their grain and grapes, should not forget those who are less fortunate, but should leave some for them, is a touching rebuke to the niggardly system of these more enlightened times. One remarkable habit, that of buying and selling, owning and profiting upon slaves, even of their own kindred,[15] seems inconsistent and cannot again enter into practice. It also, to our critical understanding, brings into severe reproach and doubt the sacred or divine authorship of the law of Moses. Jesus rectified all this.

Most of the customs of the Hebrews are fixed. The same rules established in Palestine thirty-two hundred years ago are still adhered to. It is true that at that time Judæa was a farming or pastoral country; and that the Jews of to-day, having been separated by defeat and persecution, scattered and distributed to all portions of the world, cannot continue their original pastoral and agricultural vocations and so have become merchants and money-lenders and have assumed the various methods of obtaining a living similarly to other people. It is also true that being thus isolated, having no country, and obliged to exist in the competitive world, under the competitive idea, they act among outsiders competitively.[16] This they do; and they do it thoroughly.

[14]*Leviticus* xix. 9, 10.   [15]*Exodus* xxi. 2—8. Our object in bringing the Jewish question in here, is to arrange the groundwork before bringing forward the great movements of the lowly, enslaved working people, who, as will be seen, had not only their grievance but their distinct *Plans of Salvation* from trouble, which they for ages followed.
[16]See Millman,   *History of the Jews.*

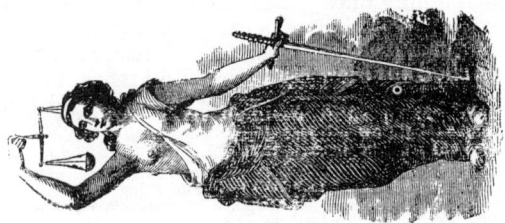

CHAPTER II.

THE INDO-EUROPEANS.

THEIR COMPETITIVE SYSTEM.

RELIGION and Politics of the Indo-Europeans Identical—Reason for Religion mixing with Movements of Labor—The father the Original Slaveholder—His Children the Original Slaves—Both the Law and Religion empowered him to Kill them—Work of Conscience in the Labor Problem.

HISTORY began to register facts and to throw its earliest light on the actions of the human race about the time that slavery began to take its leave. But enough of the slave system always remained to cast its dark shadows upon life. There had, previously to the historic record and ages before the breaking up of slavery, been an immense, an immeasurable period of time through whose trackless swamps humanity had trod; for the weak, uncertain story of a once happy reign of Neptune,[1] we are forced to ignore for want of evidence. When we reflect that there were freedmen or emancipated slaves two thousand years before the beginning of the Christian era, and that consequently the laboring classes have been struggling for four thousand years, writhing out from their slave fet-

---

[1] Plato says (*Laws*, iv. 6, Bekk., L. ed.), that a great while before cities were ever built, as is told, and during the reign of Saturn, there existed a certain extremely happy mode of government to regulate the dwelling of men.....It had all things unrestrained, yielding spontaneously.....It was governed by Dæmons of a diviner, more perfect race. Plutarch (*Numa Pompilius*), also speaks of such a time and states that Numa desired to bring back those happy days to men. Plutarch (*De Definitione Oraculorum* 18,), also says that Saturn slept on an island of the blessed. But it was in ancient Italy, Cf. Dionysius of Halicarnassus, (*Antiquitates Romanæ*, i., 34,). that the mythical Saturn and Janus chained down the god of war and closed the temples against belligerency and want. The conclusion, after all our research is, that the whole story is a myth based upon the well known longings which gave shape to thousands of Utopias and Messiahs.

ters without having yet fully succeeded, we may at least, establish a basis of conjecture as to the time it required for the laboring denizens of the ancient slave system to grow to a conception of manhood and womanhood, sufficient to break their first bonds. Of the purely slave epoch which preceded the art of annals we have little but conjecture. There must have been a comparatively high civilization at the dawn of manumissions, where history and archæology find human society and begin gracefully to transmit to us its deeds. An inconceivable space of time must have intervened. Let us attempt to make history for the laboring classes from conjectural data in order to connect the link binding the known with those dark abysses of the unknown in antiquity.

The supposed original cradle of the Aryan family from which comes the Caucasian or Indo-European type, is Central Asia. Greeks and Romans were Aryan Europeans; Arabs or Ishmaelites, Jews or Hebrews, and Phœnicians belonged to the Semitic family. We have already seen that the Semitic races, especially the Jews, were using a low and very imperfect and unsatisfactory form of the co-operative ideal in place of the Pagan or purely competitive one, as a basis upon which to build their society and their civilization. The Aryans, especially the Greeks and Romans on the contrary, built their society and their civilization upon the extreme competitive idea. The one ever was and is, mutual, interacting, loving, charitable, rigidly reverential and non-destructive; the other fierce, warlike, excessively egoistic, combative and destructive. Both brave, lofty, intelligent, capable, and susceptible of a higher development of physical type and of intellectual culture than any other branches of the human race.[2]

It appears from all the evidences that the first form of society was that of masters and slaves.[3] The extreme

---

[2] Under the ancient idea, religion which governed political as well as private habits, was exclusively based upon man-worship. Zeus or Jupiter was a man god. *Dæmons* or *Lares* were dead men, imagined, all through Pagan times to be still influential for good or evil. Cf. Pausanias, *Desciptio Græciæ*, v. 14. At Olympia the first two prayers were offered at the focal fire, always burning in honor of these dead men and of Zeus.

[3] Granier de Cassagnac, *Histoire des Classes Ouvrières et des Classes Bourgeoises*, Chaps, iii. iv. v.

ORIGIN OF BONDAGE.

lowliness of the laboring man's condition at that remote period can easily be imagined when we consider that all the children of the aristocratic household except the oldest son born of the real wife and legal mother, were totally unrecognized by law. All except this heir, were originally slaves. In fact this was the origin of slavery. The first human law was, long before being written, a law of entailment upon primogeniture. When the patrician or owner of the property, which in those times, mostly consisted of lands, died, the property did not fall to the children or by testament, as is now the case. It fell to the oldest male child. No other person of that household had any claim upon it. The deceased father may have had many other children, but these became subjects to the manor; and frequently they were very numerous.[4]

This eldest son and inheritor was, by usage of that day, obliged to bury his father within the house or court and worship him as a god. The original workingman was not even a citizen.[5] There is no lack of testimony regarding this curious custom which was really the religion and the rule or groundwork upon which stood the ancient competitive regulation of labor. Let us now trace this new family in order to get at the origin and perpetuation of human slavery.

There being in primitive ages no power as now exists, behind this new heir and administrator or despot of the paternity, he easily becomes an absolute lord or monarch. To make this unjust and wonderful civilization appear more comprehensible and home-like, we may assume familiar names. A rich farmer, one who has inherited his property from his father, dies, leaving many children,

---

[4] Fustel de Coulange, *Cité Antique*, c. vii. pp. 76—89 *Droit de Succession*. Granier, *Hist. des Classes Ouvrières*, p. 69: "Ainsi, nous pouvons dire maintenant que nous avons trouvé les premiers esclaves qui furent; c' étaient les enfants." As to the great numbers in families, see *Iliad*, XXIV. v. 495. 6. 7:

Πεντήκοντά μοι ἦσαν, ὁτ' ἤλυθον υἷες Ἀχαιῶν
Ἐννεακαίδεκα μέν μοι ἰῆς ἐκ νηδύος ἦσαν,
Τούς ἄλλους μοι ετικτον ἐνὶ μεγάροισι γυναῖκες.

So also Plutarch, *Theseus*, 3, says that Pallas had 50 children. Gideon had 70, according to Josephus, *Antiquities of the Jews*, Book V. Chapter ix. Apson had 60; Jair 30 children.

[5] Bücher, *Aufstände der unfreien Arbeiter*, S. 11. "Der beste (antike) Staat schliesst die Arbeiter vom Bürgerrechte aus; und wo sie dasselbe erhalten konnten, blieben sie stets eine misachtete und einflusslose Klasse."

boys and girls. There may be several daughters senior to his oldest son. This latter, however, because the first-born male, comes into sole possession of the paternal estate. The girls are of a sympathetic, unsuspecting nature and being also less physically powerful, they make little or no resistance. The boys are young; and being in this tender age are, after a certain amount of struggle, in shape of battles, with words and other weapons, also compelled to yield. This bully moreover to accomplish his purpose, also draws upon the superstition of the unfortunate children and hides the wickedness of his avarice behind the sanctuary of religious rites over their dead father who practiced the same cunning, force and craft before. The bully thus originated the great law of entailment upon primogeniture, and has never once loosened his grip to this day.

To resume our home-drawn, practical illustration of the origin of this ancient law of usurpation, it may be said, that not a penny can possibly fall to one of the many sisters and brothers thus cast out, although they had contributed their labor toward the creation of the estate. He becomes the supreme ruler over the property. By virtue of the arrogant law of primogeniture, ancient and hallowed as the adoration of the vestal fires, this unique successor becomes, without formality, the monarch. But his possessorship is not confined to the ownership of the real estate of the paternity. He also owns the stock and fixtures thereto belonging. Among the rest of the stock and fixtures are the brothers and sisters; both those who are pure, or born of his own mother whose character and chastity, especially in ancient times, were always beyond reproach, and also those more numerous children otherwise born.[6] These all fall to him also, as part of the inheritance! He is monarch absolute.[7] He has become a *pater familias*; and as such, has the power of his father before him. No law exists that can restrict his will.

[6] In ancient days, as shown in note 4, they were often very numerous For the law giving license to concubinage, see Gaius, *Twelve Tables*.
[7] Dionysius of Halcarnassus, *Archæologia Romana*, or *Roman Antiquities*, liber II. cap. 25; *Seven Essays on Ancient Greece*, Oxford. 1882, p. 52; "The state gave parents the power, atrocious and unnatural, to kill them; he—the father—could refuse to preserve and rear his own offspring." See likewise Aristotle, *Politic*, 4.

He cannot liberate his poor slaves;—for it is an assumed episode in prehistoric conditions that we are describing; it antedates the era of manumissions, although the same wrongs existed long afterwards. But he can punish his own slaves—his brother, sister or his child—with death. He can sell them. He can whip them and impose upon them the most cruel of tortures. Tiger or lamb is his option.

His religion is as aristocratical, as brutal and exclusive as his economic and social policy. Unlike the mild democracy infused into the worship of present civilizations, his religion cannot tolerate even the thought that all may do homage at a common shrine or adore a common Father. To allow this would be to cancel the distinction between master and slave.[8] The father of this autocrat, buried under the hearthstone, has himself become the only god whom this man may worship. Thus every nerve is active in perpetuating, glorifying and rendering aristocratic and lordly the prestige of his house.[9] The sacred altar is his father's grave over which is kept a fire that is never allowed to be extinguished.[10] His own father thus becomes his tutelary god and guardian, watching, like a veritable spook, with a jealous eye over his interests. Should this sacred fire be extinguished, the accident is punished with an ignominious death.[11] This parent-god, like the man when walking on this earth, is believed to be subject to hunger and thirst. He must consequently be fed with actual food; with bread and wine, butter, honey and the purest delicacies of the table. If this be neglected, the propitious smiles and favors which

---

[8] Fustel de Coulanges, *Cité Antique*, chap. iv. p. 33. Here this student explains the Pagan mode of sacrifice, including the whimsical old superstition of the *Lares*, or the remains of said parent after burial, to which this living heir gave offerings of food, such as milk, clarified butter, wine, ect.

[9] In Greek, this altar was called Βωμός and Ἑστία; in Latin, *Ara, Focus*—the focus of all thoughts, prayer, moral concern; the shrine.

[10] This statement is not absolutely exact: for the fires were, on certain rare occasions, renovated. See *Fustel, Cité Antique*, p. 23, Feu sacré.

[11] Centuries afterwards, when there had become many such aristocratic houses, such masters as were friendly with each other, found it necessary for mutual protection largely from the wrath of these very outcasts, to form a city of aristocratic houses. A central city-altar or focus was adopted, a central city-fire kindled and a *Vigil* or maiden watcher was stationed, to keep its fires glowing forever. Punishment of a most horrible death was inflicted upon her for letting these sacred fires die out.

prayer invokes, are turned, by the slighted and angry ghost against the perpetrators of the negligence The law of agnation or descent in the male line, rules severely in this family; and consequently the female portions of it are the especial objects of the master's power. The lord himself being supreme, may commit acts of libertinism such as would consign others to the punishment of death. Should his wife, the *mater familias*, vary from the rules of family regularity, it would place in doubt the descent of the paternity. It would cause it to become a question whether her first-born son, the inheritor, were really his own and of the pure blood—the agnate. Should the deception be so veiled as to escape the master's knowledge, there yet remains a still more terrible source of disclosure. The buried gods themselves, omnipotent and omniscient, jealous and disturbed, feeling the dignity of their noble line defiled,[12] their august prerogatives encroached upon by a pretender who might in turn at death usurp the beatitudes of the *penates*[13] and the holy altar, are aroused. Conscience in the guilty mother becomes too galling to permit of life's longer endurance and death must be the consequence after the confession, and the error rectified by the destruction of the intruder. Here is the key to that extraordinary tenacity of ancient ladies in wedlock with the noble or *gens* families, to virtue.[14] The *Lares*, or redoubtable ghosts, are, as we now begin to understand, charged with the office of chastizing such criminals ; also of watching all the thoughts, words and deeds going on in the sacred penetralia—*penates*—of the living lord's household. So egotistical and selfish is this religious culture that none but the family can pray at that altar and no one can be prayed for except members who have been in high standing. A thing so degraded as a being compelled to subsist by labor has no place there, no family, no shrine. Family initiation made it worse.

But we have only entered upon the description of this despot. His most revolting attributes are yet to be put into history. All the creatures of his household, with

[12] From this may be traced the origin of blood-distinctions still boasted of and tenaciously cultivated ; in dynasties, as divine right ; in families, as prestige. The horror against this sin was inexpressible ; and a liason with one of the outcasts rendered the crime trebly henjons.
[13] See Livy's *Lay of Lucretia*.   [14] Plutarch, *Quæstiones Romanæ*, 51.

the exception of the noble mother and her first-born male child, are slaves.[15] They may be, as we have said, brothers and sisters, or even children born to amorous coercion[16] of this thus privileged despot; yet they have no claim to anything but his sympathies. Having no legalized rights they are menials; left without education they become sycophantic and unmanly. Their food is coarse. Only the lord and lady of the house are entitled to wheat bread. They are glad to get peas and second-rate bread.[17] Should too many infants be born, a council is called and it is deliberated whether the little innocents shall be saved or killed.[18] The children being slaves, are not supposed to be supplied with a thing so dignifying as a soul.[19] The most abject superstition reigns. For a slave or a stranger to enter the apartments of this lord, is an offense, impious and unpardonable. The lord's own parents and ancestors before them for generations back, are buried under this enclosure soul and body; and their jealous *manes* or ghosts,[20] are believed to be omnipresent and on guard, with power to repel or punish the sacrilege. The manor house is situated within the holy court. The common slaves and the children constituting the true laboring element, are taught the most extreme reverence. Should they violate any of the rigorous rules they are subject to punishment; if the lord of the manor wills it, with death. Thus deep superstition, hard, unpaid labor, hard fare and degradation are enforced by the cunning wiles of priestcraft; for love of profits from labor seems to originate or urge ancient priest-power. This superstition is the more necessarily rigorous, since lack of faith is known to be dangerous, leading to sedition and rebellion.

---

[15] Fustel de Coulanges, *Cité Antique*, I. c. 1.-iv. *Antiques Croyances*. From these phenomena of the ancient family may be traced the origin of the belief in ghosts, spooks, spectres, haunted abodes etc.; *idem*, pp. 127-30.
[16] Plutarch, *Solon*, xiii. [17] Horace, *Epistolæ*, lib. II. *Epist*. 1. v. 123: "Vivit siliquis et pane secundo" Poor fare for labor continued late. Of course, where much harmony and love existed the despot could be generous.
[18] This practice held good among the Dorians even after Greeks began to acquire the art of making historical records. See Plutarch, *Lycurgus*, xvi.
[19] Homer, *Odyssey*, lib. XVII. The passage here alluded to refers to a comparatively enlightened period. As late as Plato, when emancipations and resistance had created a middle class, it was doubted whether working-people had all of the attributes recognized in true members of the human family. Cf. Plato, *Rep*. vi. 9; lxxi. *Laws*, vi; Homer, *Odyssey*, xvii. 332. Plato wanted slaves and believed in the inferiority of all laborers
[20] Cicero, *Pro Domo*; *Tusculanarum Disputationum Libri*, I. 16: "Sub terra censet ant reliquiam vitam agi mortuorum." Euri¡1des, *Alcestis*, 168; *Hecuba*.

The lord of the estate permits of no social or religious mixtures with other people or other estates. There are no tenants, no neighbors, and consequently few sociabilities. Egoism is so severe that little of the kind can be tolerated. It is master and slave; no intermediaries. Communities are unknown. Promiscuity which makes the village,[21] the community, the social gathering, the free sports of children and general merriment are interdicted by this profound solemnity based upon an adoration of, and implicit obedience in one central ruler; a man who is the inheritor; who, by virtue of this inheritance giving him power, and of this egoism giving him will, assumes, as through the countless ages his ancestors assumed, to be the sole owner in life, and the immortal to be worshiped, caressed, entreated, propitiated, glorified, after death ![22]

We have thus described, as if actually existing among us at present, a scene whose stage was once this earth;[22] whose unhappy actors were workingmen and women and whose managers were then as now, the capitalists; a scene which mankind, grace to an eternal resistance, in turmoils, servile wars, and innumerable social communes, has largely outgrown. It is a scene which no civilized society could at present tolerate. Yet it was the almost all-prevailing one among mankind of the distant past in Greece and Italy.

Lordship, therefore, was the very first condition in the establishment of society; slavery its antithesis, the second. Of the middle class occupying the great gap widely separating the lord from the slave there was none.

---

[21] The ancient house was situated within the sacred enclosure. This enclosure was divided, among the Greeks, into two parts; the first being the court. The house was in the second part. The sacred *focus* was placed near the center of the enclosure. It was consequently at the foot of the court, near the entrance of the house. The Romans had it differently, though essentially the same. The *focus* remained, as in Greece, in the center of the enclosure, but the buildings were placed around it leaving an inner court; the walls of the houses rising around it on all sides. The Greeks used to say that religion taught them how to build houses. Fustel de Coulanges, *Cité Antique*, pp. 62—85.

[22] In Greek the ἑστία δέσποινα, in Latin the *Lar familiaris*, were key-words of the ancient pagan family. Etymologically this is the origin of the term *despot*.

[23] We have not space to make copious quotations from the numerous authors whose descriptions and hints we have ransacked in search of the proof of this condition of ancient affairs; but recommend the doubtful to the following commentators and original writers: Granier de Cassagnac, *Histoire des Classes Ouvrières &c. Chapters* iii. iv. v. De Coulanges, *Cité Antique, passim;* to the *poems* of Homer; to almost any of the voluminous works of Cicero; to the *Orations* of Demosthenes; to Orelli's *Inscriptionum Collectio;* to Böckh's *Corpus Inscriptionum Græcarum;* to Euripides, *Alcestis* and especially *Hecuba, passim;* to Plato's *Creation, Protag.* 30-4, *Theæt.* 30-2, *Rep.* 21; to Pausanias, *Descriptio Græciæ;* to Macrobius, *Somnium Scipionis & Saturnaliorum Libri* and many others.

That came later. For fully six thousand years it has been growing more and more numerous until in the nineteenth century it may be said to have almost filled the great cavity and is now pressing in all directions to force the extinction of both those aged originals.

Theoretically, this middle or intermediary class betwixt lord and menial, owner and outcast, immortal and perishable, is perfect; occupying the ambrosial vales of Utopia where men are no longer struggling for existence against despotism, ignorance and death. In theory we should suppose it an altruistic state in which men looking upward to wisdom and mutual love, and backward to past ignorance and competitive greed and hatreds, would erect their society and their government upon a plan wherein neither lords nor menials could have law or foothold. Such would be the revolution realized—the revolution that began with manumissions. But practically—although many are dreaming of this ultimatum—we are far from it. Lords still exist though with milder domination and slaves yet remain though on a higher plain.

M. de Laveleye informs us that communities held lands in common for the people in times past[24] and cites an abundance of instances in proof; but while this may all be true, it is none the less true that the original condition was that of masters and slaves. Particularly was this the case with the people from whose records we extract these data —the Aryan race. It is the perfectly natural condition, explainable in the theory of development. In the Aryan, especially its Indo-European type, we see the original theory of development verified; and it comes to us from prehistoric data which philology, archæology and reason harmoniously combine to verify. What would man, primitively a wild animal, naturally do? Would he not be just like all animals? It wants only the observation of an hour to note that a group of barnyard fowls, soon after being put into a yard begin fighting for mastery or lordship; and this conflict will not stop until the strongest, cleverest chanticleer has mastered every adversary. This also

---

[24] De Laveleye, *Primitve Property*, pp. 137. In attempting to prove these notions about primitive property, this author is confronted at the outset, with the fact that he is seeking to rebut the principle of development; his village communities are a *late*, not a *"primitive"* condition.

must be said of a herd of cattle grazing on a common. The strongest steer, after a full test of its muscular forces, becomes master of the flock and remains so. With perfect truth it might be further remarked that should no individual of the herd be of the male gender, the contest for mastery will be between the heifers; thus seeming to prove the principle of the survival of the fittest without any reference to the instinct of perpetuation of species. Even plants, in their struggle for existence are constantly in the competitive field, warring with each other—the tares rooting out the wheat—until the hand of the reasoning cultivator lays low the obnoxious weeds. Thus it is shown that the principle of individual ascendency with its acknowledgement, is the original and natural one. It is the *quiritare dominium*. The law of natural selections and survival of the fittest applies without the aid of reason. Naturalists who have lavished great care and honest pains in search of proof of this philosophy in plants, animals and men,[25] have scarcely brought their investigations to bear upon that new, almost supernal power of reason, which some admit to have come later, as a result of evolution.

If we are allowed to tread the *penetralia* of this philosophy with the eye and ear of a critic we shall find in the law of natural selections the bed rock of brute competition. While beholding this with the conviction of its truth and forced to admit it as the fiat of growth, we shall see that it rests upon the toppling trestles of brute force. We shall find that the superstructure resting upon these abutments is time-worn and rotten. Its spans are becoming unsafe; its planking hoof-worn; its stringers sway with the winds of newer things and we find ourselves dizzy peering into the angry foam of progress below. As long as there are only masters and slaves the strongest brutes may survive; but when the new idea of manumission arrived which was forced upon the masters by the growth of population, the survival of the fittest changed hands. If we accept the doctrine of natural

---

[25] We here incorrectly place man above animals in deference to the egoism he has not outgrown. Especially is man to be considered and classed among animals under the philosophy of the fittest, since this very survival is mostly the result of the competitive struggle, akin to brute force and antedating the milder forces of reason.

selection based upon brute force we accept the survival of the fittest as its corollary. So long as the doctrine is so based it remains undeniably true. Reason is not there.

But with the advent of reason there came also sympathy, civilization, enlightenment; and these have already so filled the world with mutual or altruistic sentiment that the working classes of both Europe and America are now combining with a determination to drive from the world the whole brute force upon which the old theory is based. They will not longer hear to the competitive principle which holds up the shrewdest and strongest as fittest to survive. They demand the extinction of competitory force and insist upon equal opportunities for co-operation such as will result in the survival of all. They are thus ushering in the era of reason. In disenthralling their species from the competitive system of the isolated individual and establishing them on the co-operative or altruistic system they procure the revolution. They usher in the era of the survival of all and banish from the world the culture of darlings, the reign of partiality, the prestige of masters and the servility of slaves. But as force lies at the bottom of the law of natural selections and the survival of the fittest, so reason, its moral antithesis, must be the bottom rock upon which the new mutualism is founded.

We cannot leave this theoretical dissertation without some reflections upon the ghastly immorality and the return to insatiate selfishness which this new philosophy of the survival of the fittest inculcates; and must submit that it not only logically inculcates an arid dreariness of words, but has already produced and is producing withering and demoralizing effects. We shall submit that the religion of Jesus, planted by a manual laborer and forming the basis of hope upon which stands the great labor movement of our own time has been severely attacked, stamped as a calamity and trodden under foot, notwithstanding the fact that this plan of faith has been the power that openly struck the first well organized blow at the system of masters and slaves and boldly championed it as a principle; and in essence it has never since shrunk from its prodigious task toward realizing the much contested doctrine of human equality.

Viewed from a standpoint of mere comparative strength of organized muscle and brain, or of the low cunning and prowess which wrench from the weak and unwary what they do not contribute to produce, this theory of survival is undeniably logical. But these forces are the old, original ones and strictly belong to a period prior to the advent of a society enlightened and refined by reason. They are animal and are of the ages of bullies and of clubs. Why we confront such theorists is that this philosophy does not keep march with the very power that gives them insight into it—reason. The original state was egotistical, with brutal force—forcible possession. The next was arbitration, discussion, conciliation—all the struggles of reason. The former occupied an immense, unmeasured period of time, the latter has also had its vista of tedious, unhappy ages; for since the first glimmerings of history and archæology it has numbered between four and five thousand years and its millennium is still far away. It is the transition period; the passage from pure brute force and labor ordered by masters and performed by slaves with survival of the fittest, to the pure era of reason, mutual love and mutual care, with the survival of all. Such is the revolution.

Whoever, therefore, at this enlightened day, forgetting his reason, the very weapon he wields with which to grasp his inspirations, allows this aged original, because it is yet true of the beast or the plant, to usurp the domain of reason self-won in the struggle of ages,[26] returns to the dogma that because the survival of the fittest has been true of snarling beasts, of the plants and of the club-and-weapon age of men, it is also true of men in a state of reason and refinement, is going backward dragging reason with him into the caves of the troglodyte.

Let us glance at the moral effect upon the mind, of persons in search of wealth and other means of happiness natural to our lot in the competitive world. A student of evolution is constrained by perusing the pages of Lucre-

---

[26] Mr. Darwin, a thoughtful and thoroughly careful writer refrained from pushing his argument on this subject farther than it applies to energy without reason. A careful student of Darwin will perceive that he always uses the lower order of life as proof; such as plants, birds, fishes, and the other animals. He clings to this, not venturing into the domain of the reasoning power, which is alone capable to grasp the labor problem.

tius, Vogt, Spencer, Darwin and others, to view man as a creature without an immortal soul. Through the doctrine of development as explained by Darwin, men are taught to understand this perishability merely as a logical corollary of the premise itself." The theory carries with it the irrepressible deduction that if man has an immortal soul he has, himself, been the maker of it. The theory from the first, assumes that he is a creature grown from a long line of consequents, each an effect of causes natural to this world. This is evolution. It holds that motion and heat acting upon the material spread out upon this earth will of themselves, generate life; and that from cells or matrices of slime it calls protoplasm—the assumed earliest forms of life—come shape, growth and variety, some of which in time have reached as high a development as reasoning men. Nor are these ideas confined to, or the work of, the benighted and superstitious. They are gaining ground among the most thoroughly respectable and learned; so much so that it is already dangerous for the followers of the old belief upheld by Plato and Moses, to criticize or compare arguments against the ponderous weight and increasing multiplicity of proof in its support. So irrefutable is the evidence which our indefatigable diggers in science have accumlated, that from the timorous lispings of a few years ago it has become a creed for the army of science; and is claimed by naturalists, by comparative philologists and historiographers, by archæologists and others in the field of ethnical research, to be the key of the new discovery.

What then can science do for the immortal soul ? Man, certainly, away back in that night of time of which we are going to write a history, while yet an animal and brute, a *homo troglodyticus*, not yet knowing how to build a fire or hardly to wield a club, could not have possessed so noble and highly developed a thing as an immortal soul! Or if we can conceive this to be possible, what shall we think of him during the still earlier cycles of his existence in forms yet cruder and more remote ? Further than this

2: In making these reflections we do not set up a disclaimer against the theory of development. The object is to show the pernicious effect upon the mind of masses, should this theory become universally acknowledged, and taught, *before* the competitive system is superseded by the co-operative or socialistic.

we may in our play of fancy measure him at the dawn of his development of reason, which is a faculty higher but less unerring than instinct. Reason is a gift which must be guided by social laws. Not having these, man must have been a maniac; either thus, or he preserved enough of instinct to guide reason. The reason of a madman turns to cunning.[28] Cunning, we are told, is the weapon this ferocious, selfish, competing, primeval being first used to work his title clear to the realms of immortality!

Thus in reading rare records of the ancient lowly we cannot be too thoughtful or too careful when contemplating the subject of immortality. Though old in life's ephemeral span, the human race is still in the dawn of its day; and the sun has yet to rise higher and illume many a still dark chasm of our belief. The great aphorism of Lucretius:

"Proinde licet quotvis viven to condere sæcla:
Mors æterna tamen nilo minus illa manebit," [29]

though it has been parried and fought in darkness, is like that of Proudhon—"La propriété c'est le vol," still respectable; and so long as our standard cyclopedias speak of the *Rerum Natura* of Lucretius as the "greatest of didactic poems"[30] even now, when the grand sun of man's morning of life has lit up all the grottoes but that of fate and rendered radiant many a dark belief, just so long is it wisest in us to withdraw cavil, polemic and concern from a post mortem future and throw our whole religion into practical doings for the improvement of ourselves upon the mortal stage. But most especially are these words wise counsel to all engaged in a study of the labor problem.

Such is this wonderful man, says the theorist, developed from a protoplasm of slimy earth. Then up to this stage he was without a soul—an animal. He further developed to the stage of reason—mind. Cunning must then have secured for him the boon of an immortal soul; a thing

---

[28] Plato, *Laws*, vii. 14. "The boy, without being fitted by education, becomes crafty and cunning and of all wild beasts the most insolent." Plato knew the fierce nature of men and his seventh book of laws is a thoughtful code of precepts for equalizing habits among the people, and punishing with means in use for doing so. Plato even doubts the possibility of a soul in such wild creatures.
[29] Lucretius, *De Rerum Natura*, lib. III. 1088-9.
[30] *American Cyclopædia*, vol. X. p. 717, ed. of 1867.

which most people agree in believing that the reasonless animals do not possess!

This sort of speculation may appear quite innocent, even popular; for such is the freedom of thought in these days that men delight in catching at the gossamers of skepticism. Where the danger to the moral sense arises on this new philosophy, is in the fact that the revolution is not yet realized. The world is still in its competitive stage. Man is still combating with his blind egoism in the struggle for existence, It is not altruism or mutual love and care that governs his career. He is yet fighting against odds for survival; and if his fitness to win the means of life prove insufficient he does not survive, but perishes. Knowing this, he is too ready to apply his reason in the direction of selfishly actuated cunning, and thus wring out a living recklessly. One thing however, has always barred him from the exercise of dishonest cunning. It is *conscience*. From the earliest data we find man building upon conscience as the foundation of ethics. As we have shown, it began with the mother's virtue. True, it was absurdly imaginative, figuring the rage of the *lar familiaris* in case that weird omnipotent was offended by an evil deed of the living. Thus to commit an evil deed used to cause conscience to fill the imaginations of men with horrid appearances rising from the grave. Goblins and spectres of a thousand shapes. Elfins and haunting terrors appeared. Conscience was thus the origin of ghosts. Conscience, even under the most aristocratic and tyrannical religion, held base actions in check. Under the prevailing religions of the world conscience at this day holds evil doing in check. Ethics is now, as in ancient times, based upon conscience. All laws are largely the outcome of it. It is the inner counselor of outward actions and conscience of the individual must never give up its scepter so long as the competitive, egotistical state dominates. When the revolution has been accomplished, when society shall have arranged the getting of the means of life on the mutual or co-operative plan, when it shall no longer be the survival of the fittest but the survival of all, when it no longer becomes necessary to fight in the cruel, dreary old field of competition and the struggle for existence ceases, then we may find some vague grounds for imagining ourselves no longer compelled to apply the check of conscience; since wrong doing will have lost its incentive.

But now, in the height of the great competitive struggle when working people, goaded at the sight of their own labor products falling into the rapacious hands of monopolies, are again on the rally and are forming the most compact and extensive organizations that have yet existed; just at this moment when the restraining counsels of conscience are most needed to check and withhold what else may become mobocracy, with results more furious and sanguinary than the deeds of Eunus and Cleon or of Spartacus and Crixius which we are going to relate, and at the very moment the moral world seems riven and quails before the swelling legions of aggrieved labor organizing in the struggle for existence with the multifold weapons of an advanced enlightenment at their command, what do we see?

A new thing in the world. A stranger in form of a *philosophy* which denies the immortality of the soul. A codex which seeks its precedents back of religion or law, beckoning into the world a totally new scheme of dialectics. In denying the old belief in immortality it stamps the ancient conscience;[31] for what further use has ethics or morality for conscience, after the cherished hope of earning some longed-for compensation in the hereafter, has been lost?

The only conscience left to man would be that based on cunning! This invites him back to the law of Lycurgus, which made stealing a virtue but being caught, a crime. Conscience the foundation rock of religion, ancient and modern, is ground to powder by this new giant philosophy[32] whose arguments seem fortified by the chemist, the archæologist, the comparative philologist, the palæontologist, the geologist and all naturalists now devoting themselves to labors which are to prepare for a study of ethni-

---

[31] We refer mostly to that moral side of conscience which has hitherto so powerfully actuated and restrained men by force of belief in awards and punishments.

[32] Arnobius was in great doubt on the question of immortality. Lucretius, author of the celebrated didactic poem on nature, believed that the soul perishes with the body. Aristotle, now known as the greatest of teachers, could never promise anything to those inquiring of him on the problem of immortality. Darwin was equally silent on the subject.

cal science. The boldest of these claim, as we have shown, that when in the long course of evolution, man, then a brute but with a stature more erect and a cranial organism more capacious than other creatures with which the forest teemed, began to experience the first scintillations of reason, he exercised this new and growing gift for his own advantage and to secure his own personal survival; sacrificing all others for himself through prowess and strategem or cunning. Conscience came later and established ethics which has developed society, law and order and kept him somewhat restrained. Religion is the handmaid of conscience and both groped together up to the present time inseparable—neither able to exist without the other.

Thus the new philosophy finds man. Religion rests upon assumed immortality; conscience upon religion. The philosophy, by proving that belief in immortality is an illusion, that the soul is an etherial delusion, that with the decease of body comes our eternal quietus, proves also that there is no religion. The great bulwark of humanity, moral law, order, hope, restraint, is annihilated at one stroke. Conscience, resting upon religion,[33] is also shattered with it, and man goes back to his primeval cunning and brutal instincts.

Now, in coloring our description of the revolution in a history of the lowly, let us select an average workingman who has been converted to the new philosophy as thousands are—and picture the effect upon him as an agitator of the labor question.

Belief in the doctrine of development is belief either that man is without an immortal spirit or that through his own genius and cunning he has evolved or developed one out of his original beasthood, independently of an almighty power. The latter is not even pretended. Consequently immortality is denied. The belief also stamps out religious conscience; leaving in him the consciousness that, as there is no responsibility before God—there being none except insentient law which regulates the universe, the only thing to consider before the commission

[33] Conscience resting on punishments and rewards for actions in the physical world, as effects of causes, is not here taken into consideration.

of a deed, is *caution, for safety's sake;* first that the act may not recoil upon himself, and second, that he be not caught in it and discovered. These are affairs of cold reason. Concience with its compunctious concomitants, is ruled out of the affair; and rigid experimental knowledge, aptitude, tact, adaptiveness take its place. No matter how horrible the work to be undertaken, he is totally absolved from danger of punishment if cunning enough to elude the natural and the statute laws and succeed. With cold reason and in cold blood he fearlessly undertakes the deed, knowing that to succeed is to survive his victim and be happy.

Lions, dogs, wolves, hyenas, vultures are constantly doing this for they are in the world of competition and have no conscience ; and he is not a whit above them morally. Had he the restraint of religious conscience in the same field of competition, he would be lifted by it above these brutes. It teaches him the survival of the fittest and inflates his egotism with presumption that he is superior to his victim. It thus unhinges the little enlightenment which mutual co-operation and social interaction have by great agonies of effort and with the labors of conscience, sympathy and belief in immortality, brought into the world. Does it indeed, threaten our civilization ?

One will say this shocking description may apply to the workingman; but we think it too often applies practically to the most educated. It especially applies to them; for such revolting immorality seldom penetrates the ranks of laborers who from remote ages of the past have been religiously inclined and rather prejudiced in favor of religion. No tale of ancient labor can ignore its religion.

But admitting the workingman and agitator to have become a convert to this philosophy, we still have the same revolting consequences. Such consequences are now constantly transpiring. The present century is producing some reformers who are believers in the doctrine of development and are scoffers of religion. Few of them expect to live beyond their grave. Many have no conscience regarding a future punishment, and are two honest in their earnestness when they conspire against great wrongs and argue to destroy this civilization. Any person shielded from restraints of conscience by a logic which poses on the dignity and grandeur of science, may guard himself and his legions from detection by buckling on the life-preserver of cold reason, and boxing himself into some sequestered laboratory and with recondite presumption, construct infernal machines. He may sally out with these and if there come conflicts between him and unjust jurisprudence or even tornadoes of destruction, it is but the recoil of a philosophy that is driving men's conscience from the earth.

This lack of conscience is seen in the brutal treatment of poor slaves by Damophilus to which we devote a long chapter of this book. It is a want of feeling that marks the social ages of the past and rightly does not belong to modern days.

It were difficult to describe the terrible depression of moral sentiments to which a man naturally sinks under this doctrine, if really convinced by it that his own cunning, aptitude and ambidexterity are legitimate forces upon which he must depend for success and survival. Freed from the fear of punishment beyond this life, he finds that the conscience within his breast has fled. There is no everliving, responsible soul and consequently no responsibility. He finds himself completely absolved from any danger except that of failing in the attempt. He depends entirely upon adroitness or cunning. Egotism lends him faith in this; for men are enterprising and glad to undertake innocent adventures and in this philosophy every act is innocent which does not recoil upon its author. Thus stimulated and shielded he goes back to brigandage and hardened to fratricide, is willing to do devil work of whatever manner that promises to gratify greed, whim or caprice, in cajoling the transient hour. In the competitive struggle for existence, it is true, every one has the same chances but the survival falls to him who possesses the most of force, tact and cunning. Reason has not yet changed the moral aspects of things from this fighting, competitive state, to the mutually co-operative condition wherein all harmoniously agree to care for each other as the best means of caring for themselves. This great epoch is fast coming. Until its arrival men are in the competitive, transitionary state whose **progress depends** upon every possible advantage known in civilization; and one of the most powerful agents for transforming such into noble, sympathetic beings, and quickening them into the sweet emotions of love and care, is and always has been conscience. When the time arrives that reason shall have become wise, shall have massed its wayward individualism into collective solidarity, pruned off its egotism, dressed itself in robes of charity and mutual love, outgrown its benighted gropings and **adapted itself to a seat in the Christian temple of equality, then there will be time for further and more scientifically investigating the crowning problem of immortality.**

SYMBOLS OF THE ANCIENT FARM.

From an Inscription at Ravenna; age of Caesar.

CHAPTER III.

LOST MSS. ARCHÆOLOGY

TRUE HISTORY OF LABOR FOUND ONLY IN INSCRIPTIONS AND MUTILATED ANNALS.

PROTOTYPES OF Industrial Life to be found in the Aryan and Semitic Branches—Era of Slavery—Dawn of Manumission—Patriarchal Form too advanced a Type of Government possible to primitive Man—Religious Superstition fatal to Independent Labor—Labor, Government and Religion indissolubly mixed—Concupiscence, Acquisitiveness and Irascibility a Consequence of the archaic Bully or Boss, with unlimited Powers—Right of the ancient Father to enslave, sell, torture or kill his Children—Abundant Proofs quoted—Origin of the greater and more humane Impulses—Sympathy beyond mere Self-preservation, the Result of Education—Education originated from Discussion—Discussion the Result of Grievances against the Outcast Work-people—Too rapid Increase of their Numbers notwithstanding the Sufferings—Means Organized by Owners for decimating them by Murder—Ample proof—The great Amphyctyonic League—Glimpses of a once sullen Combination of the Desperate Slaves—Incipient Organization of the Nobles.

THE history of the lowly classes of ancient society must begin with manumissions,[1] although slave labor seems the most ancient. There have come to us very few traces or accounts of the slaves of high antiquity. Except some relics which have been found in caves, some hieroglyphs carved not perhaps by themselves but by masters portraying their low condition,[2] we have no landmarks to guide

[1] Granier de Cassagnac, *Hist. des Classes Ouvrières*, Chap. v.
[2] The typical strikes and uprisings of slaves do not come to us in their dreaded form except through vague, uncertain evidence, until about 600 years before Christ. See chapters on Strikes and Uprisings; *infra*.

our groping inquiry through the long night of time which lasted till the dawn of manumissions. Unlike the African slaves of modern times who were the property of a class of masters not of their own race or kindred, the ancient slaves were, in race and consanguinity, the equals of their masters; and there can be little doubt that the causes of their emancipation were in many instances, their own resistance to slavery. At present the laboring classes of the same races we are describing—the Semitic and Indo-European—are organizing in immense numbers and with skill to resist the forces which modern wage servitude inflicts; and it is therefore very similar to the great struggle humanity passed through in ancient times, to resist the oppressive system under which nearly all were born. The difference between the two struggles however, lies in the fact that the ancient one had to deal with the lowest, most debased and cruel species of subjugation which the ancient religion stamped into its tenets. Both these great struggles are of long duration. When the first was partly won Christianity came with its doctrine of equality³ and brought the struggle into the open world. It went hand in hand with the emancipation movement until chattel slavery and its vast, aged system may now be pronounced extinct throughout the civilized world. The struggle has continued; but from emancipating chattel slavery it has shifted to the enfranchisement of competitive labor.

Notwithstanding the profound learning and research devoted by M. de Laveleye⁴ in proof that the primitive condition of mankind was of patriarchal form, we find that the great slave system always prevailed among the Aryans from whom we are the immediate descendants; and indeed he sets out⁵ with a confession at least that the early Greeks and Romans never had any institutions of the communal or patriarchal nature. Prof. Denis Fustel de Coulanges makes

---

³ Granier, *Hist. des Clasess Ouvrières*, pp. 392-4; Laveleye, *Primitive Property*. Introduc. to 1st ed., pp. xxvi., xxvii. xxx., **xxxi.** Here M. de Laveleye again admits slavery to have been earlier than communism.
⁴ *Primitive Property*, Eng. trans., pp. 7-25, chap. ii.
⁵ *Idem*, p. 6. "From the earliest times the Greeks and Romans recognized private property as applied to the soil and traces of ancient tribal community were already so indistinct as not to be discoverable without careful study." M. de Laveleye might better have said such traces are not discoverable at all; and indeed, the most of the instances he cites are of a comparatively recent era, the probable development of resistance, thousand of years after the manumission of slaves had set in as a result of their strikes and uprisings, of which we get clues.

no hesitation in saying that the Aryan religion, as already described, made the first born son, by the law of entail, the owner of his own children who thus became slaves.[6] References to this old custom are very numerous in the ancient writings.[7] Under Lycurgus[8] the Spartans tried the system of communal proprietorship from the year 825 to 371 B. C. Although every deference was paid to the tenets of the Pagan religion that this celebrated code of laws established by the great lawgiver should not interfere with worship, yet worship itself being interwoven with property was seriously disturbed; because to divide among the people, the rabble, the profane, that which fell to the god who slept under the sacred hearth, or to his living son, seemed to be a sacrilege too blasphemous to endure. The scheme fell to naught. The probable fact is, that the ancient *paterfamilias*, perceiving himself robbed of his paternity, united with other patricians in similar trouble and succeeded in working the overthrow of the innovation. We propose to establish that these great innovations, like the laws of Lycurgus and many similar attempts at reform, the detailed causes of whose mighty commotions sometimes shook Rome and Greece like the eruption of a volcano, were often caused by the multitudes of secret trades and other social organizations existing in those ancient days

Historians seldom mention them. The reason for this is quite clear. This disturbing element was made up of the outcasts of society. How did it come about that there were such outcasts? The answer to this involves a detour of discovery into phenomana of evolution. Of a family of say thirty persons—there exists abundance of evidence that there were often thirty and more persons born to one patrician or lord [9]—there is but a single owner or director, the first-born son. The other children and servants by purchase or otherwise, are slaves. It was a crime to leave the paternal estate. They might be clubbed to death for dis-

[6] *La Cité Antique;*   *Leviticus,* ii. 4.
[7] Plato, *Minos,* also Servius *In Æneid,* v. 84, vi. 152.
[8] Roscher, *Histoire de l' Économie Politique,* French tr. Paris, p. 192. "He adopted a common property; education in common, eating in common, stealing authorized, commerce interdicted, precious metals proscribed, land divided equally among the citizens etc."
[9] Granier de Cassagnac, *Hist. des Classes Ouvrières,* p. 70

satisfaction with their lot but they must not leave or desert it. That entailed certain death. In extraordinary circumstances they actually did leave the bondage of the paternal estate and become wanderers or nomads. This was the probable origin of the second estate. We mean by this the freedman. Whether they obtained their freedom by revolt and bloodshed, by running away from their masters, or by emancipation as per agreement, makes little difference. In the Asiatic races of later times mentioned by Le Play,[10] they seem to have never relinquished their allegiance to some lord, patriarch or ruler. By a tenacity of habit to which we shall refer, the very most ancient customs thus sometimes come down to us. The power of human habit is astonishing. There linger to this day, in the religion worshiped by the most enlightened of mankind, many rites and forms common in remote antiquity; for although the tenets and the sentiment are no longer the same, the old rites befit themselves to the new ideas.

Desertion from this bondage is known to have been a very risky affair; because the deserter or runaway slave had not only the perils of the act of desertion to run but he also forfeited his right and title to the small hope of bliss accorded him by the gods after death. Even at emancipation the right of worship ceased,[11] and a new altar had to be erected. This was in case of marriage of a daughter when no one was injured or offended. But a deserter was treated with terrible malignity both by the father or owner and by the injured deity whose relationship in pedigree or consanguinity he severed, desecrated, disgraced by the blasphemous act. They had curious opinions on death; and religion to those ancient working people, was a part of life.[12] The fear of not being buried with the right of sepulture was greater than the fear of death itself.[13] Although comparatively no consequence was attached to a slave, yet the slave himself being by lineage and by entailment a chattel, evidently had some right to sepulture. Of what kind

---

[10] Le Play, *Organization of Labor*, chap. i. §. 9, Eng. trans., assures us that among the nomads, the direct descendants of one father generally remained grouped together. They lived under the absolute authority of the head of the family, in a system of community. Some of them are living in this method still.
[11] Fustel de Coulanges, *Cité Antique*, chap. iii.
[12] *Idem.* chap. i. p. 12 "L'opinion première des antiques générations fut que l'être humain vivait dans le tombeau ; que l' âme ne se separait pas du corps et qu' elle restait fixée á cette partie du sol où les ossements étaient enterrés."

it is difficult to determine,[14] because historians who recorded military deeds and legal transactions which in later days were considered work for noblemen, were themselves almost always of noble blood and would not mention so mean a thing as a slave who performed labor. This fact accounts largely for the scarcity of written record in regard to labor in ancient times.

Compelled by the darkness of this unwritten age of slavery which must have lasted infinitely longer than seven thousand years of whose events we catch an occasional glimpse, we first find the great philosopher Aristotle acknowledging,[15] in his startling prediction that "slave labor may become obsolete." So again Rodbertus of our own times, looking at and judging from the organized resistance of laboring men, predicts that society will outgrow wages or competitive slavery.[16] Here are two seemingly parallel cases; the one representing a condition of affairs 350 years before Christ, the other taken from actual conditions before our own eyes, in both cases, given against the stubborn will of the ruling wealthy by two of the profoundest and most daringly honest philosophers the world has produced. At the time Rodbertus von Jägetzow made this startling prediction, Germany under Bismarck, was stifling every effort of press, legislation, trade-unions and socialists, to give the dreaded fact to the world. The freedmen at the time of Aristotle were forming an innumerable phalanx of combined strength. It is not hard for students of sociology to understand why in ancient times no mention was made by historians of the wonderful organizations which then existed. But for laws necessarily recorded for the use of government and for the habit which labor unions of those times entertained, compulsorily perhaps, of inscribing their name, festivities, the tutelary saint they worshiped and the handicraft they belonged to, upon slabs of stone, there would be no means of knowing or even conjecturing the history of a transition period which launched mankind, after long centuries of struggle, out of a passive submission to abject ser-

[13] *Idem*, chap. i. *Antiques Croyances.*
[14] Later we find cremation; but only the poor who possessed no ground burned their dead. These were the outcasts supposed to have no souls.
[15] Aristotle, *Politics*, i. 4. [16] Rodbertus, *Normal Arbeitstag;* Ely, *Hist. French and German Socialisms*, pp. 176-7.

vitude into the true competitive system. We shall farther on have more to say in detail of the hatred and contempt which the ancient slave masters held toward their poor working chattels.

There was a taint upon labor. So there is now. Thus far then, there is no progress. We shall attempt to analyze the original cause of this taint upon labor and prove that the progress of to-day consists in its diminution.

Admitting the theory of development we go back to man at the dawn of reason, when he was still a beast. We even imagine a group, such as Professor Oswald Heer has pictured in the frontispiece of his masterly scientific work on the fossils of Switzerland.[17] Prowling around this group of naked human forms—some upon trees, others crawling, others walking plantigrade, or gorilla-like—we see wild animals, birds and reptiles, all in search of food. Just as the steer after a desperate encounter with its rival comes out the victor and ever holds the mastery over the rest of a herd, so the most powerful and ferocious of this group of primeval men wins with his club, his fingers, or fists the mastery over the rest. These are first impulses. They are entirely animal in character. Wild geese and ducks seek in conflict the means of knowing which of their flock shall be leader in their flight; and him of the most magnetic or muscular or intellectual powers they follow. The purely animal, then, is the form which primitive, animal man assumes. This strong master of the group is the prototype of the patrician and inheritor of the estate as thousands of years afterwards we find him lord of the manor with his slaves about him. It would be absurd to suppose that immediately at the dawn of reason, this wild animal actually assumed one of the highest types of civilization. The communistic or even the patriarchal is one of the highest forms which human beings have attempted. They have, it is true, been attempted but mostly to prove failures; simply because they were of a type even in their crudest state, too far progressed for others to appreciate and apply. The master or as we may better characterize him, the bully has always been too jealous. That Abraham and Moses tried a very low form of it, and isolated themselves so as not to

[17] Dr. Oswald Heer, *Urwelt der Schweiz*.

interfere with others, is true. But it is too well known that the Hebrews were not appreciated in their good work. Their very attempt to institute the patriarchal system even in its imperfect, half competitive form, brought against them the jealousy of the world of heathendom. It was an intolerable innovation upon the more ancient, aristocratic, brutal system of masters and slaves. And it was no mere individual, but this gigantic system which massed its powers to drive the presumptuous Hebrews from the face of the earth.

The mere animal form of government must have come first. This reasoning, says the law of evolution, must have born very brutal forms. Surely enough, so we find it at the dawn of history and at the highest discernible antiquity not only in Greece and Rome but in Egypt. It was the slave system under which the Egyptian monuments were built; and no thinking person can doubt that thousands of years of this slavery must have elapsed before the Egyptians arrived at the art of architecture in which recorded history finds them. Advancing reason had already been of millennial date ere those people could have known how to carve their hieroglyphs with nice precision upon the monuments. Again, we fail to see that these inscriptions mention any mode of a more ancient communal or patriarchal government. The simplest form of governing the primeval race must have been the one adopted; and the simplest was the one common among the animals of to-day. There was at the head of every group, or tribe, or family, a master; and him the rest obeyed, afterwards adored.

It next seems natural that surrounded by wild and fierce creatures of the waters, glades and forests, the first reasonable thing to protect this master would be to select some place of security—some rock or cave or height, whence he might go or send forth into the forests, the swamps and shores in search of fruit, roots, shellfish and game. Another thing; it is natural for man to settle permanently somewhere. This is peculiarly the case with the Aryan races. It is the form of life almost universally adopted by the Indo-Europeans. They select a seat and conquer and subjugate in all directions. This also corresponds with our proposition that the first idea was to obtain a home. With the growth of experience in the application of reason came egoism which it is said the brute does not often manifest. Now with animal prowess, a little reason and a large egoism, we have what the present labor movement calls a "boss." He is endowed with the three great attributes which our modern authorities on moral philosophy denominate *irascibility* and *concupiscence*.

Given the right of proprietorship wrung through superiority in physical power from his tribe and his children, and he unhesitatingly uses them as slaves. This the true beast cannot do, since it requires reason. The first impulse, that of cupidity, makes him a tyrant and the second, that of irascibility, fills him with cruel ferocity, accounting for the well known fact that the ancient slave-holder could and often did kill his own children.[18] The first impulse, that of concupiscence and acquisitiveness combined into one, makes him desirous to enjoy and accumulate. So his children are numerous. These two nearly allied sources of human desire or greed filled him with a rivalry to accumulate and often to sequester the stores which the toil of his slaves produced.

A third impulse, that of sympathy, being yet mostly wanting, man reasonably was thus filled with pomp and greed. These whetted his yet unbridled passions, making him ambitious to embellish his estate, caused the land to be fruitful, inspired him to build better houses, select and multiply his concubines and otherwise adorn the paternity. But the original parent-aristocrat or *paterfamilias* never until much later, desisted from the enforcement of absolute virtue of the parent-aristocrat mother or *materfamilias*.

Sympathy, it would seem came to him but tardily. Sympathy was inspired later;—brought into the world through the cult of the organizations of freedmen, after the beginning of the era of manumissions. Socrates and Aristotle recognized their powerful school of fraternal coherence and mutual love which it seems almost certain culminated in the wonderful institution known as Chistianity, destroying the old Paganism or, at least, laying the foundation for its final eradication from the world.

This picture presents a poor outlook for the slaves, who were obliged to perform the master's drudgery. They however, always had two advantages: being to the family born,

[18] Terentius, *Heauton Timorumenos*, Act III. 5; Dionysius of Halicarnassus, *Antiquitates Romanæ*, lib. II. cap. xxvi.; *Codex Justiniani*, lib. VII. tit. xlvii, *Pandectæ, (Digest)*, lib. XXVIII. leg. xi.

they owned a meagre right to some kind of burial; whereas it is known that later, the freedman could only expect cremation. To have the remains refused the noble rite of burial was a disgrace. It was a virtual acknowledgement that the person had no soul. Malefactors, runaways or deserters and freedmen so lowly as to be without protection, in other words all whom God spurned to recognize as having an immortal life, were burned or cast out to rot without honors.[19] The other advantage was that their owners were their supporters which freed slaves from the responsibilities of the struggle for bread. Still the whole picture presents a poor outlook for the slaves who were obliged to perform his drudgery. But as if they might be inclined to desert him the religious belief was so riveted upon their benighted minds that for thousands of years they did not doubt that the punishment for desertion would be a species of damnation. The slaves were taught that the most hallowed of all places was the central focus or alter of worship of the *manes* of their master. The holy and awful funeral repast had always to be partaken upon the same spot where the family ancestors lay. Thus for generations families worshiped each other at the same tomb.[20] We have already quoted from Dr. Fustel that the dread of being deprived of sepulture was greater than the fear of death itself. So fearful were the ancients, even the ancient laborers, of arousing the ire of their tutelary deities that they worshiped them by sacrifices. They even fed [21] these disengaged souls [22] and periodically furnished them with wine, milk, fruit, honey and other table delicacies which in life they had been known to prefer. These strange beliefs which were by no means confined to the Indo-European, but as Fustel de Coulanges has made clear, embraced the entire Aryan family,[23] were the

---

[19] Cicero, *De Legibus*, 2, 23, "Hominem mortuum, inquit lex XII., (meaning the Twelve Tables,) in Urbe ne sepelito neve urito...... Quid ? qui post XII. in Urbe sepulti, sunt clari viri."
[20] Euripides. *Trojans*, 381.
[21] Virgil, *Æneid*, III. 300: Euripides, *Iphigenia*, 476, "Behold, I pour upon the earth of the tomb milk, honey and wine; for it is with these that we revivify the dead;" Cf. also, Ovid, *Fastus*, II. 540.
[22] Critically, this expression is incorrect: for the ancients believed that the soul was never disengaged, but remained buried with the body in bliss. Consult Fustel de Coulanges, *Cité Antique*, liv. 1. chap. iv.
[23] In substance Dr. Fustel, *Idem*. p. 26 says: Ces croyances ne sont pas asurement empruntées ni par les Grecs des Hindous ni par les Hindous des Grecs; mais elles appartenaient á toutes les leux races, de loin reculées et du milieu de l' Asie.

prevailing ones and formed the basis of the great Pagan religion. The superstition worked so powerfully upon the benighted conscience of slaves that however severe their lot, they required a higher scale of enlightenment than could be had in these low forms of slavery before they could see their way clear to revolt. This, however came in the course of time. There is no doubt that discussion among the numerous organizations of freedmen did much toward bringing this about. The increasing number of slaves also gave them opportunity to meet and interchange opinions. In the deep gloom of abject slavery men seldom revolt. Revolt is especially rare where there is no contact with public opinion adverse to it. It is not probable, therefore, that the slaves, however bad their treatment, found themselves in a condition enough advanced in the scale of manhood to organize revolt until thousands of years of their abject servitude had elapsed. But it appears certain that revolts had been going on for a long time before we catch the earliest clues to their history.

When language had become perfected and means of mutual comprehension had come into their grasp, so that an intelligent interchange of each others feelings was had, and it became easy to express their grievances and sufferings one with another, they began to revolt. If a lord or capitalist in a paroxysm of unbridled rage, ordered one slave for a trivial offense to be strangled by the others,[24] they were compelled to be the executioners of their comrade. If his majesty raised his hand and dashed out the brains of his own child, the other children,[25] though by no means so keenly sensitive to the horror as we of our own time, would feel a common sympathy and perhaps lay up the infanticide for a future day of vengeance. When the right of sepulture was taken from them and they found that even the consolation of religion was gone, they went desperate and reckless over the imagined withdrawal, by the God they worshiped, of his blessing. In this state of mind they

---

[24] See story of Damophilos in chapter viii., on the revolt of Eunus.
[25] We have, in the ancient records, many allusions to the murder of children by the lords of the estate. See Dionyssius of Halicarnassus, *Archiologia Rhomana*, lib. II. cap. xxvi. 'Ο δὲ τῶν 'Ρωμαίων νομοθέτης ἅπασαν, ὡς εἰπεῖν, ἐδωκεν ἐξουσίαν πατρὶ καθ' υἱοῦ, καὶ παρὰ παντὰ τὸν τοῦ βίου χρόνον...., ἐάντε ἀποκτίννυναι προαιρῆται· Also *Code of Justinian*, lib. VIII. tit. xlvii. leg. x., where this right is mentioned as having once existed: "Jus (patrbus) vitæ in liberos necisque potestas olim erat permissa."

THE FIRST MERCENARY SOLDIERS. 77

must have frequently plotted together and concocted insurrections.[26] They however, did not co-operate with each other for the accumulation of wealth. This is a phenomenon of which we shall hereafter speak more lengthily. But the principle cause of the rebellions which in course of time became very common, was their increase among themselves. It must not be supposed because the master who owned all at their expense and degradation, that he could and did live in unbridled libertinism among his human chattels, who by reason of the taint on labor never had recognized family alliances among each other. However stringent the rules of tyrants over the oppressed they were never known to entirely prevail over nature. What the form of alliance between the sexes of the very ancient slaves may have been is not fully known;—whether free of formality or by the ligature of accorded right.[27] Be that as it may, the fact remains that the human race was by no means dependent for its increase upon the heads of optimate families. As was the case with the negro slaves in the Southern States of the American Republic, so in Greece and Italy the slaves multiplied among themselves. In course of time they grew very numerous. Of course, as their number increased they outgrew the actual requirements of the landed estate to which they were enfeoffed. Then they were sold to other estates or killed.[28] Later when wars occurred they become mercenaries,[29] in earlier times, under their owners, as *impedimenta* of the army; not as combatants, because they were of too ignoble birth to engage in the aristocratic vocation of war. Still later we find them assuming the dignity of combatants. Of this latter period we find clearer traces, and shall show that these mercenaries were none other than the supernumeraries from the estates, who had run away to take into their own hands the struggle for ex-

---

[26] Undeniable evidence of this is found in the great servile wars of Sicily, where Demeter or Ceres, goddess of that region was complained of by the slaves as having deserted them. See Bücher, *Aufstände der unfreien Arbeiter*, S. 53 and 54, Siefert, *Sicilische Sklavenkriege*, S. 17-18.
[27] See chapters xiii. to xx. on the *Collegia* and *Sodalicia* of Italy and the *Eranoi* and *Thiasoi* of the Greek-speaking labor unions, which produce plenty of proof that from before B. C. 600, the freedmen had their laws of marriage. The more ancient slavery is obscure in records of the social habits of the poor.
[28] Granier de Cassagnac, *Hist. des Classes Ouvrières*, p. 61.
[29] Grote, *History of Greece,—Dionysius the Elder.* Dionysius, Tyrant of Syracuse employed mercenaries, and Dion's conquest of Syracuse against Dionysius the Younger was begun with mercenary troops in B. C. 359.

istence. It is very easy to prove that there were organizations or unions of mercenaries who sold their services to princes and their generals, undertaking to accomplish certain military feats for a recompense.

But we are still treating of the workingman as a slave. The father of the family was one individual. But the family itself often consisted of fifty. Now as the only one of all these eligible to the blooded dignity of nobility was the father, what became of the rest?[30] They were not only slaves but they formed, as it were, another race. They were the plebeians, the proletariat; "hewers of wood and drawers of water." It was impossible under the extremes of this social divergence, for any communication or sympathy to be recognized between them. Even though the master was the father and the child legitimate though a slave, by the deadly inheritance of his bondage riveted upon him through immemorial usage, he dared not look up into his parent's face with the sweet, tender love of our modern consanguinity! It was a sacrilege. Equality was impossible. The number therefore, of the slave race compared with the noble, was as fifty to one. Even as late as the beginning of that powerful reform known as Christianity which may be characterized as an emancipation proclamation, the slave system was in full operation and the number of slaves enormous.

It is through that long night of slavery for the working people, that humanity received its almost indelible stamp of reproach and contempt which lingers to-day in the "taint" of labor. During the struggle of strikes and uprisings that set in after the slaves became numerous and colonies of them, either as marauders or adventurers appeared, the slave race developed many men and women of extraordinary genius and ability. We shall present an elaborate history of these as landmarks in our biography of the lowly while groping through the barren void which the historians and the literary wreckers have left us, torn in fragments or quite unchronicled in their short sighted contempt and eagerness to set forth only exploits which the ambition of their noble masters inspired. So poor was the food doled out by the masters to their slaves that they may

---

[30] The *Materfamilias* or married mother kept herself in severe seclusion so as to be above suspicion.

be said to have been fed like animals from the crib. Horace, Herodotus, Lucanus, Livy, Pliny and many others give testimony of the wretched food these poor slaves received in Greece, Egypt and Rome. Peas,[31] nuts, roots, pods, skimmed milk, very poor bread, and none made of white wheat flour.[32] Great suffering from want is mentioned in Pliny's Natural History, among the slaves of Italy. An epidemic like the black death twice broke out among them. He also states that this disease did not attack the noble or well-to-do people.[33] These great sufferings and privations caused the death rate to be so high as to decimate the ranks of the slaves thus reducing the danger always feared by the masters, of revolt and of plottings for insurrection. Aside from the curse which their lowly condition stamped upon the slaves, they were treated with ignominy and generally marked with the *stichus*[34] on their faces. The word *stigma* among the Greeks was full of reproach, not only because the scars were on the faces and bodies of these poor white men and women[35] doomed to perpetual servitude, but because it was also indelibly stamped upon their social life. Granier who produced a gem in his great work[36] for which the subsequent labor movement acknowledges its indebtedness, says of this ancient slavery: "This curse of blood is implacable. Ventidius Bassus was so fortunate as to become a consul. They said to him, you were a bootblack. Galerius, Diocletian, Probus, Pertinax, Vitellius, even Augustus had the good fortune to become emperors. They said to Galerius: You were a swineherd; to Diocletian: You were a slave; to Probus: Your father was a gardener; to Pertinax: Your father was a freedman; to Vitellius: Your father was a cobbler; and they went so

---

[31] Horace, *Ad Pisonem*, v. 249.
[32] Homer, *Odessey*, lib. VIII. c. v. 221, 222. The earth-born multitudes:
"Τῶν δ' ἄλλων ἐμέ φημι πολύ προφερέστερον εἶναι,
Ὅσσοι νῦν βροτοί εἰσιν ἐπί χθονί σῖτον ἔδοντες."
[33] Pliny, *Natural History*, XXVI. c. iii. "Non fuerat hæc lues apud majores patresque nostros."
[34] See *Comœdiæ* of Plautus: *Stichus*, "*The marked Slave;*" also Plutarch, Nicias, 29; Xenophon, *De Vectigal.*, c. iv; Diod XXXIV. *Fragment*, Dindorf
[35] Homer, *Iliad*, I. 233 "The earth-born multitude."
[36] Granier de Cassagnac, *Hist. des Classes Ouvrières;* especially in chap. v. 117; McCullagh, *Industrial History of Free Nations;—The Greeks.* This scholar quotes from Hesiod's "Ἔργα καί Ἡμέραι, v. 186., where the great poet appeals to the lords for amelioration of the people's sufferings: "Hesiod lived for many years in Bœtia where the oppression and exclusiveness of the dominant classes was as unrelenting as in Lacedæmon." *Greek Industries*, pp. 6-7.

far as to write on the marble of the statue of Augustus, in the life time of this master of the world: Your grandfather was a merchant, and your father a usurer." The same keen observer in his investigation of these ancient phenomena of slavery, makes a very important suggestion, the result, he says, of his own personal reading of the Iliad of Homer: that as there is in the whole of that celebrated poem, not one allusion to freedmen, or to the subject of emancipation; whereas in the Odyssey there appear many allusions thereto it is therefore, following the line of reason adopted by comparative philologists and historiographers in search of facts in ethnography, very reasonable to suppose that the Iliad is the oldest, and that the Odyssey came afterwards."[37] Here is a suggestion worth much to anthropologists in general; and it is to be hoped it may be cleared so as to become useful to the study of Sociology. We hear of no great spasm like that of the war of the rebellion of our own day, which produced the emancipation of the slaves. If nothing of that kind occurred between the composition of those two poems, so ancient and obscure, then it is reasonable to imagine that the emancipation was gradual; and if gradual, an unlimited time must have elapsed—perhaps thousands of years—between their composition. This alone seems capable of solving the incongruity. But it tends forcibly to show the astonishing age of slavery which may well be called the long night of suffering of our progenitors. Certain it is, however that the Iliad treats of the extremes; the lords upon the one hand and on the other the slaves. The want of an intermediary class shows its high antiquity.

At any rate, all these researches accumulate evidence showing the absurdity of a communistic or nomadic form of society having been possible among the Indo-Europeans from whom we are descended unless that tendency supervened upon the ancient system of land tenure in subsequent times. There crops out one curious association in very ancient history which, to the reader wishing to gratify his military or ecclesiastical taste is totally unaccountable; but which appears quite plain to those who study history to enjoy glimpses of the social life of the past. We refer to the aristocratic Amphictyonic Council.

[37] Granier de Cassagnac, *Hist. des Classes Ouvrières*, chap. v. p. 109

The student of the great slave system sees the absurdity of attributing this ancient series of protective organizations either to ambitious military schemes or to pure piety, although they are given to us by historians, as a system of neighbors organized to protect and perpetuate the worship of the Gods. They come down to us from the gloomy tradition of high antiquity ; and to the two first mentioned classes they are utterly incomprehensible. The sociologist however, who sees the slaves growing in numbers while the *gens*[38] remained stationary in numbers, can easily picture the causes and spirit of these leagues. They were confederations of the lords or individual owners of the patrimonies or estates. These estates, as we have seen, fell to the lords, by entail in primogeniture. The Amphictyony[39] was simply a co-operative association of the lords to defend their estates; and they most naturally, as customary with all Pagan ancients, held forth first and foremost the horrors of irreligion, knowing that the superstition of the slaves was their true stronghold, since by making it appear that attack upon or contemptuousness of the holy property was an unpardonable misdemeanor or even to utter words of conspiracy against that property remaining in the hands of the first born son, was blasphemy. This superstition thus inculcated was always, in ancient times, the bulwark of protection to the nobles. The Amphictyony existed 2,000 years before Christ, probably even much prior to that time, and grew more and more powerful, until about B. C. 700 it had grown in numeric strength and in the subtle art of self-protection so that it assumed the dignity of the Amphictyonic Council, seated itself in the holy temples of Apollo and Demeter, and had delegates who met there spring and autumn, representing twelve tribes or states of Greece and the Archipelago. Some 600 years before Christ the Amphictyonic Council had misunderstandings with its delegates and wars of extermination began. These troubles were called the holy wars. It is known that for many centuries these corporations protected themselves mutually. If one of the small neighbor-

[38] Latin "*Gens*," whence the "gentry." See Mann's *Ancient and Mediæval Republics*, chapter vi.
[39] Fiske. *American Political Ideas*. p. 72.

hoods represented in and protected by the federation was attacked or threatened, the entire power of all the others was thrown together in its defense. The article of agreement between them ran as follows: Not to destroy or allow to be destroyed or cut off from water, in peace or war, any town in the Amphictyonic brotherhood; not to plunder[40] the property of the god or treacherously extract valuables from the sanctum. Now in face of the fact that there were by this time great numbers of supernumerary slaves who had, on account of their servitude and the abuses they suffered, become reckless, fierce and ready to enter upon a life of desperate revolt, still we find writers denying that this brotherhood had any other idea than a purely religious one. To the searching sociologist it is quite clear that this organization must have been one of the very first efforts of the Indo-Europeans to form a government for the protection of property,

From incipiency this must have been the earliest form of government. But it was an aristocratic government which cast a taint on labor. It perpetuated the holiness of property which has ever since upheld the dogma of divine right of the fathers and of kings and is probably the originator of that dogma. Away back in the past, before the country had become thickly peopled and while superstition combined with rigid rules of the masters, kept down all danger of revolt among the slaves, there were no cities.[41] We have not space in this work to explain the phenomenon of the ancient city, but refer the curious to Dr. Fustel, whose work[42] cannot be perused without profit. Modern scholars are making valuable compilations of evidence showing that cities, like nearly everything else, were a natural and gradual growth.

The great Hesiod, himself a poor freedman if not a slave, may have had the Amphictyonic league and its wars in mind when he wrote:

"Men's right arm is law; for spoils they wait
And lay their mutual cities desolate."[43]

[40] The custom was to bury with the deceased father many precious articles of which he was fond in life. See Funck-Brentano, *La Civilisation et ses Lois*, on this Fetish custom and his evidence that the favorite wife was often buried alive along with the other trinkets; livre II. c. ii. pp. 114-116.
[41] Fustel de Coulanges, *Cité Antique*, liv.III. c. ii. et iii. [42] *Id.* III. c. 1
[43] Hesiod, Ἔργα καὶ Ἡμέραι, V. 161.

CHAPTER IV.

ELEUSINIAN MYSTERIES

ANCIENT GRIEVANCES OF THE WORKERS.

WORKING PEOPLE destitute of Souls—Original popular Beliefs—Plato finally gives them half a Soul—Modern Ignorance on the true Causes of certain Developments in History—Sympathy, the Third Great Emotion developed out of growing Reason, through mutual Commiseration of the Outcasts—A new Cult—The Unsolved Problem of the great Eleusinian Mysteries—Their wonderful Story—Grievances of slighted Workingmen—Organization impossible to Slaves except in their Strikes and Rebellions—The Aristocrats' Politics and Religion barred the Doors against Work-people—Extraordinary Whims and Antics at the Eleusinian Mysteries—The Causes of Grievances endured by the Castaway Laborers—Their Motives for Secret Organization—The Terrible Cryptia—The horrible Murders of Workingmen for Sport—Dark Deeds Unveiled—Story of the Massacre of 2,000 Workingmen—Evidence—The Grievances in Sparta—In Athens—Free Outcast Builders, Sculptors, Teachers, Priests, Dancers, Musicians, Artisans, Diggers, all more or less Organized—Return to the Eleusinian Mysteries—Conclusion.

DURING the long period occupying—in the case of the Indo-European race from which most of us are derived, several thousand years, there came about a differentiation in favor of the slaves. Granier in his bright exposition of this great social subject, declares slavery to have been the natural outcome of the Pagan, or family religion.[1] Fustel de Coulanges in his instructive and extraordinarily lucid work has proved every word written by Granier

[1] *Hist, des Classes Ouvrières*, pp. 39-41. *Vide* chap. iii. *passim.*

upon this daring theme, to be true.² Philosophers of our age, catching at written and unwritten obscurities which saliently obtrude upon the path of researchers groping in sociology, are getting down to real causes of events which for 2,000 years remained phenomena undeciphered. Ages upon ages have rolled and the mouldering stones and tablets, invaluable with their begrimed inscriptions, have saucily stared at science, unheeded. Furtive hints by ancient historians for centuries have mocked the lore of universities, bearing their inuendos which failed to insult the professorial sticklers to our darling notes and emendations. Great Social wars with ominous wing have been flopping and airing our ignorance as to their deep, suppressed causes. Then the downfall of the Roman empire —that of all others most inexplicable wonder—has been for twenty centuries chopped up into indigestible morsels and administered to students of history searching after great events and ecclesiastical lore. At last the student of sociology enters the field. He is philosopher enough to divest himself of the crusty film in which prejudice is encysted and manly enough to step out of the contumelious state and like a Murillo go down among the tatterdemalions and give them credit for what they were.

Society began with the bully.³ It began with unbridled irascibility, concupiscence and egoism. This creature, man, having killed or clubbed away the others, sought among the females the handsomest mate and in the best cave or hut began the family. The Aryan is not a nomad. He wants a home, a permanent residence. He is brigand enough to launch forth into all the enterprizes of plunder, but he returns to his home. This home remained his fastness which he would not quit. The land around it became his. When children came they were also his. When they grew strong and could work, his concupiscence differentiated into cupidity; and begetting many, he forced them to work. They became his slaves. If the little ones refused or otherwise displeased him his irascible impulses prevailed and he killed them. Those whom he could not spare he only punished. His irascibility made him a

² *La Cité Antique*, pp. 76-89; See also *Iliad*, xxi., *Odyssey*, xxii., *Leviticus*, xxv. 40, 41, 44, 47, 48.
³ We are forced to employ this homely term as there exists in English no other which so nearly conveys our idea.

ORIGIN OF THE PROLETARIAT. 85

tyrant, while his acquisitiveness made him rich. He became a lord. Sympathy was a stranger to his bosom though no doubt it worked an influence at an early day in moulding the nature of the family, as we know there were favorites.

He lived in the wonder-world. The phenomena of nature he could not understand. There were thunders and lightnings, but electricity was a terror which shaped a god. When this god of nature grew into shape upon his imagination his egoism coveted its glory and immortality and the bully came to imagine *himself* a god; and assumed for himself power and immortality deifying himself at death and ordaining his first-born son his worshiper and the sole inheritor of his fortune. The remuneration demanded of the son for this succession was the paternal worship and the deification and adoration of the dead father, now a saint. Egoism was thus the originator of the Pagan religion, of immortality and of the sainthood.[4]

It was a part of the genius of this cult to be aristocratic and exclusive. It inculcated divine rights of masters, of noble lords and afterwards of kings. On the other hand it was a part of the genius of paganism to have slaves. It was so exclusively aristocratic that only a very few could possibly enjoy its beatitudes. The rest were obliged to be castaways. The castaways who were debarred the favoritism of eternal life through the aristocratic burial and deification were slaves, doomed by an inheritance of expropriation and of poverty, to slavery. When they became numerous, although wretched, there now and then developed a man or woman of genius. Bereft of everything tangible, they still had minds. With minds they considered and discussed their lowly condition; with strength and ingenuity some worked themselves out of bondage and became freedmen. As freedmen they began to organize into protective associations and trade unions. Thus two distinct parties were formed.

Meantime the power of the lords or property owners increased but not so rapidly in numeric strength as the power of the outcast, and the grandees, seeing the bondmen, runaways and freedmen forming into communes, some as

---

[4] Latin *paganus*, of, or belonging to the country, *pagus*. There were then no towns or cities. These came later. Cf. *La Cité Antique, passim*.

tradesmen, some as brigands, all dissatisfied, some very dangerous, also betook themselves to organization. Thus there were two distinct classes. Which of these two classes began earliest to organize for self defense we cannot undertake to prove but reason conjectures that it must have been the outcasts. But certain it is⁵ they formed into powerful *phratries*⁶ or *curies* for mutual assistance, sometimes under religious pretenses, as in the case of the Italian *collegia*.

All along, parallel with each other through time, these two systems, the grandees or *gentes* on the one hand and the outcasts or disinherited on the other, have existed, securing themselves by mutual organization. We do not see in history much of the working classes. The principal mention made of them is in connection with slavery and the concomitant degradation of servitude. We know from certain passages in history that insurrections or slave rebellions occurred. Some of them were on a prodigious scale. Plutarch mentions instances where the masters by decree of the phratries sometimes allured large numbers of the slaves on plea of a festival or hunt and when at a convenient spot fell upon and murdered them by hundreds, merely to get rid of a dangerous element.⁷ That the servile element keenly felt the contempt in which they were regarded, crops out in the records of the remote past. We propose to give many instances.

The exclusion of slaves, freedmen and afterwards Christians from the Eleusinian mysteries gives the student of sociology an important hint to pages of the unwritten labor question; showing the reasons why the outcasts resorted to co-operation among themselves, as an only practical court of appeals to any power against oppression when aggrieved. All writers who have spoken of this celebrated and mysterious organization agree that it was very ancient. As we have found irrefutable evidences of numerous trade unions so early as the eighth and ninth century before Christ, we

⁵ Fustel de Coulanges, *Cité Antique*, lib. II. pp. 39-89, *La Famille*; Mann's *Ancient and Mediæval Republics*, pp. 22-27.
⁶ Morgan, *Ancient Societies*, p. 88: "The φρατρία is a brotherhood, as the term imports; and a natural growth from the organization into *gentes*. It is an organic union or association of two or more *gentes* of the same tribe for certain common objects. These *gentes* were usually such as had been formed by the segmentation of an original *gens*." This author sees some analogy between the ancient Greek and Roman *gens* and certain tribes of North American Indians; notably the Iroquois. Consult chapters ii. and iii.
⁷ Plutarch, *Lycurgus*; also *Lycurgus and Numa compared*.

need not trace the Eleusinian band back of that time. It is however, worthy of remark that this organization existed at a much earlier date and that, although the societies of the workmen do not as luminously come to the front on occount of this stigma which made them secret and prevented their recoguition, it is no proof whatever that they did not also exist. The organization known as the Eleusinians,[8] according to ancient authors was in full force 1,500 years before Christ. Cicero who was an admirer of all the Pagan forms that tended to hand down the exclusive splendor and dignity of the aristocratic stock, believed these feasts to have belonged to the remotest antiquity and that they lasted the longest of almost any institution.[9] Like the great trade-union movement they transmit unwritten records through an occasional slab, bearing inscriptions.[10]

The Eleusinian crusade was a celebrated and exclusively aristocratic religious festival in honor of the goddess Demeter or Ceres,[11] held at Eleusis, a large town some ten miles from Athens, in Attic Greece. It was a great outpouring from Athens, every 5 years in the month *Boedromion*,[12] lasting nine days. The great preparations made before the festival began, the extraordinary solemnity of the affair, the manner in which the Athenians attended it in a drome or chanting caravansary, gave it the appearance of a crusade. It was the origin of all well-known crusades. The attendance at this crusade was a trial of one's eligibility to the blessings of life eternal. Eleusis means a trysting place; consequently it is probable that the great games suggested the name of the place, and once established upon a projecting rock of the sea, the city afterward grew around it and in course of time held a large population. There are some touching mementoes which may be gleaned from this celebrated name. Whoever reads the bible in Greek finds frequent mention of this word in the signification of the coming of the Saviour. It is a symbolic word. Emblems in

---

[8] In later centuries the little Mysteries continued though they were not confined to Eleusis.
[9] Cicero, *De Legibus*, II. cap. XVI.; *Panegyricus* of *Isocrates*, 6.
[10] Judging from the slab of Paros they began in the fifteenth century before Christ. Larousse, *Dictionnaire Universel*, Art. *Les Éleusiniens*.
[11] Ceres, like the Pelasgic Hermes was the ithyphallic deity, having power over reproduction and the supplies of life. Cf. Encyc. Brit. vol. XI. p. 670.
[12] Βοηδρομιών, the space of time from September 15th to October 15th; from βοηρομεω, I chase with a shout. Theseus in the battle with the Amazons, chased them with cries. It is a word of great antiquity. Plutarch, *Theseus*.

those days were common; and much that is unexplained or that may yet be explained—unexplained through ignorance or neglect—comes out, by a proper interpretation of emblems.

But the Eleusinian mysteries were too absurdly exclusive to stand the erosions of what is known as progress. In perfect agreement with what we have said regarding the exclusive character of their worship, centering it upon the egoistic household name, forcing a puffed aristocracy by dint of glorifying a human creature and cutting off that glory from the many, especially those who toil, it had made itself odious and intolerable long before the advent of Christ. Yet the antiquity and greatness of the trysting scenes at Eleusis had become renowned in every well-known part of the world. All over Palestine, long afterwards the cradle of another but infinitely more democratic plan of worship, this curious practice was well-known. In Italy and Africa its fame had gone forth.

We are not speaking of the Eleusinian mysteries merely to recount a paltry historico-ecclesiastical fact. We are making a point in sociologic research. We therefore ask our reader's indulgence in comparing the social life of homespun work-people through a metaphor as opposite as the Eleusinian emblems. Yet it is no metaphor. It bears with it a bone of contention which raged for centuries, split and divided, founded heresies, sophistries, philosophies, provoked labor unions, involved work-people in communism, drew out discussion and laid the foundation of the religion of Jesus in after years. We now proceed to explain how this was done. In ancient mythology Proserpine, or as some write it, Persephone, was the beautiful daughter of Ceres the Demeter, and of Jupiter. Pluto the god of the infernal regions fell in love with Proserpine and while she was in the act of gathering flowers in a vale of Enna in Sicily, stole her from her mother, carrying her off to his nether-world home.[13] The mother though an immortal and living on the heights of Enna the Sicilian Olympus, was so grieved at the loss of her child that she came down from heaven, betook to herself the garb of mortals, became an old woman, assumed the duties of a nurse and wandered through the country,

---

[13] *Infra*, chap. viii., containing the story of Eunus and the great servile war

plying her profession for a subsistance from place to place. She went to Eleusis and there got employment. It was a job of nursing a child of the king of the place. The child's name was Demophon and under the celestial solicitude of this goddess in disguise, Metanira, the mother, beheld with astonishment and curiosity the marvelous thrift of her boy. Ceres breathed upon him the breath of life, dressed him with ambrosial ointment and at night used to purge the dross of mortality from him by immersing him in a bath of mysterious fire, with an object of making him also immortal. But one night the fond and curious mother peeped through the veil screening the immortalizing process of trans-substantiation and seeing the boy pendent in a halo of flame screamed with affright, causing the haggard old nurse to let the youngster drop deep into the consuming pit where he instantly perished. The hag then, to save herself, threw off her disguise became rehabilitated and forced the people of Eleuses to build her a temple to dwell in while still continuing her search for the lost Proserpine. Now the professional business of Jupiter was to watch the interests of mortal men. But Ceres unable to endure the loss of her stolen child and remembering the details of her husband's escape when a babe from the ferocious Saturn, struck the earth with her wand of famine. She rebelled energetically against the shape of things, and at last Jupiter came to the rescue of the innocent denizens of the earth as a professional duty. This led to the discovery of Proserpine. From her temple at Eleusis, Demeter who was the protectress of the products of labor made things uncomfortable for the people who were in her husband's care. They were stricken with malaria. Contagion spread. The ground ceased to produce and the horrors of famine engulfed them. Men prayed, sacrificed, and besought their patron gods, each *gens* for itself, and urged the further combination of gentile tribes into phratries to no effect until great Jove at last got Mercury to visit Erebus who went down into the pagan inferno where Pluto was enjoying the charms of the beautiful stolen prize. Thus the sly god got found out. This pagan inferno was Hades where Pluto was king. He, like Satan was cunning. He knew that by tempting her, as the devil a time before had tempted Eve, he could induce her to eat the forbidden fruit;—this time a pomegranite seed. Unwarily she was lured into the temptation which cost her a fourth part of each year, for the rest of her immortal existence, in the infernal abode with Pluto. The other three-fourths of the year, however, she was permitted to pass upon earth.

Such is the ridiculous story which among the ancients, was believed at the point of the poniard or under penalty of the hemlock for at least two thousand years. To cavil with its austere sanctity was a heresy costing the blasphemist his life and every hope of immortality.

Some palliation of the absurdity of this sub-terrestrial abode is furnished by the qualification that in ancient belief the world was flat, not round; and between the two flat surfaces there flowed a river with whose murky waters Erebus had something to do. On the other side, once there, the journeying immortals were ushered into view of the indescribable beatitudes of the elysium. This gorgeous *terra incognita* was not to be reached without passing the terrible cynocephalous or many-headed watchdog named Cerberus. But heaven was on the other side. Passage from this to that was the agony.

Now Ceres, the wife of the mighty Jupiter and mother of the lovely Proserpine, was the goddess of the harvests. She represented the cereals. She rode on a jagatnatha drawn by dragons. Her brow was coronated with wreaths of wheat. This rape of Proserpine by Pluto on the ragged edge, between our world of mortals and heaven became emblematic of the agonies of winter;—from autumn when the the wheat was sown, then the cold hyemal gloom of gestation in the dark borderlands, the trysting place, the hyperborean domain of hades; thence over the half congelated Styx was ferried the elastic imagination by the money getting Charon, and behold, the vernal raptures of heaven and its elysian fields appear, full of springing verdure, the land of exquisite delight!

Such was the Mythic origin of the Eleusinian Mysteries. They were weird forms of imagination, assimilating things real with things unreal and working them up into maxims, emblems and creeds, until they assumed a priesthood and became an organization of men and women knit by the tie of secrecy which nothing but the long fluctuations of progress could unbind.

THE MYSTERIOUS RITES.

What the actual performance was at the *penetralia* of the Eleusinian mysteries nobody knows. We know that they were, in their prime, symbolic of the procreative energy of nature. But they were attended with certain extraordinary rites. What were these rites? They were also conducive to the science of eternal bliss.

Who secured that bliss? In answering these two questions we must return to the kernel of our theme—the labor element. To the first one of them, the answer is vague. This we know, that the rites consisted of dramatic representations of the rape of Proserpine, daughter of Ceres, goddess of the vegetable kingdom, of the fields, and labor, who was supposed to preside over the cereals and other alimentation of man. This rape was performed by Pluto; and in its emblematic mysticisms conveys the idea not only of procreation but also of immortality of the human soul.[14] Whether more may still be contributed by science to these strange and intensely interesting rites is yet to be seen. As late as 1858 an important addition to our knowledge of the Eleusinian mysteries has been contributed in the discovery by Vlastos, at a village named Hagi-Constantios, of a marble slab containing an inscription including rules and regulations of the society.

The first day of the nine was celebrated perhaps partly in Athens or before the arrival at Eleusis. On the march from Athens to Eleusis the jealous outcasts who were excluded from the raptures of the scene, always ranged themselves in hostile array and belabored the marchers with stones and clubs, until the arrival of the procession at the temple of Megaron.[15]

The second day was called *alade mustae.* It was the 16th of *Boedromion.* It was the day of the baptism, being a march in phalanx to the sea. The procession here received their baptism and purification. The third was the day of the feasting. On the fourth day the poppey seeds were ad-

---

[14] Uwaroff, *Essai sur les mystères d' Éleusis,* 3rd. edition, Paris, 1816; Creuzer's *Symbolik und Mithologie der alten Völker;* Preller, *Demeter und Persephone* Hamburg, 1837.

[15] For a description of the temple of Megaron at Eleusis, see Guhl and Koner, *Life of the Greeks and Romans,* translated by Hueffer, pp. 48-9. The dark crypt where the mysteries were performed by the Μυσταγωγοι also the initiations, was under ground. From Aristophanes (Plato, Bekk. L. ed. *Repub.* in cap. xvii.), we learn that at the initiations they sacrificed a hog. Aristophanes, *Pax,* v. 373-5, has the passage hinted at.

ministered. This rite represented the stupefying influence of the narcissus under which the maiden Persephone was stolen away. Orpheus was the *hierophant* or priest whose duty it was to initiate eligible candidates into the mysteries. He was assisted by Erechtheis daughter of Erechtheus the smasher. It is quite likely that this initiating ceremony was some kind of violent struggle. It must have been attended by oaths of fidelity under punishment of death to any one who divulged the secret. The initiation took place in the night or in the dark crypt of the temple, as the *dadouchos* or torch-bearer was in attendance and his torch-procession represented the search for the lost daughter of Ceres. This *dadouchos* was a priest holding, as Xenophon tells us, the office hereditarily for life; and at his decease it fell to another of the same family, the *Callidae*. There was also a great sacrificial rite performed, who or what the victim, is not very clear; but the herald of the sacrifice, the *hieroceryx* was always there.[16] The new initiates were not permitted to eat flesh. Even the *hierophant* or initiating priest was required to live on low diet that passion might be restrained during the ordeal.[17] He drank a decoction of hemlock which had the effect to benumb the sensibilities, a thing exceedingly appropriate at the moment of this extatic enjoyment, where, if we are to believe Maury, a critic well credited and much quoted on this subject, all around, the voluptuous nobles of both sexes take their turns. The unscrupulus *dictionnaire universel*,[18] quoting from the above

---

[16] Creuzer, *Symbolik und Mythologie der alten Völker*,
[17] Larousse, *Dictionnaire Universel, Art. Les Éleusiniens.*
[18] "On representait dans une sorte de drame hieratique le rapt de la fille Proserpine. On passait par le veritable rencontre du sacrament." Art. *Mystères Eleusiniens*. For an account of this extraordinary symbolism among the aboriginal Americans see Bancroft's *Native Races*, III. p. 507. Is it not a possible thing that this symbolism may have come to the Aleuts and Pepiles from custom as ancient and original as the Eleusinian mysteries? Bancroft says: "The Pep'les abstained from their w ves * * * * previous to sowing, in order to indulge * * * * to the fullest extent on the eve of that day, evidently with a view to initiate or urge the fecundating powers of nature. It is even said that certain persons were appointed to perform the sexual act at the moment of planting the first seed. During the b tter cold nights of the Hyperborean winter, the Aleuts, both men and women joined hands in the open air and whirled perfectly naked round certain i ols, lighted only by the pale moon. The spirit was supposed to hallow the dance with his presence. There certainly could have been no licentious element in this ceremony, for setting aside the discomfort of dancing naked with the thermometer at zero, we read that the dancers were blindfolded, and that decorum was strictly enforced. In Nicaragua, maize sprinkled with blood drawn from the genitals was regarded as sacred food." Additionally to this fact, Bancroft says, (III, p. 506, quoting Palacio, Corta, p. 84)

author has no hesitation in hinting that the great secret which in this case was a veritable *sanctum sanctorum*, was nothing less than a wild scrambling and voluptuous erotomania, such as might happen after a feast of wine. Within these *penetralia* are thus said to have happened an exuberance of voluptuousness, a struggle to feign escape, an agony and a glory of fullest effulgence emblematically representing each, in turn, the process of nature from the time seed is sown in autumn, through the gloom and struggle of winter to the genial spring when the new cereals burst from their first verdure, to their harvest for the nourishment of man. At any rate it is ascertained as certain that there were the *course errante*, the *thalamos* or *pastos*, the veil of the *epoptai*,[19] and all solemnly conducted under the eye of the *hierophant* and Erechtheis, the priest and priestess of the mysteries. Maury[20] declares that an entrance into the fourth degree of the Eleusinian mysteries not only secured to the initiate a positive guaranty against the dreaded *supplicium* of Tartarus, or the lower hell, but it insured his felicity in this life also.[21]

This sketch of the great Eleusinian games may appear to the reader an aberration from our theme, the history of the laborers of ancient times. Not so; for it prepares the way to the student of history from a sociologic point of view, to become acquainted with the grievances the poor were forced to submit to. To be born a degraded wretch, a mere instrument, usable by a master owning one as a thing and handling that thing, its labor, its destiny as an earthy tool, is to a being possessed of sensibility and reason, a grievance. It is slavery. When this slave grows into the reasoning being he inwardly rebels against the men and the institution by which he is held in bondage. He is wise enough to foresee that his only chances of wriggling out of bondage and of securing riddance from its grievances is by some

of the aboriginal inhabitants of Honduras and Mexico: "The frequent occurrence of the cross, which has served in so many and such widely separated parts of the earth as the symbol of the life-giving, creative, and fertilizing principle in nature, is, perhaps one of the most striking evidences of the former recognition of the reciprocal principles of nature by the Americans: especially when we remember that the Mexican name for the emblem tonacaquahuitl, signifies 'tree of one life or flesh.'"
[19] Plato, *Phœdrus*, 250, c.; Böckh, *Inscr.* 1.
[20] Maury, *Histoire des Religions de la Grèce Antique.*
[21] Plato tells us of the sufferings of those who fail to obtain purgation at the mysteries. *Republic*, lib. II. cap. 7. L. edition.

institution of his own; some court of appeal. Political institutions have never given the workingman a court of appeals. The workingman has never yet had a hearing;[22] and his reason and experience both point to the terrible fact that no hearing is possible except before *his own* court of appeals. The trade union is, *per se*, a true court of appeals. We have seen that the isolated *gens* or family of nobles, when threatened by the dangers of a growing population, by pirates, by slave insurrections and feuds, organized themselves into *phratries, curias*, kingdoms, empires and thus found means of submitting their grievances to courts of justice for settlement. We have also means of knowing that the laboring element had, on the other hand, commenced the organization of their forces. Of the former there is sufficient proof; of the latter, as students in the phenomena of ancient social life, we glean here and there fresh proof from inscriptions on tablets of stone which have survived the heedless ages, enabling us to search anew the hitherto vaguely deciphered meanings of expressions of the ancient chroniclers, finding here and there trophies of inestimable worth; all going to show that the ancient laborers, although hated and hunted everywhere and very early, also formed unions and other courts of appeal against grievances. We find evidence too, that these organizations commenced very early—perhaps coeval with the political organization of the nobles, or even before.

But the labor movement of this nineteenth century surrounded by an infinitely more luminous moral atmosphere, is little likely to understand what could possibly have been the grievance of the ancient working people against the Eleusinian games. What objections men will say, could working people, ignorant as they were in those times, have had to any means of salvation soul and body, from suffering.[23] This brings the matter pertinently before us! The Eleusinian mysteries were simply a religious rite, founded amid the ignorance of an ancient period of our forefathers' existence. For that era it was enlightened. What then,

---

[22] See Bristed, *Resources of the United States*, p. 103, ed. 1818 and his reference to the dismal failure of Lycurgus in sapping the family of its loves and in encouraging cruelty.

[23] Bristed, *Idem*, p. 392, declares that all nations that have given themselves up to erratic irregularities, "every species of profligacy" have done so as a consequence of irreligion.

could the lowly who performed the world's drudgery, have encouraged, in opposition to it?

Those who thus interrogate, do so in the absence of an understanding of the question. The laboring classes, though socially degraded, had sensitive feelings. They, like their masters, were believers in the common religion and its forms. They cannot be blamed for that. But while they saw their masters favored with what they thought to be glories of religion, they found themselves utterly excluded. No one at Athens who was a slave, or his descendant could secure admittance. In far later times even christians who were the descendants of slaves and consequently mostly of the laboring element, were denied admittance. The gates, from the remotest era were arbitrarily closed against the workers who labored to produce the means of subsistence for the rich. The gorgeous telesteria, and pilasters of the great temple of Megaron, were, by the outcasts, only to be gazed upon and marveled at from a distance. The Calliades who inherited the priesthood were all of noble blood. The common rabble might get into the caravan and through the dust and din march unobserved from Athens to Eleusis. They might, as in the procession of our modern campmeeting, become inspired with the occasion and imbued with the frenzy of faith, or even dare to picture themselves worthy to participate. But the order of such a man's rank was soon manifested by the missiles, hisses, jeers and attacks against the throng, himself included, by his own people who gathered on the wayside and threw derision and vented spite in turbulence and often force against all the crusaders alike. On his arrival his case became hopeless, for a rigid examination by officers of the law soon detected his meaner rank and caused his expulsion. None but the darlings of the family constituted *gentes* were deemed fit for admission to the holy altar.

We mean by this that the working man was too low in the estimation of the devotees of the Pagan temple to be the possessor of an immortal soul.[24] Now let the questioner

---

[24] Plato, *Laws*, vi; Homer, *Odessey*. XVII. c. 322, 323; Horace, *Sermo*, I The ancient idea was that those who failed to get through the flat earth from this, the mortal side, to the other which was heaven, *Elysium*, perished. Plato the great idealist wrote (*Gorgias*, 168-73; *Phœdo*, 77, 139; *Rep*. c 13), several intensely interesting details on the wanderings and gropings of the soul on whose waxen tablet is indelibly stamped virtues and sins for Rhadamanthus and the

consider that these outcasts were human beings of the same natural stock, against whom natural laws of heredity had made no discrimination; that they were as bright, as clear, as conscious, as well developed and intelligent as their masters, were often their masters' children ; that they sometimes rose supremely to eminence despite the pitiless contempt and mountain-like obstacles they had to contend with —let the objector observe these things in a practical way and he will be furnished a true key to one cause of the dissatisfaction and counter organization of laborers of ancient times, for securing a court that might hear their appeals. The world at that period was divided into two classes, the pious and the impious,[25] which means the nobles, born of the gods and entitled to go back to the gods, and the earthborns, doomed to delve for their masters and at death go back to the earth. But although this was recognized as an old belief coming from the institution of slavery in which the most liberal of men could only acknowledge them to be more than half furnished with an immortal principle,[26] yet the intelligence of the outcasts rebelled against it. Would not men under such circumstances naturally consider this a great grievance ? In our own times, when all men are admitted to be born equal—times compared with those old days being as the dazzle of noonday to the obscurity of morning twilight—in our own free civilization the working people combine upon economic issues, their equality of right to heaven unquestioned; but those people imagined themselves suffering a humiliating grievance when the haughty disclaimer was flung into their face that they were too mean to expect either a present or a future. If then, they gnashed with anguish, or even vengeance or secretly took measures to get even with this oppression, it was but an effort to express a grievance.

We make these statements to show why in ancient times the labor movement took different phases from these we see on every hand about us. We do this because we are about to bring forward proof that there existed an opposition to

other post mortem judges to examine. Those, such as slaves supposed to have no souls, were denied even a burial. They were burned.
[25] Consult chapter 3 of Granier's *Hist, des Classes Ouvrières*, pp. 48–71. The critic should carefully study his magnificent array of notes.
[26] Plato, *Laws*, ix. half a soul; Tim, xviii. ; lxxi. Homer, *Odessey*, lib XVII; Aristotle declared that the children of the noble masters, who were born slaves could be only animated beings.

the whole philosophy based on the slave code and to the religion that denied the equality of man. The first thing is to produce proof that the working people resented their exclusion from the Eleusinian mysteries.

To do this it will be necessary to indulge in a little circumlocution, as the evidence is very vague and indirect. It is in fact, new ground. However much there may lie concealed in support of this important fact which we propose to establish, it must be confessed that such evidence lies in moldering inappreciation and neglect. Did the laboring or outcast element of that ancient era resent and combine against the system that ignored them soul and body?

We have proof that they did; but in adducing this proof hold claim to the right to draw inferences from the existence and career of as many different forms of labor and socialistic organizations as we can hunt out from the gloom of tyranny and oblivion. With this range of the whole field assumed to be conceded, we shall produce before the critic what we can find of all sorts of organizations bearing upon the point, and where the link of evidence becomes broken in the chain of chronology, shall feel perfectly exonerated for drawing upon the plausibly imaginative in order to restore that link. The fact that, as an anthropologist we are undertaking to write a history of ethics from a standpoint of sociology, entitles us to a right to scientifically use all the strategy of comparative testimony. By these remarks is meant the trade union, the co-operative society, the burial society, the society for social amusement among the lowly, the agrarian foment, the social wars, even to some extent the sophist and Pythagorean socialism, the ascetic Essenianism and finally the grand culmination of all, Christianity. All these strictly belong to the true social history of the ancient lowly; for all their membership was originally of freedmen and slave origin.

In order to answer the question properly it is necessary to glance a moment at the social history of the Grecian peninsula. As early as 1055 B. C. there had been a horrible murder or massacre of the Helots or slaves and their descendants at Sparta. It was in the mythical ages; but great events even among the poor and ignorant have a certain faculty of transmitting their history through tradition. It has come down to us through poetry and song, through hints of ancient history, through honest Plutarch, and we are assured as to the assassinations which were from time to time perpetrated upon the defenseless working people of that time. We also know that these poor creatures who were to the body politic of those people what the bones are to the body, had unions for self protection. Still further it is known that they enjoyed the right to organize. It has been ascertained that the slaves themselves actually possessed protective societies[27] and considering the free and intelligent classes whence they were derived it is quite natural that they should have possessed them. Especially is this possible among the helots or slaves of Lacedæmon. They were, as we have seen, slaves by inheritance, often their wealthy masters' own children. They were prisoners of war, forcibly reduced to that wretched condition by being beaten in the war with Helos; and later in the great Messenian war, when Sparta became the victor in that conflict, those brave, proud, ingenius Greeks along with all of the two above mentioned classes, were humiliated, subjugated, degraded to the

[27] It is known that they did at a later period; Cf. Lüders, *Die Dionysischen Künstler*, S. 22 & 47. This author mentions a very interesting inscription (Böckh, *Corpus Inscriptionum Græcarum*, I. p. 417), that has come to light, at or near Pergamus, which shows that slaves belonged to the *eranoi* or union of mechanics. On page 46, Lüders says "Bezeichnend für den Charakter des Vereinswesens der späteren Zeit ist es, dafs auch Sclaven nicht allein an einem Eranos sich betheiligen, sondern auch unter sich ein religiöses Collegium mit Unterstützungscasse bilden druften. Für den von Sclaven benutzten Eranos bieten zahlreiche Beispiele die unlängst in Delphi gefundenen Freilassungsurkunden. Das Collegium Rhodischer Sclaven zu Ehren des Zeus Atabyrios (Διὸς ’Αταβυριασταί τῶν τᾶς πόλιος δούλων"). So also in p. 47, Lüders further corroborates the facts that slaves belonged to the unions: "Dass aber Vereine von einiger Bedeutung auch Sclaven zur Bedienung hatten, ist natürlich; Kraton hatte als Priester des von ihm gestifteten Collegiums der Attalisten testamentarisch dem Thiasos unter anderem Tempel- und Hausgeräth auch Sclaven vermacht. Auf den Reliefs aus Nicäa haben wir in den um das Mahl bes häftigten und in den Musicirenden Personen Sclaven erkannt." On page 22, Lüders has already mentioned this Kraton, in proof of the membership as slaves: "Kraton, günstling der Attalen und hochangesehnes Mitglied und Priester der grossen Synodus Dionysischer Techniten in Teos, hatte nach seiner glänzenden Aufnahme an dem Hofe von Pergamos dort aus dem Verbande der Künstler einen Verein von Thiasoten zu Ehren der Pergamenischen Könige gestiftet, dessen Mitglieder sich Ατταλισταί nennen." Farther on in the same page, he shows that Kraton made the union a present of his own slaves when he died; probably, as Foucart shows that they sometimes did, (*Mém. sur l'affranchissement des esclaves par forme de vente à une divinité* p. 28), in order to set them free. "In seinem Testamente endlich, von dem uns, so wie von jenem Briefe, ein Fragment erhalten ist, vermacht er dem Verbande eine ansehnliche Geldsumme, damit sie aus den Zinsen ihre Opfer und festlichen Zusammenkünfte bestritten den Statuten gemäfs (καθὼς ἐν τῇ νομοθεσίᾳ πρὸς ἑκάστων διατέταχεν). Das Mobiliar des Verein hauses, das Geschirr zu den Opfern und Mahlzeiten und der feierlichen Pompe, das in dem erhaltenen Theile des Testament aufgezählt wird, hinterliess er dem Verein nebst einer Anzahl Sclaven zu dauerndem Besitz.

same servile condition. But although the body was bowed down to servitude, the mind remained to play its fancies, to plot and plan, to concoct in secret; and language was also theirs—a facile tongue—rich in versatility of idiom; full of thrilling nuance and touching charm. The powerful physique was there, the love of adventure, the Greek cravings for a better lot, with fortitude, dash and intrepidity which form the gallant characteristics of that grand people—all these the workingmen of high antiquity possessed. More than this, they had intelligence enough to know that the cruelties they suffered were unjust. If then, we hear through the scintillations of the fragments that there were uprisings, social turmoils and wars, we know them to have been the natural outcome of such a state of things, and nothing to be wondered at.

Now we have promised to adduce proof that there were unions of Greeks who resisted the public insult of the great Eleusinian mysteries which denied to the slaves and their descendants, the freedmen, all hope of happiness here and hereafter.[28] We simply desire, in order to clear up the vagaries, to consider, in our inquiry, the whole of Greece at a time.

Scanning the social condition of the slaves from evidence, we find plenty of assurance that they belonged to the state. The state leased them out. The state, from the primitive family, was organized for purposes of defense.[29] The family first possessed the slave. Slaves became more numerous than families. They did all the labor and were allowed no privileges. So they rebelled. Some ran away, hid in fastnesses, became dangerous brigands. They became organized. Then the rich families organized themselves into fratries and other forms. As the slaves had belonged to the families, so now they belonged to the fratries. This means that as the slaves were before private property, so now they, or some of them, became public

---

[28] Plutarch, *Theseus*, speaks of the demagogue Menestheus who, about 1186 before Christ rose up against the tyranny of the aristocrats at Athens, with the claim that the people also had a right to be initiated into the Eleusinian mysteries. Even at that remote period there must have been between the poor and lowly and the rich and lordly, great struggles regarding this grievance.

[29] Morgan. *Ancient Society*, chap. ii : Drumann, *Arbeiter und Communisten in Griechenland und Rom*, S. 24: "In Epidamnis gab es keine Hanwerker als die öffentlichen Sklaven."; "Das Handwerk ist daher verrufen und verachtet." S. 26: Aristotle, *Politic*, ll. 4, § 13.

property, This was a political sequence upon the organization of the families into fratries and the consolidation of the fratries into the state. Of course the rich family still kept as many servants as it needed; but large numbers remained with the public domain. These state slaves formed into organizations.[30] From the earliest mythical accounts down to 58 years before Christ we find evidences abundantly proving that the law gave work-people the especial right to organize not only in Rome but also in Greece. The celebrated Law of the Twelve Tables which specified the manner of organization of workingmen, is declared by the commentators to be a translation from the Greek laws of Solon.[31]

The Twelve Tables clearly set down the arrangement, ordaining that the trade unions should remain in obedience to the law of the state. The unions followed the law, and Gaius wrote the law thus fixed, so plainly that Justinian incorporated it into the digest. A fragment of the law of Solon[32] shows plainly that trades unions were common and tolerated by that lawgiver. A strong cumulative evidence that the slaves belonging to the state were enormously organized into protective association, is found in the fact that they succeeded in their insurrections against the masters. An important example of these slave insurrections is given of the miners.[33] In Attica they once rebelled, and marched upon the town near the silver mines, occupying the castle of Sunion. These people were called "*thetes*" or "*demoes*."

In Athens the fact of their manumission did not make them anything above mere earth-borns. They could develop genius, become teachers, philosophers, poets and business men. Sometimes they rose to positions of wealth, even themselves becoming master-builders, and some of them were the greatest sculptors and painters the world ever produced; but the taint of servility was born in their blood. Phidias the most celebrated sculptor, ancient or modern, was a descendant of the slaves. He was

---

[30] Lüders, *Dionyschischen Künstler.* S. 46; Wescher-Foucart *Inscriptions de Delphes*, pp 89, 107, 139, 244, giving abundant evidence
[31] Gaius, *Digest*, lib XLVII. tit. xxii lex. 4; Plutarch, *Numa*.
[32] Granier, *Histoire des Classes Ouvrières &c* pp. 283-7.
[33] Consult the Encyclopedias, *Articles* on *Slavery*; also for instances of Asiatic slaves joining the rebellion of Aristonicus, see *Infra*, chapter ix.

really a freedman. He built the *propylae* of the Parthenon, and with his skillful hand made the beautiful and colossal statues of Athena and the wonderful chryselephantine statue of the Olympian Zeus. Parrhasius, one of the finest painters, who transmitted to the Italian schools the art of delineations, was, in all probability a freedman. Demosthenes in his terrible vehemence pronounced Æschines a son of a freedman. That alone probably had a strong tendency toward deciding the great case against Æschines, whose mighty genius, though the outcome of lowly parentage, well-nigh brought to the scaffold the greatest orator of ancient or modern days. In these bright years of our nineteenth century, such scurrile slurs as Demosthenes hurled against his enemy, which were used to incite contempt, would be thought an insult upon the act of labor. Innumerable were the marvels of genius among the Greeks, and as innumerable the deprecatory innuendoes, the cowardly jealousies, the surreptitious revenges that were seated and sealed in the accident of birth. Much of the greater and lesser broils may be attributed to it.

Our object in this divergence is to give, from a reading of the past, in the spirit of sociological research, the fact that the lowly of the Greek population were organized to a large extent, against this scathing grievance, the taint of labor.

That the slaves belonged in great numbers to the state is seen by any one who consults the law of Lycurgus.[34] It must be most distinctly understood that the great law of Lycurgus was intended only for the development and enjoyment of the two favored classes of Lacedæmonian society—the Spartans and Pericœci. He belonged to the Eurystheneid line of Spartan kings. An aristocrat by birth and according to Herodotus, living about a thousand years before our era, he would not permit the third class or working people even to taste of the advantages of his system—otherwise almost a perfect socialism if we except its heathenish immodesty and blood-thirst. The land he divided into 9,000 lots for the Spartans who were

---

[34] Plutarch, *Lycurgus*: "It is not worth while to take much pains as to riches since they are of no account; and the Helots (slaves) who tilled the ground, were answerable for the produce mentioned." And a few lines farther on: "So much beneath them they estimated every thought of mechanic arts as well as wish for riches."

fewest in numbers, 30,000 lots for the Periœci or Laconians who were more numerous in proportion. The poor Helots or work-people and descendants from slaves got nothing although their proportionate numbers were three to one. This hegemony of Greece incorporated into itself the most degrading slavery to be found in the world's history. Lycurgus although to his favorite people perhaps in many respects a model, was towards those he arrogantly assumed to be beneath him—the laboring class—the model of a monster. His system of the ambuscade[35] disgusted even Plato, who was a believer in slavery. Plato's great heart turned away in loathing from such a stupendous abomination. The ambuscade, a diabolism that should blacken any age, could exist only in a country where calm, cold-blooded contempt gets the better of the warmer emotions. In looking over the lofty but ghastly eloquence of Cicero, whose implacable contempt for the working people in later times cost him his life, we have the nearest parallel to inveterate hate.

No historigrapher can hereafter afford to neglect the inhuman butcheries perpetrated by the ambuscade; since they differed from the massacres of Stone Henge, of Saint Bartholomew, of the Incas, of the Mamelukes, of Wyoming, in being consummated at moments of profoundest peace; at moments when the innocent victims were wrapt in the fiendish assassins' service, sweating in the fields, at the mill, with the flocks, on the provision market, producing, garnering and distributing the food, the clothing, the shelter which their heartless butchers were consuming without gratitude, to invigorate their veins whereby to accomplish such treacheries!

Just before reciting these horrors let us revert to the victim. He was primarily the slave by the ancient family law of entail and primogeniture. The shackles of abject servitude were first inherited through the humiliating law of entails which fixed the heir of the patrimony, the first born son, as a lord to be served, worshiped, immortalized, and blessed; his children to be chattels, subjected, forced to labor, distrusted, branded and cursed.[36]

[35] For more on the *Cryptia*, see Plutarch, *Lycurgus*.
[36] Fustel de Coulanges, *Cité Antique*, livre 2. *La Famille*; Granier de Cassagnac, *Histtoire des Classes Ouvrières*, chap 3.

Next, after this primary calamity came the slaves of war; whole communities taken, carried off by the captors and degraded to slavery and its concomitant curse,[37] as in the case of the Messenian war with Sparta. Lastly the slave trade;—three great ancient systems. Under these he suffered torments which no pen of mortal will ever portray. He was known by his dress, sometimes going in rags equivalent to nudity, in gangs under a brutal boss. Sometimes, in this condition, man along with woman, destitute of means of being decent, dragging the long day among the fields and flocks; dogskin hats and sheepskin breeches, which survive longest the wear of the wearer, and often totally nude. They were each flogged once a day as an admonition, though having committed no offence and forbidden to learn the manly arts. They were obliged to stoop and crouch in piteous obsequiousness to these drivers lest jealous tyranny interpret their upright posture to be an assumption of the estate of manhood.[38] Such was the condition of the workingman of Sparta which, above all other countries whereof we discover a historic trace, was the most pitiless toward the slave. And the most shameful phase of this confession is the cruel fact that all this was precept of the Lycurgan law!

We must return to the *cryptia* or ambuscade of the law of Lycurgus. These Helots or working people, state-slaves of Lacedæmon, lived and performed much of their labor in the rural districts. The law of Lycurgus provided for the election, annually, of five magistrates or overseers, called *ephori*, whose function was to strengthen and heighten the principles of democracy that the happiness of the people might be equalized. Plutarch's doubts as to whether Lycurgus instituted the *ephori* seem to be dispelled by his acknowledgment that both Plato and Aristotle thought so.[39] One of the functions of this institu-

---

[37] Ælian, *Historia Varia*, I. 1.; Athenæus. *Deipnosophistæ*. vi; Xenophon *Memorabilia*, 8, 6, § 2 ; Bücher, *Aufstände der unfreien Arbeiter* S. 36 ; All of these authors also Livy give evidence on the enslavment of men taken in war.
[38] "The Ephori indeed, declared war against them! Against whom? Why poor, naked slaves who tilled their lands, dressed their food and did all those offices for them which they were too proud to do for themselves." Cf. Plutarch, *Lycurgus*, note in Langhorne's tr.
[39] Plato, *Republic, Dissertation on Lacedæmon*; Aristotle, *Politic*. v. ascribes their origin to a later period of the law's existence than that of the lawgiver's lifetime. Nevertheless they are the outcome of the great law of Lycurgus.

tion for the promotion of popular democracy was to see that the ambuscade was well carried out. All that was meant by the term *people* was the people who owned the land, either by parcel or as government property together with the slaves and other chattels of that property. This means that the really worthless and indolent non-producers were the people. The useful majority of the inhabitants, the working population, were entirely ignored, contemptuously denied every vestige of participation in this much boasted government, although there exists abundance of evidence that they were naturally intelligent and as worthy as their masters, of enjoying the product of their labor in this state of democracy.

Instead of this, the ephori ordained that a certain number of young men from among the aristocrats should, at their command, arm themselves with daggers, and provided with a sort of knapsack with provisions, secretly sneak off into the mountains and jungles.[40] The distances these legalized assassins were required to go varied very much. These youths had governors who had the power to order them to do as the ephori should determine. The governors, whenever the ephori voted a new slaughter of the working people, called together the smartest and most able bodied of these young men, armed them with daggers, sharpened and gleaming for the occasion.[41] At the same time the inhuman overseers whom we may with due propriety call bosses, in accord with a technical signification fully adopted by the prevailing labor movement of to-day, were ordered to see to it that the toilers should be without arms or means of any kind with which to defend themselves when suddenly set upon by the amateur Spartan soldier, dagger in hand. With all these odds against them the poor, unsuspecting, half naked working people were driven by the bosses, as usual into the field, the mill, the kitchen and the various places of service wherever required to eke the drudgery of a sun-and-sun summer day of toil. Meantime the assassins were laying in wait in the vicinity for their prey. It was a manly sport! The law of Lycurgus made more compulsory than any other code on earth, the provisions of manly

[40] Plutarch, *Lycurgus*, where these horrors are related.
[41] Thucydides, *De Bello Peloponnesiaco*, liber IV. 80.

gymnastics. This was one of them. It was sport!" By
the exercise of this manly sport the youth's blood flowed
stronger, his muscles grew, his body waxed athletic; he
digested with a better relish the food his blood-begrimed
victim had in the morning prepared for him before his
murderous weapon slashed and pierced her gentle heart.
We quote from Plutarch. No one ever speaks illy of Plutarch. His means of knowing facts were better than ours,
and his kind nature even in the barbarous age in which
he lived, revolted against the consistency of such a democracy. He says:"
"The governors of the youth ordered the shrewdest of
them from time to time to disperse themselves in the
country, provided only with daggers and some necessary
provisions. In the day time they hid themselves and rested
in the most private places they could find; but at night
they sallied out into the roads and killed all the Helots
they could meet with. Nay, sometimes by day, they fell
upon them in the fields and murdered the ablest and
strongest of them."⁴⁴
These are specimens of authentic history of the lowly
as they have passed through a transition period of unnumbered centuries, from abject slavery to a Christian
democracy which recognizes all men as equal and provides
for them precepts for equal enjoyment. But before quit-
ting these chambers of cruelty and carnage it remains our
sad duty to recount what modern historians well know,
but seldom divulge—the great assassination. It happened
during the Peloponnesian war. This account comes from
the trusted and reliable historian Thucydides, who lived
at the time and made it his business for many years to
keenly observe what transpired, during that long and
tedious struggle of seven and twenty years. The story is
briefly told by him. Dressed and reflected upon in our
own way it appears in substance as follows:

During the great Peloponnesian war, one of the most
renowned in antiquity, the forces of the army sometimes
became decimated and it was necessary to recruit them

---

[42] K. O. Müller in *Die Dorier*, denies this; but the evidence is too strong against him. Again, Müller's opinion regarding their "aboriginal descent" has been completely overturned.
[43] Plutarch's *Lycurgus*.
[44] *Idem*; Cf. tr. of the Langhornes Vol. I. pp. 63-4.

from whatever source possible. When, therefore, there were no more soldiers to be had from among the Spartans and Periœci or recognized citizens, the military authorities were obliged to call out the laboring men who, at the time of the Peloponnesian war, were three to four times more numerous than the non-laboring class. This in ancient times was always a humiliation. War was the noble occupation, labor the ignoble one. To ask a person in disgrace to assist the nobles out of trouble was equivalent to humiliating confession. If then, the laborer, in a great emergency was marshaled to the rescue, the only way to blot out the stain such a humiliation entailed was to enfranchize this warrior from social thraldom and thus stanch the blot by elevating him from the fetters of bondage. If further, the bondsman after performing the service manfully, redeeming his masters by bravery and valor, earning his liberty by saving their lives and preserving their realm from wreck, could be secretly murdered after such decree of manumission was administered, it would save the proud masters many a disagreeable jeer, painful wince and blush of shame when reminded that their existence and happiness was due to the daring and fidelity of a hated menial who still shocked their pride with his presence.

It came to pass that this humiliating expedient was indispensible to save the nation from irretrievable ruin and thousands of the enslaved laborers were marshaled and drilled into the army. They were not allowed to bear heavy arms; that would have been a still greater disgrace. So they bore light arms and bore them gallantly. After serving through many a tedious campaign probably of years' duration, after winning victories in many a skirmish and in many a field and earning the full measure of their promised reward, after seeing the Lacedæmonian armies victorious at every hand and the great war prosperously advancing toward triumph for the southern Greeks, there were brought before the military tribunal for dismissal over two thousand workingmen who had proved truest in arms and been adjudged worthiest of liberty. Their faithful hands had valiantly borne the standard of an ungrateful country. Their strong hearts had never flinched either before their sullen discipline or the cleaving blades of the combatants. Their fiery zeal and fearless blows had won the victory and earned the liberty which, before this august council, proudly they heard pronounced. Over 2,000 slaves who toiled for masters were thus regularly enfranchised and marched into a temple or other enclosure or field—no mortal knows or ever will know what—to take the oath of freedom. But the anxious wives and children waited and wept long before these brave men came to gladden their hovel homes. For here we come to the recital of one of the darkest pages of history. Still more painful is this page because blotted. Too foully blotted for perusal; since, aside from a ghastly blood-stain that smirches its story in mysterious gloom, it is written in the almost undecipherable hieroglyphs of reticent shame. Thucydides blushes for this lurid page;[45] but unlike the unmanly historians of the past who have cringed in the presence of truth which could not port the flattery of lords and masters of high degree, he bravely told us all he knew. And what he knew is enough to make the blood run cold.[46] Besides, it comes to us subscribed to by Plato,[47] Aristotle[48] and Plutarch,[49] on whose minds, if we catch aright their words, this massacre we are going to relate made an impression so strong as to waver the tone of these great philosophers' belief in slavery[47] and seriously color their dialectics.

[45] Thucydides during the Peloponnesian war for the hegemony of Greece, commanded a division of the Athenian marine force; but being out-generaled at Amphipolis by Bra-idas went for twenty years into exile and during that time used his wealth and talent writing the celebrated history which has come down to us.
[46] Thucydides, *De Bello Peloponnesiaco*, liber IV. cap. 80. "Καὶ ἅμα τῶν Εἱλωτῶν βουλομένοις ἦν ἐπὶ προφάσει ἐκπέμψαι, μή τι πρὸς τὰ παρόντα τῆς Πύλου ἐχομένης νεωτερίσωσιν· ἐπεί καὶ τόδε ἔπραξαν, φοβούμενοι αὐτῶν τὴν νεότητα καὶ τὸ πλῆθος (ἀεὶ γὰρ τὰ πολλὰ Λακεδαιμονίοις πρὸς τοὺς Εἵλωτας τῆς φυλακῆς πέρι μάλιστα καθεστήκει)· προεῖπον αὐτῶν ὅσοι ἀξιοῦσιν ἐν τοῖς πολεμίοις γεγενῆσθα σφίσιν ἄριστοι, κρίνεσθαι, ὡς ἐλευθερώσοντες, πεῖραν ποιούμενοι καὶ ἡγούμενοι τούτους σφίσιν ὑπὸ φρονήματος, οἵπερ καὶ ἠξίωσαν πρῶτος ἕκαστος ἐλυθερούσθαι μάλιστα ἂν καὶ ἐπιθέσθαι. Καὶ προκρίναντες ἐς δισχιλίους οἱ μὲν ἐστεφανώσαντό τε καὶ τὰ ἱερὰ περιῆλθον ὡς ἠλευθερομένοι. Οἱ δὲ οὐ πολλῷ ὕστερον ἠφάνισάν τε αὐτοὺς καὶ οὐδεὶς ᾔσθετο ὅτῳ τρόπῳ ἕκαστος διεφθάρη."
[47] Plato, *De Republica*, *Dissertation on Model State*.
[48] Aristotle, *Politic*, V.
[49] Plutarch, *Lycurgus*, cap. 28. This massacre occurred under Brasidas, in B. C. 424. Ælian, *Historia Varia*, I. 1, says that in Greece the superstitious belief everywhere prevailed that these cruelties to the poor slaves caused a judgment from heaven upon the Spartans, in form of an earthquake, B. C. 467, by which 20,000 people lost their lives. This must have been before the massacre described and proves the frequency of those horrible deeds of the Ephori and their tutored and organized assassins. For later comments on this earthquake at Sparta and the superstitious terrors believed to come from their cruelty to slaves, see McCullagh, *Industrial History of Free Nations*, I. p. 6.

THE MYSTERIES

This much is known that during the time these 2,000 or more soldiers were going through the ordeal of being garlanded, crowned, distinguished and conducted to the temple of the gods to receive their first beatitude, their blessing and reward for bravery, the ephori were busily and secretly making out a declaration of war, arming the valorous young men and giving them instructions to crawl cat-like upon them with the assassin's daggers! No more is known; for here the page is torn beyond recovery. But enough is known. The happy braves all disappear forever. Naught but a dark and spectral mystery broods over this page of history. The workingmen had received the emoluments of their hire at the hand of an assassin democracy!

The careful student of history from a standpoint of social science may pick up evidence that to some extent even the Helots were organized. Facts continually crop out in the records showing that these degraded doers of Spartan labor under the law of Lycurgus, unable to resist the exactions, raised insurrections against their tormentors, and that they sometimes got the better of them. In almost every other part of Greece they are known to have been organized into many forms of associative self-support by which they were able to command more respect. We return to Athens.

The fact must not be lost sight of that at Athens as everywhere among the Aryans, there were two distinct classes by birth—the nobles, claiming to be descended from the gods, and the earth-borns who went back to earth. The first would not work if they could possibly avoid it; at least this may be said of the men. The latter did most of the work; not only the menial drudgery but the skilled labor of building the magnificent temples and other public edifices whose imposing ruins are still a wonder of the now living age. To the credit of woman in high life be it said that sometimes the *materfamilias* spun and wove, according to some testimony of Plato. There are two important facts to be considered: In Greece, Rome and elsewhere in Europe and western Asia, northern Africa and the islands, the working people greatly outnumbered the non-workers. In Greece they were three and four times more numerous. Again, they were often chattles of that state. The land belonged to the state and the laborers who tilled the land went with it. This as we shall see, became in Italy, under the generous laws of Numa, a great benefit for them which they enjoyed for about 500 years. In Greece the land also belonged to the state; but the cruel law of Lycurgus which was instituted 1,000 years before Christ and held good, as Plutarch tells us for 500 years, treated the poor creatures with such flagitious absolutism that they could never enjoy so well as did the Roman laborers, the boon of their own organization.

The law of Lycurgus was pernicious in its inculcation of the two moral elements of Plato; those of irascibility and concupiscence without sympathy. When a master owns a slave from whom he expects to receive labor product, he finds it for his own advantage to treat him well; otherwise he would not receive the full product of the man's labor; but when the land belonged to the state and the slaves also, this personal responsibility was smothered with it. Thus hatred and contempt, attributes of Plato's irascible impulse, constituting one of the bases of moral philosophy, were for ages allowed to develope in the breast of the Spartan. Again, concupiscence or desire, being common or national under the Lycurgan law, was averted from its natural competitive course by a communism of gratification without responsibilities and a communism of participation; and these with idleness and all the depravity which such deteriorating influences entail, lowered Spartan morality below the plain of sympathy. This unfeeling and inhuman condition of the public mind became a natural result ultimately destroying the otherwise unhindered plan of Lycurgus.

Had the law of Lycurgus provided for absolute equality of *all* men, slave and noble alike, had its communism applied to all on exactly equal footing, the common ownership could have been carried out by the state with greater general happiness and all the cruelty which depraved Spartan life would have been saved to the credit of a splendid people. But that would have been a death blow to the Pagan religion, itself based upon egoism and possible only under a system of lords and slaves. Thus, with the exception of the taint of labor and its concomitant wrongs to the human race, the ancients began radically. They began by having the family egoism of the primordial hearthstone—the first ownership—subdued into common ownership of land and even of children; and had they banished that hideous curse, the taint of labor and added to their other and truly virtuous methods of self culture, the enobling, healthful and thrift-bearing practice of impartial economical labor as a necessary requisite to sanity and wealth they would have taught the world a lesson of advancement instead of one in degeneracy and shame. The same must be said of Athens and the other Grecian states except that none of them are known to have been so cruel and heartless as the Spartans under the Lycurgan law.

We have thus sufficiently shown the grievance borne by the ancient working people inciting and goading them to organization. It now remains to be proved that the Greeks of this class, were actually in a substantial state of combination, especially the Athenians, during the existence of the Eleusinian games near Athens; a point which throughout the chapter has been the subject in kernel, of our inquiry. This substantiated, we have a startling clue to the causes from a sociological standpoint, of two historical phenomena: the social wars and the advent of our era.

Every recent investigation reveals fresh slabs or drags from the depths of time, earth and oblivion something in proof. Dr. Schliemann, quotes a passage of Homer which shows an explanation comprehensible to us in no other way than that there existed an understanding at that ancient day, between the lower people. A peddler came to the palace with a gold collar set with amber beads, and Homer sang a beautiful verse describing the knowing look that the young prince saw exchanged between the man and the servant woman in the hall while the queen was admiring the amber necklace.[50] These were the nods and winks

[50] Schliemann, *Tiryns; The Pre-historic Palace*, p. 368, containing the passage from Homer. This also suggests that the working people, including house servants, were secretly in league at Mycenæ and that the league reached as far as Phœnicia.

ἠλυθ' ἀνὴρ πολυΐδρις ἐμοῦ πρὸς δώματα πατρός,
χρύσεον ὅρμον ἔχων, μετὰ δ' ἠλέκτροισιν ἔερτο·
τὸν μὲν ἄρ' ἐν μελάρῳ δμωαὶ καὶ πότνοα μήτηρ
χερσίν τ' ἀμφαφόωντο, καὶ ὀφθαλμοῖσιν ὁρῶντο,
ὦνον ὑπισχόμεναι· ὁ δέ τῇ κατένευσε σιωπῇ·
ἤτοι ὁ καννεύσας κοίλην ἐπὶ νῆα βεβήκει."

of the secret society which were observed but could not be read by the lad. This was in the second millennium before Christ.

Granier, who must have been a great hunter of facts, observes that slavery was originally of the family; not of violent origin,[51] precisely what Dr. Fustel de Coulanges has since proved beyond refutation of the most probing commentators seeking contrary evidence.[52] Of course history gives ponderous testimony that violence was a source of enslavement; but that was not the origin. When our era opened it brought with it an inestimable boon; a pearl of great price; the utter extinction of social class [53]—nothing less than the long sought revolution. Dr. Cliffe Leslie in an introduction to M. De Laveleye's "Primitive Property," observing the progress of this greatest of all the revolutions which he rightly sees is yet far from being realized though nearly all civilized races have repudiated the curse of slavery, takes the entirely correct view with regard to ownership after the momentous but gradual revolution is past.[54]

It is known that in early Greece the *hetairai* and the *hetairoi* were female and male associates of the laboring class, and that they had their legalized association for mutual benefit. From very early times they used their associations, not only for mutual protection against oppression but also for mutual improvement and pleasure.[55]

The celebrated jugglers were mostly members of an organization under whose auspices they used their jugglery as a trade wherewith to gain a living. These are of almost incredibly ancient origin and in Greece many of them were descendants of Egyptian slaves. It is not difficult to prove that at an epoch since which an æon of time has

[51] *Histoire des Classis Ouvrières*, p. 33: "In conclusion, everything leads in the plainest manner to the belief that slavery had no other beginning than that of the family entailment of which it constituted an economic part."
[52] *La Cité Antique*, liv. II. chap. vii. pp. 76–89.
[53] Paul, *Epistle to the Gallations*, chap. iii. verse 28; "There is neither Jew nor Greek, there is neither bond nor free, there is neither male nor female; for ye are all one in Jesus Christ."
[54] *Primitive Property, Introduction*, p. xxi. "The owners of property are on the eve of becoming a powerless minority; for the many, to whom the whole power of the state is of necessity gravitating, see all the means of subsistence and enjoyment afforded by nature in the possession of the few." Cliffe Leslie.
[55] Guhl and Koner, *Life of the Greeks and Romans*, pp. 268–269, showing Greek customs and manners at a *symposion*. Other evidence testifies to there being a secret organization at these feasts, which conducted the ceremonies. See also Lüders, *Die Dionysischen Künstler*, *passim*.

rolled over the human race, those jugglers were plying their profession the same as at a much later era in which we find them at Athens.[56] The professional business of these jugglers and tumblers was to amuse the people; and there are abundant inscriptions and pictures to be found on vases and other pieces of pottery which show that they worked hard to earn their money. These were specimens of the slave system which marks the despotic rule, and existed first. All remote antiquity bears evidence, in prehistoric inscriptions and inkings of different nature, of many slaves, and that labor was degraded." The slaves being first, there came about an era of manumissions. Freedmen entered upon the scene bearing the taint of slave labor and were obliged to resort to all sorts of industry and wit to make a living; and among other methods adopted to secure that end, they entered into mutual alliances with each other for common assistance through trade organizations. There were great numbers also of the *communia mimorum*[58] or unions of comic actors who in a similar manner got a living by amusing the people. Strabo speaks of them[59] and Böckh gives the Greek of an interesting institution of this kind.[60] Mommsen gives the law recorded in the digest from Gaius, which afterwards suppressed most of these societies.[61]

A curious union was that of the *Urinatores*, men whose business at Rome was to dive in the Tiber and probably

---

[56] "An attempt has been made to mathematically measure this vast eriod of time by calculating from the depth of mud of the alluvial Nile, at wh ch objects have been found, by L. Horner, on *The Alluvial Land of Egypt*, and result published in the *Phil. Transactions*, 1858, p. 75, which gives 12,000 years, at the assumed rate of deposit of three and five tenths inches per 100 years at Memphis, from the fragments of vases found 70 feet under ground." Sir Gardne Wilkinson, *Ancient Egyptians*, vol. I. pp. 8-9., note, *paraphrased*.
[57] Cf. Bancroft, *Native Races*, vol. IV. *Antiquities*, pp. 305-6, showin that l the remote past of Central America, inscriptions exhibiting the most despotic conditions were produced, probably thousands of years before the discovery of the present nomadic races who were found in a semi-communal state. At Pr lenque are inscriptions on the ancient walls showing conditions coeval with the earliest European monarchism. A king garbed in fine military attire, and the everlasting slaves on bended knees and in humble suppliance. They a e freely drawn, with art superior to Egyptian, being in *bas reliefs*, in stucco on the wall of the palace.
[58] Mommsen, *De Collegiis et Sodaliciis Romanorum*. p. 83: "Commui 'a mimorum Romanorum et in nomina et in institutis τὰ κοινὰ τῶν περὶ τὸν ὀνύσσ τενιτῶν referunt, quæ apud Græcos ampla et plurima fuerunt."
[59] Strabo, *Geographica*, XIV. 643, 28.
[60] *Corpus Inscriptionum Græcarum*, nos. 349 and 2931.
[61] Mommsen; *De Coll. et Sodal. Romanorum*, p. 84. Great numbers of these societies existed about the Hellespont and among the Ionian Islands.

also into the public baths in search of things lost by the grandees while boating or bathing.[62]. At Naples, Nice and other places on the sea these divers had unions and no doubt possessed skilled men who succeeded in restoring the valuables after the wrecks of triremes, and other craft.[62] Especially were these unions a benefit to community at Syracuse, the Piræus and Byzantium, where these and other unions abounded in great numbers. Mommsen on the law of Solon also declares that there were both sacred and civil communes,[63] and he further states that all such societies were not only permitted, but they possessed at that early period (B. C. 600), the right of perpetual organization. The probability is that these organizations had existed from a much earlier epoch than that of Solon; but having never done any harm at Athens and the Athenians being a much more sympathic people than the Spartans, they were never molested. So long as the trade unions of the world, ancient and modern, have restricted themselves to mere pleasure, religion, and frugality, they do not appear to have been harshly dealt with; but so soon as they ventured to consider and act upon the subject of politics, which of all others, was most necessary to their welfare, they became objects of hate and of repression. Especially was this the case in ancient times; because politics like war, was a noble calling. Petty frugality, and crude convivial, as well as burial ordeals were too trifling and mean in the eyes of the nobles to attract attention.

There was at Athens a class of public servants.[64] They were not real slaves although public property, and treated as menials; never being allowed to participate in the slightest degree in the principle of government and yet they actually performed all the routine labor of the government. At the time we hear of them through public records and through inadvertent mention by historians, they seem to resemble freedmen. They received a small salary to keep them alive, and their business was to keep

---

[62] Orellius, *Inscriptionum Latinarum Selectarum Amplissima Collectio*, No. 4115: "Ti. Claudio Esquil. Severo Decuriali lictore.................sportulæ viritim dividantur præsertim cum navigatio scapharum diligentia ejus adquisita et confirmata sit. Ex decreto ordinis corporis piscatorum et urinatorum totius alvei Tiberis quibus ex SC. coire licet." The inscription was found in Rome.
[63] "Notabilis est hoc loco lex Solonis, ex qua sacra civiliaque communia non alio jure fuerunt quam quo societates ad negotiationem præditionemve consti tutæ." Mommsen, *De Collegiis et Sodaliciis Romanorum*, p. 39.
[64] Consult Dr. Hermann, *Political Antiquities of Greece*, paragraph 147.

the books and do the various duties of a public office under government.

They had their protective unions. Being clerks, and constantly in presence of polite people, they made a genteel appearance and were apt in the civilities of court. But like all their class they also had a grievance. They were treated as menials because they were not "blooded;" and consequently could not pit their natural genius and ability against that of their masters who conducted the public offices and who belonged to noble stock. "It was required that Archons and priests should prove the purity of their descent as citizens for three generations."[65] The business of the Pagan temple was a part of the state affairs; and consequently priests in those times were public officers. Priests were politicians. One of the qualifications of the Archons or rulers was to have a good record that they attended to religious ceremonies. Ostracism, banishment and death were among the punishments designated by the law for neglecting these duties of citizenship; and the least whisper against any of the gods or the regulations of the Pagan religion was blasphemy. This explains the causes of that great difference in station which existed without regard to the business qualifications of the men. Smart workingmen without rights, or any claim to rights, were often required on a mean salary to do all the work of both departments of governments without being entitled to the least benefit in either, while a tyrant and sensualist held all control and honor like some modern sinecurists of our offices. There is evidence that this exclusivism was regarded by the poor workmen as a great grievance; but their exclusion from free participation in religious rights and especially from membership in and access to the Eleusinian mysteries was the greatest one. Against these grievances they were organized in secret.

Dionysius of Halicarnassus mentions a society of the *Thiasotes* or Greek labor unions, the members of which had for their patron deity the goddess Minerva through the noble family of the Nautii, who brought the image of Minerva away from the Trojans to Italy.[66] Here it ap-

---

[65] *Idem*, §. 148. The δοκιμασία, or scrutiny into the antecedants of candidates, is here explained.
[66] Dionysius of Halicarnassus, *Antiquitates Romanæ*, VI. 69.

pears that the union was not permitted to worship their goddess directly but had to approach her through a noble family. By worshiping the borrowed proxy they got access indirectly to the object of their reverence. This statement is valuable as it sheds light upon what in those early times is thus proved to have been felt as a grievance; and shows that it was imperative on the part of the unrecognized working people to organize and take counsel with each other on what they considered a most important matter, the right of worship, from which they were excluded on account of their reputed meanness of birth. The existence or non-existence of the soul depended upon it. Dirksen in his Twelve Tables points to Gaius in proof that the *hetairai* and the *sodales* were one and the same organization;[67] the former being in Greece and the latter in Italy. He further states that a comparison with the law of Solon proves that they were tolerated and their actions encouraged, if not regulated by him. The Twelve Tables are now known to be contemporaneous with, if not a translation from the law of Solon; and the law of Solon was a paraphrase of the still more ancient law of Amasis an Egyptian king.

Nor was this organization common to Rome and Greece. Granier says: "Trades Unions existed since the time of Solomon, and among the Greeks from the time of Theseus."[68] In the time of Joshua, B. C. 1537-1427, they are spoken of. We have evidence regarding an organization that attempted a resistance to the overbearing nobles, in time of Agis I. These were Helots. The insurrection did not succeed, for it appears that the king caused their murder in large numbers. Agis I. was one of the mythical Spartan kings and is believed to have reigned more than a thousand years before Christ. This great massacre of the helots took place 1055 years before Christ. Traditionally the event came down to the era of writing as something mysterious and terrible. When at last, it entered the chronicles of historians it was dim in detail and being a subject which gave pain instead of pleasure —one of those servile episodes which early history appears

[67] They had in Greece the σύσσιτοι (communists), who **ate at the common table**, the ὁμόταφοι (burial societies), the θιασῶται (disciples of the doctrine of mutual love).
[68] Granier de Cassagnac. *Histoire des Classes Ouvrières*, chap. xii.

to have preferred to leave unwritten—we unfortunately have only a few faint records which have struggled through the mists of high antiquity and gleam darkly through sullen tradition and venturesome historic jottings upon us. But the murder of the helots by order of Agis I. is spoken of by many authors as having occurred B. C. 1,055 or thereabout. After that event they became *adscripti glebae*, public property attached to the soil.

The student of history from a standpoint of sociology, would, however, be glad to obtain more light upon that event; because we want to know what was the origin of the Aristotelian philosophy and the surroundings that motived it.

Of all the philosophies or systems of arrangement as a basis of enduring polity, the chrematistics of Aristotle, properly understood, is sure to be that which any and all great labor movements cannot but adopt. The sociologist, who intelligently scans the evolution of our race on the enormous scale in which things are presented to him by the vicissitudes of the lowly and downtrodden poor who have fed and enriched the non-laboring few from earliest ages, cannot but wonder how a rich and fortunate man, an aristocrat, a believer in slavery, a dialectician, and one who spurned the menial, who counciled and advised the mightiest of monarchs, could have settled down in the conclusion that there is only one way of getting at truth and that is by beginning at small things and through them, in tireless investigation and experiment, learn to know and improve. Yet all who study the logic of this man, as laid down by him, are irresistibly led to traverse the very path which he opened with the keen edge of his slashing knife of reason. He "discriminated between the several faculties;—the nourishing, feeling, concupiscent, moving and reasoning powers of animal organism and attempted to explain the origin of these powers within the body, and build his morals and politics on the peculiarities of human organization."[69] Everything according to Aristotle, if we would positively know, must be founded on close observation of facts. His *eudaimonia* was attained only through the bliss that rewards mind or reason when it achieves

---

[69] *American Encyclopædia*, Art. *Aristotle*.

LABOR A SOURCE OF A THINKER'S SUCCESS. 117

truth by indefatigable experiment and experience. He would have men acquire all knowledge by study of humble facts, and lay down therefrom a true basis of political economy. Nothing, not even the servile race, the slaves, the freedmen, the workingmen, was so mean but Aristotle could enrich his mind by studying it.

Here lies concealed from all eyes except those of the student of man from the standpoint of sociology, a phenomenon. Why did Aristotle adopt opposite conclusions from Plato, his old master? Plato believed largely in the theory that only the unseen gods dwelling in the etherial abodes, could impart to man absolute knowledge. Aristotle dared believe and teach that knowledge could only be had by observation and experiment with little things; for they were the beginnings. The poor workingman, then infinitessimally little as Aristotle believed him, was the beginning, being the author of labor product and consequently worthy of observation and study. This was the first encouragement the unappreciated maker and producer of all means of life ever received from a philosopher.[70] In all ages the workingman has been an unobserved factor. He is of the earth; this he has himself acknowledged, whatever claims the idler may have filed in his own behalf to the contrary. Being of earth, he digs and cultivates it and from his labor springs the fruit which when ripe and harvested is eaten and enjoyed by the idler. He built edifices which have survived the decompositions of time and his master enjoyed them. But more important and more obscure are the fine details he performed which, though often considered too mean to mention, were in reality as now, the very bulwark of human existence and though too obscure to attract attention were in reality the foundation of all nourishment, achievement, history and knowledge. The great philosopher saw this. He studied nature; and the workingman, recognized as an element of nature, was watched by him. The numerous mutual societies and unions of resistance existing about the philosopher came in for a share of investigation and

[70] It has been stated that Aristotle plagiarized Kapila and certain other East Indian teachers and authors of great learning, having obtained their books while on his celebrated scientific journey of researches with the emperor Alexander the Great. The question is however, obscure. He certainly followed some of the ideas of Anaxagoras, Kapila and others.

were seen to be the deeply underlying fundament of all whence the whole superstructure of society rose. Without the little, and humble, too unappreciated producer the world would be a wilderness of forests and wild beasts Hence, as all came from humble toil, so the toil of investigation and experiment, however mean and unworthy the rich might esteem it, was the very most necessary of all things to resort to in order to arrive at truth, improvement and correct government. This is the basis of the philosophy of Aristotle. The world is following it to-day, led by labor; and the myriad links of invention, and discovery in experimental progress, are in exact harmony with the recommendations of the Stagerite of the Nymphæum.

There are some curious episodes in the life of Plato, which the ordinary reader, without system and without knowledge of the little details of life of the age he lived in, overlooks. What was the trouble with him at Syracuse? Nearly four hundred years before Christ, Plato, after varied travels, after he had written his "Theætctus," and his "Statesman," and was well-known to have decided against the workingmen, to have pronounced them too vile to merit a better fate than bondage, and to have declared that the proper form of government was that of aristocrats and slaves, we find him at Syracuse, spurned by Dionysius, waived from his presence, and consigned to the billingsgate that fed the great city with fish.[71] To be sent away from the tyrant's presence when his sole mission was to teach his majesty the honeyed sweets[72] of his then famous philosophy, was bad; but to be relegated to the city's *ban-lieues*, among the brobdagnagians, and hear their ridicule, was worse. But they must have been especially disagreeable to him since he well knew that their raillery was directed against him. They were of the lowborn, with little education and no urbanity; he was of the great *gens* family, a very Ariston, of pure stock, boasted of, among all Athenians. But they had wit and sufficient means of knowing facts, to be informed that he was the proud teacher of aristocrats, that he did not teach

---

[71] Grote, *Plato and the other Companions of Socrates.*
[72] "At Platoni quum in cunis parvulo dormienti apes in labellis conssedisent responsum est, singulari illum suavitate orationis fore; ita futura eloquentia provisa in infante est." Cicero, *De Divinatione*, I. 36.

the lowest of the people but that he believed with the citizens of Sparta and of Athens that their slavery and humiliation were just. We also have found some evidence that these people were organized. They belonged to the four trade unions, viz: the mercenaries,[73] the *caudicarii* or boatmen and sailors, the *piscatorii*, fisherman and the *fabri*, artisans. There must also have been unions of the tax gatherers; at any rate in later times, for Cicero mentions *vectigalia* in connection with Verres who was governor in Sicily.[74]

This last fact is one very interesting to know; for it sheds fresh light upon that memorable episode in the life of Plato. The unions, finding that the tyrant Dionysius had taken an affront at Plato, and hating him themselves, were willing to conspire with the king against his life. It was probably an organization of the *caudicarii* whom Dionysius engaged to carry him off to Italy and their greed to make a living out of the affair was probably what saved his life. Instead of killing him as they were probably paid to do, they received an offer in Italy for him alive, which they accepted and sold Plato as a slave. He was afterwards ransomed by his friend Dion and returned to Athens a wiser man. We are not informed as to what influence this experience had upon the great philosopher; but there are gleamings which illume our conjecture that his illustrious disciple, Aristotle, who always opposed his theories, took care to enrich his store of wisdom from the circumstance.

In early times, while the world was yet too ignorant and inexperienced to understand the advantages of arbitration and of subsisting upon peaceful rather than warlike measures, brigandage was common. It existed by international permission or common consent. The only industrial system then known was that conducted by the trade unions; for according to the regulations of Solon and king Numa, even the slaves were many times managed by overseers who were under pay of the unions. The rich citi-

---

[73] Grote, *Hist.* p. 79. The mercenary soldiers especially hated Plato who had acted the friend of Dionysius. The latter had cut down their pay, p. 86), in consequence of which they had struck. They were all organized. Cf. also, Grote's Plato, and Livy, XXV. 33.

[74] Cicero, *Verres.* II. 3, 7: "Quoniam quasi quædam prædia populi Romani sunt vectigalia nostra atque provinciæ."

zen believed it a disgrace to labor. He made his wealth or cap work for him. Among other chattels were his slaves. But he was too high to personally conduct the labor of slaves. This was done, to a large extent, by those who were not ashamed to perform labor. Of course, then, these overseers were descendants of slaves. They were the freedmen, who on receiving their manumission struck out for themselves; and for safety and success formed themselves into unions for mutual assistance and resistance against competition, danger and abuse. Among the multitudes of occupations they assumed are found, especially with the Grecians and Syracusians, the Phœnicians and the people inhabiting the Grecian Archipelago, that of brigands and the mercenaries. Both the brigands and mercenary systems were closely leagued into unions which upheld each other in the vicissitudes of the struggle for life. The whole system of the warlike patrician families both in Greece and Rome may be said to be one of brigandage. What is arming a multitude of idle men, disciplining them to the use of weapons and marching them into a neighboring country to destroy the products of industry but brigandage? Yet ancient history is a constant repetition of this predatory and cruel system. It was brigandage.

Among the sufferers from this system were oftentimes the working people; some of them slaves, but many also freedmen, belonging to unions. They were thus torn from their peaceful occupation. Possessing the long experience of association they naturally utilized this their only means of gaining a living, by becoming brigands. They turned their trade unions into bandities and learned to estrange themselves from habits of industrious peace and assume the fierce modes of marauders. They exchanged the workshop for the jungles, the mountain fastnesses, the caves and thus became fighters and guerrillas. A remarkable case of this desperation is seen in that extraordinary man Spartacus, the gladiator, of whom we shall give, in a future chapter, a complete and exhaustive history, in investigating the terrible results of Roman repression of trade unions by the conspiracy laws. It is enough here merely to mention that this tendency of ancient labor organization to reverse their habits, forsake the peaceful in-

THE TRADE UNION A STATE INSTITUTION. 121

dustries which they loved, and wander away in organized clubs seeking subsistence through plunder, was by no means a fault as such actions are now considered; for otherwise they would have immediately been seized by the conquering legions and sold into slavery. In those precarious times, therefore, brigandage was no crime, although to be caught was slavery or death. But it added a fierceness to the social aspect of the human race.

The Eleusinian mysteries caused a great deal of dissatisfaction and feud by reason of their severe, aristocratic exclusiveness which often wounded the pride even of the haughty patrician families of Attica, and we now return to them as our legitimate theme. In our chapter on the system of trade unions farther on we give a detailed description of the ancient labor unions and evidences of their immense number which we have collected, partly by our own travel and observation, partly by personal interviews with the great authors of Archæological works and partly by ransacking with much patience and labor every written statement which original law and history, together with the criticism of modern and ancient authors thereon, have contributed to illume this dark page of the social past.

The ancient trade union, both under the law of Solon and of Numa Pompilius, was a state institution! The land taken by conquest belonged to the state, together with the family religion and all its magnificent temples of worship. The great buildings of the cities were property of the state; most of the slaves who cultivated the soil under the direction, exclusively, of the trade union, were also property of the state. This made a social state—an almost socialistic state—and in many respects more social than political; but entirely spoiled by the terrible social distinctions of rank.[75] The religion, based upon heredity and superstition combined, was an extraordinary tissue of errors, greatly increasing the common misery of the people by flaunting in their faces the insult that none but

---

[75] Millar, *Origin of Ranks*, Basil. 1793. chap. vi.; Granier, *Hist. des Classes Ouvrières*, pp. 484–493. In his 18th chapter, Granier cites the rescript of Antoninus Pius: "Dominorum quidem potestatem in servos suos inlibitum esse oportet, nec cuiquam hominum jus suum detrahi." Ulpian, *De Officio Proconsulis*, lib. VIII; *De Dominorum Sævitia*. This power of the masters over their slaves was thus later transferred to the state.

the high-born citizen, eligible to the Eleusinian mysteries, could be sure of heaven. There could be no peace of mind while such a grievance existed; for it not only goaded the greater part of the people as an insult but distracted them with fears. It is a prominent characteristic of the Aryan race to believe in religion and build up institutions of a religious nature; and it will probably remain so unless some physical discovery be made throwing positive light against the theory of immortality. At the same time the Indo-Europeans were—precisely as they still are—an extremely democratic people by nature. A religion, then, based upon the most absurdly aristocratic dogmas could not, without great conflict maintain itself among the equality-loving Indo-Europeans. Jesus Christ during his visit among us established the remarkable idea that God was no respecter of persons; that all men were created equal; that although the *elysion* and *tartaros* or the heaven and hell were the same, the eligibility to gain the one and fly the other depended not upon stock, birth, fortune, but behavior. The revolution was then begun. When we understand from a standpoint of scientific sociology the phenomena of the past thus connected with the ancient struggles of the lowly, there bursts forth before our vision a glory of light sweeping away hitherto insurmountable difficulties to the analysis of certain vague and obscure points in history.

It is now, after having opened these facts thus far, in order to set down two theorems: The first is, that *the greater the organization of the working classes for mutual protection and resistance the higher the standard of enlightenment in the communities they inhabit.* In other words the intensity of enlightenment in civilization may be measured and compared by the numeric proportion of the laboring people arrayed in organized resistance against ignorance and oppression. The second theorem may be construed to read that *the higher the enlightenment, the more complete is the extinction of social ranks.*

We are also now ready to make an announcement which no person can consistently deny, to wit: that the era covered by the ancient trade unions is that known, sung and celebrated as the "Golden Age." It is not only the era of military, but pre-eminently of social, and in

Greece, of intellectual prosperity. The great literary era of the Romans occupies the latter half of the celebrated golden era. It lasted from the days of Numa Pompilius who encouraged the free organization of Roman trade unions which was about 690 years before Christ, until the year 58 B. C. when Cæsar ordered the conspiracy laws.[76] In Greece from the time of Solon about 592 years before Christ it continued down to her conquest by the Romans.

Thus the economical prosperity of both Greece and Rome is proved to have covered those centuries which were favored with the right of free organization. We shall now proceed to touch upon the actual deeds of these unions and show as we have the evidences that the superb architectural works whose august ruins still amaze the beholder were, to some extent at least, the handiwork of those trade unions, backed by that phenomenal, and to the present age, incomprehensible social state which never sold its lands, religion, jurisprudence or ornaments to others, nor allowed them to be overridden by monopolies. The labor of land culture—which produced and distributed among all people their food—of manufacturing arms and equipments for the armies, of provisioning the armies while on the march and at rest, of manufacturing and repairing the household furniture, of image-making, which appears to have been a considerable industry and of constructing architectural works, was largely assigned to the labor unions during the golden age.[77] Numa discouraged warfare, but made specific arrangements governing the artisan class;[78] and at the *Saturnalia* obliterated the lines of distinction between the nobles and the common born. He distributed the artisans into nine great mechanical fraternities. Flavius Josephus[79] gives an elaborate and highly interesting account of the building of the temple of Jerusalem by Solomon. Suffice it to say here, that the employer, Hiram, who was engaged by Solomon to come with his skill and skilled force all the way from Tyre a distance of about 100 miles, to design and construct this

---

[76] Suetonius, *Cæsar*, 42: "Cæsar cuncta collegia præter antiquitus constituta distraxt."
[77] Granier, pp. 284–323, all through.
[78] Plutarch, *Numa*, cap. xvii.; also *Lycurgus, and Numa Compared*.
[79] Josephus, *Antiquities of the Jews* book XII. cap. ii.; also *Hist. of the Jews*, book VIII.

magnificent edifice, was, so to speak, a boss or chief over a trade union, which through him, took one of the largest and most imposing contracts known in ancient or modern times; and it is a very interesting example of the intelligence and extraordinary enterprise of the Phœnicians. We are not among those eager *creduli* who jump at conclusions, and ready to suppose that this Hiram was the founder of the celebrated ancient fraternity of "Free Masons." On the contrary, the institution was old when Hiram brought to Solomon the 3,200 foremen and the 40,000 artificers who built this gorgeous temple of which Josephus so glowingly speaks. But this immense work being a religious undertaking, conducted by a political decree and under state control, and furthermore being a Semitic, not an Aryan enterprise and consequently free from the mean, rank exclusivism characterizing and belittling the source-history of all their great works, was able to rise and carry with it some lucid *scintillae* as to the manner of its erection. The great temple of Solomon furnished posterity a slight glimpse at the order of Free Masons; being a landmark merely observable in an obscure night of time. Its ruins may, therefore, be truthfully classed, by the student of sociology, as archæological proof of the ancient trade union movement. By this, the mind of the general reader may better understand the source of that all-pervading cloud which so unfortunately shuts us off from the clues—to say nothing of the history —regarding the construction of one of the most magnificent works of sculptured masonary ever produced. The religio-political institutions, based on the antithetic origin of birth and its entailments of rank, prevented the workingmen from rising into recognition, or transmitting beyond their own generation any detailed knowledge as to how those structures rose. The powerful archon Pericles, of Athens, furnished us an illustration of this. He wanted to build the Parthenon. Now Pericles, the statesman, building a church, shows that no difference existed between church and state, since belief was compulsory under law. The Parthenon was the grandest edifice of either the ancient or modern world.[80] Although Pericles was a

---

[80] Guhl and Koner, *Life of the Greeks and Romans*, pp. 25-28.

noble, of the family of the Pisistratidæ, yet we know that he was the intimate friend of Phidias. So we are informed that Solomon enjoyed the acquaintance of Hiram. This might be, though Phidias and Hiram were both of mean extraction, according to the estimation of ranks. But their superiors admired them for their genius alone. A wonderful contrast projects from a coincidence of the late mediæval age, consisting in Raphael's intimacy with Pope Leo X., for at the time of Raphael, Christianity with its inexorable moral erosions had gnawed away much of the ancient ranks, and had begun to invite an absolute equality; whereas, in the more ancient times, under the dominion of the Pagan faith, it could not be more than admiration and acquaintance. In the same manner, Pericles, who was the master political genius of his age, could admire and keep an acquaintance with Aspasia, a lady of the lower rank, but he could not raise her by any gift of title to a higher one than that in which she was born.

It is almost certain that in the construction of the Parthenon, Ictinus was to Pericles what Hiram [81] was to Solomon. Ictinus,[82] we are told, was chief architect, and with the assistance of Callicrates and Phidias who worked on the chryselephantine statue of Athena, had charge, as chief architect, of the Parthenon. It appears [83] that Phidias took the entire control of all the building enterprises of Athens and also, probably of the temple of Eleusis; for Ictinus built the fane of this temple. We are now centering upon the interesting point of our investigation. It took Phidias, Ictinus and Callicrates ten years to design and complete the new Parthenon, the most magnificent and imposing structure of ancient or modern times. More fortunate are we in having Josephus and other authority for the temple of Solomon whereon not only the chief architect, but 3,200 foremen and 40,000 masons of the great "body" or masons' fraternity were engaged.[84]

At the Piræus there existed, at the time of the building of the Parthenon, great numbers of trade unions,[85] under

[81] Care should be taken not to confound Hiram the artificer with his friend Hiram the king. [83] Guhl and Koner, *Idem*, p. 25.
[82] Pausanias, *Hellados Periegesis, (Description of Greece)*.
[84] Josephus, *Antiquities of the Jews*, book VII. chap. ii, In latin the "body" *corpus*, was a legalized workingmen's society, the same as *collegium*. See Orelli, *Inscr.* Vol. III. Henzen, p. 170, of supplement index.
[85] See Chapter I. of Lüders *Dionysische Künstler*, pp. 14–18.

a provision of Solon engraved on wooden scrolls and kept in the Acropolis and the Prytaneum, which were legalized organizations and whose recognized business was to work for the state. Now with the multitudes of trade unions existing all around, at Athens, at the Piræus, at Eleusisis it supposable that the three directors built the parthenon in ten years? Instead of the 3,200 foremen and 40000 men as at Jerusalem, there were probably at Athens 4,000 foremen and 50,000 masons, sculptors, draftsmen, hod carriers, laborers and others too numerous to detail. We find that this great public work was finished 438 years before Christ, just at the time when the golden age of labor was at its zenith of glory both in Greece and Rome.

It was the golden age of art and economic thrift. It also corresponds exactly with the stretch of time during which the trade unions under the laws of Solon at Athens and of Numa at Rome were in fullest force, granting and encouraging organization of the working people, which was used by them for protection and for resistance to all dangers that might beset them.

It is thus shown that while a serious grievance existed among the working people of ancient Greece, in form of an exclusivism denying them the right to save their souls by becoming members on equal footing in the Eleusinian order, there also existed a vast organization or confraternity which, then as now, afforded them opportunities for meeting in secret and discussing this grievance. It is scarcely necessary even to conjecture whether they did or did not use these advantages for such discussion. Human nature is alike in all ages. When the conspiracy law, or law of Elizabeth, was annulled in 1824,[86] permitting the people to organize in England, they immediately took advantage of every opportunity trade unionism afforded, wherewith to discuss their grievances. The growth and intelligence of the ponderous labor movement in the United States is largely due to the discussion which is constantly taking place in their secret unions. We venture that the same thing occurred in the times we are describing; because it could not well have been otherwise. Where the grievance exists and the opportunity to meet

[86]Thorold Rogers, *Six Centuries of Work and Wages*, p. 438 As to the nature of the act of Elizabeth, see *idem*, pp. 398-9. Cf. Porter's Progress of the Nation.

and discuss it exists, it is not in the order of nature among intelligent beings, to resist it. We are fortunate enough to have found statements upon the subjects of trade unions transmitted to us through great authority. Gaius, who wrote a digest of law on the Twelve Tables, has a passage which has been preserved and so important is it that both Granier and Mommsen refer to it as conclusive evidence that the law of the Twelve Tables providing for the right among working people to organize and enjoy trade unions, was to some extent a translation from Greek tables of the code of Solon.[87] In this passage are mentioned many organizations taken from the Greek text inscribed on the scroll of the law of Solon and also on the tablet of the Twelve Tables. The *Thiasotai* then were precisely in Greek what the *Collegia* were in Latin. The sailors' unions here mentioned were the same which we speak of elsewhere as existing in large numbers at the Piræus or seaport of Athens which was distant from the metropolis only five miles. The organizations of the stone masons, the marble cutters, the carvers, the image makers of wood mineral and ivory, and others, were located within the city. Some of these unions, probably the image makers, pretended more religious piety than others; but the fact is,[88] that all of them were combined for mutual aid and resistance against grievances. Under the law, so long as they did not corrupt the statutes of the country ("*dum ne quid ex publica lege corrumpant,*") they were not only allowed to career unmolested but were even protected by this provision of the great lawgivers.

This brings us face to face with two proven facts: that

[87] *Digest*, lib. XLVII. tit. xxii. leg. 4; "Sodales sunt qui ejusdem collegii sunt quam Græci ἑταρίαν vocant." Again: "Sodalibus," ait Gaius, "potestatem facit lex (duodecim Tabularum) pactionem quam velint sibi ferre, dum ne quid ex publica lege corrumpant." Sed hæc lex videtur ex lege Solonis translata esse; nam illuc ita est: "Ἐὰν δὲ δῆμος, ἢ φράτροες, ἢ ἱερῶν ὀργίων, ἢ ναῦται, σύνσιτοι, ἢ ὁμόταφοι, ἢ θιασῶται, ἢ ἐπὶ λίαν οἰχόμενοι, ἢ εἰς ἐμπορίαν. Ὅτι ταύτων διαδῶνται πρὸς ἀλλήλους, κύριον εἶναί, ἐὰν μὴ ἀπαγορεύσῃ δημόσια γράμματα." Both Mommsen (*De Collegiis et Sodaliciis Romanorum*, p. 85,) and Granier, *Hist. des Classes Ouvrières*, p. 291, quote this remarkable passage from the Digest. The unions here mentioned in the Solonic law are the *Brotherhood* the *Priests of the Communes*, the *Sailors*, the *Co-operators*, the *Burial Fraternities;* and the regular trade unions or θιασῶται such as were organized in the categories of Numa

[88] Mommsen, *De Collegiis et Sodaliciis Romanorum*, p. 35, "Ut igitur de interpretatione verbi a XII. Tabulis adhibiti non constet, Gaii verba ad omnia collegia pertinere certum est neque ulla ratio reddi videtur posse, cur collegia opificum legum ferendarum jure caruerint sacris sodalitatibus concesso." See also Lüders, *Die Dinoysischen Künstler*, passim. These points are overwhelming in proof that the Greek and Roman trade union systems were nearly identical.

during the renowned era of Grecian architecture, *belles-lettres*, philosophy, sculpture, paintings—all work of laborers—there also flourished a great labor movement; just as now in England, in Germany, in France, in the United States and Canada, during the most brilliant period of all human enlightenment, ancient or modern, there flourishes an enormous social organization for self-help and for resistance against grievance endured by working people. It also proves the correctness of our theorems that the greater the organization of the laboring people against grievances the higher the enlightenment, and the higher the enlightenment the more complete the extinction of social rank; consequently the intensity of human civilization viewed on the largest scale, is, under the competitive system, to be ascertained by the prevalence or non-prevalence of these organizations, acting as mutually self-aiding forces and as tribunals or courts of appeal from the grievances their members are liable to suffer. How ineffable, then, the arrogance of a paltry few! What must have been the character of resistance during the times of which we speak? Evidently very crude. At the present day there is much system; a general interlinking of union with union, no matter how wide apart, for a quite clearly expressed common cause. Not so anciently, although we have an inscription at Pompeii to prove that in B. C. 79 there existed an international union. Their grievances were greater than now, because social equality was contemptuously and most openly put down. The law recognized them as having no more claim to citizenship than dogs. Now, in Germany, France, almost everywhere, the working people are voting.

Whoever, in reading the "Ancient Assemblies,"[89] for a moment imagines that those celebrated gatherings included the slaves or freedmen, should read more carefully. It is the *freemen* who are meant, not freedmen. The difference was simply infinite, even in enlightened Attica; for freedmen were descendants of the ancient slaves. They never were citizens, could not vote, could not hope, except in cases of great genius like that of Phidias, to be decently

---

[89] Schömann, *Hist. Assemblies of the Athenians, passim*. This book will clear up any error readers may entertain who doubts whether the working class was allowed a voice in legislation.

spoken to; and even as such they were obliged to obtain some special decree from the Areopagus in order to detach themselves from this scathing odium of rank. Being so mean, so lowly, while the patricians, the grandees, the freemen were descendants of the nobility in the direct lineage of the gods, it followed that the gods also contemned them. Consequently two-thirds of the population of Greece were without a soul. If they claimed to have souls they knew that the only place for them was Tartarus or hell; certainly not heaven; for that was the abode of the gods who spurned them on account of their lowly birth. Better cultivate the belief that they had no souls at all! This to them, terrible reflection, was probably the origin of the ancient philosophy of annihilation.[90] The philosophy of extinction of the sou' must have consumed a share of the discussions of those ancient mechanics in their secret meetings. They built the magnificent temples which glowed with genial warmth of the solemn and haughty religion, only for the heaven-born, repelling with sullen frowns the earth-born designers and finishers of their collonades, vaults and sculptured images. No merely political institution could possibly separate so widely one class from another as did that arrogant religion which not only instituted slavery of the laboring people but denied them an immortal soul and the beatitudes of heaven.[91] There is now no grievance of this kind in civilized existence—although economical and social dissatisfaction remains. The new religion is rapidly extinguishing the dogma of distinctions in birth, as well as the dogma that "the earth-born have no immortal existence."[92]

Narrowing the array of evidence into our legitimate field, we find in Eleusis a target at which millions are peering with a mingling of longing, of envy and of hate. They are

[90] Consult Lucretius, *De Rerum Natura*; also Arnobius, who wrote the famous *Adversus Gentes*. Arnobius was not fully convinced of Christianity; and at the same time his mind was evidently so enlarged by it that he could not reconcile it with the older Pagan belief in the nether post-mortem abodes. He was however, religiously inclined and was reluctantly drawn to Christianity which obliterated all lines by declaring the equality of all mankind. Between these awful doubts Arnobius seems never to have come to a belief in an immortal existence. Pliny the celebrated naturalist was a believer in the doctrine of Lucretius that there is no existence hereafter. Cf. Cuvier in *Bibliog. Universelle*.
[91] Granier, *Hist. Whole argument*; Fustel de Coulanges, *Cité Antique*. No intelligent person can read these invaluable works without understanding our meaning.
[92] Whatever science may or may not develop regarding these debatable theories is not the part of this disquisition to consider. We simply give the facts at command, as to the difference between the grievances discussed by the organizations of then and now.

the two-thirds of the population of the country—the laboring ranks. There, upon a lovely range of rock and lawn stands the old Pelasgian city of Eleusis, populous and thick-studded with their own *eranoi* and *thiasoi*, labor unions whose members are the strong-muscled men of Greece. It is the eve of autumn, the great quinquennial *Boedromion* which from traditions brought mystic meanings picturing the fierce amazons in flight before the conquering giants of Theseus. It is the last half of shimmering September whose delicious zephyrs float the gossamers above the sea.

All the world knows that on the morrow thousands upon thousands of people are to leave the Athenian metropolis behind them and commence their crusade to the Eleusinian feast. They are the eligibles, the citizens, the freemen. Not a being from among the laboring and lowly class can be permitted hardly to join the great procession. Fond of privilege but barred its enjoyment they gather in their best rags, upon the scene and form in a standing multitude along the line of march. No care has ever been bestowed upon their education and they are in consequence, rough, perhaps boisterous and insulting. As the procession moves along they pelt the crusaders with sticks and stones.[93] They feel the deep disgrace of their exclusion and are animated with unhappy feelings and hatred and revenge. They turn their eyes toward the magnificent temple of Megaron, built[94] by their own hands, of marble quarried from the rock near by.[95] It is pre-eminently the most majestic work of their handicraft, standing solemn and alone like a mysterious winged creature, striking awe by its very presence and as though a ghostly apparition which had surged from the dark pits of the sea.[96] To the left loomed up a view of

[93] When, as the fable goes, Ceres left king Celeus and went to the old temple, Iambe, her female slave, ridiculed her. Ever afterwards at the αγυρμος or day of march at the crusades, the lower or excluded classes met on the wayside with stones, clubs and ridicule.
[94] Consult Rose, *Inscriptiones Græcæ Vetustissimæ*, pp. 187-190.
[95] *Idem*, p. 187, note ; "E duro quodam marmoris genere (quale prope Eleusiniem invenitur.") Likewise the description of the great temple, by Guhl and Koner, *Life of the Greeks and Romans*, pp. 47-49.
[96] "Prope oleam erat puteus aquæ salsæ (θάλασσα Ερεχθηίς) quam sub flatum noti surdo murmore fluctuum instar strepere, narrabant Athenienses. Ipse silicet Neptunus hanc voraginem aperuerat tridente, cujus adhuc vestigium in saxo vivo expressum restabat. De fonte salso noli dubitare. Nam et alius in arce fons aquæ amaræ qui etesiarum flatu — sub ortum caniculæ — impleri, postea considere solebat, *Clepsydra* dictus." Ister. Ap. Schol. Aristophanis, Av. 1693, p. 63. Though this superstition may have been based at the acropolis, it is evident that the horrors of it came from old Eleusis : besides Erechtheis was the priestess in charge of the Eleusinian initiations.

the noble *pronaos* whose fluted columns towered high, holding their graceful architraves, and culminating in those exquisite Corinthian capitals of the pilasters, celebrated throughout the world for the beauty and richness of their carvings. Their own Ictinus, guiding their own, or their ancestors' toil had built the huge, but forbidding *telesterium* and conclave where those mysterious initiations and degrees were conferred; not upon them, but upon those born worthy of the honor. Their own Xenocles was the master mason who had led them through a labyrinth of toil which produced the lordly, throne-like *anactoron* were dwelt the immortal Ceres. Their own master sculptor, Metagenes had directed their skillful hands through the mazes of sculpture which produced those soft and charming friezes, and reared the upper columns on which rest the vast entablatures with their architraves and frettings. Led by such masters who have come down to fame as the genius of classic architecture, wage-earners had delved for more than a decade of years to fashion the home of the *Mystagogoi*, those favored priests who repulsed them with bitterest scorn and all others who could not bring proof that for three generations at least, they had never disgraced themselves by the social blight of labor. These were the thanks the ancient lowly received for building those enduring and exquisite monuments of art.

No wonder then, that as the procession moved down from the acropolis to the sea, the outcasts, uncultured, unrefined, enslaved, treated the haughty initiates with brickbats and jeers. There were quarrels about this grievance; but so dark has the historian been upon the subject that we are unable to obtain further positive data than these we quote. But what we do know sheds light upon the causes of a great change which in course of time came into the world; a change that planted the seed of revolution. It was a religio-political state based upon legalized pretentions, and assumed absolute rights of less than one-third of the entire population of the Indo-European world and the absolute non-recognition and social, political and hierarchical ostracism of the other two-thirds of the population on whose labor they depended for their food, clothing, shelter and worship.

A word more may suffice to close this chapter. Our object in saying so much has been to exhibit the double grievance suffered by the religious as well as the social and economic tyranny of ancient society over the laboring people. From the time labor organizations began, until the era of the sophists, no one can tell the ages that elapsed. The sophists and philosophers began their work in Greece five centuries before Christ. They were revolutionists so far as they dared go. The general movement of Plato and Aristotle must though conflicting, certainly be regarded as one of the most remarkable of the world. It worked enormously in the direction of preparing mankind for the revolution—the change from a condition of slavery of the useful laboring masses to one of complete social, political and spiritual recognition and equality. Plato was a slave owner. He was so proud that he disdained to accept money for his services as a teacher, preferring to accept presents from the wealthy young students under his charge —the reverse of what in our own times is considered proper. Had Plato thus lived and acted just before our modern war of the rebellion he would have been called a slave-driving hypocrite by abolitionists at the North, and a canting moralist by the people at the South. He was of neither party. Even the workingmen of his own times hated him. What he did was probably equilibrated both between sympathy and diplomacy, largely tempered by sympathy and conscience and on the whole, working all the radical good which the times would permit. The world is better for this celebrated advocate of slavery having lived; for on the whole, though he could not see any way possible of expunging this horrid social ulcer of slavery from his republic, his sympathy got the better of acquisitiveness and like all the teachers of that era, he melted the brutal spirit which in Sparta instigated such inhuman cruelties toward the laboring class. All over Attica they were treated with comparative tenderness and consideration and though they suffered the grievances we have described, yet they shared the age of philosophy and art as an age peculiarly their own in organization and plenty. It was their Golden age of equality. We do not mean exact equality or similarity in the physical and intellectual sense; for nothing could be more absurd. We mean by it the extinction of those aristocratic lines which pride, egoism and greed had so long held as a basis of religion and of state.

CHAPTER V.

STRIKES AND UPRISINGS.

GRIEVANCES CONTINUED. PLANS OF ESCAPE.

First Known and First Tried Plan of Salvation was that of Retaliation—The Slaves test the Ordeal of Armed Force—Irascibility of the Working Classes at length arrayed against their Masters—Typical Strikes of the ancient Workingmen—Their Inhuman Treatment—Famous Strike at the Silver Diggings of Laurium—20,000 Artisans and Laborers quit Work in a Body and go over to the Foes of their own Countrymen—The Great Peloponnesian War Decided for the Spartans, against the Athenians by this Fatal Strike.

In ancient Greece, Sicily and Rome there occurred great and disastrous strikes. The character of the elements causing these disturbances varied greatly from that of the modern strikers. Quite the reverse of our modern, the ancient strikers were either slaves or freedmen descended from such, and in a condition of extreme lowliness but often so intelligent that notwithstanding the odds against them they sometimes out-generaled their masters and obtained for a long period of time, even years, against wealth, priesthood and military force. The reasons for this we have already explained but may appropriately repeat. The slaves and freedmen were mostly men of their masters' own blood. They were of the same race, color and natural intelligence. They used the same languages, were accustomed to the same roads and fields, knew the cliffs, grottoes, forests and jungles; and there being no firearms or other instruments of destruction which in our modern warfare throw the balance of power into the hands of the most disciplined rather than the most numerous, they sometimes triumphed for a time by dint of numbers.

During the Peloponnesian war a great strike of the working people occurred in and about the silver mines of Laurium,[1] B. C. 413. It may be well here to enumerate some of the grievances inciting them to this desperate resolve which they knew perfectly well beforehand, would, unless they succeeded, terminate in their death by tortures of the most inhuman artifices the maddened cruelty of greedy money-getters could invent. Nearly all the slaves and other working people, laborers and artificers engaged in this enormous strike, were intelligent people. Some were persons who were slaves by the misfortune of birth;[2] others were prisoners of war reduced by violence to slavery. Still others were slaves as merchandise brought to the mines by the vicissitudes of traffic; and lastly and worst, there were large numbers who were convicts, condemned to work in the mines under the lash of brutal hireling overseers of contractors[3] who worked these mines on leases from the government to which they paid one twentieth of the proceeds. It was a great grievance to the intelligent workingmen to be goaded by the knowledge that he was a social monstrosity.[4] Men now recoil at the sight of a slave because he is the rare relic of an institution which human wisdom and sympathy have outstripped, outlived, outgrown in the glori-

[1] Thucydides *De Bello Peloponesiaco*, VII. 27: "Ἀφίκοντο δὲ καὶ Θρᾳκῶν τῶν μαχαιροφόρων τοῦ Διακοῦ γένους ἐς τὰς Ἀθήνας πελτασταὶ ἐν τῷ αὐτῷ θέρει τούτῳ τριακόσιοι καὶ χίλιοι, οὓς ἔδει τῷ Δημοσθένει ἐς τὴν Σικελίαν ξυμπλεῖν. οἱ δ' Ἀθηναῖοι, ὡς ὕστερον ἧκον, διενοοῦντο αὐτοὺς πάλιν ὅθεν ἦλθον ἐς Θρᾴκην ἀποπέμπειν. τὸ γὰρ ἔχειν πρὸς τὸν ἐκ τῆς Δεκελείας πόλεμον αὐτούς, πολυτελὲς ἐφαίνετο· δραχμὴν γὰρ τῆς ἡμέρας ἕκαστος ἐλάμβανεν. ἐπειδὴ γὰρ ἡ Δεκέλεια τὸ μὲν πρῶτον ὑπὸ πάσης τῆς στρατιᾶς ἐν τῷ θέρει τούτῳ τειχισθεῖσα, ὕστερον δὲ φρουραῖς ἀπὸ τῶν πόλεων κατὰ διαδοχὴν χρόνου ἐπιούσαις τῇ χώρᾳ ἐπῴκειτο, πολλὰ ἔβλαπτε τοὺς Ἀθηναίους καὶ ἐν τοῖς πρώτοις χρημάτων τ' ὀλέθρῳ καὶ ἀνθρώπων φθορᾷ ἐκάκωσε τὰ πράγματα. πρότερον μὲν γὰρ βραχεῖαι γιγνόμεναι αἱ ἐσβολαὶ τὸν ἄλλον χρόνον τῆς γῆς ἀπολαύειν οὐκ ἐκώλυον· τότε δὲ ξυνεχῶς ἐπικαθημένων, καὶ ὁτὲ μὲν καὶ πλεόνων ἐπιόντων, ὁτὲ δ' ἐξ ἀνάγκης τῆς ἴσης φρουρᾶς καταθεούσης τε τὴν χώραν καὶ λῃστείας ποιουμένης, βασιλέως τε παρόντος τοῦ τῶν Λακεδαιμονίων Ἄγιδος, ὃς οὐκ ἐκ παρέργου τὸν πόλεμον ἐποιεῖτο, μεγάλα οἱ Ἀθηναῖοι ἐβλάπτοντο· τῆς τε γὰρ χώρας ἁπάσης ἐστέρηντο καὶ ἀνδραπόδων πλέον ἢ δύο μυριάδες ηὐτομολήκεσαν, καὶ τούτων τὸ πολὺ μέρος χειροτέχναι, πρόβατά τε πάντα ἀπολώλει καὶ ὑποζύγια· ἵπποι τε, ὁσημέραι ἐξελαυνόντων τῶν ἱππέων πρός τε τὴν Δεκέλειαν καταδρομὰς ποιουμένων καὶ κατὰ τὴν χώραν φυλασσόντων, οἱ μὲν ἀπεχωλοῦντο ἐν γῇ ἀποκρότῳ τε καὶ ξυνεχῶς ταλαιπωροῦντες, οἱ δ' ἐτιτρώσκοντο. Xenophon *De Vectigal.* IV. 25.

[2] Granier de Cassagnac, *Histoire des Classes Ouvrières*, chap. iii.

[3] Plutarch *Nicias and Crassus Compared*, 1.

[4] Drumann, *Arbeiter und Communisten in Griechenland und Rom*, S. 24; Böckh, *Public Economies of the Athenians*, p. 263, for instances of men owning great numbers of slaves: See also Böckh s *Laurische Silberbergwerke in Attika*, passim.

NO SUNDAY FOR WORKINGMEN. 135

ous race of enlightenment. Even at that **early age the** slave's servitude was the source of his own intelligent disgust; for covered as he was with the indelible brands and scars of systematic mutilation, and decrepit in premature age through blows and strains of violence and overwork, his mind remained unimpaired, often edged to consciousness of its own incompatibility with this state of degradation. The poor creatures were never allowed to eat white bread.[5] There were no Sundays for them. Of the 365 days they were forced to delve 360. Sometimes the government owned them and subbed them with the mines themselves to the contractors, following the plan of Xenophon,[7] who sometimes thus worked great numbers at a time. Often, however, the rich contractor himself owned laboring men with whom to operate the mines. Thus Nicias owned a thousand slaves,[8] Mnason also owned a thousand.[9] The ancients appear to have had a species of passion for seeing acts of brutality and cruelty.

Wakes are of great antiquity. Originally they were public fights on the occasion of the death of an important member of a *gens* family, in which the combatants were his slaves so unfortunate as to have survived him. All the family, its slaves and their children, perhaps also the community not allied by blood, were summond to see what in our refined age would not only be repellent cruelties, but intolerable ones—a fight to the death, of slaves of the deceased, with daggers and clubs.[10] The first combat on record of this kind occurred in B. C. 264, arranged by the brothers Brutus.[11] But authors agree that the practice comes from much more remote antiquity; and mention of it is made here to prepare the reader to understand some of the causes

---

[5] Granier, de Cass. *Hist. Ouvrières*, p. 98, who gives references.
[6] Bücher. *Aufstände der unfreien Arbeiter*, S. 96; Xenoph. *Memorab*. lll, 6, 12. For 360 days in the year those poor working people, male and female, had to drudge. Xenophon. 4, 16; Böckh, *Silberbergwerke*, S. 125.
[7] Xenophon, *De Vectigal*. cap. iv.
[8] Bücher, *Aufstände, etc.* S. 96; Drumann *Arbeiter und Communisten*, SS. 11-23.
[9] Böckh, *Public Economies of the Athenians*, p. 263. The celebrated plan of Xenophon for replenishing the Athenian treasury (*De Vectigal*. cap. iv.) was to have the state put 60 000 of its own slaves on the state silver mines of Laurium, to be leased to contractors. He even gives figures on the presumable income from this plan of relief to the state.
[10] Friedländer, *Darstellungen aus der Sittengeschichte Roms*, II. 216.
[11] Guhl and Koner, *Life of the Greeks and Romans*. We give references to modern authors so that readers not conversant with the original languages may get them and satisfy themselves.

lurking at the bottom of the evil of ancient strikes and uprisings. Gibbon relates the horrible story of the Syracusian, L. Domitius.[12] One of the poor, innocent slaves during his prætorship, one day while assisting in the chase, killed a wild boar of enormous size and very dangerous. The daring deed got noised about until it reached the ear of Domitius who ordered the slave to be brought to him as he desired to see so brave a man. The poor creature appeared before this fellow, humbly expecting a trifle of praise so seldom the lot of the Syracusian slave. To his horror, however, this monster's first question was, what kind of weapon or means were employed by him in performing the deed. The answer was a javelin. "Are you not aware that the javelin is a weapon for gentlemen; and that for so mean a creature as a slave to use the weapons of men, is death?" Turning to his soldiers he said, "take this slave away and crucify him." The trembling wretch was actually crucified upon the spot. The heart sickens at the contemplation of our descent from such a type of monsters!

Bücher notes[13] that single contractors often worked 300 to 600 slaves in the silver mines of Laurium and that convicts who were government property were sometimes sold to the contractors who exploited their labor in their own name.[14] Sometimes intelligent men in those days were half slaves and half free, being enfeoffed by livery of seizin, no doubt, if unambitious of freedom, enjoying thereby some advantages over those entirely out in the competitive world. Such men were paid a per diem, varying from 3 to 7 *oboli*, or from 10 to 19 cents for their labor.[15]

Callias the friend of Cimon, B. C. 460, became wealthy, managing mines. All or nearly all the mines were, with the ancients, the property of the state. The state contracted the working of the mines to enterprising business men who often hired slaves to do the work. These contractors were often men of noble blood. The sense of the social structure being against conducting or managing one's own business.

[12] Gibbon, *Decline and Fall of the Roman Empire*, Vol. I. p. 48. N. Y., 1850: Böckh, *Silberbergwerke*, S. 122–3, adds testimony to this hardheartedness of the ancients, referring to Plato who, for his perfect state, wanted only Greeks exempt from slavery.
[13] *Aufstände etc.*, S. 96.
[14] Böckh, *Abhandlung der Historisch-Philologischen Classe der Preussischen Akademie der Wissenschaften*, 1814–15.
[15] *Id. Public Econ. of Athenians*, p. 164.

Only the slaves and other workmen, those who actually performed the work, were doomed to suffer the odium of labor. Any business man who could get a bond, could take from the state a portion or the whole of a mine; and sometimes even the slaves themselves were to be had of the state. In this case, the complete outfit was contracted for by the individual, who had no further care than to manipulate products and gains. Callias and Cimon had either contracts for or ownership in the mines of silver at Laurium, located to the southeastward of Athens about 30 miles.[16] Their names appear also, but vaguely in connection with the Pangæus mines in Thrace. It is known that Thucidydes the celebrated historian owned mining property in Macedonia. He was a rich slave owner and optimate. One Sosias a Thracian contractor hired from Nicias a thousand slaves, at an *obolus* per day each.[17] Hyponicus rented or hired as many as 600 slaves to these contractors and received, as Xenophon tells us, a *mina* daily for their labor. Philemonides for 300 slaves got half a *mina*.[18]

Public servants were not always free. Wages in the time of Pericles stood about as follows:[19] for a common laborer who carried dirt, 3 *oboli*,[20] or $10\frac{1}{2}$ cents per day. A gardener got 14 cents; a sawyer of wood, one drachm, or 19 cents; a carpenter received sometimes as high as $17\frac{1}{2}$ cents while millers in the grain mills received 15 to 18 cents. Scribes or copyists no more. The architect of the temple of Minerva got no more than the stone sawyer and others only as much as the common laborer. His name was Polias. Bœckh says he received one drachm or exactly $17\frac{1}{2}$ cents. The *hypogrammateus* or secretary to the superintendent of public buildings got only 5 *oboli* or about 15 cents.

The fares for traveling conveyances were also very low. In fact, the clerks and public officials of every kind were government subjects who received low salaries and worked long hours. Their life was a constant drudgery. The superintendents themselves were officers of family or blood. They were citizens; but the dignity of their position restrained them from receiving any recompense.

---

[16] Plutarch, *Cimon*. Cornelius Nepos, *Cimon;* "non tam generosus quam pecuniosus, qui magnas pecunias ex metallis fecerat."
[17] Xenophon, *De Vectgal.* §. 4, 14; Plutarch, *Nicias*, 4.
[18] Xenophon, *Id.* 1, c. § 15.   [19] Böckh, *Pub. Econ. Athen.* p. 164.
[20] An obolus was 3½ cts, a drachma 19.

STRIKE AT THE SILVER MINES.

Thus in Greece, Rome and everywhere throughout antiquity, such were the oppressive conditions that the intelligent among the working classes, goaded by their sufferings, were on the alert, sometimes for revenge, sometimes for objects of amelioration, but oftener from sheer, reckless despair, and ready to strike out in bloody rebellion against their master.

With this statement on general causes of strikes we proceed with the story of the greatest of all, belonging purely to this category of human resistance, to be found either in ancient or modern times.[21] It may be plausibly conjectured that this great strike in turning the tables against the Athenians and thus deciding the celebrated Peloponnesian war against them and the little democracy that had grown up in the Athenian civilization and refinement, went far toward suppressing the true progress of the human race.[22]

The silver mines of Laurium, 30 miles south from the city of Athens, were among the resources of Athenian wealth. They belonged to the government. The methods of obtaining the precious metal was by arduous labor, without much of the modern machinery. Diodorus describing the Egyptian mines between Captos and Cosseir, pictures the sufferings of the poor convicts and barbarians working there;[23] and Bücher says that was also the case with those working the Laurian mines.[24] According to this, men and women in great numbers who had committed some crime [25] against the state or otherwise, were dragged into the subterranean cavern, stripped entirely of their clothing, their bodies painted, their legs loaded with chains and in this frightful condition, set at work drilling the rock, breaking it in pieces and carrying it to the mouth of the shaft. Outside the mine were smitheries, machine shops for making stamping mills, water tanks and courses for washing the metal, wagon shops for making and repairing vehicles of conveyance and other conveniences necessary for so great an industry, employing great numbers of slaves and freedmen for carrying on the works.

---

[21] The greater uprisings are known, not as strikes but as servile wars; although we sometimes confound them with strikes.
[22] Drumann, *Arbeiter und Communisten in Griechenland und Rom*, S. 64.
[23] Diodorus *Bibliotheca Historica*, V. 38.
[24] Bücher, *Aufstände der unfreien Arb.* S. 96.
[25] Compare Plutarch. *Nicias and Crassus Comp. Init.* Plutarch here avers that the workmen under Nicias were often malefactors and convicts.

These mines of Laurium were in operation when the Peloponnesian war broke out, B. C. 432, between the Spartans and Athenians, which lasted 27 years. Thucidydes speaks as though the offer held out to the workmen employed as slaves by the Athenians, of 18 cents per day uniformly, was a very tempting one.[26] They were poor dependents, some slaves, some freedmen, some convicts, subjected to abuse, thrown pell-mell together, driven to hard work, poorly fed, those within the mines, naked and suffering, and utterly destitute of that feeling known to us as patriotism, although many of them were Athenians.[27] During this obstinate struggle the Lacedæmonian forces, B. C. 413, approached as near to Athens as Decelea, a garrisoned frontier town in Bœtia held by them, where they established themselves over against the Athenian lines. The distance between Decelea on the borders of Boetia and Athens is only about 20 miles. The Athenian *ergasteria* or workshops were manned in part by slaves.[28] So, whether in the shops and arsenals at Athens, or in the silver mines of Laurium, both of which, during war time, were indispensable for supplying money and arms, the sinews of production were not quickened by that peculiarly inspiriting urgent known to us as patriotism. Labor hated alike home, fatherland and employer. When war broke out the laborer, instead of turning his power and genius to swift production of engines for hurling missiles of destruction among the invaders of his country, sought in the vortex of fierce disturbance, some fissure of retreat from the monstrous cruelties of bondage.

Thus in this pivotal contest between the Spartans and Athenians, compared with the Spartans' treatment of the Helots or Lacedæmonian slaves, the Athenians with all the horrors that have been pictured, were mild, we find the grievance intensified beyond endurance. Compared with Spartan suavity, philosophy and moral advancement, the Athenians were as civilization to barbarism; for Sparta had never questioned the claims of Pagan aristocracy and Lycurgus had built upon it in all its austere presumptiveness a ring or community of about one-third the population and damned the remaining two-thirds to a stage of slavery

[26] Thucydides. *De Bello Peloponnesiaco*, VII. 27, already quoted. p. 107.
[27] Bücher. *Aufstände d. unfreien Arb.* S. 21.
[28] Drumann; *Arb. u. Communisten in Griechenland u. Rom*, S. 64; "Auch in den Fabriken, εργαστερια, sah man nur Sclaven."

very little better than that of naked convicts described by Diodorus in the gold mines of Egypt.[29] Yet notwithstanding the brutal example the poor slaves had just witnessed, of Spartan treachery, in assassinating 2,000 brave helots a few years before,[30] some knowledge of which they must certainly have possessed [31] we find the poor Athenian workmen readily accepting an offer by the Spartans and joining them in great numbers against their own fatherland.

Undoubtedly this was a very dangerous exploit of the strikers and could not have succeeded without some organization. But we are left in the dark regarding most of the details. No doubt the near approach of the Lacedæmonian forces and the demoralization of the Athenians as well as their ingratitude, together with the arrogance of Cimon and the revenges of Alcibiades, might have had much to do with it.

This great strike must have been plotted by the men themselves. We are, through the two or three brief references to it, given us by the historians,[32] left to infer that it must have been well concerted, violent and swift. The inference is unequivocal that in 413, B. C. 20,000 miners, mechanics, teamsters and laborers suddenly struck work; and at a moment of Athens' greatest peril, fought themselves loose from their masters and their chains. These 20,000 workmen made a desperate bolt for the Spartan garrison newly established at Decelea on the borders of Bœtia. The strike must have been the more desperate on account of the offers held out to them by the enemy. One of the offers was that they should be provided with work which they should perform on their own reckoning; but that they should pay only a part of it to their masters or employers. At this lay, by industry and patience they could not only live better but could "lay by a certain sum with which to

---

[29] Diodorus, *Bib. Hist.* III. 11, V. 38.
[30] Thucydides, IV. 80, massacre of the Helots, B. C. 424, *ut supr*, p. 106 sq
[31] Witness the intimate undercurrent of .e ephony during the great uprisings of Eunus, Aristonicus, Athenion and Spartacus; and the same was repeated during the anti-slavery rebellion in the United States, with same mysteriously accurate information.
[32] Thucydides, *De Bello Pel.* VI. 91. VIII. 4, VII. 27; Xenophon, *De Vectigal.* 4. 25; Drumann, *Arb. u. Comm.* S. 64; Bücher, *Aufstände. unfreien Arbeiter,* S. 21: "Im Jahre vor Chr. 413 schlugen sich 20,000 A henische Fabrikarbeiter zu den Lakedamoniern, ein schwerer Schlag für den Lau is den Bergbau." Böckh, *Laurische Silberbergwerke,* S. 90-1, also mentions it.

buy themselves free. Unaccustomed to plenty and suddenly thus provided with enough to eat and drink, they naturally gave themselves up to indulgence to some extent for Dr. Drumann tells us that many of the slaves lived better than the freedmen themselves, though we have no account of their dissipating.[33] The statement of Dr. Bücher, that this strike of the workmen of Athens was a heavy blow to the mining operations of the Laurian silver diggings, confirms the importance of this immense uprising in Attica. The sudden loss of 20,000 workmen, inured to the hardships of mining life, and drilled to the mechanical niceties of the assays for the money supply, of the wagon works, and of the armories at Athens where most of the sabers, slings, daggers, javelins, campaign wagons and other *impedimenta* of war were constructed, is known to have been a serious set-back to the progress of the Peloponnesian conflict. But while it disheartened the Athenians it proportionately encouraged and delighted the Lacedæmonians; and as the latter were not of the party of progress but engaged in invidious activity against the Athenians, at that time the most democratic and advanced people in the world, it acted directly against the evolution of mankind. No one pretends to deny that the Spartans, boasting of the hegemony of their youth and their consequent warlike prowess, were mad with jealousy against the wondrous work of Athenian philosophy, letters, fine art and polish;—the very adornments, theoretical and mechanical,

[33] Drumann, *Arbeiter und Communisten in Griechenland und Rom*, S. 64. "Der grösste Theil der 20,000, welche im peloponnesischen Kriege in Attica zu der spartanischen Besatzung in Decelia entliefen, kam aus Fabriken. Mitunter wurde ihnen gestattet, für eigene Rechnung zu arbeiten, und ein Gewisses theil an ihre Herren abzugeben; so konnten fleissige und sparsame eine Summe erübrigen und sich loskaufen; manche machten mehr Aufwand als die Freien." Bücher says, S. 21: "Wo viele Sklaven derselben Nationalität in einer Stadt zusammen lebten, sagt Platon, (legg. VI. p. 777), geschähe grosses Unheil, was doch nur auf wirliche Aufstände mit all ihren Gräueln zu deuten ist." So also at Rome the feeling was against the poorest class and aggravated by a fear of their mutinies. Cato the elder was a hard-hearted slave-driver as Livy, (XXXIX. 40), coolly hints, without seeming to imagine that brutal treatment of a menial was inhumanity. Macrobius, *(Saturnaliorum Libri*, I, xi. 2, 25-30,) says that in Rome so great was the cruelty of citizens to the laboring class that God himself protested: "Audi igitur quanta indignatio de serui supplicio caelum penetrauerit. anno enim post Romam conditam quadringentesimo septuagesimo quarto Autranius quidam Maximus seruum suum ueberatum patibuloque constrictum ante spectaculi commissionem per circum egit: ob quam causam indignatus Iuppiter Annio cuidam per quietem imperauit ut senatui nuntiaret non sibi placuisse plenum crudelitatis admissum." Thus cruelty with other grievances caused them to revolt. Of course, those who were already free were still more fortunate. It is curious that the law was such that the slaves remained slaves even after winning the strike.

142　STRIKE AT THE SILVER MINES.

which have in course of subsequent ages succeeded in ridding the world of slavery. Yet we find in this great strike 20,000 workingmen revolting and turning their muscle against their own comparatively progressive institutions, thus doing all in their power to aid the Spartans in subduing this growing Athenian intelligence. Of course we cannot blame them for resistance; for it raised them, although it doomed their cause. The brilliant Athenians were, after a struggle of 27 years, defeated and the Spartans succeeded in re-establishing the old, jealous, conservative paganism—that deadliest enemy of freedom, the nursery of slavery, the home of priestcraft and of aristocracy, ever inculcating belief in divine right of few against many.

Not far from Decilea on the Athenian seacoast, about five miles to the southeastward of the Laurian silver mines, was the little mining city of Sunion. There was an old castle at this place, which, like that in the forest of Sicily,[34] was under the ægis of a powerful divinity who recognized the workingman and protected him, whatever his deeds or his guilt, so long as he could hold himself within its walls.

It was about the close of the first Labor war of Eunus of Sicily that another enormous and horribly bloody strike occurred in the mines of Laurium.[35] The men undertook and carried out the same plan as that of Decelia, and struck work to the number of more than a thousand.[36] It must have been a memorable and shockingly sanguinary event. Sunion was the stronghold of the silver mines.[37] By the appearance of things as presented to us in the meagre details given, no improvement for the comfort of the miners had ever been introduced since the great strike of Decelea. The poor creatures were still suffering under the lash, delving 360 out of the 365 days in the year, naked, men and women indiscriminately tugging under the clubs of heartless foremen and directors, the same as ages before,[38] That these poor

---
[34] See Second Sicilian Labor War, chap. xi. where it is related that the strikers were actually shielded by the god of the castle, and no one dared to disturb them until they had organized that mighty rebellion.
[35] A full account of this strike-war occurs in chap. x. pp. 201-241 q. v.
[36] Augustin *de civ. d.* III, 26, tells us also of a great uprising of the miners in Macedonia.
[37] Böckh, *Laurische Silberbergwerk*, S, 90.
[38] Athenæus, *Deipnosophistæ*, VI. p. 271: quoting E. Poseidonius, the continnator of the *Histories* of Polybius says: " Καὶ αἱ πολλαὶ δὲ αὗται Ἀττικαὶ μυριάδες τῶν οἰκετῶν δεδεμέναι εἰργάζοντο τὰ μέταλλα. Ποσειδώνιος γοῦν ὁ φιλόσοφος καί ἀποστάντας φησὶν αὐτοὺς καταφονεῦσαι μὲν τοὺς ἐπὶ τῶν μετάλλων φύλακας, καταλα-

BLOODY MUTINY AT SUNION.

people, many of whom were freedmen had their labor organizations is proved beyond a shadow of doubt. Böckh comments upon the passage of Demosthenes against Pantætus,[39] showing a quarrel of the contractors in the mines with the trade unions. These quarrels were frequent occurrences in those days. It might have been some similar trouble that caused the uprisings we are describing, although it occurred in later times.

More than a thousand of the miners one day simultaneously struck work and proceeded in a body to the protecting castle of Sunion where they claimed and secured protection from the divine guardian that watched over this holy institution.[40]

Should any one complain of us for dragging religion into our history of the ancient lowly, their folly will here be seen. It is another of the numerous instances showing that labor, politics and religion were all institutions of govern-

---

βίσθαι δὲ τὴν ἐπὶ Σουνίῳ ἀκρόπολιν καὶ ἐπὶ πολὺν χρόνον πορθῆσαι τὴν Ἀττικὴν. Οὗτος, δὴν ὁ καιρὸς, ὅτε καί ἐν Σικελίᾳ ἡ δεντέρα τῶν δούλων ἀπόστασις ἐγένετο. See also Böckh, S. 123.

[39] See Demosth, *Agt. Pant.* 966–7. The *eranoi* mentioned were the veritable trade unions, corresponding with the Roman collegia, the French jurandes and the English trade unions. The *thiasoi*, as we persistently explain, were that branch of the *eranoi* which had in charge the entertainments and solemnities. We have already shown that slaves often belonged to the unions. Foucart, (*Associations Religieusues Chez Les Grecs*, p. 121 and 219, *inscription* No. 38), mentions an important inscription showing that one Xanthos a Lycian slave belonging to a Roman named Caius Orbius, founded a temple at the mines and consecrated it to the moon god. This moon god in return for the favor protected the slaves. The slab bears evidence from which we quote the first six lines as follows:

Ξάνθος Λύκιος Γαίου Ὀρβίου καθείδρυσα τὸ ἱερ ὀντοῦ Μηνὸς
Τυράννον, αἱρετίσαντος τοῦ θεοῦ, ἐπ' ἀγαθῇ τύχῃ, καὶ μηθένα
ἀκάθαρτον προσάγειν, καθαριζέστω δὲ ἀπὸ σκόρδων καὶ χοιρέων
καὶ γυναικός, λουσαμένους δὲ κατακέφαλα αὐθημερὸν εἰσπορεύεσθαι, καὶ ἐκ τῶν γυναικείων διὰ ἑπτὰ ἡμερῶν λουσαμένην κατακέφαλα εἰσπορεύεσθαι αὐθημερὸν, καὶ ἀπὸ νεκροῦ διὰ ἡμερῶν δεκα.

The remarks of Foucart in the text, p. 121 are: "Celui qui, vers le deuxième siècle après notre ère, introduisit dans l'Attique le culte de Mên, était un esclave lycien, employé par un propriétaire romain aux travaux des mines. C'était le dieu lui-même qui, dans une apparition ou dans un songe, l'avait invité à élever le temple. Aussi le fondateur a-t-il pris soin de répéter, dans les deux inscriptions, qu'il exécutait le désir de Mên; c'était mettre ainsi sous sa protection le règlement qu'il édictait: Moi, Xanthos, Lycien, appartenant à Caïus Orbius, j'ai consacré le temple de Mên Tyrannos, pour me conformer à la volonté du dieu." We would like to ask how a poor slave working in the mines could found, erect and consecrate a great temple so solid that its ruins and inscriptions remain as testimony to this day? Foucart in his desire to prove that all those inscriptions were purely religious and nothing more, forgets that a slave so lowly could do no such thing. He was simply managing officer of a great trade union so Democratic that social distinctions were unknown to it. This eranos erected the temple.

[40] Schambach, *Der Italische Selavenaufland*, S. 5: "Um 620 a. u.–134 v. Chr. empörten sich die in den Laurischen Silberberken arbeitenden Sklaven, tödteten ihre Wächter, nahmen das Kastell von Sunion ein und verwüsteten Attika lange Zeit.

ment. Let the reader imagine a thousand workingmen safely protected from the most deadly enemies, by a god! But not only for a day or two were they thus screened from the wrath of armed soldiers who had orders to spear every one of the strikers the instant he was seen outside the sacred pale, but for months this continued and there were battles fought and frequent and successful sallies made by the workingmen all under the protecting arm of the god.

The strikers killed their overseers, rushed into the town, took possession, got the temple to sleep in, organized themselves for combat, took the arms from the armories, and for a long time laid waste the country on every side, remaining masters of the stronghold within. The mayor of the city, one Heraklitos,[41] after their rage was probably spent, succeeded in defeating them when in all probability the usual brutalities of wholesale crucifixion were enacted and nearly every one put to death. This is the more certain because at this time, B. C. 133, the Romans were not only masters of all Greece, but their contractors were operating the silver mines at Laurium, for which kind of employment they had a peculiar fondness.

Another strike and bloody stampede of a similar kind took place at the gold mines of Pangætus in Macedonia, which was of sufficient magnitude to get into the history of Augustin, and Schambach mentions it as another important occurrence.[42]

[41] Orosius, V. 9: "In metallis quoque Atheniensium idem tumultus servilis ab Heraclito prætore discussus est."
[42] Schambach, *Der Italische Sklavenaufstand*, S. 5: "Auch die griechsche Welt wurde in ähnlicher weise, wenn auch in geringerer Ausdehnung, heimgesucht. Nach Augustin de civ. III, 26 verwüsteten kurz vor dem Ausbruche des ersten sicilischen Sklavenkrieges empörte Sklavenbanden Macedonian und die anstossenden Gebiete.

CHAPTER VI.

GRIEVANCES.

LABOR TROUBLES AMONG THE ROMANS.
MORE BLOODY PLANS OF SALVATION TRIED.

THE IRASCIBLE PLAN in Italy—Epidemic Uprisings—Attempt to Fire the City of Rome and have Things common—Conspiracy of Slaves at the Metropolis—Two Traitors—Betrayal—Deaths on the Roman Gibbet—Another Great Uprising at Setia—Expected Capture of the World—Land of Wine and Delight—Again the Traitor, the Betrayal and Gibbet—The Irascible Plan a Failure—Strike of the Agricultural Laborers in Etruria—Slave Labor—Character of the Etruscans—Expedition of Glabro—Fighting—Slaves Worsted—Punishment on the dreadful Cross, the ancient Block for the Low-born—Enormous Strike in the Land of Labor Organizations—One Glimpse at the Cause and Origin of Italian Brigandage—Laborers, Mechanics and Agriculturers Driven to Despair—The great Uprising in Apulia—Fierce Fighting to the Dagger's Hilt—The Overthrow, the Dungeon and the Cross.—Proof Dug from Fragments of Lost History.

STRIKES and labor mutinies are known to have occurred at Rome. There was one of a desperate nature in the year 417, B. C., while Lanatus, P. Lucretius and Spurius Rutilus were tribunes under the consuls Vibulanus and Capitolinus.[1] This was during the Peloponnesian war and the fact that it occurred about the same time with the great strike of the 20,000[2] miners and artisans at Athens, shows that the assertion made by the investigation of the United States Bureau

---
[1] Livy, *Annales*, lib. IV. 45.
[2] Authors differ a little as to dates. The difference is agreed to within three years; i. e. B. C. 413 for the Athenian and 417 for the Roman strike.

of Labor, that panics and depressions are simultaneous and somewhat epidemic in character, is true.³ This remarkable phenomenon will repeatedly exhibit itself as we proceed. Livy states that in the same year the city of Cumæ in Campania, long inhabited by the Greeks, but located only a short distance to the southward of Rome, had been taken.⁴ Undoubtedly some of the conspirators whose story we are about to recount, were Greeks. Syracuse, a Greek-speaking city, being brought into contact at the same time by the novel adventures of Nicias and Cimon, must have afforded the slaves an opportunity of hearing the news of the great strike pending at Decelea. On the whole, judging from the established fact that strikes and uprisings among workingmen are nearly always contagious, it may safely be set down as probable that these historical events were simultaneous. At any rate, the warning words of Macrobius, that "the more slaves the more enemies"⁵ would have been applicable to both Greeks and Romans; for though delivered subsequently, they were always true.

Enthused by some subtile agency, whether of emissaries from secret societies, or straggling travelers or pirates bringing exaggerated accounts from Greece, or whether goaded to the act by their own misery neither of which will ever be explained, we know that in the night, in the year 417, according to our own reckoning, or 419 according to Bücher,⁶ the slaves in a conjuration they had previously concocted, arose and attempted to fire the city of Rome. Their hatred was not only against their bonds *per se*, but also extremely intense against the aristocracy who, ever since the time of their beloved king Servius Tullius, B. C. 578–534, had oppressed them through both fear and jealousy. Tullius was the 6th Roman king; and of all others since the great Numa the most friendly to the poor and lowly. His sympathy was the stronger for his having once been a slave himself. He restored the arrangement of Numa that had regulated their trades and economic relations. He upheld the old trade organization. As to the slaves, it is probable

³ Consult *First Annual Report of the United States Bureau of Labor*, 1886, pp. 15 and 290 refering to panics and depre sions.
⁴ Liv. lib. IV. cap 44. fin. Cumæ was also the birthplace of Blossius the rich labor agitator, q. v. chapter on Aristonicus.
⁵ Macrobius, *Saturnaliorum Libri*, I. 11.
⁶ Bücher, *Aufstände der unfreien Arbeiter*, S. 94.

that he also greatly assisted them. All who could count upon enough freedom, he organized. He added to the first class of Numa's system two centuries.[7] This was recognizing in them some power of defence and an element of dignity. When this good man died, the nobility, mad with jealousy, overturned some of the laws and regulations he had established. Even during his life, such was their hatred that they plotted an indiscriminate slaughter in which many poor working people fell victims. Before he died, he caused to be engraved or otherwise chronicled, a constitution which greatly favored the slave population and the freedmen; but it was swept out of existence by those who succeeded him.

To clearly exhibit the state of human credulity in ancient times as well as to trace the origin of the proletarian theory of Saviors and the prevalent beliefs in immaculate conceptions, it may here be stated that Servius Tullius was imagined a descendant of a slave on his mother's side and of a god on his father's. This may really and consistently with the Pagan faith have been perfectly true; because according to that religion any *paterfamilias,* or head of a noble *gens* family was a god and there was a law giving him privilege to have children by his female slaves.[8] All strikes and uprisings had been easily subdued under Servius Tullius. The massacre of the slaves alluded to was not in the least, so far as we have information, instigated by him, but by the jealous nobility who could not bear to see a favor shown the poor whom they despised. After King Tarquin acceded to the throne and the good work of Tullius was destroyed, they seem to have revived their old uneasiness; and no doubt many uprisings actually took place which have never been mentioned in history. Thus, 143 years elapsed before the occurrence of the scene we have introduced. The intelligence regarding this horror is exceedingly meagre. Livy simply relates that the happiness of the Roman people was this year disturbed, not by a defeat of the army this time, but by "a great dan-

---

[7] Orelli, *Inscriptionum Latinarum Collectio,* nos. 1803, 2448, 4105; Livy, I. 43; Drumann, S, 154; Plutarch, *Numa,* 17.
[8] Granier, *Hist. des Classes Ouvrières,* p. 70. But the best proof of this is Dionysius of Halicarnassus, lib I.. Consult also Bombardini, *De Carcere et antiquo ejus Usu,* quoting the law: "Romulus permisslt maratis jus vitæ ac necessitudinis in uxores suas indulgere."

ger." He characterizes it indeed, as prodigious.⁹ Thus though all the particulars are not given the probabilities are, that it was a memorable affair.

A certain number of slaves of Rome formed a conspiracy to secretly set fire to the city in the night. The plan was to fire the houses in many places at once. Then, when the buildings were ablaze, they expected a stampede of the people as sometimes occurs at a burning theatre or church, on which occasion there settles a horror and a craze, the people losing their wits and thus falling an easy prey to a few well organized ruffians who, with a stern leader are able so shrewdly to command and manage as to demolish, plunder and make off with much that the flames leave unconsumed. This was the intention of the Roman slave conspiracy. They made their plans to throw the city into a vast confusion and at a point when flames and fright combined to perfect the moral chaos, to seize the arms from the armories and whatever else was available, put the citizens to the sword, set their fellow slaves free, and having completed the work of devastation, take possession of the property, occupy the citadels and the capitol and settle down in the enjoyment of the women whom they did not propose to hurt in their general massacre of the men. In the act of carrying out this prodigious carnage they where betrayed by two of the conspirators as is commonly the case in such attempts. As a result the ringleaders were seized by the officers of justice and crucified.[10]

It is very singular that Livy, usually elaborate when dwelling upon an important event, should so peremptorily dismiss this subject which he introduces as one of the historical events of Rome in which the Roman people, as it were, through the protecting power of their god Jupiter, narrowly escaped. How many or how many thousands were crucified, excepting the two who exposed the conspiracy to Jupiter,[11] is not stated. We recall this to mind with the more interest, since later uprisings like those of Eunus, Aristonicus and Spartacus were followed by the

---

[9] Liv. lib. IV. 45: "Annus felicitate populi Romani periculo potius ingenti quam clade insignis" Cf. Dionys. Halicar, excerpt xi.
[10] Dionysius of Halicarnassus, *Aechæol. Rhomaike*, xii. 5.
[11] *Idem*, IV. 45: "Avertit ne.and.i consilia Jupiter, indecisque duorum comprhenensi sontes poenas dederunt."

execution of thousands upon the cross. The two traitors were richly rewarded with money and freedom.[12]

Bücher reckons the year in which occurred another uprising in the heart of Latium, Italy, to have been B. C. 194. It was a very dangerous strike of slaves. The old Pomptine swamps in ancient times near the mountain city of Setia were infested with the runaway slaves, who to exist, were obliged to sally out from their glades where they hid by day, and played a rôle of brigands. All about the swamps on the higher levels, the soil was celebrated for productiveness. Setan wines were renowned for their relish. The city itself was between these marshes and the mountain cliffs, affording the brigands an immense range of forests, rocks, acclivities and jungles, which could be used as fastnesses when the pursuers or the weather would not permit the fugitives to live in the marshes below. Of course the little fortified Setia full of good things, but maintained by the labor of slaves, was an object of envy and a moral stumbling block to this order of submission within, and their cupidity or vengeance without. There were also numbers of other small cities and towns in this region. The encroachments of the rich *gens* families upon the *ager publicus* or public lands, which under the laws of Numa and Servius Tullius had been cultivated by the small farmers, sometimes by unions of farmers and as it were, in a socialistic way, had driven out the happy olden days and flogged into their places the horrid slave system of cultivation. Here, at the foot of this spur of the Appenines, as in the valley of the Guicus about Pergamum and the exquisite plateau of Enna,[13] the greedy slave owner had fastened upon the limbs of his human chattels the clanking chains of enforced bondage and declared a lockout of the former guilds who worked the government lands on shares. That they had no other right to these lands than that of lawless might we shall in our chapter on Spartacus, sufficiently portray.[14]

These landlords, it is conceded by every one who has given attention to the subject,[15] acted in every way the

[12] *Idem*: "Indicibus dena milia gravis æris, quæ tum divitiæ habebantur, ex ærario mumerata et libertas præmium fuit."
[13] See detailed accounts of the great uprisings of the workingmen at these places, chapters, vii.—x.
[14] Chapter xii.   [15] Drum. *Arb. u. Comm.* S. 152-3.

part of high-handed land pirates, in seizing the farms from the former lessees of the government of Rome. Without doubt these, maddened by their outrageous deprivations, instigated many a revolt of the slaves who had, as chattels, and under the bitterest urgents of lash and threat, been forced to take their places. It was a time when a third of the honest, hard working population were being literally choked away from their means of earning a living for their families.[16] There is no lack of information regarding the grievances of either the slaves impressed into the labor they hated, or the former tillers, locked out from the labor they loved. It is therefore without wonder that we hear of the outbreak or strike of B. C. 198. The numerous bands of slave bandits prowling among the swamps and mountain fastnesses formed an alliance[17] with the slaves within the city, who were as dissatisfied with their shackles as were the degraded agricultural wretches delving outside. The collusion spread from Setia to Praeneste 35 miles to the north and to Circeji a few miles beyond. About the time the conjurators were ready to make their deadly dash, was the moment when the people of Setia were to have a gala-day. What sort of festivity is not exactly clear. But judging from the popularity of the gladiatorial games not only at Rome but at that time, also in most of the provincial cities, it perhaps may be plausibly conjectured that the plays alluded to by Livy were the horrible butcheries of the arena. This public event afforded the conspirators an opportunity. Their plan was to take advantage of the enthusiasm of the games when least the populace were on the alert, crash upon the people, plunder the town, seize weapons and munitions necessary; then striking for the town of Norba, commit the same violence there, murder the masters and most of the other patricians and proceed to other cities in the vicinity repeating the carnage at each place until they gained the mastery of the world! Under the allowance of instruc-

---

[16] Plut. "Tiberius Gracchus," makes a plaintive comment on their sufferings.
[17] Büchner, "Aufstände d. unf. Arb." S. 28.

tion the slaves of that period enjoyed, this impossible
scheme should not seem absurd; since they doubtless had
little knowledge or conception of a world stretching beyond their vision and experience.

Again the traitor. Setia was under the prætorship of
C. Cornelius Lentulus. Just at the outbreak of the strike,
but whether during the tumult of a bloody fray we are
uninformed, two of the conspirators lost courage and betrayed the plot. Livy says: "The object was, when Setia
was once in their hands, by the combined result of murder and sudden tumult to first seize and similarly serve
the cities of Norba and Circeji. Information of this terrible plot was carried to Rome and laid before the Prætor, L. Cornelius Merula, by two slaves who arrived from
the scene before daybreak and in systematic order exposed the anticipated operations of the insurrectionists."[18]

Instantaneous action was now necessary at Rome. The
Senate was in a few minutes convoked. The two Roman
consuls for that year, (B. C. 198), Sextus Ælius Pætus and
T. Quinctius Flamininus, were absent with their commands in Gaul and elsewhere; so Merula one of the four
ædiles or tribunes of the people, was called to the task of

[18] Liv. XXXII. 26. "Quem ad modum Gallia præter spem quieta eo anno
fuit, ita circa urbem servilis prope tumultus est excitatus. Obsides Carthagi-
niensium Setiæ custodiebantur. Cum iis, ut principum liberis, magna vis ser-
vorum erat. Augebant eorum numerum, ut ab recenti Africo bello, et ab ipsis
Setinis captiva aliquot nationis eius empta ex præda mancipia. Cum conjurationem fecissent, missis ex eo numero primum qui in Setino agro, deinde circa
Norbam et Circeios servitia sollicitarent, satis iam omnibus præparatis ludis qui
Setiæ prope diem futuri erant, spectaculo intentum populum adgredi statuerant,
Setia per cædem et repentinum tumultum capta, Norbam et Circeios occupare.
Hujus rei tam fœdæ indicium Roman ad L. Cornelium Merulam prætorem urbis delatum est. Servi duo ante lucem ad eum venerunt, atque ordine omnia
quæ acta futuraque erant exposuerunt. Quibus domi custodiri iussis, prætor
senatu vocato edoctoque, quæ indices adferrent, proficisci ad eam conjurationem
quærendam atque opprimendam iussus, cum quinque legatis profectus obvios
in agris sacramento rogatos arma capere et sequi cogebat. Hoc tumultuario de-
lectu duobus milibus ferme hominum armatis Setiam, omnibus quo pergeret
ignaris, venit. Ibi raptim principibus conjurationis comprehensis fuga servorum
ex oppido facta est Dimissis deinde per agros qui vestigarent * * * * * * * * *.
Egregia duorum opera servorum indicum et unius liberi fuit. Ei centum milia
gravis æris dari patres iusserunt, servis vicena quina milia æris et libertatem;
pretium eorum ex ærario solutum est dominis. Haud ita multo post ex eiusdem
conjurationis reliquiis nuntiatum est servitia Præneste occupatura. Eo L. Cornelius prætor profectus de quingentis fere hominibus, qui in ea noxa erant, supplicium sumpsit. In timore civitas fuit obsides captivosque Pœnorum ea mo-
liri. Itaque et Romæ vigiliæ per vicos servatæ, iussique circumire eas minores
magistratus; et triumviri carceris lautumiarum intentiorem custodiam habere
iussi; et circa nomen Latinum a prætore litteræ missæ, ut et obsides in privato
servarentur, neque in publicum prodeundi facultas daretur, et captivi ne minus
decem pondo compedibus vincti in nulla alia quam in carceris publici custodia
essent."

suppressing the conspiracy. At this impromptu meeting of the Roman Senate it was ordered that Merula should take the field in person. There being at that instant very few regular troops at command, no time was lost in waiting orders to mass them, and it appears that he set out immediately with few, gathering militia as he proceeded on his way to Setia; for it appears that before reaching the scene of the danger the number of his forces reached 2,000 men. No particulars are given regarding the attack on the conspirators. We have no information as to whether there occurred a conflict. We are informed that the ring leaders of the conspiracy were arrested; also that the slaves were thrown into great confusion. Livy states that the town of Setia was the place where many hostages from the Carthagenian army were kept. The battle of Zama between Scipio and Hannibal, B. C. 202, had resulted disastrously to those old enemies of Rome and these hostages were kept by the conqueror as a pledge against further hostilities. Being penned in together, they also naturally joined the conspiracy and the ring-leaders referred to by Bücher, may have been some of the veritable warriors of the great Hannibal now pining in custody as hostages around the barracks of Setia.

But here again, as in the story of Spartacus, the excellent history of Livy is broken off and lost. How much of the real story is missing may never be known. But for the epitome or heading of this book we should be left in the dark entirely as to the results; but there is a passage in this which states that 2,000 of the conspirators were arrested and slaughtered.[20] Judging from the usual method of servile executions, it might be inferred that the captured like those of Spartacus, Eunus and Aristonicus, were crucified upon the gibbet. It is more probable however, since some of them were Carthagenian veterans, that part of them were crucified and the remainder butchered; because it was against the Roman code of honor to hang veteran soldiers or others than those of the servile race, upon the ignominious cross. Jesus a religio-political offender was crucified by the Romans in a Roman pro-

[19] *Aufstände d. unfreien Arb.* S. 29.
[20] Liv, lib. XXXII. *Epitomy*: "Conjuratio servorum, facta de solvendis Carthageniesium obsidibus oppressa est: duo milia necati sunt.

vince, not because of his offence, which might have received a nobler or less ignominious punishment, but because he was a workingman, not a soldier; and consequently ranked with the servile class in contradistinction to the noble class of the *gens* family, of the Pagan religion.

The uprising was suppressed after a struggle, the duraation and the particulars of which are left for our curiosity to surmise. But the causes of the grievances among the slaves were too profound to be easily stamped out. Merula and his legions, their reeking sabers and victory-boasting tongues, their tales of gibbet and dagger-to-the-hilt, the agony of woe and death, had scarcely had time to settle into the first lull; the perpetrators of the treachery which discovered the plot had but received their reward [21] by order of the Roman Senate, when news came that from the direction of Præneste the spirit of insurrection was again rife—this time in and about that city—and that a plot had been disclosed among the slaves who again in great numbers were caught making a singular spring in hopes of making themselves masters of it. Again their design was baffled. The Roman forces were once more sent out with orders to exterminate the slaves. The same prætor, L. Cornelius Merula, was soon on the warpath and as before, the inexperienced proletaries, among whom were many Punic hostages with their slender preparations and want of arms, could stand no ground with their powerful enemy. A battle must have been fought of considerable importance, and the result was certainly a disaster to the slaves and Carthagenian hostages and prisoners to whose secret machinations the blame is principally attributed by Dr. Bücher, also Livy himself by implication.[22] The number of poor wretches who suffered on the scaffold reached 500, making 2,500 public executions, besides the number not given in either case who were killed in the conflicts before being overcome. A great turbulence was caused thoughout the community.

Strong vigilance was now instituted at Rome to protect the smaller places from a recurrence of those dangers which had stamped their terror upon the inhabitants. The triumvirs ordered a closer guard to be kept over the

[21] "Egregia duorum" &c. Liv. XXXII. cap. 26.
[22] Livy, *Idem*; Büch. *Afifstände &c.* 29: Allgemein mass man geheimen Umtrieben der punischen Geisseln und Gefangenen die Schuld bei."

great underground prison called *carcer lautumiae*,[23] where those taken prisoners were placed. It was ordered that the Carthagenian hostages be degraded to the condition of slaves to work for private individuals and disallowed further privilege of being seen any more in public or having any more enjoyment in the open world. The shackles in which the prisoners were chained, were ordered to weigh not less than 10 pounds. The prison in which they were thenceforth to be forever kept was the public *carcer*, a description of which may now be interesting.

"There was a place" says the Italian jurist Bombardini,[24] "in the ancient Roman prison, called the Tullian cell, whither you descend by a ladder to the distance of 12 feet, into a damp hole, excavated in the earth. It was walled in on all sides and vaulted overhead having the sections adjoined. It had a putrid odor and a frightful outlook." But this is but the beginning, (B. C. 650-500,) of what it had developed into, by the time of which we speak. (B. C. 198). Long before this the prisoners here were at work. "Their masters saw them but rarely; their food was lowered to them through breathing holes, also their straw and scanty clothing."[25] Varro likewise tells of the *latomia* or quarry and the ergastulum called the *prison Tulliana*.[26] At any rate the public prison still to be seen, was a deep and spacious excavation under the Capitoline Hill, which had been made by prison labor. The object of the ancients in setting prisoners at work was twofold. First, vengeance rather than correction, as in our days of comparative enlightenment. Secondly, economy; for the ancients had the contract system with all its brutalities and horrors. The stone quarried out of these diggings furnished good building material and the holes thus left made prisons for the workmen who quarried it. Thus, in course of ages Rome became what Pliny called the *Urbs pensilis*,[27] or city hanging in the air. Most of these stu-

---

[23] Bombardini, *De Carcere et antiquo ejus Usu*, cap. iii.
[24] *Idem*, Cap. iii, p. 746 of *Thesaurus Grœvii et Gronovii, Supplement*.
[25] Maurice *Hist Politique et Anecdotique des Prisons de la Seine*, pp. 1-4.
[26] Varro, *De Re Rustica*, cap. iii, 8 speaks of them and of the popular opinion that these holes were nurseries of serpents. Cf. Prudentius, *Hymn* V.
[27] *Nat. Hist.* Speaking in another place (lib XXVIII 4,), Pliny thinks they were dug by Tullus Hostilius: "L, Piso primo annalium auctor est, Tullum Hostilium regem ex Numæ libris eodem. .... multi vero, ma na-rum rerum fata et ostenta verbis permutari. Cum in Tarpeio fodientes delubro fundamenta, cap it humanum invenissent, missis ob id ad se legatis

pendous catacombs are still to be seen in a more or less perfect state of preservation. Like the vast catacombs of Paris, they were originally stone quarries; then some of them differentiated into sewers, *cloacae*, some into public prisons, some into subterranean workshops, *ergastula*. The person condemned, if of low rank without family or money, was sent *ad opus publicum*, to the public works. "It was a place into which people were snatched; excavated from sharp rocks, immensely deep; a huge cutting or grotto quarried in the depths with passages interrupted by great, sharp-cornered rocks between which the victims' bodies squeezed. Projecting crags bristled as they sprang forth from the walls in darkness of midnight and frowned horribly over the abyss—a place of all others, from which the person doomed, when once thrown in, never afterwards saw the light of day."[28] Of course the convicts were furnished with lamps to light their steps and hands at work.

The reader is now left to judge for himself as to the justice or injustice of the causes lurking at the bottom of all ancient strikes.

We are again grateful to Dr. Karl Bücher, who reminds us of the account sparingly given by Livy, of another great uprising, B. C. 196, among the agricultural laborers of Etruria.[29] This noble country stretched from the Tiber on the south to the Ticino on the north. The rapturous landscapes of the Arno, the many beautiful Appenine lakes and mountains were Etruscan. No land ever subjugated by Rome possessed more agricultural or mineral wealth. Its original inhabitants possessed the refined civilization whence Rome took most of her prosperity. Bold, inventive, mechanical, progressive, the Etruscans ill-brooked the fetters of slavery fastened upon them like gyves by the greedy land grabbers who took possession of the soil, somewhat in the manner of the land owners of Great Britain and Ireland at the present time. The descendants of the ancient Etruscan stock held much of the land,

Etruriæ celeberrimus vates Olenns Calenus præc'arum id fortunatumque cernens, interrogatione in suam gentem transferre tentavit," etc. For a description see Prudent us *Hymn* V.
[28] Eutrope? *Epit. Rom. Hist. Era of Tarquin.*
[29] *Aufstände d. unf. Arb* S. 29.
Granier, de Cass *Hist. Classes Ouv.* chaps. xiii. xiv. ; Orell. nos. 3346; 3347, 9673, 1239, *of Inser. Lat. Col.* See also within account of the *Vectigalaia*

as free agriculturers and to them the government had long farmed it on shares, thus securing to the laborers a good living from the proceeds and to the government a good revenue which was paid, not in money but in kind, the rent tax being collected through the celebrated system of the vectigalia.[30] The slave system of the rich lords, who, without a tittle of right by law, and indeed in direct defiance of the precedents established by Numa and Servius Tullius, as well as the Licinian law, which, through the intrigues of the great proprietors had, from its passage, remained a dead letter, was now becoming a terrible scourge.

Indeed, in after days, Tiberius Gracchus on his way to Spain, passed through Etruria and found to his horror that once populous land in the hands of a few lordly masters who had completely locked the original agriculturers out and supplanted them with slaves. The scene of slavery and woe so stirred the blood of this noble Roman that he devoted his remaining life to the great agitation which is famous to this day as the agrarian movement with the bloody commotions that attended them, resulting in his own assassination. Such was the terrible condition of human slavery at that time, B. C. 196. In fact the slave system had to a large extent, driven out the once free and prosperous labor not only of Etruria but also of lower Italy, Sicily, Asia Minor, large parts of Greece, Spain and the smaller islands; and Rome was becoming the fattening pen of the arrogant grandees who lived in degenerate profligacy upon the lash-enforced drudgery of millions of slaves. Perhaps in telling these portentous truths to the world in the light of a social historiographer, we are among the first to discover the germ of a deeply hidden virtue in the revolt whose history occupies but eight poverty-solemnized lines in the great history of Livy. But to the student of sociology even this poor sketch brings back to us the profound wisdom of Anaxagoras and Aristotle who taught that all knowledge, all virtue and all progress eminate from humblest origin and that we can have nothing permanent or perfect except through investigation and experiment involving the severest trials. And although the poor slaves fell in thousands by the lash, the dungeon,

[30] *Aufst. d. unf. Arb.* "Trotzdem gelang es ihm nicht ohne heftigen Kampf die einzelen Haufen zu zerspringen."

the cross and although hundreds of years elapsed before the bonds of their slavery were broken yet who shall say their dying agonies here did not contribute to the cumulous of forces which at last swept their fetters away?

L. Furius and Claudius Marcellus were consuls at Rome when this agrarian uprising occurred. Their offices of state requiring their attention, the prætor, M. Acilius Glabro had in charge the "peace of the community." Little is known of the details of this uprising. The slaves were inhumanly oppressed and ready to accept desperate conditions if they held out the least promise of success in freeing them of their sufferings. On the other hand, the old cultivators had for centuries lived in ease upon the public lands and their organizations interlinked with those of the *collegia* and *sodalicia* which were just then being treated with severe censure and even threat by the Roman citizens who managed legislation. Efforts were begun about this time to suppress most of the labor organizations. The wealthy who were engaged in driving out free agricultural labor and supplanting it by that of slaves on the plantations, were particularly bitter against free labor, both in city and country.

When the news of the uprising reached Rome, Glabro immediately set out with one of the two legions of soldiers at command. By the appearance of things, the organization was not complete among the insurgents. The slaves, as Livy calls them in his sweeping terms, but more probably also the disaffected part of community generally and now locked out—those who formerly tilled the land on shares and also the slaves themselves—all of whose cause was common, met Glabro hilt to hilt and in a bloody battle were overcome. Bücher surmises that though the Romans were victorious, it was not without a heavy battle.[31] Great was the number of fallen workingmen and the number of those of their ranks taken prisoners was still greater. The leaders of the revolt were scourged and hung upon the cross. The remaining slaves were given up to their merciless masters to receive at their hands a double portion of hardships in the future. The freedmen engaged in this insurrection would, under the Roman custom of

[31] Livy, XXXIII. cap. 36: "Ex his (the strikers) multi occisi multi capti: alios verberatos crucibus adfixit, qui principes conjurationis fuerant, alios dom inis restituit."

treating enemies taken in battle, be sold as slaves or held as criminals and sent to the quarries and mines to linger for life at hard labor; for Bücher here correctly states that only under extraordinary circumstances did the Romans ever treat with lenity their captured enemies and the slave insurgents of all others, are known to have received the most relentless measure of malignity at their hands.[32]

One of the countries in which Spartacus was best received and from among whose people he obtained the largest number and the best volunteers who accepted with gratitude his offers of freedom, was Apulia. It was that rich, well watered, pastoral tract lying to the north and bordering on the Tarentine gulf. About 120 years before the great and memorable war of Spartacus broke out, these fine lands lying between the eastern slope of the Appenines and the Adriatic, were prey of the slave system. "Where earlier, the industrious farmers had thrived in happiness and plenty, herdsmen now in lonliness drove and herded countless flocks of cattle and sheep belonging to Roman Senators and knights."[33] Apulia being on the opposite side of the mountains from Rome and most of the opulent cities of Italy, was a region topographically suitable for robbers, both of land and sea. To the west were the mountains, whose rocks and forests afforded shelter for men of desperate nerve. The introduction of servile hands through the slave trade which had driven free labor from the agricultural and pastoral regions of Italy had naturally been followed by a variety of desperadoes whose bands at the time of our story, infested the whole stretch. He also surmises with much intelligence that these organized gangs were not without a distinct purpose in working for their fellow men, and our own inspection satisfies us that a philosophy or culture had from high antiquity existed for the redemption of the poor everywhere.

In another chapter we shall show the relationship between the societies of *Dionysoi* and those of the *Bacchantes*. Indeed there appears little difference between them. In both words, one Latin, the other Greek, we have

[32] Büch. *Aufst. d. unf. Arb.* S. 31.
[33] Lüders, *Dionys. Künst. passim.*

the same meaning. They were in Greece, in the islands, in Asia Minor and Palestine, mostly organizations of artificers or skilled mechanics;[34] but because they held festivities and conducted them on methods peculiar to themselves as well as because they were working people, they were looked upon with suspicion. No author of antiquity or orator could speak with respect of the bacchanals. We know by the inscriptions that they had many societies at Rome and in the provincial cities. Cicero and Livy spurn them. No doubt the obloquy they suffered drove them into these fastnesses and made them, by sheer compulsion, assume suspicious attitudes. However this may be, we find Livy associating them with another great strike or uprising of the workingmen which occurred B. C. 185-184, in Apulia and along the coast between there and Bruttium.

It was during the days of the stern Cato's power, in the consulship of Appius Claudius Pulcher and M. Sempronius Tuditanus.[35] The so-called province of Apulia was in the care of the prætor, L. Postumius. This man's watchground was Apulia and the shores of the gulf of Tarentum. A few years afterwards the famous Spartacus led his army o rebel workingmen, consisting of volunteer gladiators, shepherds, bacchantes and slaves, to Metapontem, where he spent the memorable winter of B. C. 73-72.[36] Too just to allow disorder, too wise to permit even a draught of w'ne to be drank in carousal, too good to give his loved soldiers the bridle, this modest gladiator here proved himself the terror of the haughty Romans and a prototype of modern military virtue, genius and discipline. And this town was in the very valleys of the scenes of our present story.[37] Livy, as is usual with ancient historians, when speaking of the uprisings of the oppressed working classes makes short work of his story. We linger upon his stingy descant because of the peculiarly interesting associations connected with the mightier revolt of the great gladiator chieftain, one hundred and ten years afterwards upon the same spot.

There had been many cases of dissatisfaction, some of which had reached the ears of the vigilant Romans.

[34] Livy, XXXIX, cap. 29.
[35] Consult chapter xii of this work.
[36] Büch. *Aufst. &c.* S 31.
[37] Livy, XXXIX. 29, and 41.

Great organizations among the enslaved shepherds and drovers were heard of. A case was reported in which detachments of half starved cowboys and ploughmen threw away their bondage, knocked down and garroted their overseer, seized his knife, his sword and club and made their way to the mountain caves and jungles whence with desperate revenge and want, they returned reinforced to plunder and sack their master's goods. It got so that the government highways were unsafe; and in ten years from the time of our last story of the strike in Etruria, 192-182, another enormous "slave conspiracy" had been found to exist.

As soon as reliable news of this reached Rome, L. Postumius[38] the prætor, or as the same informant names him "propraetor" in another place,[39] instantly marched with a large force of troops to the scene.[40] The prætor had previously had charge of all Apulia and Bruttium. He had the watch of all the Adriatic coast from Rhegium to Mt. Garganus, east of the Appenine range and most likely also a considerable force of troops stationed at different points where Roman *praesidia* or garrisons existed.[41] This is self-evident; since the senators and knights owning the lands and the slaves who worked them were also military officers as well as lawgivers and it was easy for them to legislate for placing the standing army where it should best protect their gluttonous acquirement of wealth.

The details of the manœuvres, skirmishes and battles gone through with before the climax was reached, are left unwritten. But there can be no doubt that a battle was fought; because, of the total number of the insurgents taken, no less than 7,000 were condemned to the mines and of the great number who were captured many were executed which means, of course, crucified.[42] Those who were caught were certainly sent either to the mines, *ad metallum*, to the Roman prison, *carcer Tullianus*, or to the quarries, *lapicidinae*. But the most probable thing is,

---

[38] Livy, XXXIX, 41, ad fin: "L. Postumius propraetor, cui Tarentum provincia evenerat, magnas pastorum coujugationes vindicavit et reliquas Bacchanalium quæstionis cum omni est cura."
[39] Bücher. *Aufstände der unfreien Arbeiter*, S. 31, note 2.
[40] Weisseκborn. *Com on Livy*, xxxv. 20
[41] Livy, XYYIY. 29, ' De multis sumptum est supplicium."
[42] *Idem*, cep. 41: "Partim comprehensos, Romam ad senatum misit, in carcerem omnes a P. Cornelio conjecti sunt."

that there being so many, they were distributed according to their adjudged guilt, in the three prisons.⁴⁸ The horrors of either of these three places have been described. But this awful retribution inflicted upon the poor struggling workingmen and their suffering families by the military arm of Rome, protecting slavery the most brutal and demoralizing institution that ever cursed the nations of the earth or whetted the appetites of the greedy by locking out honest laborers from their natural employ, failed to stifle the hopes of those hardy mountaineer farmers whom tyranny had turned into brigands. Bücher renders a word of comment on Livy's short-cut information, to the effect that those who escaped, re-organized their banditti in a distant point and began anew their work of pillage, which he characterizes as having become the plague of the times—a plague which was in effect, the foundation of that terrible brigandage, never suppressed in Italy until in recent years. This, then is the origin of those terrible "bacchanalian orgies"—the innocent workingmen, long organized in the unions or guilds " for self-protection and co-operation entirely under the laws and sanction of Numa and Tullius in the old, happy days of Rome's golden economies, now driven and dispersed to the wailing winds of her night of slavery!

Noble writers of the very ancient past have spoken kindly of the Bacchantes both of the Greek and Latin-speaking races of mankind, and lately Böckh, the archæologist who has done more than any other man to reveal the true status of ancient life and has uncovered many errors which policy and prejudice have cultivated, openly acknowledges that he finds no element of harm or of wrong intention in the bacchanalian organizatian among Greek-writing Societies of Asia Minor, and his invaluable evidence we shall bring forward in a subsequent chapter, because he fixes his opinion from the unerring evidence of the stones bearing inscriptions from their own hands.

Hesiod the poet and celebrated master who lived probably more than a thousand years before Christ and came of the lowly stock, was the first known labor agitator. His greatest poem, "Works and Days," full of pleadings for the

⁴⁸ For an elaborate description of the trade unions under Numa, also on Servius Tullius and Clodius, see chapters xiii.—xix. of this work.

poor, is the first book on the labor question. He may be styled the father of the emotions of pure sympathy, because the earliest witness.

But already at his time there were thousands of labor societies that were discussing with him this great problem and with him practically building a cult of co-operation full of the tender sympathies of human brotherhood and of mutual support.

CHAPTER VII.

DRIMAKOS.

A QUEER OLD MAN OF THE MOUNTAINS.

Strike of Drimakos, the Chian slave—Co-operation of the Irascible with the Sympathetic—A Desperate Greek Bondsman at Large—Labor Grievances of the ancient Scio—Temperament and Character of Drimakos—Vast Number of unfortunate Slaves—Revolt and Escape to the Mountains—Old Ruler of the Mountain Crags—Rigid Master and loving Friend—Great Successes—Price offered for his Head—How he lost it—The Reaction—Rich and Poor all mourn his Loss as a Calamity—The Brigands infest the Island afresh since the Demise of Drimakos—The Heroön at his Tomb—An Altar of Pagan Worship at which this Labor Hero becomes the God, reversing the Order of the Ancient Rights—Ruins of his Temple still extant—Athenæus—Nymphodorus—Archæology—Views of modern Philologists.

WE are indebted to the geographer and historian Nymphodorus Siculus for an account of a very remarkable strike and maroon-like revolt of slaves in the island of Scio. This island—the ancient Chios—which lies in the Greek archipelago at a distance of 7 miles from the coast of Asia Minor, contains an area of little more than 500 square miles. It has, from high antiquity, been celebrated for the ever varying beauty of its scenery, its perpetual verdure, its forests that are inaccessible to civilized life, its countless streams and streamlets whose pure waters rush from calcarious steeps and fall into the tiny rivers or the sea.

Chios is aged as the primeval home of the Pelasgians and the Leleges of Cyclopean fame and antiquity, and consequently is Greek in its remotest sense. It was of all lands most accursed with slavery.[1] While the Peloponnesus and Attica recruited their slave ranks with their own sons and daughters and their prisoners of war, Chios betook herself to the disgraceful slave traffic to secure her recruits—a custom undoubtedly borrowed from her neighbors, the Phœnicians. What the tale of startling uprisings and shocking cruelties of these struggling people would be if told, we know not;[2] for we are obliged to let all knowledge lapse in the æons of an unwritten past and patiently wait until the era of our story, accidentally recorded by Nymphodorus, a geographer, as having transpired a short time before his day.

Judging from this we are able to fix its date,[3] not at about 250 years after the birth of Christ as surmised by Dr. Bücher, but at a very much earlier period. We follow the story of Nymphodorus, who received this informa-

[1] All over Greece and especially in Chios in Ionia there was constant fear of slave rebellions. Plato (*Republic* ix. 5 fin. and in very many other passages), mentions this fact as a constant terror in those days.

[2] The indications are that there constantly occurred in those times mutinies among the working people. Many of them were prodigious. Dim information of one in Southern Greece is found, which occurred between 300 and 400 years before Christ. The cruelty of masters was so great that when an earthquake destroyed 20,000 people it was believed to be their punishment for cruelty. The all-prevailing fear of being murdered by slaves is frequently hinted at by Plato. To read the eleventh chapter of the first book of Macrobius is really worth the attention of the thoughtful. It is replete with evidence that anciently there was a strong anti-slavery movement. Macrobius, (*Saturnatiorum*, l. xi. 7–9. Eyssenhardt), says: "Vis tu cogitare eos quos ius tuum uocas isdem seminibus ortos eodem frui cælo, æque uiuere, æque mori? Serui sunt: immo homines. Serui sunt: immo conserui, si cogitaueris tantund m in utrosque licere fortunæ. Tam tu illum uidere liberum potes quam ille te serunm. Neçcis qua ætate Hecuba seruire cœperit, qua Crœsus, qua Darei mater, qua Diogenes, qua Plato ipse? Postremo quid ita nomen seruitutis horremus? seruus est quidem, sed necessitate, sed fortasse libero animo seruus est. Hoc illi nocebit si ostenderis quis non sit. Alius libidini seruit, alius auaritiæ, alius ambitioni, omnes spei, omnes timori." Again *(Idem* 13–14*)* come the prophetic words: "Non potest amor cum timore misceri. Unde putas adrogantissimum illud manasse prouerbium quo iactatur totidem hostes nobis esse quot seruos? Non habemus illos hostes sed facimus, cum in illos superbissimi contumeliosissimi crudelissimi sumus et ad rabiem nos cogunt peruenire deliciæ, ut quicquid non ex uoluntate respondit iram furoremque euocet." But it was fear rather than compassion that forced our hard-hearted forefathers to talk in this strain.

[3] Schambach, *Italische Sclavenaufstand*, I., S. 5; refers to this slave insurrection in the following clearly expressed language: "Auch das riche Chios war zu derselben Zeit B. C. 134, der Schauplatz einer wilden Sclavenempörung, die erst nach mehreren Jahren unterdrückt wurde. Athenæus VI. He seems to have no doubt as to the era of the story of Drimakos being identical with that of the great servile wars. But what time did it begin? This is the important question. Athenæus says or intimates that Drimakos was in the vigor of manhood when he began the revolt; but he was an old man when he died and up to the last the malcontents held their ground. Now if we agree with Schambach that his " zu derselben Zeit " meant the end of the period, or thereabout, we must add at least 30 years to allow him to become and old man which makes the rebellion to have begun about the year B. C. 364.

HOW WE COME TO KNOW THE FACTS. 165

tion directly from the Chians themselves, from whom he must have received his data while visiting the island and its inhabitants in search of information for his book which was a description of the coast of Asia minor and the multitude of islands, large and small, that stud the Archipelago.

The islanders recounted to Nymphodorus that a slave named Drimakos had lived and died in those parts, whose history was remarkable. Consequently this Sicilian Greek, whose errand was knowledge, became curious to know about the strange man Drimakos and all the particulars, in order to embellish the chapter of his " Nomima Asias" or customs and habits of the Asians—in other words, his descriptive geography. And now that our attention is fastened upon so weird an object as a runaway slave with drawn dagger, bolting from his pursuing owner and climbing a crag to a mountain den with a dozen abolitionists as desperate as he, we pause to ask, who is this Nymphodorus?

Alas such curiosity is rewarded with the aggravation of a mystery! We know nothing of Nymphodorus. We only know that he lived and wrote in his geography a description, not only of the island of Scio as it was before the time of Christ, but also of the customs and usuages that were practiced by its inhabitants; and interspersed in his work there was many an incident, description and story, one of which was this tale of Drimakos, the runaway slave. We know that this priceless literary gem, like the noble but lost chapters of Diodorus, and Sallust, of Livy, of Fenestella, Dion Cassius, Theophanes, Nicolaus Damascenus, Cæcilius Calactenus and a wealth of others with their flood of facts, come to us only in the secondhand and oblique mention of others who read them before they were destroyed; or sometimes in multilated fragments of the originals which escaped the vandals who perhaps thought that by robbing posterity of facts that disclosed the beastliness of their institutions they might confer a favor upon the sin as well as the sinners whose power they fawned upon and flattered. At any rate the work of Nymphodorus is lost; and the question remains: who is Nymphodorus and what about Drimakos the Chian runaway slave?

The fact is, Athenæus,[4] an Egyptian of antiquity, saw and read this book of Nymphodorus the geographer, and in his "*Deipnosophistae* or Banquet of the Learned," a *pot pourri* or hodge-podge of science, history and anecdote, reproduced for us the essential facts concerning this affair of Drimakos, which was no little incident to make light of, but a vast insurrection of slaves, like that of Eunus and Spartacus, involving a lifetime, with bloody wars and a great and terrible and successful struggle of "outlaws" against society. It is Athenæus, the middleman then, not Nymphodorus, whom we must follow and carefully scan, picking every word down to the bone, to get the meat of his language; always suspicious enough of translations to avoid them entirely, especially when exhuming such literary mummies as those wrapped and preserved in chemicals musty with the taint of labor.

Nymphodorus in his lost work on the customs and usages of the Asians,[5] says it was not long before his time that the facts concerning Drimakos occurred. But although no doubts exist regarding the truth of the general facts, nobody is clear as to the exact time of Nymphodorus. Whether the insurrection of the Chian slaves was a spasmodic affair, belonging to one lifetime, or whether the episode of Drimakos was simply one incident distinguished for its magnitude and duration among many that for ages were constantly occurring, is a problem.[6] We shall present the facts as given in the *Deipnosophistae* of Athenæus carefully adhering to the points in the text and seasoning the story only to befit the character of our pages for the general reader. But there seems to be no evidence to confute our theory that Nymphodorus wrote his story at least a century before Christ, and that the true age of Drimakos was that of the other great slave rebellions which began to rage about a century and a half before Christ.

[4] Most chronologists make Athenæus to have lived about A. D. 250. Dr. Bücher, therefore, must certainly be entirely incorrect in putting the date of the work of Nymphodorus at "Mitte des dritten Jahrhundertes nach Christo; *Aufstäde der unfreien Arbeiter*, S. 22, since Athenæus himself lived before that time. We are fully confirmed in the opinion that Drimakos' uprising was contemporaneous with that of Eunus of Sicily and Aristonicus of Pergamus, and was an outcrop of that great agitation.

[5] Νόμιμα Ασίας. The island of Chios was only separated from the continent of Asia by a strait 7 miles wide, and easily visible from the main shore. For a good description of this island. see Eckenbrecher: *Die Insel Chios*, Berlin, 1845.

[6] Pauly's *Real Encyclopædia*. Vol. V, S. 193, contains an article from Westermann, discussing the probable time of Nymphodorus, q. v.

From the story as related by Athenæus it does not appear that Drimakos escaped from his master amid scenes of blood-shedding, but that those horrors were reserved for the immediate future. He was then a young man of great sternness and determination, shrinking from nothing he had set his mind upon, and too nervous and sensitive to bear the galling humiliations of slavery. He was also a man of sympathies, and felt for his fellow slaves as well as himself. In such a frame of mind he could not but have felt deeply for the thousands of poor creatures who had been bought or kidnapped from their native homes and brought to this island to be sold like animals and here forced to delve under the merciless lash. Most of the labor of land culture and mechanics, all the household drudgery, as well as the attendance upon arrogant lords and ladies, and the office work of the government, was performed in those days by slaves; and Chios was no exception.

Like Achæos, Cleon, Athenion and Spartacus, the desperate young man broke his bonds by some violent effort. It may have been the immediate result of a quarrel with his master or his overseer, or perhaps a conspiracy of a handful of fellow bondsmen as in the case of Athenion or Spartacus; perhaps a stampede after a battle with clubs and butcher-knives. One thing we know upon such points in general: masters were on the alert at all times, having little confidence in their human chattels, and kept them under guard, often chained at night and in many places, branded.

When Drimakos arrived in the mountains with his band of runaways, he found in the clefts of rock and among the sun-warmed ledges, suitable fastnesses wherein not only to hide in safety but to sleep, and obtain repose. Hunters and other mountaineers had been there before them and built an occasional cabin. With the rocks and fragments they erected more, and with axes and perhaps saws and other tools, covered them and constructed for themselves rough seats and tables. But food was only to be had in the granaries and houses below, in the richly cultivated valleys, and in the distant city they had left.

Here the masters were up in arms, ready for an expedition in pursuit of their escaped bondsmen. The word went vigorously forth that they must be retaken, either dead or alive. On the other hand while preparations were making for a grand pursuit, other slaves took flight and centered to the mountain fissures of Drimakos, now their acknowledged leader.

How they got their first supply of provisions we are unaware, but they certainly did not starve. The same question might in the absence of these particulars also be asked as to how they were supplied with arms with which to do battle with their pursuers. What we know is that they were the recipients of good luck; partly through their own courage and partly through a combination of circumstances which favored them from the start.

The whole truth is, they, like Eunus and the smiling goddess Demeter, or Spartacus and his fortune-telling wife, who foretold prodigies of happiness, had also their Messiah, soothsayer, prophet and warrior in the person of Drimakos, whom they implicitly obeyed and worshiped with a superstitious awe; and so long as the enthusiasm of this belief in him as a Savior remained untarnished, their heaven-inspired dash and valor were insurmountable and their prowess was unscathed. Moreover there prevailed a superstition among the slave-owning Chians themselves, against slavery and especially this class of slave-holding practiced on the island of Chios. In proof of this we quote from Athenæus the following:

"Nymphodorus, it is thus seen, has furnished us with the account; but I find that in many copies of his history Drimakos is not spoken of by name. Yet I cannot imagine that any of you are ignorant of what Herodotus, that prince of historians, said regarding the Chian, Panionios, and what righteous punishment he underwent for having castrated three boys and sold them.[7] Then again Nicol-

---

[7] Herodotus, *Historion*, viii. *Urania*, 105-106. The horrible story of revenge is thus told by Herodotus and tersely illustrates the almost inconceivable brutality and cruelty of slavery or of the greed which inspired it. " Ἐκ τουτέων δὴ Πηδασέων ὁ Ἑρμότιμος ἦν· τῷ μεγίστη τίσις ἤδη ἀδικηθέντι ἐγένετο πάντων τῶν ἡμεῖς ἴδμεν. ἀλόντα γὰρ αὐτὸν ὑπὸ πολεμίων καὶ πωλεόμενον ὠνέεται Πανιώνιος, ἀνὴρ Χῖος, ὅς τὴν ζόην κατεστήσατο ἀπ' ἔργων ἀνοσιωτάτων. ὅκως γὰρ κτήσαιτο παῖδας εἴδεος ἐπαμμένους, ἐκτάμνων, ἀγινέων ἐπώλεε ἐς Σάρδις τε καὶ Ἔφεσον χρημάτων μεγάλων. παρὰ γὰρ τοῖσι βαρβάροισι τιμιώτεροί εἰσι οἱ εὐνοῦχοι πίστιος εἵνεκα τῆς πάσης τῶν ἐνορχίων. ἄλλους τε δὴ ὁ Πανιώνιος ἐξέταμε πολλοὺς, ἄτε ποιεύμενος ἐκ τουτέων τὴν ζόην, καὶ δὴ καὶ τοῦτον. καὶ οὐ γὰρ τὰ πάντα ἐδυστύχεε ὁ Ἑρμότιμος, ἀπικνέεται ἐκ τῶν Σαρδίων παρὰ βασιλῆα μετ' ἄλλων δώρων· χρόνον δὲ προϊόντος πάντων τῶν εὐνούχων ἐτιμήφη μάλιστα παρὰ Ξέρξῃ. 106. Ὡς δὲ τὸ στράτευμα τὸ Περσικὸν ὅρμα ὁ βασιλεὺς ἐπὶ τὰς Ἀθήνας ἐὼν ἐν Σάρδισι, ἐνθαῦτα καταβὰς κατὰ δή

ANCIENT ANTI-SLAVERY DISCUSSION. 169

sus the peripatetic as well as Poseidonius the stoic both wrote in their histories that the Chians were afterwards enslaved by Methridates, tyrant of Cappadocia, and bound hand and foot, were given over to their own slaves. Surely the gods were angry with the Chians."[8]

Nor was this superstition against all kinds of chattel slavery confined to the island of Chios. The people of Attica and different parts of Greece were tormented with conscience on account of their unjust system of slavery and the ever-recurring revolts of their slaves; and the Lockrians, who never tolerated slavery, taunted them for their wickedness.[9] But the revolts of the slaves themselves, and the growing number of the *psomokolaphoi* or runaways and the consequent loss to their masters, together with the desperate, often bloody deeds of these runaways whetted their sins and inflamed their fears lest the gods should frown upon them as the upholders of this national abomination. Add to all this the further and significant fact that the freedmen all around them were in sympathy with the slaves and were often organized into powerful unions which sometimes even permitted the slaves to membership.[10] Especially was this the case

τι πρῆγμα ὁ Ἑρμότιμος ἐς γῆν τὴν Μυσίην, τὴν Χῖοι μὲν νέμονται, Ἀταρνεὺς δὲ καλέεται, εὑρίσκει τὸν Πανιώνιον ἐνθαῦτα. ἐπιγνοὺς δὲ ἔλεγε πρὸς αὐτὸν πολλοὺς καὶ φιλίους λόγους· πρῶτα μέν οἱ καταλέγων ὅσα αὐτὸς δι' ἐκεῖνον ἔχοι ἀγαθά· δεύτερα δέ οἱ ὑπισχνεύμενος ἀντὶ τουτέων ὅσα μιν ἀγαθὰ ποιήσει, ἢν κομισάμενος τοὺς οἰκέτας οἰκέῃ ἐκείνῃ· ὥστε ὑποδεξάμενος ἄσμενον τοὺς λόγους τὸν Πανιώνιον κομίσαι τὰ τέκνα καὶ τὴν γυναῖκα· ὡς δὲ ἄρα πανοικίῃ μιν περιέλαβε, ἔλεγε ὁ Ἑρμότιμος τάδε· "Ὦ πάντων ἀνδρῶν ἤδη ֽμάλιστα ἀπ' ἔργων ἀνοσιωτάτων τὸν βίον κτησάμενε, τί σὲ ἐγὼ κακὸν ἢ αὐτὸς ἢ τῶν ἐμῶν τις ἐργάσατο, ἢ σέ, ἢ τῶν σῶν τινα, ὅτι με ἀντ' ἀνδρὸς ἐποίησας τὸ μηδὲν εἶναι; ἐδόκεές τε θεοὺς λήσειν οἷα ἐμηχανῶ τότε· οἵ σε ποιήσαντα ἀνόσια, νόμῳ δικαίῳ χρεωμενοι, ὑπήγαγον ἐς χέρας τὰς ἐμάς, ὥστε σε μὴ μέμψασθαι τὴν ἀπ' ἐμέο τοι ἐσομένην δίκην." Ὣς δέ οἱ ταῦτα ὠνείδισε, ἀχθέντων τῶν παίδων ἐς ὄψιν, ἠναγκάζετο ὁ Πανιώνιος τῶν ἑωυτοῦ παίδων τεσσέρων ἐόντων τὰ αἰδοῖα ἀποτάμνειν· ἀναγκαζόμενος δὲ ἐποίεε ταῦτα· αὐτοῦ τε, ὡς ταῦτα ἐργάσατο, οἱ παῖδες ἀναγκαζόμενοι ἀπέταμνον. Πανιώνιον μέν νυν οὕτω περιῆλθε ἥ τε τίσις καὶ ὁ Ἑρμότιμος·"

[8] Athenæus *Deipnosophistæ,* Lib. VI. cap. vii.
[9] Athenæus, *idem;* Böckh, *Public Economy of the Athenians,* mentions it.
[10] See Lüders, *Die Dionysischen Künstler* S. 46–47, also S. 22. We have however given Lüders' views and proof (see p. 98 and note 27) in full in another chapter, q. v. The evidence as to slaves being sometimes members is overwhelming. Foucart, *Associations Religieuses Chez Les Grecs,* pp. 5–6 says: "Il en était tout autrement pour les thiases et les éranes. Non-seulement ils étaient ouverts aux femmes mais encore les étrangers, les personnes de condition ou d'origine servile y avaient accès. Ce dernier point est d'une grande importance, fort heureusement, les témoignages des monuments épigraphiques sont assez précis pour l'établir avec une entière évidence. Il serait inutile de citer toutes les inscriptions qui en donnent la preuve; j'en ai seulement choisi quelques-unes, pour montrer que cette composition était la même dans les différents pays. Les exemples sont assez nombreux pour qu il soit permis d'étendre la conclusion aux cas mêmes où la preuve directe fait défaut, et de regarder l'admission des femmes, des étrangers, des affranchis et des esclaves, comme un caractère commun de toutes ces associations." Foucart further shows that freedmen and freed-

among the Greek-speaking slaves—far more so than among the Romans—and in these society meetings they all, bondsmen and freedmen alike, under protection of their secret *eranos* or union, discussed their sufferings and perhaps also concocted their plots of salvation. Thus, from all sources—the inner-consciences, the frowning gods, the slaves' own grievances and the constantly recurring strikes maintained by runaways and bloody battles—greedy capitalists were reminded of this abomination which they were hugging, even in ancient days.

The words of Nymphodorus plainly tell us that in the Island of Chios revolts and escape to the mountains were of common occurrence. His words reproduced in the banquet of the learned by Athenæus make the matter plain. We give them below in a note from the old scholiast latin version of 1557, as they introduce the story in plain words.[11] The reader is now fully prepared by this description of the surroundings to comprehend the story of Drimakos whom we left in the mountains with his followers, busily at work with saws and axes building rough cabins and meditating a desperate swoop upon the city they had left, that they might seize a part of the grain and stores which their own former labor and that of their fellow bondsmen had created. This expedition was well planned. Of this we have assurance in the words of

woman got their freedom many times through their organization. Under the head "Affranchis ou esclaves," p. 7, he cites inscriptions whose epigraphs clearly explain that slaves were members in Rhodes. We have elsewhere shown that the ancient states owned slaves. They were known as public servants. "Une inscription de l'île de Rhodes mentionne une société religieuse composée des esclaves publics de la ville (voyez p. 112, note 4). La mutilation du monument enlève à ce témoignage une partie de sa valeur. Mais l'examen des noms propres qui se rencontrent dans les autres inscriptions prouve que ces associations admettaint les affranchis et probablement même les esclaves." On page 112, cited by Foucart occur the words: "Un fragment d'inscription, restitué par Keil d'une manière hardie, mais, à tout prendre, vraisemblable, montrerait la composition particulière de la société qui se plaçait sous le patronage de Zeus Atabyrios. Elle aurait été formée des esclaves publics de la ville de Rhodes, et c'est l'un d'eux qui aurait exércé le sacerdoce. Ὑπὲρ Διοσαταθυριαστᾶν τῶν τᾶς πόλιος δούλων, Εὐαι. .ενος γραμματεὺς δαμ ὁσιος ἱερατεύσας Διὸς 'Αταθυρίου . . . τῶν κυρίων Ῥοδίων ἀν έθμκε Δ ιῖ 'Α ταθυρίῳ . . . . Philologus, 2d suppl., p. 612." It seems exceedingly strange that this learned author should lack the power of penetration so far as to continually make a hack of a pet idiosyncrasy regarding these innumerable organizations having been strictly religious orders. The fact is, as we continually show, braced also by epigraphists like Mommsen and Böckh that they were *bona fide* labor societies compelled under vigorous laws to cover their real object with the shield of the Pagan faith.

[11] "Haec igitur de illis scripsit Nymphodorus in Asiæ Navigatione, Chiorum servi ab ipsis dominis aufugientes in montes sublimioraque, ipsorum devastantes multi simul coacti sunt. Est enim ipsa insula aspera multisque arboribus referts." Athenæus, VI., chap. vii., (*Natalis de Comisibus, Veneto*, 1556).

Athenæus who says that Drimakos was not really the aggressor but that the Chians sent an expedition into the fugitives' retreat, and that the latter being favored and well generaled, came off victorious. This means that the Chians were decoyed into ambush by Drimakos, attacked, cut to pieces, their arms captured and the slaves left complete masters of the field. In other words, there was fought a bloody battle, even a succession of battles, and of such terrible cruelty that even the heart of the stern Drimakos was melted with sympathy and he soon sought a council of arbitration to put a stop to the ruthless effusion of blood. But this did not occur until sometime after the first decisive contest with the masters was fought.

When, by this and other victories, the slaves found themselves in full possession of their caverns, and their new home supplied with provisions, their soldiers with arms captured from the defeated masters, and their numbers much augmented by incoming detachments of runaways from all parts of the island, they began to think of discipline and order. Drimakos was made king, commander-in-chief and despot; and he began to exercise an iron rule over his subjects nearly as severe, but more just than that of their former masters.[12] Having vanquished the armies of the masters in repeated and bloody battles, causing a state of things which may have lasted for years —since both the duration and dates are forgotten by our historian—the slaves continued to get their provisions from the granaries, barns, farms and stores, in the following extraordinary manner:

A council or conference was called by this victorious man of the mountains, whereat the Chian masters were invited to participate with him and his victorious legions on equal terms, under a flag of truce. When the generals and magistrates of the city and the rebels met, king Drimakos made a speech which contained a covenant of arbitration, perhaps unheard of before or since. We give

[12] The latin version Athen, VI. chap. viii. *Natal. de Com. Ven.* 1556, tells it in these words: "Paulo ante nostra tempora famulum quendam, narrant ipsi Chii, profugisse atque in ipsis montibus habitasse, qui cum esset bellicosus animoque virili fugitivorum servorum Dux ac imperator declaratus erat, non aliter atque reges solet exercitus cum sepius postea Chii copias in eum eduxissent, nihilque facere possent, ubi eos Primacus (sic enim servus nominatur) frustra interior conspexit, sic ad ilios locutus est." The gist of his speech we give in full, *Vide Supra.*

the substance of his proposition in his own words, in order to show that singular examples of co-operation and arbitration have been tried in the remote past:

"An oracle has been consulted and our revolt has, from the start, been upheld by the gods. We shall never lay down our arms. We shall never again submit to the drudgery of bondage. We are fixed in our own minds and act under counsel of the Almighty. Nevertheless if you follow my advice and adhere to it in the strictest faith, after signing this pledge and contract, the war may be terminated and the further effusion of blood dispensed with; then we can mutually live in peace and enjoy tranquility on terms which will be full of prosperity to the whole state of which we all are members."

The Chians who had been humbled by their defeats and losses consented to an armistice of war, thus recognizing for the slaves the dignity of a public enemy. They found it a convenience, doubtless against their will, to submit to propositions of reason. Drimakos then explained his plan:

"What we want is enough to subsist upon;—no more. In future, when hunger and need inspire us, we shall visit your granaries, flocks and stores and take what we require but always by weight and measure. The weights and measures are to be these which we have brought you and exhibit before your eyes. Here also is a signet[13] with which we propose to seal up your storehouses and granaries after taking from them what we require, as by this means you will be able to distinguish our work from that of common robbers. Regarding the slaves who in future shall escape from you to our camp, I shall rigidly investigate the causes of each man's running away, weigh his story carefully, and after submitting his case to an unbiased examination, if he be found to have suffered injustice at your hand, proving that he has been treated wrongly by you, I shall protect him. If on the contrary, the runaway slave be found not to have had a sufficient cause, I shall return him to his master."

Drimakos, it is seen, thus recognized and upheld slavery as an institution, only punishing its abuses. This fact

---

[13] By the word used in Athenæus meaning signet or seal we are probably to understand a contrivance of some kind for locking up the storehouses and granaries—locks and keys

HIS METHOD OF INTERPROTECTION. 173

corresponds with the ancient opinion that slavery was right; a thing not at all to be wondered at, considering the prevalence of this aged institution and the inculcation of the competitive system through its massive religious and political machinery, based upon an unscrupulous ownership alike of men and things, by the ancient law of entailment and primogeniture. We do not find that the slave system was ever publicly and boldly and philosophically denounced as an institution. But it is certain that t was fought in the secret unions and communes until esus daringly came out in open discourse against it and founded Christianity upon the new basis of absolute equality of man, which was essentially, as the results have proved, a revolution or upturning of the entire system of paganism and its heathenish discrimination between the grandee and his human chattels; and to him must be ascribed the authorship of the idea of unconditional emancipation. But while Drimakos could not unscrupulously war with slavery as an institution his course is exactly in ine with the great movement of his day which in other chapters we are describing[14] in these arguments. He betrays himself in the foregoing speech to have been, like Eunus, a soothsayer, or prophet, or Messiah, such as the innumerable *sodalicia* and *thiasoi*, or labor unions everywhere possessed.[15] He, like Spartacus, Blossius, Eunus, and the rest, was infused with this strange, everywhere-prevailing idea of some Messiah coming to the redemption of the poor slave. All the slave runaways were superstitious, and used in good faith and in harmonious consistency with their creed, this nympholepsy of the Messiah, long before the real Messiah came.[16]

These conditions of Drimakos were readily agreed to by the Chian capitalists, who were not in a condition to refuse. In consequence, so soon as the stipulations were formally signed they went into effect and the slave-king for many years had only to send his troops boldly and openly on their strange marauding adventures, always tak-

---

[14] See chapter xxii and elsewhere, on *Trade Unions* which adduces proof that the freedmen arose out of slavery through their own efforts and argued up the idea from their own narrower basis.
[15] Consult Lüders, *Die Dionysischen Künstler*, Foucarts, *Associations Religieuses* for the Greek, and Mommsen. *de Collegii et Sodaliciis Romanorum* for the latin unions, *passim*. [16] See Bücher, *Aufst. d. unf. Arb. S.* 79.

ing quantities by weight and measure as agreed upon, and always locking up the storehouses and granaries when they left them. The result was a mercy to the whole island which had been hitherto infested with robbers. It is not stated, but left to be inferred from the sequel, that Drimakos drove all other robbers from the island; for we know that his armed force, now legalized, acted as a sort of police to the whole personality and property of the people, slaves included. He adhered with severity to the stipulation of the agreement and when runaways appealed to him for protection he instituted a strict investigation of their case; those not having been maltreated being always sent back to their owners. This of course had the effect to cause masters to treat their slaves with kindness and never to overwork or otherwise abuse them, lest they incur the terrible wrath of the god-favored umpire seated on his throne among the crags and eagles-nests of the mountains. On the other hand the would-be runaways were surer to reflect cautiously before making the attempt, being in deadly fear at the just judgment of the despot before whom they were to be arraigned for trial immediately after their suit before him for protection. Thus the revolted slave became not only an absolute ruler, king and general-in-chief of the slave population, but also, in some respects, a judge in a court of justice with a standing army at command to enforce his decisions—an umpire over the whole population, bond and free.

Years rolled by and Drimakos felt old age approaching, yet did not flinch from what he considered the dignity and honor of his plan of justice. He remained at the helm, punishing or rewarding like a czar, until he was old and feeble and weary of a lengthier existence. He had a friend in the person of a young man, also a psomokolophos or runaway, who probably deserved this appellative for being pliant and perhaps a little parasitical and given to the recipiency of tit-bits in payment for flatteries ingeniously brought to the old man's ear. He, like many of the other slaves, was a native of a distant land, having when very young been kidnapped or taken a prisoner of war, and as a victim to the vicious slave-trade, sold to the planters of Chios. He was one of those young fugitive slaves who had proved his grievance under the investigation, been accepted, retained and trusted. Drimakos loved him and confided in his youthful honesty.

Meantime the Chians, unsatisfied with what they regarded as their burden, offered a large reward in gold to whomsoever should bring them the head of Drimakos. This they did against their true interests; since at that moment while under the eagle-eyed justice of this weird old judge in the mountain cliffs, their true interests were being more reasonably and economically subserved than ever before or afterwards, as the sequel of this story bears record. Perhaps the old man in his peevishness was grieved by their ingratitude in offering a bounty on his head. At any rate, we are told that he grew weary of his hoary hairs and enfeebling senectitude, and resolved that the ungrateful masters should pay the bounty and take the consequences whether of pleasure or of regret. In other words he resolved to send them his head and make it bring its price in gold!

In our own days of comparative sympathies and sensibilities a resolution like this could scarcely emanate from any person other than a madman; and our first judgment, shocked at the bare conception, is that no horror so appalling could have been devised by anything saner than some idiocracy of an errant brain. But 2,000 years have softened the human mind which, though yet cruel and sometimes even savage, is so comparatively tender that it pronely misjudges the motives and the drastic will which impelled some acts of our progenitors.

Drimakos resolved to shuffle off his mortal coil. Calling to him the friend whose name our informants have not transmitted to us, he spoke to him in the following characteristic words:

"Boy, I have brought thee up nearest to me, ever with the emotions of confidence and love more than that felt for all others of mankind. Thou art child and son and all that to me is dear. I have lived out my span. I have lived long enough; but thou art still young and hast blood and hope and sprightliness, and there is much before thee. Thou shalt become a good and brave man.

"Son, the city of the Chians is offering to him that bringeth them my head a sum of money and promising him his freedom. Therefore thy duty is to cut off my head, take it to them, receive thy reward, return home to thy fatherland and be happy."

The innocent youth at the thought of such an ungrateful and sickening atrocity, refused for the first time to obey his benefactor, and struggled hard to change the old man's determination, but in vain. Having resolved, he was inexorable. When the youth found him fixed in his horrible resolution and knew by long acquaintance with him that it was unalterable, he allowed himself to be persuaded.

The slave-king laid his head upon the block and the youth cleft it with the axe of the executioner!

Having buried the body of his friend and patron, the youth took the head to the city, received its price, his freedom and an amnesty and departed for his home with wealth and distinction.

The Chians did not long rejoice over their boasted capture of the head of the land-pirate. Soon after he was dead the runaway slaves with whom the rocks and forests of that rugged country was infested, being no longer under the restraint of the ever vigilant Drimakos, returned to their wonted habits of pillage by land and piracy by sea. The Chians were poignantly reminded of the error they had committed in their harsh measures against the powerful but just chieftain, who, for many years had held the discontented and warlike freebooters under control. The fugitive slaves re-began their work of robbery and devastation. Readopting their former habits of plunder based on revenge as well as want, they ceased to be an organized body following a stipulated arrangement like that which so long had existed between Drimakos and the Chian people, and became a desperate gang of land pirates and outlaws.

The treachery of the Chians in securing the removal of Drimakos thus recoiled upon themselves in shape of a calamity. They remembered the prophetic words of the martyred chieftain, that the gods had espoused the cause of the poor slaves and were angry with their masters. A feeling remembrance, kindling a high degree of respect for him now set in, and both combined to produce a veneration which caused them to erect a tomb or mausoleum over his grave, which the Greeks called a *heroon*, and he became the object of hero worship. This was no less a structure than a temple dedicated to Drimakos, the now deified hero.

Such was the sublimity of the subject that this *heroon* or temple arose so splendid and enduring that its ruins[17] remain to this day and have been the object of study by archæologists and other students from more than a dozen points of view.[18] The superstitions of the times now came in play in the flexible imaginations of these people. They persuaded themselves that they often saw in the gloom of night the ghost of Drimakos, now as before their friend, as, bony-fingered and spectral, it appeared to warn the Chians of some foul plot his fellow runaways and brigands were concocting against their lives and property. And many a time were the lurking filibusters thus checkmated in their manœuvres, ambuscades and sallies, and many a time defeated in their bloody designs by the wan and stalking ghost of Drimakos. Curiously enough this superstition was mutual between bond and free; for the brigands themselves worshipped the *manes* of Drimakos as their hero also; and always first brought to his mausoleum the richest trophies of their marauding expeditions before dispersing to their caverns with the rest.

So weird and romantic does this tale of the wild men of ancient Scio sound that we have hesitated before allowing it to contribute its enriching lessons and charms, lest it prove unable to bear the criticism of our learned but skeptic readers. But when our eye at last caught the smiling assurances of its trustworthiness from savants like Dr. Karl Bücher, and other learned teachers of philology, and from their pen we obtained the bracing words that not the slightest doubt[19] exists as to the credibility of the story, we ventured to bring it forth upon its merits as another instance of labor's hardships and struggles for existence.

[17] Consult Stark bei Hermann, S. 40, 16.
[18] See Ross Travels in the islands; *Inscription de Scio*, No. 72..
[19] Bücher. *Aufstände der Unfreien Arbeiter*, S. 23. "Mag man einzelne Züge dieser Geschichte romanhaft finden, es bietet sich auch nicht der leiseste Grund an ihrer Echtheit zu zweifeln, und selbst wenn die klugen chiischen Kaufiaute sie zur Erklärung des Heroöns und als Abschreckungsmittel für ihre Sclaven er funden hätten, bliebe sie darum weniger ein treues Spiegelbild vorhandener Zustände."

CHAPTER VIII.

VIRIATHUS.

A GREAT REBELLION IN SPAIN.

The Roman Slave System in Spain—Tyranny in Lusitania—Massacre of the People—Condition before the Outbreak—First Appearance of Viriathus—A Shepherd on his Native Hills—A Giant in Stature and Intellect—He takes Command—Vetillius Outwitted—Captured and Slain—Conflict in Tartessus—Romans again Beaten—Battle of the Hill of Venus—Viriathus Slaughters another army and Humiliates Rome—Segobria Captured—Arrival of Æmilianus—He is Out-generaled and at last Beaten by Viriathus—More Battles and Victories for the Farmers—Arrival of Plautius with Fresh Roman Soldiers—Viriathus made King—More Victories—Treason, Conspiracy and Treachery Lurking in his Camps—Murdered by his own Perfidious Officers—Pomp at His Funeral—Relentless Vengeance of the Romans—Crucifixion and worse Slavery than before—The Cause Lost.

The successful issue to Rome, of the third Punic war by which Carthage, agreeably to the inveterate apothegm of Cato: *"delenda est Carthago,"* the land of the terrible Hannibal was chopped to pieces and its inhabitants butchered or sold into slavery, caused an enormous amount of suffering to the human race.

Not only did the spirit of greed cause Roman land speculators to press the enforcement of the slave laws which seized prisoners and consigned them to the most cruel wholesale bondage in Asia-Minor, Italy and Sicily, but it extended this mischief also into sunny Spain.

ENFORCED BONDAGE AND REBELLION. 179

One of the main causes of the rebellion of inner emotions of the celebrated Tiberius Gracchus against Rome, goading him to become the champion of a reform in favor of the poor, was the wretchedly enslaved condition of the working people in all countries under Roman domination. Their terrible condition in Etruria was no worse than in Numantia in Spain. He had seen the indescribable suffering at Carthage, when nearly the entire population were either put to the sword or sold in slavery. Spain was on the verge of rebellion everywhere. Roman conquest had but a few years before, stricken Epirus a fruitful land eastward from Italy. Paulus Æmilius tore from the farmers of this region upwards of £2,000,000 of their savings in gold, and after the battle of Pydna, seized no less than 150,000 people by order of the Roman senate. These people, nearly all farmers and other workers, were dragged from their homes and sold for slaves. Seventy cities were sacked and destroyed.

Towns, villages, cities on every side, as well as farms and small industries, with their unions and communes, were reduced to a desolate waste, and the people, who were still alive, whether suffering under the lash of masters in a foreign land, or gasping under tyranny at home, were burning with bitterness, revengefulness, hatred and other lurking passions, and sinking into degeneracy, recklessness and poverty.[1]

Such was also the miserable status of affairs in Spain in the year B. C. 149, when our story of Viriathus begins. Old Lusitania before the Roman conquests, was a populous and enterprising country. There were associations, of the Lusitanian laboring people, which under some favorable rules had existed so long that they had become rich. Traces of their enterprise are still to be seen in form of temples, bridges and roads. It appears to have been in their days of highest glory that Rome, with a blackening curse of human slavery, struck this beautiful, sunny clime and its contented, happy and prosperous people.

Our story begins with a perfidious piece of treachery of one Servius Sulpicius Galba, who commanded the Roman army of invasion in Spain. Like Verres in Sicily, Galba

Plutarch, *Paulus Æmilius;* Livy, XL. 25-28; Wallace, *Numbers of Mankind.*

seemed to have no moral respect for humanity. He worked his plans to secure the confidence of these people and when the opportunity arrived, perfidiously murdered them in great numbers, seized and dragged others into slavery and robbed their country of its gold with which he afterwards, in spite of old Cato's efforts to have him punished, bought himself free from the sentence of the law at Rome. Soon after these outrages of Galba, Rome withdrew many of the soldiers from Spain and the people rallied with greater determination than ever, to retrieve their losses. They were mostly farmers and mechanics, and men of strong, well established principles.

Among those who had the fortune to escape from the last massacre of Galba was a young man named Viriathus. He is represented by Diodorus as almost a giant in stature[2] and a person born to command. He was endowed by nature with the rare faculties of honor and truthfulness, while at the same time leading the life of a hunter, a shepherd and finally of a border warrior in defense of himself and his kindred. An excellent description of Viriathus is left us by Diodorus in a short fragment of his histories which have been fortunately preserved. This fragment, while it represents him to have been a robber, extols at the same breath his honor for distributing the plunder among his men.[3] Livy speaks of him as a man of warlike qualifications, having had experience as a mountaineer.[4]

The charge against him, of being a lawless bandit is no longer maintained by authors, since the the circumstances under which he careered, show of themselves, that he did

[2] Diodorus, *Bibliotheca Historica*, lib. XXXIII. Eclog. V. of *fragmenta*: "Οὐριάτϑου κυρήσαντες, μεγάλα ‛Ρωμαίους ἔβλαψαν. ἦν μὲν οὖν οὗτος τῶν παρὰ τὸν ὠκεανὸν οἰκούντων Λυσιτανῶν, ποιμαίνων ἐκ παιδὸς, ὀρείῳ βίῳ κατέστη συνήθης, συνεργὸν ἔχων καὶ τὴν τοῦ σώματος φύσιν· καὶ γὰρ ῥώμῃ, καὶ τάχει, ηαὶ τῇ τῶν λοιπῶν μερῶν εὐκινησίᾳ, πολὺ διήνεγκε τῶν' Ἰβήρων. συνείθισε δὲ αὐτὸν τροφῇ μὲν ὀλίγῃ, γυμνασίοις δὲ πολλοῖς χρῆσθαι, καὶ ὕπνῳ μέχρι μόνου τοῦ ἀναγκαίου. καθόλου δὲ σιδηροφορῶν συνεχῶς, καὶ λῃσταῖς εἰς ἀγῶνας καθιστάμενος, περιβόητος ἐγένετο παρὰ τοῖς πλήθεσι, καὶ ἡγεμὼν αὐτοῖς ᾑρέθη, καὶ ταχὺ σύστημα περὶ ἑαυτὸν λῃστῶν ἤθροισε, καὶ προκόπτων ἐν τοῖς πολέμοις, οὐ μόνον ἐθαυμαστώθη δι' ἀλκὴν, ἀλλὰ καὶ στρατηγεῖν ἔδοξε διαφερόντως."
[3] Idem, *Excerpt* de Virt. et Vit. pag. 591: "῞Οτι Οὐιριάτϑος ὁ λῄσταρχος ὁ Λυσιτανὸς καὶ δίκαιος ἦν ἐν ταῖς διανοιαῖς τῶν λαφύρων, καὶ κατ' ἀξίαν τιμῶν τοὺς ἀνδραγαθήσαντας ἐξαιρέτοις δώροις, ἔτι δὲ οὐδὲν ἁπλῶς ἐκ τῶν κοινῶν νοσφιζόμενος, διὸ καὶ συνέβαινε τοὺς Λυσιτανοὺς προθυμότατα συγκινδυνεύειν αὐτῷ, τιμῶντας οἱον εἰ τινα κοινὸν εὐεργέτην καὶ σωτῆρα."
[4] Livy, *Epitom, of Historiarum*, Libri, LII. "Viriathus in Hispania primum ex pastore venator, ex venatore latro, mox justi quoque exercitus dux factus, totam Lusitaniam occupavit."

nothing which any patriot would not be bound to do in defense of home, family and friends. What the ancient authors seem to be prejudiced against him for, is the fact that, like Athenion and Spartacus, he was poor and that he belonged to the lowly and strictly laboring class. But even with the excusable charge against him that he was a robber, we find very few who do not speak highly of him as a great leader and a man of uncommon justice.

The only thing Galba and Lucullus seem to have been able to think of, when sent from Rome into Spain, was to plunder at an unlimited cost of suffering and blood. Cheating, deceiving, working deeds of treachery against the people and amassing gold was their single object; and to get the gold from Spain and carry it as their own personal property to Rome, was their bent and determination.[5]

Among the few Lusitanians who escaped from the last massacre of Galba, was Viriathus. He adroitly forewarned himself and a few friends, of a treacherous plot, just at the moment of its consummation and with difficulty extricated himself, although great numbers of innocent people were murdered or enslaved. His opportunity was now at hand, and he informed the shattered remnant of the band, of which it appears he was at the time, little above the rank and file, that if they would entrust the future command of their forces to him, he would lead them out in safety. In a speech he told them that they were too confiding; that the Romans were utterly devoid of all instincts of truthfulness or honor, and that the only tactics in future to be pursued must be based upon the idea of treating them as enemies; that whatever the hypocritical pretence of either the Roman senate, or its inhuman emissaries that Spain was in need of protection, the truth at the bottom was, that Rome wanted the whole of this fair and fruitful land, its productive mines, its waving grain fields, its fisheries, timber forests and gems, for her great

[5] Applan, *Iberia*, 60; Livy, *Epitome*, XLIX. remarks that Cato was stern enough to have Galba punished but the trial came to naught; the infamous traitor had too much gold at command: "Quum L. Scribonius tribunus plebis rogationem promulgasset, ut Lusitani, qui, in fidem populi Romani dediti, a Ser. Galba in Galliam venissent, in libertatem restituerentur, M. Cato acerrime suasit. Exstat oratio in Annalibus eius inclusa. Q. Fulvius Nobilior, et saepe ab eo in senatu laceratus respondit pro Galba. Ipse quoque Galba, quum se damnari videret, complexus duos filios praetextatos, et Sulpicii Galli filium, ° dus

VIRIATHUS.

lords; and she only wanted these inestimable resources worked for such arrogant darlings of her aristocracy, not by free labor but by that of slaves, subjugated through plots and systematized perfidy. Give me, said Viriathus, the unlimited command of your brave warriors and I will rid the land of our fathers of these mortal foes.

The speech won the distinguished sympathy of the governors. The tall mountaineer received the full command of the army; and now begins one of the most remarkable series of successes, wrought amid difficulties, cruelties and transient triumphs, to be found in the history of Rome. These extraordinary contests lasted, according to various authors from eight to twenty years.[6]

After the departure to Rome of Galba and Lucullus, with their gold, a prætor or governor, named Gaius Vetilius was entrusted by the Romans, with the care of the Spanish possessions; and Viriathus thus left the flocks under his care in the mountains and valleys of his home to take permanent charge of the broken and disheartened army which had regained some spirit, however, on account of the evacuation of their territory by Galba, and began marching down into the fertile valleys of Turdetania.

Vetilius met them promptly, and before the new commander could organize his troops, or perhaps before he really got command, gained a victory, driving them back and forced them to agree to, and almost conclude an unconditional surrender. This was perhaps the auspicious

---

[6] We here give the several authorities for the duration of these wars, from the massacres of Galba to the assassination of Viriathus consecutively as follows:
Appian, *Historia Romana, Iberia*, 63, put it at about 8 years: "Ὁ δὲ ἐς ὀκτὼ ἔτη Ῥωμαίοις ἐπολέμει· καὶ μοι δοκεῖ τὸν Οὐριάτθου πόλεμον, σφόδρα τε ἐνοχλήσαντα Ῥωμαίοις καὶ δυσεργότατον αὐτοῖς γενόμενον, συναγαγεῖν, ἀναθέμενον εἴ τι τοῦ αὐτοῦ χρόνου περὶ Ἰβηρίαν ἄλλο ἐγίγνετο."
Livy, *Historiarum*, Liber, LII. *Epitom.* "C. Vetilium praetorem, fuso eius exercitu, cepit: post quem C. Plautius praetor nihilo felicius rem gessit: tantumque terroris is hostis intulit, ut adversus eum consulari opus esset et duce, et exercitu." This mention is found by a careful study of the different commands, to make the duration to have been about 14 years.
Justin, XLIV. 2, says 10 years; while Diordorus makes it to appear about 11 years, and Orosius, *Historiæ Adversus Paganos*, V. 4, about 8 to 10 years.
Eutrope, *Breviarium Rerum Romanorum*, IV. 16, evidently takes his statement from Livy; for aside from putting the wars of Virathus at 14 years, he uses almost the same language in describing the man : "Quo metu Viriathus a suis interfectus est, cum quatuordecim annis Hispanias adversum Romanos movisset. Pastor primo fuit, mox latronum dux, postremo tantos ad bellum populos concitavit, ut assertor contra Romanos Hispaniae putaretur."
Vallejus Paterculus, *Breviarium Historiæ Romanæ*, lib. II. cap. 90 declares the duration of the wars with Viriathus to have been 20 years and undoubtedly Mommsen in putting it at 8 with Appian, is entirely wrong.

moment at which Viriathus first showed himself and made his speech, as we have just recounted.

This hardy Spaniard, on getting the reins firmly into his hands, introduced a method of tactics little understood or anticipated by the Romans. He made an unexpected revolt against the stipulations of capitulation then being drawn up, accompanying the same with a dash of his troops, and by a series of twists and turns in which the swiftest of the Spanish cavalry were brought into play, succeeded in extricating the little army so entirely from the grasp of Vetilius that he effected a retreat into a rocky woodland, and there safely spent the night in rest and needed refreshment, and the following day in religious purifications according to the Spanish creed.[7] The flight, according to Appian, and others, was accomplished by dividing the army into several parts, each under the command of a trusted leader, with orders to reunite at a given point, and with 1,000 horses under his own command he covered their retreat, first galloping to the rescue of one and then the other. In this manner they all reached Tribola in safety, after holding their pursuers in check for two days by means of various expedients of consummate ingenuity in which he took advantage of the wild and rugged shape of the land.[8]

All this time he was marching southward toward the strait of Gades, to the ancient Carteia. Vetilius could illy brook the escape of his game which so short a time before he believed to be in his hand. He made a desperate effort to frustrate the splendid retreat of the Spanish army, but Viriathus decoyed him into an ambush at the foot of the Hill of Venus where a celebrated battle was fought, which Appian and others graphically describe.[9]

It was a deep gorge, thick-set with briars, rocks, forest trees and other obstructions, which puzzled the best army

---

[7] Appian, *Historia Romana, Hispania*, 62 : Frontin, *Strategematon*, lib. III, xi. § 4 : "Viriathus, cum tridui iter discedens confecisset, idem illud uno die remensus securos Segobrigenses et sacrificio cum maxime occupatos oppressit."

[8] Appian, 62, 20-25, of Mendelsohn: " Ὡς δ' εἴκασεν ἀσφαλῶς ἔχειν τῆς φυγῆς τοὺς ἑτέρους, τότε νυκτὸς ὁρμήσας δι' ὁδῶν ἀτριβῶν κουφοτάτοις ἵπποις ἀπέδραμεν ἐς Τριβόλαν, Ῥωμαίων αὐτὸν διώκειν ὁμοίως οὐ δυναμένων διά τε βάρος ὅπλων καὶ ἀπειρίαν ὁδῶν καὶ ἵππων ἀνομοιότητα."

[9] Consult also Dion Cassius, *Historiæ*, LXXVIII. p. 33, Wess.; Frontin, *Strategematon*, lib. III. cap. 10, refers to this as one of the great strokes of strategem: "Viriathus disposito per occulta milite paucos misit, qui abigerent pecora Segobrigensium : ad quae illi vindicanda cum frequentes procurrissent simulantesque fugam praedatores persequerentur, deducti in insidias caesique sunt."

unaccustomed to mountain life but which least tormented a man like Viriathus, whose life had been that of a hunter and shepherd among glens and precipices.[10] It was about the time when Viriathus, after his three days retreat, was entering the town of Tribola, that Vetilius and his men made a desperate effort to seize him. Some of the Spanish detachments were out reconnoitring when they were set upon by a heavy body of Romans in the ledge, and after many hours of severe fighting the Romans lost their general and gave way with a loss in killed of about 5,000 soldiers—a half of their entire force. It was soon afterwards discovered that Vetilius had met one of the hardy mountaineers, and in a hand to hand encounter had been taken prisoner by him.[11] Most writers agree that the Roman general was mortally wounded in this encounter. It was a great and bloody victory.

Immediately after the triumph of Viriathus at the Hill of Venus, an immense number of slaves and free tramps whose condition was worse than that of slaves, came into the camp from all quarters, to offer themselves as soldiers; and although we do not find much in the fragments of history left us on this rebellion, yet it cannot be doubted that a very large army was called into being; and this was probably the prime secret of the continued train of successes attending the career of the insurgents.

There was another army in Spain, subject to Rome, consisting of Spanish militia and mercenaries, or perhaps freedmen who had been impressed into the Roman service. These, 5,000 strong, on the arrival of the news of the disaster to Vetilius, struck out in a rapid march from their quarters on the river Ebro.

The eye of Viriathus was however on the lookout for them. He marched a large force to waylay, and prevent them from joining the enemy who had by this time so far recovered as to show an army of 16,000 men, now marching toward Gades the old Tartesssus. He met them at some convenient place and in a second battle destroyed them so completely that nothing was left of the force

[10] Diodorus, *Bibliotheca Historica*, XXXIII. Eclog. V. "Συνείδισε δὲ αὐτὸν τροφῇ μὲν ὀλίγῃ, γυμνασίοις δὲ πολλοῖς χρῆσθαι, καὶ ὕπνῳ μόνον ἀναγκαίον· καθόλου δὲ σιδηροφορῶν συνεχῶς, καὶ θηρίοις καὶ λῃσταῖς εἰς ἀγῶνας καθιστάμενος, περιβόητος ἐγένετο παρὰ τοῖς πλήθεσι, καὶ ἡγεμὼν αὐτοῖς ᾑρέθη, καὶ ταχὺ σύστημα περὶ ἑαυτὸν ᾐστῶν ἤθροισε."

[11] Appian, *Historia Romana*, idem, 63.

BATTLE OF THE HILL OF VENUS.

worthy of being henceforth considered an auxiliary to the Romans.

All these manœuvres, victories, and vicissitudes occupied the year; and by the time the Romans were snugly fortifying themselves in Tartessus, news of the defeat of the armies and death of the governor arrived at Rome. Gaius Plautius was dispatched to the scene with a large reinforcement of 13,000 men, consisting of 10,000 foot and 3,000 horse.

But in the meantime, Viriathus was realizing his highest glory socially and politically, among his own people. He redeemed from its bondage, and reoccupied, the whole province of Karpetania; and large as the Roman army was, they dared not make an attempt against him. He was made a king and given powers and position which became princely but not magnificent; for he refused to accept anything but his wonted frugal fare. He only claimed to be an honest shepherd and workingman. They married him to a lady of high estate and wealth but all he would accept was herself, leaving to those who were flattered by gew-gaws, the shallow pleasures of jewels and gold. His only ambition was to divert his natural gifts from a profession of intrinsic value in the field of labor, to that of the military camp, until he should redeem his people from slavery and danger into which they had been forced by the Roman conquests. He was witty and bright, and he surpassed his fellows in physical stature. An indefatigable worker, he always slept in full armor and fought in the front ranks; and even at the moment of highest triumph ever refused to indulge in intemperance of any kind.[12]

After the arrival of Plautius, as prætor or governor from Rome, with the large force of 13,000 men, as we have mentioned, and time had been taken to reorganize the broken remnants stated by Appian to number 16,000 men, an expedition was arranged to bring the daring revolter to punishment. But in the first dash, Viriathus attacked his detachment of 4,000 and almost exterminated them. In a succession of engagements and strategems Plautius was so completely hacked to pieces that he retired in midsummer into winter quarters, at a safe distance from the now dreaded Spaniard. This disaster to the Roman prætor was so complete that he never recovered from it, and was afterwards driven into exile and disgrace.

The next general sent out from Rome against Viriathus was the son of Paulus Æmilius, who a few years before had dragged into slavery 150,000 people, after the battle of Pydna, in Epirus. His full name was Quintus Fabius Maximus Æmilianus. He brought with him an army of 15,000 foot soldiers and a cavalry force of 2,000, which added to those already in Spain but now in a demoralized condition must have aggregated a force of little less than 50,000.[13] Fabius Maximus pitched his camp at Orsona, not far from where the city of Seville now stands, and remained there until the next year, closely watched by Viriathus.

This Roman governor seems to have left the command to a person less capable than himself whose name was Quinctius; for the Spaniard lured him into some conflict which seems to have been deadly. Appian is not clear as to what it was, but speaks of the shrewd manœuvres of Viriathus, and of a battle, the results of which were the loss of many, by hard fighting. The inference is, that both Æmilianus and Quinctius were defeated and destroyed; for we next hear of the arrival from Rome, of another general, Quintus Servilianus, a near relative of the same Æmilius Paulus.

This general brought with him two whole legions and ten elephants from Utica, a town northward from Carthage in Africa. This new force, in addition to the elephants, consisted of 18,000 foot and 1,600 horse.[14] Servilianus had little difficulty in marching with this army through several of the districts which had been reconquered by Viriathus. He took many of the leaders of the rebellion, and had at one time as many as 500 killed for taking part in the revolt. Great numbers were sold into slavery. Those caught, who were found to have turned against the Romans, were cruelly treated by having their hands cut off.

[13] Appian, *Historia Romana, Iberia*, 65: "Καὶ παρὰ τῶν συμμάχων στρατὸν ἄλλον αἰτήσας, ἧκεν ἐς Ὀρσωνα τῆς Ἰβηρίας σύμπαντας ἔχων πεζοὺς μυρίους καὶ πεντακισχιλίους καὶ ἱππέας ἐς δισχιλίους."

[14] Appian, *Historia Romana*, idem, 67: "Ἅπαντας ἐς μυρίους καὶ ὀκτακισχιλίους πεζοὺς καὶ ἱππέας ἐξακοσίους ἐπὶ χιλίοις. ἐπιστείλας δὲ καὶ Μικίψῃ τῷ Νομάδων βασιλεῖ πέμψαι οἱ τάχιστα ἐλέφαντας, ἐς Ἰτύκκην ἠπείγετο, τὴν στρατιὰν ἄγων κατὰ μέρος."

ASSASSINATED BY HIS OWN MEN.

At length Viriathus, who was watching his opportunity, caught the old Roman at the siege of the town of Erisane, and after a severe contest defeated him. Driven to a rocky ledge in an angle from which it was impossible to escape, the victorious Spaniards had him completely in their power.

Here, at the zenith of a long list of brilliant successes, virtually closes the glory of Viriathus. He was so foolish as to let his sympathies get the better of his judgment.

So complete was this victory over Servilianus that he was glad to treat on any terms; and the surprising sequel is, that the terms offered by Viriathus and accepted at Rome were so mild. The Spaniard was to be acknowledged king over his native country of Lusitania, and henceforward to be regarded as a brother or ally to the Romans!

Of course this furnished Rome another period of time to recuperate and concoct new schemes of treachery. This she did, by sending the perfidious Cæpio to take the place of Servilianus, and he was not long in bribing the friends of Viriathus to turn against their long trusted master and murder him in his sleep.

An enormous, far-sounding wake accompanied by gladiatorial orgies of shocking ferocity, was held over his remains. The date of this great revolt in Spain is fixed at 149 years before Christ. This disgraceful triumph of Cæpio was followed by the enslavement of innumerable peasants, traders and working people, and the end was worse than the beginning.

If we are to believe Vellejus Paterculus, the great wars of Viriathus against the Roman slave trade—for it was nothing less—lasted about 20 years; and taking all things into consideration, it could not have been a shorter time, although belittled by the historians. Mommsen is anxious to make it appear but 8 years, agreeing with Appian. In the account of Spartacus, written by Vellejus, we found this historian's statement as to the great numbers of that general's men, to perfectly agree with the circumstances in the case, although it throws a flood of light, clearing up and making perfectly reasonable, the details of that great war; and showing it to have been one of the most prodigious conflicts ever known. Yet great efforts seem to have been made to suppress the history of Spartacus, and modern authors appear surprisingly anxious to perpetuate the suppression of it.

VIRIATHUS.

The whole affair of Viriathus was caused by a treacherous, wholesale effort on the part of the Roman *gens*, or lords, to reduce Spain to slavery, to choke her liberty-loving people down to chains, unpaid, enforced labor, turn her fruitful lands into slave-worked plantations and stock-farms, *latifundia*, as in Sicily, and thus build up an arrogant landed aristocracy. The immense and long-continued resistance of this humble workingman held that powerful race of optimates in check; and it proved one of the principal reasons of their having never succeeded in brutalizing the Spaniards as they did the less fortunate people of Sicily.

The great gladiatorial wake given in the honor of the murdered Viriathus adds no glory to his name that can descend to an age of sympathy, such as would now embrace his cause; nor could such a scene have been sanctioned, even at that comparatively feelingless era, by the hero himself, could his noble spirit have looked down upon it. It was simply an expression of contemptible hypocrisy that lay concealed in Roman politicians of that day. They often took this hideous method of diverting the human mind from plans of salvation which had been adopted by the murdered heroes.

We have no adequately extended accounts of this special scene, but know those horrors to have been popular among Romans at that time; and we are safe in taking, as a basis of description, the steel engraving of such a gladiatorial event drawn by Heck for the German Encyclopedia.[16]

Circling round on the raised seats of an amphitheatre, appears the vast, applauding multitude, as is still seen in the bull-rings of Spain. To the extreme right is an African horned-horse (gnu), in a spasmodic plunge to unseat his athletic rider, a man who is being dragged to the ground by a tiger, its teeth fastened in the wretch's back.

Away back amid the dust and smoke of the conflict are discerned forms of animals and men swirling in the vortex of rage, fear and death. A leopard has killed a naked man and floored another; and farther on, a hippopotamus is crashing through an indistinguishable heap of women,

[16] *Bilder Atlas zum Konversations-Lexikon.* III. A. 2, Tafel 15, Fig. 1; Leipzg 1849-1851.

men, dogs, panthers, dead or dying, some fighting to the last. Closer by, a nude Goliath, his arrows now useless, is wrenching the jaws of some wild beast with his sinewy hands while his other victim, a wild, ox-like monster twice his size, lies underneath the struggling fighters in the final agony.

A little to the left and fairly out in the arena, is seen a ferocious lion rearing high his expressive face to the beholder—a face beaming with dæmoniacal intelligence, as if mingling a malignant laugh with rage—holding his full main erect and one huge paw raised to strike a Bengal tiger whose wreaking teeth and lips are thereby, and with apparent reluctance, forced from sating hunger on the quivering flesh of a beautiful, half-naked woman, prone and dying in the awful qualms of pain and terror.

Above her, half dead with horror, her tiny bare arms extended toward the dying friend, her sweet face fraught with agonies of despairing love and suppliance and fright, but with not the slightest signs of resistance—true to that pleading womanhood that has ever been the controlling power of preservation with our race—stands, in a flowing *chlamys*, an exquisite female form confronting these frenzied monsters ogling, and ready to grapple each other over the expiring body of her friend. And all this time the hilarious shouts of the half-crazed betters and winebibbers—"the people"—seem to be made audible, by the visible outward signs of hand-clapping and the waving of handkerchiefs and banners.

But these are mere features of this appalling scene. At the feet of the terrorized woman lie the vanquished forms of two stalwart men in total nudity, and as if fallen in the desperately chivalrous acts of defending the now dying one. Between their bodies, sprawling on his back, lies a mangled lion; and on the loins of the man at the left, an African tiger of proportions huge and with maw distended, is cutting off a hideous python as though, by some deathinstinct, to prevent itself from being throttled in the serpent's squeeze.

A score of the more innocent animals now encounter the eye; some are zebras, some gazelles, and a number are of the ursine brood, dead and dying, as if marked out for the first prey to this sanguinary conflict. Then, between an ugly rhinoceros and a behemoth whose ghastly teeth **part to let the light** into his cavernous mouth, fight, as if in **mutual compact** for some reciprocal benefit, a muscular **human** champion and a Bengal tiger, the one with the **rhinoceros, the** other, the river-horse; while high above them **all dart the** forked tongues of two jungle serpents—boas **or pythons**—of mouths and coils so huge that labyrinth-**like, their** lengths are lost in the whirl of the dust and **confusion.** Above this chaotic cyclone towers a gigantic **elephant which,** having parried by a final blow with his **proboscis, a** panther that is slipping lifeless from his back, **re-engages** with his immense tusks an attacking lioness, **and by** murdering the two, succeeds in saving for a **transitory** moment, his rider, a large, nude, human creature **who,** ghoul-like, seems wrestling betwixt the exhilarations **of a fleeting** triumph and the horrors of a portentous **foreknowledge.**

With **tail erect,** horns poised, and with fierce, bloodshot **eye impatient** for the onslaught, is seen a bull rushing at **a brace of** wild beasts in deadly grapple farther to the left; **and a coil of** snakes in the angle closes the furious excitement.

There does not exist the flimsiest argument to support the idea that these human victims were not working people. Most of them were prisoners taken by the Romans during the wars of Viriathus and held for vengeance until this ghastly opportunity to wreak it arrived. The women too who defencelessly, as we have described, shared the horrible game whose moral effect upon the sight-seers was more to madden their blood-thirst than melt the heart into an anguish of pity and of chivalrous indignation, were often—in this case wholly—faithful creatures who, like many grand female characters of our modern days, had, along with Viriathus **and his followers, seized** the noble cause of human liberty.

CHAPTER IX.

EUNUS.

GRIEVANCES. MORE SALVATION ON THE VINDICTIVE PLAN.

THE IRASCIBLE IMPULSE in its Highest Development and most enormous Organization—Greatest of all Strikes found on Record—Gigantic Growth of Slavery—General View of Sicilian Landlordism and Servitude before the Outbreak—Great Increase of Bondsmen and Women—Enna, Home of the Goddess Ceres, becomes the Stronghold of the Great Uprising—Eunus; his Pedigree—He is made King of the Slaves—Story of his 10 Years' Reign—Somebody, ashamed to confess it, has mangled the Histories—The Fragments of Diodorus and other Noble Authors Reveal the Facts—Cruelties of Damophilus and Megallis, the immediate Cause of the Grievance—Eunus, Slave, Fire-spitter, Leader, Messiah, King—Vengeance—The innocent Daughter—Sympathy hand-in-hand with Irascibility against Avarice—Wise Selection by Eunus, of Achæus as Lieutenant—Council of War—Mass-meeting—A Plan agreed to—Cruelty of the Slaves—Their Army—The War begun—Prisons broken open and 60,000 Convicts working in the *Ergastula* set free—Quotations—Sweeping Extinction of the Rich—Large Numbers of Free Tramps join—Another prodigious Uprising in Southern Sicily—Cleon—Conjectures regarding this Obscure Military Genius—Union of Eunus, Achæus and Cleon—Harmony—Victories over the Romans—Insurgent Force rises to 200,000 Men—Proof—Overthrow and Extinction of the Armies of Hypsæus—Manlius—Lentulus—The Victorious Workingmen give no Quarter—Eunus as Mimic, taunts his Enemies by Mock Theatrical, Open-Air Plays in the Sieges—Cities fall into his Hands—His Speeches—Moral Aid through the Social Struggle with

Gracchus at Rome—Arrival of a Roman Army under Piso—Beginning of Reverses—Crucifixions—Demoralization—Fall of Messana—Siege of Enna—Inscriptions verifying History—Romans Repulsed—Arrival of Rupilius—Siege of Tauromanion—Wonderful Death of Comanus—Cannibalism—The City falls—Awful Crucifixions—Second Siege of Enna—Its 20,000 People are crucified on the Gibbet—Eunus captured and Devoured by Lice in a Roman Dungeon—Disastrous End of the Rebellion or so-called Servile War.

THE enormous growth of slavery just before the beginning of the Christian era was the cause of several of the most gigantic and bloody uprisings the world has ever known. Those convulsive episodes invariably arose from maltreatment of workingmen and women. Dr. Bücher, whose delineations we so often quote, shows that the necessary workmen for supplying slave material to man the great estates which the Roman lords, about this time were grasping from the original cultivators who farmed the government land on shares thus turning them out of house and home, were bought and sold as common goods at ridiculously low prices.[1]

In B. C. 103 there were at Rome scarcely 2,000 persons owning property considered taxable; such was the enormous monopoly of the public lands and of other property by a few.[2] These few property owners were proportionally richer and their management of the army and of the legislature, for suppressing uprisings of the outcasts and the enslaved proletaries was so much the more unlimited. The freedmen who had many organizations for protection which for centuries they had enjoyed when slaves were comparatively few, now found their unions, their business, their homes and freedom undermined and supplanted by countless hordes of slaves as prisoners of war, victims of the prodigious slave trade going on between Rome and foreign markets. When Tarentem was captured, B. C. 209, there were sold 30,000 war prisoners.[3] In B. C. 207, af-

[1] Bücher, *Aufstände der unfreien Arbeiter*, S. 85-86; "Tit. Liv. XLI. 28: Sempronii Gracch. consulis i per o auspicioque legio exerci usque populi Ro a ii Sardiniam sub g t. In ea provincia hostium cæsa a t capta sui ra octoginta milia." We elsewhere quote in our copious footnotes the sources whence modern authors derive he r figures.
[2] Strabo *Geographica*, xiv. 668; Apul jus, IX

ter the battle of Metaurus, 5,400 were captured and sold. In B. C. 200 at least 15,000 were siezed and sold. In B. C. 137, the event of the return of Tiberius Gracchus from Sardinia, the fact that 80,000 men, women and children had been either killed or sold into perpetual slavery, was brought to light. Because Gracchus, whose grand nature, though a military commander, revolted against such atrocities and sought reform, he was set upon by a mob of inuriated legislators and wealth-owners, and murdered in he streets of Rome. Such was the enormous mass of the Sardinian slaves that prices fell to a ridiculously low ebb becoming a laughing stock and the proverb got abroad: "cheap as a Sardinian." After the siege of Perseus there were 70 cities destroyed and 150,000 people sold at the different slave markets.⁴

This fearful condition of human slavery set into Greece still earlier. By a similar monopoly of land and of other property by the few, it came to pass that in the great city of Athens of 515,000 souls, only 9,000 (B. C. 300) could be allowed political rights graded and franchised by family and property.⁵ Other mention puts it at 21,000 souls or citizens.⁶ At the same time, when there were 21,000 propertied or blooded citizens and 10,000 strangers under protection of the city, there were 400,000 slaves.⁷ But as Athens at that time (B. C. 309,) counted 515,000 persons, we come into a knowledge of the fact that the remaining 84,000 were the plebeian or freedmen population.

The great city of Corinth whose census B. C. 300, gave only 40,000 "souls" had a slave population of 640,000 who of course, according to Plato⁸ and other aristocrats, could

³ Liv. XXVII. 16: "Milia trigenta servilium capitum dicuntur capta.
⁴ Liv. XLV. 24; Plutarch, Æmelins Paulus, 29.
⁵ Diodorus Siculus, XVIII. 18; Plutarch's Phocion, 28.
⁶ Bücher. Aufstände, S. 84.
⁷ Athenæus, Deipnosophistai, quoting Ctesicles,
⁸ Plato. De Legibus vi. in dissertation on the immortality of the soul: Phædo passim; especially 74, 125, 7, 8, 9. Bekk.: Phædrus, 51-85; Republic, vii. 1-4, where the working-people are allotted half a soul, vi. 9 : deformed by their craft and servile; So Timæus, xvii. shows how souls are a growth, lxxi. ad fin; Laws, ix. 8, fin; Statesman, 46: Yoking those who wallow in ignorance to a race of servile beings. The meaning here is that such as labor are undivine; i. e. not fully furnished with souls. Soul is in two parts, mortal and immortal, Statesman, 46, Timæus, 71, Laws, vi. 19; Nothing healthy in a slave's soul, says Plato, and quotes the Odyssey, XVII. 332-333. where far-thundering, aristocratic Jove deprives the slave of half his mind, soul or upper nature.

not possess souls because too mean to be honored by the gods with a thing so noble; and this accounts for their not being enumerated in the census of the city. They appear to have been too lowly to belong to the numbers of mankind.[9]

Notwithstanding this fearful condition of despotism we find that the Locrians in south Italy had no slaves, being organized communists. From the first settlement of this rich country by the Pythagoreans no slaves are known to have existed until after the Roman conquests;[10] and consequently the culture among them of equal rights when it came to clash against the enormous spread of slavery by the cruel conquests of Rome, no doubt urged the great epidemic of uprisings which form the subject of this and other chapters of the present work.

It is somewhat surprising, in the full face of these facts and the agonizing struggles of competitive warfare upon which these brutalities existed, that men still ask in wonder regarding the causes of downfall of the Greek and Roman empires! Another veritable *renaissance*, this time comprising sociologic research and comparative history, is at our threshold, destined to clear up many a point that for want of a true knowledge of the problem of labor has, through the ages, lain obscured midst the shortcomings of scorn and the musty vellum of histories and of laws.

In Sicily the condition of affairs was shocking. This fruitful island, which as early as B. C. 210, had been conquered by Rome and turned into a Roman province, was an especial offering to that hideously cruel system of slavery which Roman character, above all others, seemed by nature most suited to develop with the blind attributes of barbarity. As an instance of their grasping concentration of Sicilian property into few hands we quote authorities to the effect that Leontini had but 88 landed property holders; Mutice but 188; Herbita 257; Agyrium 230. The property owners of whole cities could be counted by the dozen.[11] All Sicily was overrun with slaves by birth

---

[9] Xenophon, *De Vectig.* IV. 14; Athenæus V.; Böckh, *Laurische Süberb.* 122-4, all give accounts of great slave owners.
[10] The Locrians had no slaves which seems to be regarded by Plato as something phenomenal: *Timæus*, ii. Bekk.; Böckh, *Pub. Œkon. Athn.* also declares that they had no slaves. Not only did the ancients have vast numbers of slaves (see *Encyc. Brit.* vol. xx. p. 140), but there were many freedmen at a very early age. See Homer, *Odessey*, XI. 480.
[11] Bücher, *Aufst. d. unf. Arb.* S. 39.

and slaves of the auction shambles. The original inhabitants were dispossessed and driven from the land or remained as slaves. The small farmers had been either annihilated or crowded together in little towns to eke out a wretched existence under the terrors of intimidation, or had been dragged down to bondage.[12] Great numbers of Syrians who from their mountain homes where they were inured to brisk physical activities, were brought over by the Romans in chains, to till the lands as slaves. Such was the extent of slavery everywhere.[13] Greece at that time was being conquered and her hardy warriors humbled to slavery, sent in great numbers in chains to Syracuse to be transported to the fruitful lands which in the days of Verres were styled the granary of Rome.[14] The Roman conquests of the Carthagenians and the victories over Hannibal were followed by the greater cruelties for their having been dearly won. Thousands of Africans hardened to army life in the Punic wars, were sent into Sicily as slaves to dig the soil for the proud Roman occupants of that land.[15] Only the fattest portions of land were cared for, the new possessors' idea being only gain. Strabo declares that so far as the æsthetic was concerned all was a barren waste. There were many beautiful and fruitful valleys and some plateaus which had long been celebrated for fertility and fine landscape.

Among the wonderfully fertile and paradisaical plateaus of Sicily was that of Enna, the seat of the greatest proletarian strike, insurrection or bond and free labor war of of which history, tradition or inscriptions give an account in any country of the globe.

This great strike or labor mutiny of Enna in Sicily took place, according to the conclusions of Dr. Bucher,[16] between the years 143 and 133 before Christ, lasting 10 full years. During a period of three years the Syrian slave-king Eunus, from Apamea near Antioch but a few leagues

[12] Diodorus S culus, XXXIV. ragment i . 3, 4 and elsewhere, Dind.
[13] Drumann, *Arb. u. Komm.* S. 24; "In Epidamnos gab es keine Handwerker als die öffentl chen Sklaven.'
[14] Diod. i. 1. 2; i. 27; Columella, *De Re Rustica*, 1. 6, 3, 8, 15, 16,
[15] Strabo, *Geog.* VI.; Büch. S. 40.
[16] *Aufstände d. unf. Arb.* S. 121-128, *Excurs*. As to the name, notwithstanding Dr. Siefert. we follow the Gr ck E'vva, though some Romans wrote "Henna."

to the northward of Nazareth, held sway over all of the central districts of Sicily; and from the most reliable evidence he reigned, after his coalition with Cleon in B. C. 140, for seven more years, over the whole island of Sicily.

Introductorily to this extraordinary fact, proving the great power and vigorous leadership of some of the ancient labor agitations, it will be necessary to bring upon the scene a brief description of the place, the prevailing social conditions and an outline of the character of the men.

The three leading men who originated and managed this great servile war, were Eunus, Achæus, and Cleon. Their two enormous armies, aggregating 200,000 soldiers were united in B. C. 140, when Eunus was proclaimed the monarch over Sicily entire.

We thus introduce these three branded, enslaved workingmen to the reader. We say branded and mean in the expression by no means a figure. They were not only branded, as at the moment we write, leaders of this labor movement are branded, with obloquy, black-list and stigma of men at the helm of public literature. They were literally and indelibly branded with hot irons.[17] Large numbers of quotations from the authors most explicitly prove that all slaves were branded; and the field workers were not only branded on the forehead and limbs, but often on the body; and since they were obliged, like the helots of Sparta, to go mostly naked, these disfigurations were summer and winter exposed to view and not only was their disgrace stamped upon them forever but their chances of escape from bondage utterly destroyed.

Once on the very spot where this great outbreak of the slaves and freedmen occurred, the plateau valley of Enna, there lived a very rich man named Damophilus. He possessed legions of slaves whom he forced under sting of the lash, to work naked upon his farms. His wealth of acreage, "latifundium," consisted in part of stock farms. These teemed with herds of cattle and other animals which in those times throughout Europe were a large source of

[17] Büch. S. 42, "Dass Alle gebrandmarkt, nur die Feldarbeiter auch gefesselt waren." Consult the following ancient and modern works: Diodorus, XXXIV. frag. ii. 1, 27, 32, 36; Florus, III. 19; Marquardt, V. i. 186; Mom. "Römische Geschichte;" Mom. "G. I." no. 845; Siefert, "Erst. Sicilisch. Sklavenkrieg," S. 12: Plato.

Roman wealth. One day a few of his poor, naked slaves, shivering in the chill winds of the mountain height upon which Enna stood, came to him and beseechingly implored a few rags to cover their bodies and shut out the cold which added to their sufferings. Their daring plea was answered by this cold-hearted capitalist with something like the following cutting leer: "Don't wandering tax-gatherers tramp the country naked and must'nt they give their clothes to those who want them? Would'nt I be taxed a customs duty on the rags I gave you?"[18] With that Damophilus ordered the shivering wretches to be tied to the whipping post and warmed up with a sound flogging, then sent back naked to their labor of caring for their master' flocks of a thousand animals.

Under such intense aggravations what else could be expected than a secret organization of the thus abused and degraded laborers who worked the lands? This question comes the more cogently as we realize that large numbers of them were as intelligent or more so than their own masters. Just at this epoch, as already shown,[19] all over Greece, Syria, Palestine, Asia Minor and the islands of the Archipelago vast numbers of trade unions and social societies existed among the freedmen and some among the slaves. We also know that when the Romans seized upon newly conquered countries they likewise seized the people, bond and free and sold them into slavery. Large numbers of these unfortunates were organized unionists, accustomed at home to the art and secret of practiced combination.[20] Another still more important cause of the terrible strike which resulted from such ill-treatment was a similarity of language. All Sicily was Greek. The Greek was the principal tongue spoken in Syria and even Phœnicia and other portions of Palestine at and before the time of Christ; although a bad Hebrew was the popular idiom. All the island inhabitants near by spoke the pure Greek. It also was spoken in Magna Græcia or Lower

[18] Diod. frag. ii. 38, Dind.
[19] Chapter xx. *Infra,* on trade unions citing inscriptions, laws &c. in evidence. Diodorus, XXXVI. frag. 6 Dind. tells us that not only slaves but many freedmen were engaged in these mutinies and strikes causing great tumults and confusions.
[20] Compare Lüders, *Dionysische Künstler,*; Also Foucart, *Associations Rel.* throws much light upon the subject of their religious beliefs.

HOME OF CERES, GODDESS OF LABOR.

Italy. Thus with intelligence, with a practiced knowledge of social combinations, with a sense of their wrongs made keen by the memory of happier days, with the true blood of the proud Greeks coursing more or less through their veins and finally but most practically, with the powerful Greek tongue uniformly at their command, they undertook that immense strike-rebellion amidst certain advantages which must go far toward clearing away the phenomena of its transient success.

The slave grievance rapidly grew into a movement for resistance in and around Enna, the little pastoral city, famous for its temple of Ceres whence Plato had carried Proserpine, the daughter of that goddess to whom shepherds, planters and especially working people had from a high antiquity looked, for her gifts of prosperity.[21] Thus here we find the link completing the chain of curious interest connecting the history of the Eleusinian mysteries with that of the ancient labor movement. Those laboring people were religious; but about this time they were bitterly complaining that Ceres their favorite goddess had forsaken them.[22] Enna was the original, ancient seat and citadel or throne of the great goddess Demeter, called in Latin *Ceres*. She was the protecting immortal who in the Pagan mythology, seated in her temple on the heights of Enna in the island's center, shielded all Sicily from famine. Her name had spread to foreign lands and she was worshiped in Attica and Syria. Thousands came on annual pilgrimages to Enna to worship at the temple of Ceres; and great feasts to her were here regularly celebrated, because she was believed the mother of the world and the fructifying goddess of all nutritious, fruit-bearing seeds of agriculture, especially the cereals. Near that city lay, at the time of our story the meadow and by it the stream and the spring and grottoed rock where her beautiful daughter[23] Persephone or Proserpine, whilst gathering flowers, was stolen by Pluto and long hidden from her distracted mother. The meadow was bedecked with a grand carpeting of roses, hyacinths and violets and the soft zeph-

[21] See chapter iv. on the mythical legend of Proserpine's abduction. the Eleusinian mysteries and the grievance of the proletarian outcasts.
[22] Bü her, *Aufstände*, S. 52
[23] Consult *Encyc. Brit.* Art. *Ceres ; La Rousse*, *Dict. Univ.* Art. *proserpine*. Much literature is extant confirming these statements.

yrs of summer were aromatic with their odors. All the landscape was adorned with nature's tempting vegetation. Many a tiny lake with pure, clear waters peeped from between the hills and hillocks of Enna and rich, well cultivated lands on every side were, and had for centuries been the pride of Sicily.[24] Wheat and other cereals had long prospered with such success that the place had obtained a celebrity. And yet, midst all these magnificent offerings of nature we see this region a scene of the most brutal and greed-cursed slavery to be found in the annals of that insatiate institution.

Antigenes is the name of one of a joint stock company whose business at that time was traffic in human beings. He certainly owned a city residence at Enna and kept his slaves about the house.[25] Among these was a man who, born and brought up in Apamea near Antioch, Syria, had more than probably been a leader of an "eranos"[26] or a "thiasos" in his native home. This is made the more probable by his being a pretentious prophet and Messiah while in a state of bondage at Enna. It was the wonderful Eunus; the magician, fire-spitter, wonder-worker, prophet and the plotter of the hugest slave insurrection of ancient or modern times; slave-king of Enna, then king of all Sicily and commander in chief at one time of over 200,000 soldiers; —the man who, with his sagacious generals, faithful and true, beat army after army of the Romans, sent years in succession, to meet his slave and freedmen troops and who in the teeth, as it were, of Syracuse and of prouder Rome, actually reigned in humane splendor, apparently beloved and respected, for a period of ten years; constituting a veritable epoch of history, though nearly lost and quite unrecognized through the taint of labor. We shall confine ourselves to a relation of all the facts and particulars to be had, based upon the evidence quoted and which per-

[24] Strabo, "Geog." VI.: Consult the exquisite picture of the landscape given by Dr. Bücher, "Aufstände" etc. S. 52.
[25] Diod. XXXIV frag. ii. 5, Dind.
[26] "Id." frag. ii. 1, 5, "seq." For fuller description of these trade or labor unions see chapters xiii.—xx. Eunus, Cleon and Athenion were all born near the home of Jesus.
[27] Büch. S. 54: "Er war ein grosser Magier und Wunderthäter, der zu den Göttern in nächster Beziehung stand und nicht nur im Traume von ihnen die Zukunft erfurh, sondern auch in wachendem Zustande sie leibhaftig vor sich sah."

haps, no person on thorough criticism, will be able to controvert. Eunus was a prophet. He pretended to work miracles,[27] and was one of the ancient Messiahs.

But we must not suppose that he was a weak minded man because he knew how to blow fire from his mouth or because he vaunted presages which often came true. He was in all probability an extraordinary man, full of shrewd wisdom, endowed with almost superhuman courage and certainly with great judgment and patience in selecting his generals and in giving and indulging, to keep them in place and power while holding to himself supreme control.[28] When a slave he foretold that although the goddess Demeter or Ceres had apparently forsaken the poor, yet she was revealing herself in dreams to him and promising her might to their deliverance.[29] So certain was he of theocratic interference that he told of his mediatorial powers not only to his fellow working people but even to his master and to all the lords and ladies, who, to beguile their evening hours, used to invite or more probably, order him to recount the results of his nightly interviews with the august goddess. Pretending that as she was also the patron deity of Syria his native land, he maintained that she revealed herself to him with an assurance that he was to become a king and deliverer. Even these supernatural things he told to Antigenes at these banquets amid the laughter and derision of the skeptical guests. His ingenuousness worked upon their curiosity and their invitations were apparently made with a purpose of amusement during their orgies of wine and gluttony. Their sport, he however, seems to have overlooked, taking their vein of merriment or ridicule in a manner peculiar to himself

From what followed, it cannot be imputed to Eunus that he was weak minded. He promised Antigenes to except and spare him on the day of wrath—an obligation which he religiously kept and faithfully carried out.

The cruelties of Damophilus,[30] who caused his working hands to be whipped, struck deeply into the sensitive feelings of thousands of other men. They were able to come together, secretly or otherwise to discuss their sufferings

---

[28] Diod. *Idem*, fragment ii. 5. 6.
[29] Diod. XXXIV. 5, 6, 7, and 8 of frag. ii.
[30] *Idem*, XXXIV. frag. ii. 34, 35. Dind.

and form their plot. Dr. Bücher understands from gleanings of the Vatican and other fragments that the plot originated with the slaves of Damophilus.[81] It is however, quite certain that what came to pass was spontaneous resulting from a combination of grievances and a strong religious belief in Eunus. The other slaves of Antigenes also took part.

Damophilus and his yet more cruel wife Megallis, appear to have been models of ferocity. Their young and beautiful daughter was the exception. Megallis was in the habit of whipping her female slaves to death with her own hand. It was like a mania people sometimes possess, for delighting in scenes of suffering. Endowed with unlimited power through the Roman laws and usages, to do as she pleased, she suited any action to fancy and gloried in tearing the poor life from her helpless victims. Nor was the ferocity of her husband much less. The incident we have recited was probably one of leniency compared with many that remain untold, Certain it is, that his atrocities together with those of his wife toward her defenceless female slaves are what decided this great uprising.

But we have the extremely pleasing assurance that the feeling which those slaves entertained toward the kindhearted daughter of this ferocious pair—a young maiden whom they all loved—proved her palladium; for with the greatest tenderness they guarded and spâred her through the scenes of blood.[82]

Plans of a great revolutionary revolt were soon decided upon, and collusion with Eunus secured the sympathy of the city slaves. These arrangements were then communicated to those in the country.

The plot was thus completed and the moment set. All had enthusiastically determined to break loose by a desperate struggle, from their unendurable tortures and dauntlessly brave the storm with all the consequences this perilous action entailed. They had worked themselves up to believe that their goddess would be propitious.

By preconcerted arrangement, four hundred slaves assembled at the setting in of night, in a field near the cita-

[81] Bücher *Anfttände &c.* S. 55.
[82] Diod. XXXIV. ii. 39: "Ὅτι κατὰ τὴν Σικιλίαν ἦν τοῦ Δαμοφίλου θυγάτηρ ......Ἑρμείας, ἀπήγαγον εἰς Κατάνην πρός τινας οἰκείους."

del of Enna. They quickly organized a meeting. They then each took a sacred oath to persevere in their enterprise and hold fast together. The little multitude came armed. Their weapons each had obtained as best he could. All were armed with courage and with anger; and each determined to defend his new liberty to the death. They marched up to the Enna heights under a leader who used all his prodigious arts and legerdemain, gesture, and fire-spitting, to encourage them and prevent a panic. Without meeting resistance they gained admission through the gates, into the city.

There were the millionaires with the ladies, the temple of the goddess, the theatre, the place of entertainment. The insurgents instantly took possession of the streets and as they marched, singled out their well known victims. Rich men and women who long had held unbridled power over hitherto helpless slaves, now saw the danger as they felt their guilt. Pitiless was the retributive reaction of the enraged and surging mass. They brained their owners; and those who had made sport of their leader Eunus, likewise bit the dust. All slaves and prisoners found in dungeons and in irons were set free.[33] A terrible scene followed. Children were torn from their mothers' arms, and women ravished in presence of their husbands, who, bound in cords, could make no resistance to this fiendishness. Scenes of death were everywhere enacted; for from the onset of this bloody work, the slaves, stinging with a keen memory of their sufferings,[34] enjoyed with a peculiar glee which fills the savage, the opportunity, each with cuts and gashes to cross out his ghastly account. To a thus quickened lust of vengeance, there rushed a remembrance of the cruelties of Damophilus who gloated on the bruises of his clubs and the sting of his whips, and of Megallis, his wife, who had whipped to death her female servants. It was an hour of vengeance. All centered upon this sweetest morsel of the savage;—summary retribution. Blood of the now helpless rich flowed freely amid the yells of the naked slaves whose brands and scars gleamed hideously by the fires of the burning houses of their fallen masters. Great numbers of slave-holders paid their former acts of indiscretion with their lives.

[33] Diod. XXXIV. frag. ii. 12.   [34] Id. Sec. 49

A TERRIBLE SCENE OF CARNAGE.

Large numbers of slaves who were kept in service within the city and who had previously been prepared for the crisis, now joined the insurgents, swelling their forces and making the capture of the city complete.

We have in other pages [35] shown that in nearly all trade unions, especially the branch of them known as the *thiasoi*, they seem to have had an officer whose duty it was to foretell, work miracles and do other sage things, such as in those early ages of the world were not only common, but were thought necessary. The idea of a Messiah or deliverer sent from heaven to ransom the lowly from their everywhere prevailing misery permeated all their organizations. [36] Eunus therefore, in his pretentions, but copied from thousands.

The hours of grateful vengeance sped on the breezes of that truculent lullaby. Object after object of their detestation and hatred was dragged forth and amid screams for mercy, relentlessly silenced with knife, flames and bludgeon until before the fury waned the pitiful wails of the slaughtered grew faint through sheer extermination.

But one there was who yet remained uncaptured and unpunished. This was Damophilus. On consultation it was ascertained that he was cowering in his pavillion, a little distance from the city. The insurgents sent thither a detachment with orders to bring him in alive. By this time the rage of the slaves had begun to assuage. They brought their great abuser before Eunus in the auditorium of the theatre, whither they adjourned to hold a trial of his case. Damophilus, covered with wounds and bleeding, his arms pinioned, his fine dress torn and soiled, was dragged before the stil. maddened crowd, his wife Megallis with him, both trembling in fateful expectancy of their doom.

The rich man was granted an opportunity to answer and spar the scathing accusations that were heaped upon him—bitter reminders of his mercilessness to them when the power was his to abuse them. But Damophilus coyly and cunningly met each accusation with words clothed in ambiguity and dazzle and parried off their bitter bluntness by his affected utterances of honeyed words. He was

[35] Chapter xviii. and elsewhere.   [36] Foucart, *Associations Rel.*

making inroads upon their sympathies when Zeuxes and Hermias, two powerful Greek slaves, who had themselves, in other days been victims of his cruelty, rushed between him and hope, one with a dagger and the other an axe. These men were keenly sensible to the progress Damophilus was making on the susceptibilities of his tatterdemalion jury; and fearing lest his mellifluous explanations should overcome them and that they might thus commit the absurdity of punishing thousands less stamped with cruelties and turn loose the deep-dyed monsters whose atrocities were the immediate cause of the revolt,[37] they crashed down the aisle of the theatre, advanced upon him weapons drawn and put a violent end to this mock trial of their foe by beating out his brains upon the spot. Diodorus relates that one of them stabbed him with a knife in the side and the other chopped off his head with the axe. Nor was this all. The terrified Megallis, who must have seen the reeking knife and the merciless guillotine by which her husband had fallen, heard his pleadings for an extension of life and with horror beheld his ghastly punishment, was delivered up, bound hand and foot, to the tender mercies of her female slaves little less instinctively savage than their male companions frenzied with woman's hatred and still goaded by memory's spectres of their own mothers and daughters perishing under the lash once wielded by this most pitiless enemy, the now supplicating Megallis' own hand. Little could be hoped for under such circumstances. Mercy was impossible. The horrified and shrieking lady was, like Damophilus, arraigned for mock trial before a horde of nude and blood-grimed women, taunted until each imbittered one requited herself with censure and derision, with dallying flings and a satiety of jeers such as only wild women avenging a wounded love, possess the genius to consummate. When all these preliminaries were ended, Megallis was seized by a dozen muscular females, stripped of her finery and undoubtedly her clothes, dragged to the pinacle of a lofty crag in which the mountain city of Enna abounds. All effort of the shrieking, fainting woman to writhe out of their clutching fingers fast fixed upon her throat and body were unavailing

[37] Diod. frag. li. 14, Dindorf.

and fruitless. They drew her out upon the projecting prominence yawning over the abyss well known to the shuddering unfortunate as the Golgotha of miscreants and recalcitrant slaves. From these frowning crags eagles and ominous night-birds were wont to startle the listener with their screams. Legends of horrors of this fatal rock were told by mothers as early inculcations to their babes. This wretched victim may have also more than once contributed her ingenuity descanting upon its boding gloom and terrors as she lavished it on the torture of her now avenging chattels.

But all this sentimentalism suffices nothing in presence of so ghastly a reality as the death that now frowned, and stared this quivering mother in the face. The unimpressible avengers were not to be frustrated by the moans and sobs which formed a part of the solace of their grievances. When they had dragged her to the very brink they no doubt made her undergo some of the prevailing formulas of death and then plunged her headlong down the precipice where she was battered to a jelly upon the sharp flints of the dell below. Such, according to Diodorus, Strabo, the modern critics and some tale-telling inscriptions, was the fate of an ancient millionaire and his wife whom great prosperity had rendered void of all the amenities and lovliness of civilized life.

There yet remained one member of that fate-stricken family—the daughter already alluded to; a young lady of both tender age and heart.[18] This damsel had from her babyhood shown exceeding sympathy and kindness toward the female slaves in their misfortunes. Never had she taken part in her mother's cruelties. She had, on the contrary, shown them the tenderest commiseration; and her many little offerings during their sufferings, had often gone far in the direction of healing a breach between fate and despair. Those whom the master's love of vengeance had left bound and often chained in dungeons of the *ergastulum*, with which ancient slave farms were cursed, she had comforted and administered to. Could such kindness be now forgotten? Could the remembrance of this child-benefactress, even in that awful vortex of violence, be overlooked? Could conscience be stifled even midst butcheries

[18] Diod. frag. 89.

whose mocking carnival made death a satire upon empty ideas of right and wrong? Or could such a pretty thing as sympathy wedge itself in amongst the howls and turbulence that shook this scene of oblivion and of death? Yes. A love which was stamped into their fierce, rough natures still lived and warmed them like a sunbeam, forcing itself foremost, even into this terrible qualm reacting against morality. Not a ruthless hand was laid upon her trembling form. Speechless unanimity prevailed on the question of sparing her life. All would spare and protect a faithful friend. On consultation Hermias, one of her father's executioners, was chosen leader of a picked band who soon after performed the perilous task of escorting her safely to the distant city of Catana, the home of some relatives near the sea.

We have in this episode another instance substantiating the opinion heretofore expressed, that the emotion of sympathy has been a growth in the breast of the crushed and humiliated classes, fledged from their schools of mutual love or commiseration and common support. Poor people are themselves the makers of most of the sympathies which they enjoy. Even the daughter of Damophilus grew in sympathy at the sight of misery. However rude the crust screening from view our inner nature, that nature never had, under Pagan control, much sympathy allowed it. Sympathy seems clearly to have been a growth out of a vast association in many parts of ancient Greek and Roman states and did not thrive among the opulent. Concupiscence with its cupidity and irascibility were the pillars on which rested the ancient paganism and its aged competitive system; and though the majorities who were of the working class possessed enough of the latter in its crudest form, yet they had little greed or avarice. They in fact, developed sentiments of a reverse nature. They longed for a socialism that would breed sympathy with its mutual love and care. Diodorus, one of our informants on this subject of the slaves of Enna, in referring to their treatment of the daughter of Damophilus and Megallis, says: "These slaves on strike demonstrated, in showing no sympathy or mercy to those who had been their masters and in delivering themselves up to their own violence and wrath, that what they did was not the mean promptings of barbarity, but a just retribution or punishment for the injustice which had been done to them;"[39] bold words indeed, but just and true; and the student of sociology may now divine the reasons why that brave publicist has lain for 2,000 years in obloquy, with his wonderful tales and descriptions in tatters among the rubbish of the vaults, or later, in the literary sepulchres of the Vatican.

It appears that this theatre which had been the scene of the fury we have described became the focus of deliberation after the frenzy of their vengeance had subsided and the more serious matters connected with the future began to force themselves upon their reflection. They saw that as soon as the news of their action reached Rome, the scornful power which for ages had thrived by conquest and its booty of lands and slaves, there would spring up an immense army to suppress them. They had the sagacity to foresee that their only hope was in a strong army well equipped and disciplined, powerful enough to cope, even with the forces of Rome. It further appears from the evidence that so deep had been the foresight and so long the communings on this matter, so secretly had the whole uprising been concocted, that all things necessary to this resistance were well-nigh prepared beforehand; and the general appearance with its sequel demonstrate that the central idea of a tumultuous feast of blood and dissipation and of subsequent demoralization and gluttony was far from them. But it cannot be denied that they had already determined to throw down the slave system of which they were victims and upon its ruins build up a social fabric which should deal equitably and humanely by all. To one acquainted with the vast and inexhaustable power of Rome, this dream of the poor slave socialists would have seemed an absurd machination of the fancy. But on the other hand they were on an island with whose rocky cliffs, caverns, forests and by-paths they were well acquainted. They wanted to build up a kingdom of men and women emancipated from slavery and economic want with their leader Eunus, on the throne. They held good to this resolution.

Eunus was elected king.[40] It does not appear that their

[39] Diod. XXXIV. fragment ii. 39.   [40] *Idem*. frag. ii. 14.

choice of him was on account of any military tact which he had shown as their leader nor on account of his superior capacities of any kind, unless it was that of working wonders. This however, was extremely necessary in the mind of superstitious men, as were most of the ancients, especially the laboring class who, in their unions among the freedmen, often kept a sorcerer who knew how to spit fire, dawdle with the little oracles and pronounce prophecies. Even the rich had their *magi* or fortune-tellers and their *haruspices*, as well as higher priests who often decided the turn of conquests by the simple consultation of an oracle. Eunus could blow fire, tell wonders, pretend and prophecy; and Eunus was elected king. Again, the name *Eunous*, the benificent, was considered a harbinger of deeds certain to bring forth good.

King Eunus, on receiving his crown, rose equal to the majesty of his new estate. He assumed all the oriental bearing of kingly dignity. He established the offices of state with such splendors as he could command. There was given him for a queen a female slave who like himself, hailed from Apamea in Syria—probably old playmates. Such was the happy one to be raised to the queenship. To crown himself in still more royal imitation of the dignities of his fatherland he named himself Antioch.

From the moment Eunus began his reign he appears to have been successful. Full details are wanting. From Cicero we have hints [41] that the temple of Ceres or Demeter was preserved with scrupulous care, as well as all the property belonging to it. No doubt however, he changed the officers of the temple from high priests to vestal virgins, supplanting the old by a choice of his own people.

Bücher thinks [42] that his administration from first to last, considering all circumstances peculiarly connected with the character and notions of the Semitic and Aryan races with whom he had to deal, showed more than usual fitness. He understood the theory of government. It is certain that at Enna there was one of those cavern prisons, such as had been dug by Dionysius the tyrant at Syracuse. We know that those pestilential subterranean

---

[41] Cicero. *Verres.* iv. 50, 112
[42] *Aufst.* S. 59: "Mehr als gewöhnliche Befähigung." Siefert. S. 18: "Man wählte ihn zum könig ....weil er den Aufstand begonnen hatte."

dungeons existed in great numbers, called by the Romans *ergastula*, in many parts of Italy and Sicily. They were often underground workshops like the quarries—the horror of the ancient slave. Florus and Diodorus combine in the statement that more than 60,000 fighting soldiers of the great rebel army were convicts turned loose from these prisons[43] during the war. Eunus incarcerated a large number of the rich in the holes at Enna and it may be presumed that the old prisoners were first discharged to give room for the new. A council of war was held and it was decided to put all these many prisoners to death. This was the result of a mass meeting of the faithful and unfaltering to Eunus, as a forewarning of the certain result of taking part in any effort to escape, or of mixing and intriguing to restore the old government. Few of the old rule people were left alive except the free mechanics who could make arms; and even they were compelled to work in fetters. To those who had invited Eunus to a seat of mock honor on account of his pretended powers in legerdemain and gifts of divination at their symposiums and for the amusement of guests, and whom he had promised their lives in case he realized his heaven-offered kingdom, he held good his word. He also saved them their fortunes.[44] They were spared by a royal decree and the mandate was sent them in true regal form. He also saved the temples and other holy property.[45]

At length Eunus called a council of permanent government. First of all was chosen Achæus. "He was, in a formal manner made *consiliarius* of the faithful." The ancient author who leaves us these choice fragments of history[46] suffixes his opinion that Eunus in making choice of him as lieutenant and counselor general, showed wonderful ability and prudence. This man understood and deeply sympathized with the Syrian element of which the slave population of Enna by conquest was largely composed. But he was moreover endowed with extraordi-

---

[43] Florus, *Epit. Hist Rom.* III. 19, § 6; "Hoc miraculum primum duo millia ex obviis, mox jure belli refractis ergastulis, sexaginta amplius millia fecit exercitum."
[44] Diod. XXXIV. frag. ii. 42; "Τῶν ὅλων δε τοῖς ἀποστάταις καταστὰς κύριος."; Bücher, *Aufst.* S. 59; Siefert, *Sklavenk.* S. 17.
[45] Cic. *Verr,* iv. 50, 112.
[46] Diod. *Id.* frag. ii. 42.

nary wisdom and unscrupulous will-power in expedients, where emergencies required it. He was capable of fearlessly organizing, on the inspection of a circumstance, a resistance powerful enough to shatter the peril whatever it might be ; and he had the judgment and force of character to push it to its immediate and successful results. He was bold enough to plainly tell to Eunus his misgivings and impart to him the truth; and that dignitary had wisdom and a sufficient amount of common sense to hear him with composure and acquiesce in his views. A perfect agreement was the result.

Dr. Bücher gives it as his opinion that Achæus was one of the thousands of unfortunates who had been reduced to slavery through the Roman conquest of Achaia, B. C.146, or about 3 years before.[47] Achaia being in the heart of the Greek Peninsula, on the gulf of Corinth, near and including the great city of that name, was of purest Greek; and Greeks in those days were mighty men. But the brutal fiat of Roman conquest had recently swept over the whole Grecian territory and buzzard-like, swallowed up her famous provinces and cities and sold her braves into slavery. We thus find circumstantial evidence that Achæus had the sagacity, acumen and intrepidity of his race. So well pleased was the slave-king with Achæus that he made him a present of one of the fine houses of his former millionaire masters.

The success of the great insurrection from henceforth is to be attributed in large measure to Achæus, general-in-chief. In three days he had armed and equipped no less than 6,000 soldiers and had them ready for the expected armies from Rome which all well knew would soon arrive by forced marches to put down the rebellion. As all these slaves knew the awful consequences of defeat, we may imagine the incentives which prompted their activity in making ready for coming conflicts.

The outside agricultural places soon began to be heard from. They consisted of heterogeneous ranks—a motly mass, who, rushing from their work on hearing the news of the revolt, straggled into the new head-quarters from far and near. They streamed into the town, each with a

[47] *Aufst. d. unf. Arb.* 8. 60.

butcher-knife, an axe, a sickle, a pitchfork of iron or wood. Slings were weapons with which the numerous shepherds were best practiced; and they knew their use with fatal effect. Inspired with a hope of liberty at any price or agony of effort, they were ready to stake their lives under perilous odds for a chance at winning it.

There were at that moment no troops of the Roman legions in Sicily. The only immediate forces to be feared by the workingmen were the militia from the different cities. There had occurred no dangerous strikes among the slaves for many years here, and in consequence, Rome had not, as in Etruria, on the Tarantine gulf and elsewhere, provided a standing army kept stationary under a prætor for the express purpose of suppressing the ever-recurring rebellions of labor [48] which were not only in this nation troublesome but had proved themselves at Sparta and Athens a great source of danger. Besides this, Rome was busy quelling similar disorders nearer home. The only available force at hand was the militia.

Meanwhile the insurgents were recruiting a powerful force by tapping every resource that offered a promise of strength. Among others, as already noticed, the great cavern jails were full.[49] All through the country these workhouses whether underground, in towns or out on the farms, were broken into and emptied, the prisoners ransomed and those able to bear arms welcomed to the army of resistance.[50] Our principal resource whence we extract these facts is Diodorus Siculus, who wrote elaborately on the subject, often giving minute details; but being an honest man and writing of his own native country, committed what in his times seems to have been the error—though no fault of his conscience—of telling the truth. We in consequence, as students of sociology must charge against that slave-holding aristocracy,[51] all mutilation of his history, especially those paragraphs delineating the Roman disaster

[48] Liv. XXIX. 17, 41, XXXII. 26 XXXIII. 36.
[49] Diod. XXXIV. frag. ii. 36 : "Καὶ τούτων τοὺς μὲν πέδαις δεσμεύωσι εἰς τὰς συνεργασίας ἐνέβαλλε." Damophilus had also made them work in the fields while chained.
[50] Diod. frag. ii. 25 26.
[51] A similar outrage has been committed upon Livy's history of Spartacus proved by the epitomies or la er headings XCV. XCVI. & XCVII which have survived the wreck We give further details of th s disaster together w th that of Sallust, farther on.

which followed; for although some clauses are left complete others are bereft of their treasures of priceless information. A large portion of the details, amounting in all, to chapters, has apparently been sequestered through the vandalism of contemporaneous censorship and the inestimable manuscripts disrupted from their historical chain covering at least ten years of this eventful rebellion which went far toward shaping the actions of men and preparing the world for the advent of a different culture.

At any rate we have a statement that not less than 60,000 prisoners were delivered from the ergastula[52] and we know that these also joined the rebellion. Everywhere were the slave-holders murdered, and in proportion as the more desperate ones were delivered from bondage and fetters, the search all over the island to find and exterminate them became more industrious. On the eastern side of Sicily were magnificent fields of wheat and different grains and a large amount of pasture lands stocked with cattle and sheep and bearing prodigious quantities of wine and olive oil. The slave hordes now free, swept over this country, murdering and destroying all before them, notwithstanding the efforts of Achæus at restraint. The story of Cambalus, a wealthy citizen of Morgantion in the upper districts of Symæthus, is told[53] as an exception to the usual prudence of this commander: This nobleman while on a hunting excursion came across a band of these prowlers. Alarmed at his close proximity to the dangerous men he turned and ran toward the city, following the high road. When near his own home he met his father on horseback going toward the danger, who immediately dismounted and begged the son to mount and save himself by flight. While thus in filial and paternal love, tarrying, neither deciding to take to flight, the freebooters came up and killed them both.[54] But Achæus generally forbade such strong measures. Wherever he heard

[52] Florus, *Epit.* III. 15, elsewhere quoted.
[53] Mannert, *Geog.* IX. 2; Cato, *De Re Rustica,* 6; Columella, *De Re Rustica* III. 2.
[54] Dr. Bücher, *Anfstände der unfreien Arbeiter,* S. 61, extracts the story in full: "Gorgos, mit dem Beinahmen Kambalos, ein durch seinen Reichthum und Edelmuth bekannter Bürger von Morgantion im Gebiete des oberen Symäthus zog auf die Jagd aus und stiess auf eine Sklavenbande. Er floh die Strasse zur Stadt zurück und begegnete bald seinem Vater der zu Pferde des Weges kam Dieser stieg sofort ab und flehte den Sohn sein Le en zu retten. Der Sohn hinwieder den Vater; und während sie so in dem Wettstreite kindlicher Liebe und väterlicher Zärtlichkeit sich erschöpften, erschienen die Aufrüher und erschlugen beide."

of atrocities committed by his men he is said to have exerted every energy to prevent their recurrence, appealing to the danger should the Romans gain the upper hand. The rebels began to comprehend that something nobler than mere rage was wanted. They soon began to be more careful of the stores of grain and other necessaries. They also spared a large number of the small cultivators who had not been active in injuring them.

There were also great numbers of freedmen, now little better than beggars; for as most farm labor since the new impetus of the Roman slave system had set in, was performed by slaves, they were obliged to beg because they had no work. These wretched tramps, perceiving their opportunity, soon began to organize in secrecy.[55] The great war now raged in earnest. The new force of beggars who hitherto had been roaming in a demoralized condition do not seem to have done credit to the slaves; for while they turned their hands to destruction of property and delivered themselves up to gluttony, their faults were all laid to the slaves. By this circumstance we are made aware that the actual status of intelligence was higher among the slave population than the tramps, who had become demoralized and degraded through discouragement and suffering.

It was a long time before the Romans, tormented with the terrible struggles of the proletaries at that moment raging in Italy over the agrarian question, could awaken to a full sense of the situation. There was certainly some provincial government at the time, for mention is made to the effect that Roman prætors[56] then had the province in charge; but they were both too much enfeebled by their enormous wealth at Syracuse or the dissipation concomitant to it and by their being practically without a force sufficient to the emergency. The insurrection seems not to have been uniform in different parts. In those days it took some time for slaves to communicate with each other; and when that was accomplished there must be time to ponder over the dangerous experiment and prepare for action; but it is known that almost everywhere in, and

[55] Diod. XXXVI. frag. v. speaking of the second war (see chapter XI.). expressly states that it was not the slaves alone but also freedmen. So also Florus III 19: "Cum liberis (nefas!) et ingenuis, dimicatum est."
[56] Bücher. Aufst. S. 61–62.

close about the cities, the uprising was general; for everywhere the slaves ran away from their masters and hurried to join the Ennian army.

Achæus in a short time found himself master of a well equipped army of 10,000 men. He devoted his energies to drilling these raw troops and teaching them their new business. We are wanting details for showing the exact dates, but the events of which we speak, according to the close examination of all material by Dr. Bücher, make it between B. C. 143 and 140.[57] Repeated skirmishing took place between Achæus and the advance guards of the Roman prætors but as often the latter were totally overthrown. Undoubtedly many great and terribly bloody battles were fought.[58] Certainly the results were disastrous to the Romans; for the territory of Eunus' kingdom gradually enlarged stretching over upper Symæthus and eastward down to the sea. It also struck northward and extended for a considerable distance to the west. But we hear of nothing having occurred in the south, up to this point.[59] There was however, a great uprising there, soon to be heard of The signal successes of Achæus had become noised abroad. Slaves everywhere were waiting for a leader. A new and almost distinct strike was preparing to burst forth southward near the coast, among the productive fields and pastures long celebrated for stock-breeding, especially that of draft animals and fine horses. Along this seaboard no harbors appear. The land lies in plateaus, with precipitous steeps overhanging the Mediterranean; but the levels above and the occasional valleys, are exceedingly fruitful.[60] It was the celebrated Agrigentum. Along the southern coast of Sicily at that time few inhabitants existed. The old places which had once been occupied by the colonists from Megara and Rhodes had been long depopulated.

Acragus, well remembered by the Romans as having

[57] *Idem, Excurs,* "über die Chronologie des s.cilischen Sclavenkriege und Verwandtes" S 121-129. Here Bücher gives data (which we follow,) showing that it must have been B C 143-140 or the first two years before the army of Achæus amounted to 10,000 men.
[58] D od. XXXIV, frag. ii. Dind.
[59] Bücher, *Aufst* S. 62. W. mostly follow Bücher's admirable tracings of the war from this point.
[60] Strabo, *Geog.* VI.; Cicero. *Verr* II. i. 28; D'Oroille, *Sicula*, p. 289 Plin. *H. N.* VIII. 64.

CLEON. 215

withstood, during the Punic wars all those terrible vicissitudes and had long been inured to hardships, still maintained itself and a good share of its population. It was a rich portion of the island and large numbers of the land owners possessed and exploited slaves who became so numerous that they performed all the labor leaving none for the freedmen who were thus reduced to the condition of roaming tramps and beggars. Some men owned 500 [61] in the earlier days and there still existed very rich men in the city, holding large portions of land and many human creatures as chattels. Here was the seat of a recorded instance of the prevailing cruelties: One Polias, having invited to dinner an equally heartless slaveholder, who was unwilling to allow his slaves rest long enough to sleep, called together his own, especially the women and children, and like the animals, fed them nuts and dried figs—the only nourishment they were allowed for supper.[62]

It is not to be wondered at then, if the slaves whenever opportunity offered, ran away from such masters and sometimes became cunning and dangerous brigands.

Another desperate character of this war was Cleon, called in Livy, "Gleon," a Cilician by birth,[63] from the town of Comana in the Taurian region of southern Asia Minor. It appears that he and his brother, called "Coma" by Valerius Maximus in his *Memorabilia*,[64] were runaway slaves who, having betaken themselves to the mountains drove a marauding business in the general interest of their fellows still in bonds. Here they plied the arts of the *latrocinia* or highway robbery, and stood ready to espouse the rebellion of Eunus which was now creeping toward their confines. Another theory of Cleon is that like Spartacus, he had elsewhere learned to be a robber but had been seized by a Sicil-

---
[61] Siefert, *Sicilische Sklavenkriege*. S. 38.
[62] Stobæus, *Floril*. LXII. 48; Cf. Bücher. 64.
[63] In his note 2, S. 64, Dr. Bücher refers to Cleon's birthplace, as follows "Diod. fr. 2, 43: ἐκ τῶν περὶ τὸν Ταῦρον τόπων. Nach § 20 hiess sein Bruder Komanos (Coma bei Valer. Max. IX, 12, 1 ext. ist offenbar ein Schreibfehler statt Comanus), woraus mit ziemlicher Sicherheit zu schliessen, dass Komana die Vaterstadt der beiden Brüder war. Ob aber an die pamphylische oder on die kappadokiche Stadt dieses Namens zu denken sei, muss unentschieden gelassen werden. Letztere, inmitten des Antitauros am Saros gelegen, war eine Hauptstätte des den syrischen Dienten verwandten Cultus der Ma (Artemis Taurica) Strabo XII. p. 585; man wurde dann den Beweggrund für den raschen Anschluss Kleons an Eunus in religiöser Superstition zu suchen haben.
[64] Diod. XXXIV. frag. ii. 20 & 43.; Valerius Maximus, IX, 1.; Sief. it. 18

ian corsair and brought over to this place where he was sold in slavery and set to work herding horses in the pastures, whence he escaped and made himself the terror of the region, playing his old pranks with success. But this theory fails to account for his brother.

By some means Cleon, who had a strong band ever on the alert, heard of the great movement of Eunus at Enna. The distance was certainly not so great but that they could have held correspondence; especially after the forces of Achæus had, by victory after victory over the prætorian militia, cleared the obstacles away.

Cleon on hearing the particulars of the insurrection, ran up the flag of open rebellion and offered freedom to all slaves who should espouse his cause. The mighty name he had already won went far toward deciding innumerable slaves. Everywhere these Agrigentine bondsmen responded to the shrill bugles of Cleon. As fast as they came into camp he armed and drilled them for service. Battles must have followed for we find him in possession of the city. The two most powerful captains of the rebellion now stood over-against each other, both having won battles, undoubtedly important ones; for as our details are missing and the leading points preserved, we are left to our imagination in making up the links in the chain of history. It was now the hope of the rich owners that these rough commanders would, though at first victorious, soon have a falling out; that jealousy would prove a quicker means of ridding them of their now terrible enemy than their own opposition; for such were the proportions of this uprising that Cleon soon counted upwards of 70,000 men.[65] With such an army it was reasonably conjectured that he would not long submit to a subordinate position under Eunus. Bücher in assuring us that the reverse was the case,[66] suggests that the cause of the perfect harmony known to have existed may have been Cleon's superstitious faith in the infallibilty of Eunus as a mediator for poor humanity between God and man;

[65] Livy, LVI. "C. Fulvio Consuli mandatum est, hujus belli initium fuit Eunus servus, natione Syrus; qui contracta agrestium servorum manu et solutis ergastulis justi exercitus numerum implevit. Gleon quoque, alter servus, ad septuaginta millia servorum contraxit, et copiis junctis adversus populi Romani exercitum bellum sæpe gesserunt."
[66] Bücher, *Aufst*, S. 65.

it being fully believed that he was a Messiah.⁶⁷ This might have done much, but the fact that they knew that in the absence of perfect harmony their own lives would certainly be speedily lost, together with their cause, is the more probable solution to this problem. Cleon accepted a position of what, in our military terms, may be called a brigadier-general, of the grand army under Eunus, or rather under Achæus, lieutenant-general to Eunus; and the force assigned him was only 5,000 men.

The two armies of the great mutiny against capital became thus consolidated into one. It is stated by Livy that in Agrigentum alone there were 70,000 men under arms;⁶⁸ and we have seen that Achæus already had a large, victorious force. Thus the combined armies steadily grew in numbers and discipline. This immense force was divided up between many leaders; Eunus being the commander-in-chief with Achæus and soon afterwards Cleon, the two principal lieutenants.

The armies stretched from Enna to Agrigentum and a wing extended south and eastward to the sea—perhaps as far eastward as Syracuse. Soon after these arrangements were accomplished the new prætor arrived in Sicily with an army of well equipped Roman soldiers consisting of 8,000 men. How many stragglers of those demoralized forces whom Achæus had often punished and dispersed, came to swell the freshly landed army of this prætor, L. Plautius Hypsæus,⁶⁹ does not appear. But Dr. Siefert, on the strength of a statement of a fragment, says that no regular troops accompanied Hypsæus from Rome.

Hostilities south now became general. The Roman did not have long to wait. A force of 20,000 slaves probably of both Achæus and Cleon met him, fully inspired with the supernatural powers of their fire-spitting king, as well as burning with old hatred and a desire to settle accounts with their enemies. A great battle was fought. Hypsæus was utterly routed and ruined; and the rebels were left masters of the field.

⁶⁷ Florus, III. 19, 4: "Syrus quidam nomine Eunus fanatico furore simulato dum Syriæ deæ comas jactat, ad libertatem et armas servos, quasi numerum mperium concitavit; idque ut divinitus fieri probaret, in ore abdita nuce, quam sulphure et igno stipaverat, leniter inspirans, flammam fundebat."
⁶⁸ Liv. LVI. *Epit. ad fin.*; See quotation in note 65.
⁶⁹ Diod. frag. ii. 18. This is probably a remnant of a full statement mostly lost.

The news of this additional victory spread rapidly and those slaves who had hitherto hesitated, now flocked to the insurgent army, soon swelling it to the almost incredible magnitude of 200,000 men. The language of our information is, however, too assuring to warrant us in dallying over doubts; for not only do the ancient authorities give these figures but we also find the strong reinforcement of the modern philological critics who make no hesitation in pronouncing it to be true.[10] The people at Rome entertained hopes that the force under Hypsæus would be of sufficient strength to put down the rebellion; but as time wore by, straggling remnants of the shattered army verified a dismal fear that great disasters had befallen them; otherwise the gloomy news of the expedition was lost.

Other expeditions soon followed the sad one just mentioned. As we know that in a similar rebellion by Spartacus some 70 years later, the armies of Rome were large, so in reason, we cannot imagine them to have been small in Sicily. Time and other despoilers have deprived us, it is true, of many details, in histories we know to have been written. But enough remains to attest the enormous proportions of the Sicilian labor rebellion and the success that everywhere attended the arms of the workingmen. C. Fulvius Flaccus, consul, appears next to have come to the scene; his colleague Scipio Africanus going to Numantia. This commander was however, preceded by a certain Manlius, mentioned in the fragments of Diodorus referred to. He, like his predecessors was annihilated. There can be no doubt that this word applies here in its literal sense. So complete was the extinction that scarcely a human being ever returned to convey intelligence of the disaster to Rome. Then followed Lentulus, afterwards Piso and Rupillius. Whenever the Romans gained an advantage by dint of superior military skill they lost it through the overwhelming and ever increasing numbers of the slaves, who in addition to their own manufacture of arms and munitions of war which they forced the freedmen-mechanics [11] of Sicily to accomplish for them, turned all the splen-

[10] Büch S. 65: "Bald betrug sie gegen 200,000 Leute;" also S. 126 "Nicht lange nachher beläuft sich die Zahl der Aufständischen insgesammt, Soldaten. Sensenmänner, und Ungerüstete, auf 200,000, 'und in vielen Kriegen kämpfen sie glücklich, seltener erleiden sie Niederlagen.'"

did weapons wrested from the defeated warriors of the
Roman nobility to their own uses and grew invincible.[71]
 No prisoners were spared. Eunus had undoubtedly resolved upon this plan from the first. He killed Antigenes
his owner, also Python, with his own hand, both of whom
he had promised a "cheap deal," and spared the friends of
the festivities as we have related, only as a mater of faith
with his word. He had opened all the dungeons of the
ergastula which confined many who labored in those grottoes. What more could they want of those disgusting
holes? No. With them there was no lingering prisoner.
To be taken prisoner was to die—a ferocious necessity!
Besides these barbarous economics, they possessed the
remarkable negligence of the Romans which had struck
into Sicily at the time of the defeat and final evacuation
of the island by the Carthagenians, in B. C. 210. Everywhere the walls of cities and other fortified places were
battered down, and left mouldering in disuse and everywhere was found unhindered admission to the cities, the
storehouses and the citadels.[73] Much of the success of their
phenomenal marches was attributed to the supernatural powers of king Eunus.
 They believed themselves invincible; and as time wore
on, year after year of undiminished prosperity apparently
fortified this belief. Eunus once led his victorious forces
before one of the few fortified places that attempetd to
withstand him and to the besieged inhabitants spoke with
bitter irony, denying that he was even the cause of the
trouble, or his men in rebellion. On the contrary, they
themselves by their former atrocities, had driven them to
a compulsory step which they little desired to take. In
full consciousness of their enemy's helplessness and the
stinging remembrance of their former sufferings, they
made a great show of their triumphs, parading the now
emancipated revolutionists in pompous formality and for-

[71] This fact must be considered as applying to a certain
number of freedmen denominated by the modern labor organizations *Scabs*, who had made themselves obnoxious by an obsequious catering to masters; for we find that a few years later
(see *Athenion*, chapter x.) there were great numbers of free
artisans who espoused the cause of the slaves and took up
arms gladly in the defense of a common cause.
 [72] Bucher, *Aufst.* S. 66 "Wurde auch einen kleinen Erfolg
errungen im nachsten Augenblicke raffte sich der Aufstand
mit doppeltor Wuth zusamen and drang unaufhaltsam und
grausam, wie alle socialeu Kriege, weiter."
 [73] Consult Diod. XXXIV. frag ii. 45.

cing the reluctant to hear the history of the causes of it,[14] through mock theatrical representations in mimic composition, as was practiced in Syria the fatherland of Eunus. This practice referred to by Diodorus,[15] no doubt has reference to the great labor unions called the *eranoi*, or better, their branch, the *thiasoi*,[16] a part of whose duty was to provide entertainment for the members. It is known that mimic entertainments of a histrionic character were frequently among the programs of amusement. "There was" says Dr. Bücher, "more than one bitter drop spilled into the bowl of misery at such seiges; since overturned riches, unbridled rapine, purposeless power, appeared to gentlemen to be the cause of tneir destruction; it was in fact, a practical lesson against the will of these compulsory listeners to mimic tragedies, which, like every other lesson where the spirit is against its learning, is fruitless and unheeded."[17]

The bitter and bloody conflict of this great mutiny of the working people of Sicily had now been raging about 6 years with the prophet of Antioch at its head. The military force of Rome such as she could spare, had been exhausted again and again in efforts to regain her foothold in Sicily, but in vain. The slaves were at last masters of the island. Here, by a most fortunate circumstance, the lacerated history of Diodorus remains so unbroken in this particular link as to explicitly transmit this truth; and in words which cannot well be misunderstood.[18] Diodorus, though his veracity has long lain in abeyance, has outlived his calumniators, and great savants, having proved the truth of statements by his pen which for many centuries lay in ridicule, are now searching for them as being those most valuable in critical use.

Besides the cities mentioned, there were many on the east coast of the island which also, one by one, joined the army of the revolutionists. Some of them, it is known, were taken by force. Others offered themselves to the conquerors, partly through their own wish, partly from a

[14] *Id.* frag. ii. [15] *Id.* 34.
[16] See Lüders, *Die Dionys. Künstler*, Tafeln I-II. Also *Infra*, chap. xvii.
[17] *Aufst. d. unfreien Arbeiter*, S. 67.
[18] Diod. xxxiv. frag. ii. § 25. "Οὐδέποτε στάσις ἐγένετο τηλικαύτη δούλων ἡλίκη συνέστη ἐν τῇ Σικελίᾳ, δι᾽ ἥν πολλαὶ μὲν πόλεις δειναῖς περιέπεσον συμφοραῖς, ἀναρίθμητοι δὲ ἄνδρες καὶ γυναῖκες μετὰ τέκνων ἐπειράθησαν τῶν μεγίστων ἀτυχημάτων, πᾶσα δὲ ἡ νῆσος ἐκινδύνευσε πεσεῖν εἰς ἐξουσίαν δραπετιῶν."

dread of sack and pillage.[79] Among these were Tauromanion and Catana, the place of refuge for the daughter of Damophilus and Megallis. As to Syracuse,[80] the great and long celebrated capital of Sicily, seat of the former proud tyrants, home of Dion, Plato's friend, and center of the mechanical sciences of Archimides, the city whose hills were quarried and pierced into horrid dungeons—the suffocating latomies, where workingmen by thousands, uncomforted and forgotten, had worked and smothered for painful centuries to the delight of monsters such as Dionysius ;—as to this formidable theatre of the *lapicidinae*, we are so far informed as to be able to say with a degree of certainty, that also this haughty mistress of the Mediterranean fell before the rebel arms.[81]

Messana to the north, had been least abusive to these people when in bondage, and in consequence was spared. Yet even Messana made a strong resistance ; for situated on the strait separating Sicily from Italy, an important pivotal position by being almost as much Italian as Sicilian, it at last gave way.[82]

The capture of this important seaport and stronghold was the immediate cause of the uprising or strike of the slaves and other working people, in large numbers, over on the Italian side, of which we give an account in another place.[83]

[79] Strabo. *Geog.* VI; Diod. frag. ii. 20, Orosius, V. 9.
[80] From Diodorus we have one tattered fragment (ii. 9,) which makes it probable that Syracuse also fell into the rebels' grasp.
[81] Elsewhere we have endeavored to show that there existed some unexplained reason for Plato's strange experience among the fishermen of Syracuse and the motives of Dionysius in banishing him thither. Plato was hated by the workingmen. The fishermen among whom he was relegated certainly were organized; and they were in sympathy with the mercenary soldiers on strike because Dionysius reduced their pay. We herewith reproduce the words of Dr. Bücher in his text pp. 66–8 and footnote 4: "Eunus war zuletz fast Herr der ganzen Insel geworden*** wahrscheinlich selbst Syrakus &c. Diod. frag. 9: τοῖς καταφαγοῦσι τοὺς 'ιερωμένους ἰχθῦς οὐκ ἦν παῦλα τῶν κακῶν· τὸ γὰρ δαιμόνιον ὥσπερ ἐπίτηδες εἰς παραδειγματισμὸν τοῖς ἄλλοις ἅπαντας τοὺς ἀπονενοημένους περιεῖδεν ἀβοηθήτους· οὗτοι μὲν οὖν ἀκολούθως τῇ παρὰ θεῶν κολάσει καὶ τῆς διὰ τῆς ἱστορίας βλασφημίας τετευχότες ἀπέλαυσαν τῆς δικαίας ἐπιτιμήσεως. Das Bruchstuck gehört hierher schon wegen der in seiner Nachbarschaft stehenden fragm. der Exc. Vatic., welche sämmtlich auf den Sklavenkrieg Bezug haben. Bei den "heiligen Fisnen" kann nur an die der Arethusa auf Ortnygia gedacht werden von welchen Diod. V, 3 Folgendes erzählt: ταύτην (τὴν Ἀρέθουσαν) οὐ μόνον κατὰ τοὺς ἀρχαίους χρόνους ἔχειν μεγάλους καὶ πολλοὺς ἰχθῦς, ἀλλὰ καὶ κατὰ τὴν ἡμετέραν ἡλικίαν συμβαίνει διαμένειν τούτους, 'ιεροὺς ὄντας καὶ ἀδίκτους ἀνθρώποις. ἐξ ὧν πολλάκις τινῶν κατὰ τὰς πολεμικὰς περιστάσεις φαγόντων. παραδόξως ἐπεσήμηνε τὸ θεῖον καὶ μεγάλαις συμφοραῖς περιεβάλετο τοὺς τολμήσαντας προσενέγκασθαι. περὶ ὧι ἀκρεβῶς ἀναγράψομεν ἐν τοῖς οἰκείοις χρόνοις
[82] Orosius, *Historiarum Libri Adversus Paganos*, V. 6, 9; Julius Obsequens, *De Prodigiis*, I. 1. [83] Consult chapter ix. *Infra*.

The terrible scuffle into which Rome was drawn, during these momentous times, together with the murder of Tiberius Gracchus,[84] in B. C. 133, show how this mighty people were paralyzed by the labor problem of that century. But with the death of this powerful tribune and faithful friend of the poor, the fortunes of the victorious Eunus crumbled. The real but hidden cause of the comparatively unobstructed career which had now held him king of Sicily fully 10 years, was probably not Rome's inability to cope with him in military force and tactics; it was her social and political demoralization. It was an interregnum of wills;—whether paganism should continue its reckless course against nature, against justice, against human development, and cover the earth with slaves, or whether a revolution against it should, in defiance of its haughty and despotic predilections and unbridled greed, be submitted to. When we look back at the astonishing conquest of Eunus and of his generals and men from this point of view we shall see the waves of the phenomena of Rome's final downfall then and there begun, roll back, together with many another dark political obscurity.

Gracchus was not yet dead, but still in the vortex of his anti-slavery land agitation, spurred on by Blossius his devoted friend. C. Calpurnius Piso was one of the consuls chosen for that year. On him devolved the command in Sicily. He arrived at Messana with a large force and finding it in possession of the slaves, laid siege to the city. After a severe storming the place fell into the hands of the Romans. As many as 8,000 slaves were slain and the prisoners captured were all crucified. Piso was a man of much nerve and business energy, combined with judg-

[84] Plutarch. *Tib. Gracchus*, 9-14; Appian, *De Bellis Civilibus*, lib. I. 9:
'Μέχρι Τιβέριος Σεμπρώνιος Γράκχος, ἀνὴρ ἐπιφανὴς, καὶ λαμπρὸς ἐς φιλοτιμίαν, εἰπεῖν τε δυνατώτατος, καὶ ἐκ τῶνδε ὁμοῦ πάντων γνωριμώτατος ἅπασι δημαρχῶν, ἐσεμνολόγησε περὶ τοῦ 'Ιταλικοῦ γένους, ὡς εὐπολεμωτάτου τε καὶ συγγενοῦς, φθειρομένου δὲ κατ' ὀλίγον ἐς ἀπορίαν καὶ ὀλιγανδρίαν, καὶ οὐδὲ ἐλπίδα ἔχοντος ἐς διόρθωσιν. 'Επὶ δὲ τῷ δουλικῷ δυσχεράνας, ὡς ἀστρατεύτῳ, καὶ οὔποτε ἐς δεσπότας πιστῷ, τὸ ἔναγχος ἐπήνεγκεν ἐν Σικεγίᾳ δεσποτῶν πάθος ὑπὸ θεραπόντων γενόμενον, ηὐξημένων κακείνων ἀπὸ γεωργίας. καὶ τὸν ἐπ' αὐτοὺς 'Ρωμαίων πόλεμον, οὐ ῥᾴδιον, οὐδὲ βραχὺν, ἀλλ' ἔς τε μῆκος χρόνου, καὶ τροπὰς κινδύνων ποικίλας ἐκτραπέντα. Ταῦτα δὲ εἰπών, ἀνεκαίνιζε τὸν νόμον· Μηδένα τῶν πεντακοσίων πλέθρων πλέον ἔχειν. Παισὶ δ' αὐτῶν, ὑπὲρ τὸν παλαιὸν νόμον προσετίθει τὰ ἡμίσεα τούτων· καὶ τὴν λοιπὴν, τρεῖν αἱρετοὺς ἄνδρας, ἐναλλασσομένους κατ' ἔτος, διανέμειν υοῖς πένησι.' Wordsworth. *Fragments of Early Latin*. p. 221. We have in the preceding chapter, giving an account of the great epedemic of strikes and uprisings which were occurring almost everywhere in the Roman territory, caused entirely by a profound and honest dissatisfaction among the laboring people.

ment. In addition to this, he must have had a large army. All we possess of the facts are hints touching the main events; the particulars are left to be drawn by inference. Certain it is that his force was large enough to assure him in the bold adventure of attacking Enna; and judging by comparison with the magnitude of the Roman armies afterwards sent to subdue Spartacus,[85] he could not have had fewer than 75,000 or 100,000 men. Considering the results positively known, it may be no boldness to presume that his army was at least 80,000 strong.

The insurrectionary armies on the other hand, were, without doubt, greatly demoralized by their hitherto unfailing successes. They were now no longer slaves, but a host of ignorant and superstitious freedmen regaling unhindered in wantonness and luxury, having had 10 years of security, constantly under the delusion that king Eunus, if not himself an immortal, was at least in daily intercourse with Ceres, whom nobody dared imagine to be less than the powerful protecting goddess of that island. Thus fortified in delusions confirmed, they had in course of these ten years of good fortune, begun to relax their vigilance, leaving to the supernatural, the power which alone their own strong, well-directed arms could accomplish. Things were in consequence, now in perfect readiness for Rome to triumph over the rebellion.

Piso, instead of waiting to skirmish with the generals of Eunus, marched directly to his stronghold. It was a bold strike; and affords us an excellent exhibit of his courage and judgment. He was no communist; and an instance proving this is recorded which clearly shows that socialistic theories were being discussed in those ancient days, by rich and poor: In the fierce struggle which resulted in the murder of the Gracchi, this same Piso said to one of these stanch advocates of the rights of labor, as he railed against the growing spirit of equality threatening extinction to the proud Roman *gens* and making inroads upon the tribunes and the senate: "It is not with my will and consent that you desire to divide your property; but should you do so I shall demand my share."[86] The slaves were socialists, enjoying their booty in common; and it

[85] See chapter xi. *below.*
[86] Cicero, *Tusculanarum Di-putationm Libri* III. 20, 48.

could not be expected that any leniency would be shown them by Piso.

According to our authority, Piso, after the capture of Messana, turned his campaign directly toward Eunus' citadel on the heights of Enna. A captain of cavalry led his force too incautiously and got into an ambush laid by the mutineers where he met with some loss in arms, men and horses. Piso singled him out as a coward. He was humiliated, and barefoot and almost naked, obliged to stand before the tent as a watch, forbidden to speak with his comrades or to enjoy his baths. Those left of the defeated cavalry were ordered to give up their horses and go into the company of slingers.[87] The object of this severe measure was to thoroughly impress the Roman soldiers with the almost deadly results to them, of a failure through disobedience or lack of bravery. On the other hand, both leaders and rank and file were rewarded for an act of valor. Valerius Maximus[88] also tells a story of Piso's own son, who for having performed some meritorious act in this campaign, was awarded a gold cross weighing three pounds, which he was requested by his father to preserve and wear after he had returned to Rome and it had been publicly presented. This had the effect to fill the minds of all with emulation, adding dash and intrepidity while doubtless dispelling a superstitious fear of the long victorious slaves.

At last the Roman legions arrived before the walls of Enna and immediately laid siege. We are indebted to Dr. Bücher's invaluable dissertation, referring us to Dr. Böckh's inscriptions often used by us; for without his mention we might have missed certain palæographs that shed light upon the otherwise unwritten pages of Piso's siege of Enna.[89] On the northern steep of the city is a great rock from which the slave women flung headlong the living form of Megallis, wife of Damophilus.[90] To

[87] Valerius Maximus, *Fact. Dict. Mem.* II. 7. 9. [88] *Id.* IV. 3, 10.
[89] Büch. *Aufstände.* S.74. note 1 reads: "Ritchl. P. L. M. VIII. 1: *Corp. Inscriptionum Latinarum.* (Böckh) [no. 642 sq. vgl. Nitsch a. a. O. Seite 249. Aus dem zweiten Sicilischen Aufstande: *Corp. Inscr. Græc.* Böckh, No. 5570, 5687, 5748, z. Th. mit dem Namen des Athenion. No. 5748 aus Leontini mit der Aufschrift APAMEO geht vielleicht auf dem APAMEER Eunus. *Corp. Inse. Lat No* 646. Sq. stammen wohl aus dem Fechterkrieg." We however subjoin the remark that Diodorus mentions Athenion as having likewise been of Apamea—a point which the learned philologist may have overlooked.
[90] See current chapter, page 215.

this day there are occasionally found, on and about this rock, balls from the Roman catapults which were hurled at the walls of the beleaguered city during that siege,[91] These relics of Roman projectiles have the name, L. Piso inscribed upon them; as they are found in quantities,[92] the circumstance goes far to attest the prodigious magnitude of the siege, as well as the great length of time that must have been consumed before the place fell into the Roman consul's hands. In fact, it did not fall before the sword of Piso. He was, in some mysterious manner, repulsed; being probably many times attacked and repelled by the sorties of Cleon. At last he is found in the narrative back on the east coast having without a shadow of doubt, been driven there by the slave-king.

In B.C. 132, P. Rupilius was chosen consul at Rome. As just hinted, Piso had met with some unchronicled disaster at the hands of the stubborn rebels of Eunus, who had in their turn, taken the offensive and surged him back to the sea.[93] Rupilius had already held office in Sicily under a joint stock company and had made a large fortune in the capacity of a land speculator. During his official life there he had acquired a good knowledge of the roads and principal objective points of the island.[94] It was this same Rupilius who, with Popilejus Lænus, urged and in some degree consummated the persecutions of Gracchus, whose revival of the ancient Licinian law and whose socialistic oratory had enraged the land and slave-holding aristocracy

---

[91] Böckh. *C. I. L,* nos. 642, & 646? *C. I. G.* 5570, 5687, 5738; Eitehl. *Plautus,* VIII. 1. Böckh, *C. I. L.* 5748 gives the word APAMEO 1, e: "Eunus of Apamea." It may mean Athenion of Apamea, however; but both were powerful labor agitators.
[92] Pliny, *N.H.* VII. 56; Cic. *Tusc.* IV. 17, 40; *Lael.* 10, 20, 73, 69.
[93] Büch. *Aufst. D. unfr. Arb.* 8. 78.
[94] Valerius Maximus, *Factorum Dictorumque Memorabilia,* lib. VI. 9, 8; Siefert *Erster sicilisch. Sklavenkrieg* S. 35, note 57, "Pseudoascon. in Verr. II p. 212: P. Rupilius quondam ex publicano factus consul. Valer. Max. VI, 9, 8 erzählt sogar, dass er ursprünglich, ein Diener der Staatspächter gewesen sei: P. Rupilius non publicanum in Sicilia egit, sed operas publicanis dedit Idem ultimam inopiam suam, auctorato sociis officio, sustentavit —Er war ein Freund des jüngern Scipio Cic. Lael. 19. Als Consul führte er zu Anfang seines Amtsjahres mit seinem Collegen Popillius Laenas die Untersuchung gegen die Mitschuldigen des Tib. Gracchus (Cic. Lael. 11, Val. Max. IV, 7, 1) Nach Vellei. Pat. II, 7 wurde er wegen der Strenge, mit welcher diese Untersuchung geführt wurde, gleich Popillius vor Gericht gezogen, während andere Schriftsteller nur von der Verfolgung des Letztern durch C. Graccus sprechen. Vgl. *Pauly's* RE. V. 1900. Er endete später plötzlich aus Aerger und Schreck über die misslungene Bewerbung seines Bruders um das Consulat. Cic. Tusc. IV, 17. Irrthümlich nennt übrigens Florus III, 19 den Perperna als den Besieger der Sklaven."

of Rome to a high pitch and caused his murder by a mob of the nobility the year before, while Piso was vainly besieging Eunus at Enna. Such a man would therefore, naturally be selected by them as a proper person to confide in, if sent to quell the great uprising of their chattels in Sicily. It does not appear however, that Rupilius assumed command of Piso's army immediately on his election to the consulship. But that he superseded him [95] is certain; for his trouble with the unreliableness of his own troops is spoken of by a number of the old writers. [96] A son-in-law of Rupilius, Q. Fabius, commander-in-chief of a division of Piso's army, had been defeated at Tauromanion on the eastern coast of Sicily, losing the citadel, a stronghold of much value. This had proved a triumph to the revolutionists. But it appears to have been re-taken by Piso in some subsequent struggle. [97]

Rupilius on assuming command, found Tauromanion again in the possession of Cleon and Eunus. As a punishment, Fabius was deprived of his command and compelled to quit the island. Rupilius then resolved to lay siege to Tauromanion. The besieged fought desperately and by an exhibit of courage and impetuosity threw back the Roman forces, driving them into a corner. Still Rupilius was not overcome. Rallying, he attacked the defenses of the slaves and checked their opportunity to do great damage. He then closed them in and began the process of starvation with all the malignant obstinacy of a Roman warrior. How long the siege lasted is not quite apparent; but in time, the provisions began to disappear. Hunger at last made its gaunt and ghastly tread into the abodes of the besieged, turning brave men into cannibals and making life a lottery by adding a horror of the carnivore to the pang of death. The poor wretches first attacked their own children and devoured their flesh; and then with the true beastliness of the gunæcophage, they

[93] Büch. S. 74. [94] Valer. Max. VI. 9, 8.
[95] Diod. frag. li. § 20. [96] Valer. Max. IX. 12; Oros. V. 9; Flor. III. 19.
[97] Id V. 11, 7, 3 ;Flor. III. 19.
Diod. XXXIV. frag. ii. 20. Κατὰ δὲ Σικελίαν ηὔξετο τὸ κακόν, καὶ πόλεις ἡλίσκοντο αὐτανδροι καὶ πολλὰ στρατόπεδα ὑπὸ τῶν ἀποστατῶν κατεκόπησαν, ἕως 'Ρουπίλιος ὁ 'Ρωμαίων στρατηγὸς τὸ Ταυρομένιον ἀνεσώσατο 'Ρωμαίοις, καρτερῶς μὲν αὐτὸ πολιορκήσας, καὶ εἰς ἄφατον ἀνάγκην καὶ λιμὸν τοὺς ἀποστάτας συγκλείσας, ὥστε ἀρξαμένους ἐκ ποίδων βορᾶς καὶ διελθόντας διὰ γυναικῶν μηδὲ τῆς αὑτῶν ἀλληλοφαγίας μηδ' ὅλως φείσασθαι.

sated their wolfish appetites on the flesh and the innocent blood of women and other adults who could not fight.[98]

Tauromanion was commanded by Cleon's brother, Comanus. In a moment of extreme desperation the latter, half dead with the grip of famine made an attempt to escape. He was however, detected issuing from the walls of the doomed city. Arrested and led before his hated enemy, the inexorable Rupilius, he was questioned regarding the power of his comrades within the fortifications, their objects and hopes of escape. The hour of the bold man of terrors had come. Never deigning an answer, with an almost unheard-of force of will, the man, after a wild moment's pause and a withering stare, covered his head with his mantle, drew in his breath, and by a superhuman struggle at self-command, refused to breathe again, dying amidst and before the astonished gaze of, Rupilius and his guards![99]

Finally the Romans succeeded in battering through the lower wall a gap and thus forced an entrance. But there yet remained an excellent and almost impregnable citadel into which the besieged took refuge as the Romans entered the breach. Here again they safely held themselves for a time, until through a treachery of one of the commanders, the Romans were admitted.

The scene which followed must be imagined; it cannot be described. With a spirit of relentless vengeance Rupilius tied the helpless, writhing prisoners fast, until his soldiers could have time to erect a multitude of gibbets; then in the frightful manner of all Roman criminals nd the proletarian outcasts, they were hung upon the ignominious cross. Afterwards their bodies were hurled down all precipices which formed an escarpment of the citadel.[100] Little indeed is preserved of this awful martyrdom but a variety of broken gems corresponding with the main body of our narrative, are extant, which leave us the conjecture that its language falls short of the ghastly truth.

It is fair here to state on the other hand that a similar cruelty and want of feeling characterized the men in rebellion. Their vote at the first deliberative council de-

[98] Diod. frag. li. § 20; Oros. V. 9.
[99] Val. Max. IX. 12, exc. 1.
[100] Compare Siefert, S. 22 with Bücher, S. 75.

claring for the butcher-knife policy was an edict inhuman and unworthy of a cause so exalted as that of freedom. Nor do we, except under the sagacious Achæus, find that they once deviated from this cruel and almost internecine policy which may have tended to harden the spirit in Rupilius, of revenge, retaliation and ferocity.

Rupilius, having now partially quenched a blood-thirsting spirit on these victims, marched directly for Enna. On his arrival he found the place an almost natural fortress, as difficult to storm as Tauromanion. Upon one side a similar precipice formed a natural wall, impregnable under any assault. The only thing practicable was to besiege the place, wait until the enemy's stores gave out and apply for a second time, the process of starvation. Cleon, the hitherto unconquerable commander-in chief, held the fort. Eunus and his retinue had also gone back thither, before the siege of Tauromanion opened. Achæus is lost sight of. He is mentioned as dead; but from what cause is unknown. Comanus had fallen at Tauromanion. At the siege, there frequently occurred sorties of bodies of volunteers who would sometimes dash with precipitation from within the walls, cutting, wounding and taking prisoners, numbers often of the consul's best men. In one of these sallies Cleon, the intrepid chief, now mainstay of the already worn out and fainting slaves, was the leader in person. The number of the party this time proved insufficient to cope with the force which Rupilius detailed against them and in an effort to extricate them from the peril Cleon himself, in a hand to hand conflict, fell mortally wounded, a prisoner of the Romans, and expired.

When the news of the death of this loved and trusted leader came to the ears of Eunus and his people, a general gloom overspread the city. Courage was shattered. The king himself lost hope. His faith forsook him and he shrank in horror and despair. Now followed the work of that perfidious, cruel, with ancient workingmen's organizations, ever-present pest, the traitor. As at Setia, at Sinuion, at Tauromanion, so here at Enna, this dangerous gorgon of insidiousness and villainy was at his post with fair words and foul intrigue ready to work his deadly poison for the enemy and against a friend and thus the keys to the gates of the city were soon after the death of Cleon, delivered to the workingmen's implacable foe. Enna fell into the hands of the Romans.

The wholesale slaughter of the people, all of whom were captured, is an untraced horror. All that we are told by the hints left in fragments of its historians and seen in later commentaries, is that 20,000 of them, including the catastrophe of Tauromanion, bit the dust. The multitude of soldiers, of the aged, of women and children who suffered by sword and cross in other parts of Sicily, may be easily imagined. But at Enna the crucifix for weeks was a busy demon of retribution. A sullen gleam of joy seems to have lit the workers of revenge and to have made the glare of the firebrands of torture and the sobs and moans of the helpless in their hour of agony so cruelly prolonged, moments of a true elysium to the maddened aristocracy with souls steeped in competition whose glaives wreaked as they slashed from heart to heart of these vanquished representatives of labor.[101]

Eunus who had, during his day of fortune, given himself up to luxury and perhaps gluttony, had probably become demoralized and with him many others.[102] A whole people, suddenly changed from abject slavery and degradation into affluence, becomes in turn, the arrogant master, the owner, lord; and enters and occupies a condition utterly unnatural to their expectations, however well it may conform to their tastes. The result is voluptuousness and degeneracy. The ten years' uninterrupted reign of Eunus may have resulted in jealousies and internal distempers. How Achæus came to his end is unknown; but suspicion points to some fatal feud between him and Cleon.

The great army of 200,000 soldiers[103] at the time of the junction of Achæus and Cleon is no longer in view upon the arrival of Piso and the first siege of Enna. Where were these legions, invincible at the outbreak of the war? What had occurred internally?

Eunus lost all hope and courage at the death of Cleon; and as Rupilius entered, shrank from his kingly seat and fled with a thousand guards, equally bereft of courage,

[101] Siefert, 22: "Die Sklaven wurden unter Martern getödtet, meist von den hohen Felsen gestürzt. Auch hier (bei Henna) wurden Tausende nieder gehauen; die Gesammtzahl der in Tauromenion und Henna getödteten Sklaven betrug über zwanzigtausend," [102] Büch. S. 76.
[103] Diod. XXXIV. frag. ii; Siefert, S. 29; Büch. S. 65. Bücher and Siefert are agreed in putting the number at 200,000. Livy, Cleon alone, 70,000.

hoping to escape to an inaccessible cleft or hiding place in the mountain. This rift of rocks wth its trembling contents was soon discovered by a straggling party of Roman troops. Physical force was at an end and the omnipotent powers of the humiliated prophet were now all that his adherents had to fall back upon for succor. The Romans approached and commenced furiously the work of arrest. Seeing that the goddess had withdrawn her arm of protection, the guards of Eunus, rather than suffer the horrors of the cruel and ignominious crucifixion, fell to mutual extermination and by a desperate inter-suicide, robbed the gibbet of its prey. Eunus with his cook, his baker, his bath attendant and "king's fool," [104] having no courage for mutual self-destruction, hid in a deep crevice of the crag. Thither the inexorable Romans followed and dragged them out. They then hung his kitchen mates upon a cross.

As to Eunus, he was first taken to the dungeon of Morgantion, under guard; afterwards, according to Plutarch, to Rome, (probably the *carcer Tullianus*, or one of the underground Mamertine caves) where in excruciating misery, covered with vermin and seething in filth, darkness and terror, he ended his extraordinary life.[105]

Rupilius was a man too thorough to leave his work unfinished. He sent powerful detachments into every part of Sicily wherever his scouts brought intelligence of any group of rebels still at large. Great numbers of them were seized, brought into head-quarters and thence taken

---

[104] Diod. XXXIV. frag. ii. 22.
[105] Diod. XXXIV. frag. ii. 23. Dind. "Καὶ παραδοθεὶς εἰς φυλακήν, καὶ τοῦ σώματοςαὐτοῦ διαλυθέντος εἰς φθειρῶν πλῆθος, οἰκείως τῆςπερὶ αὐτὸν ῥᾳδιουργίας κατέστρεψα τὸν βίον ἐν τῇ Μοργαντίνε;" Livy, *Epit*. XC: "Capitur, carcere a pediculis devoratur;" Plutarch, in Life of Sylla. 37, says; "This abcess," speaking of Sylla, "corrupted his flesh turning it all into lice." * * * "We are told that among the an ients, Acastus, son of Pelias, died of this sickness; and of those that come nearer our times, Al·men the poet, Pherecydes the divine, Callisthenes t e Olynthian who was kept in close prison, and Mucius the lawyer. And after these we may take noti e of a man who did not distinguish himself by anything laudable, but was noted in another way, it may be mentioned that the fugitive slave Eunus, who kindled up the servile war in Sicily and was afterwards ta en and carried to Rome, died there of this disease;" Siefert 22 "Mit 4 seiner Diener, dem Koch. dem Bäcker, dem Badesklaven und dem Lustigmacher ward er in einer Höhle gefangen Er starb im Gefängniss an der Läusekrankheit entweder zu Morgantion oder Rom." According to Prudentius (Hymn V,) the ancient cavern ; riso ns were constructed with an object to roduce as much torture as possible. Other ancient authors agree in conveying the idea that human ingenuity was taxed t o ent such hells.

to the many Dionysian quarries or *lapicidinae*, dungeons for which Sicily was famous, and those found guilty of direct participation in the uprising were crucified. But these latter were the most numerous share. All the rest were re-delivered to their masters to receive worse treatment than before.

Such was the first servile war in Sicily; the **greatest** labor rebellion or strike, on record in any country or at any time. It was a most suggestive matter; being inspired by, based upon, animated, from its inception and all through by grievances against the conditions regulating labor and relying upon the superstitious idea of a Messiah, fervently believed, among the ancient poor, to be their promised deliverer.

Meeting of Achaeus & Cleon. — See page 217.

CHAPTER X.

ARISTONICUS.

A BLOODY STRIKE IN ASIA MINOR.

FREEDMEN, BONDSMEN, TRAMPS and Illegitimates Rise against Oppression—Contagion of monster Strikes—Again the Irascible Plan of Rescue tried—Aristonicus of Pergamus—Story of the Murder of Titus Gracchus and of 300 Land Reformers by a Mob of Nobles at Rome—Blossius, a Noble, Espouses the Cause of the Workingmen—He goes to Pergamus—The *Heliopolitai*—The Commander of the Labor Army overpowers all Resistance—Battle of Leuca—Overthrow of the Romans—Death of Crassus—Arrival of the Consul Paperna—Defeat of the Insurgents—Their Punishment—Discouragement and Suicide—Aristonicus strangled, Thousands crucified and the Cause Lost—Old Authors Quoted.

THE great uprising or strike, partly of slaves and partly of freedmen, artisans and farmers at Pergamus and in its vicinity, was to some extent the result of the abortive slave revolution in Sicily just described. It is interesting to the student of sociology, but especially so to the student of social life in antiquity, in many respects, if for no other reason than that it occurred but a short distance from Palestine with its Nazareth, its Jerusalem, its thousand memorable scenes that 163-166 years afterwards cradled and founded the mightier, more imperishable revolution of Christianity which aimed the final blow at slavery.

Pergamus, on the river Guicus, was, at the time of this story, a beautiful city, already ancient in years and vicissitudes. Attalus III., a son of Eumenes, a freaky, cruel and jealous monarch, ruled the place from B. C. 138 to 133, when at his death he transferred it without a con-est to the Romans; so that it was a Roman possession when our story begins. The official news of this testament of Attalus was delivered to the delighted Roman Senate in the early fall of B. C. 133. There had been a great turmoil in Rome, occasioned by the abortive attempt of Titus Gracchus to restore the Licinian law, making it a crime for any person to hold more than 500 acres of land. The entire aristocracy had combined with the most unscrupulous and desperate resistance against Gracchus; and that same year had murdered him for daring to propose a measure which might curtail their arrogant and altogether illegal seizure and appropriation of the public domain, *ager publicus;* thus building up a landed aristocracy. The poor people, freedmen and slaves, had been intensely interested in the results of the commotion, which in the assassination of Gracchus by the lords and the overthrow of his noble measure, had been a disaster to them. Finally the defeat of Eunus and his army of revolutionists in Sicily, at that moment accomplished by Rupilius, added to the woe of the entire plebeian class. But now, as if this misfortune was not enough to fill their cup of bitterness, the news arrives from Asia Minor, a country in which the trade and labor unions were more splendidly organized than almost any other part of the world,[1] that Pergamus and the whole rich province of Eumenes and his successors, was, without a struggle, turned over to the greedy Romans, with its beautiful and fertile valleys of the Guicus and tributaries, to become the scene of human slavery and its extended horrors. Already this terrible institution was planted there, competing with free labor. But this free labor is proved by the inscriptions to have been so well organized and so self-sustaining that it could exist under almost any government except that of the conquering, trampling Romans. The news, then, that Pergamus had been deeded to Rome, without even consulting her people, was a mournful shadow which the proletarian class, if we judge by what followed, certainly interpreted to mean the doom of liberty and organization. Plutarch thinks that human slavery and its booty had much to do with this strange transaction, which afforded Gracchus a chance to argue for an immediate

[1] See chapters xix. and xxi.

distribution of money and lands, left in the testament of
the dead king, among the poor, under this new agrarian
measure which had actually passed and become a law.'
Of course such a proposition only exasperated the Roman
lords to the frenzy which burst into a tumultuous mob
and ended in that eloquent, well-meaning tribune's violent
death, followed by a great insurrection or mob of the
Roman lords and the murder of over 300 work people at
Rome. There has been considerable comment by the historians and others, as to the legality of the testament of
Attalus,[3] who at the time of his death is thought by his
strange conduct to have been insane.

Attalus had a half brother named Aristonicus, a natural
son of Eumenes by a woman of the place who was a daughter
of a musician whom probably the royal family had employed. According to a clause in the law of succession it
appears that this person, now a strong, ambitious and vigorous man, was the real heir apparent to the throne, although only half noble and the other half plebeian by
birth. He certainly submitted with a bad grace to the
arbitrary testament of the dead king, which, it was suspected, had been accomplished through intriguing Roman
lawyers often seen hovering about the palace.[4] Aristonicus entered his claim to the throne immediately after the
tyrant's death. He entered into the new project with
energy. Nor was he without friends. The largest part of
the kingdom favored his pretention. There were many
cities of some dimensions lying in the valleys of the river
Gaicus and its tributaries, nearly all of which determined
for him from the start as their future king. By the appearance of things Aristonicus was not only one of the
common people but very popular among them. Like the

[2] Plutarch, *Tiberius Sempronius Gracchus*, 14, Oros. V. 8. Gracchus had not
met his fate when Eudamus delivered the testament of Attalus to the Romans.
[3] Livy, *Epitom.* LVIII., LVIX. which give us enough to show that Livy also
wrote the history of this great mutiny which he calls a bellum servile. Oros. V.
6, 10. Strabo, XIII. Sallust, IV, *Historiarum Populi Romani Libri*, fragments
'Eumenem, cujus amicitiam gloriose ostentant. initio prodidere Antiocho paci.
nercedem; post Attalum custodem agri captivi sumtibus et contumeliis ex
ege miserrumum servorum effecere: simulatoque impio testamento, filium ejus
Aristonicum, quia patrium regnum petiverat. hostium more per triumphum
luxere: Asia ab ipsis obsessa est: postremo totam Bithyniam, Nicomede mortuo,
iiripuere, cum filius Nusæ, quam reginam appellaverant. genitus haud dubie
sset." Büch. *Aufs*. S. 103.
[4] Diod. XXXIV., *frags*. ii. and iii. Oros. V. 10. Strabo, XIV. p. 646. Polyl
XXX. 2

rest, he was a castaway. Rome haughtily refused to recognize his claim. A number of cities like Colophon, Myndum, and thickly populated places as Samos, even if they wished to side with him, were afraid of the Romans. To secure them it was necessary to use armed force. Aristonicus soon found himself at the head of a considerable army and also a little navy consisting of a number of ships. From the palace he had obtained some money and with it he hired Thracian freedmen as mercenaries, a common practice of those times. Besides these, many of the soldiers were those who formerly had done duty for his brother.

The Ephesians, seeing the turn things were taking sent a fleet against him which completely destroyed his little squadron near the coast opposite Cyme. Aristonicus now determined to depend upon trying his fortunes by land.

Great numbers of slaves having heard of the success of Eunus in Sicily, and fearing, as well they might, that the occupation of Pergamus by the Romans would result in their worse degradation, were ready to welcome the new adventurer. The organized freedmen had cause for still greater fears. It was at the commencement of those days of persecution of trade unions by the Romans which culminated B. C. 58, in a law for their suppression.⁵ The workingmen of antiquity possessed means of conveying intelligence of their hopes, fears and methods from one center or post to another; and it is ascertained that in this war of the pretender to the throne of Pergamus, large numbers, not only of slaves, but also of freedmen joined his army, although it was always known as the servile war.

In the interior he found the slaves already in rebellion. They had raised in a great insurrection, murdered their masters, taken possession of their estates⁶ and were organizing an army when Aristonicus appeared before them making overtures for their mutual assistance. He offered them their freedom and a respectable place in the army. He promised them that on the result of success he would build up a state based on their ideal of freedom and equality as had been advocated in the meetings of the unions.

⁵ See chaps. xii to xviii, containing full accounts with foot notes of proof reference.
⁶ D'od. XXXIV, *frag.* iii.

The *eranoi* and *thiasoi*[7] existed in great numbers on this coast of Asia Minor, especially at Cyme, Pergamos and Samos. These, in common with those in Greece, Syria, and the islands, had established a culture of democracy. The promise made to these confiding people was that they should have the enjoyment of their rights guaranteed them and should be made full citizens; their state which the new monarch was to govern for them was to be the "sun" among nations and they were to be the ennobled, dazzling citizens of the sun, *Heliopolitai*. Such a condition bespoke almost the opposite of what they had ever seen in human government. The old groundwork of Greek government was one of lordship and bondsmen, dividing mankind by a gap so wide that it could scarcely be passed by leaps of fortune or aptitude. Yet they seem to have been able to comprehend the force of these promises. The discussions they had previously had in their societies had prepared them to receive and appreciate the promise. On the other hand they were to work with an obedient will and help the new king to establish himself on the throne. Dr. Bücher[8] points out that the dazzling idea of becoming such citizens of the sun was what enraptured and won the slaves of Enna and all Sicily over to Eunus during the great servile war. The more ancient Syrian religion had been that of sun-worship, and their sun-god was equivalent in power and importance to the Greek Jove.[9] The Syrians had an idea that their sun-worship was done to a sun-god and goddess; the god being equal to Jupiter and the goddess to Demeter or Ceres. So we hear of Eunus pretending to be the chosen representative of Ceres, who made the sun warm the fruits of the earth. Like the Greek gods who dwelt on the height of Olympus the *ouranos* or vaulted dome of heaven, so Adad and Atargatis, the sun-god and goddess of the Syrians,[10] had their celestial home on the plateau eminence between the twin mountains of Lebanon, at the source of the Orontes, whose waters swept the foot of Antioch. Sun and earth

---

[7] For *eranos* and *thiasos*, the ancient Greek-speaking labor unions, see chap. xix. *infra*.
[8] *Aufstände der Unfreien Arbeiter*, S. 106. "Der name der Heliopoliten weist darauf hin, dass es derselbe war durch welchen Eunus seine Syrer fanatisirte."
[9] Macrobius *Saturnaliorum Libri*, I, 13, 10, Eyssenhardt, 1868: "Assyrii quoque solem sub nomine Jovis, quem Δια Ἡλιουπολίτην cognominant, maximis cerimoniis celebrant in civitate quæ Heliopolis nunc ipatur"
[10] Strabo XII.

HIS FIRST VICTORIES. 237

are within their power which is all that is glory, goodness and light. Thus these poor enslaved beings, stunted by hard labor and sufferings, either as slaves under the master's lash or as freedmen whose organizations are threatened or broken up, and whose business is lost—they being already in a state of insurrection—quickly grasped the offer of Aristonicus and became his soldiers.

Thus began another great strike or uprising of the labor-class; this time in far off Asia Minor, that was destined to add one more link to the already immense concatenation of circumstances leading to the great revolution of Jesus. But it may be looked upon as a most necessary thing in the stubborn logic of a *fiat*, in order that mankind might be taught the utter fallacy of any vengeful policy based upon the purely irascible, combating the acquisitive or concupiscent impulses of human nature.

Aristonicus began the war with slaves and freedmen as soldiers, in a manner similar to that of Eunus. His object was to become a king over a socialistic state. We are not aware of the number of cities that refused him, but it must have been considerable.[11] These he stormed and on forcing an entrance, plundered and treated with cruelty. The first city taken was Thyratira; the next Apollonis—large towns built by the Atalæ and Seleucidæ.

Conquest followed and city after city fell into the hands of the pretender and his rebel army. This successful campaign continued until we find them in possession of the entire kingdom. Nothing is imparted to us in regard to whether the neighboring slaves rebelled against their masters, in imitation of these proceedings at Pergamus.

At Rome, little or nothing was done during the year B. C. 133-132, to quell the new uprising in Asia. The great city was still trembling midst the cyclonic billows of the Gracchan revolt. The new servile wars at Rome and Capua, excited to a high pitch by the affair of Gracchus and his agrarian law was a dangerous rekindling of the war of Eunus. Titus Gracchus during this period was assassinated, as we shall soon relate, and a large detachment of the Roman army was still absent in Sicily under Rupilius, putting down the

---

[11] Sallust wrote a full history of the war but his details are all gone. Nothing of his valuable history remains except fragments, some of them so broken as to contain only half a line.

immense social upheaval recounted in the preceding chapter.

Thus, for a short time Rome had no time to turn attention toward her new territory of Pergamus bequeathed her by Attalus III. When the news, however, reached the city that the pretender was earnestly and successfully making headway and with the armed proletaries, rapidly achieving their object, the Romans awoke to a realization of the truth. But wherever the promise of booty showed itself they were seldom known to lie negligent or apathetic.

The two consuls for the year 131 were P. Licinius Crassus Mucianus and L. Valerius Flaccus. According to an old usage, Licinius Crassus was the Pontifix Maximus, and as such, through a religious superstition, could not leave Italy. Pagan religion also interposed against the other consul taking the field; he being *Flamen Martialis* to his colleague. There arose a dispute among the senators, and the illustrious name of Scipio Africanus was brought up for the general command of the expedition. But this plan was rejected and it was at last resolved to send Crassus, who had been one of the ardent friends of Gracchus and his land reform, and for this reason was beloved by the common people. Another reason for preferring him for the command of the expedition was, that he was not only master of the Greek but also spoke its Asiatic dialects; and having exhibited talent as an orator, he was believed to possess a variety of abilities necessary to insure success.[12]

He set sail from Rome during the early part of the year, with his whole army and the navy constituting in all a large force, and with a prosperous voyage on the Mediterranean arrived safely in the harbor of Pergamus.[13] He had no other idea than to make himself master of the new legacy of Pergamus; for it does not appear, because he sympathized with Gracchus and the Italian proletariat, that he even understood or cared in the least, for an almost exactly similar state of suffering and somewhat similar movement in Asia. The question of sympathy with the poor seems to illy befit the objects of the commander of the expedition

---

[12] Valerius Maximus VIII, 7, 6: "Jam P. Crassus, cum in Asiam ad Aristonicum regem debellandum consul venisset, tanta cura Græcæ linguæ notitiam animo comprehendit, ut eam in quinque divisam genera per omnes partes ac uumeros penitus cognosceret. Quæ res maximum ei sociorum amorem conciliavit, qua quis eorum lingua apud tribunal illius postulaverat, eadem decreta reddenti." Cic. Phil. XI, 8, 18.

[13] Gell. I. 13, 11.

ARRIVAL OF BLOSSIUS

against Aristonicus. It would seem that the impulses of tenderness he had manifested for Gracchus and the Italian poor and his rising power shown by his election might have played a deal in deciding upon Crassus against Scipio to get him out of the way.

On landing, Crassus had interviews with Nicomedes, king of Bithynia; Mithradates, king of Pontus; Ariarthes, king of Cappadocia and Pylæmenes of Paphlagonia; all of whom were seriously alarmed about the labor agitation, expecting similar uprisings would take place in their own territories; and they were probably trembling in view of the danger. They all eagerly joined with the Romans in their effort to put down the rebels. Each pledged himself to contribute a strong force of troops.

On the other hand, Aristonicus, in addition to his proletaries, had also engaged another body of soldiers, consisting, of Thracian mercenaries. Phocæa, one of the finest cities supported him and many others staked their interests in him. But his best piece of fortune was meeting with Blossius of Cumæ, a stoic, who infused with the spirit of the movement of Gracchus and also of Eunus of Sicily, had risen in Asia Minor as advocate of the rights of mankind and become a social reformer.[14] Plutarch tells the full story of Blossius. We reproduce his and other points.

A man named Blossius from the Italian *municipium* of Cumæ, subject to Rome, who, it appears, was an educated patrician, for some cause unexplained became greatly charmed by the majestic eloquence of Gracchus and his extraordinary defense of the poor working population of Italy. What inspired him to it may be conjectured to have existed in some degree independently of an enthusiasm for one man. The city of Cumæ was itself a home of labor unions.[15] It was about that time also that persecutions, frowns and threats had set in against labor organizations of every kind. Roman aristocracy had lived to see the steady growth of human liberty and was shrewd enough to perceive that trade unionism was a potent factor in its promotion. Labor unions took a political shape notwithstanding the severe

[14] Plutarch, *Tiberius Gracchus*, 17, 20; Valerius Maximus, IV. 7, 1; Cicero, *Læl.*, 11, 37.
[15] Orellius, *Inscritionum Latinarum Collectio*, Nos. 2,263, 6,422, 6,463, 5,158, 131. These figures refer to slabs of stone on which are found inscribed the registers of collegii or trade unions. Cumæ must have been a hive of unions at that time.

laws against them. To head off these tendencies of organized labor, existing not only in Cumæ but everywhere, the Roman lords were combined almost to a man, heart and soul and with malignant determination, to destroy them. To do this the more effectually they appealed to the avaricious instincts of the so-called citizen class, portraying the immense individual wealth which might be developed from the great accessions of stock and farm lands falling to the Roman arms through conquest. This wealth was already in many places being realized and the power to be used for its development was *human slavery*. The slave power was the muscle of the subjugated tillers of the land. But to accomplish this there must be rigorous laws for suppressing free labor. Gracchus, who had seen the horrors of slavery in Etruria while once traveling through that country on business, had determined to devote his life to the rescue of the slaves and threatened freedmen. Blossius saw him and they became intimate friends.

On the morning of the fatal patrician mob, "Gracchus," says Plutarch, "who was a grandson of Scipio Africanus, set off for the Forum of Rome when he heard that the populace were gathering there; but not without a presentiment of ill omen. A brace of snakes had laid eggs in his highly ornamented helmet. The chickens from whose entrails the *aruspex* was to forshadow his augury, refused to come from their coop and eat. Two black ravens were seen fighting on the roof of a house and one of them rattled a stone down at his feet."[16] All these were bad omens[17] which to those superstitious people proved so disastrous by prostrating their faith, hopes and consciences in many an hour of trial and caused disasters more terrible than their enemies themselves. The boldest of the comrades of Gracchus were staggered. Further than this, when he left the threshold of his home, Gracchus had stumbled and hurt his toe so badly that it bled profusely. Blossius was with him, and it seems was the spokesman of the train.

Gracchus, like many another leader among the ancients, shrank at this array of ill omens, but Blossius dissuaded him from his timid design of returning by the following per-

---
[16] Plutarch, *Titus Gracchus*.
[17] Fustel de Coulanges, *Cité Antiqv*, is the best work we can refer to for an explanation of the influence of superstitions in ancient times. For the superstitions themselves, see Julius Obsequens, *de Prodigiis, passim*.

suasive speech: "For Tiberius Gracchus, grandson of Scipio Africanus and tribune of the Romans, to be scared at a crow, and disappoint the people who are assembled to receive his aid, would be an unendurable disgrace. His enemies would not alone laugh at such a blunder but they would malign him to the common people as an insolent tyrant." Friends also now came to herald the fact that a great number of people were gathering and were impatient of his arrival and that all was calm.

The outcome of it was that Gracchus yielded, but was soon beset by one of those terrible mobs of Roman nobles and their hirelings, denounced as an ambitious schemer who wanted nothing but the votes and support of the rabble and intended to make himself tyrant of Rome. They set upon the defenceless man and murdered him with kicks and clubs.

So great was the faith of Blossius in Gracchus that when afterwards asked if he would have burned the capitol had he been commanded by him to do so, he replied that Gracchus was too wise to have made such a command, but supplemented it when pressed with the daring answer that he should have obeyed.[18] Blossius, notwithstanding the treason, escaped and was not pursued, probably because he was thought to be infatuated. He now bent his course toward Asia Minor [19] and joined his learning and influence to the insurrection of the freedmen and slaves, under the leadership of Aristonicus.

We now return to the career of Publius Crassus, a relative of the Gracchi—Caius, the brother of Tiberius Gracchus, having married his daughter Licinia. As mentioned, he had no sympathy whatever with the emancipation movement which was then raging over the known world, excepting

[18] Cicero, *Lælius*, II, makes this account almost exactly similar with that of Plutarch, or of Valerius Maximus *De Amicitia*, VIII vii 1: ' Nam cum senatus Rupilia a Lænati consulibus mandasset, ut in eos qui cum Graccho consenserant, more majorum animadverterent; et ad Laelium, cujus consilio praecipue consules utebantur, pro se blossius deprecatum venisset, familiaritatisque excusatione uteretur, atque is dixisset. Quid site Gracchus templo Jovis Opt. Max faces subdere jussisset: obsecuturusne volentat illius, propter istam quam jactas familiaritatem, fusses? Nunquam istud inquit. Gracchus imperasset, satis, imo etiam nimium; totius namque senatus consensu damnatos mores defendere ausus est Verum quod sequitur, muito audacius, multoque periculosius; compressus enim perseveranti interrogatione Laeli, in eodem constantiae gradu stetit; seqne etiam hoc, si modo Gracchus annu sset, facturum respondit.

[19] Valerius Maximus, *idem* note of Thyss. "Tiberium et Caium, fratres, ob gravissimas seditiones, quas in podulo suis legibus excitabant, nostes a Senatu fuisse judicatos, et utcumque a nobilitate caesum; alterum a Nasico, alterum ab Opimio. Quo tandem caeso, Blossius ad Aristonicum regem confugit. Profligatis deinde rebus Aristonici, mortem sibi concivit."

so far as that of Rome proper was concerned. He landed at or near Pergamus and formed an alliance with the princes of the Pergamenian kingdom and the kings of Bithynia, Pontus, Cappadocia and Paphlagonia, engaged as many native soldiers as possible and with his own army and the auxiliaries, made an assault upon Leucæ, a strongly fortified city. A protracted siege must have followed; for he was there fighting in the following winter, when his consulship had nearly expired. He was laying his plans to leave for Rome when entrapped and surprised by the arrival of heavy reinforcements for Aristonicus. Crassus was forced to give battle and was totally defeated. He was himself surrounded by the enemy and taken prisoner. Treated no doubt, with severity, and discouraged if not distracted, he sought death rather than disgrace; and one day, infuriating one of the Thracian mercenaries by a punch in the eye with his riding whip, the latter plunged his sword through his body and killed him on the spot.[20] The head of the dead Roman general was cut off and the body taken to Smyrna and buried.

In the meantime, at the *comitia* at Rome, M. Paperna had been elected one of the new consuls for the year 130. The news of the turn of military things in Asia Minor cast an alarm at the home government and Paperna was fitted out and soon on his way with an army large enough to crush the forces of Aristonicus at a blow. Arrived in Mysia and receiving the particulars of the disaster of Crassus at Leucæ he betook himself to the spot where the slaughter occurred. The time of year when he arrived must have been March or late in February; for Aristonicus was yet at winter quarters.

Before the latter could prepare himself for resistance, Paperna fell upon him by surprise. A great battle ensued in which Aristonicus was totally overthrown. With the

[20] **Valerius Maximus, III. ii. 12,** *De Fortitudine:* "Militis hujus in adverso casu tam egregius tamque virilis animus, quam relaturus sum imperatoris. P. enim Crassus cum Aristonico bellum in Asia gerens, à Thracibus, quorum is magnum in præsidio habebat, inter Eleam et Smyrnam exceptus, ne in ditionem ejus perveniret; dedecus, accersita ratione mortis, effugit. Virgam enim, qua ad regendum equum usus fuerat, in unius barbari oculum direxit. Qui vi doloris accensus, latus Crassi sica confodit: dumque se ulciscitur, Romanum imperatorem majestatis amissæ turpitudine liberavit. Ostendit fortunæ Crassus, quam indignum virum tam gravi contumelia afficere voluisset; quoniam quidem injectos ab ea libertati suæ miserabiles laqueos prudenter partier ac fortiter rupit, datumque se jam Aristonico, dignitati suæ reddidit." Cic. Legg. III. 19, 42; Strabo XII.

shattered remnant of his army he fled to Stratonicæ but was doggedly followed by the Romans who surrounded the place and starved him to a capitulation. With most of the slaves he fell a prisoner to the Romans.

Paperna's time being about to expire—the manœuvres, cross marching and other vicissitudes of the campaign having absorbed the summer—Aristonicus, with a portion of his rebel soldiers and officers, was conveyed back in irons to Pergamus. Paperna pressed his design to take his distinguished prisoner, as well as the Pergamenian treasure bequeathed by Attalus III, back to Rome, before the arrival of the new consul should deprive him of his laurels; since it was often the habit in such cases, where the counsulship lasted but a year, for the new comer who had done nothing, to bereave the real winner of his honors, if the latter's works were incomplete. Just before Aquilius the new counsul appeared on the stage, Paperna was taken sick at Pergamus, and died.[21]

A word remains to be said as to the probable fate of the poor slaves and freedmen who formed the principle part of the army of revolution. Almost nothing is left us on this point. Aristonicus it is known, was taken by sea to Rome in chains and strangled in the cell of his prison, B. C. 129. His ardent and faithful friend Blossius of Cumæ, seeing his cause, and lifework, thus ground to powder between the millstones of Roman power, desired no longer to live. In his philosophy of human equality which this defeat had practically extinguished, death seemed preferable to a lonely existence and he put an end to himself.

But what of the rank and file? It would seem by the silence itself of historians and the otherwise unaccountable delay of Paperna at the scene of his victory—delay which brought his departure for Pergamus late into the following fall although the battle was fought in the early spring—nearly the entire summer had been consumed in the horrible work of crucifying the unfortunate working-people who,

---

[21] Valerius Maximus, III. iv, 5: *De Humili Loco Natis.* "Non parvus consulatus rubor M. Perperna, utpote qui consul ante quam civis; sed in bello gerendo utilior aliquanto reipub. Varrone imperatore. Regem enim Aristonicum cepit, Crassianæque stragis punitor extitit. Cum interim cujus vita triumphavit, mors Papia lege damnata est. Namque patrem illius, nihil ad se pertinentia civis Romani jura complexum, Sabelli judicio petitum, redire in pristinas sedes coëgerunt. ita M. Perpernæ nomen adumbratum. falsus consulatus, caliginis simile imperium, caducus triumphus, aliena in urbe improbe peregrinatus est."

through that battle, had lost their cause."² Could there have remained to us one faithful copy describing the scenes of vengeance ²³ and the dangling corpses left rotting on the gibbets of Stratonicæ in Carea, we should then have a chronicle of things perfectly harmonious with the brutal nature

---

²² Plato, *Laws*, book IX. chap. 9, in giving his directions regarding the treatment of a slave who is a murderer or accessory to the crime, lays down the rule that if a freeman or citizen commit homicide he shall be turned over to the murdered man's relatives, who have the power to redeem him for money, for good previous conduct, or through the intercession of his friends. If however, the crime be committed upon a citizen by a slave, such offender is to be handed over to the relatives who are to torture or otherwise punish him without limit, as they please: the only proviso being that the torture or punishment *shall not stop short of death*. This is Plato's state of the "Blessed"—lenient in comparison with the existing laws—and as the customs of the Greek-speaking Asians and islanders were fully as severe as those of the Athenians and fellow countrymen of Plato, it cannot be supposed that anything less than death could have befallen the victims of Paperna. The following is Plato's law; which we give in English: "If a slave kills his master in a passion, let the kindred of the deceased use the murderer in whatever manner they please, and be clean of the acts, so long as they do not by any means preserve the life of the slave." But in the same law Plato rules that this happy republic shall "let him who kills his own slave, undergo a purification." (Translation of Burges). Surely a human low-born was considered inferior to a dog, for that animal was often exempt by reason of his irresponsibility!

²³ That this was a genuine labor rebellion there seem to be no grounds for doubt. Dr. Bücher, *Anfstände der Unfreien Arbeiter*, S. 107-8, in the following significant language brings forward the question of the prevailing ideas of those people, especially the laboring class, whose organizations were being seriously threatened by these events: These *Attalic* societies had always hitherto been not only befriended but protected by the Pergamenian kings. We quote the words of Dr. Bücher on the *Dionysian Communists:* "Die letztere bestand darin, das sich die Feiernden durch Weihen und Sühnungen, durch üppige Tänze unter dem Klang der Flöte und der Handpauke in sinnberückenden Taumel und wilde Begeisterung versetzten, in der sie sich zur Gottheit emporzuschwingen, Wunder sehen und verrichten zu können meinten. Wenn gerade damals diese Kulte auch im eigentlichen Griechenland in einer grossen Zahl von geschlossenen Vereinen und frommen Bruderschaften gepflegt wurden (S. 34. 92), so ist das, was ihnen Verbreitung verschaffte, nicht sowohl das Zaubermeer eines schrankenlosen Sinnenrausches, in das sich ein unbefriedigtes, überreiztes Geschlecht so gern versenkt, als vielmehr die diesen Genossenschaften eigenthümliche, der socialen Anschauungsweise der Hellenen fremde Gleichstellung aller Mitglieder, mochten sie Griechen odor Barbaren, Männer oder Frauen, Freie oder Sklaven sein. Darnach ist die Bezeichnung, Bürger der Sonnenstadt, zu beurtheilen; sie schied die Anhänger des Aristonikos als die gläubige Gemeinde des Adad von den Ungläubigen, die verbrüderten Armen und Elenden von ihren feindlichen Bedrängern, wie wir den von Eunus auf dem Schild gehobenen Namen der 'Syrer' demzufolge auch nach der religiösen Seite werden zu nehmen haben, als das Kennzeichen der Anhänger der Atargatis." This Atargatis was the veritable goddess Ceres, protectress of labor, of whom we have already spoken so much in our chapters on the Eleusinian Mysteries, and on Eunus and Athenion of Sicily. Several coincident circumstances crowd themselves into this connection, to-wit: This is the prolific, original soil of the early Christian church. The apostles must have used these half-smothered communes, ready in advance, perforce their own previous cult, to embrace any new idea that promised relief; for the rebellion having failed, all the free farmers, mechanics and laborers were dragged down to slavery; and their condition was, at the beginning of our era infinitely worse than it had ever been before. Again, this very spot together with the adjacent islands, is to this day the repository of innumerable inscriptions—the marvel of Archæologists—which begin to be the subject of contention among scholars who are averse to recognizing such a thing as a labor movement, and who are consequently nonplussed regarding anything other than that

of the Romans and bearing the reflex of probability, in the similar pictures of horrors which, in every other case we have described, were painted by the historians' pen, as in letters of blood, warning all workingmen of the ghastly wages of rebellion. We are left no personal description even of the hero of this great uprising which involved 3 years of savage fighting, many drawn battles with the Asians, the siege and taking of several fortified cities, and the defeat and disastrous overthrow of one large, well-generaled and thoroughly equipped consular army of Rome. All we know is the short but numerous and fully corroborated statements given as cold and feelingless facts, by chroniclers of different periods, different nationality, sentiment and language. To suppose this to have been an exception to the deeply fixed habit of intimidation and condign vengeance of the Romans, or that these rebel workmen were treated with more lenity than those who had espoused the cause of Eunus and Cleon, or were to espouse in the coming struggles of Tryphon and Athenion or of Spartacus and Crixus, would be to admit that unheard of departure of the Romans from a fixed principle. No; the scenes of blood-spilling which followed the downfall of Aristonicus were appalling. But that very blood was the seed of a sect which soon afterwards, near that very region, bore fruits destined to destroy the Pagan system of slavery and to rear a new one based upon kindness, forbearance, mutual love, brotherhood and recognized equality of the human race.

own debatable grounds regarding their origin as well as their immense numbers. What were they; who were they; whence are they? Our answer is that they were nothing other than labor societies, which for hundreds of years had been legalized at Rome, in Greece, in Egypt. (See Herodotus, II. 164-8 and 177, which makes it almost certain that Solon carried his law from Eygpt), everywhere; but which the then existing anti-labor hostility at Rome, caused by the greed of Roman land and slave speculators and their politicians, was in a desperate struggle to subdue, by a measure (which they finally passed), known in modern times as *conspiracy laws*. After this hostility set in, the poor creatures were obliged in conformity to some law, to shield themselves by the cloak of ostentatious religious rites, graved into their inscriptions; **and it is here that the arch æologists are misled.**

CHAPTER XI.

ATHENION.

ENORMOUS STRIKE AND UPRISING IN SICILY.

SECOND SICILIAN LABOR-WAR—Tryphon and Athenion—Greed and Irascibility Again Grapple—The War Plan of Salvation Repeated by Slaves and Tramps—Athenion, another remarkable General Steps Forth—Castle of the Twins in a Hideous Forest—Slaves goaded to Revolt by Treachery and Intrigue of a Politician—Rebellion and the Clangor of War—Battle in the Mountains—A Victory for the Slaves at the Heights of Engyon—Treachery of Gaddæus the Freebooter—Decoy and Crucifixions—Others cast Headlong over a Precipice—The Strike starts up Afresh at Heraclea Minoa—Murder of Clonius a rich Roman Knight—Escape of Slaves from his *Ergastulum*—Sharp Battles under the Generalship of Salvius—Strife rekindles in the West—Battle of Alaba—The Propraetor punished for his bad Administration—Victory Again Wreathes a Laural for the Lowly—A vast Uprising in Western Sicily—Athenion the Slave Shepherd—Another Fanatical Crank of Deeds—Rushing the Struggle for Existence—Fierce Battles and Blood-spilling—What Ordinary Readers of History have not heard of—Fourth Battle; Triokala—Meek Sacrifices by the Slaves, to the Twins of Jupiter and Thalia—March to Triokala—Jealousy—Great Battle and Carnage—Athenion Wounded—He escapes to Triokala and recovers—Fifth Battle—Lucullus marches to the Workingmen's Fortifications—Batte of Triokala—The Outcasts Victorious—Lucullus is lost from View—Sixth Battle—Servilius, another Roman General Overthrown—The Terrible Athenion Master of Sicily and King over all the Working-People—Seventh and Final Field Conflict—Battle of Macella—Death of Athenion—Victory this Time for the Romans—End of the Rebellion—Satyros, a powerful Greek Slave escapes to the Mountains with a Force of Insurgents—They

A CONGRESS OF RUNAWAY SLAVES. 247

are finally lured to a Capitulation by **Aquillius who treacherously breaks Faith** and consigns them as **Gladiators to Rome**—They fight the Eighth and last Battle in the Roman Amphitheatre among wild Beasts—A ghastly mutual Suicide—The Reaction—Treachery of Aquillius Punished—The Gold-Workers pour melted Gold down his Throat.

An enormous and memorable uprising or strike, both of slaves and wage workers of antiquity, occurred in Sicily, beginning 29 years after the close of the war of Eunus, which ended B. C. 133, bringing the date at B. C. 104.

As in the account we have given of the first servile war of Eunus, Achæus and Cleon we have followed the admirable chronology and other points of Dr. Karl Bücher, so in this second war, we follow the splendid elaboration of Prof. Otto Siefert, the learned doctor-professor at the college-gymnasium of Altona.[1]

It has already been observed that there existed among the ancients, an occasional asylum where slaves and freedmen driven to straits by the cruelty of others, could in emergencies, flee and hide in security, under the protecting ægis of a certain divinity. There existed such an asylum in Sicily. It was located on the sombre shores of two small lakes westward from Syracuse in the interior. The asylum was built in honor of the *Palikoi*, twin children of Jupiter and the nymph Thalia. The legend is, that out from the surface of one of the lakes a hideous column of sulphurous waters sprang high into the air like a fountain, causing an unendurable smell and a deafening roar.[2] Here stood a temple or Pagan convent and asylum. All around was the hideous forest. In view near by was a craggy mountain-steep where dwelt elves and urchins,

---

[1] Siefert, *Sklavenkriege auf Sicilien*, Altona, 1860, S. 24-40, *Brochûre*. We quote his note 69, S. 36, on the sources of information whence we derive our knowledge of this uprising, and the duration of time it occupied, as follows: "Quellen deeses zweiten Sklavenkrieges sind: Florus, *Epitom. Historiarum Romanarum*, lib. III. cap. 19; Dion. Cass. Exc. Peiresc. 101, 104; Diodor XXXVI. Liv. LXIX. Die Dauer: ὁ μὲν οὖν κατὰ Σικελίαν τῶν οἰκετῶν πόλεμος διαμείνας ἔτη σχεδόν που τέτταρα τραγικὴν ἔσχε τὴν καταστροφήν. M.'Aquillius beendigte ihn im J. 99, nachdem er 101 als Consul den Oberbefehl übernommen hatte; als der Krieg ausbrach, war Licinius Nerva Proprætor, nach ihm kommandierten L. Lucullus und C. Servilius: also begann die Empörung im Laufe des Jahres 104. Euseb. Arm. setzt irrthümlich das Ende um 4 Jahre später an auf Olympiad, 171, 2, (95)." The events being obscure though thrilling and often highly romantic, we shall reproduce *verbatum* many of the paragraphs of these and several other highly respectable contributors to the history.

[2] Aristotle on *Wonders*, 57. Diod. Sic. XI. 88-90. Παλικων λιμνη. It seems to have been a forest marsh or swamp.

demons of the mountain and of the wailing woods. Satyrs and wizzards danced the mad antics of fury to the æolian strain of their harps; while Thalia, mother-goddess of the twins, smiled on them as their idyllic muse; and her guardian command hushed the frenzied winds and waters, and balmed their sulphurous odors with the breath of encouragement.[3]

This was the spook and goblin-haunted asylum where, in the summer of B. C. 104, a large number of naked, hardworked and sweat-begrimed slaves gathered together for the protection of the institution. They were stragglers from Syracuse who had undergone an examination of their eligibility to life and liberty.

What was the deep motive which inspired so strange a visitation as this, coming unheralded to the old castle at the swamps of the twins?[4] The workingmen had, as it were, of their own spontaneous instincts, centered there for safety! A full explanation of this is a history of one of the most desperate and sanguinary rebellions recorded in history.

Marius was one of the two consuls of Rome in B. C. 104. In order to help him carry out the war measures which had been determined upon, the Roman Senate had authorized him to secure troops by conscription from the conquered provinces. Sicily, ever since the Punic

[3] Diod. XI. 89 Ἐπεὶ δὲ περὶ τῶν θεῶν τούτων ἐμνήσθημεν, οὐκ ἄξιόν ἐστι παραλιπεῖν τὴν περὶ τὸ ἱερὸν ἀρχαιότητά τε καὶ τὴν ἀπιστίαν καὶ τὸ σύνολον τὸ περὶ τοὺς ὀνομαζομένους κρατῆρας ἰδίωμα. Μυθολογοῦσι γὰρ τὸ τέμενος τοῦτο διαφέρειν τῶν ἄλλων ἀρχαιότητι καὶ σεβασμῷ, πολλῶν ἐν αὐτῷ παραδόξων γεγενημένων. Πρῶτον μὲν γὰρ κρατῆρές εἰσι τῷ μεγέθει μὲν οὐ κατὰ πᾶν μεγάλοι, σπινθῆρας δ' ἐξαισίους ἀναβάλλοντες ἐξ ἀμυθήτου βυθοῦ καὶ παραπλήσιον ἔχοντες τὴν φύσιν τοῖς λέβησι τοῖς ὑπὸ πυρὸς πολλοῦ καιομένοις καὶ τὸ ὕδωρ διάπυρον ἀναβάλλουσιν. Ἔμφασιν μὲν οὖν ἔχει τὸ ἀναβαλλόμενον ὕδωρ ὡς ὑπάργει διάπυρον, οὐ μὴν ἀκριβῆ τὴν ἐπίγνωσιν ἔχει διὰ τὸ μηδένα τολμᾶν ἅψασθαι τούτου· τηλικαύτην γὰρ ἔχει κατάπληξιν ἡ τῶν ὑγρῶν ἀναβολή, ὥστε δοκεῖν ὑπὸ θείας τινὸς ἀνάγκης γίνεσθαι τὸ συμβαῖνον. Τὸ μὲν γὰρ ὕδωρ θείου κατάκορον τὴν ὄσφρησιν ἔχει, τὸ δὲ χάσμα βρόμον πολὺν καὶ φοβερὸν ἐξίησι, τὸ δὲ δὴ τούτων παραδοξότερον, οὔτε ὑπερεκχεῖται τὸ ὑγρὸν οὔτε ἀπολείπει, κίνησίν τε καὶ βίαν ῥεύματος εἰς ὕψος ἐξαιρομένην ἔχει θαυμάσιον· Τοιαύτης δὲ θεοπρεπείας οὔσης περὶ τὸ τέμενος, οἱ μέγιστοι τῶν ὅρκων ἐνταῦθα συντελοῦνται, καὶ τοῖς ἐπιορκήσασι σύντομος ἡ τοῦ δαιμονίου κόλασις ἀκολουθεῖ· τινὲς γὰρ τῆς ὁράσεως στερηθέντες τὴν ἐκ τοῦ τεμένους ἄφοδον ποιοῦνται. Μελάλης δ' οὔσης δεισιδαιμονίας, οἱ τὰς ἀμφισβητήσεις ἔχοντες, ὅταν ὑπό τινος ὑπεροχῆς κατισχύωνται, τῇ διὰ τῶν ὅρκων τούτων ἀναιρέσει κρίνονται. Ἔστι δὲ τοῦτο τὸ τέμενος ἔκ τινων χρόνων ἄσυλον τετηρημένον, καὶ τοῖς ἀτυχοῦσιν οἰκέταις καὶ κυρίοις ἀγνώμοσι περιπεπτωκόσι πολλὴν παρέχεται βοήθειαν. Τοὺς γὰρ εἰς τοῦτο καταφυγόντας οὐκ ἔχουσιν ἐξουσίαν οἱ δεσπόται βιαίως ἀπάγειν, καὶ μέχρι τούτου διαμένουσιν ἀσινεῖς μέχρι ἂν ἐπὶ διωρισμένοις φιλανθρώποις πείσαντες οἱ κύριοι καὶ δόντες διὰ τῶν ὅρκων τὰς περὶ τῶν ὁμολογιῶν πίστεις καταλλαγῶσι. Καὶ οὐδεὶς ἱστορεῖται τῶν δεδωκότων τοῖς οἰκέταις πίστιν ταύτην παραβὰς· οὕτω γὰρ ἡ τῶν θεῶν δεισιδαιμονία τοὺς ὀμόσαντας πρὸς τοὺς δούλους πιστοὺς ποιεῖ. Ἔστι δὲ καὶ τὸ τέμενος ἐν πεδίῳ θεοπρεπεῖ κείμενον καὶ στοαῖς καὶ ταῖς ἄλλαις καταλύσεσιν ἱκανῶς κεκοσμημένον.

[4] Id. See note above. "Μυθολογοῦσι γὰρ τὸ τέμενος τοῦτο διαφέρειν τῶν ἀλλωνάρχαιότητι καὶ σεβασμῷ, πολλῶν ἐν αὐτῷ, παραδόξων γεγεγημένων."

CAUSES OF THE TROUBLE. 249

wars had been one of these provinces. Almost every human creature not possessing the blood of a *gens* family in this *palaestra* of suffering was now a slave.[5] The condition, bad enough before, was rendered worse if possible, by the ghastly defeat of the 200,000 slaves, in their uprising and war of rebellion under Eunus a generation before.[6] But it was for Nicomides, king of Bithynia, in far off Asia Minor, to kindle the war-fagots. Bithynia though a kingdom of some independence was nevertheless a satrapy of Rome; and the order of Marius the consul, that Nicomides should levy troops out of his dependency, for the Roman army, could not be carried out for the reason that the rapacious Roman tax-gatherers known as publicans[7] had sold almost everybody into slavery and it was degrading, and contrary to all law and rule of antiquity except in the severest emergencies, to make soldiers of slaves. This made the *senatus consulti* a dead letter. Rome was vast in actual dominion at this time and any law touching one part, generally held good also for any other. It was found on test that also in Sicily, the majorities were slaves and that, like Nicomides, so also Nerva, propraetor over Sicily under Marius, was cut off from the hope of supplying his quota of troops for the Roman army.

What was to be done? On an investigation it was found that most of the workingmen best able to bear arms, were slaves. Again, their owners were unwilling to hear to their being set free. It would be a loss of property. These clubbed together and pooled their money, being politicians enough to know that an offer of a bribe would

---

[5] Diodorus Siculus, *Bibliothecæ Historicæ Reliquæ*, XXXVI. iii. 1, 2, 3: "Κατὰ τὴν ἐπὶ τοὺς Κίμβρους τοῦ Μαρίου στρατείαν ἔδωκεν ἡ σύγκλητος ἐξουσίαν τῷ Μαρίῳ ἐκ τῶν πέραν θαλάττης ἐθνῶν μεταπέμπεσθαι συμμαχίαν. Ὁ μὲν οὖν Μάριος ἐξέπεμψε πρὸς Νικομήδην τὸν τῆς Βιθυνίας βασιλέα περὶ βοηθείας· ὁ δὲ ἀπόκρισιν ἔδωκε τοὺς πλείους τῶν Βιθυνῶν ὑπὸ τῶν δημοσιωνῶν διαρπαγέντας δουλεύειν ἐν ταῖς ἐπαρχίαις. Τῆς δὲ συγκλήτου ψηφισαμένης ὅπως μηδεὶς σύμμαχος ἐλεύθερος ἐν ἐπαρχίᾳ δουλεύῃ καὶ τῆς τούτων ἐλευθερώσεως οἱ στρατηγοὶ πρόνοιαν ποιῶνται, τότε κατὰ τὴν Σικελίαν ὢν στρατηγὸς Λικίνιος Νερούας ἀκολούθως τῷ δόγματι συχνοὺς τῶν δούλων ἠλευθέρωσε, κρίσεις πρίρεις προθείς, ὡς ἐν ὀλίγαις ἡμέραις πλείους τῶν ὀκτακοσίων τυχεῖν τῆς ἐλευθερίας. Καὶ ἦσαν πάντες οἱ κατὰ τὴν νῆσον δουλεύοντες μετέωροι πρὸς τὴν ἐλευθερίαν."
[6] Diodorus, XXXIV. *frag.* ii. 18.
[7] The *publicani* must not be confounded with the *vectigalarii* as tax collectors. The latter were workingmen with a plebeian society. The publicans were blooded, grasping aristocrats, belonging to the *equites* and were, according to Cicero, the "flos equitum Romanorum, ornamentum civitatis, firmamentum rei publicæ" (Pro Plano.), words characteristic of this boasting aristocrat. The publicans scattered horror and destruction everywhere. See *New Testament*, also Smith's *Dictionary of the Bible*, art. "*Publicans*."

have the desired effect upon the proprætor Nerva.⁸ Nerva, it appears, took the bribe; but in doing so, performed some queer diplomatical gymnastics in order to glide away from a semblance of blame and thus unintentionally set the whole island into an uproar. He had first published a proclamation requiring all slaves who believed themselves entitled to emancipation, to come and receive their liberty. This was under a new law just enacted by the senate at Rome. The law was suited to the emergency and was indited to read that subjects must no longer be seized by the publicans and sold for taxes; and that those who had been thus sold should be entitled to appear before city officials of their vicinity and receive their liberty.⁹

Now what was the governor to do? The slaves to the number of 800, having become aware of this by the proclamation actually calling them in and eager for liberty, had escaped from their masters, probably by running away and were already thronging around the propraetor in impatient expectancy of the promised papers of emancipation, hoping to join the Roman army and thus become free and honored men. Alas! No such happiness was in reserve for them. The miserable liar, ready to grasp his bribe even at the expense of sullying conscience with malfeasance in office, when the banded slave owners thickened around him pressing on all sides, issued another edict to the slaves advising them to go back to their masters with the treacherously perfidious supplement that he would stand between them and all harm.

Struck down with horror, the poor wretches, feeling that in their surreptitious escape they had partly taken the initiative in procuring their own freedom and knowing the dreadful extent of vengeance which awaited them on their returning to the now exasperated masters, betook themselves as stated, to the citadel of the twins at the lakes of the *Palikoi*. And well they might; if we may believe the words of Florus who of all other writers had the least sympathy for the slaves in rebellion.¹⁰ Yet Florus

⁸ This statement is made on the strength of Dion Cassius (*frag.* 101), who intimates as much in speaking of the sums pooled by the slave owners.
⁹ Diod. Sic. *Bibliotheca* XXXVI, *frag.* iii. 2. as quoted in note 5, q. v.
¹⁰ Florus, *Epit. Rerum Romanorum*, lib. III. cap. XIX. S. 1, speaking of the first servile war says: Utcumque etsi cum sociis (nefas!) cum liberis tamen et ingenuis dimicatum est. This word *nefus* characterizes the struggle as a blasphemy.

describes them as prisoners in chains. All over Sicily there existed prisons called in Latin *ergastula*, in Greek *ergasteria*, where slaves were kept in custody over night in irons. Some were forced to work in these dens; but most of them were marched out in the early morning to their grinding labors on the farms.[11] During the servile war 20 years before, Eunus attacked these horrid slave-pens and set fully 60,000 of the manacled slaves at liberty.[12] These immediately joined his great army of revolution, swelling it to such an extent that the slaves were victorious in many battles.

What took place at the asylum in the forest of Jupiter's twins we are but imperfectly told. They conspired;[13] though as in the case of every strike of the ancient slaves, so also here, our histories are riddled to fragments. But enough has been preserved from the ruthless vandal's hand to make clear what we shall with confidence relate. A most bloody and devastating war soon burst forth, spreading, in a few days over nearly all of Sicily.

There is a town now called Scillato but in those days the Sicilian Greeks knew the place by the name of Ancyle.[14] Here a massacre announced and kindled the first flames of war. Thirty slaves organized under a leader named Oarius, broke chains in the night, set upon their masters and murdered them in their sleep. Later in the same night, probably through the action of the first thirty, 200 more slaves were delivered from their shackles, or at least from bondage, and the whole neighborhood was made hideous by scenes of terror which they enacted. It was at the slopes of the Nebrode heights not far from the town of Engyion. A fastness crowned the height which, like

[11] Flor. 19. "Hic ad cultum agri frequenta ergastula, catenatique cultores."
[12] *Idem.* c. 6 "Hoc miraculum primum duo millia ex obviis, mox jure belli refractis ergastulis, sexaginta amplius millium fecit exercitum." See war of Eunus chap. IX.
[13] Diod. XXXVI. *frag.* iii. 8. Dind. says: Οἱ δ' ἐν ἀξιώμασι συνδραμόντες παρεκάλουν τὸν στρατηγὸν ἀποστῆναι ταύτης τῆς ἐπιβολῆς. Ὁ δ' εἴτε χρήμασι πεισθεὶς εἴτε χάριτι δουλεύσας, τῆς μὲν τῶν κριτηρίων τούτων σπουδῆς ἀπέστη, καὶ τοὺς προςιόντας ἐπὶ τῷ τυχεῖν τῆς ἐλευθερίας ἐπιπλήττων εἰς τοὺς ἰδίους κυρίους προςέταττεν ἐπαναστρέφειν. Οἱ δὲ δοῦλοι συστραφέντες, καὶ τῶν Συρακουσῶν ἀπαλλαγέντες, καὶ καταφυγόντες εἰς τὸ τῶν Παλικῶν τέμενος, διελάλουν πρὸς ἀλλήλους ὑπὲρ ἀποστάσεως. Nothing however, can be clearer than this fragment of Diodorus. The slaves, screened from harm by the hospitable old temple, had leisure to organize their rebellion on a prodigious scale, which they accomplished with effect.
[14] Siefert, *Sicilische Sklavenaufstände*, S. 36, note 71, points to Cicero, *Verres*, III. 45, who writes it "Incilienses," and concludes: "die Stadt ist auf dem Nebrodengebirge in der Nähe von Engyion zu suchen."

the asylum of the *Palikoi* offered the slaves security. Here they fortified themselves, received allies, sent strong and fearless scouts to cut the bands and set their fellows free and thus in a few days so augmented their force that by the time the Roman prætor made his appearance with an army to put down the *emeut*, they were strong enough to offer front.

This first organized resistance of the slaves was however, destined to meet with disaster through treachery. A man named C. Titinius Gaddæus probably of Roman and possibly of noble stock, prowled, in those days, about this country, in the capacity of a marauder. He was an escaped convict, having a considerable time before been condemned to death for certain crimes. With a banditti of freebooters of his ilk, he stole about at night, hiding by day in the inaccessible fastnesses of the mountain and thus by robbery and deceit, gained a precarious living, always on the alert for an opportunity and always destitute of conscience. The proprætor, Licinius Nerva who was the cause of the disaffection among the slaves, sought, and probably by promises of exoneration secured, the alliance of this freebooter who subtly set about making the friendship of the slaves then watching an opportunity to destroy the militia which Nerva had levied to put down the trouble. Gaddæus succeeded in decoying the slaves into an ambush and by arrangement turned the poor wretches over to the Roman governor who crucified some of them and others he killed by casting headlong from a high precipice to be dashed to jelly upon the rocks.[15]

Nerva now believed the trouble to be over. He was even foolish enough to disband his forces, consisting mostly of militia whom he discharged from further service and sent to their homes. But the slaves seem to have been on the alert; perhaps encouraged by the utter want of generalship shown by Nerva. The question now arises in the mind of the reader how poor, enslaved, ignorant creatures many of whom were in fetters, could have been able to rebel at all; much less keep a correspondence with others sufficiently to know what was going on at different points. The answer must be, that they felt themselves in

[15] Diod. XXXVI. iii. 6, *fin.* Dind. των δ' ἀποστατῶν οἱ μὲν μαχόμενοι κατε-κόπησαν, οἱ δὲ τὴν ἀπὸ τῆς ἁλώσεως δεδιότες τιμωρίαν ἑαυτοὺς κατακρήμνισαν.

a desperate condition and combined their entire energy and intelligence to greater effect than may be naturally imagined. Men engaged in such desperate adventures think nothing of turning night into day; and like the similar case with us in recent days, they may have had secret outposts and means of communication.

At any rate, the Roman general had hardly disbanded his force when the war-cloud gathered in another part of the island. A rich Roman knight named P. Clonius,[16] who possessed estates, such as were celebrated in history as the *latifundia*, was murdered by his slaves near Heraclea Minoa on the southeastern coast of Sicily. This murder was perpetrated by a band of 80 desperate men who concocted their conspiracy during the lull and broke from the *ergastula* helping each other by signal, to free themselves. The number in the revolt rapidly increased. The governor, Licinius Nerva, was now in a helpless condition, without an army. The slaves rushed in every direction, freeing each other, and pitched tent on the banks of the river Alaba[17] coursing at the foot of the Mons Caprianus, to the number of over 2,000 men. This, however, occupied some time, during which Nerva succeeded in mustering a considerable force which he marched or transported by water to the scene of war.

The distance from Syracuse to Heraclea Minoa is not far from 95 miles in a straight line westward but following the road or the shortest route by sea around the Portus Odysseæ and past Agrigentum, it could not be less than 130 miles.[18] To convey his army and *impedimenta* thither and fix his headquarters at Heracleia, occupied so much time that it must have been toward the spring of B. C. 103, before anything serious transpired.

On a favorable position, the two adversaries drew up in line of battle. The name of the Roman commander was M. Titinius,[19] whose forces summed up the largest

---

[16] Diod. XXXVI. iv. 1, *init:* "Τῶν δὲ στρατιωτῶν πρὸς τὰ οἰκεῖα ἤθη ἀπολυθέντων, ἧκόν τινες ἀπαγγέλλοντες ὅτι Πόπλιον Κλόνιον, γενομενον ἱππέα Ῥωμαίων, ἐπαναστάντες οἱ δοῦλοι κατέσφαξαν ὀγδοήκοντα ὄντες, καὶ ὅτι πλῆθος ἀγείρουσι."

[17] Diod XXXVI 4. "ἐφεξῆς δ᾽ ἐγένοντο τῶν δισχιλίων οὐκ ἐλάττους." This force of 2,000 men was collected within 7 days.

[18] In relation to Nerva's route Diodorus says nothing.

[19] Iod. XXXVI. 4. 3. Bind. says: Μάρκον Τιτίνιοι. Nevertheless we are constrained to think Titinius the same person who had betrayed them, *i. e.* Titinius Gadæus

number that the Roman prætor, with the addition of 600 men drawn from the fortress of Enna, was able to muster. On the whole, relying on the superior armor and other equipments of his own men, compared with the destitute condition of the workingmen, who depended upon butcher-knives, sickles, clubs, slings and whatever they could grasp, the Romans seem to have had the advantage. But the rebels besides being full of that courage which desperation inspires and anxious to meet a hated foe, had also the most advantageous position. No details of this battle have come to us further than that it was a fierce and bloody encounter; the slaves fighting desperately following charge with charge, dealing such ponderous blows against their adversary, composed partly of raw militia, that the latter gave way, or were killed on the spot. The rout of the Romans now became general. A panic seized them. They cast away their arms and ran for life. The slaves grasping their weapons, pursued and hacked those whom they could to pieces, scoring a signal victory.

The strike which hitherto had manifested itself in murmuring and an occasional outburst, now assumed warlike proportions. Section after section of the island broke away from their masters and joined the gathering army. The force under drill, soon after the battle at the Alaba river is reported to have been 6,000[20] strong; all well equipped with the best of arms which they had taken from the enemy. Greatly encouraged by this first victory, they set about organizing in earnest. More fettered slaves who were working in chains were cut loose from the *ergastula* or work-prisons. These glad to escape, joined the rank and file, and being the most desperate and brave made reliable soldiers in the insurrection.

A mass meeting was now called for the election of a leader. There was a certain character who had signalized himself as a man of great energy, named Salvius. This man had been the principal in the movement which had consummated the assassination of the Roman knight Clonius, at Heracleia Minoa ending in the defeat of the proprætor

---

[20] Diod. XXXVI. iv. 4: "Καὶ πολλῶν καθ' ἡμέραν ἀφισταμένων, σύντομον καὶ παράδοξον ἐλάμβανον αὔξησιν, ὡς ἐν ὀλίγαις ἡμέραις πλείους γενέσθαι τῶν ἑξακισχιλίων. Ὅτε δὴ καὶ εἰς ἐκκλησίαν συνελθόντες καὶ βουλῆς προτεθείσης πρῶτον μὲν εἵλαντο βασιλέα τὸν ὀνομαζόμενον Σαλούιον δοκοῦντα τῆς ἱεροσκοπίας ἔμπειρον ἶναι καὶ ταῖς γυναικείαις θέαις αὐλομανοῦντα."

Licinius[21] Nerva at the battle of the Alaba river. Like Eunus, the slave-king of Enna in the war of the strikers, which had ended 29 years before, he was a prophet, a worker of incantations, a flute-player, and dispensed supernatural and wonderful doings among the credulous slaves and freedmen. A slave himself, of superior bearing and gift of command, he was elected by acclamation as king.[22] King Salvius immediately on assuming power, turned his attention to organization and order. He taught his wild and often gross-mannered men that success does not come from savagery and rapine nor from destruction of property by laying waste the country and its fruits; and brought them to understand that an unbridled career is dangerous. The army was divided into three divisions, under his three picked warriors as commanders, and marched off at different angles into the country with the order to reunite at a given point, at a given time, bringing with them provisions. The plan succeeded exactly. At the appointed time and place the three divisions again united, having collected from the dairy and stock farms so large a quantity of sheep, cattle, horses, grain and other supplies that the question of want for the army which had also greatly increased, was settled for a long time to come.

Great numbers of horses had come into the hands of Salvius. A force of cavalry was organized 2,000 strong, undoubtedly well equipped. The army grew to the majestic proportions of 20,000 foot besides the cavalry—in all 22,000 combatants.[23] With activity this force was drilled to discipline and fitted for receiving the approaching Roman army. King Salvius after completing preparations for a campaign, set off on a march toward Morgantion situated on the coast of Sicily, near the mouth of the river Symethus. Morgantion was a fortified city with a citadel; and had been the seat of a terrible conflict between the slaves and the Romans in the war of Eunus.[24] The rebel chieftain hurriedly conveyed his large army

---

[21] Diodorus, IV. 4. characterizes Salvius as a Slave who knew the arts of prophecy and could play the flute or horn. He was a favorite with women and possessed the mysterious arts of slight of hand. See note 20, *fin.*
[22] Siefert, *Sicilische Sklavenkeiege,* S. 27. "Indess zeigte Salvius d:ch eine grössere Befähigung für seine Stellung, als sich nach seinem früheren Leben erwarten leiss."
[23] Diod. XXXVI. *frag.* iv, §§ 7, 7, 8, Dind.
[24] ee chap. ix., on the Servile war of Eunus.

thither, a distance from Heracleia **Minoa** of about one hundred miles. The Roman prætor knowing that greater mischief was meant, had in the meantime collected an army, partly from Italy, partly from Sicily, as well as of stragglers who had survived the last disaster—in all, amounting to 10,000 men. With this force he marched day and night in order to arrive at Morgantion before the rebels could reach the place. This he appears to have succeeded in doing but found nobody but the women and children of the slaves; for the men, aware of the near approach of Salvius and his army had escaped to a hiding haunt which they frequented, by a gate or other means of egress through the walls, during a dark night. Salvius now determined to give his enemy battle. He led his troops in solid phalanx and good order against the prætorian army, making the attack with such a shock as to stagger him by the onset. It appears from a remark made by Diodorus that the prætor must have had slaves as a part of his force; for Salvius, taking advantage of some opportunity, gave the soldiers of the Roman army to understand that they would be freed if they threw down their arms. As a result the Roman troops began to throw away their weapons and save themselves by flight. A panic was thus created and the rout became general. Salvius pursued and succeeded in taking 4,000 Italians and Sicilian Greeks, while 600 were killed on the spot.[25] Large quantities of arms fell into the hands of the again victorious rebels, together with all the munitions of war that were stored in the magazines. The victory before Morgantion was complete. Quantities of armor and campaign equipments were taken, together with provisions for maintaining the siege of the city itself. Certain it is, that after the battle, the Roman prætor retired within the fortress of Morgantion with his remaining troops, and by promising the slaves the boon of lib-

[25] Diod. XXXVI. iv. 7. "Οἱ δ' ἀποστάται ἐξαίφνης ἀντεπιθέμενοι, καὶ ὑπερδέξιον τὴν στάσιν ἔχοντες, φνης ἀντεπιθέμενοι, καὶ ὑπερδέξιον τὴν στάσιν ἔχοντες, βιαίως τε ἐπιρράξαντες, εὐθὺς ἐπὶ προτερήματος ἦσαν· οἱ δὲ τοῦ στρατηγοῦ ἐτράπησαν πρὸς φυγήν. Τοῦ δὲ βασιλέως τῶν ἀποστατῶν κήρυγμα ποιησαμένου μηδένα κτείνειν τῶν τὰ ὅπλα ῥιπτούντων, οἱ πλεῖστοι ῥιπτοῦντες ἔφευγον. Καὶ τούτῳ τῷ τρόπῳ καταστρατηγήσας τοὺς πολεμίους ὁ Σαλούιος τήν τε παρεμβολὴν ἀνεκτήσατο καὶ πορίβήητον νίκην ἀπενεγκάμενος, πολλῶν ὅπλων ἐκυρίευσεν, Ἀπέθανον δὲ ἐν τῇ μάχῃ τῶν Ἰταλιωτῶν τε καὶ Σικελῶν οὐ πλείους ἐξακοσίων διὰ τὴν τοῦ κηρύγματος φιλανθρωπίαν, ἑάλωσαν δὲ περὶ τετρακισχιλίους."

erty, which indeed all those poor creatures were fighting for without really knowing how, inspired them to such valiant resistance against their fellow slaves outside, that for a long time no progress was made by Salvius in getting possession of the city and Dr. Siefert is in doubt whether he accomplished it at all.[26] But this doubt proceeds from a misunderstanding of the historical fragment of Diodorus, from the point of view of the actual genius of this theme. Diodorus who so long has been misunderstood, knew perfectly well what he was saying when he told us that Salvius when his army had grown to be 30,000 strong sacrificed, after the conquest of Morgantion, to the twin heroes—the very immortals who had protected him a short time before, at a short distance from there, in the Asylum of the poor and unprotected slaves. At their forest asylum, amid the roar of waters and the fumes of sulphur and gloom and loneliness, these twin sons of Jupiter and Thalia had entertained and protected them with the ægis of divinity and it was now in order, at the moment of conquest and victory to sacrifice to them in purple and splendors, in repayment.[27]

Another reason why the Roman prætor lost Morgantion is that he had been treacherous to the slaves under his command, promising them, as we have stated, that if they fought bravely against their fellows outside, they should have their freedom. This they did valiantly but the perfidious governor again lied them out of this much longed for and expected boon. Whereupon accepting the offer of Salvius to spare all who would throw down their arms, they joined their fellow rebels.[28] Thus again the Romans were forced to open their eyes and behold Sicily,

---

[26] Siefert, *Sicilische Sklavenkriege*, S. 27. "Morgantion aber zu nehmen gelang ihm vorerst doch nicht." "Ob in Folge dessen die Stadt fiel, ist aus der erhaltenen Berichten nicht mit zuverlässigkeit ersichtlich."
[27] Diod. XXXVI. vii. 1. Παλικοι." The exact words which seem to have been misunderstood, are; "Ὁ δὲ τὴν Μοργαντίνην πολιορκήσας Σαλούιος, ἐπιδραμὼν τὴν χώραν μέχρι τοῦ Λεοντίνου πεδίου, ἤθροισεν αὐτοῦ τὸ σύμπαν στράτευμα, ἐπιλέκτους ἄνδρας οὐκ ἐλάττους τῶν τρισμυρίων, καὶ θύσας τοῖς Παλικοῖς ἥρωσι, τούτοις μὲν ἀνέθηκε μίαν τῶν ἁλουργῶν περιπορφύρων στολὴν χαριστήρια τῆς νίκης, αὐτὸς δ' ἀναγορεύσας ἑαυτὸν βασιλέα, Τρύφων μὲν ὑπὸ τῶν ἀποστατῶν προσηγορεύετο." The language is unmistakable. Still Dr. Siefert thus muses: "Doch können sich diese Worte auch auf den Sieg über Licinius Nerva beziehen, und so ist es wohl, da πολιορκήσας nicht füglich für ἐκπολιορκήσας genommen werden kann." But the whole phrase reads plainly that Salvius was master of the situation
[28] Siefert, *Sicilishe Sklavenkriege*, S. 27. "Unbegreiflicher Weise versagte der Prætor diesen Versprechen die Bestätigung und trieb dadurch den grössten Theil dieser Tapferen in das Lager der Aufrührer."

their "granary of the world," south and east, in the hands of surging, pitiless slaves in the terrible attitude of rebellion.

Lilybæum and Segesta or the old Ægesta stood on the Mediterranean sea; the former at the western extremity, the latter northward in the *sinus Segestanus*, 25 miles apart. This new scene of the slave rebellion opens 150 miles or more from that of the battle grounds of Morgantion. No newspapers, no railroads, no telegraphs to convey news particulars or rumors of events. How then, in a reign of suppression and terror among maddened masters with their whips, chains, *ergastula* and crucifixion-gibbits and their optional use, could all the slaves of Sicily, even those of the farthest extreme, have known, understood, reciprocated with each other, midst these awful tumults of self-enfranchisement?

On one of those western farms of Sicily there writhed in the fetters of compulsory labor, a man named Athenion —a slave, yet born with all the proud and lofty impulses of manhood. Florus who, unlike Diodorus, spoils his histories with unkind allusions,[29] unmindful of the desperate acts he himself might have resorted to under similar treatment, speaks bitterly of him but in his words of vituperation gives us valuable facts. This man's name was Athenion. He was a Cilician by birth;[30] but having a superior bearing and faculty of command, had charge of 200 herdsmen on one of the great stock farms of that productive region of Sicily. His family and those of his men and fellow slaves were kept at work in the slave pens or *ergastula*, as distinctly stated by Florus. Athenion and his men over whom he officiated as boss or overseer, feeling that a time had come to strike the blow for liberty and, as we are obliged to surmise, posted regarding the doings of King Salvius, far to the other extremity of Sicily, determined to make a desperate trial to obtain freedom from servility and degradation.[31] He imparted his plan to a

---

[29] *Epitom* III. 19. "Athenio pastor, interfecto domino, familiam ergastulo liberatam sub signis ordinat. Ipse veste purpurea, argenteoque baculo et regium in morem fronte redimita, non minorem, quam ille fanaticus prior, conflat exercitum; acriusque multo, quasi et illum vindicaret, vicos, castella, oppida diripiens, in dominos, in servos infestius, quasi in transfugas sæviebat."

[30] "Athenio Cilex." See Dind. paraphrase of Diod. XXXVI. v. 1. Cilicia was on the borders of Syria in Asia Minor but a few miles from Palestine. He hailed from near the stage of the greater movement 100 years later.

[31] Diod. XXXVI. v. 1-4.

few of his men. The result was that at an appointed time the 200 slaves attacked their owners—two millionaire brothers—killed them, ran and cut the fetters from their families in the slave-prison, set them free, everywhere sounding the bugles of rebellion, and set about arming and drilling the men who came running into the quarters from all directions, begging for enrollment. In five days there were more than a thou-and slaves under arms, with Athenion as leader.

Athenion was another man of wonders, and he now began to assume the unnatural powers of Messiah, king, fortuneteller, star-gazer and prophet. The result of such manœuvres of course, was to confirm the ignorant slaves at his command, in the belief that he was initiated into the favors of the gods. They elected him king of the rebel government. Apparently aware of the methods of Eunus and of Salvius; and judging in his own way the errors of their plans, Athenion blocked out a plan of his own, unique and farsighted. He refused to except all the slaves who came flocking into his army, mad with the delirium of revenge, desperate in risks, and eager for war to the knife. He examined them and accepted only those whom he judged most powerful, obedient and fearless. All the rest he sent back to their old employment with orders to cultivate the land and multiply the stock and other land products,[32] lest there come a famine which would be more destructive to the army than an enemy from Rome. He set himself up as a star-gazer and proclaimed to his men that he read in the stars how he was to be the king over all the Sicilians. Under these auspices the army had swollen to 10,000 men. We are distinctly informed that he was vain enough to strut about considerably, with fine purple and sporting a silver cane;[33] but the kind-hearted reader, in view of the shrewd policy of this conduct, may see fit to forgive a poor branded slave, whose only clothes probably had hitherto been his naked skin.[34]

The first campaign of Athenion was against the forti-

[32] Many of these farms however were now entirely in their own hands, the owners having been killed.
[33] Flor., *Epitom.* III. 19. "Ipse vesta pupurea, argenteoque baculo"
[34] Diod. XXXIV. frag. ii. 38, tells the story of the slaves of Sicily branded to the bone, whipped because they dared ask for a few rags to protect them from winter.

fied city of Lilybæum which he attacked with his 10,000 men. The siege continued for some time without success; and he concluded, with much wisdom, Dr. Siefert says,[35] to raise the siege, saying that the gods were so unfavorable to the taking of Lilybæum that a disaster was about as certain as a victory. The wisdom of thus desisting from this attempt to carry the city by siege, Dr. Siefert does not state. Still it is self-evident, resting upon Athenion's probable information of the arrival from Mauritania of a large detachment of men which king Bocchus, a dependent of Rome, had dispatched to the rescue of Lilybæum. Even as it was, the shrewd slave-king with all his efforts to vacate did not succeed without his being attacked on the night of their landing, by the Moors and suffering considerably. Athenion who seems to have depended upon his gifts of imbibing counsel from supernatural sources,[36] did not expect so much from the fortified cities as did Eunus and Cleon, whose terrible starvation when hemmed in and besieged by the Romans at Morgantion and Enna, was still fresh in the memory of many. Here he seems to have been wise. He afterwards found that those fortresses if left to themselves, conquered themselves, as it were, by strifes and turmoils of the citizens with their slaves who were plotting to get away and join the insurgents under arms. In consequence, the rebels had no fear of the cities joining the Roman forces; since they had all they could attend to, keeping mischief in quell at home. The whole country, however, was soon in possession of the strikers.

A new source of the insurgents' strength now devel-

[35] Siefert, *Sicilische Sklavenkriege*, S. 27-28: "Der Sterndeuterei kundig, hatte er in den Sternen gelesen dass er König über ganz Sicilien sein werde; deshalb suchte er den geordneten Zustand auf der Insel, die er schon als sein Eigenthum ansah, aufrecht zu erhalten. Ein Angriff auf das feste Lilybaeon, den er mit zehntausend Mann unternahm gelang zwar nicht, diente aber doch dazu, den Glauben an seine Sehergabe zu bestärken. Als er nämlich mit grosser Klugheit die Belagerung aufzuheben beschloss, unter dem Vorgeb n, den Göttern ge alle diese Unternehmung nicht und man könne eine Niederlage nur durch raschen Abzug vermeiden, trat schon das Verkündete ein. Ein Korps maurischer Hülfstruppen, welches der neue Bundesgenosse der Römer, König Bocchus von Mauretanien, unter Anführung des Gomon den bedrängten Lily betanern zugesendet hatte, machte sofort nach seiner Landung einen nächtlichen Angriff und fugte den schon im Abmarsch begriffenen Truppen des Athenion nicht unb deutenden Schaden zu."

[36] Cf. Bucher. *Aufsände der Unfreinen Arbeiter*, S. 78. "Man darf sich die Schwierigkeiten, welche den Führer einer Sklavenbewegung erwarteten, ja nicht als gering vorstellen."

oped itself. The poor free people, whose condition was oftentimes worse than that of the slaves themselves, came in great numbers and joined the phalanx of the slaves.[37] They were ground to powder between the masters and the slaves. Not unfrequently their miserable condition was such that they resorted to violence of themselves; and many being organized in unions as we have shown, they were a source of turmoil.[38] Thus these combined sources of power made up a large army which Dr. Siefert, shrewdly catching a most important statement of Florus and carefully paraphrasing the torn fragments of Diodorus and Dion Cassius, sets aside the contradictory statement of Cicero, thus resuscitating and making tangible what must clearly have been two terrible battles involving the acknowledged overthrow of two Roman prætors, one after the other.[39]

[37] Diod. XXXVI frag. vi. Dind. There is materital extant sufficient for an interesting and instructive essay on the ancient tramps of Sicily and other countries. So interesting is this account of the ancient tramps that we present Dindorf's paraphrase of Diodorus in full on the tramp question: "Ingens vero tum rerum confusio, et malorum quod dicitur, Ilias Siciliam universam occuparat. Non enim servi tantum, sed etiam ex liberis egestate afflicti omne rapinarum et flagitiorum genus committebant, et quicunque offerrentur, servi aut ingenui, ne quis perditam illorum malitiam enuntiaret omnes impudenter trucidabant. Ideo quotquot in urbibus se continebant, vix illa quæ intra pomeria essent, pro suis habebant: quæ vero extra, aliena exlegique violentiæ mancipata judicabant. Multa insuper alia a multis contra normam æquitatis et humanitatis per Siciliam audacter peragebantur." But this historian does not stop here. The tramps who were freedmen who, on account of the newly imported cheap labor of the slaves, were suffering from want of means, unable longer to find employment, had grown desperate to the last degree, and tearfully dangerous. Fragment xi. continues the description of those terrible days and desperate men as follows: "Non enim servi dumtaxat rebelles Siciliam vastabant, sed etiam ingenui, quotquot nec prædia uec agros possidebant, ad latrocinia et rapinas conversi, catervatim per regionem discursabant, et, paupertate simul et mala mente impulsi, armenta et pe ora abigebant, fruges in villis conditas diripiebant, et obvium quemque nullo discrimine, servum an ingenum, obtruncabant ne quis esset qui eorum furorem ac facinora indicaret. Quumque in Sicilia justitum esset, eo quod nullus prætor populi Romani jus dicebat, cuncti liberrimam licentiam nacti impune debaccabantur: proinde nullus non locus infamis erat rapinis ac latrociniis ac vi perditorum hominum in ditissimi cujusque fortunas secure invadentium. At ii, qui p ullo ante fama atque opibus clarissimi inter cives suos fuerant, tunc fortuna subito commutata non modo a fugitivis per summam contumeliam compilabantur, ed prætera injurias et insolentias hominum ingenuorum perferre cogebantur. Quocirca universi vix illa, quæ intra pomœrium erant, pro suis habebant: quæcunque vero extra urbium muros erant posita, ea aliena et prædonum violentiæ obnoxia existimabant Denique per singulas urbes atque oppida ingens confusio ac perturbatio juris judiciorumque erat. Nam perduelles, quum agrum omnem agminibus suis occuparent infensi dominis satqua inexplebili cupiditate flagrantes, itinera omnia intercludebant. Qui vero in urbibus supererant adhuc servi, ægri ac defectionem animis spirantes, terrori dominis erant."

[38] Siefert, idem, S. 28: "Diese besitzlosen Freien übten oft nach ärgere Gewaltthaten aus als die Sklaven. Es herschte eine masslose Verwirrung und Gesetzlosigkeit eine Κακων Ιλιας, wie Diodor sagt." See Diod. XXXVI. frag vi. init.; also our note 37 above.

[39] Cicero, Verres, II. 54, gives it as follows: "Athenionem qui nullum oppidum cepit." Of course: for he had determined wisely from the start, not to molest the towns Siefert however, idem, S. 36, remarks in note 76: "Bei

The truth as to the lost histories of this bloody war is made up by a short but clear statement in Florus' Epitome of Roman history, and for perfect fairness we propose to use the old *recensio* and notes of Fischer and Duker. Florus, being an aristocrat of an exalted *gens* family, either of the proud Julian or of the Annæan stock, enjoying the family prestige of the Cæsars, whose instincts, true to the genius of the Pagan world could muster no sympathy and hardly a contemptuous pity for so mean and degraded a creature as a slave, would surely not have confessed, in writing his epigrammatical story of Athenion, to more than the truth. His sense of humiliation as he confesses the terrible flagellations which his country received during the servile wars, comes repeatedly to the surface in his pages, betraying the feelings of moral nausea; and he confesses no more humiliations of his family and race than truth compels. Yet Florus distinctly tells us that Athenion utterly destroyed two Roman prætors, or at least their armies and camps.[40] This is perfectly consistent with the general contour of the story. A Roman leader possibly Lucullus, who afterwards fought Salvius, with a probable force of Moors under some commander sent out by King Bocchus, had arrived in time to save Lilybæum from the assault of Athenion. When their fleet unexpectedly appeared, Athenion retired at night but was attacked and somewhat damaged before making good his escape. The rebel commander now prepared himself for a general engagement with the allied armies of Lucullus and Bocchus.

It is, therefore, not until after the battle of Triocala that we can apply the statement of Florus regarding Athenion:

Cicero ist der Zweck der Erwähnung wohl ins Auge zu fassen." See *Supra*.
[40] Florus, *Epit. Rerum Romanarum*, lib III. cap. 19, §. 11. "Athenio pastor ..... sæviebat. Ab hoc, quoque Prætorii exercitus cæsi, capta Servilii castra, capta Luculli" (castra). In note h. Fischer explains as follows: "*Servilii Castra, Capta Luculii.* Alios Annales habuit Florus; nam ex nostris, C. Servilii et C. Licinii Luculli castra non modo non capta fuisse, contra vero, et a Lucullo victore semel, et a servillo tantum non repressos fuisse servos manifestum est." This is as we surmised Florus had at his command at the time he wrote, works of history which at present do not exist at all as here suggested by Fischer. By the defeats of Athenion are only meant those occurring at Triocala and the previous repulse though not a defeat which he had suffered on his withdrawal from Lilybæum. We now turn to the Duker comments §. 11. p. 919 Delphine classics and this : "Ab hoc quoque Diodorus, lib. XXXVi. tribuit hæc Salvio cuidam, cui Athenio, velut imperator rigi, audiens fuerit." True, Diodorus says Salvius was victorious over a prætor but it was on the extreme east coast and the prætor was neither Ser Cius nor Luculius but the propraetor, P. Licinius Nerva. Nothing is safer than to follow Siefert. q. v. Seite 59.

"This man putting on raiment of purple, sporting a silver cane, his forehead coronated in the manner of kings, not less fanatical than the fellow Eunus before him, inflamed his army and melted together their sympathies so that they were even far more bitter; and then, as if to vindicate this predecessor's actions, raved over towns, castles, villages, tearing them to pieces, inciting the slaves against their masters and causing them to turn traitors and join his hordes. Thus he met and captured the camps of Servilius and likewise those of Lucullus." These are the plain words of Florus, who though whimsically proud, was honest. Accepting them we proceed; for he framed this statement from historical sources now not extant.

We now return to the movements of Salvius, the slave-king of Sicily, whom we left after the battle before Morgantion, in possession of the whole country, having beaten the propraetor, Licinius Nerva, and consummated a great sacrificial solemnity to the honor of the twins of Jupiter in whose asylum they had from the first been protected. This worthy flute-player, Messiah and prophet, had in the meantime not been idle. The army of picked men was now augmented to a force of 30,000, and by direction of Salvius, concentrated into one solid army-corps. The union of these men was effected at or in the vicinity of Leontini, in the fruitful valley of one of the many beautiful rivers which fall into the Mediterranean from the mountains. Here on the occasion of another ovation in thanks and honor to the *Palikoi* or twins, for propitiating the victories, the slave-king assumed the robes of royalty and the more resounding name of Tryphon;[41] ordering that henceforth he should be known by that name. The next thing was to select a situation whereat to establish himself. With this intention he now resumed his march back to the spot where the first decisive battle had been won.

Salvius, alias Triphon, appeared at the stronghold of Triocala on the upper waters of the Alaba river where were combined sweet waters, fruit, wine, oil and all the profusion of vegetable and animal plentitude. Here was improvised for him a palace. Athenion, the rival slave-

---

[41] Büch. *Aufst* S. 78, says his real name was Diodotus Tryphon and cites Wesseling.

king was summoned to appear, and brought with him 3,000 men, leaving 7,000 or more in the field, under proper leaders. Siefert thinks the object of Tryphon in sending for Athenion was to put him in chains through impulses of jealousy.[42] At any rate, Athenion was arrested and for this treachery Tryphon afterwards paid with bitterness; for retribution was at hand. Nevertheless, the fortifications which had been designed went on to completion. The place was surrounded by a wall and dykes 5,000 feet in length and became a large market place. Triphon chose for himself a council and lictors in the manner of the Romans. These strode about on guard with their bundles of whips and their hatchets in hand, attired in jewels and purple.[43] While this was going on Athenion, the bravest and wisest of the two slave-kings, lay in chains, waiting for his opportunity. It came.

The year B. C. 103 witnessed in Rome the fitting out of the propraetor L. Licinius Lucullus who with an army of Romans and Italians 14,000 strong arrived in Sicily. On landing the force was augmented by 800 Bithynians, Thessalians and Acarnanians, 600 Lucanians led by the bold Cleptius and 600 others of different extraction. This formed a total of 16,000 men. But it must by no means be reasoned from this statement that there was no considerable army of the defeated and scattered ranks of Nerva and the Moors, to be collected by Lucullus wherewith largely to augment his army in Sicily itself. Undoubtedly the combined army of Lucullus when in readiness for the great battle which we are going to recount, numbered 25,000, many of whom were experienced veterans. With this large army, many of whom were Romans, the governor boldly marched across to within a mile and a half from Triocala which he intended to besiege and take by storm. Like Rupillius before, he was provided with thongs and gibbet-makers, to crucify the slaves who should fall into his hands

[42] Siefert, *Sicilische Sklavenkriege*, S. 29 "Welche Grunde ihn hierzu bewogen hatten, ist nicht klar; sicher jedoch, dass Triphon in ihm einen heimlichen Nebenbuhler sah den er sobald sich eine günstige Gelegenheit bot, verhaften und in Gewahrsam bringen leiss."

[43] Diod. *idem*, vii. 4; Ἐξελέξατο δὲ καὶ τῶν φρονήσει διαφερόντων ἀνδρῶν τοὺς ἱκανούς, οὓς ἀποδείξας συμβούλους ἐχρῆτο συνέδροις αὐτοῖς· τήβενναν τε περιπόρφυρον περιεβάλλετο καὶ πλατύσημον ἔδυ χιτῶνα κατὰ τοὺς χρηματισμούς, καὶ ῥαβδούχους εἶχε μετὰ πελέκεων τοὺς προηγουμένους, καὶ τἆλλα πάντα ὅσα ποιοῦσί τε καὶ ἐπικοσμοῦσιν ἐπετήδευε βασιλείαν.

BATTLE OF SCIRTHÆA.

But Tryphon whom we left in a fit of narrow jealousy putting Athenion, the best of the rebel generals, in chains and behind bars, hearing through scouts of the near approach of a great army of Romans and their allies, made haste to consult this rival king and ascertain his views. Athenion advised him not to risk a siege but to confront the Roman in the open field and offer battle.

Tryphon who well knew the judgment of Athenion as a commander and the great influences he possessed over his troops, of whom he had in his own right fully 10,000, acquiesced; and the combined armies of the two kings, in all 40,000 men, marched northward to a place called Scirthæa" and there pitched in line of battle. Opposite at a distance of a mile and a half lay the Roman legions. The offer of battle seems mutually to have been accepted; but which of the two antagonists gave the onset cannot be clearly ascertained. Here stood on the one hand, a great army of 40,000 desperate slaves, flushed with half a dozen victories, burning with the memory of their previous sufferings and anxious for revenge. Their commanders had a sufficient taste of the luxuries of freedom to make them desperate and they were not wanting in the certain knowledge of the terrible fate which awaited defeat. To them and their braves alike, this murderous conflict meant liberty and continued luxury, or else death in the battle-field or upon the ignominious cross. On the side of the Romans, every man knew that defeat by a base legion of runaway slaves was of itself a scandal which reflected alike upon the general and the soldier. The proud senate made it dangerous for him who could not return to the capital with the blood and, as it were, the scalp of the last slave who had dared to defy its arrogant and overbearing prowess. Besides this, there yet remain untold the incentives for the prætors to enrich themselves by plunder—a boon which defeat would deprive them of.

With these contrasting urgents, involving hopes and plans which were to furnish the foundations of history of progress or retrogression for the human race, the two great armies fell into mortal grapple. After a certain amount of sparring and skirmish between the outskirts,

⁴⁴ Dird. XXXVI. *frag.* viii. 2, 3, 4 and 5. Paragraphs 3 and 4 contain the description of the battle as we give it. q. v.

the main body of each army closed in with an unwavering clash of arms under which the combatants fell in thousands.⁴⁵ Amid the battle, while the terrible plunges of maddened men with thrusts and din were at their height of fury, Athenion, mounted on a prancing steed, rushed, at the head of a detachment of his cavalry 200 strong, with a certain frenzy which sometimes characterizes life energies when wrought to a tension of reckless excitement. He lunged into the enemy's center, striking down everything before him. No doubt this was a rash action, however magnificent it may seem to the critic of military exploits ; for although he made his hated foe tremble with the shock, he received three blows so stunning, though not fatal, that his fellow-slaves on seeing him fall, feeling that in him as in a god, resides alone the genius of victory, fell into a panic. When the soldiers of Athenion shrank back the cry of victory must have been raised by the Romans ; for Diodorus tells us that half the slaves, in number 20,000, were either killed or taken prisoners, but that the remaining 20,000 fled back to their defences at Triokala under command of Tryphon who survived. Siefert's suggestion that the rebels lost courage scarcely appears well founded.⁴⁶ We not only find the slaves again in possessing of their fortress of Triocala with Tryphon, but we are told that the rebels kept it; and we are without assurances that they were either captured or driven away. Nor was the gallant Athenion lost to them; for after the catastrophe which may have closed with the sunset, on this great and bloody battle, this hero, taking shelter from harm under cover of night, arose and so far returned to reason and strength that he crawled safely back to the fortress of Triocala with the rest. Thus, considering the severe punishment suffered by the Romans, the fact that they did not pursue, that it was nine days before they arrived before the fortifications of Tryphon and Athenion, and ventured, battered and shattered up to the

⁴⁵ Nach einigem Geplänkel kam es zum geordneten Angriff, dessen Erfolg lange herüber und hinüber schwankte." Diodorus, XXXVI, frag. 8 3, says, "Τὸ μὲν οὖν πρῶτον ἐγίνοντο συνεχεῖς ἀκροβολισμοί. etc." This skirmishing with light armed troops introduced the general battle.
⁴⁶ Siefert, *Italisch. Sklavenkriege*, S. 29: "Da unternahm Athenion mit zweihundert auserwählten Reitern einen Angriff, durch den er Alles vor sich niederwarf. Unglücklicherweise aber wurde er mitten in diesem Erfolge durch drei Wunden kampfuntählig gemacht worauf die Sklaven, muthlos gemacht, flohen," Diod. XXXVI. frag. viii. 4, who informs us that Athenion when struck down 'eigned death until night, when he escaped.

BATTLE OF TRIOCALA.

gates of the rebel fortress, in fine, that they failed altogether of taking the place and experienced thereafter nothing but defeat, is strong circumstantial evidence that Scirthæa was a drawn battle on both sides.

Nine days after the Battle of Scirthæa the army of Lucullus appeared in front of the town of Triocala. How many men his army now mustered or how many of the former officers like Cleptius still adorned his ranks, is not definitely given. But they had within the nine days so far recovered from the severe punishment they had received, as to be at least endowed with the boldness to altogether underrate the strength and spirit of their adversary.[47]

Meanwhile Athenion was rapidly recovering from his injuries received at the battle of Scirthæa and was, as we are led to understand by the evidence left us, so far restored that he appeared with all his former valor and vigor. Dr. Siefert who talks about the lost courage of the working men,[48] naturally enough catching the idea from Florus, says that they now mustered courage to attack the Romans.[49] Our opinion is, reasoning from appearances which confirm the valiant fighting force, such as must appear to every candid, unbiased reasoner, shows the rebels to have crippled the Romans at the great battle of Scirthæa 9 days before; and that they did not lose courage, but doggedly held their own throughout. Certain it is that another obstinate battle was fought before the fortifications of Triocala. The Romans made the first attack but were received apparently in open field by the rebels. A conflict followed in which the entire strength of both armies was brought to bear. The loss on both sides was very serious. But in this second scene of blood the victory was with the workingmen. Lucullus was completely driven from the field, his camps taken by storm[50] and his army so scattered from place to place that he seems never to have recovered, but fell to plundering like the slaves and freedmen themselves, appropriating

---

[47] Diod. *frag.* viii. 5.
[48] We can no longer say slaves. A large proportion of the rebel army was now composed of freedmen, mechanics, laborers, etc.
[49] Siefert, *Sicilische Sklavenkriege*, S. 29. "Als Lucullus endlich 9 Tage nach der Schlacht zur Belagerung der Veste schritt, war der ershütterte Muth schon wieder belestigt."
[50] Florus, lib. III. cap. XIX. "Lucullo capta castra—vicos, oppida, castella diripiens," referring to Athenion. Siefert, S. 29, speaking of Lucullus, says; "ja sein Lager soll sogar von den Sklaven erstürmt worden sein." See note 76 where Siefert refers to Cic. *Verr.* II. 5%; "Athenionem qui nullum opidum epi" remarks: " Pei Cicero is der Zweck ins Auge zu fassen."

the funds entrusted to him, to his own use and with defeat, avarice and demoralization was rendered *hors de combat* altogether.

What had in the mean time been going on between the two rival slave-kings, Tryphon and Athenion, no one can tell. We only know that the former, after the battle of Triocala had died [51] and that Athenion had been elected king over all the rebels, including slaves and freedmen. Perhaps a dark deed of revenge or of jealousy may have been committed; more humanely let us foster the conjecture that Tryphon had lost his life in some valorous charge which secured the victory to the slaves, in the desperate battle we have just recounted.

The year B. C. 102 had thus rolled by and not only was another large prætorean army of the Romans annihilated but the rebels with Athenion, their veteran general at their head, were complete masters of Sicily.

Rome under this extraordinary condition of things, sent C. Servilius, B. C. 102, with another prætorian army under orders from the senate to leave no means untried whereby to stamp out the rebellion. This Roman commander and prætor must have landed his army at Massana on the so-called *Etruscum fretum*, now the Straits of Messina; and judging from appearances the first battle may not have occurred at a long distance from there. It is not certain but that the Romans marched in a southwesterly direction for many miles into the interior before the two armies met. We only know that the combatants sought and found each other and that there was another encounter; of course, one of those fierce and internecine struggles in which great numbers of brave men are occasionally mowed down, but whose numbers, memory and place are, for shame, pitched into the dark grottoes of oblivion. Florus shuffles the fact over to posterity with language provokingly crisp and indicative of mortification and distaste;[52] Cicero denies;[53] Dion Cassius[54] is in tatters at the Vatican; Diodorus lies

---

[51] Diod. XXXVI. 1. " Τελευτήσαντος δὲ Τρύφωνος, διάδοχος τῆς ἀρχῆς δ 'Αθηνίων καθίσταται, καὶ τοῦτο μὲν πόλεις ἐπολιόρκει," etc.
[52] Flor. *Epitom. Populi Romani.* III. 19. "Athenio -vicos, oppida, castella diripiens"
[53] Cic. *Verres*, II. 54. "Athenion qui nullum oppidum cepit." This however, we think innocently refers to the fact that Athenion's policy was from the first, not to take the fortified towns; since Eunus and Cleon in taking this course had lost their cause.

contorted into the tell-tale mutterings of his fragments;[54] Livy leaves only the paltry exordium of his epitomies.[65] But enough of these is still extant, together with the circumstantial evidence such as the disgrace by the Roman Senate, of the defeated prætors and their exile for life, and continued ravages of the war for years; all these verified facts prove the words of Florus, to the effect that Servilius and Athenion met in some undescribed and mortal fray; that the proud slave-king won a complete victory; and that labor from its points of irascibility and vengeance was once more vindicated. Such is not only our own rendering of the real meaning of the vague words left us but they are as conscientiously read by others.[56]

After this important and probably great battle which was the fifth in number since the outbreak of the war and which from our authority we may call the battle of Florus, the Roman general, either disheartened or prone to enrich himself like his predecessors, with plunder and malfeasance, or still more probably, being utterly annihilated, left the strikers with Athenion at their head, complete masters of the field. They ravaged and laid waste the country on every side, destroying castles, towns and cities. Athenion next turned his wrath toward Messana. Reaching it by forced marches, he stealthily at night surprised the inhabitants of that city as they were engaged in its outskirts celebrating the sacrifices to their gods, and cut them to pieces, taking quantities of plunder which he made off with. But he steered shy of the city itself, keeping apparently in mind the danger of being hemmed in, and the dreadful results which, in the previous rebellion under Eunus, had caused the great catastrophe.

Athenion after marching through the northeastern portions of Sicily[57] gathering wealth by plunder, struck a westerly tack and the next we hear from him, is at the ancient walled

[54] Dion Cassius, *excerpt*, 101. Peiresc; Diod. XXXVI. ix. 1 and 2.
[55] Livy, *Epitome*, LXIX. *fin*. "M. Aquillius proconsul excitatum confecit."
[56] Siefert, *Italische Sklavenkriege*, S. 30. "Athenion, der nach dem inzwischen erfolgten Tode des Tryphon, König der Sklaven geworden war, trat ihm (Servilius) mit grosser Kühnheit entgegen und schlug ihn aus dem Felde; nachdem auch das Lager des Servilius einmal genommen war, wagte dieser sich nicht mehr zum Kampfe hervor, und Athenion konnte ungehindert das land durchstreifen, kastelle und kleinere Städte einnehmen."
[57] Much obscurity enshrouds both the history and topography of this place Livy, lib. XXVI. 21, speaks of the place as being obscure. "Secutæ defectionem earum Hybla et Macella sunt ignobilioresque quædam aliæ." This mention refers to B. C.

town of Macella supplied with a castle or citadel. It is situated southeastward of Segesta and not more than 40 miles to the eastward of Lilybæum. Here he established and fortified himself, B. C. 101, the third year of the war; supplying his army with the products of the fruitful country around him.[58]

During this time C. Marius and M. Aquillius had been elected consuls at Rome, and it was resolved to send a full consular army to Sicily and thus put an end to the war at once. Accordingly Aquillius, during the year 101, arrived in the island with a consular army consisting of a large force of veteran Romans and other soldiers. The terrible handling which the people of Sicily who had remained hostile to Athenion, had received, made them eager to grasp this new offer of succor; and it cannot be doubted that large numbers of the defeated fragments of the armies of Lucullus and Servilius were mustered in, swelling the consular army to a host. Aquillius proved, for the first time, a match for the redoubtable strikers.

Whether the Romans landed at Messana or at the port of Ægesta in the vicinity of Macella where the army of Athenion lay, is not easy to determine. The distance from the Ostia or port of Rome by water, direct to Ægesta, or to Messana is by fifty miles in favor of a landing at Ægesta; and to have gone by way of Messana would have cost the consul a march of 150 miles from there to Macella, on the head waters of the Scamander, over a country already laid waste by the army of his foe. We cannot but assume that these two desperate generals met at, or near Macella; for Diodorus tells us that Athenion, true to his old resolution never to let the Romans hem him into a walled town, marched out in full force to meet him.[59]

A great battle was fought. When the two chiefs espied each other, they rushed together in mortal duel.[60] Athenion,

[58] Ptolemy the ancient geographer mentions it as being in the interior of the island. See *Universal Geography*, III. 4, 14. Whereas Polybius, I. 24: κατά τε τὴν ἐκ τῆς Αἰγέστης ἀναχώρησιν Μάκελλαν πόλιν κατά κράτος εἷλον. This puts the place far to the west near Athenion's possible birthplace; Dion Cassius, *Exc.* 104: Χωρίον δέ τι Μάκελλαν εὐερκὲς τειχισάμενος, etc. Siefert imagines this to refer to the town in the neighborhood of Messana. Polybius is however right; in proof of which we refer the critic to Arrowsmith's *Orbis Terrarum Veterum Descriptio*. Lond. 1822.

[59] "Athenion stellte sich dem Aquillius in offener Feldschlacht entgegen." Siefert, S. 30. Florus, III. 19, but he may have referred to the successful sieges by Aquillius of the fugitives after their defeat.

[60] Dion Cassius, frag. 104.

almost exactly like Spartacus at his last and great battle of Silarus, struck out for his illustrious antagonist, determined with his own hand, to wreak vengeance and thus cross out accounts with Rome's highest and proudest source of power. The men were equally brave and gifted in the sabre's use. How long the duel lasted is not told; but we are distinctly informed that this time it was the slave-king's turn to receive the mortal thrust.[61] Aquillius was a tiger in combat and though he received heavy blows on the head and in his breast he was the fortunate of the two combatants.[62] Athenion, pierced and dying, fell bleeding at the consul's feet.

Again, as at the battle of Scirthæa, the warriors of Athenion lost courage at the fall of their beloved leader, who this time was finished and never rose to their rescue as before. All but a fragment of 20,000 workingmen were killed or taken prisoners. These fled to the mountains close at hand, but were followed by Aquillius with so much energy that in two years time they were nearly exterminated.

Manius Aquillius afterwards wrote at Capua an inscription which is still extant and quoted in the archæological collection of Orelli, to the effect that when he was prætor in Sicily he had busied himself hunting down runaway slaves and had returned to their masters as many as 917 of them.[63] This very interesting inscription sheds a flame of corroboratory light upon that immense uprising and substantiates the history of the affair, as we have extracted it from the fragments. It also adds to history the statement that the Sicilian slaves had reinforcements from Italy.[64]

The awful scenes of crucifixion [65] as in the case of the re-

---

[61] Diod., XXXVI. x. 1, which corresponds with Siefert. S. 30, "Athenion stellte sich dem Aquillius in offener Feldschlacht entgegen, fiel aber in derselben durch die Hand des Consuls, der selbst an Kopf und Brust verwundet wurde."

[62] Diod. XXXVI. x. 1. Καὶ πρὸς αὐτὸν δὲ τὸν βασιλέα τῶν ἀποστατῶν Ἀθηνίωνα συμβαλών, ἡρωικὸν ἀγῶνα συνετήσατο. Καὶ ταῦτον μὲν ἀνεῖλεν, αὐτὸς δ' εἰς τὴν κεφαλὴν τρωθεὶς ἐθεραπεύθη.

[63] Orellius, *Inscriptionum Latinarum Collectio*, No. 3, 308. "Eidem prætor in Sicilia fugivos Italicorum conquæisivei redideique dominis DCCCCXVII."

[64] Shortly after this war another broke out in Italy which lasted some time; but although it was of so much importance that several of the historians wrote valuable descriptions of it in their books, the vandals succeeded in destroying the pages and we have only some fragments left in an almost illegible form. We have however, in chapter viii. succeeded in picking out many of the prominent events of the Italian slave and freedmen or tramp war of this era, q. v.

[65] The evidences for this are indeed vague except by inference. Florus, III. 19, says *Supplicium*," which with him and Livy always implies the worst. But that almost every one of the captured rebels was crucified, must, by implication be accepted even almost without evidence, other than the well-known, implacable, inexorable Roman Law, which hung such malefactors of the servile race upon the ignominious cross.

bellion 30 years before, were now rehearsed and many a captured slave perished on the cross.

But there still remained at least one strong man named Satyros who, with the other bold lieutenants of Athenion, fell to marauding and in spite of the efforts of the proconsul prolonged the struggle[66] for two years. Satyros and his men were however, in B. C. 99, all captured and taken to Rome, under the promise solemnly conferred by the Roman general, that as a condition of capitulation they should be exempt from punishment and treated with honor as prisoners of war. The perfidious wretch had no sooner gotten the prisoners in safety to Rome, than he offered them to the aristocracy as the basis of a great triumph or ovation which he claimed, as an honor to the hero who had suppressed the rebellion. The poor creatures were dragged into the arena on a given day, and told that instead of liberty, their horrible doom was to amuse the ladies of Rome and others, who for love of show frequented the amphitheatre to view the bloody contests of gladiators. Not only were they destined to this but they must fight wild beasts like slaves. The great auditorium was crowded with spectators, among whom beat true hearts for humanity and fairness. A characteristic of the great gladiatorial games always had been and still was at that time, that of democracy. All classes, rich, poor, the eminent and the lowly alike had seats; and as there was at that moment a fierce war of tactics raging between the labor organizations and the aristocracy and as a strong partisanship existed against Aquillius and every one of the prætors who had been sent out against the slaves and freedmen fighting for liberty in Sicily, it was very natural that such a party would numerously attend the great ovation, if for nothing more than to pick up points against this aristocrat whom they hated.

When the convicts arrived in chains, trembling with disappointment and broken hearts and like the wild lions, tigers and hyenas they were to fight, found themselves

---

[66] Livy, LXIX. *Epit. ad fin.* "M. Aquillius proconsul in Sicilia bellum civile excitatum confecit. Marius was one of the consuls of this year, and Diodorus tells us that Aquillius was the other. This looks doubtful. Rome was at that moment involved in the fierce agrarian agitations: Cf. *id,* "et cum legem agrariam per vim tullisset," etc. True, Livy may refer to his proconsulship as being the extension of his service in Sicily through the next two years, (B. C. 99), as the war did not close for 2 years after the battle. Again this may rectify the discrepancy in Aquillius' inscription. See note 61.

thrust loose and suddenly given knives and other weapons, they all mutually, in presence of the great throng frenzied with wine, nervously betting, many in anticipation of beholding blood spurting from their naked forms, solemnly agreed to become each others' mutual exterminators.

Satyros led the mutual fratricide. Seizing their weapons they rushed upon each other with all the fury to which they had for 5 years been wont. The audience were thrilled and astonished. The heroic fellows, one after another, fell, gashed and pierced with their own daggers; while the remaining warriors, girding their courage by the excitement and din, drove the knife deep into each others' brave hearts. All had fallen and lay gasping, the hot blood draining their bodies of both spirit and vitality. Satyros, the powerful Greek, was still upon his feet. Without faltering he drove his weapon deep into his own breast and thus triumphantly expired.

This magnificent stroke of courage recoiled badly against the perfidious Aquillius who had treacherously lied them out of their lives. The word rang out that the glory of these brave men's fall was infinitely grander than that of the wretch whose vanity was to be puffed by an ovation.[67] A reaction then and there set in against the fellow and one L. Fufius, soon afterwards brought suit against him for extortion and malfeasance which was so energetically pressed that the great orator Antonius had to be engaged to save his life. He was retained for the trial and succeeded only by seizing Aquillius, and tearing open his clothing during an impassioned gush of eloquence, and exhibiting to the people the wounds which he had actually received in the duel with Athenion at the battle before Macella.[68] But even this did not save the fellow's life; for where there lurks an enemy in public opinion there also lurks a means. Aquillius who afterwards fell a prisoner to Mithridates was taken to Pergamus and in a horrible manner was tied back down upon a stone and held there while the gold melters poured a ladle full of melted gold down his throat.[69]

[67] Viele meinten, grösser sei der Ruhm der Gefallenen als der Ruhm des überlebenden Siegers." *Sicilische Sklavenkriege*, S. 31.
[68] Livy, *Epitome* to book LXX. "Cum M. Aquillius de pecuniis repetundis cauam diceret, ipse judices rogare noluit. M. Antonius, qui pro eo perorabat, tunicam a pectore ejus discidit, ut honestas cicatrices ostenderet, indubitantur absolutus est."
[69] Pliny, *Nat. Hist.* XXXIII. 14. "Nec jam Quiritium aliquo, sed universo nomine Romano infami, rex Mithridates Aquilio duci capto, aurum in os infudit.

274   *ATHENION.*

Lucullus and Servilius, the prætors whom Athenion had defeated and driven from Sicily, as we have related, were also both accused of robbery and malfeasance in office and banished from Rome into perpetual exile."

[70] It is hardly to be wondered at that early commentators misunderstand the true principles involved in this great war, or that they misapply the true facts in the case. Both Granier and O'Brien fail to comprehend at all that there existed a socialistic cult of great but secret influence which had a powerful effect upon the minds of the men involved in all those troubles. Granier, *Histoire des Classes Ouvrières*, p. 496, characterizes them as "bandits," as follows: "Un trait fort ceractéristique, et qui fut commun à Eunus et à Athénion, c'est qu'en se révoltant ils n'eurent ni l'un ni l'autre l'idée d'abolir l'esclavage et d'établir l'égalité. A peine au milieu de leurs armées, ils se hâtèrent d'oublier qu'ils avaient le cou pelé par la chaîne, et de goûter avec délices les prérogatives de la seigneurie, D'abord, ce qui est facile à croire, les châteaux, les villages, les villes, furent mis au pillage." So Mr. James Bronterre O'Brien, an honest and kind-hearted writer who devoted his life to his fellow-men, amid persecutions, likewise misunderstands the ancients. He says (*Rise, Progress and Phases of Human Slavery*, p. 31), speaking of upholding the dignity of human nature, that in these conflicts "there was nothing of the sort. The harsh conduct of masters and the violation of workhouse rules were the motive power of each revolt." The fact is that the workhouses he mentions were, as we have shown, dungeons, often underground and intolerable hells; and those poor people were chained down in them, and in the morning marched in chains to the fields. The systematized workhouses with which these writers become confounded, were those of the later Augustan age. To get into the *ergastulum* of Sicily or Italy before the emperors, was a serious thing, and we know of no rules whatever in Sicily restricting the master's will. He could kill his slave or keep him without rule. Mr. O'Brien and M. Granier de Cassagnac are both entirely wrong in saying that there was neither premeditation nor purpose in these great revolts. They charge against Eunus and Athenion that " they began forthwith to ape the pomp and the circumstance of their oppressors." Every action of Eunus and of Athenion on the contrary, was incontestably pre-determined; and the fire-spitting prestigiation of Eunus and Satyros, as well as the purple and silver staff of Athenion, were indispensable to inspire their uncouth, superstitious soldiers with feelings of awe and reverence, necessary to order and discipline. In fact this was the key to their success.

CHAPTER XII.

SPARTACUS.

THE IRASCIBLE PLAN TESTED ON AN ENORMOUS SCALE.

RISE, VICISSITUDES and Fall of a Great General—The Strike of the Gladiators—Grievances that led to the Trouble—Growth of Slavery through Usurpation of the Land by the arrogant Optimates—What is known of Spartacus before being Sold into Slavery—Bolt of the 78 Gladiators from the *Ergastulum* of Lentulus at Capua—Escape of the Runaways—How they seized Weapons—Vesuvius—First Battle—Battle of the Cliffs —Rout of Clodius—Second Battle—Destruction of a Prætorian Army—Battle of the Mineral Baths—Great Increase of the Rebel Force—From a petty Strike it assumes the Proportions of Revolution—Fourth Battle; Hilt to Hilt with Varinius—Destruction of the Main Army of the Romans—Winter Quarters of Spartacus at Metapontem—Honor, Discipline and Temperance of the Workingmen—Proofs by Pliny and Plutarch—Coalition with the Organized Laborers of Italy— Uses of Gold and other Ornaments Forbidden--Wine Banished—Great Numbers Employed in the Armories of Spartacus—Fifth Battle—Battle of Mt. Garganus—Ambuscade of Arrius—Overthrow and Death of Crixus—Sixth Battle— Spartacus Destroys the Consular Army of Poplicola—Seventh Battle—Great Conflict of the River Po—Overthrow of Cassius and Defeat of the 10,000 Romans—Spartacus, now Master, assumes the Offensive—Eighth Battle—Lentulus Defeated; Great Army nearly annihilated—Mortification and Terror of the Romans—Ninth Battle—Mutina—Proconsul Cassius again Routed in a Disastrous Conflct with the wary Gladiator—Spartacus now obliged to contend with the Demon of Insubordination—Crassus elected Consul—Reverses Begin—On down to Rhegium—Sedition, Treachery, Betrayal —Workingmen's own Jealousies, Insubordination and Lack

SPARTACUS.

of Diplomacy cause their final Ruin—Tenth Battle—Scaling of the Six-Mile Ramparts by Spartacus—Battle of Croton—Destruction of the Seceders, Granicus and Castus—Obstinate Fighting—Spartacus arrives and checks the Carnage—Petelia, the Eleventh Battle—Victory—Twelfth Battle; Silarus—Last and most Bloody Encounter—Spartacus, stabbing his Horse, Rushes sword drawn, in search of Crassus—Heaps of the slain—Dying like a King—End of the War—The great *Supplicium*—Pompey and Crassus, emulous of meagre Honors—Inhuman Cruelties—Awful Wreaking of Vengeance on the Cross—Dangling Bodies of 6,000 Crucified Workingmen along the Appian Way—Thousands of Others crucified—Utter Failure of the Irascible Plan of Deliverance.

As physical science informs us of convulsions in nature called by geologists, the Permian age which brought the palæozoic era to an end and left, after its prodigious upheavals, the calm in which we live, so historical fragments and palæographs inform us of great social cataclysms immediately preceding the immense calm that began to envelop human society during the reign of Augustus, rooted into it by the visit and labors of Jesus. The desperate social upheaval here referred to—the last in the line—was that of the gladiators under Spartacus, B. C. 74–70.

In introducing this mighty conflict of Spartacus—the greatest and last of all the ancient struggles coming into our categories of the "irascible" against the "concupiscent," and undertaken by labor, in its plan of salvation from the horrors of slavery and suffering—we find it necessary to sketch an outline of the condition which matters were in during the century preceding the advent of Jesus, who was the next reformer in chronological order.

Of all the methods of systematic cruelty practiced upon the ancient lowly, that of the gladiatorial games excelled; and it is our duty, in order that the reader may see the whole truth laid bare, which actuated this rebellion, to quote a few specimen descriptions of that ferocious amusement, from the authors and the slabs. Athenæus, quoting the lost work of Nicolaus Damascenus, describes in unmistakable language, the horrible custom common at that time. He says it was a common thing for rich men to invite guests to dinner and after the wine and other intoxicating stimulants began to madden them, to introduce gladiators into some ring or private amphitheatre. As these poor creatures, driven by the foreman to fight, cut each others' throats, boisterous applause and laughter at the scene were indulged in. Sometimes beautiful women were thus forced to attack and butcher each other in the same manner as the men. Large sums of money were paid for these innocent victims, for no other purpose than to toy with this inhuman passion in the male and female guests, for beholding atrocities of this ghastly nature while they wallowed in inebriate and lascivious beastliness. Often small children were driven naked into the arena, given knives, and forced, for the amusement of these truculent nobles, to struggle in the awful qualms of danger and death until the little innocents, one or more, fell dying in their bath of blood.[1]

Gladiatorial games, as we have shown in our chapter, on amusements, were the real origin of wakes; and of this we possess the evidence of Valerius Maximus. Some 264 years before Christ, two brothers named Marcus and Decimus Brutus, on the death of their father, a lord of a *gens*, possessing slaves, held in his honor and at his funeral, a gladiatorial combat. There being no amphitheatre at that early date, the Forum Boarium was used, and a permit was granted by the city. Appius Claudius and M. Fulvius were the consuls.[2] One need not wonder that a license was granted to butcher workingmen by a monster like Appius Claudius. He hated them and was strug-

---

[1] Schambach, *Der Italische Sclavenaufstand*, S. 7-8, quotes in proof of this, Nicolaus Damascenus, indirectly as follows: "In dem gewaltigen Geschichtswerke des Nicolaus Damascenus wurde der Sklavenkrieg in 110, Buche gehandelt, aus dem uns bei Athen, IV, pag. 153 F. (fragm. 84 bei Müller fragm. hist. graec. III, pag. 417) ein Fragment erhalten ist, welches in der von M. gegebenen lateinischen Uebersetzung, die ich der Allgemeinverständlichkeit wegen statt des griechischen Textes hier gebe, folgendermassen lautet: Nicolaus Damascenus, Peripateticae sectae philosophus, libro historiarum decimo supra centesimum Romanos scribit inter coenandum gladiatorum paria committere solitos, his verbis: gladiatorum autem spectacula non solum in publicis conventibus et amphitheatris edunt Romani, invecto ab Etruscis more, sed etiam inter epulas. Itaque amicos ad coenam invitant interdum, tum ut alia, tum ut duo triave gladiatorum paria dimicantia iis exhibeant. Igitur postquam vino ac dapibus sese ingurgitarunt, introduci jubent gladiatores: quorum ubi quis jugulatur, universi convivae plaudunt eo spectaculo exhilarati. Quidem etiam in testamento jussit mulieres formosas, quas emerat, ferro inter se dimicare; alius item pueros impuberes, quos in deliciis habuerat. Sed populus eam atrocitatem detestatus testamentum eorum irritum esse jussit. Das Ganze macht den Eindruck, als habe es zur Motivirung des Aufstandes gedient."

[2] Valerius Maximus, *De Spectaculis*, 7; "Gladiatorium munus primum Romae datum est in foro boario. Ap. Claudio, M. Fulvio Coss. dederunt M. & D. Bruti, funebri memoria patris cineres honorando. Athletarum certamen à M Scauri factum est munificentia."

gling to suppress them and their unions even at that early time. Thyse, who arranged the Lugdunum edition of Valerius Maximus, adds that slaves were sacrificed on funeral occasions of such men.[3] The origin then is fetish and belongs to, and must, like many other inhuman rites, and practices, be charged to religion.

As an instance that gladiators were the game of priests and priestcraft not only at Rome, but even in North America among the less ancient Aztecs, we may cite Bancroft, on the Nahuas. He says, speaking of the feast of Xipe: "The next day another batch of prisoners called *oavanti*, whose top hair had been shaved, were brought out for sacrifice. In the meantime a number of young men also named *tototecti*, began a gladiatorial game, a burlesque on the real combat to follow, dressing themselves in the skins of the flayed (human) victims."

The story of these victims is told on the preceding page as follows: " Let us now proceed with the feast of Xipe. We left a part of the doomed victims on their way to death. Arrived at the summit of the temple each one is led in turn to the alter of sacrifice, seized by the grim, merciless priests, and thrown upon the stone; the highpriest draws near, the knife is lifted, there is one great cry of agony, a shuffle of feet as the assistants are swayed to and fro by the death-struggles of their victim, then all is silent save the mutterings of the high-priest as high in air he holds the smoking heart, while from far down beneath comes a low hum of admiration from the thousands of upturned faces."[4]

This picture almost exactly corresponds with the gladiatorial horrors of the time of Spartacus at Rome, Capua

[3] Thysii, *Recensio nova Lugd. Batavorum*, 1651: "Gladiatorum munus. Origo Glad atorum à re funebri. exemplum ab Hetruscis, At fortasse Hetrusci ipsi à Græcis Undecunque exemplum, causa tamen and origo funus. Nam quoniam olim animas defunctorum humano sanguine propitiari creditum erat, captivos vel alto ingenio servos mercati in exsequiis immolabant. Postea placuit impietatem voluptate adumbrare. itaque duos paraverant. armis quibus tunc et qualiter poterant eruditos, mox edicto die feriarum, apud tumulos erogabant. Hæc muneris origo. Atque Gladiatores illi à busti cineribus Bustuarii dicti. *Lipsius Gladiatorum munus*. Vulgo, gladiatorum, quod gladiatorium Livio aliisque dicitur, non enim gladiatorum munus illud erat, sed ejus qui gladiatores pugnantes populo exhibebat." pp. 170-171.

[4] Bancroft, *Native Races*, Vol. II, pp. 358-359. These horrors were extracted from the histories of Las Casas, Clavigero, Gomera and others. The Christians were far ous against the practice and broke it up for which they have been maligned. There seems indeed no doubt that in breaking it up they committed faults; but the great anti-slavery movement of Las Casas, which warred against every cruelty, freed Mexico from these two pests long ago.

and hundreds of provincial towns all over Italy. Where history fails the inscriptions come to the front with their irrepressible language, making up the gaps. These are seemingly innumerable. A peculiar character resembling the Greek *theta* expresses the violent death of the gladiator mentioned on the slab. Orelli's catalogue entitled *Res Scenica* teems with them.[5] As a rule they may be considered epitaphs; for after the dead gladiator had been dragged off the sands his body was generally given up to his friends, some of whom were organized in the numerous unions, and hence the occasional laudatory words on his character, his affection for his family, his skill in the use of weapons.

But nothing is more certain than that these poor people had a mutual or reciprocatory terror of these scenes which were almost sure to terminate only with their lives. When M. Valerius Lævinus died B. C. 200, his sons forced fifty of the old man's slaves to begore his grave with their blood. Flaminius, 25 years later, on the occasion of his father's death, caused 74 gladiators who had been hired for the service, to balm with their blood his ghost about to be deposited under the sacred hearth. The emperor Trajan once ordered a vast gladiatorial orgie lasting 123 days. Not less than 10,000 gladiators were

---

[5] Orellius, *Inscriptionum Latinarium Selectarum Collectio*, Nos. 2,551. "Poetelius, Syrus lanista ad Aram Forinarum . . . . . ubi negotiatorem familiæ gladiatoriæ habes; 2,552 is a slab on which are lettered certain data about one Cornelius Frontin; how he won liberty at the great games and liberty for his children. It was found on the Appian Way and catalogued by Mur. No. 620, 4; 2,554; 2,555 is one of which considerable mention has been made: "Inscriptiones gladiatoriæ in Opere musivo Romæ asservato apud Marini, *Atti.* 1, p. 165." It is two inscriptions in one, recording the death by the steel of both, "Astianax. vicit. Kalendio death), Astianax, Kalendio (death or killed). Quibus pugnantibus Simmachus ferrum Maternus habilis misit." So No. 2,556, remarkable inscriptions discovered at Pompeii, showing that gladiators fought with wild beasts Romenelli, *Viaggio a Pompeii.* Rome, I, p. 82. Another (No. 2,545), tells in the words of an epitaph, more than a chapter of history. A gladiator had fought eight times in these games before he fell, and so skillfully had he despatched his fellow adversaries whom the betters had pitted against him that he received floral decorations and much applause. But we have not space to mention more than a few of the extremely numerous specimens. As to the average years which gladiators lived we find these data carefully figured by Schambach from the inscriptions of Orelli as follows: " Ueber sein Alter " (meaning the age of Spartacus) "ist uns zwar von den Alten nichts berichtet; trotzdem macht dieser Punct noch nicht die grözten Schwierigkeiten. Das man zu Fechtern vorwiegend Leute in jungen oder mittleren Lebensjahren wählte, ist natürlich; die erhaltenen Sepulcralinschriften auf gefallenen Fechter bestätigen dies. Wir finden in den Inscr. lat. ed Hagenb. et Orelli folgende Todesjahre verzeichnet) 22 (nr. 2,572), 27 (nr. 2,592), 30 (nr. 2,571), 46 (nr. 2,590). und schwerlich wird das zuletzt angegebene Lebensjahr öfters überschritten sein Wir werden also nicht weit fehl gehen, wenn wir uns Spartacus als einen Mann zwischen 30 und 40 vorstellen." *Italischer Sklavenaufstand*, S. 15-16.

obliged to fight and die in the combat for the worse than beastly gratification of that degenerate humanity.

At Capua, Pompeii, Præneste, Ravenna, Alexandria in upper Etruria, even in Gaul and among the Germans, these games of gladiatorial carnage were fashionable. Commodus upheld them, Domitian extended them, and finally, and to their shame be it said, even the Christians themselves left the noble principles and precepts of their master and for the paltry baubles of adulation and of imperial favor, fell back into the ghastly heathenism of the amphitheatre.⁶ But fortunately for future civilization, this did not occur until the cult of the so-called early Christians had firmly taken root among workingmen, the terrible system's victims; and even to this day it is this element that alone is manfully fighting and resisting cruelty.

De Quincey, in his characteristic language, tells the story of Caligula who took delight in feeding the wild animals of the amphitheatres with the quivering flesh of human beings. He brings his story in, incidentally, as an instance as follows:

"On some occasion it happened that a dearth prevailed, either generally of cattle, or of such cattle as were used for feeding the wild beasts reserved for the bloody exhibitions of the amphitheatre. Food could be had and perhaps at no very exorbitant price, but on terms somewhat higher than the ordinary market price. A slight excuse served with Caligula for acts the most monstrous. Instantly repairing to the public jails and causing all the prisoners to pass in review before him *custodiarum seriem recognoscens*, he pointed to two bald-headed men, and ordered that the whole file of the intermediate persons should be marched off to the dens of the wild beasts. 'Tell them off' said he, 'from the bald man to the bald man.' Yet these were prisoners committed, not for punishment, but trial."⁷

From the earliest times of which history gives any record, brigandage or marauding was not only common but in many countries quite popular.⁸ It was the natural outcome

---

⁶ Guhl and Koner, *Life of the Greeks and Romans*, pp. 554-566.
⁷ De Quincy, *Ancient Histories and Antiquities*, pp. 88-9.
⁸ Carey, *Principles of Social Science*, Vol. I p. 189. Rent is original brigandage differentiated by refinement. "Opportunity makes the robber, and the most daring among them becomes the leader of the band. One by one, the people

of the competitive system, forcing the patricians or *gens* families of high-born rank, to co-operate with each other, and in Greece, to form interprotective *fratries*, in Rome, *curies*,[9] which may be regarded as first evidences of that differentiation that made nations out of isolated families.[10] Much of this marauding spirit was the result of their abuse practiced against slaves whose intelligent sensibilities to maltreatment they little understood. Although those slaves had neither social or political liberty they had minds and strong physical vitality.[11] These they often used in self defense. It was not uncommon for them to take control of their own lives, escape into the mountains whose caverns and jungles afforded them protection, and organize nightly expeditions against those whom they considered their common foe. Some of them became bold and chivalrous bandits. Only on extremely rare occasions does their history appear in the writings of the chroniclers of their times probably because of the contempt for them as being mere property, which was entertained by the ruling society, whose interests the historians were often forced to serve.

Historians were mostly of the aristocratic or noble stock; because, as their business was to record the deeds of heroes, the laboring race was considered too insignificant to do that work. So in earlier times soldiers were of nobler stock than workingmen, for the same reason. Thus we find in almost every instance, that historians were of noble blood, while sculptors, architects, poets and teachers were descendants from the slaves.[12]

---

who desire to live by their own labor are plundered; and thus are they who prefer the work of plunder enabled to pass their time in dissipation. The leader divides the spoil, and with its help is enabled to augment the number of his followers, and thus to enlarge the sphere or his depredations. With the gradual increase of the little community, he is led, however, to commute with them for a certain share of their produce, which he calls rent, or tax or *taille*."

[9] For an interesting discussion of the *gentes* or gentiles which we designate the *gens* families, see Morgan's *Ancient Society*, Chapter II, pp. 62-70.

[10] Florus, lib. III, cap. 20. §1, (Fisher) denies this, unable to understand the possibility of equality by merit. "Nam etsi ipsi (meaning slaves as compared with gladiators) per fortunam in omnia obnoxii; tamen quasi secundum hominum genus sunt." (Note C).

[11] Fustel de Coulanges, *La Cité Antique*, p. 118, chap. X. "La signification vraie de *familia* est propriété: elle désigne le champ, la maison, l'argent, les esclaves, etc." The word thus developed politically and covered cities and nations

[12] Granier, *Histoire des Classes Ouvrières*, chap. XVI. Also chap. XI, pp. 243-244; Lucian, *Somnium*, §. 6-9; Consult Drumann s remarks *Arbeiter und Communisten in Griechenland und Rom.*, S. 29-30. Miller, *Origin of Ranks*, chap. VI, p. 243: "The ancient institution by which every one who is able to bear arms

Among the most remarkable of the workingmen of ancient days whose genius revolted into rebellion against the servile condition, was Spartacus. Judging from piecemeal evidence, scantily, and we might also say, stingily announced by the historians of his time, the deeds of Spartacus, for valor, for success, for magnitude, and for the terror they struck into the hearts of the proud Romans, were equal if not superior to those of Hannibal. The more our investigation of the darkened facts reveals the sagacity and purity of this man, the more profound becomes the respect and the more intense the admiration for him by all true lovers of gallantry and freedom. In fact, there are interests astir in the human breast which must lead to a more searching acquaintance with the fountains at the social *penetralia* of the times, that bubbled forth under his terrible hand and shook the social and political world from center to surface, paling the senators and tribunes at Rome.

Spartacus was, in all respects a workingman. He had no ornamental initials attached to his name, such as betoken any claim to privileged ancestry. It was simply Spartacus.[12]

---

is required to appear in the field at his own charge." This of itself precludes the lowly who have no such economical means, from being soldiers, and shows the entire absence in the early ages, of the now prevailing socialistic mode of 'evying and supporting armies by the state. See also Guhl and Koner, *Life of the Greeks and Romans*: "The contempt against trades expressed by Cicero is further illustrated by the fact of tradesmen being with few exceptions debarred from serving in the legions;" Drumann, *Idem Römischer Abschnitt*, S. 106, sq. *Dichter*, confirms the statements that poets, artists and other workers were of the lowly class.

[13] Flor.,III, 20, 1. "Bellum Spartaco duce concitatum quo nomine appellem nescio." Mommsen, *History of Rome*, vol. IV, p. 102, Harpers' ed., tries, because his deeds were of so prodigious a magnitude, to make him a member of a noble family of the Spartocids; but the name he trumps up to serve this silly conceit is not Spartacus all; it was *Spardokos*, and the family was far from the home of our hero while the time of their career was equally distant. Mommsen's exact words translated are: "Spartacus, perhaps a scion of the noble family of the Spartocids which attained even to royal honors in its Thracian home and in Panticapæum, had served among the Thracian auxiliaries in the Roman army, had deserted and gone as a brigand to the mountains, and had been there recaptured and destined for the gladiatorial games." Schambach makes this vaguely conjectural, and succeeds only in repeating the well-known fact that in Thrace the name Sportox, Sportokos and Spardokas was about as common as our name Smith. He says, *(Italische Sklavenaufstand*, S. 15): "Dass Spartacus von Geburt ein Thraker gewesen, darin stimmen alle Nachrichten überein; Plutarch fügt noch hinzu, er habe einem Nomadenstamme angehört. Eine thrakische Stadt gleichen Namens wird von Stephanus von Byzanz, s. v. erwähnt; aus Thuc. II, 101 lernen wir einen Glied des odrystschen Königshauses kennen, das den Namen Σπάρδοκος führt. Durch Inschriften und Münzen ist uns bezeugt, das in dem bosporanischen Herrscherhause der name Σπάρτοκος öfters vorkam. Vgl. Böckh corp. inscr. gr. II, 91. Möglich, das auch unser Spartacus in seiner Heimat den Rang eines Häuptlings schon bekleidet hat."

CAUSES LEADING TO THE REVOLT.

Like all other prominent persons without the prestige of high rank to build from, Spartacus rose by his own genius. He arose amongst his fellow slaves in the year 74 before Christ. This was precisely the time corresponding with the movement of the Roman Senate to suppress the right of organization;[14] and serves as additional evidence that the suppression of organization among working people was followed by a great struggle. The first appearance of Spartacus appears to have been sixteen years before the law was passed suppressing the ancient right of organization.[15] It seems evident, that threats against the *Jus coeundi*, or law permitting free organization, were, at the time Spartacus makes his appearance, being pushed, with great fury by the nobility, on the slim pretext that they were corrupting the politics as well as the general morals of Rome.[16] But we know from the accounts of the Gracchi that a furious dissention was all along, raging against the unions and in favor of the suppression of the law engraved upon the Twelve Tables which permitted free organization; and the fierce hatred of the patrician minority of the Roman people, who were assuming and monopolizing the public lands contrary to the Licinian law—a dead letter—had by no means died out.[17] The fact is, that although this great social feud had not cropped out in the time of the appearance of Spartacus so as to be much mentioned in any record of the time, yet

---

[14] See account of this suppression together with the efforts of Clodius and Cicero for and against it, in chapter xiii. *Trade Unions.*

[15] Mommsen, *De Collegius et Sodaliciis Romanorum*, p. 73. *De legibus contra collega latis*. "Usque ad finem sæculi septimi liberum jus coeundi mansit." The year *Ab Urbe Condita* 700. Sæculum septimum, was B. C. 58.

[16] Mommsen says that Asconius refers to the year 65 before Christ in the following words: "Frequenter tum etiam coetus factiosorum hominum sine publica auctoritate malo publico fiebant . . . . . . propter quod postea collegia pluribus legibus sublata sunt," Of course these "societies of pretentious men without authority" to which Asconius refers, are the trade and other labor unions. (Ascon., *In Cornel.* p. 75.)

[17] Centralization of wealth upon individuals was at this time about at its highest pitch. Formerly even the lords sometimes worked on these farms. Pliny can hardly believe it, though he enumerates many, *Nat. Hist.* XVIII. 3. Plutarch, *Solon*, also speaks of it. But working with one's own hands in Agriculture had disappeared by the time of Spartacus and everything was now done by slaves and freedmen See Wallace, *Number of Mankind*, p. 123, referring to Plutarch, *Solon*. Solon finding that the very poorest freedmen who, if they did not get work, were seized and sold, took their part and must therefore be classed among the earliest labor reformers on record. Not only Spartacus but great reformers at his time and before were seized and sold into slavery. See *Encyclopædia Britannica*, Vol. XX, p. 653, 9th edition. Agathocles tyrant of Syracuse after murdering 10,000 of the people of Segesta had sold the rest into slavery. B. C. 307. Schambach, S. 1-2. *Zahl der Sklaven.*

it was there, ready to be kindled into flame at any moment and by any daring adventurer.

The most terrible enemy of the plebeians, or, as we prefer to call them, the working classes, was Cicero,[18] whose sense of justice was confined to his own interpretation of laws favoring the privileged class, or *gens* families. Strange to say, in the year 70 B. C., he was in the act of prosecuting Verres, the prætor of Sicily, for acts of rapacity which it was feared would again cause the servile war to flame forth in that island; a subject concerning which we shall soon have more to say; but a short time afterwards we find him violently lampooning the workingmen at Rome in his defense of the laws restricting their organization. We also find him slurring Clodius, whose powerful eloquence succeeded in vindicating them for a time and in bringing odium upon his name. Studying the causes of the servile war of this period from a consultation of the changes which occurred in the Roman law, and bearing, at the same time, a close scrutiny of the chronicled events such as are sparingly afforded by historians, together with such as we find engraved on the tablets of the unions before and after the promulgation of the restrictions to labor organizations, we cannot but see that the wide-spread disaffection called the servile war of Spartacus [19] must have been largely caused by the law prohibiting and threatening to prohibit free right of combination.

Though little is known of the birth of Spartacus, the legend goes that his father whom he much loved was also a captive slave; and that the young son of 15 years, as he held the head of his dying parent, chained and nailed to the trunk of a tree, is conjured by the old man to avenge his death [20] and that, like Hannibal, he then and there vowed vengeance upon his powerful enemies,[21] and in consequence his terrible spring at Rome in riper years was in obedience to promise. All this must, for want of proof, be re-

---

[18] As evidence that Cicero hated the plebeians we have in many places, quoted his own words in our copious annotations, q. v. in chapters on *Trade Unions*.

[19] Florus, III, 20, *init*, ennobles it with the appellation, "Bellum Spartacium."

[20] Vela, the Italian sculptor executed a group of statues portraying this scene which was set up in London in 1862. *Dictionnaire Universel*, Art. *Spartacus*.

[21] "Serment de Spartacus; groupe de marbre de M. Barrias, Solon de 1872. Spartacus ainé euchâiné et cloué á un tronc d'arbre vient d'expirer etc." See *Dictionnaire Universel*, Art *Spartacus*.

DESCRIPTION OF THE GREAT GLADIATOR. 285

garded as romance. But we come to the recital of more solid facts.

Spartacus, in the year B. C. 74, was a man of giant frame, handsome, of white complexion with an abundance of dark ringlets, and possessed of an affable bearing, winning and yet severe in its magnetic aptitude for command. He was young for one of his experience, knowledge and judgment of the world. He had been a shepherd on his native plains in Thracian Greece.[22] While engaged at this bucolic calling he made companionship with other young men unfitted for this dreamy life. They attached themselves to habits of the numerous mountaineers who sallied from their cabins at convenient times and attacked Roman soldiers who often marched through the country during those days of war and invasion. At any rate, we first find him at Capua, a city situated about twenty miles north from Naples. We also have evidence[23] that he had been captured in Thrace, taken forcibly to Capua as a prisoner and on account of his powerful physique and peculiarly fine appearance, was trained in a school of gladiators by the master teacher of athletic games, Lentulus Batiatus. Capua was then a considerable city of Italy. It was celebrated for its extravagance and luxury. In the heart of an exceedingly fertile region, its indolent patrician inhabitants had usurped the *ager publicus* which during the happier days of the golden age of Rome had been farmed by labor unions or colleges under the celebrated provisions of Numa Pompilius and Solon.[24] The *ager publicus* was the public land. It was property in common which belonged to the State.[25] The Licinian Law, or the memory of the defunct statute having this title, was at that moment a bone of contention. Spurius Cassius long before the Twelve Tables were engraved or the decemvirate created, had made a strong effort in behalf of the unions, or order of the united la-

---

[22] See *International Encyclopædia;* La Rousse, *Dictionaire Universel,* Articles, "*Spartacus;*" Schambach, *Italische Sklavenaufstand.* V. 15. "Dass Spartacus von Geburt ein Thraker gewesen, darin stimmen alle Nachrichten überein." Consult also Florus, III, 20; Appian, I. 116-121. Orosius, *Historiarum Adversus Paganos,* VII.

[23] Plutarch, *Crassus,* 8.

[24] Digest, lib. xlvii. tit. 22, leg. 4, and the law of the Twelve Tables there spoken of by Plut., *Numa,* xviii.

[25] See Licinian law and the Agrarian conflicts, Plut., *Titus Gracchus.* Also the *Encyclopædias,* Art. *Agrarian Law*

borers, one of the great branches of that labor organization indirectly provided for by Numa. The co-operators or amalgamated societies for victualing the inhabitants of Rome were necessary to the life of the state.[26] Their business had been to attend to the farming of the *ager publicus* or lands belonging to the state. It is an unhappy characteristic of individual wealth, however, to love the boasted social gulf separating them from labor; and as certain individuals grew enormously rich and politically powerful they committed encroachments upon the ancient system of supplying the people with provisions as it were, by communistic means. The trade unionists or socialists were gradually encroached upon by these wealthy *gentes*, or patricians who pushed slaves out upon the *ager publicus*, driving off the unionists and their system by slow degrees, substituting for them abject and degraded toil, and maddening the *collegia* or unions who took advantage of their organizations to discuss this grievance, a political as well as a social one.[27] There were at Rome good men as well as bad among the rulers in power. At all times these are to be seen in Roman history. Spurius Cassius, a consul, got a law passed restoring these lands, which had been arbitrarily taken possession of, because he found that the wrong had already begun, in his early time to produce poverty. But the patricians arrogantly ignored the measure, or rather fought it down. Great estates manned by slaves appeared on the public domain to which the optimates had no right whatever, except that of superior force, prestige and tact. Thus, on the one hand, in many places, especially in the particular territory south

---

[26] See "*Victualers*," in chap. xvi, pp. 889-400. Also consult Granier, *Histoire des Classes Ouvrières*, chap. xii, explaining how the trade unions were employed by the Roman government.

[27] In addition to our own copious figures on the importation of slave—in other words cheap labor, we quote Schambach as follows: "Von diesen ruckweisen Ueberschwemmung mit frischen Menschenkräften abgesehen, wurde der regelmäszige Bedarf auf dem Wege des Handels gedeckt. Fort und fort wurden aus dem Norden, aus den Gegenden am schwarzen Meere, aus Syrien und Libyen eine Menge von Sklaven durch Händler nach Italien importirt. Lange Zeit war Delos der Hauptsitz dieses Handels; zur Zeit der höchsten Blüte (um 100 v. Chr.) sollen an einem Tage oft 10,000 Sklaven hier abgesetz sein. Selbstverständlich war auch Rom ein wichtiger Platz für den Sklavenhandel. Auf welche Weise der Händler in dem besitz seiner Waare gekommen, darnach fragte man nicht; Menschenraub zu Wasser und zu Lande, selbst Menschenjagden, wie sie heutzutage noch in Afrika an der Tagesordnung sind, waren nichts Ungewöhnliches, wenn auch die grosze Masse gebrachten, als ein Opfer heimischer Fehden, durch Tausch oder Kau. in dem Besitz ihrer derzeitigen Herren gekommen sein mochten." *Der Italische Sklavenaufstand*, S. 2.

and east of Rome, of which Capua was a fruitful center, the ancient *collegia* or labor organizations were gradually driven together into cities, and the slaves of conquest and slaves of birth from the *gens* who were everywhere numerous, were forced [28] to delve for rapacious masters, without remuneration, under the tyrannical lash of foreign mercenary drivers.[29]

The same state of things continued until the time of Appius Claudius, one of the Roman decemvirs, whose business as a decemvir was, *per se* to carry out the law of Cassius, restoring the public domain to the people. What was this decemvirate created for? History is exceedingly explicit and unanimous in stating the functions of the decemvirate—*decemviri legibus scribendis*.[30] They were created for the express purpose of carrying out the law of the Twelve Tables, one special provision in which was to encourage the organization of the free labor element; which organization, as a business compact, was to till the *ager publicus* on shares and furnish the people food and other necessities therefrom.

Appius Claudius must, especially from a standpoint of sociology, ever be regarded as one of those black and morally nauseating buzzards at which an occasional glimpse is had by the disgusted sensibilities of the virtuous as they climb down the ladder of time. He was, in a most strangely surreptitious manner, the arch enemy of the very measure he was elected to defend! In war, his best soldiers the *mercenarii*, forsook him. In morals, he was a cruel and villainous libertine and his rape of Virginia,[31] under pretense that she was one of the "miserable proletaries" who bore the taint of labor and that therefore, the laws of chivalry and of common decency did not reach her case, together with the terrible death of the poor girl at her father's hand, ended in bringing the tryant to prison and a violent end.[32]

---

[28] Consult Strabo, VI. p. 250, see also Lüders' *Dionysische Künstler:* "Der von den Tarentinern gegen die Römer zu Hülfe gerufene Pyrrhus hatte, um den verweichlichten Bürgern anzuhelfen, nichts Eiligeres zu thun als die Syssiten in zukunft zu verbieten, (page 12). Also Schambach's *Italischer Sklavenaufstand,* VI, S. 17.

[29] For accounts of the enormous slave populations of different eras, see Schambach, *Italischer Sklavenaufstand,* I, 1-4. Bücher, *Aufstände der Unfreien Arbeiter,* S. 26, 36, 65, 84. Drumann, *Arbeiter und Communisten,* S. 24, 156, 64 and our own chapters.

[30] Livy, III, 33.   [31] Livy, III, 55, 56, 57. Dionys. of Harlicarn.

[32] Livy, *Libri Histortarum,* III. 57. "Et illi carcerem ædificatum esse, quod

The inimical inroads upon the *ager publicus*, and the consequent ruin of the common people instigated by Appius Claudius and his band of patrician adherents created so great a defection among the plebeians that in B. C. 366, the famous Licinian law, *de modo agri* was called into being by Stolo a low-born himself. It was, in reality, a regulation instituting a system of small holdings; for under it one of the consuls was to be a man of the people and no one rich or poor could be allowed more than 500 acres of the public land. This celebrated law, of Licinius Stolo, a plebeian, which may be regarded as one of the primitive causes of those great social wars and agrarian contentions such as brought Rome to her phenomenal decline, was also doomed to defeat. By the time of the revolt of Spartacus we find, on every side of the metropolis, the grandees occupying the land, living in luxury, while the land which for many centuries had been cultivated by the comparatively free laborers or freedmen, was now laboriously worked by degraded slaves, ready to revolt and watching their opportunities for revenge.

We are now prepared to resume the thread of our narrative. Young Spartacus, a workingman, in every sense,[32] by birth from an earth-born family, by accident of capture and by sale as a slave, was assigned to the exciting and dangerous labors of a gladiator. His task was the revolting one of amusing the non-laboring grandees, their ladies and fashionable pets, the indolent and proud, who languidly sought in the game, the wager, the bagnio, the amphitheatre and its bloody combats, a gratification of their passion for these scenes of ancient life. The ruins of the great marble-faced amphitheatre of Capua where Spartacus is supposed to have killed many of his own comrades in misfortune, are still an object of attraction to travelers.[34] Capua was at that time a large city. It lay on the Volturnus, a beautiful river of Campania flowing from the Samnian Appenines westward into the Mediterranean

---

[32] Iomicilium plebis Romanæ vocare sit solitus. Proinde, ut ille iterum ac saepius provocet, sic se iterum ac saepius iudicem illi ferre, ni vindicias ab libertate in servitutem dederit: si ad iudicem non eat, pro damnato in vincula duci iubere. Ut haud quoquam improbante sic magno motu animorum, quum tanti viri supplicio suamet plebi iam nimia libertas videretur, in carcerem est coniectus,"

[33] Dr. Schambach's effort to prove him to have had a recognized family, is without foundation in fact.

[34] See Rinaldo, *Memoria Istoriche Della Citta di Capua.*

through mountain gorges, valleys and plains, watering some of the most fruitful lands of that magnificent peninsula. These delightful and fruitful fields had been the *ager publicus* since 363 years before Christ; but like many of the vast estates of the republic, had by the time of our hero, become private manorial grounds tilled by slaves.

Spartacus had previously had some military experience of a low order;[35] for it is certain that he was a prisoner, having deserted the alliance in which he was treated as a servant—a humiliation his spirit was too proud to bear—and being recaptured, was sold into slavery.

There was at Capua, in addition to the amphitheatre, a school, probably of importance enough to secure for its enterprising proprietor, Lentulus Batiatus, a considerable income. Plutarch expressly states that most of the gladiators were Thracian Gauls, and further exonerates Spartacus from having come to this fate, by any crimes he had committed.[36] He was forced there by the injustice of his master. It seems to have been the opinion of Sir Edward Bulwer Lytton, that Roman gladiators were superior to the Gaul or other imported contestants at the Pompeian, and of course, the Capuan amphitheatres; and we are to infer from him that Roman vigor and strength were superior to all other even at the metropolis of Rome. But we must ever bear in mind that this Roman blood was native; that although it was servile by heredity through long generations from plebeian parentage as the element of outcasts, yet it was actually Roman blood; while the Thracian element was actually of Greek blood, and that in consequence a gladiatorial fight between a Thracian Greek and a Roman stirred up the Roman spirit of emulation on grounds of national pride; since they fancied

---

[35] "Il avait servi dans les légions comme auxiliaire, mais trop fier pour accepter une servitude déguisée sous le nom d'alliance, il avait déserté à la tête d'une troupe de ses conpatriots, mais repris et vendu son courage et sa force étaient employés en qualité de gladiateur." La Rousse, *Dictionnaire Universel*.

[36] Plutarch, *Marcus Crassus*, 8: "Δέντυλον τινὸς Βατιάτου μονομάχους ἐν Καπύῃ τρέφοντος, ὧν οἱ πολλοὶ Γαλάται καὶ Θρᾷκες ἦσαν." Florus *Annales*, III. 20: ..... "quippe cum servi militaverint, gladiatores imperaverint, illi infimae sortis homines, hi pessimae, auxere ludibrio calamitatem." So also Schambach, *Italische Sklavenaufstand*. VI, S. 18-19, who puts the proportion one third Thracians and two-thirds Gauls in the armies of Spartacus: "Zum Oberanführer wählten sie jetzt den Thraker Spartacus, zu Unteranführern die beiden Gallier Crixus und Œnomaus. Mit grosser Wahrscheinlichkeit dürfen wir aus diesen Wahlen in Bezug auf die Zusammensetzung des Haufens den Schluss ziehen, das etwa ein-drittel Thraker zwei-drittel Galliern gegenüberstanden, ein Verhältnis, welches sich auch in weiteren Verlauf der Ereignisse nicht wesentlich ändert."

they beheld in the bloody duel a recapitulation of the more serious conflicts with Pyrrhus or Mithridates. We know that on occasions of the games at the amphitheatres, when Romans were to meet Gauls or Greeks, the advertisements were more pronounced and the betting ran ruinously high among the rich·frequenters of the ring. Undoubtedly Spartacus, who spoke Greek and Latin with facility, was aware of this. He had, as a scholar under Lentulus Batiatus, either in the open functions or at rehearsals, severely punished, by his giant muscular force and mastership of the art of swordsmanship and pugilism, many wretches whose lot like his own was to measure strength and science alike with friend and foe.

But although of prodigious courage, aptness and physical energy, Spartacus was humane and generous; and his nature revolted against the hideous character of his employment. He loved the memory of his native hills and valleys. His central desire was to reach home and spend in quiet the remainder of his eventful life. Besides, his wife, also a Thracian Greek, was ever at his side with her loving tones of encouragement. Plutarch says that she was possessed of the gift of divination. He relates that Spartacus when taken prisoner was first brought to Rome to be sold. While there, a serpent was once, as he slumbered, discovered twinning caressingly about his head and locks; whereupon on inquiry by superstitious people, as to the import of this strange action of the gods, she answered in her public capacity as retainer to the orgies of Bacchus, that this conduct of the friendly reptile betokened that her husband would rise to be great and formidable, and die happy! [37] Unfortunately for the Romans he rose to be formidable to say the least.

[37] Plutarch, *Marcus Crassus*, 8; "It is said when he was first brought to Rome to be sold, a serpent was seen twisted about his face as he slept. His wife, who was of the same tribe, having the gift of divination, and being a retainer besides to the orgies of Bacchus, said, it was a sign that he would rise to something very great and formidable, the result of which would be happy. This woman still lived with him, and was the companion of his flight." According to Tacitus, however, she was a German; for in his Germaniæ, a curious chapter occurs in her praise setting her forth as an example of the heroism of the ancient German women. We quote the excellent statement of Schambach on this point: *Italische Sklavenaufstand*, V, S. 16: "Was des Spartacus frühere Lebensschicksale anlangt, so steht fest, dass er eine Zeit lang unter den Hilfstruppen im römischen Solde gestanden hat, vielleicht in dem Heere des Proconsul P. Claudius, der die noch freien Stämme der makedonischen Thraker unterwerfen sollte. Hier hat er sich wahrscheinlich jene genaue Kenntniss des römischen Herrwesens erworben, welche die unerlässliche Vorbedingung zu

But whatever the vicissitudes of Spartacus at Rome, it is certainly at Capua, many miles from the eternal city, that we must introduce him. He must have been sent to the Capuan school of gladiators to be trained in the science of those ferocious combats with an object of being sent back to Rome prepared *ad gladium* or *ad ludum*,[38] for the amphitheatre which afterwards, at the Coliseum became the scenes of brutalities and abominations, such as the world has seldom witnessed. Neither are we prepared to state whether Batiatus the *lanista* or "butcher-master" of Capua, was to prepare him for the full-armor games of the *hoplomachi* or for the deadly Thracian dagger duels "to promote the pleasure of gentlemen."[39] But for whatever exact purpose he was designed at the arena they were doomed to disappointment.

At Capua there was at that moment an organization of the *unguentarii*[40] who furnished, it is said, all Italy with perfumes of the richest quality and who in carrying on this trade under the rules of their *collegium* or labor union realized, so long as the ancient law applied in their case, a good living as wage earners. Considering the amount

seinen zuküftigen Siegen war. Nach Florus ist er sodann desertirt u. Strassenräuber geworden, als solcher gefangen und unter die Gladiatoren verurtheilt. Mit dieser Ueberlieferung stimmte indessen Appian I, 116, ἐκ δὲ αἰχμαλωσίας καὶ πράσεως ἐν τοῖς μονομάχοις ὤν nicht überein, und auch ein Fragment Varro's bei Charis. I, p. 108, Innocente Varro de rebus urbanis tertio, Spartaco innocente conjecto ad gladium spricht gegen Florus. Dass er mehrmals seinen Herrn gewechselt, ehe er in des Cn. Lentulus Batiatus Fechterschule nach Capua kam, scheint aus Plut. *Crass.* 8; ὅτε πρῶτον εἰς 'Ρώμην ὤνιος ἤχϑη hervorzugehen. Plutarch erzählt auch noch die Sage, dass nach seiner Ankunft in Rom sich eine Schlange im Schlaf um sein Haupt gewunden und dass eine thrakische Wahrsagerin dies dahin gedeutet habe, 'er werde gross und furchtbar und bis an sein unglückliches Ende glücklich sein,' eine Prophezeiung, die in ihrem letzten Theile an Allgemeinheit nichts zu wünschen übrig lässt.

38 To be killed by decree of law, or to be saved after three years of service, in successful competitive fights. Very few *ad ludum* gladiators, ever came out alive.

39 Florus, *Annales*, III, 20, §8; "Nec abnuit, ille de stipendario Thracæ miles, de milite desertor; inde latro, dein in honore virorum gladiator."

40 *Unguentarii*; see chapter xix, on *Trade Unions*, Capua is also the seat of the curious historical inscription of Aquillius, (Orelli, *Inscriptionum Latinarum Collectio*, No. 3, 308), which speaks of the 917 runaway slaves restored by him to their masters, during the great Sicilian Slave war (chap. xi., Athenion), which could not have been inscribed more than about 17 years before. We therefore quote the inscription entire as it furnishes evidence of what must have been the state of feeling with working people at the time the war with Spartacus broke out at Capua: " M Aquillius, M. F. Gailus. procos viam fecei ab regio ad Capuam et in ea via Ponteis omneis meiliarios tabellariosque poseiuei hince sunt Nouceriam meilia Captuam XXCIII, Muranum IXXIII cosentiam CXXIII Valentiam CLXXX. ad Fretum ad statuam CCXXXI regium CCXXXVII, suma Af Capua regium meihaCCCXXI. Et eidem praetor in Sicilia fugiteivos. Italicorum conquaesiuei redeique homines DCCCCXVII eidemque primus fecei. Ut de agro poblico ara toribus cederent paastores forum aedisque poblicas heic fecei."

of demand for such an article in the most extravagant and luxurious era of Roman wealth, we must infer that the business employed a large number of people. But just at this moment the senate at Rome was seriously contemplating the suppression of the trade unions. We know that this contemplated suppression was desperately resisted both by the unions and some of the tribunes of the people and other men of power; and if we are to suppose that the men were as keenly on the alert in those days as they now are, we cannot but imagine that their influence if not their numbers, were lent toward kindling this servile war. For this reason if for no other, it is highly important that we should know this story.

The auspices were all favorable to Spartacus while at Capua, who, together with 200 of the Thracian, Gallic and Roman gladiators, plotted a measure for escape. The plan was to stealthily secure the knives and other articles to be found in the kitchens and eating rooms of the institution, and with these, make a rush in a body for the principal doorway which was guarded by Roman soldiers.[42] Just before the appointed moment arrived, however, a certain person enrolled in the conspiracy let his courage forsake him; or it may be, was bribed by secret detectives to reveal the truth. However this may have been, a dash by the officers of the law was suddenly made for the arrest of the insurrectionists, which would have succeeded had not Spartacus put his utmost efforts forth to prevent it—being actually ahead of time. As it was, 78 of the most trustworthy and daring burst through the door into the street and thence out of town. The 78 men[43] had succeeded in providing themselves with long

---

[41] Appian *Historia Romana.* **I. 116**: "Τοῦ δ' αὐτοῦ χρόνου περὶ τὴν Ἰταλίαν μονομάχων ἐς θέας ἐν Καπύῃ τρεφομένων, Σπάρτακος Θρᾷξ ἀνήρ, ἐστρατευμένος ποτὲ Ῥωμαίοις, ἐκ δὲ αἰχμαλωσίας καὶ πράσεως ἐν τοῖς μονομάχοις ὤν, ἔπεισεν αὐτῶν ἐς ἑβδομήκοντα ἄνδρας μάλιστα κινδυνεῦσαι περὶ ἐλευθερίας μᾶλλον ἢ θέας ἐπιλείξεως, καὶ βιασάμενος, σὺν αὐτοῖς τοὺς φυλάσσοντας ἐξέδραμε, καὶ τινῶν ὁδοιπόρων ξύλοις καὶ ξιφιδίοις ὁπλισάμενος ἐς τὸ Βέσβιον ὄρος ἀνέφυγεν." Plutarch, *Crassus,* **8,** (Langhorne,) says: "One Lentulus Batiatus kept at Capua a number of gladiators, the greatest part of which were Gauls and Thracians; men not reduced to that employment for any crimes they had committed, but forced upon it by their master. Two hundred of them, therefore, agreed to make their escape. Though the plot was discovered, threescore and eighteen of them, by their extreme vigilance, were beforehand with their master, and sallied out of town, having first seized all the long knives and spits in a cook's shop."

[42] Florus, *Annales,* III. 20, puts it at 30: "Cum triginta haud amplius ejusdem fortunae viris, erumperunt Capua." Plutarch says 78; and this best agrees with others.

FIRST BATTLE. 293

knives and any other things they could lay hands on which could be used as weapons.[43]

The first battle was fought with the troops of the garrison at Capua, and if we are to credit the hints of Plutarch the conflict must be considered both the opening battle and victory of Spartacus. The Capuan troops, after the escape of the seventy-four, attacked them, as they gained the gates and passages into the open road; but by some dexterous charge were defeated by the gladiators and compelled to return empty-handed to the garrison. They took the main road, presumably the Appian Way, which, leading from Rome through the city of Capua, joins the Via Aquilia about five miles to the south of this place. The Via Aquilia, parting from the Appian Way to the right, leads almost directly to the foot of Mount Vesuvius, a distance from Capua of nineteen or twenty miles. It was on this march that the fugitives met some wagons loaded with a quantity of daggers, swords and knives which they were taking to the city. These weapons were to be used by gladiators in the arena; and it is not unlikely that they were intended for these fugitives' own use at the Capuan amphitheatre. Implements so much needed were, of course, instantly seized, though not without a fight. Thus equipped they reached a mountain ledge in safety. On personal inspection of the place we are inclined to conjecture that Spartacus and his friends first reached the northeasterly base of Vesuvius, or that part which is now the fragment of the volcano [44] and known as the "Somma," whose separate peak five miles eastward from the crater is called the "Punta del Nasone" and is nearly 4,000 feet above the sea which is visible to the westward. At that time, before the eruption, it must have been 5,000 or 6,000 feet high.

[43] Plutarch, *Marcus Crassus*, 9, in relating these things speaks very bitterly against them, as being mere barbarians: "Καὶ πρῶτον μὲν τοὺς ἐκ Καπύης ἐλθόντας ὠσάμενοι, καὶ πολλῶν ὅπλων ἐπιλαβόμενοι πολεμιστηρίων, ἄσμενοι ταῦτα μετελάμβανον, ἀποῤῥίψαντες, ὡς ἄτιμα καὶ βάρβαρα, τὰ τῶν μονομάχων." Florus and Cicero put the number of the first gladiators down as low as possible : "Cum Spartaco minus multi prima fuerunt. Quid tandem isti mali in tam tenera insula non fecissent?" Cicero, *Ad Atticum*, Liber VI. *Epistola*, 2. Florus, *Annales*, III. 20, §. 1, declares there were scarcely more than 30 who escaped with Spartacus: "Spartacus, Crixus, Ænomaus, effracto Lentuli ludo, cum triginta haud amplius ejusdem fortunæ viris eruperunt Capua." Consult also Frontin, LXXIV. 1, 5, 21; Vellejus Paterculus, II, 30, 6.

[44] Vesuvius was not known to have ever had an eruption at that time. Appian, *Historia Romana*, I. 116, only says: "ἐν τὸ Βέσβιον ὄρος ἀνέφυγεν." Plutarch

Here the fugitives took refuge among the crags and wild vines that overhung the mountain side. It was at a point where there was but one approach, that they fixed their first resting place. This was a projecting table-rock which shelved forward over a craggy precipice embowered in the foliage of wild grape vines." Here, on a crag rising perpendicularly over an immense chasm, the little band pitched their tents. They held a council of war and elected Spartacus commander-in-chief and Crixus and Œnomaus," his lieutenants. Spartacus, now in full command, immediately began to exercise those gifts of genius, foresight and power which have covered one of the most brilliant military pages in the history of either ancient or modern times."

As might be expected, the people of Capua were filled with terror at the escape of the gladiators." There was a feeling of shame and humiliation based upon the fact that the rebels were slaves. To combat with equals had ever been the pride of Rome; but to bring her noble arms to bear against a thing so low and hateful in the scale of being as a servile revolt was, from a social point of view, a national degradation and a disgrace.

Nevertheless, the report reached Rome that the gladiators under Spartacus, the prophetic giant, had revolted and escaped to the mountains, and a large detachment of troops, who were probably stationed at Capua, was sent

who must have borrowed from Sallust (See Schambach, S. 9), is our principal source for these details

[45] La Rousse, *Dictionnaire Universel*, Art. *Spartacus*, see also Plutarch, *Marcus Crassus*, VIII., IX.

[46] Flor., III, 20, §. 1. "Spartacus, Crixus, Œnomaus, effracto Lentuli ludo, cum triginta haud amplius ejusdem fortunæ viris,"

[47] Schambach, *Der Italische Sklavenaufstand*, V. S. 15: "Plutarch sagt im Leben des Crassus cap. 8: οἱ πολλοὶ Σπαρτάκειον πόλεμον ὀνομάζουσι und Florus, der die sicilischen Sklavenkriege 'bellum servile' nennt, setzt über das *zwanzigste* Capital des dritten Buches die Ueberschrift '*bellum Spartacum*,' bringt den italischen Sklavenkrieg also in eine Katagorie mit den andern *grossen* Kriegen (wie dem bellum Hannibalicum, Sertorianum Mithridaticum), in denen ein Mann so vorwiegend als die Seele des Kamfes erscheint, dass dieser nach ihm benannt zu werden verdient. Zwar finden wir bei den römischen Autoren vorwiegend andere Bezeichnungen, z. B. bellum servile (Augustin de c. d. III, 26, Ampel. c. 41, 45), servilis tumultus (Caes. b. G. I, 40), bellum fugitivorum (Front), 'hoc fugitivorum et ut verius dicam gladiatorum bellum' (Oros.); aber allen diesen Benennungen liegt die Absicht zu Grunde, den verhassten Führer der Aufständischen nicht wider Willen zu Nachruhm zu verhelfen."

[48] In further proof that originally the *paterfamilias* had the right to enslave or even kill his children, see Canon Lightfoot, on *The Collossians*, p. 312, quoting the *Digest*, 1. 6. "In potestate sunt servi dominorum: quae quidem potestas juris gentium est: nam apud omnes peraeque gentes animadvertere possumus dominis in servos vitae necisque potestatem fuisse."

SECOND BATTLE. 295

out under the command of the Roman prætor, Clodius Glaber, to subdue them.[49] One account gives the number of this force at just 3,000 men. Clodius appeared at the base of the precipice during the day, knowing that the rebels were on the height above him. The army, however, took up its quarters at one side of the acclivity to the ascent of which there was but one approach. This they guarded to prevent the gladiators from escape in the night.

Now was the time for the wily Spartacus, whose band was without suitable arms for a contest. The duel was to consist in the measure of comparative wit. When evening came Spartacus and his men who during the day had taken vines and of them woven ladders sufficiently strong to hold the heaviest man and long enough to reach the foot of the overhanging precipice back of whose capstone the band lay intrenched, let themselves down in such silence as not to awaken the suspicion of the slumbering army. All descended the ladder empty-handed in this manner, except one man who remained to lower the arms; after which he also climbed down and thus all succeeded uninjured, in reaching the plain below, at a point least suspected by the Romans,[50] Profound silence reigned. The proud prætor and his 3,000 men were now but a few steps from where stood those desperate slaves who well knew that one slip or false action might end their lives.

Spartacus, ranged his men in a manner to surround the Roman encampment. When all was ready the startling whoop of onset was given and the gladiators centering in, apparently in large numbers, with their terrifying warcry and death-dealing weapons, completely routed those whom they did not kill upon the spot. The rout of the Romans was complete and the rebels remained masters of their baggage and arms, 74 Roman cohorts being killed on the spot.[51]

[49] Compare Florus, III. 20, 4. "Clodio Glabro, per fauces montis vitigineas." See Schambach, *Italischer Sklavenaufstand*, VI. S. 19. Also *International Encyc.* Art. *Spartacus*, Livy, *Epitome*, XCV., gives the name of the Roman legate as Claudius Pulcher." Appian says Varinius Glabrus, I. 116. . . "καὶ πρῶτος ἐπ' αὐτὸν ἐκπεμφθεὶς Ὀυαρίνιος Γλάβρος." But he gives us very little of this first strategical manœuvre and battle, and passes on to the greater conflicts which followed,
[50] Plutarch, *Marcus Crassus*, 8: Frontinus, I. 5, 22.
[51] Frontinus, I. 5, 21. "Cohortes gladiatoribus quatuor et Septuaginta ces-

SPARTACUS.

The result of this second success was electrifying. On the part of the Romans, public sentiment was filled with humiliation and disgust. Arrangements were immediately made at Rome to send a powerful force, under a leader in whom they had confidence; and Publius Varinius, a prætor, was sent south at the command of a large body of troops ably supported by two lieutenants, Furius and Cossinius. The prætor had so much faith in Cossinius that he made him his assistant and chief counselor.

Spartacus, who had gained this decisive victory at the precipice of Vesuvius, was cool and calm, full of the sense of his responsibility and still unwavering in the child-like desire to reach safely his native home, far to the northward, across the Adriatic. He had the ripe judgment to foreknow that the Romans when aroused were invincible.

But resolutely suiting the opportunity to the circumstances, he issued a proclamation of emancipation and protection to all the slaves who should join his force. Multitudes of cattle-drivers, shepherds, herdsmen and others whose condition had been degraded by the land-holders to slavery, appeared before him offering their allegiance. They were accepted and armed with implements wrested from Clodius, at the ambuscade of Vesuvius. The entire force under Clodius Glaber, being only given at 3,000 there could not have been arms enough for more than that number, unless some of the volunteers furnished their own weapons. This might have been the case; but to offset the argument that the servile auxiliaries used other than the dignified military armor, we have a passage in Plutarch, declaring that at the first skirmish against a detachment from Capua where the gladiators were victorious they threw away their knives as things "disgraceful, dishonorable and barbarous."

His wish was constantly to secure arms, and naturally; for immediately on the defeat of Clodius Glaber, the renegade force of 78 gladiators from Capua swelled into an

gorint;" See also Flor., III. 20: "Nihil tale opinantis ducis, subito impetu castra rapuere." Schambach, *Italischer Sklavenkrieg*, S. 20, says: "Alle Nachrichten stimmen nemlich darin überein, dass die Fechter an Zahl unendlich viel geringer waren, Frontin I, 5, 21 gibt sogar an, es seien noch die 74 allein gewesen: verum etiam ex alio latere Clodium ita terruit, ut aliquot cohortes gladiatoribus quatuor et septuaginta cesserint. Der Angriff gelang vollständig, die römischen 'milites tumultuarii' räumten fliehend das Feld und liessen **ihr Lager mit allem** Gepäck im Stich, das eine Beute der Empörer wurde."

THIRD AND FOURTH BATTLES.

army of 10,000 "men of great vigor and very swift runners." and Spartacus "covered them with armor, some heavy, some light for picket duty."[52] As the cities of Herculaneum and Pompeii were but a few miles distant to the south and west, it is quite possible that he realized not only arms but many volunteers from that quarter. The indomitable rebel now set himself about drilling his men into military service. The wretched *ergastuli* were changed into free men who assumed military dignity,[53] from the moment of their desertion from their masters thus realizing immediate participation, without having to linger upon the anticipations of promise. With 10,000 desperate soldiers under rigid drill he soon felt himself capable to cope with a prætorian army. Nor had he long to wait.

The Roman prætor, Publius Varinius, as already stated, was in the same year, B. C. 74, sent with a large army to put an end to the trouble.[54] He had two lieutenants, Furius and Cossinius. Varinius placed much confidence in Cossinius as a man of uncommon judgment. But the combined wisdom of both was not enough to induce the Roman army to keep together; for Furius was sent with a strong detachment of 2,000 men against the " common robber."[55] Spartacus, perceiving the Roman army divided into two columns, fell upon the weakest line, that of Fu-

[52] Plutarch, *Marcus Crassus;* Florus, III. 20, 3, also speaks of the 10,000 as follows: "Servisque ad vexillum vocatis, cum statim decem amplius millia coissent hominum." Plutarch, *Marcus Crassus,* correctly applies this estimate after rather than before the battle of the ambuscade.
[53] Smith's *Dictionary of Greek and Roman Antiquities,* Art. *Spartacus.* The runaways resorted to all sorts of expedients to obtain arms and munitions. See Florus, III. 20, 6. "Affluentibus in diem copiis, quum jam esset justus exercitus e viminibus pecudumque tegumentis, incouditos sibi clipeos; e ferro ergastulorum recocto gladios ac tela fecerunt." So also Appian, *De Bellis Civilibus,* I. 116-117: "Μετὰ δὲ τοῦτο Σπαρτάκῳ μὲν ἔτι μᾶλλον πολλοὶ συνέθεον, καὶ ἑπτὰ μυριάδες ἦσαν ἤδη στρατοῦ, καὶ ὅπλα ἐχάλκευε, καὶ παρασκευὴν συνέλεγεν, οἱ δ' ἐν ἄστει τοὺς ὑπάτους ἐξέπεμπον μετὰ δύο τελῶν."
[54] Appian, *De Bellis Civilibus,* I. 116. "Μεριζομένῳ δ' αὐτῷ τὰ κέρδη κατ ἰσομοιρίαν ταχὺ πλῆθος ἦν ἀνδρῶν, καὶ πρῶτος ἐπ' αὐτὸν ἐκπεμφθεὶς 'Οὐαρίνιος Γλάβρος, ἐπὶ δ' ἐκείνῳ Πόπλιος 'Ουαλέριος, οὐ πολιτικὴν στρατιὰν ἄγοντες ἀλλ' ὅσους ἐν σπουδῇ καὶ παρόδῳ συνέλεξαν (οὐ γάρ πω 'Ρωμαῖοι πόλεμον, ἀλλ' ἐπιδρομήν τινα καὶ λῃστήριῳ τὸ ἔργον ὅμοιον ἡγοῦντο εἶναι), συμβαλόντες ἥττωντο. 'Οναρινίου δὲ καὶ τὸν ἵππον αὐτὸς Σπάρτακος περιέσπασε· παρὰ τοσοῦτον ἦλθε κινδύνου 'Ρωμαίων ὁ στρατηγὸς αὐτὸς αἰχμάλωτος ὑπὸ μονομάχου γενέσθαι."
[55] Horace, *Carmina,* liber III. Carmen. 14, lines 18-20;
"Et eadem Marsi memorem duelli,
Spartacum si qua potuit vagantem
Fallere testa."
Cornelius Tacitus, *Annales,* lib. III. cap. 73, speaks of the successes of Spartacus as shameful applying the epithets "robber and deserter." "Non alias magis sua populique Romani contumelia indoluisse Caesarem ferunt, quam quod desertor et praedo hostium more ageret, ne Spartaco quidem post tot consularium exercituum clades inultam Italiam urenti."

rius, and with an impetous dash, broke through his main
body, routing and destroying nearly the entire detachment. The larger force however remained, commanded
by Cossinius, the legate and confidential adviser of the
commander-in-chief. That worthy, doubtless, incredulous
regarding the abilities of the man he was to cope with, so
far forgot the rigorous vigilance of war as to indulge in
the tempting baths of Salenæ. The eagle-eye of Spartacus bent upon the prey. While the Roman was thus
luxuriating, the gladiators rushed with fierce rapidity and
like a thunderbolt struck the spot, and very nearly succeeded in seizing Cossinus in the bath. He escaped, however, with precipitation, but his army was attacked by
surprise, routed, large numbers killed and Cossinus himself in attempting to restore order was slain in battle
which covered the field with the dead. The conquering
legions followed up the victory and made themselves masters of the camps of the Roman army.

The report of this victory at the Baths of Salenæ spread
like wildfire through the land. Slaves rushed into the
camp of the rebels, offering their services in exchange
for freedom. The newly gotten arms were transferred
from the Romans to the sun-baked and brawny hands of
the rebels. The drill and military manœuvre went rigorously and with great system forward in their camp; and
while the hopes of the unsophisticated bondmen beat
high the pride of the Roman nobility and citizens was
mortified and crushed.

Varinius[56] with the remnant of his army, consisting of
the greater fraction of the original force, was in the vicinity, or at least, not very far from the scene of the last disaster in which Cossinius met his fate. There are no data
extant which give the full accounts of this encounter. To
the student of sociology it must be announced with keen
regrets that the entire three books of Livy covering the
space of time between 74 and 71 B. C., are, with the exception of the epitome of books, XCV., XCVI. and
XCVII., completely lost. A discovery of the lost authorities would indeed be a rich legacy to the science of sociology. Exactly similar is the fate of the great *Libri His-*

[56] Publius Varinius according to Plutarch, although Appian says Varinius Glabrus.

toriarum, of Sallust."⁷ Of all writers on ancient history, Sallust and Livy rank among the most plain-spoken and manly. By the epitomies and fragments still extant we know that these missing histories of the servile war were elaborately written; and judging from the careful study and insertion of figures, speeches and other literary condiments which spice their narrations we should, had they not perished, be supplied with a flood of new details regarding this servile war. Those inestimable jewels are, however, lost, unless some Niebuhr arises to rescue them from their dusty shadows. The triumphs of Spartacus were an unendurable stigma upon the Roman name, and the shame which the successes of gladiators and slaves inflicted, though it could not be effaced from memory, could be expunged or obliterated by destroying the books and by acts as barbarous as that which afterwards lined the drives for miles both sides of the Appian Way with the crucified followers of this general.

Spartacus soon after made a formidable onset upon Varinius, who was overthrown, showing this to have been a great battle. Much obscurity hangs over this engagement.⁵⁸ Could the whole truth be revealed we should perhaps be presented with one of the world's bloodiest struggles; for we are informed by Plutarch that about this time the army of Spartacus had greatly swollen, and Appian declares it to have reached 70,000 men. The Roman general was overthrown. He lost all his troops, his horses, baggage, and his prætorian fasces. In fact he was annihilated; for we hear no more of him.

⁵⁷ See Schambach's *Italischer Sklavenaufstand*. II. S. 6. This keen observer and critic considers Sallust's history to have been far the most authentic and complete of all. He says: "Am meisten zu bedauern haben wir den Verlust des grössten Werkes des Salustius, welches den Titel führte libri historiarum populi Romani. Salustius war von den römischen Autoren, die eine Geschichte jenes Krieges gegeben haben, derjenige, welcher den Ereignissen selbst nicht nur zeitlich am nächsten stand, sondern auch die meiste historische Glaubwürdigkeit hat. Vermöge seiner Stellung im Staate und seiner weitreichenden Verbindungen war er im Stande die besten Nachrichten zu geben, und mit einer anziehenden charakteristischen Darstelluug verband er Methode und Kritik. Seine Historien waren sehr ausführlich."

⁵⁸ " Dans un combat desastreux il (Varinius) perdit ses troupes, ses baggages, son cheval, et jusqu' aux faisceaux prétoriens " (La Rousse, Art, *Spartacus*). See also Michaud, *Bibliographie Universelle*, Vol. 40, pp. 18-21, wherein we are reminded of the extraordinary allusion by Tacitus *(Germaniæ.* cap. 8), of the wife of Spartacus having been a fortune-teller. She accompanied her husband through his remarkable career. Her name was *Aurinia* and Tacitus supposes her to have been a German. See *Infra*, ¡ , 313 note 73 Appian, 116, *fin.*, confirms the statement that Varinius lost many of his troops and his colors.

Spartacus from this time was adorned with the regular accompaniments of a Roman pro-consul. With a great army he overran the territory of Campania, ravaging and sacking Nola, Nuceria and Cora; then crossing the Samnian line into the province of Hirpinius he seized what he wanted from Compsa on the Via Numicia. Crossing the Appenines he marched his army southward into the rich peninsular division of Lucania. Here in the great fertile plains, between the mountains and the Tarantine Gulf, he was absolute master. His arms extended still farther southward over the domain of Bruttium in Magna Græcia.[59] In fact the destruction of the Varinian army had placed the rebels in complete possession of this whole portion of Italy. Here were pitched the winter quarters, B. C. 74–73.[60]

But Spartacus well knew that he must not follow the voluptuous plan[61] of Hannibal who, one hundred and forty years before at Capua, among the same valleys of which he was now master, and after the strikingly similar battle of Cannæ, had allowed his Carthagenian braves to be spoiled by luxury and wealth. Fixing his quarters at or not far from the city of Metapontum,[62] which lay on the Tarantine gulf between the rivers Acalandrus and Casuentus, where the alluvial bottoms filled those parts of Italy with harvests of the cereals and the vine, Spartacus estab-

---

[59] Appian, *Historia Romana*, I. 117, *ss.* "Τὰ δ' ὄρη τὰ περι Θουρίους καὶ τὴν πόλιν αὐτὴν κατέλαβε, καὶ χρυσὸν μὲν ἢ ἀργυρον τοὺς ἐμπόρους ἐσφέρειν ἐκώλνε, καὶ κεκτῆσθαι τοὺς ἑαυτοῦ, μόνον δὲ σίδηρον καὶ χαλκὸν ἐωνοῦντο πολλοῦ, καὶ τοὺς ἐσφέροντας οὐκ ἠδίκουν. ὅθεν ἀθρόας ὕλης εὐπορήσαντες εὖ παρεσκευασαντο, καὶ θαμινὰ ἐπὶ λεηλασίας ἐξῄεσαν. Ῥωμαίοις τε πάλιν συνενεχθέντες ἐς χεῖρας ἐκράτουν καὶ τότε, καὶ λείας πολλῆς γέμοντες ἐπανῄεσαν."

[60] Schambach, *Italtscher Sklavenaufstand*, III, S. 13, makes the war to have commenced in the summer of B. C. 74, which we follow, *Idem*, S. 20, Schambach draws from the Vatican fragments of Sallust as follows: "Nachdem Spartacus alle Elemente der empörung, welche Campanien darbot, an sich gezogen wandte er sich in andere gegenden. Leider sind wir über die Route, die er einschlug, nicht genau unterrichtet; doch dürfen wir an der Hand der vatikanischen Fragmente des Salust mit denen Orosius übereinstimmt, annehmen, dass er sich zunächst quer durch die Halbinsel an die Küsten des adriatischen Meeres wandte, von wo er dann die Richtung nach Süden einschlug und nach Lukanien gelangte. Wenigstens berechtigen uns die Fragmente des Salust zu der Annahme, dass Varinius, von dem weiterhin die Rede sein wird, in Picenum den Aufständischen gegenüber gestanden habe. Auf diesen Marsche eroberten sie Annii Forum und vielleicht auch Avellae, dessen Einwohnerschaft sich ihnen wenigstens zum Schutze ihrer Mark entgegenstellte. Dass auch hier die Sklaven ihren Weg mit Mord und Brand bezeichnet haben, ist wohl gewiss."

[61] Plutarch, *Marcus Crassus*, 9–10, Smith's *Dictionary of Greek and Roman Biography.* Art. *Spartacus*, Sallust, Fragm. *Historiarum*, III, *idem*, Gerlach ed., p. 254 Pliny *Nat. Hist.*, XXXIII. 14.

[62] Cf. La Rousse, *Dictionnaire Universel*, according to which the camp of Spartacus was near Thurium, q. v.

lished himself for the winter, astonishing his historians by an ordeal of tactics and a discretion which the wisest and most virtuous might follow at the present day. As explained in our account of the Roman *collegia* or social organizations, all Italy was at this period covered with social societies of protection, of resistance and for convivial and burial purposes.[63] To make coincidence more striking to the student of sociology, it may be explained that it was at just this critical moment that the Roman politicians who for centuries had been invidiously watching the rise and progress of the social movement under the law of Numa Pompilius, were busily discussing a measure for the wholesale suppression of the great social movement, root and branch. This law for their suppression did not succeed, on account of the powerful interference of the tribune Clodius, until the year 58 B. C. But we are not without evidence that everywhere the unions of labor were all this time on the alert, expecting the calamity and preparing for revolt. These unions were innumerable.[64] Italy and Greece were honeycombed with them.[65] Another proof[66] that this remarkable conquest of Spartacus in the industrial centers of Italy actually revived the organizations or turned their membership to his use, is seen from a slur in Cicero, the bitter hater of everybody who was too poor to live without manual toil. Speaking of them he says: . . . . "not only those ancient labor unions have had their right of organization restored to them, but, by one gladiator, innumerable others, and new ones, have been instituted." These words from such high authority, shed a blaze of light upon our conjecture that Spartacus was working in collusion with the disaffected labor unions which had either been suppressed or their existence threatened, as is plainly proved, at that time.[67] Thus Cicero becomes our most valuable and re-

[63] Cf. chaps xiii, to xix., *infra*, on Trade and other labor organizations among the ancients.
[64] Cicero who was incensed at the success of Clodius whose eloquence restored the right of organization to the workingmen, says: "Collegia non ea solum quæ senatus sustulerat restituta, sed *innumerabilia* quædam nova ex omni fæce Urbis ac servitio concitata." Cic. *In Pisonem*, 4, 9.
[65] "L. Julio C. Mario Coss, quos et ipsi Cicero memoravit SCto collegia sublata sunt." Cf. Mommsen, *De Collegiis et Sodaliciis Romanorum*, p. 73.
[66] Cic., *Pro Sesto*, 25, 55. "Ut collegia non modo illa vetera restiturentur sed ab uno gladiatore innumerabilia allia nova constituerenter." This inimitable satire, was, in all probability flung at Spartacus who had then been dead only a few years.

SPARTACUS.

liable historian by his utterances at the bar, in the senate and his epistles. We must make the importance of this matter excuse prolixity and repetition. Speaking of these very times but apparently not suspecting the extraordinary concatenation of circumstances which we use in evidence of our conjecture, the great archæologist Mommsen, explicitly states, concerning the ancient conspiracy laws of this period which we conjecture contributed much to the so-called servile wars, that they were of two sorts. "Thus I have two points to note here: In the first, I do not think that the Clodian trade unions contained slaves as members; for I think the pure trade organization of skilled workmen did not admit slaves. They were societies for religious purposes.[68] Then the law of Clodius must be looked upon as touching only the city of Rome; as Cicero says: '*ex urbis faece*'—out of the slums of the city of Rome. It was of such that Clodius would conscribe and classify. The fact is, innumerable unions of the servile race, as their relics show, were scattered over all Italy, derived from ancient times, under the protection of the provincial cities."[69]

We are told that the young general after fixing his quarters snugly for the winter, instituted a rigorous drill of his troops. According to Pliny he denied them the use of gold and silver lest they should become demoralized by handling these vitiating treasures.[70]

One thing is certain during his sojourn in Lucania: he set all the slaves free and declared such work to be his mission.[71] He also garrisoned the cities, although it is claimed that some of them he plundered. He committed no acts of brutality. He forced his soldiers to abstain from intemperance.[72] He was humane to his prisoners.

---

[67] See Ascon, *L. C.*, speaking of Clodius: "De collegiis restituendis novisque instituendis quæ sit ex servitiorum fæce constituta."
[68] Here Mommsen is mistaken, and he later on admits that they used religion as a cloak to screen them from the rigid laws.
[69] Mommsen, *De Collegiis et Solaliciis Romanorum*, pp. 77-78. The text is as follows: "Qua ratione conscriptio instituta sit et ad quaenam collegia haec lex maxime pertinuerit, iam exposui. Itaque duo tantum habeo adhuc adnotanda; primum cum servi in collegiis Clodianis essent, non esse cogitandum de collegiis opificum, quae servos admisisse non arbitror, sed de sacris tantum; deinde Clodii legem ad Urbem tantum spectavisse, cum Cicero cellegia et *ex urbis faece* constituta dicat et Clodium in foro conscripsisse et decuriavisse."
[70] "Quibus deliciis veneunt tam aurea quam aurata, cum sciamus interdixisse castris suis Spartacum, ne quis aurum haberet aut argentum. Tanto fuit plus animi fugitivis nostris." Pliny, *Nat. Hist.* XXXIII. 14.
[71] Cf. *International Encyclopœdia*, Art. *Spartacus*.

FAITHFUL WIFE OF SPARTACUS. 303

For once we have a record of a skillful soldier, a loving husband, a humble workingman and a gentleman.

We are in possession of several very reliable evidences that Spartacus was married and that his wife shared his prison and military life. Plutarch is our authority for the first and Cornelius Tacitus for the latter. Not only was she faithful to him but she certainly became a celebrated pattern of fidelity, making herself by deeds of a true heroine, an object of praise to so great an extent that Tacitus holds her up as an example of the heroic character of German women. Her name was Varinia.[73] "The most terrible guerilla chieftain recorded in history was unstained by the vices of his conquerors."[74]

Spartacus had among his men, a large number of skilled workmen who belonged to unions. Among them were members of the *Fabricenses*,[75] armor makers; of the *Castrensiarii*, sutlers who took contracts under the old rule of Numa to supply the soldiers with provisions; *fabri*, workers in hard metals; *caligularii*, soldiers' boot makers or army cobblers and many other mechanics whom he engaged and employed in the manufacture of arms and other details of supplying his army. There was the great order of the *Vectigalarii*[76] which had been created by Numa, upheld by the Twelve Tables, and for 500 years employed by the Roman government and all the *Municipia* of Italy as collectors of the revenues from the incomes of the public domain, but which had lost their employment through the usurpation of the *ager publicus* by land monopolists and their system of slave labor.

---

[72] Plutarch, *Marcus Crassus*, (Langhorne,) says: "But they (meaning the obstinate slaves against the orders of Spartacus) relying upon their numbers, and elated with success, would not listen to his proposal. Instead of that, they laid Italy waste as they traversed it."

[73] Tacitus, *Germaniæ*, 8. "Memoriae proditur quasdam acies inclinatas iam et labantes a feminis restitutas constantia precum et objectu pectorum et monstrata comminus captivitate, quam longe impatientius feminarum suarum nomine timent, adeo ut efficacius obligentur animi civitatum, quibus inter obsides puellae quoque nobiles imperantur inesse quin etiam sanctum aliquid et providum putant, nec aut consilia earum aspernantur aut responsa neglegunt. vidimus sub divo Vespasiano Veledam diu apud plerosque numinis loco habitam, sed et olim Auriniam et compluris alias venerati sunt, non adulatione, neque tamquam facerent deas." It is said that this "Aurinia" was the wife of Spartacus.

[74] Smith's *Dictionary of Roman Biography*, Art. *Spartacus*.

[75] Orell., *Inscriptionem Latinarum Collectio*, Nos. 4,079, 4,083, and *infra Armorers*, chapter XV. pp. 372-88, *Trade unions*. There are many inscriptions showing that the blacksmiths, armorers and other iron and metal workers existed at that time in lower Italy, under the *collegia* or trade organizations.

[76] Orell., *Inscr. Lat. Collectio*, Vol. II. of *Collegia, Corpora, Sodalicia et cet*, pp. 227 246 Also index, Vol. III.

These he furnished with work and wages, by sending them *en revanche*, to collect from the rich who had usurped the lands, the provisions and money for his army and its expenses. Thus Spartacus, in the granary of Italy became the master workman of all the secret unions of trades and laborers; and we have no evidence disproving the immense popularity to which he unquestionably arose among the wage earners.

The army by this time, which must have been the early spring of B. C. 73, was swollen to 120,000 [17] men, armed and well equipped, in readiness to battle with the mightiest force Rome could muster. With this splendid force he now meditated a daring attempt on Rome.

But one great misfortune now began insidiously to exhibit itself. His army, especially that division of the Gauls under Crixus, his hitherto faithful lieutenant, began to show signs of jealousy. Of all the fratricidal passions that curse and wither the hopes and career of the organizations of labor, jealousy is the most venomous and deadly. Born of the human spirit, it runs in lurid juices as of the cobra's fangs, and strikes death under cover of fascination. With the adder's blindness it envenoms the atmosphere by puffs, mistaken for zephyrs and balm, and to the innocent like Spartacus it throttles the spirit with the dark moral shadows of doom.

Had this insidious spectre not appeared, the army of the gladiators and workingmen might perhaps have succeeded, to some extent, in a desperate march on Rome and thereby—although its conquest was out of the question—some wise negotiation might have succeeded in much permanent good to the proletaries. But the exact opposite was in the end the result. The plan of this campaign was not carried out.

The camp at Metapontum was constantly visited by

[17] Cf. Smith's *Dictionary of Roman Biography*, Art. *Spartacus*; Schambach, *Der Italische Sklavenaufstand*. Appian makes it to have been 120,000; and Spartacus seriously contemplated an invasion of Rome, he says, cap. 117, lib. I: "Ὁ δὲ Σπάρτακος τριακοσίους Ῥωμαίων αἰχμαλώτους ἐναγίσας Κρίξῳ, δώδεκα μυριάσι πεζῶν ἐς Ῥώμην ἠπείγετο, τά ἄχρηστα τῶν σκευῶν κατακαύσας καὶ τοὺς αἰχμαλώτους πάντας ἀνελὼν καὶ ἐπισφάξας τὰ ὑποζύγια, ἵνα κοῦφος εἴη· αὐτομόλων τε πολλῶν αὐτῷ προσιόντων οὐδένα προσίετο. καὶ τῶν ὑπάτων αὐτόν αὖθις περὶ τὴν Πικηνίτιδα γῆν ὑποστάντων, μέγας ἀγὼν ἕτερος ὅδε γίγνεται, καὶ μεγάλη καὶ τότε ἧσσα Ῥωμαίων." This was after the battle of Garganos and the death of Crixus. See *infra*. So Julius Obsequens, *vide* Lycosthens, *De Prodigiis*, 118: "Armorum horrendo clamore" (from Capua) "centum millia hominum consumpta Italico civilique belle relato est."

MODESTY OF HIS AMBITIONS. 305

merchants who purchased brass and iron and other goods on a large scale. We are told that it presented the spectacle of a great fair.

Spring came and it was learned that three consular armies, fully equipped, were on their way to meet the forces of the rebels; and Spartacus took up his line of march northward, keeping the shores of the Adriatic. The object of this movement was to reach the Alps, cross them and disperse the army at the point where the Gauls might return in safety to their homes to the northward and the Thracians might take to the right and thus reach their homes in Thrace.[78] It appears that Crixus and Œnomans had remained with Spartacus at the winter quarters but that there was a quarrel. The evidences

[78] No writer disagrees from the main statement that the central and longing idea of Spartacus was to reach his native home and again enjoy the occupations of peace. Plutarch, *Marcus Crassus*, 9, says : " By this time he (Spartacus) was become great and formidable. Nevertheless his views were moderate, He had too much understanding to hope the conquest of the Romans, and therefore led his army to the Alps, with an intention to cross them, and then dismiss his troops, that they might retire to their respective countries, some to Thrace and some to Gaul." Granier, next to Florus and the English Encyclopædists, the most merciless of the commentators, says : *Histoire des Classes Ouvrières et des Classes Bourgeoises:* " Spartacus, qui était un homme dont le cœur valait mieux que la condition, n'avait qu'une idée ; il voulait qu'on franchît les Alpes, qu'on gagnât les Gaules, et qu'une fois là, chacun reprit le chemin de son pays. La stratégie des consuls et la mutinerie de ses compagnons l'empêchèrent de réaliser son projet. Schambach defends Spartacus against the generally accepted libels and slanders afloat in Rome and which acted as a palliative subduing the galling fact that the haughty nation was humbled by a low-lived gladiator: " Hält es doch Florus für nöthig sich mit den Worten 'magnitudo cladium facit, ut meminerimus' zu entschuldigen, als er den Namen des Anführers in einem der sicilischen Aufstände anführt! Aber mit der ansicht, den Mann einfach todt zu schweigen, begnügte man sich nicht ; man befleckte sein Andenken durch erfundene Verbrechen und machte seinen Namen zu einem Schimpfworte, und selbst Männer wie Cicero und der ältere Plinius haben sich von den stimmen des grossen Haufens hierin nicht zu emancipiren vermocht. Uns, die wir keinen Grund haben, Spartacus als grimmigen Feind zu verabscheuen, liegt die Verpflichtung ob, seine Person in das richtige Licht zu stellen und gegen unverdienten Tadel zu vertheidigen," (Schambach, *Der Italische Sklavenaufstand*, S. 15. Dr. Drumann in Vol. IV. S. 74, sq. of his great History of Rome *(Römische Geschichte)* gives Spartacus this just tribute: "Die Natur hatte ihn zum Helden und Herrscher geschaffen, durch klugheit, Muth. Freiheitsliebe und Mässigung ragte er über seine Gefährten hervor ; er brachte das allmächtige Rom zum Zittern, als er die Ketten zerbrach, und begehrte auch jetzt nichts, als frei zu sein ; die Grausamkeiten seiner zügellosen Schaaren kommen nicht auf seine Rechnung, sofern sie nicht gegen die Unterdrücker gerichtet waren: nur gegen die Römer, in deren Spielen er sich und die Menschheit entehrt fühlte, die ihm nicht einmal die Flucht gestatteten, ihn und die Uebrigen einzufangen suchten, um sie an das Kreuz zu nageln, kannte er kein Erbarmen. Auch auf einer Höhe, wo Alles um ihn her den Schwindel befiel, blieb er besonnen ; er wollte Rom nicht zerstören, weil er nichts Unmögliches wollte ; die Vorhersagungen seiner thrakischen Gattin über die ihm beschiedene Grösse verblendeten ihn nicht ; aber die Sklaven verwirrten und vereitelten seinen Plan " The inquisitive student of Spartacus may al o consult a fragment of Varro, Charis. I. p. 108: "Spartaco innocente conjecto ad gladium." American Encyclopædia, Vol. XIV. p. 829, acknowledges that: "His own desire was to secure the freedom of the slaves by taking them beyond the Alps ; but they, eager for plunder, refused to leave Italy."

also tend to prove that Crixus and a large detachment of the Gauls separated from the main army on the march northward. Œnomans also had a falling out; for it seems he undertook an expedition to the westward of the main army under Spartacus on the march through Picenum near the Adriatic Sea. This expedition of Œnomaus was undertaken contrary to the wishes of Spartacus and to gratify a desire for plunder. This lieutenant was met by Gellius [79] commanding one of the three consular armies sent out by the Romans, and in the battle which followed, he was killed, his army routed and those soldiers who escaped were glad to get safely back to their general-in-chief who never ventured a battle without knowing beforehand that he had some chances in his favor.

But Crixus who was weak enough to be jealous in such a dangerous emergency was too weak to be victorious over the Romans. He rashly ventured a battle at the foot of Mount Garganus in Picenum, with his large detachment of the army, amounting to 35,000 men.[80] It is likely that he was drawn into an ambuscade by Arrius who commanded the third consular army of the Romans. Crixus in his speech to the soldiers before the battle braced his men with assurance that it was " better to die manfully in the attempt of freedom than to be butchered

[79] Orosius, *Historiarum Adversus Paganos Libri*, V. "Œnomaus enim jam superiore bello fuerat occisus." Schambach, *Italischer Sklavenaufstand*, S. 19, acknowledges the obscurity in which the facts regarding this lieutenant of Spartacus are enveloped : "Jener Œnomaus muss bald gefallen sein ; Crixus, der als der erste nach Spartacus erscheint, spielte seine Rolle länger."

[80] Livy, *Liber*, XCVI. *Epitome*, gives the number destroyed at 20,000 including Crixus. "Q. Arrius, prætor Crixum fugitivorum ducem cum viginti militbus hominum cecidit." Appian, *Historia Romana*, 117, *init*. "Καὶ τούτων ὑπὸ μὲν θατέρου Κρίξος, ἡγούμενος τρισμυρίων ἀνδρῶν, περὶ τὸ Γάργανον ὄρος ἥττατο, καί δύο μέρη τοῦ στρατοῦ καὶ αὐτὸς συναπώλετο αὐτοῖς· Σπάρτακον δὲ διὰ τῶν Ἀπεννίνων ὀρῶν ἐπί τὰ Ἄλπεια καὶ ἐς Κελτοὺς ἀπὸ τῶν Ἀλπείων ἐπειγόμενον ὁ ἕτερος ὕπατος προλαβὼν ἐκώλυε τῆς φυγῆς, καὶ ὁ ἕτερος ἐδίωκεν. ὁ δὲ ἐφ᾽ ἑκάτερον αὐτῶν ἐπιστρεφόμενος παρὰ μέρος ἐνίκα. καὶ οἱ μὲν σὺν θορύβῳ τὸ ἀπὸ τοῦδε ὑπεχώρουν·" Sallust, *Frag. Historiarum*. We quote the following fragment to show the desperate fighting of the slaves presumably at this battle with Crixus—"ingre, tante setui debacchoratur, nefandum in modum perverso vulnere et interdum lacerum corpus semianimum omittentes, alii in tecta jaciebant ignes, multique ex loco servi, quos ingenium socios debat, abdita à dominis aut ipsos trahebant ex occulto, neque sanctum aut nefandum quicquam fuit irae barbarorum ac servili ingenio : quæ Spartacus nequiens prohibere, multis precibus cum oraret, celeritate nuntios." In the next fragment we see the plans of Spartacus thwarted and Crixus on the eve of his overthrow and death: "Aliquot dies contra morem fiducia augeri nostris cæpit, et promi lingua. Qua Varinius contra spectatam rem incaute motus novos inccgnitosque et aliorum casibus percussos milites jam, neque tam magnifice fumentes prælium, quam postulaverant. Atque illi certamini conscii inter se juxta seditionem erant. Crixo et gentis ejusdem Gallis at que Germanis obviam ire et ultro offerre pugnam cupientibus contra Spartaum."

for a Roman holiday." The unfortunate Crixus, less discreet than intrepid rushed into the din of strife and in a furious battle which occupied the day was slain and his army defeated with great loss.

The routed soldiers, however, had one comfort. They could go back to their general better qualified through the lesson, with confidence in their sagacious chieftain whom they had deserted. Even this rebuke did not entirely quell the terribly revolutionary character of his insubordinate troops.

Spartacus now started over the Appennines in forced marches northward toward the river Po, dogged every inch of the route by the large consular armies of Rome under C. Cornelius Lentulus and Gellius Poplicola, the two consuls and Q. Arrius the prætor, who commanded the third consular army. But he sustained no losses. Every time the enemy ventured a battle he was sure to be hacked and punished by the terrible columns of the now veteran proletaries.[81]

Spartacus appears to have bent every energy toward making a permanent escape from Italy. In the struggle to make headway, the sallies of the enemy in flank and rear were always met by the wary gladiator with a shock which stupefied and annihilated them; and in this manner he contested every attack, watching with a judicious eye every movement of the several Roman armies, for opportunities to inflict the heaviest blows.

At last, in one of his wily manœuvres he succeeded in alluring Poplicola and his large army into a place suitable, as he believed, to make a general attack. We are a little undecided as to where this bloody battle took place. There are data to the effect that Spartacus now had 70,000 men in solid column.[82] But most of the great histories being lost, the lesser writers of those times perhaps

[81] Flor., III. 20, 10. "Inde jam consulares quoque aggressus, in Appenino Lentuli exercitum percecidit: apud Mutinam Caii Cassii castra delevit."

[82] It is probable that the rebel force was still stronger than this; for Appian puts it at 120,000 while yet in Thuria. Vallejus Paterculus, however, seems to carry the idea that it was less: "quorum numerus in tantum adolevit utque ultimo dimicavere acie XL millia hominum se Romano exercitui opposuerint." But his scholiast edition finds fault with these figures, as absurd and refers to Eutropius who says 60,000. Orosius and Livy, who make the rebel force about this time to have been a medium between 120,000 (Appian's statement) and 40,000 (that of Vallejus), concluding that the "C." of the latter author must have been changed in vicissitudes of so many ages into an "L," and that it originally read XC. millia or 90,000.

ashamed of what they considered a humiliation and disgrace, rush over the less prominent events, mentioning only in an obscure manner, certain points.

The tactics of Poplicola were to harass the flank while Lentulus kept his army in the front of Spartacus who took no further notice of the latter than to keep him from doing mischief. When at last, Spartacus saw his opportunity, burning with a desire to avenge Crixus, who had fallen at Mt. Garganus, he gave his men the long coveted order of attack.

A great and bloody battle was fought. All day the glitter of helmets and the clash of swords told the horrid tale of death. It was a rencounter of Greek and Gaul and Roman —representatives of the bravest lands of ancient days.

Phalanx by phalanx, the proud army of Poplicola gave way before the intrepid assaults of the laborers. No sooner did the Romans begin to weaken and bend than the carnage redoubled. Spartacus made good every opportunity and crashed upon the now broken columns of his adversary. Thousands of the Romans fell dead and dying. A few escaped. Night brought the slaughter to a sullen close.[84] The victorious legions of Spartacus returned to their tents to rest. Large numbers of prisoners had fallen into their hands, among whom were many haughty Roman knights. Spartacus with bitter irony soon afterwards forced them to fight as gladiators in the funeral games which he celebrated with pomp to the manes of Crixus.[85]

Thus we have an account of the fifth battle won by this

---

[83] Florus, III. 20, 12, is greatly grieved at this humiliation; "a quo pulsi, fugatique (pudet dicere) hostes in extrema Italiæ refugerunt."

[84] "Sur la route il rencontra et écrasa deux armées consulaires, deux autres prétoriennes et arriva enfin tout combattant et toujours victorieux sur les rives du Po, dont les eaux débordées lui barrèrent le chemin." La Rousse, Art. *Spartacus.* Plutarch, *Crassus*, tr. Langhorne, IX. says: "Lentulus, the other consul, endeavoured to surround Spartacus, with his forces, which were very considerable. Spartacus met him fairly in the field, beat his lieutenants, and stripped them of their baggage." Scraps from the earliest and best authors serve where the thread of the story is lost; and indicate the truthfulness of the history. Sallust has one as follows, which though badly mangled, seems to relate to this severe contest: * * * "M or Trequii præter s r ciem necessariam haud multo secus quam ferro noceri poterat. At Varinius, dum hæc aguntur à fugitivis, ægra parte militum autumni gravitate, neque ex postrema fuga, cum severo edicto juberentur, ullis ad signa redeuntibus, et qui relinqui erant per summa figitia detrectantibus militiam. Quæstorem suum C. Thoranium ex quo præsente vera facilime noscerunt, * * * commiserant, et tamen interim quum volentibus numero quatuor."

[85] Florus, III. 20. " Qui defunctorum quoque prælio ducum funera impera

FIFTH BATTLE. RETALIATION. 309

extraordinary genius. The episode of his avenging the death of Crixus by forcing the proud Roman leaders to descend to the debasing *ergastulum* and meet in gladiatorial combat and with the weapons of dishonor they had previously forced Crixus and Spartacus to wear, bears at once a tinge of melancholy and perhaps of gratification even to the most enlarged minds.

Not only the consuls but also two prætorian armies were completely routed by the tiger-like springs of Spartacus [86] during this phenomenal march northward in quest of his boyhood's home. It is indeed interesting to know that his wife accompanied him in his wanderings.[87] There seems to be a simplicity and tenderness which contrasts with the magnitude and the ferocity of his adventurers; something unique and almost enchanting is felt as one follows him step by step along his thorny path.

After routing and annihilating these prætorian armies,[88] we next find him face to face with the large army of Lentulus near the river Po.

Spartacus seems now to have assumed the character of a fugitive, so desirous was he to make his escape. Time had been given for the remnants of the Romans, shattered but not destroyed at the battle with Poplicola, to join the army of Lentulus, now augmented to larger numbers than any body of troops Spartacus had yet encountered.

There was a prætorian, or "third consular army" mentioned by Plutarch. Livy mentions Cassius as a pro-consul and C. Manlius as the prætor.[89] This would imply that two battles were fought between the two great pitched battles of Poplicola and of Lentulus, the regular

---

[86] toriis celebravit exequiis, captivosque circa rogum jussit armis depugnare: quasi plane expiaturus omne præteritum dedecus, si de gladiatore munerator fuisset." So also modern commentaries; See Smith's *Dictionary of Greek and Roman Biography*, Art. *Spartacus*. The *American Encyclopædia*, Vol. XIV. 1867, page 823, makes no hesitation in placing this humiliating episode as an event of the war, "At the head of 70,000 men he triumphed over two consular armies in 72, and forced his Roman captives to fight as gladiators at the funeral games which he celebrated."

[86] See Pomponius Mela. 21; Livy. *Epitomies*, XCV. XCVI. XCVII; Diod. XXXVIII. 21. Orosius, V. 24, 25. Cf. also considerable in the writings of Cicero, and in the various English and German *Encyclopædias*; these however, with few exceptions are childishly erroneous, contradictory and lamentably incomplete.

[87] Plutarch, *Crassus*, where we find this assurance.

[88] Cf. Smith's *Dictionary of Greek and Roman Biography*; La Rousse, *Dictionaire Universel*, Art. *Spartacus*, and Tacitus, *Germania* 8, where we find that her name was Aurinia.

Livy, *Epitom*. XCVI. "C. Cassius pro-consul et Cn. Manlius prætor male adversus Spartacum pugnaverunt."

consuls. Cassius who was prætor in the northern portions along the Po, with a large army of at least 10,000 men, gave battle to Spartacus just before the latter reached this river. It was a deadly encounter, and though the conflict raged with fierce determination on the part of the Romans, they were no match for the now invincible gladiator and his veterans who gained one of the most telling triumphs of the war.[90] It was between these two bloody engagements and in this region that Spartacus spent the winter of B. C. 72–71.

The army of the gladiator now increased.[91] We should be almost totally confounded without Livy's Epitomies of wrecked history at this juncture of the war, and could scarcely proceed. It is through these made clear, that after the defeat of Cassius and his 10,000 near the Po, as related by Plutarch, the really great battle spoken of, where Spartacus met Lentulus "fairly," was Livy's great carnage,[92] told in words too plain to admit of misunderstanding.[93] Plutarch says: "the two consuls having consolidated their troops in the country of Picenum, fell upon Spartacus in full force. He, however, gave them battle and with great slaughter nearly annihilated them." This fills two missing data. We are all along told that Spartacus, while near the river Po, before these "great defeats" of the "two consuls and their two prætorian armies," was a fugitive, anxiously striving with all his military tact, to escape from Roman territory. Now, however, we have authors augmenting the army of Spartacus.[94] We find him with a vast and well drilled, well disciplined, well fed and highly elated army of 120,000 men.

A march upon Rome was frustrated by the desire of plunder; although it is stated that Spartacus did not dare to make the attempt.[95]

---

[90] Plutarch, *Crassus*, 10. "He (Spartacus) then continued his route towards the Alps, but was opposed by Cassius, who commanded in that part of Gaul which lay about the Po, and came against him at the head of 10,000 men. A battle ensued, in which Cassius was defeated, with great loss, and saved himself not without difficulty." So Livy, *Epitome* of liber, XCVI. *et supra*, note 90.
[91] Plutarch, *Crassus*, 10.
[92] Livy, *Epitome*, XCVI. "Idcirco duo consules, junctis copiis in agro Piceno ei concurrerunt. Sed illa (Spartacus licet eas magna clade profligasset."
[93] Schambach, *Italischer Sklavenaufstand*, S. 8, concedes the scholiast view. Livy did not write the epitomies to his books, but thinks that they are faithful to the original contents.
[94] Livy, XCVI. of *Epitomies*, of the lost books. Appian, I. 117.
[95] Livy, *Epitome*, XCVI. "Ad Urbem ducre non est ausus."

SIXTH AND SEVENTH BATTLES. 311

This great battle between Spartacus and the combined armies of the two consuls, Lentulus and Poplicola, took place a long distance south of the Po, near where Spartacus had defeated the first consular army under Poplicola; for it was in the territory of Picenum, nearly 200 miles from the river. The army of the proletaries was now about 100 miles northeastward from Rome and was marching southward. This arrangement of data brings the statement of Plutarch in line and clears up the whole jumble. The story of Cassius and his defeated army of 10,000 was Plutarch's battle of the Po. Spartacus then taking the offensive, marched southward into Picenum, where he fought the great battle of Picenum—the *magna cladis* of Livy.

Great consternation now prevailed at Rome. The news of the disaster to Lentulus and Poplicola and their splendid armies was regarded as a calamity. Indignation raised to its highest pitch and was only equalled by mortification and shame. A gladiator,[96] and slave, who, all his lifetime had been a poor man, earning a scanty living by manual toil, had combined audacity with genius, gathered the menial hordes[97] that worked the estates of haughty landlords and in eight battles, at hand-to-hand combat and at the test of strategem, endurance, valor and prowess had worsted, overthrown and annihilated the patrician gentry of Rome.[98]

Lentulus was recalled and disgraced. His humiliation has always been a mystery to readers of history. The true light of the affair has been shut out—so dark was the history of this matter kept for ages from the reader's mind.

Spartacus was maligned by everybody; and public sentiment turned a smile in his favor into a heresy and intimidated the favorable opinions and conversation of the people as well as blockaded the will and the pen of historians.

Spartacus, everywhere victorious was, after the great

[96] Florus, III, 20. "Tandem etiam totis imperii viribus contra mirmillionem consurgitur."
[97] Livy, *Epitome*, XCV. "Res proseræ, et assolet, statim invenerunt socios, multosque pastores, durum et pernix genus."
[98] Cicero, *Ad Atticum*, VI. 22. "Cum Spartaco—duce fugitivorum, qui bellum servile commovit, et vel cum quingentis prædonibus jam satis mali facere potuit."

battle in Picenum, forced to proceed southward by his foolish soldiers who, puffed [99] with success, were wanting in obedience and could not participate in the dream of Spartacus to retire to the pastoral charms of his native land. We next find him marching to Thuria, with a vast army and great quantities of plunder, with the intention of passing the winter of 72-71, B. C. But another victory was yet to be won before the army could reach its winter quarters—the battle with Mummius in Picenum.[100]

It was now nearing the time of the Roman Comitiæ, or the assembly of Roman citizens for voting for new officers. Among these officers consuls were to be elected. But so great was the terror which Spartacus had inspired that no candidates were to be found. This phenomenon is explained by the fact that whoever should be elected consul would have to go in person to meet the dreaded gladiator. Finally, after much hesitation, Marcus Licinius Crassus, consented to be nominated and of course, received the full vote and confidence of the people.

Accordingly, Crassus, prepared for the campaign against the great guerrilla chieftain with eight full legions of Roman soldiers mustered for the occasion. But the fragments of the defeated armies of Poplicola and Lentulus, together with the prætorian forces, also shattered by Spartacus, were now returning to the metropolis in a straggling, demoralized condition. All these were soon joined to the new army of Crassus.[101]

The new confidence which this election of Crassus inspired caused a great number of young Roman gentry to volunteer, and we may be certain that the eight legions were full. A full Roman legion of that era consisted of 6,000 men which makes 48,000 for the new army of eight legions.

[99] Cf. Smith's, *Dictionary of Greek and Roman Biography*.
[100] This account is given in Plutarch's *Life of Crassus*. Mommsen, *History of Rome*, here breaks the story of Spartacus and his victories into a tangle of unintelligible data, although its thread is seen to be quite clear, with a little pains.
[101] Appian, *Historia Romana*, I, 118: "Τριέτης τε ἦν ἤδη καὶ φοβερὸς αὐτοῖς ὁ πόλεμος, γελώμενος ἐν ἀρχῇ καὶ καταφρονούμενος ὡς μονομάχων. Προτεθείσης τε στρατηγῶν ἄλλων χειροτονίας ὄκνος ἐπεῖχεν ἅπαντας, καὶ παρήγγελλεν οὐδείς, μέχρι Λικίνιος Κράσσος, γένει καὶ πλούτῳ Ῥωμαίων διαφανής, ἀνεδέξατο στρατηγήσειν, καὶ τέλεσιν ἐξ ἄλλοις ἤλαυνεν ἐπὶ τὸν Σπάρτακον." Plutarch says: "No sooner were the senate informed of these miserable proceedings, than they expressed the greatest indignation against the consuls, and gave orders that they should be superseded in the command, Crassus was the person they pitched upon as a successor, and many of the nobility served under him, as volunteers, as well on account of his political influence and from personal regard."

From the start, there must have been at least 100,000 men sent out under Crassus against the rebels, which force kept constantly increasing to the end.

Returning to Spartacus, we find evidence [102] that while at the zenith of his popularity between the Po—which he did not cross—and Picenum, he offered inducements to all who would cast off the yoke of despotism, to join. That the slaves took the offer of freedom is evident from the number, which commentators venture to put at 120-000, and which we positively know soon greatly augmented. Many of the higher classes spurned offers to co-operate because they "disdained to join slaves;" although they hated the Romans. [103]

When Crassus arrived in Cis-Alpine Gaul, near the city of Mutina, where the army of Spartacus lay, he studied closely the traits of his antagonist and concluded to adopt the tactics of Fabius who had previously been successful over Hannibal, by worrying him and not giving battle. After harassing Spartacus in rear and flank for some time he sent the pro-consul, C. Cassius Longinus, around on the other side with orders to be watchful and goad the enemy, without hazarding an engagement; but the fox-witted gladiator, with apparent indifference, allured this Roman into an idea that he could safely go beyond his orders, and attack a wing of the workingmen who were in reality, impatient for the fray.

At a weak moment, least suspected and least watched, Spartacus gave the welcome order of battle. The shout went up and with it came the force of the onset. Cassius was crushed by the unexpected blow and completely routed. The field of Mutina covered with the slain, remained with the workingmen.

Spartacus, slowly continuing his march southward, harassed and tormented by Crassus who was too good a commander to venture a general engagement, studied every opportunity to catch the Roman at a weak point. [104] Op-

---

[102] Cf. Larousse, *Dictionaire Universel*, Art. *Spartacus*, based on the remarks of Plutarch.

[103] These gems giving the finishing touches of the story, are taken from isolated fragments of the broken histories so badly mutilated indeed, that we should be loth to pass upon them, did not our inferences coincide with those of others who have taken great pains to get the kernel of the theme.

[104] "Le général Romain se borna de couvrir le Latium, n' osant hasarder battaille contre le terrible gladiate r et se contenta á le harceler et le faire misérable, par ces lieutenants, invariablement battus quand ils avaient la témérité

portunity soon came. The propraetor, Cn. Manlius, was caught at an unguarded moment and in a terribly bloody conflict of which we have only a sullen and lugubrious mention by historians, was torn to atoms by the charge of a heavy detachment of Spartacus.

The condition of the Roman army was now that of terror. After the defeat of Cassius at the city of Mutina and of Manlius at a point southward, we find Spartacus, still harassed by Crassus, in the rich valleys of Picenum, the scenes of the next and ninth battle in which the gladiator chieftain was conqueror. Crassus posted himself here, in advance of the workingmen, for the purpose of intercepting their march southward.

Mummius, one of the most trustworthy lieutenants of Crasus, was sent round to the flank of the enemy, with orders to continue strategical manœuvres; and was strictly charged to follow him, but not to hazard a battle. Mummius had more courage and conceit than discretion or obedience. He proved to be precisely the man whom Spartacus wanted. The foxy gladiator now dallied with ruse and incantation and finally decoyed the whole force, consisting of 12,000 men into an assailable point. This whole manœuvre seems to have been deeply laid inasmuch as it contained an admixture of flattery. At any rate, however ambidextrous the incentive, the decoy on the one hand and the ambition on the other, prevailed.

Just when Mummius believed he was in the act of ridding his country of a loathsome foe, a wild war-whoop of the mirmillions burst out along the lines. Spartacus at the enemy's vulnerable points gave the order of attack. This time it was many against few. Mummius was overslaughed. "His whole army completely routed. Many were killed upon the battle field. Others terrified, cast away their arms and saved their lives by flight."[106]

Again the arms of Spartacus were victorious. Mummius was annihilated.[107] Disaster again convulsed the ægis of slaveholding, degenerate Rome, whose haughty men, many of whom owned at that moment from 1,000 to

---

de livrer combat." La Rousse, *Dictionaire Universel*, Art. *Spartacus*.
[106] Plutarch, *Idem;* Appian ; Mommsen and some of the *Encyclopædias*.
[107] Cf. *International Encyclopædia*, Art. *Spartacus*. Although we give reference to original authority there is a variety of readings and of opinions ; and we therefore cite contemporaneous writers and recommend them to the reader.

TENTH BATTLE. MUMMIUS RUINED. 815

10,000 slaves each, were freshly reminded by every victory of Spartacus, of the doom of their crumbling institution, sacred, as one of the pillars of the paganism they worshiped for a religion. Crassus had cause to be severe. Plutarch adds that: " He severely reprimanded Mummius who had escaped unhurt. He armed the few survivors anew, insisting upon their giving bond of fidelity to the new arms given them. He took 500 of the most cowardly, divided them into 50 platoons and these into decades, one of whom was by lot, put to death; in this way recalling an ancient military usage of punishment. This kind of punishment in fact, is the mark of the greatest infamy; for as the execution is public, in sight of the whole army, circumstances that are awful and affecting follow."[108] But this horrible chastisement came late. Spartacus had again been victorious.

But two causes now set in to cast shadows over the glory of the conquering gladiator. His own ignorant and foolish soldiers began again to show signs of insubordination, elated by their never failing successes. They wanted to plunder and feast upon the fat of the land; and while they were actually becoming demoralized and dissolute in their extraordinary experience of victory, their new enemy Crassus was growing wiser and surer in his harrowing experience of defeat. These two causes combined to bring the terrible lion to his end.

Crassus, after this ferocious specimen of the cruelty of war, attacked Spartacus, and drove him to the sea.[109] But

---

[108] Plutarch, *idem;* Appian, *Historia Romana,* I. 118. " Καὶ τῶνδὲ μὲν αὐτίκα διακληρώσας, ὡς πολλάκις ἡττημένων, ἐπὶ θανάτῳ μέρος δέκατον διέφθειρεν. Οἱ δ' οὐχ οὕτω νομίζουσιν, ἀλλὰ παντὶ τῷ στρατῷ συμβαλόντα καὶ τόνδε, καὶ ἡττημένον, πάντων διακληρῶσαι τὸ δέκατον, καὶ ἀνελεῖν ἐς τετρακισχιλίους, οὐδὲν διὰ τὸ πλῆθος ἐνδοιάσαντο. ὁποτέρως δ' ἔπραξε, φοβερώτερος αὐτοῖς τῆς τῶν πολεμίων ἥττης φανεὶς αὐτίκα μυρίων Σπαρτακείων ἐφ' ἑαυτῶν που στρατοπεδευόντων ἐκράτει, καὶ δύο αὐτῶν μέρη κατακανὼν ἐπ' αὐτὸν ἤλαυνε τὸν Σπάρτακον σὺν καταφρονήσει." Sallust, *Historiarum Populi Romani, libri.* Recensio of Anton. Thysius, old Lugdunum edition, p. 502, has a sadly mutilated scrap; "Sorte ductos fusti necat:" and the learned editor in a note explains as follows: "*Sorte ductos fusti necat,* Puto legendum, eductos, accipiendumq; de severa ac militari Crassi disciplina, qua idem in fugitoribus coërcendis usus, ex duabus Mummianis Legionibus contra edictum Imperatoris in hostem (Spartacum) pugnare ausis, profligatisque; quingenpit primos, unde initium fugæ factum fuerat, sorte eductos decimari præcetos. Quod vetus supplicii genus intermortuum, ac desitum jampridem, postliminio in castra Romana reductum a Crasso." According to Sallust they were killed with clubs.

[109] Appian I. 118, fin: " Νικήσας δὲ καὶ τόνδε λαμπρῶς ἐδίωκε φεύγοντα ἐπὶ τὴν θάλασσαν ὡς διαπλευσούμενον ἐς Σικελίαν, καὶ καταλαβὼν ἀπετάφρευε καὶ ἀπετείχιζε καὶ ἀπεσταύρου." Mommsen, *History of Rome,* Vol. IV. p. 106.

SPARTACUS.

this signal victory mentioned by Appian, is denied by Plutarch in the following terms: "After thus chastising his men, he (Crassus) led them against the enemy. But Spartacus turned back and retired through Lucania to the sea."[110]

Spartacus marched his army southward along the Adriatic to embark for Sicily across the straits of Messina. There is strong circumstantial evidence that privateers of the Mediterranean assisted Spartacus; and if we judge from this point of view, a new light is thrown upon the history of his career. No written records, however, exist proving this, and for want of it we follow the story as it is told.

If the pirates, so-called, refused to help him, thus clearly working in the interest of Rome, as Mommsen suggests, why should Rome have immediately instituted a man-hunt against them? Tacitus has some remarks favoring our theory that the pirates were faithful to Spartacus. Another potent question is, how did the gladiator get the great army of 300,000 men? Did not the privateers ship them over from Sicily? We shall refer to these things later.

This new move of Spartacus to reach Sicily is called by some, his last stroke of genius. It was an original one. There had been, some 27 years before, a great rebellion of the slaves in Sicily [111] and at this moment, when Spartacus approached that fair isle—the granary of Rome—it was suffering from the most inhuman exactions, by order of Verres, the insatiate and avaricious despoiler, whose greedy havoc was soon afterwards opposed by Cicero. The slaves and property owners alike, were goaded by this man's rapacity to the verge of rebellion against Rome. Had Spartacus succeeded in crossing safely with his army the chances are that the goaded people would have gladly

---

[110] Plutarch, *Life of Crassus.*
[111] See chapter xi *supra.* The strange words of Cornelius Tacitus, *Annalium*, liber, XV. cap. 46; referring to Spartacus and the Roman flotilla against the pirates, show how fearful was the danger, and they seem to advert to the link of friendship existing between them and Spartacus: "Per idem tempus gladiatores apud oppidum Præneste temptata eruptione praesidio militis, qui custos adesset, coërciti sunt, iam Spartacum et vetera mala rumoribus ferente populo, ut est novarum rerum cupiens pavidusque. Nec multo post clades rei navalis accipitur, non bello (quippe haud alias tam immota pax), sed certum ad diem in Campaniam redire classem Nero jusserat, non exceptis maris casibus. Ergo gubernatores, quamvis saeviente pelago, a Formiis movere; et gravi Africo, dum promunturium Miseni superare contendunt, Cumanis litoribus impacti triremium plerasque et minora navigia passim amiserunt."

THE PRIVATEERS LEND A HAND. 317

joined him in overwhelming numbers, if for nothing else than to rid themselves of this insatiable Roman governor whose exactions, to satisfy personal greed, well-nigh brought Sicily to bankruptcy and ruin.[112]

On his arrival at the sea opposite the Sicilian shore, Spartacus who had formed this plan of crossing over with his entire army for the purpose of recruiting from the ranks of the slaves, negotiated with the freebooters or brigand mariners, as they are mercilessly called in the histories, who from ancient times ransacked the coasts for plunder.[113]

They exhibited a quality of perfidy, perhaps against Rome—although the historians show that it was against Spartacus—which actually resulted in their being swept from their trade; for soon after the suppression of the servile war which they are represented to have been too treacherous and disingenuous to sustain, the Romans sent an expedition against them which certainly was a continuation of the great man-hunt ending in their own extermination.[114] If Spartacus could have accomplished this magnificent strategical feat and realized his scheme of passing the winter in Sicily where the terribly-oppressed and down-trodden slaves would have deserted in vast numbers and extricated themselves from their otherwise hopeless servitude, he might, allowing him his wonted success, not only have beaten Crassus, but also the armies of Pompey and Lucullus when they afterwards arrived.

In fact, we know not what would have been the final result upon the human race—indeed, we are loth to speculate; for under the humane management of Spartacus it might have resulted in a permanent recognition of the honor and merit of human labor which was in those times denied.

It is enough to repeat what history relates, that the selfish, dishonest and treacherous pirates took the proffered gold of Spartacus but failed to land him in Sicily; for though his army enormously increased, yet his failing to

[112] Cicero, *Verres, passim*. Here Cicero gives an eloquent account of this man's extortious. Cicero assumed the cause of the people vs. Verres and succeeded in obtaining a verdict.
[113] Heeren, *Peuple de l' Antiquité*, Vol. II. pp. 170-173 of the French translation.
[114] Liv., XCVIII. "L. Metellus prætor in Sicilia adversus piratos prospere rem gessit." *(Epitome);* Vellejus Paterculus, *Abridgment of Latin History, Book* II. c. 31.

get there probably disconcerted and squeezed him betwixt the mill-stones of peril and hope, leaving him heart-broken and defeated. It was the knell of Spartacus. What further the historian can trace of this great general and most marvelous genius is but the description of prodigious spasms and writhings of a dying giant.

Crassus, watching from a distance these defeated manœuvres of the gladiator, conceived the idea of imprisoning him in the narrow neck or point of the promontory of Bruttium or Rhegium, by throwing up a line of circumvallation across this miniature isthmus with an object of hemming the proletarian army in and besieging it during the winter. The writer of the article in the Great French Universel Dictionary declares that Crassus was positively afraid to give the enemy an honorable battle.[115] Spartacus, regarded this enormous line of retrenchments with contempt. It was an earthwork reaching from sea to sea, being, as Plutarch tells us, "36 miles long, fifteen feet high and a wall above this of considerable height—a work great and difficult."

It was now the winter of B. C. 71-70. The supplies for the army of the proletaries were disappearing. Something must be done. Spartacus watched his opportunity, bent on retreat which involved an escape from this trap. One dark wintry night amid the roar of a storm, while the forces of Crassus lay chilled, and torpid, least alert and fitted for surprise, the army of the slaves, at the command of their leader, burst from the bivouacs and sword in hand scaled the intrenchment, filling it with earth and wood, and in spite of all resistance passed over and gained the free plains beyond.[116] Thus commenced the admirable re-

---

[115] Speaking of Spartacus he says: "Telle ètait, cependant la terreur qu' il inspirait encore, que Crassus entreprit de l' enfermer dans la presq' île de Rhegium, par une fosse d'un retranchment de 15 lieus de longeur! Le chef des esclaves temoigna son profond mépris pour cet immense travaille èt pour des ennemis qui n' osaient plus l' attaquer en face; puis quand les vivres commenceraient de lui manquer, il combla une partie de la tranchée pendant une nuit orageuse, força les lignes der Romains et manouvra librement dans la Lucanie, ou il extermina encore les troupes des deux leutènants de Crassus qui oseraient l' inquieter dans sa retraite." La Rousse, Dictionaire Universel, Art. Spartacus.

[116] Appian, Historia Romana, I. 119: Σπάρτακος δὲ ἱππέας ποθὲν αὐτῷ προσιόντας περιμένων, οὐκέτι μὲν ἐς μάχην ᾔει τῷ στρατῷ παντί, πολλὰ δ' ἠνώχλει τοῖς περικαθημένοις ἀνὰ μέρος, ἄφνω τε καὶ συνεχῶς αὐτοῖς ἐπιπίπτων, φακέλους τε ξύλων ἐς τὴν τάφρον ἐμβάλλων κατέκαιε, καὶ τὸν πόνον αὐτοῖς δύσεργον ἐποίει. Αἰχμάλωτόν τε 'Ρωμαῖον ἐκρέμασεν ἐν τῷ μεταιχμίῳ, δεικνὺς τοῖς ἰδίοις τὴν ὄψιν ὧν πείσονται μὴ κρατοῦντες." Mommsen, History of Rome, IV. p. 107: "but in a dark winter night Spartacus broke through the lines of the enemy, and in the spring of 71

treat of Spartacus—a retreat which for fine generalship combining fertility of expedient, quelling insubordination within, and overcoming obstacles without, may yet, when more carefully studied and better known, come to be regarded as one of the true models in warfare. The Roman general now thoroughly frightened, wrote to Rome for more help.[117]

It appears that after the failure of Spartacus to reach Sicily, a revolt of prodigious extent took place in his army. A body of probably over 50,000 men separated from the main army. They vaunted that Spartacus was a coward; dared not meet the Roman general; that they would not longer be restrained from giving the hated enemy battle. They accordingly appointed as their commanders two of the most boasting of the malcontents, Gannicus and Castus, and demanded of these inexperienced captains to be led to battle.[118] They then provoked the army of Crassus to an engagement. When Spartacus, whose wearying sym-

---

was once more in Lucania." Plutarch, *Crassus*, tells the same story, while Schambach, clearly shows it to have been the spring of 70.

[117] Appian, I. 119–120: " Οἱ δ' ἐν ἄστει Ῥωμαῖοι τῆς πολιορκίας συνθανόμενοι, καὶ ἀδοξοῦντες εἰ χρόνιος αὐτοῖς ἔσται πόλεμος μονομάχων, προσκατέλεγον ἐπὶ τὴν στρατείαν Πομπήιον ἄρτι ἀφικόμενον ἐξ Ἰβρίας, πιστεύοντες ἤδη δυσχερὲς εἶναι καὶ μέγα τὸ Σπαρτάκειον ἔργον. Διὰ δὲ τὴν χειροτονίαν τήνδε καὶ Κράσσος, ἵνα μὴ τὸ κλέος γένοιτο Πομπηίου, πάντα τρόπον ἐπειγόμενος ἐπεχείρει τῷ Σπαρτάκῳ, καὶ ὁ Σπάρτακος, τὸν Πομπήιον προλαβεῖν ἀξιῶν, ἐς συνθήκας τὸν Κράσσον προσκαλεῖτο." Crassus much frightened, certainly sent for and obtained both the army under Pompey, victorious in Spain and that of Lucullus from Asia Minor, victorious in the Mithridatic war. See also La Rousse, *Dictionaire Universel*, Art. *Spartacus*: " Crassus écrivait au senat afin qu'on envoyât pour le seconder, Pompée alors de retour d' Espagne, et Lucullus qui revenait d' Asie. Mais il repentait bientôt de cette démarche et recherchat les occasions de terminer la guerre afin d' avoir seule l' honneur."

[118] Plutarch, *idem*, is one of our best witnesses on this great battle: "He resolved, therefore, in the first place, to attack the troops which had revolted, and formed a separate body, under the command of two officers named Cannicius and Castus. With this view, he sent a corps of six thousand men before to seize an eminence which he thought would be of service to him but ordered them to conduct their enterprise with all imaginable secrecy. They observed his directions; and, to conceal their march the better, covered their helmets and the rest of their arms. Two women, however, who were sacrificing before the enemy's camp, discovered them, and they would probably have met their fate, had not Crassus advanced immediately, and given the enemy battle. This was the most obstinate action in the whole war. Twelve thousand three hundred of the enemy were killed, of which number there were only two found wounded in the back; the rest died in their ranks, after the bravest exertions of valour." Livy, whose valuable history of this great war is lost is fortunately quoted by Frontinus, *Strategematon*, II. 5, 34, out of the 97th, the book of the *Annales Ab Urbe Condita*, as follows: "Triginta quinque millia armatorum (fugitivorum a Crasso devictorum) eo proelio interfecta cum ipsis ducibus (Casto et Gannico) Livius tradit, receptas quinque Romanorum aquilas, signa sex et viginti, multa spolia, inter quae fasces cum securibus." This makes the numbers actually killed to have been 35,000. Undoubtedly this is the more accurate estimate; it also shows the enormous magnitude of the army of Spartacus.

pathies echoed his foreknowledge of the certain result, perceived this movement, he evidently gave up all for lost and resolved to die, bravely combating for his cause. Crassus met the seceders and a terribly bloody battle took place near Croton, on the banks of a lake in lower Lucania, whose waters, Plutarch says, are " sometimes pure and sometimes salt." The contest was extremely severe. Plutarch wrongly describes it as the greatest of the war. It was long before the army of the seceders gave way. Not a man flinched. Of the heaps of slain none were wounded in the back; all falling in the ranks performing the bravest acts of valor. At last, overcome by numbers they were forced to yield a little, giving the Romans an advantage which they took and killed 12,300, or as Livy, quoted by Frontin, probably more correctly puts it, 35,000,[19] of the seceders, on the spot; nor would any of the proletaries have survived the slaughter had not Spartacus, by a forced march, arrived in season to interfere and put an end to the bloody work. But Ganicus and Castus were among the slain.

Crassus on the whole, had made little to be proud of by this last encounter; for his forces were much more numerous than the seceders. Besides he certainly lost a large number of men in the contest, and perceiving that its effect was only to heal the mutiny and knit the rebels together into an indissoluble brotherhood by teaching the dangers of their temerity, he began to fear that Spartacus, now rapidly marching northward, was earnestly meditating an attack on Rome.

The army of the proletaries, still hugging the shores of the sea, was now nearing the Tarentine gulf on its march northward toward the port of Brundusium in its second attempt to reach Sicily by sea. Just after cross-

[119] Frontin, in his *Strategematon*, or *Military Science*, liber II. cap. v. 34, *De Insidiis*, instances this battle as one of the prominent examples of military tactics; and gives the great conflict in a new and interesting dress: "Crassus, Bello Fugitivorum apud Cantennam (Catanam) bina castra comminus cum hostium castris vallavit. Nocte deinde commotis copiis, manente praetorio in maioribus castris, ut fallerentur hostes, ipse omnes copias eduxit et in radicibus praedicti montis constituit; divisoque equitatu praecepit L. Quintio, partem Spartaco obiceret pugnaque eum frustraretur, parte alia Gallos Germanosque ex factione Casti et Cannici eliceret ad pugnam et fuga simulata deduceret, ubi ipse aciem instruxerat: quos cum barbari insecuti essent equite recedente in cornua, subito acies Romana adaperta cum clamore procurrit. XXXV milia armatorum eo proelio interfecta cum ipsis ducibus Livius tradit, receptas quinque Romanas aquilas, signa sex et XX, multa spolia, inter quae quinque fasces cum securibus."

ing the river Strongoli, or Neæthus of the ancients, and in the very ancient town of Petelia, the Roman forces under the command of L Quintius, one of the officers of Crassus and the quæstor, Tremellius Scrofa, came up with the intention only of harrassing him in rear and flank, according to the express orders of Crassus who adhered to the Fabian tactics. Spartacus on being attacked by a few skirmishers in the rear, suddenly wheeled a large detachment upon the Romans who were not prepared, and succeeding in routing them so completely that the quæstor who was wounded, barely escaped with his life. It was another great victory.

But Crassus, who was a good judge of effects, soon perceived that it was the cause of reviving among the slaves the malignant spirit of insubordination. They were again so inflated with success that they threatened to rebel; and their miserable conduct forced Spartacus to take an opposite direction from that which he chose to march, causing a disaster by hurrying them onward to final downfall. Plutarch declares that the insurgents after this victory became so arrogant and mutinous that they drew swords and insisted upon being led against Crassus' army in open field. They demanded to be marched through Campania to Rome; and Spartacus was not long afterwards forced to give orders to march toward the now trembling capital. Yet notwithstanding this insubordination he could but admire their bravery and knew their impetuosity when led to battle. Plutarch in speaking of their valor at the battle of the seceders where, according to Livy, no less than 35,000 of the rebels were slain, says that they died manfully, only two of the killed being found wounded in the back. "The rest had died in the ranks, after the grandest exhibit of bravery." Spartacus, aware of the approach of Pompey from the direction of Rome, on the one hand, and of the expected landing of Lucullus at Brundusium, on the other, and knowing the folly of hope against these three great veteran armies combined, struck a forced march for Brundusium, thinking still to secure the co-operation of the privateers in transporting him to Sicily, before Lucullus hove in view. Though he could rely upon his soldiers' bravery he foresaw that a general engagement must be fatal.

Thus we begin to comprehend the strange reticence of the historians regarding the fresh allies of Crassus, now actually centering together. The old stigma upon the touch of a creature of lowly condition by an optimate of Rome is apparently the cause of the suppression of all histories which gave the details. There is one authority, however, which brings some of these marvels to light. This is Vellejus Paterculus whose History of Rome was early mutilated in all the manuscripts except one, which survived until it was printed late in the Middle Ages. Armed with this, we see better to follow the thread of this great rebellion to its close, and can thus correct some very misleading errors of modern writers.

The whole army of the proletaries moved to the seaport of Brundusium, where it was hoped to obtain ships and sail to Sicily. But here Spartacus was met and assailed by Lucullus at that moment in the act of landing his whole army, recalled by the senate of Rome to help Crassus. Whether much fighting took place we are not informed; but foiled again in his designs by sea, he turned northward, harassed and goaded by the veteran army from Asia in full force.

In these returning legions of Lucullus, was a man who was soon afterwards destined to play an extraordinary rôle, in favor of the proletaries, and to lose his life in their defense. It was Clodius, a brother-in-law of Lucullus, general-in-chief. Wealthy, of noble blood, educated, and one of the most eloquent lawyers of those days—a man who restored to the poor workingmen their right of organization, and who in doing this, crippled the mighty Cicero and brought him to disgrace, exile and final death. But we leave his extraordinary story for other pages of our history to recount. Suffice it here to say that the indescribable scenes of suffering and of horror which he was eye witness to in this campaign shaped his life-course ever afterwards, in favor of the lowly.[120]

[120] Publius Clodius was of patrician blood. See Lippincott's *Biographical Dictionary*, Vol. I, art. *Clodius*. "Demagogue of a very profligate character of the patrician house of Appius Claudius Pulcher; served in Asia under Lucullus his brother-in-law; became a violent enemy of Cicero who had appeared in evidence against him; raised several bloody riots against the friends of Cicero when they proposed and passed a decree for his restoration B. C. 57" (see Cicero, *Pro Milone*); Drumann, *Geschichte Roms*. The *Encyclopædia Britannica*, refusing to mention him under a special article-heading, calls Clodius "a worthless demagogue,"

LAST EFFORT TO ESCAPE. 323

Lucullus, according to good authority, **drove the gladiator from the shipping and dogged him in the rear at every step.**[121] Pompey was present with the whole of the large army which he had successfully commanded in Spain. These facts we know; for if we do not find mention of actual participation of these two freshly-arrived Roman generals and their veteran legions, as being engaged in the great and final battle of Silarus, we certainly find them engaged in the man-hunt which was instituted on the same day. Plutarch also hints at the fact.

In apparent deference to Crassus, who was the real commander of the three combined armies, the history-manglers have evidently seen fit to trifle with the truth in leaving no mention of Pompey or of Lucullus in the last great conflict. And especially pointed does this suggestion become when we take into consideration that neither of these two generals was desirous of having his name mixed up with so disgraceful a thing as a victory over what went current under the name of a mob of gladiators.

It is thus made certain that the workingmen were hemmed in between these three experienced consular and veteran armies of Rome, in a mountain pass at the head

---

while acknowledging that he "assailed Cicero with a formal charge of putting citizens to death summarily without appeal to the people," obtaining a decree from the people for his banishment 400 miles from the city. Under the title "*Milo,*" the *Pugilist* and murderer of Clodius, the *Encyclopædia Britann.* says: "P. Clodius, the leader of the ruffians who professed the democratic cause was his personal enemy, and their brawls in the streets and their mutual accusations in the law courts lasted for several years " Thus Clodius, the champion of trade unions and organized labor is called "leader of the ruffians" who were the working people of Rome. The Lippencott *Biographical Dictionary,* Art, *Cicero,* says of Cicero: "His enemy, Clodius, who became tribune of the people in B. C. 58, and who was supported by Cæsar and Pompey, now manifested his vindictive malice against Cicero by a law which he proposed: that whoever has put to death a Roman citizen without form of trial shall be interdicted from fire and water." The fact that Cicero had committed such murders is proved by the actual passage of this law and his being sent into exile and his house on the Palitinate Hill publicly burned, thus consummating his terrible disgrace. We fail to see in these stern measures of Clodius in punishing murder, and in upholding the aged and respectable law permitting the organization of the working people, anything that would not be considered humane and respectable in the highest degree, if repeated right in our own blazing civilization.

[121] Appian, 120, of book I. says : . . . . "Πομπηίου, πάντα τρόπον ἐπειγόμενος ἐπεχείρει τῷ Σπαρτάκῳ, καὶ ὁ Σπάρτακος, τὸν Πομπήιον προλαβεῖν ἀξιῶν, ἐς συνθήκας τὸν Κράσσον προυκαλεῖτο. ὑπερορώμενος δ᾽ ὑπ᾽ αὐτοῦ διακινδυνεύειν τε ἔγνω, καὶ παρόντων οἱ τῶν ἱππέων ἤδη ὥσατο παντὶ τῷ στρατῷ διὰ τοῦ περιτειχίσματος, καὶ ἔφυγεν ἐπὶ Βρεντέσιον Κράσσου διώκοντος. ὡς δὲ καὶ Λεύκολλον ἔμαθεν ὁ Σπάρτακος ἐς τὸ Βρεντέσιον, ἀπὸ τῆς ἐπὶ Μιθριδάτῃ νίκης ἐπανιόντα, εἶναι, πάντων ἀπογνοὺς ἐς χεῖρας ᾔει τῷ Κράσσῳ μετὰ πολλοῦ καὶ τότε πλήθους· γενομένης δὲ τῆς μάχης μακρᾶς τε καὶ καρτερᾶς ὡς ἐν ἀπογνώσει τοσῶνδε μυριάδων, τιτρώσκεται ἐς τὸν μηρὸν ὁ Σπάρτακος δορατίῳ, καὶ συγκάμψας τὸ γόνυ καὶ προβαλὼν τὴν ἀσπίδα πρὸς τοὺς ἐπιόντας, ἀπεμάχετο, μέχρι καὶ αὐτὸς καὶ πολὺ πλῆθος ἀμφ᾽ αὐτὸν κυκλωθέντες ἔπεσον."

waters of the river Silarus. It is also certain that Spartacus, if not his whole army, now knew perfectly well that the doom was near; they had by this time all become frenzied for the approaching butchery.

As one of the most bloody and terrible battles the world has ever known was fought here, it is fitting to pause in order to minutely describe the scenes and to array our evidence, obtained with great difficulty, regarding the numbers of the contestants, the date of the battle and the carnage during its rage, and afterwards during the man-hunt instituted by the Romans—the whole constituting a cruel and awfully bloody page not to be found in the annals of history, and which to the people at large, and even to the students of our universities, must be regarded as a chapter of news.

There were in the combined armies of Crassus, Pompey and Lucullus, undoubtedly more than 400,000 men, most of whom were experienced veterans, thoroughly hardened to the combat and to all the rigors of the military camp.[122]

In addition to the significant words of Florus regarding Rome and her massing the entire force against the insurgents, we have the auxiliary argument of reason which shows that it could not possibly have been otherwise; for evidence is not wanting that the force of Spartacus at the battle of Silarus, was no less than 300,000 strong. His army which at the battle of Picenum is acknowledged by Appian to have been 120,000 in number, by some unrecorded means which we conjecture to have been the collusion and co-operation of the privateers bringing men from Sicily, had grown to the imposing total of 300,000. Vellejus tells us this, in [123] honest fig-

---

[122] The conjecture that there were 400,000 soldiers in the combined Roman army at the battle of Silarus is not based upon circumstantial evidence. Florus, whose words are never regarded with distrust, tells us distinctly that after the destruction of Lentulus and Poplicola, and the humiliating retaliation by Spartacus, of the gladiatorial combat in honor of Crixus, the fallen comrade, these words: "Then, indeed they (the Romans), with their entire powers massed, bore down upon the gladiator. Tandem etiam totis imperii viribus contra mirmillionem consurgetur." Accordingly we find the Romans soon sending posthaste for all the old veteran armies; one of which was in Spain victorious over the powerful Sertorius, and the other in Asia, equally triumphant over Mithradtes. All surged together against Spartacus. See Florus, *Annales*, III. 20.

[123] Our accidental discovery of this invaluable information may be worth relating: The unreasonable figure of 40,000 given in our own version of Vellejus, in view of the great combined forces admitted by Plutarch, Appian and Florus

ures; although they have been garbled by a merciless translator and made to read 40,000. This cheat would have actually prevailed but for the accident already mentioned, of the preservation of a MSS. copy from which the *editio princeps* was printed soon after the invention of that art, and a copy of which is still to be seen at the Vatican.[124]

Supplied with these important figures, so long held back, but so perfectly reasonable—since they straighten out the incongruities which meet the reader who sees the vast multitudes of the Roman legions positively known to be now centering in—we find ourselves in a condition, otherwise crippled in absurdities and discrepancies, to make a better description of the contest.

Time was given for the army of Spartacus to make long

---

against Spartacus led us to suspect that an immense error lurked in the history of the battle of Silarus. Ransacking for more light we ran against the reference to Dr. Schambach's *Italischer Sklavenkrieg*, which we procured from Europe after much delay. Page 11, *Quellen zur Geschichte* has the following: "Vellejus ist für uns wenig wichtig. Wir erfahren durch ihn nichts, das uns nicht auch sonst bekannt wäre, mit Ausnahme der Zahlenangabe, dass von 300,000 Sklaven in dem letzten Kampfe noch 40,000 übrig gewesen seien. In dem Wenigen, was er gibt, lässt sich ihm eine Unrichtigkeit nicht nachweisen." This not only explained the reasonable facts, but also vouched for the truthfulness of Vallejus. Setting out afresh on the hunt for the exact words of the *editio princeps*, we at last found a copy of the Lugdunum edition containing the MSS. text in a note.

[124] During and before the *renaissance* there appears to have been a not inconsiderable dispute among scholars over the figure CCC, *millia*, to be seen in the *editio princeps* of Vallejus, on account of this figure having been altered to XL. millia. We therefore give the rendering with its falsified figure, and follow it with the remarks of the Lugdunum editor written some 200 years ago, together with the perfectly trustworthy quotation from the *editio princeps* Vellejus, interpolated by a fraud, is currently made to say these words about Spartacus.

"Fugitivi e ludo gladiatorio Capua profugientes, duce Spartaco, raptis ex ea urbe gladiis; mox, crescente in dies multitudine, gravibus variisque casibus adfecere Italiam quorum numerus in tantum adolevit, ut qua ultimo dimicavere acie, XL. millia (in the original manuscript written by Vallejus himself CCC. millia) hominum se Romano exercitui opposuerunt."

The remarks of John Campbell upon this interpolation are given in a note, very guardedly, as follows:

"Ut nihil hic mutandum putem, facit maxima scriptorum dissentio. Quorum in hoc numero diversitatem scire qui desideret adeat eruditissium Treinshemium ad Flori liberum III. cap. 20, Vossius." Farther on, same note: "XL. Alii hunc numerum plurimum augent. Inter quos is qui minimum est Eutropius. Hic sexaginta millia virorum ab iis collecta fuisse scribit. Apianus vero ad C. ac XX. millia extendit. Orosius, Livii epitomator, medium tenuisse videntur. Itaque vix ambigo, quin in Vellejio fit XC. Millia hominum Vossius. Nimis exiguus numerus, in quo variant scriptores, *Princeps Editio*, CCC. millia homnum " Signed Heinsius.

In the Hudson edition (Oxaniæ), the text is the same as above; but the note regarding Heins is quoted as follows: Note 5; " XC. legendum esse non ambiguit Voss. An XC. aut C. millia hominum scribendum dubitat Heins, QUIA EDITIO PRINCEPS CCC. MILLIA HABET HOMINUM."

This is sufficiently positive to settle the number of the army of Spartacus at the battle of Silarus, at 300 000 men, because it is the same wording of Vellejus himself who lived near the very spot and whose father probably commanded a division of cavalry at the battle.

marches westward toward Rome, in obedience to the demands of his mutinous soldiers. A straight cut from Brundusium to the battle-field could not have been less than 100 miles; as it was on the head waters of the Silarus in a nearly direct line from that seaport and Rome. As we have evidence of his having been repulsed by Lucullus at Brundusium, we can understand how he was followed by him all along this march. Crassus likewise, if not in the act of constantly provoking him, as we are inclined to suspect, was in the mountain pass of the Silarus when he arrived and pitched camp by its side.

The combined hostile armies now lay over against each other for a considerable time. Fortifications were drawn by both and the activities on the Roman side, of centering in, were given both time and force. We now find the two contestants face to face, each tempting the other to make the first dash. It was, according to Dr. Schambach's estimate—which we adopt as the most accurate—as late as February of the year 70 before Christ. The war had been raging about four years. But although winter, it is not in our power to know whether it was cold weather. Probably not; for the winters are generally mild in these portions of Italy.[125]

One day Crassus ordered his soldiers to dig a trench and while thus engaged the gladiators made an advance, upon them. It proved the commencement of the great battle.[126] From a simple skirmish both armies gradually closed into the deadly fray and the combat became more and more furious. They eagerly welcomed the battle with reckless feelings of despair, knowing that their hour had come, yet staking their hopes upon another great and decisive victory.[127]

Heroism, love of conflict, intrepidity and fearlessness

[125] Plutarch, *Crassus*, mentions severe coldness a month or two before when Spartacus ran the blockade in Rhegium. But that was a night squall. Besides the battle of Silarus occurred near the opening spring. This agrees with Schambach, S. 13.

[126] Plutarch, *idem*, 12. 'Crassus therefore hastened to give that stroke himself, and with the same view, encamped very near the enemy. One day, when he had ordered his soldiers to dig a trench, the gladiators attacked them as they were at work. Numbers came up continually on both sides to support the combatants; and at last Spartacus seeing what the case necessarily required, drew out his whole army." *Trans. of Langhorne.*

[127] La Rousse, *Dictionaire Universal*, speaking of the gladiator says: troupe était affolée de succese."

of death were frenziedly seated on their hearts; but until now, recklessness had been a stranger in the camps of Spartacus; and when this came, foreknelling the desperate ultimatum, all mutually realized the approach of dissolution and were ready to drink the intoxicating potion which brave men taste midst the furious lunge of steel.

Thus a skirmish between the advance guards of both armies brought on the general engagement. Spartacus who was goaded by a hatred of the Roman leader, for some time stood off at a distance, eyeing the contest. Brigade after brigade fell into the murderous vortex. At length Spartacus issued his general order of battle and at the ring of his war clarions the two angry armies closed up bringing on the ferocious conflict.[128] They brought their chieftain his horse; but the gladiator, like Warwick, drew from its sheath his sword and with one blow of his strong arm, killed the excited steed; then shouting onward to his men, uttered the farewell speech of Spartacus to his soldiers. " Victorious I shall find horses in plenty among the enemy; defeated I shall no longer want one." Then poising himself he rushed for Crassus with his steel high in air and fell upon the ranks of his adversary in personal combat. " It was a fierce struggle. Long after the victory was hopeless Spartacus was traced by heaps of the slain who had fallen by his hand, and his body was lost completely in the awful carnage which closed that day of blood."[129] Plutarch says that he aimed to kill[130] Crassus; and toward this mark through darts and javelins he pressed, and over windrows of the dead, rushing in quest of his foe, whom, indeed he did not reach, but he killed two of his centurians. When all who made with him this mad and desperate plunge had fled or fallen, the terrible gladiator remained fighting with unflinching gallantry until he fell, covered with many wounds and so completely cut to pieces that his body was never found. Even Florus who had no language sufficiently bitter with which to malign him, says " he died like a Roman em-

---

[128] Appian, I. 120: " Γενομένης δὲ τῆς μάχης μακρᾶς τε καὶ καρτερᾶς ὡς ἐν ἀπογνώσει τοσῶνδε μυριάδων, τιτρώσκεται ἐς τὸν μηρὸν ὁ Σπάρτακος δορατίῳ, καὶ συγκάμψας τὸ γόνυ καὶ προβαγὼν τὴν ἀσπίδα πρὸς τοὺς ἐπιόντας ἀπεμάχετο, μέχρι καὶ αὐτὸς καὶ πολὺ πλῆθος ἀμφ' αὐτὸν κυκλωθέντες ἔπεσον."
[129] Smith's *Dictionary of Greek and Roman Biography*, Art. *Spartacus*.
[130] Plutarch, *Crassus*, 12.

peror."[131] His forces appear to have fought manfully until the death of their leader, when the lines gave way and a hideous carnage followed. The Romans gave no quarter. Sixty thousand workingmen fell in this glorious defeat—glorious in the appreciation of all who admire feats of sublimest valor; but alas, a defeat which for centuries riveted the chains of the servile race.

We paraphrase Appian for the following, on the close and consequence of this terrible scene: The butchery by the Romans surpassed the power of counting, for it covered many thousands. The body of Spartacus lay dead on the field. Great numbers fled to the mountains after the battle, and Crassus pursued them. They, however, reorganizing themselves into four divisions fought back, until all were destroyed except 6,000 who were crucified upon the high-road from Capua to Rome.

These "many thousands" slaves who escaped to the mountains as here reported by Appian were the 40,000 of Vellejus, in his *editio princeps* which we have used on the assurance of Dr. Schambach.[132] This would make the number of men who fell in the battle after and before the death of their leader and including the carnage of the route, when no man was spared and no quarter given, to foot up 260,000—an immense number—but when we reflect that there raged an internecine spirit breathing only vengeance and void of feeling throughout the great Roman army, and contemplate the possible strokes of such swordsmen, under orders to exterminate their now defenseless victims, these numbers are not surprising.

A few more words and the tragedy is told. Such were the numbers of the brave veterans of this great revolt who fell in the gigantic contest on the banks of the river Silarus.[133] In the mountains, during the pursuit great num-

[131] "**Spartacus ipse in primo agmine fortissime dimicans, quasi Imperator, occisus est.**" (Florus, liber III. cap. 20).
[132] Heinsius distinctly says that Vellejus put the number of the army of Spartacus at 300,000, from which total 40,000 escaped: "qua *editio princeps* habet XL. e CCC. milia hominum." So Schambach in *Der Italische Sklavenaufstand*, S. 11, *Quellen zur Geschichte*, says: "Wir erfahren von Vellejus——dass von 300,000 Sklaven in dem letzten Kampfe noch 40,000 übrig gewesen seien." The two accounts of Appian and Vellejus Paterculus do not at all disagree. Appian, I. *idem*: "Ὅ τε λοιπὸς αὐτοῦ στρατὸς ἀκόσμως ἤδη κατεκόπτοντο κατὰ πλῆθος, ὡς φόνον γενέσθαι τῶν μὲν οὐδ᾽ εὐαρίθμητον Ῥωμαίων δὲ ἐς χιλίους ἄνδρας, καὶ τὸν Σπαρτάκον νέκυν οὐχ εὑρεθῆναι. πολὺ δ᾽ ἔτι πλῆθος ἦν ἐν τοῖς ὄρεσιν, ἐκ τῆς μάχης διαφυγόν· ἐφ᾽ οὓς ὁ Κράσσος ἀνέβαινεν."
[133] For a description of the Silarus and the surrounding region see Strabo, *Geographica*, V. cap 4.

bers more fell, and 6,000 were taken prisoners of war. The remainder of the great army who after the defeat, and the death of their beloved and faithful leader, endeavored to escape, was indeed small.

According to Appian, the pursuit was made by Pompey who must have participated in the battle. This grasping egotist easily finished the massacre and then vaunted that he had been the principle in putting down the rebellion; thus adding to the proof that all the three Roman armies were massed. Great numbers of the fugitives were overtaken and crucified. Every one of the 6,000 who fell prisoners at the battle of Silarus and in the mountains was hung on the cross along the Appian way; and for months their bodies dangled there to delight the vengeance-loving gentry who, on their drives to and from the cities of Rome and Capua, rejoiced to behold such sights as in our time would provoke the shame and contempt of the world.

Slavery from the downfall of Spartacus, the last emancipator, had an unhindered sweep in Rome and her provinces until Jesus, 100 years later, founded or brought into the open world the culture of the communes hitherto compulsorily secret, that mankind at birth are naturally free and equal—a culture which is based upon peace and submission; the antithesis of the plans of Eunus, Athenion, Spartacus and all revolters. This plan was original in Jesus, and it has prevailed; for chattel ownership of man by man has, under his open culture, disappeared from the earth. Rome became "a model of rapacity, dishonesty and fraud; having in her period—almost a thousand years, produced scarcely a dozen men whose names have descended to posterity with an untarnished fame."[134]

But if Spartacus, whose acts were in Italy, might be called a Roman, he certainly may be included in the list of names of the untarnished famous; for his nature was gentle though his character was marked and equal to the dignity of grander victories than came into the list of the Scipios or the Cæsars—since he fought entirely for a principle, dying as his wife had predicted of him, happy in the enthusiasm of an exuberant, manly swoop of nerve and muscle, grand, if not gigantic, amid the dismaying fury of enemies of liberty and of law.

[134] Carey, *Principles of Political Economy*, Vol. I. p. 247.

Immediately after the destruction of Spartacus and his army, another great man-hunt was instituted, similar to those we have described in the chapters on Viriathus, Eunus and Athenion. It lasted six months, raged with merciless atrocities and was followed by another exterminatory man-hunt against the pirates who, if we are to believe the histories which have been permitted to survive, were the true friends of the Romans, because they treacherously refused to assist the insurgent army to cross into Sicily. But as we have already stated, this story looks extremely flimsy and must be considered with caution; as the fact remains well vouched for that Rome fell upon the pirates and privateers with a powerful fleet commanded by Pompey himself and succeeded in less than a year, in annihilating them so completely that ever afterwards the Mediterranean was cleared of these maritime desperadoes.[135]

No fewer than 1,000,000 slaves are reported by Cæcilius Calactenus to have been crucified and otherwise slain in the combined wars of the slaves who rebelled against the huge and inhuman slave system of the Romans. This estimate, repeated with reserve by Dr. Schambach,[136] comes to us not from Calactenus direct, for his valuable histories are, like the others, lost; but it is transmitted indirectly by Athenæus, whose quotations from the lost books are more and more highly prized.

But alas! Of what utility were all these outbreaks of human irascibility with their awful details of blood and extermination? True, one comfort clings: To die in the desperate attempt for freedom was better than to live in the griping coils of slavery. But "an eye for an eye and a tooth for a tooth" brought no relief for downtrodden humanity. It never has, it never can, it never will. The still lingering idea of a semi-belligerent force organized on the strike plan, so long as it does not choose the weapons

---

[135] For the law commissioning Pompey to the work of exterminating the pirates, see Vellejus, *Historia Romana*, liber II. cap. xxxi.; and for a description of the work itself, Appian, I. 121; Pliny, *Historia Naturalis*, VII. 25; Tacitus, *Annales*, XII. 62; XV. 25, *Bellum Piraticum*.

[136] Schambach, *Italischer Sklavenaufstand*. S. 5. "Die Zahl aller in diesen und anderen minder bedeutenden oder uns zufällig nicht überlieferten Aufständen getödteten Sklaven giebt Athen., wahrscheinlich nach der übertriebenen Berechnung des Cäcilius von Kalakte auf etwa eine Million an." These doubts regarding the number would have been dispelled had the learned doctor reflected that the number of lives lost in the war of Spartacus alone exceeded half that sum. A quarter of a million of slaves were killed in the last battle and in the man-hunt which followed. No doubt several millions were killed in all.

of overt war, and sedulously abstains from military or other violent means of resistance and self-defense, may be in conformity with the reasonable methods of relief; it is unquestionably consistent with the modern age and yields the rough polemic and the intellectual jar which surges and jostles men into a conception of arbitration and political unanimity. But humanity in the awful and relentless conflicts we have described, of which this revolt of Spartacus was the last and the typical example, has had enough of the destructive, enough of the irascible, enough of extermination. Let us profit by these examples, and no longer remain regardless of the better and more promising plan of another master, and the next to succeed. This great preceptor constantly taught the working people "that they resist not evil;" and his are the precepts prevailing all through the civilizing inculcation of " good for evil," until, after a bi-millennial trial of the brutal instincts, the oppressor now perceives and is being constrained to acknowledge that "an injury to one is the concern of all."

Whoever has the curiosity to observe the results of these defeats upon the Roman people will find that all the blood that was shed had no influence whatever toward refining human feelings. About this time the amphitheatre began in earnest to supersede the older games of the Roman circus. The revolts had kindled up a fresh spirit of vengeance, and popular conversation inflamed the hideous passion for sights in the gladiatorial ring.

These revolts had moreover taught the Roman politicians and all those who catered to power, that the slave system which made bondsmen of prisoners of war taken by tens of thousands in the great conquests of the past hundred years, were a desperate and dangerous element in the land. But a people filled with grudges as were the Romans, after this terrible succession of revolts which have been described, could think of no mild, humane methods of getting rid of the dangerous slaves.

To see them thrown to the wild beasts and eaten alive or to train them for the ghastly habit of cutting each others' throats upon the sands of an amphitheatre, was to their truly ferocious character the natural way of getting rid of them. This in part answers the inquirer's question as to the cause of the rapid and phenomenal decline of morals at Rome.

The comparatively innocent circus waned in favor of the arena. Vast amphitheatres were constructed in towns and cities everywhere. Blood-money reigned triumphant.

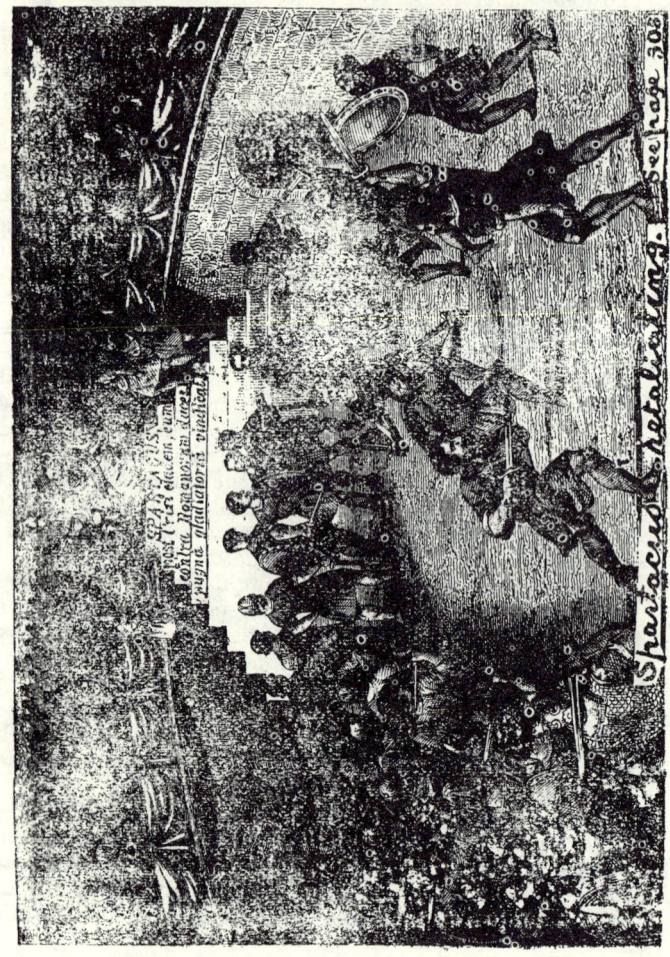

CHAPTER XIII.

ORGANIZATION.

ROME'S ORGANIZED WORKINGMEN AND WOMEN.

ORGANIZATION OF THE FREEDMEN—The *Jus Coeundi*—Roman Unions—The *Collegium*—Its Power and Influence—What the Poor did with their Dead—Cremation—Burial a Divine Right which they were too Lowly to Practice—Worship of borrowed Gods—Incineration or Burial and Trade Unions combined—Proofs—Glance at the Inner social Life of the ancient Brotherhoods—State Ownership and Management—Nationalized Lands—Number and Variety of Trade Unions—Struggles—Numa Pompilius First to Recognize and Uphold Trade Unions—Law of the 12 Tables taken from Solon—Harmony, Peace, Ease, steady Work. Prosperity and Plenty Lasting with little Interruption for 500 Years—Bondmen fared worse.

WE have spoken of certain organizations among the working people of ancient times. That these existed is no longer denied. In Rome they were mostly freedmen. But what inspired their combination into secret orders does not appear plain to those who study the past for the sake of gratifying a taste for great events. Neither do those who study it for purposes of gleaning points in philosophy and religion as commonly understood, obtain any correct idea of them. The ancient contempt rooted in the taint of labor which slavery inspired is yet too strong; and there still lingers too much of the old spirit of paganism to allow of interest, or hardly of curiosity. This must answer the astonished student of sociology who asks why so much ignorance on the subject of those ancient societies.

Again, we have alluded, in a previous chapter, to the fact that writers and speakers of those days were extremely chary of information regarding them. The cause of this was identical with that which inspires the same thing here amongst us now—disdain. From 1870 until 1886, a period of sixteen years, little was known to the masses of society of the vast organization amidst us, down in society's core, except that now and then a strike, like a volcanic eruption, shook the moral and financial surface. Yet in that period the most splendid vehicles of knowledge ever before known, existed. There was an organized policy, mixed with contempt, silently preventing even a wayside mention of these phenomena. When in 1886, a decided stand taken by Mr. Powderly, pleasing the press which may have expected to see defeat and disaster of the great collectivity, flung the door of the mighty dungeon ajar, and a knowledge of their numbers and power burst out, the people were overwhelmed with surprise. How much easier then, was it, in that barbaric age, without mechanical means of transmitting truth, even had historians, poets and philosophers been inclined to do so, to close the doors against curiosity and the love of learning.[1]

We begin by the broad statement that from the earliest times at which anything is known of them, although they were sunk in ineffable contumely, they yet enjoyed one boon —the right of combination. Strange to say, no conspiracy laws are to be found; at any rate among the Romans,[2] until about the time of the emperors.[3] These rights of organization in very ancient times, extended all over Europe so far as is known.[4] Some of the first gleamings of this may be gotten from the authors. As early as Numa Pompilius'

[1] Mommsen, *De Collegiis et Sodaliciis Romanorum*, p. 31. "Si quærimus de loco collegiis opificum in rebus publicis apud Romanos concesso. Sed id ipsum quæritur, an quærere liceat: est enim altissimum de hac re apud auctores silentium." Here Mommsen admits that the profoundest silence reigns among authors, in regard to these unions, and refers for his proof to a stone (vide Orell. *Inscr.* 4,105) bearing an insription of a union. This was a union of musicians that existed at Rome. The inscription runs thus: "M. Julius Victor, ex collegio Liticinum Cornicinum." Mommsen alludes to this find in proof of the fact that working people had organized Unions of musicians.
[2] In page 52 of the Consular report of Mr. James T. Dubois, U. S. Consul at Leipzig, published by the State Department in 1885, at Washington, there is a reference to the attempted suppression by Tullius Hostilius of the *Collegia Opificum*; but that they continued to thrive he acknowleges in the next paragraph. A close inspection shows that they were by no means suppressed.
[3] Mommsen, *De Col. et Sodal. Ramanorum*, cap. iv. §10, p. 73.
[4] Gruter, *Inscriptiones Antiquæ Totius Orbis Romenorum*, 399, 4. 431, 1. "Omnia corpora Lugduni licite coeuntia." Cicero, *Pro Sexto*, 14, 32, says: "There was no town in Italy, no colony, no prefecture, no board of tax collectors at Rome, no trade union, not holding common cause with one another." This was during his struggle to suppress them.

time, perhaps 700 years before Christ, they are known to have existed in great numbers. This king tolerated them; and there exist some curious data respecting the system which he invented for their regulation.[5] He ordered that the entire people including the working classes, be distributed into eleven guilds. This statement of Plutarch is however regarded by Mommsen as incorrect. The latter, after investigating the data given anterior to Plutarch, concludes that it must have been eight classes instead of eleven. At that time there were distinct trades, embracing all the arts of remote antiquity. While this may be true that eight was the number of categories there certainly is agreement among authors as to about that number.[6] It would appear by their complete privilege of combination and their apparently perfect recognition by this wise king who reigned probably 700 years before Christ, that at times there must have been a great deal of skill among the artisans. Skilled mechanics were needed to make all the armor of those warlike times. During the reign of Numa Pompilius which lasted thirty-nine years the trade unions must have made great advancement.[7] Indeed, considering the harsh treatment they afterwards received at the hands of the Roman emperors in later years, beginning B. C. 58, we are left to infer that for nearly 700 years of the best life of Rome these labor organizations flourished uninterruptedly.[8] According to Plutarch, this ancient king so favored the idea of labor organizations that he made their particular case the very basis of a great reform. Plutarch tells us that he closed the temple of Janus for forty-three years,[9] and all this time there was perpetual peace. The working people are known

---

[5] Mommsen, *De Coll. et Sodal. Rom.*, p. 78, says: The relics of innumerable communal associations of ancient times, are seen scattered all through Italy, as found among the inscriptions of the Italian towns. See also Plutarch's *Life of Numa*, much quoted by writers.
[6] Pliny, *Naturalis Historia*, XXXIV. 1. "Æqualem Urbi auctoritatem ejus declarat, a rege Numa Collegio tertio ærariorum fabrum instituto." Again XXXV. 12. "Numa rex septimum collegium figulorum instituit."
[7] Dirksen, *Zwölf Tafeln*, says: "Der römische Staat vergönnte ursprünglich lediglich den Gewerben, die den Bedürfnissen des Krieges und des gottesdienstes zunächst fröhnten, seinen unmittelbaren Schutz und eine selbständige Communalverfassung."
[8] Mommsen, *De Coll. et Sodal. Rom.* p. 33. "Jus coeundi fuit antiquis temporibus omnibus concessum."
[9] Plut., *Numa and Lycurgus compared.* "The primary view of Numa's government which was to settle the Romans in lasting peace and tranquility, immediately vanished with him; for after his death, the temple of Janus, which he had kept shut as if it had really held war in prison and subjection, was set wide open, and Italy was filled with blood."

to have had their golden era during the reign of this great lawgiver.[10] If for no other reason than this, the reign of Numa Pompilius must ever be regarded as one of the most valuable, and fraught with richest lessons to the human race. It is true that this is not so considered by students of history from a standpoint of great historic events, or of religion and philosophy as ordinarily understood, but the student of history from the purely sociological basis may justly regard this reign as one of the marvels of the world. We are at a loss to understand how Plutarch, with his clear mind and honest motives, could have compared Numa with Lycurgus. But Plutarch was not a socialist. He did not understand the immense world of meaning rolled up in the mystic deeds of Numa, whose reign, had it proved a failure, he himself would not have praised.

But Numa's reign was by no means a failure. It was a decided departure from the customs of those ancient days, because it completely discountenanced the warlike ambitions of other rulers and cultivated the arts of peace. To carry out such a policy it was necessary to have industry made respectable and stand boldly to the front, and be in every way protected.

But the trades were already organized. He did not organize them that we know of, but simply accorded them free privileges to organize themselves. He classed his people of all grades by a method of his own and in that classification made a place for the workers whom he was wise and manly enough to recognize. Before the time of Numa the working people had never been recognized that we are aware of. His distribution of the entire industrial class into eight or nine grand divisions or trades,[11] does not probably imply that there was no greater variety than this, but it was probably merely for the sake of convenience.

We are not to suppose, because the free right of combination was given the working people by king Numa, that

---

[10] ——— "Ἐν δὲ ἡ διανομὴ κατὰ τας τεχνας, αὐλητῶν (flute players), χρυσοχοων (gold workers), τεκτόνων (carpenters), βαφέων (dyers), σκυτοτόμων (shoemakers), σκυτοδεψῶν (tanners and curriers), χαλκέων (braziers), κεραμέων (potters), τας δε λοιπὰς τέχνας εις ταὐτὸ συναγαγὼν ἐν αυτῶν ἐκ πασῶν ἀπεδείξε σύστημα." (Plut. Num. 17).

[11] Mommsen, *idem*, p. 29. Hæc si expendimus, videmus Plutarchum fortasse etiam Florum totum populum non opifices tantum in IX classes distribuere, quod etsi absurdum est, notandum tamen, cum inde nonum collegium ortum esse videatur."

this carried with it all the immunities belonging to other people. Caste remained. They were still looked upon as degraded creatures. It was for the Christian era to declare the absolute equality of men. But this right of free combination, *jus coeundi*, was certainly used to an enormous extent as a means of working up a state of things and a spirit of freedom or self-constituted public opinion among working people, fitting them by slow degrees, to consider themselves equal to others. The right of combination during this remarkable reign, having been prominently and thoroughly established, it remained so for over 600 years; and we are told explicitly that no interruption occurred until 58 years before Christ, for both the efforts of Claudius and Tarquin to suppress them entirely failed.

At that date much of the outcast and industrial population of Rome had become well organized and workingmen were, as we shall see, beginning to exercise a powerful political influence. They had been violently attacked by Cicero and other proud aristocrats and nobly and successfully defended by Clodius and a number of other Roman officers of high rank; and a fierce and terrible hatred attended with clearly discernible political manœuvres, was growing into an issue on the advent of the Cæsars.

Lord Mackenzie [12] says that "the earliest legislation deserving of notice was the celebrated code of laws called the Twelve Tables." Yet so far as the treatment of our special subject—that of the strictly laboring people—is concerned, these were but the simple recording of the old rules of Numa Pompilius and of Solon. In our opinion Numa had borrowed his notions regarding the organization of the working population mostly from the then existing state of labor organization in Egypt, Asia Minor and Attica.[13] We have repeatedly shown every development among them to have been a traceable growth. Monarchs and lawgivers when clothed with power could arrange these habits of their subjects into words and forms but the people themselves had already been using them from immemorial times.

Solon, as early as B. C. 580 established laws permitting

[12] Roman Law, pp. 5-6.
[13] Gaius, XII. Tables explained by Dirksen. Mom. *de coll.* etc., p. 39. "Not abilis est hoc loco lex Solonis, ex qua sacra civiliaque communia etc.

laboring people to organize; and made it compulsory upon boys to learn a trade.[14] If the father of a family of working people neglected to do this he could not compel his sons to support him in his old age. Both Solon and Numa legalized the organizations of working people and gave them the full right of combination. Lycurgus, on the contrary,[15] as we have seen, wanted no emancipated slaves. He was an upholder of military despotism. All labor being a degraded and disgraceful entailment, must, under the laws of Lycurgus be performed by the abject, groveling slaves. Thus in the Peloponnesus, trade unions got no encouragement whatever, which accounts for the paucity of stone tablets found in lower Greece, bearing inscriptions commemorative of the labor unions. Northern Greece, the islands, Asia Minor and Italy, on the contrary, abound in these suggestive mementos of ancient labor organization, an account of which the historians of those periods have sedulously left barren.

All this proves that while labor was grudgingly tolerated as a necessary means of life to the gentile classes of both Greece and Rome, it was never recognized by either as respectable or hardly decent; if we except that of agriculture and the nearest it ever came to any recognition was during the wise and happy reign of king Numa Pompilius who extended every encouragement to its organization and died leaving it a veritably abiding institution as his laws intended.

He actually took salient and very suggestive steps toward filling up the social gap separating the high-borns from the low-borns of Rome. He instituted that at the Saturnalian feasts which occurred every December as a harvest thanksgiving or carnival, all ranks of a social character should be forgotten; that figuratively no slave, no social distinction, no arrogance should exist. Thus labor, for a moment each year, was raised up and the social arrogance of wealth and birth leveled down, to a par with each other. But it must not for a moment be imagined that the working people of either Greece or Rome ever

---

[14] Plut. *Solon;* Herodotus, *Euterpe,* cap. 177, gives us a hint making it probable that trade unionism existed in Egypt in the time of Amasis who upheld it: ‘Νόμον δὲ Αἰγυπτίοισι τόνδε Ἀμασίς ἐστι ὁ καταστήσας· ἀποδεικνύναι ἔτεος ἑκάστου τῷ νομάρχῃ πάντα τινὰ Αἰγυπτίων, ὅθεν βιοῦται· μὴ δὲ ποιεῦντα ταῦτα, μηδὲ ἀποφαίνοντα δικαίην ζόην, ἰθύνεσθαι θανάτῳ.

[15] Plut. Lycurgus and Numa compared.

arose to be considered by the *gens*, or patrician stock as anything more than plebians who were outcasts by birth, and though often the children of patrician fathers, yet through the ancient religio-political law of primogeniture, or the sacred law of inheritance, were relegated into bondage whence they never escaped except through gradual development by manumissions, and finally through the mighty all-levelling proclamations of Jesus which theoretically and at last practically overthrew every distinction.

But we shall more elaborately treat this grand and extraordinary episode in human development in our sketch of Jesus, from a business-like or secular point of consideration, as a subject of inquiry into sociological phenomena.

We now return to Lord Mackenzie's statement that "by the decemviral code"—meaning the Twelve Tables—"the plebeians gained a considerable step toward the adjustment of their differences with the patricians, but it was nearly 80 years before these differences were settled by the admission of the plebeians to the supreme offices of the state."[16]

In the first place, this "considerable step toward the adjustment of differences" was taken under king Numa, 118 years before the Twelve Tables were engraved upon the slabs. In the second, the very first decemvirs were composed of such tyrannical usurpers and aristocrats as Appius Claudius, who, although they had the laws adjusting the differences between patricians and plebians engraved upon eleven Tables, yet they prevented the latter from realizing their benefits. Another thing must be continually borne in mind, that under the sway of the Pagan or competitive religion, which was the foundation of law and social order, any absolute equality between patricians and plebians was impossible from beginning to end; and no assertion that the adjustment of differences was ever gained by any means can be considered correct. The difference between them always remained; but under the gracious adjustment of Numa and of Solon, afterwards inscribed in Latin from a Greek translation, in a formal law upon the Twelve Tables at Rome, the right of organization first came to the freedmen, in letters. Nor does this right of organization apply to the slaves, who still

[16] Mackenzie, *Roman Law*, p 7.

existed in great numbers. On the contrary we show, in our sketch of Spartacus and repeatedly elsewhere, that the rapacity of the Roman lords and middlemen finally became so great that they bought up slaves, redoubled their numbers, encroached upon the common farm lands and upon manufactures with cheap slave labor, each owning great numbers of slaves,[17] and finally under Cæsar, succeeded in procuring conspiracy laws which suppressed the trade and many other species of organization, opening the way by sheer aggravations, for the advent of a completely new order of things in the repudiation of paganism entirely, and the embrace, mostly by these wretched slaves and persecuted freedmen, of a totally new religion which built upon the workingmen's fundamental principle that all are born free and equal.

Thus it becomes evident that writers who speak of the three forms of Roman law afterwards known as the *leges populi*, the *plebiscita* and the *senatus consulti*, must, if from a standpoint of social science, be very careful not to count the two-thirds of the entire Roman population, who were abject slaves,[18] enjoying neither freedom, respect, right of resistance or organization whatsoever.

The great trade organization received their first serious blow through the law which suppressed open work and drove them into secret conclave, counter manœuvres and diplomacy. We have said that historians carefully avoided any mention of these troubles. This is true; but the labor turmoils open to the students of sociology the true meaning of certain slurs occurring in the speeches and epistles of Cicero and others, the import of which can be explained in no other way.[19] We must constantly hold uppermost the

---

[17] Crassus owned 500 slaves, see Plut. Crassus, 2. C. Cælius Claudius owned according to Pliny, no fewer than 4,116 at a time, ".... quamvis multa civili bello perdidisset, tamen relinquere servorum quatuor millia centum sedecim." *Nat. Hist.* XXXIII. 47. Great numbers of slaves existed in antiquity. See Wallace, *Numbers of Mankind*. p. 54, sq. Immense population during the slave era, pp. 294-303. Also pp. 91 and 97; Athenæus V. 20. Ancient Census and remarks of Hume, *Ancient Populousness* declaring that Athenæus does not reckon the children. Æmilius Paulus after the battle of Pydna, B. C. 167, destroyed 70 cities of Epirus taking the value of 10,000,000 dollars in gold and 160,000 people as war-slaves to Rome and the provinces, Wallace p. 300 and Livy, XLV, c. 14. See Seneca. *De Tranquilitate*, 8; Vast numbers in Crete see Lippincott, *Pronouncing Gazetteer of the World* art. Crete. They were mostly slaves and freedmen; Plato *Laws* vii. 11. Countless Myriads of Women they call Sauromatides.
[18] Cf. Wallace,*Numbers of Mankind*, p. 61. Liv. lib. 6, cap. 12.
[19] Cicero, *Pro Sesto*, 25: "Collegia non modo illa vetera contra SC. restituerentur sed ab uno gladiatore innumerabilia alia nova conscriberentur." This

causes of the Christian idea skipping southern Greece in its westward course and planting itself at Rome and everywhere among the already existing communes, with a view of determining a solution to this phenomenon in the great social field already prepared there by these organizations. King Numa by no means originated the union of the trades at Rome. He simply permitted and encouraged what already existed. We now proceed to give some facts in regard to them. Although the king distributed the working people into eight or nine classes we are not to suppose that there was no greater variety of handicraft in his time. There are still extant slabs and stones found in different places in Italy, notably at Rome and what were ancient towns and cities south and east of Rome, bearing inscriptions which indicate that large numbers of trades were plied in very ancient times.

The *Collegium* a veritable trade union was originally an organization of working people for mutual aid and protection. During the 39, or as Plutarch puts it, 43 years of Numa's reign we hear of no contortion or prevarication of this word from that correct and original sense. But after his death, when the temple of Janus was reopened and wars and their harvests of brutality and repression disturbed the serenity of labor making the mechanics watchful of their interests, they somewhat changed their outward appearance but not their character. For instance, a trade union of to-day is often a protective, an insurance and a burial society. So it was then; but amid the turmoils, suspicions and dangers of war it often became convenient, in order to suit appearances to be exclusively religious. The Pagan religion was at that time popular. Each of the great popular, aristocratic families or *gens* had a tutelary saint or other object of worship, and it was very convenient for the trade union to dedicate itself to one of these tutelary deities; not only to elicit favor from the great patrons but also because they were themselves religiously inclined. Thus the colleges, although they maintained their practical economic or trade union object of mutual advantage in a business sense, often passed for religious institutions; and we have abundant

fling was probably hurled at Clodius with a bitter reference to Spartacus. Cf sketch of Spartacus, chapter XI.

evidence of this, not in the written histories but in the inscriptions which now begin to exhibit in a new and significant manner, their character and career.

The ancient *collegia* or working people's fraternities in Italy were not confined to the male sex. In later eras of the empire they existed in great numbers as the inscriptions show. Some of them were composed partly, and a few are known to have been composed entirely of women.

The learned archæologist, Johann Casper Orelli, has devoted 89 octavo Latin pages [20] to the enumeration of a collection of stone inscription-bearing tablets on which in ancient days, were engraved the wills of the deceased, the tutelary gods worshipped by the members, sometimes even the manner in which they came to their death, the degree of conjugal affection in which they had mutually lived together and many other little particulars shedding important and interesting light upon their mode of living [21] in those ancient days—events left almost totally blank on the pages of history.

Gruter, another archæologist of great patience and erudition, has given us an immense collection [22] of ancient inscriptions, many of which are accompanied by his own readings; thus laying the foundations for simplifying the keys to the study of sociology, and enriching the mind by a knowledge of ancient customs.

The archæological works of Raffaello Fabretti have also furnished us a large amount of material, while Theodore Mommsen has applied his usual care and judgment in making clear much of that which otherwise we might have overlooked.

The *collegium funerarium* was the burial society. After gathering all the information at our command, we are constrained to conclude that it much resembled the great system of friendly or burial societies of Great Britain at the present day. They existed in large numbers, especially at Rome; and in later times, after the passage of the laws of repression they were mostly exempt, because religious. Of this we shall speak later.

[20] Orellius, *Incriptionum Latinarum Selectarum Amplissima Collectio*, pp. 274-360 of Vol. II. *Sepulcralia*,
[21] No 4,352 Orel. reads: "Numisinæ conjugi castissimæ et incomparabili adfectione feminæ cum qua vixit ann. XVII., Mens. XI., Dieb. XVII."
[22] Gruterius, *Inscriptiones Antiquæ Totius Orbis Romanorum*.

From the prodigious labors of Muratori we also obtain several valuable contributions,[23] especially so on account of examples he gives, of genuine trade unions, inscriptions of which he took from Cis-Alpine Gaul, that were written early in the Christian era.

Rose, a learned Greek scholar [24] and antiquarian, wrote a work from which we find much evidence in support of our theme, especially regarding the high status in skill of workmen in ancient days; and the splendid work of Guhl and Koner entitled "The Life of the Greeks and Romans," fortunately well translated into English further intensifies our wonder at the high perfection to which the labor of antiquity had brought the arts and architecture.

From the analytical works of August Böckh, we have deduced considerable, proving that the organizations of the proletaries were by no means confined to Italy.[25] If Cicero could say they were "innumerable in all Italy," Athenagaros might also have said they were equally abundant throughout the peninsula of Greece and the Ionian Isles. The writers we refer to find tablets of stone in all these countries, some of them, excusably enough, engraved with words often wrongly spelled, sometimes in words suggestive of the prevailing lingo, perhaps even slang language which slaves and their descendants, the freedmen, almost always without education, would naturally make use of, which is of itself exceedingly interesting, bringing the working people of ancient Rome, Greece and Asia freshly down to us, as it were, in their work clothes, their tools in hand, and their careless vernacular exactly as used in every day life.

In announcing our remarks on the ancient *Sepulcralia* or burial societies, we cannot do better than refer to the popular scientific research on the origin of the plebians, by Prof. Fustel de Coulanges. This author, while not appearing to understand that they might have been partly derived from the outcasts of the patrician family, relegated by the *paterfamilias* into slavery, admits fully as much.[26] Every student of the facts recognizes that the

[23] Muratoins, *Antiquitates Italicæ, Medii Ævi*, 6 vols. Milan, 1,744.
[24] Rose, *Inscriptiones Græcæ Vetustissimæ.*
[25] Böckh, *Corpus Inscriptionum Græcarum*. 3 vols Berlin, 1853, folio.
[26] ' Nous sommes pourtant frappé de voir dans Tite-Live, qui connaissait' les vieilles traditions, que les patriciens reprochaient aux plébéiens non pas d être issus des populations vaincues, mais de manquer de religion et même de famille.

great plebeian class of the ancient population was originally derived from the outcasts of the family and that they were, as a religio-political consequence, without a religion, without a home, without even a recognition or count among the citizen population [27] and without marriage rites. They were consequently all illegitimates.[28] These are stupendous facts, little understood by people of this day.

These were great grievances which they had to bear. They built up among themselves a religion of their own, had secret organizations and burial societies which often served as a shield to their trade unions, from the law.[29] They were regarded by Cicero as wild beasts;[30] and he invariably speaks of the organized proletaries with scathing contempt. Just after the death of Spartacus, while the senate was endeavoring to pass a law for the suppression of labor organizations, Claudius Pulcher, who to "curry favor with the plebeians,"[31] changed his name to Clodius, and boldly came to the front in defense of the labor unions. In spite of all the efforts of Cicero against him Clodius actually succeeded not only in preventing the passage of restrictive laws against the trade and other organizations, but secured the enactment of several others, greatly favoring the proletaries who had been covertly using their secret burial societies and mutual aid communes as organizations of resistance. Cicero was greatly

---

Or, ce reproche qui était déjà immérité au temps de Licinius Stolon et que les contemporains de Tite-Live, comprenaient à peine, devait remonter à une époque très ancienne et nous reporte aux premiers temps de la cité." (Fustel de Coulanges, *Cité Antique*, p. 278).

[27] *La Cité Antique*, p. 322: "Les hommes de la classe inférieure formèrent entre eux un corps," and again p. 278: "Le peuple comprenait les patriciens et leurs clients ; la plèbs était en dehor."

[28] *Idem*, p. 278-9: "C' était renoncer a une religion. A jontons encore qu.. le fils né d' un marriage sans rites, était réputé bâtard, comme celui qui était né de l'adultère, et la religion domestique n' existait pas pour eux." So with the ancients religion and citizenship were one and the same thing.

[29] Mommsen, *De Collegiis et Sodalicus Romanorum*, p. 4. "Tanta vero fuit sodalitatis religio, ut publicis etiam legibus sodales prohiberentur, quominus eam læderent."

[30] "Fera quædam sodalitas et plane pastoritia atque agrestis Germanorum lupercorum : quorum coitio illa sylvestris ante est instituta, quam humanitas atque leges." Cicero, *Pro Marco Coelio*, 11.

[31] See *American Encyclopœdie, Article Clodius*. Were it not that this article was written in the same spirit of aristocratic bias of patrician history, it would have to be pronounced by the student of sociology as scurrilous. The truth is, Clodius was at heart, a noble, wise and exceedingly able tribune. He was one of those in the army of Lucullus, who took part in the suppression of Spartacus. After his overthrow 6,000 of the proletaries were brutally crucified on the Appian way lining that avenue for miles with this horrid spectacle. From that time Clodius was the staunch lawyer of organized labor.

incensed at this.[32] It is clear that Cicero, who was intensely aristocratic, drew down upon him, in his prodigious defense of the *gentes* and the correspondingly aggravating raillery against the organized workers, the hatred and revenge of the laboring element of Rome, who, driven to straits, took up the political issue and even took up arms. These studies are exceedingly interesting, inasmuch as they reveal to us that Rome at that time—less than 100 years before Christ, was very populous, that much the larger share of her population consisted of the proletaries both slaves and freedmen, and that the freedmen and some of the slaves were organized; and finally that this organization, whether in shape of burial or of trade unions, was the cause of political contention, which grew rapidly into vast commotions and a civil duel between the gentiles and the proletaries. Cicero, the mortal foe of the latter, was constantly inveighing against them[33] until his death. In fact, it will be easily shown that the great orator came to his death directly in consequence of his bitter complicity in these labor convulsions, always taking sides against them.

A curious fact is observed, in looking over Orelli and Gruter's list of inscriptions of the burial societies, showing that among the poorest the practice of cremation was common. The order had niches or recesses attached to the grounds frequented by them for their meetings; and being too poor, in fact disallowed the noble rite of burial and its attendant family worship, they were obliged to burn the bodies of the deceased and preserve their ashes in pots called *ollæ cinerariæ*.[34] The poor fellows, having no religion of their own, denied that honor by the privileged classes who lived upon their labor, and often being

[32] Cic., *Pro Sexto* We render as follows: "This Clodius has chosen this name instead of Aurelius for his tribunal labors to curry favor with the organized slaves - men enlisted from the streets arranged in companies, cheered on by his moral stimulus to arms, to pillage."
[33] Mommsen says: "Compluribus locis Cicero invehitur in P. Clodium restitutis, lege sua collegiis ann. 58 ante Christ. nova collegia ordinantem." *(De Coll, et Sodal. Rom*, p 57.)
[34] Fg. Orelli, *Inscr.* No. 4,358. *Sepulcralia*, reads: " D M. M. Herennius a plowman and Herennia Lacena writen in their son's own handwriting. The pot containing the ashes stands on left side of the monument," etc., etc. So again Guhi and Koner, Life of the Greeks and Romans, pp. 378-9, figs 401, 402 and others with descriptions. These represent the celebrated *Comlumbaria* of which Gorius wrote an elaborate work, illustrated with engravings. Fig. 402 snows not only the niches in which stand to this day the cinerary urns, but also the urns themselves. One *columbarium*, the *Vigna Codina*, has 425 such niches in nine rows, p 479. A small marble over each urn gives the name. These are the burial places (see p. 377) of the slaves and freedmen.

of the same original stock and consequently of religious tendency, were in the habit of borrowing from the *gens* families some tutelary deity in whose name to worship. This, it appears, they had always maintained the right to do. When Christianity came a few years afterwards, with its new and absolutely democratic religion and its mutual co-operation more nearly fitted to their case, they embraced it in great numbers.

Mommsen mentions some regulations in the laws governing the burial societies; among others is one against suicide.[35] It was a law for preventing suicide by appealing to their pride in a decent burial; and prohibited any money being taken from the communal fund wherewith to defray the funeral expenses of the suicide.

After the passage of the conspiracy laws, B. C. 58, the unions continued to exercise their wonted habits in defiance of the laws of suppression. Two causes lie at the base of this fact; there were by this time wealthy business men in the organizations who controlled social and political influence, although themselves of plebeian stock. This is one cause. Another is, that the organizations, when they felt the knife of persecution, withdrew themselves from public view and became intensely secret. Where the organizations were for religious purposes they were not suppressed; but there was a special regulation fixing it so that they could simulate, or use religion as a cloak.[36] It is very unfortunate that the ancient laws of the Twelve Tables were not preserved so as to have come down to us as engraved. They are known to have been placed in the most conspicuous part of the Roman forum. It was the oldest of the three written systems of Roman Law[37] having been established B. C. 452. It is, moreover, now supposed to have been almost identical with the Greek law; the provisions, so far as the labor communes are concerned, being alike for the Greeks and Romans. It appeared to Gaius to be a translation, and seems to have

---

[35] Item placuit, quisquis ex quacumque causa mortem sibi adsciverit, ejus ratio funeris non habebitur." (*De Coll. and Sodal. Rom.* p. 100.)
[36] Mommsen, *Idem,* p. 87; "Ipsa illa simulata religio senatum promovit ut jus coeundi tolleratt." The clause of the law appears to except or exempt those aged associations known to be beyond suspicion: "Sub praetextu religionis vel sub specie solvendi voti coetus illicitos nec a veteranis tentari oportet." (Lex 2, *Dig. de extr. crim.* xlvii, ii.
[37] Mackenzie, *Roman Laws,* p. 5-7.

been the identical law of Solon who is known to have given the free right of organization to the proletaries of Athens.[38] Our opinion is that these Tables of laws favoring the laboring classes, had become so obnoxious to the Roman *gentes* that they determined to rid the forum of its presence, thus virtually annulling the laws.

Large numbers of burial associations existed and it is repeatedly acknowledged that they often acted as a shield to the real trade unions under the garb of religion, notwithstanding the law. Mommsen describes a burial society at Alburnum in Lucania the notice of which was found inscribed on a *libellus* with some words spelled wrongly: "Artimidorus Apollonii, magister collegii Iovis Cernani et Valerius Niconis et Oflas Menofili, quæstores collegii ejusdem, posito hoc libello publice testantur." Then follow the laws of the society prescribing the use of the common fund. Mommsen, however remarks:[39] "It is clear that this mutual relief society of Cernanus, although bearing or holding up the name of a god, was nevertheless instituted, in order to give the funeral benefit, collected within a certain time and under the law, to the heirs of the deceased." This means that under the semblance of the burial society, they substantially met as a mutual aid commune—perhaps a trade organization. Again, aside from the opinion of Mommsen, always reliable, we have Asconius for positive testimony that frequently the sacred societies, of which the burial societies were a part, were suppressed on suspicion that they were discovered by the police to be engaged in carrying out the business of those trade or other organizations on which the conspiracy law had laid its hand.[40]

[38] Cf. Granier, *Histoire des Classes Ouvrières*, p. 325. "Nous avons fait voir d' ailleurs que la loi romaine des Douze-Tables sur les corporations contenait les mêmes dispositions que la loi grecque, à ce point qu' elles ont paru à Gaius être la traduction l' une de l' autre." The words of Gaius (*vide Digest*, lib. XLVII, tit. xxii. leg. 4. will be found quoted in our note 87, page 127. On page 290, note 1, Granier speaks of the intimate relations between Athenian and Roman trade unions as follows: "Du reste, si le texte de Plutarque pouvait laisser quelque doute sur le fait des jurandes athéniennes, un fragment de Gaius sur les Douzes Tables, conservé par le Digeste, dit que la loi sur les corps des métiers parait avoir été empruntée aux lois de Solon sur la même matière; et là dessus Gaius cite le texte même de la loi de Solon, dans lequel il est statué que les membres des métiers peuvent s' ériger eux-mêmes en corporations en respectant les lois de l'État."

[39] Mommsen, *De Collegiis et Sodaliciis Romanorum*, p. 94.

[40] "Frequenter tum etiam cœtus factiosorum hominum, sine publica auctoritate, malo publico fiebant . . . propter quod postea collegia sancta et pluribus legibus, sunt sublata." (Ascon. *in Cornel.* p. 75.)

ORGANIZATION.

By far the most numerous and powerful of the organizations of proletaries or outcasts among the ancients were the genuine trade unions.[41] Had it not been for the ancient habit, probably established by the lost law of the Twelve Tables, of inscribing [42] more or less of the objects, dates, names of leaders or organizers, and name of the tutelary deity under which they chose to worship—being proscribed from the privilege of worship of their own—we should be altogether without data regarding the vast trade societies which from immemorial times existed in Greece and Rome and in the provinces over which those nations ruled. We have sufficiently explained the causes of this organization. It may be well, however to sum them up in this manner:

First in ancient times all lands not belonging to the *gens* estates but achieved by conquest, were common property of the state. The people relied upon the products of these lands for their subsistence. This was true of people of all ranks, whether the haughty *gentes* or the degraded slaves. Many subsisted upon the fruits of the common lands. King Numa, admitting this, was wise enough to create, or rather recognize an already existing system of trade or business-unions, the special function of which was to till the lands and divide and distribute the products. Nothing could be more sensible and nothing more practical than to give the soil-tillers their organizations under protection of the state—and this means under a species of subvention or common guarantee. It must not be forgotten that by a law of ancient religion there were two distinct classes—workers and non-workers or the privileged and the non-privileged classes. They were so distinct that Dionysius of Halicarnassus declares that the latter were not even counted with the people or enumerated in the census as human beings; a fact which has caused much astonishment to the writers on ancient populousness; some counting them in and some not; thus producing figures so ridiculously at variance and contradictory that nobody pretends except approximately, even to conjecture what the ancient population was![43]

[41] The more numerous slaves are here excepted.
[42] We are, as yet, without the words of the law rendering it binding upon the communes to set up and inscribe a marble, or other stone slab. It was probably lost with the Twelve Tables. Also the similar law of Solon.
[43] Cf. Wallace on the "Numbers of Mankind." Edinburg, 1753, p. 28

Thus for many centuries, the lands of the ancient Romans, called *ager publicus* was common or public property, tilled by the proletaries, many of whom were organized into unions legalized by the arrangements of the Twelve Tables which was merely a literal ratification of the plan of Numa Pompilius, dividing the workers into nine species of craft and allowing each the autonomy of an organization. This shifted from the shoulders of the state or land-owner the care and responsibility of cultivation, while it elevated the proletaries to the practical dignity of that work. It was not the plan of small holdings by isolated families but of small holdings by isolated communes, which in turn, were amenable to, and under the general direction of the state, or common proprietor.

It cannot be said that this really great and wise system ever attained to a wide extent. The idea seems to have been clear to the workingmen and they carried it into force to some extent, but were always met with fierce opposition. The manner in which the state obtained its share of the proceeds or usufruct of these lands was by the *Vectigalarii*, the celebrated union of tax collectors who, instead of using money, took the tax "in kind;" which means that they went to the farmers, *agricolæ*, after the harvests and with wagons, brought to the *Municipium* or town in whichever district they were stationed, the share of the proceeds of the common land due the city people —grain, wool, fruits, pease, beans and whatever the land produced. The grain thus collected was turned over to the organization of the united *pistores* or millers, to be ground; thence to the united bakers, *panifices* to be made into bread. So with regard to everything. The almost phenomenal simplicity and universality of this great plan of the ancients is accounted for only by the fact that there were two classes so widely separated that the very touch of a proletary was supposed to pollute. In consequence of this wide distinction the merchant, who was also a workingman, could not become a monopolist because he was obliged to be a unionist which naturally recognized him at a par with his peers. This was a direct result of the crude communism which legalized trade unionism had

"Slaves who were of so little account under the ancient governments."—"Free citizens who alone had a voice in the public councils."

created and upheld for many centuries not only at Rome
but all over Italy and in many parts of Greece.

Very gradually however, some merchants succeeded in
becoming rich." On the other hand, as we prove in our
sketch of Spartacus, the older slave system which still
continued under the law of Lycurgus in Sparta, underwent a revival in Italy. By the plan of Numa Pompil-
ious, which was the true ancient trade union system, there
was no way for an aristocrat to conduct business of
any kind without polluting himself by contract with the
proletaries. He could, by owning the slaves, job them to
managers of genius, themselves of the laboring class, some
to a boss farmer, some to a miller, some to a wagoner, some
to a manufacturer, and thus, without himself touching his
own property, gratify his desire of profit, indirectly,
through the labor of his slaves. We are told that Crassus bought up as great a number as 500 slaves at a time;
that Nicias owned 1,000; that Claudius owned as many as
4,116 and Athens owned and hired out no less than 100-
000 slaves!" But these things did not occur in Italy until
the decline through Roman hostility, of the seven centuries of trade unionism, which began in high antiquity, and
which had been acknowledged and incorporated as an industrial system of the state under Numa, nearly 700 years
before Christ and did not give up its foothold without one
of the most terrible and protected agrarian and servile
struggles recorded or unrecorded in the vicissitudes of
the world. Nor must the remark be forgotten that during all the centuries through which this trade unionism
existed the golden era of prosperity and general happiness
was at its highest so far as labor was concerned.

But this prosperity and happiness will be better understood as we enumerate, one by one, the links of trade
unions which formed the great chain of industrial weal.
While we are doing this it may be well to keep constantly
in mind the suggestion, together with its proofs, that labor organization for protection, co-operation, resistance
and mutual improvement is always the best standard by

" Consult Drumann, *Arbeiter und Communisten in Griechenland und Rom*, p.
31: " Es verminderte die geringschätzung nicht mit welcher man auf die Arbeiter
sah, dass mehrere berühmte Männer durch ihre Geburt oder durch ihre früheren
Beschäftigung diesem Stande angehörten."

⁴⁵ For these statistics, see Bücher, S. 35-9. Schambach, *Italische Sklavenaufstand*, S. 1-3. Siefert, *Sicilische Sklavenkriege*, S. 10-14.

which to measure the intensity of true civilization. When the law forbidding these organizations struck the proletaries, one-half a century before Christ, their decline began; and this decline was a powerful cause of the fall of the Roman empire.

The old system of abject slavery pre-existing in the higher antiquity, gradually reappeared with the great Roman Conquests and usurped the foundations of the happier unions with its malignant concomitants of degraded labor under the lash of an overseer on the one hand, and with its millionare politicians, schemers and voluptuaries on the other. Corruption followed. Hope fled with liberty. Thrift disintegrated into pestilential reservoirs of vice. Rome fell into a mass of corruption.

It is not at all strange, nor to be wondered at that the poor who constituted the laboring class, should keenly feel their degrading exclusion from the Eleusinian Mysteries. Nor is it at all to be wondered at if we find Plutarch reciting to us his account of what must have been a gigantic uprising of these people 1,180 years before Christ, under Menestheus, as under Aristonicus in Asia Minor, 1,047 years afterward they rose against similar social degradations. Heaven to those poor people was a boon much nearer and more visible than at the present day. They imagined the earth to be flat. On this side all were mortal; on the other immortal. Some of the immortal happy had power to come from the other side to this. Here from Mount Olympus they assumed charge of the welfare of mortals. Many believed the flat earth so thin that rivers meandered from one to the other. Between the two surfaces there were surging floods of horrid smoke and steaming, lurid waters or pits of fiery asphaltum for the wicked, as well as bright, purling streams sparkling and cool for the just, leaving the banks and plains that were covered with verdure and peopled with enchanting birds and game.

Let the mover of the modern labor agitation who treats with scorn the author who mixes religion with a history of the ancient, reconsider. He must go back to them as they really were, poor down-trodden, superstitious, credulous and ignorant of facts while misled by priests. They believed heaven was so near by lineal measure that they often imagined they could hear the melodious voices of the blessed on the other sides; yet while they had nothing on this side to live for and their grasping imagination overheard and dwelt upon a future world beyond this "vale of tears," they found themselve shut out from all hope. The workman in the modern field of labor agitation certainly has but a gloomy foretaste in anything further than his future natural life. His predecessors have gone before with the axe and sickle of reason and past experience, tools of the thus intellectual pioneer. Their incomputable toil has, with investigation and experiment, with repeated millions of practical works, cleared away the mythic film of priestcraft and superstitious belief. The earth is now a globe. The miner knows this; for the deeper he descends the more unendurable the heat. Who wants now to descend to heaven? Who wishes to go to the other side, to China—a race groveling, mortal and inferior, rather than that of the ancients, beautiful soraphic, melodious, immortal. Who now wants to visit the ouranus of old Plato in the vaulted dome of heaven ? Who wants to rise when everybody knows that instead of a region of the immortal happy the farther one mounts the more uninhabitable, more frigid more stifling the ethers of space ? Labor's own skillful hand has caused all this metamorphosis in the human mind and forced it and is still forcing it out of its ignorant soarings and credence-ravings down to a cognizance of the earthly things that are.

No, we must picture the life of the ancient lowly as it really was in all its cushioned imagination, in all its yearnings to get there by the beautiful river, its green carpets on the other side where the wicked ceased from troubling and the weary were at rest; and those otherwise incomprehensible, religio-practical associations can be understood and their full function appreciated only by our throwing off our own prejudice and contemplating them as they really were. This we propose to do.

INSCRIPTION AT LANUVIUM. 353

L. CEIONIO. COMMODO. SEX. VETULENO. CIVICA. POMPE- IANO. COS. A. D. V. IDUS. IUN.

Lanuvi in Municipio in Templo Antinoi in Quo L. Caesennius Rufus
In the temple of Antinœ, city of Lavinia, where L. Cæsennius Rufus

Dict. III. et patronus Municipi conventum haberi jusserat
spokesman and guardian of the town, ordered an association formed, through

per. L. Pompeium
L. Pompey

F . . . . um, QQ. Cultorom Dianae, et Antinoi, Pol-
and F . . . . . under tutelary care of Diana and Antinœ, promising to con-

licitus est se
tribute towards it

in annum daturum eis ex liberalitate sua Hs. Xv. M. N. usum
out of his purse within a given year a sum of $600 for use of the union.

Die natalis Dianae Idib. Aug. Hs. CCCC. N. et die natalis An-
On Diana's birthday, the *Ides* of August, and birthday of Antinœ, $16 more.

tinoi V. K.

Decemb. Hs. CCCC. N. Et praecepit legem ab ipsis con-
In the month of December, $16. He also prescribes a law regulating the

stitutam sub tetra-
the union which is

stilo Antinoi parte interiori perscribi in verba infra scripta.
written on the inside of the 4 columned pillar in words as recorded below:

M. Antonio Hibero P. Mummio Sisenna Cos. K. Ian. Collegium
During the consulship of M. Antonius Hiberus and P. Mummius Sisenna the

Salutare Dianae

Et Antinoi constitutum, L. Caesennio L. F. Quir.
mutual benefit society of Diana and Antinœ was organized by

Rufo Dict III. IDEMQ. PATR.
L. Cæsennius Rufus, its recognised patron.

KAPUT   EX. S. C. P. R.
Designation.   Written by order of the Præfect.

Quibus coire convenire collegiumque hebere liceat. Qui stipem
It is permitted that all wishing to organise themselves, may do so.

menstruam conferre volent in Funera II in collegium coeant neq.
Any one desiring to pay monthly dues of 8 cents to the Funeral fund may

sub specie eius collegi nisi semel in mense coeant conferendi causa,
attend the meetings twice a month if the objects of such meetings be the

unde defuncti sepeliantur
burying of the dead.

Quod faustum felix salutareq. sit imp. Caesari Traiano Hadriano
Whatsoever is favorable, happy and healthful for the emperors, Trojan, Adrian

Aug. totiusque
and the whole house of the Cæsars,

domus August. nostris collegioq. nostro; et bene adque in-
will also be good for us and our society; and we should perform well and

dustrie contraxerimus, ut
industriously our duty that we may

exitus eorum honeste prosequamur. Itaq. bene conferendo
honestly reach the end. So ought we universally to agree, that we may

universi consentire
grow old in union.

debemus, ut longo tempore inveterescere possimus.

Tu qui novos in hoc collegio intrare voles, prius legem perlege et sic
O thou who wouldst bring initiates into this union, read well these rules, that

intra, ne postmodum queraris aut controversiam relinquas.
thou leavest no controversy with thy heirs!

LEX COLLEGI.
Law of the Union.

Placuit universis, ut quisquis in hoc collegium intrare voluerit,
Be it ordered in presence of all men: That whosoever may desire to join this

dabit kapitulari nomine.
union shall give to the Secretary-Treasurer

HS. C. N. et vini boni amphoram; item in menses sing. A.
his address, an initiation fee of $4, and a flagon of good wine; and like-

V. Item placuit, ut quisquis mensib.
wise 4 cents monthly dues. It is ordered that

continenter non pariaverit et ei humanitus acciderit, eius ra-
whoever fails to settle dues continuously for months, remaining a member

tio funeris non habebitur,
by grace, will not have the right of burial, even

etiam si testamentum factum habuerit.
though he may have willed to the association his property.

'tem placuit quisquis ex hoc corpore N. pariatus eum decesserit
Be it ordered that whoever dies, not in arrears to the order let his $4, be re-

sequentur ex arca HS. CCCC. N. ex qua summa decedent
turned from the treasury as expenses of burial.

exequiari nomine HS. I. N. qui ad Rogus dividentur. Exe-
One sesterce shall be divided at the funeral pile. But the ceremony must

quiæ autem pedibus fungentur.
be performed on foot.

INSCRIPTION AT LANUVIUM. 855

Item placuit, quisquis a municipio ultra miliar. XX. decesserit
Be it ordered, that whenever a member dies at a distance of 20 miles from the

et nuntiatum fuerit, eo exire debebunt electi ex corpore N.
city, it shall be reported, a permit taken and 3, elected from among the

homines tres, qui funeris ejus curam agant et rationem po-
members, be sent to see to it. Should it be found that there was any de-

pulo reddere debebunt, sine dolo malo. Si quit in eis fraudis
ception, then as much as four-fold the amount shall be exacted as a fine,

causa, inventum fuerit, eis multa esto quadruplum.
by reason of such injustice.

Quibus sing. nummus dabitur; hoc amplius viatici nomine citro
Those to whom money is given, are to receive it as follows: If it be more

sing. HS. XX. N. quod longius quam intra mill. XX. de-
than the 20 miles, the sum shall be for each, 20 sesterces. But if the

cesserit et nuntiari non potuerit, tum is qui eum funeraverit
member dies at a greater distance than 20 miles, and it cannot be an-

testato tabulis signati sigillis civium Romanorum VII. et
nounced, then, whoever attends to the funeral must send an account,

probata causa, funeraticium ejus; satio dato ab eis nemenem
signed and bearing the seal of 7 Roman citizens; and when the case

petiturum, deductis commodis et exequiario, e lege collegii
has been proved, and the funeral expenses found reasonable, no one

dari sibi petat.
objecting, his pay shall be disbursed from the treasury if he asks it.

A nostro collegio dolus malus abesto neque patrono neque patro-
Let there be no craftiness in our union. Neither patron nor patroness mas-

næ, neque domino neque dominæ neque creditori ex hoc col-
ter nor mistress, nor even credi tor, shall make any demand, account

legio ulla petitio esto nisi qui testamento heres nominatus est.
or claim whatever, or anybody else, except him who is elected heir.

Si quis intestatus decesserit, is, arbitrio quinq. et populi funerab
If any one die without children, five sesterces shall be given & all attend.

Item placuit, quisquis ex hoc collegio servus defunctus fuerit, et
Be it ordered that whoever dies a member, being a slave, and his body is

corpus ejus a domino dominave inquietate sepulturæ datum
unwillingly given up for sepulture by master or mistress who will not

non fuerit neque tabella, ei funus imaginarium fiet.
permit a registration, an imaginary funeral shall be held.

Item placuit, quisquis ex quacumque causa mortem sibi adsciverit,
Be it ordered that whoever commits suicide from any cause, for this reason

ejus ratio funeris non habebitur.
no funeral can be held.

Item placuit, ut quisquis servus ex hoc collegio liber factus fuerit
Be it ordered that whatever slave is set free by this union, he shall contrib-

> is dare debebit vini boni amphoram.
> ute a flagon of good wine.

Item placuit, quisquis magister suo anno erit ex ordine albi ad
It is ordered that whatever manager who during his year, shall not attend the

> cænam faciendam, et non observaverit neque fecerit, is arcæ
> ceremony nor observe, nor perform functions, shall pay a fine of 30 ses-
>
> inferet HS. XXX. N. et insequens ejus dare debebit et is
> terces into the treasury and the place shall be forfeited to his suc-
>
> ejus loco restituere debebit.
> cessor.

ORDO CENARUM VIII. ID MAR.
Order of the feasts, on the 8th., Ides of March :

NATALI CÆSENNI . . . . PATRIS V. K DEC.

NAT. ANTONOI IDIB. AUG NATALI DIANÆ ET COL-

LEGII XIII. K. SEPT. JAN. NATALI L. CÆSENNI

RUFI PATR. MUNIC.

Magistri cænarum ex ordine albi facta quo ordine homines qua-
The managers of the feasts established by the order, will place the men, 4 at a

> terni ponere debebunt: vini boni amphoras singulas, et
> time, in their order: each contributing a flask of good wine and a loaf of
>
> panes A. Ii qui numerus collegi fuerit et sardas numero
> best bread, and each, four pickled sardines served hot in proper
>
> quatuor strationem caldam cum ministerio.
> dishes.

INSCRIPTION AT LANUVIUM.

Item placuit, ut quisquis quinquennalis in hoc collegio factus fuerit, a sigillis eius temporis, quo quinquennalis erit, immunis esse debebit, et ei ex omnibus divisonibus partes duplas dari. Item scribae et viatori a sigillis vacantibus partes ex omni divisione sesquiplas dari placuit.

Item placuit, ut quisquis quinquennalitatem gesserit integre, ei

ob honorem partes sesquiplas ex omni re dari, ut et reliqui recte faciendo idem sperent.

Item placuit, si quis quid queri aut referre volet, in conventu referant, ut quieti et hilares diebus sollemnibus epulemur.

Item placuit, ut quisquis seditionis causa de loco in alium locum transierit, ei multa esto HS. IIII. N. Si quis autem in obprobrium alteralterius dixerit, aut tumultuatus fuerit, ei multa esto HS. N. Si quis quinquennali inter epulas obprobrium aut quid contumeliose dixerit, ei multa esto HS. XX. N.

Item placuit, ut quinquennalis sui cuiusque temporis diebus sollemnibus ture et vino supplicet et ceteris officiis albatus fungatur, et diebus natalium Dianae et Antinoi oleum collegio in balineo publico ponat antequam epulentur.

The remarkable features of this college are that under the guise of piety, and of being a burial and mutual benefit society, it was used to emancipate slaves. That it was a trade or labor union is shown by its being devoted to securing good places to work.

Everywhere the severity of the law is apparent. Rome had a mortal fear of labor riots and uprisings and hence the many fines which stood as a constant menace, acting as a check against insubordination. It was difficult to obtain a privilege or charter to organize one of these labor unions, and consequently where they possessed one, it was prized as a gem of great value; which may account for their great age, found in some cases to have been four or five hundred years.

The love of the Latin race for pleasures is observable all through. They used this great union or commune for that purpose; but they are seen in these rules and regulations, to have held uppermost a peculiar system of culture tending toward ultimate emancipation from the lowly and restricted condition in which they were held by the law and the police.

CHAPTER XIV.

THE CATEGORIES.

THE GREAT ECONOMIC ORGANIZATIONS.

ANCIENT FEDERATIONS of Labor—How they were Employed by the Government—Nomenclature of the Brotherhoods—Categories of King Numa—Varieties and Ramifications—The Masons, Stonecutters and Bricklayers—Federation for Mutual Advantages—List of the 35 Trade Unions, under the *Jus Coeundi.*

NUMA POMPILIUS, the first king after Romulus, recognized trade unions even before Solon of Athens, who followed rather than led in this scheme as a measure of political economy.[1] They had, however, already existed, perhaps thousands of years before receiving any recognition at all. One of the first of importance legalized by these lawgivers was the fraternity of builders.

They were called in Greek, the *technicai* and in Latin *tignarii.* It is evident from Plutarch, that he intended this word to include also the mason.[2] If, however, all the building trades were organized into one body or union, they were very different from trade unions of our day. Besides, had Plutarch intended to convey the idea that all the building trades were united into one under Numa he would, it seems to us, have used the still more comprehensive Greek term *technites* which expresses it. Again its Latin synonym found by Mommsen, proves that Numa's

---

[1] Plutarch, *Numa* 1. Numa followed Romulus to the throne, about 690 years before Christ Plutarch's suggestion that he might have personally known Pythagorus and that he had been brought up among the Pythagorean Greek settlements of Italy which were communistical in character looks exceedingly plausible.

[2] See Wm. Langhorne's tr. of Plutarch, *in Numa.*

union was that of workers in metal and wood.[3] In those times the mountains back of Rome produced dense forests, which were not swept away by machinery with the rapidity of modern art. The people, on account of wars, want of medical science, comparative abstinence from marriage, dissoluteness of the rich, hardships of the poor, did not multiply rapidly. In consequence the forests produced new trees as fast as they were cut away by the workmen. Rome was mostly built of wooden houses; and no doubt there was an abundance of work for the carpenters. All the great public buildings were constructed by trade unions for the state, direct—that is, with contractors or middlemen, and the carpenters' union used to take charge of the woodwork. The *Ager publicus*[4] had to be furnished with houses for the Gentry. Honorary seats were made by these *fabri tignariorum*, such as the splendid *bisellia*[5] or cushions of the gods. The fine villas of wealthy gentlemen[6] who had a custom of turning public moneys and lands to their own account were work of their art. In fact this was common from the highest antiquity before the division of the *gentes* into *curæ* and tribes. Thus it was not considered a breach of political rule to divert the public funds, to a certain extent, to the building or repairing of their own fine residences; And this work was performed by the builders' unions.

There were two names under which the wood-workers of the building trades were known. These were the *dendrophori*, mentioned in the code of Theodosius[7] as

---

[3] Mommsen, *De Collegiis et Sodaliciis Romanorum*, pp. 29 30. "Inter classes primam et secundam interjectæ erant centuria fabrum tignariorum et centuria fabrum ærariorum, sive, ut Dionysium (VII. 59) seqnamur: δύο λόχοι τεκτόνων καὶ χαλκοτύπων καὶ ὅσοι ἄλλοι πολεμικῶν ἔργων ἦσαν χειροτέχναι.

[4] We prefer to use this Latin term because it saves explanatory words necessary to qualify the meaning of the English word "land." It means common lands belonging to the government, on which the workingmen had no claim as citizens. The propensity of the Roman building trades to organize in protective societies is richly illustrated in an article written by Mr. Rogers and forming a chapter in a large work on labor edited by Mr. Geo. E. McNeill, Bost. 1887, entitled "*The Building Trades*," Mr. Rogers. (pp. 335-7), shows that this proclivity of the ancient Romans for organizing into communes was never lost even in far off Kent, sticking to the English people to this day, furnishes a formidable argument against the assumption that the Saxon Rule absolutely superseded that of the earlier inhabitants.

[5] Fabretti *Inscriptiones Antiquæ Explicatic*, p. 170, 324. p. 227, 604. Grut. 675, 3. Also Orell, No. 4,055.

[6] Our own word "gentleman" is directly derived from the Latin word *gens*, or high and respectable family. If we call the human race an "Order," the *gentes* may be considered a "genus."

[7] Codex Theodosii, 14. 8. Also Orell, *Incriptiones Latinarum Collectio*, Nos.

veritable trade unions, and the *tignarii* who were the true carpenters and joiners. As we construe the signification of these two terms from the stone monuments and slabs on which they are found engraved and not as found in the dictionaries, we conclude that the *dendrophori* must have been the heavy lumbermen and framers. They cut and hewed the heavy timbers both for buildings and ships; while the *tignarii* did the lighter work. One thing is certain; they both occur together in many of the inscriptions.¹ This class of trade unions was considered necessary to the welfare of the state; and was exempted from being suppressed when, in B. C. 58, the conspiracy laws were put in operation by Cæsar; although so much suspicion rested upon them that they were watched with a jealous eye by the officers of the law and as appears, much of their former vitality was crushed out. They had existed from the time of Numa in Rome, and of Solon at Athens, in full strength and vigor. At the time of their suppression by restrictive laws nearly all the Grecian territory, especially that of Attica, including Athens, the Piræus, Eleusis and all the populous towns where they are known to have existed in great numbers, belonged to Rome, then mistress of the world.

It must have been a very strange experience for a great people to undergo. Here was a system of manufacture and repairs of immemorable age, authorized by the most highly esteemed lawgivers, one of whom was one of the seven wise men of Greece. It had been known by the chronicles for fully 600 years, and, though it performed duties which by the haughty and foolish were considered degrading, and upon which there rested a taint, yet it was an important institution, taking charge of indispensable affairs of public as well as of private life. All at once it was suppressed. That the result was a dangerous convulsion cannot be wondered at.

Gruter cites a college of *dendrophori*² who used to build

3,741, 4,082, 3,349, 7,336, 7,145, 3,888, 5,113, 4,055, 6,037, 7018, 7,018, 6,031, 6,073, 6,590, 911, 4,109, 7,194, 7,197, 4,069. Each of these 19 numbers represents a *collegium* or trade union of wood-workers. The inscriptions were found in as many places nearly as there are numbers.

⁸ Orell. 4,084, "Collegium Fabrorum Navalium . . . . . Tunc ea ipsa conditione fabr. Tig. Pisaurensium." Pisaurum was an Umbrian town at the mouth of the navigable Pisaurus, *Inscr.* 4,160 Faber Tignariorum and Coll. Dendrophorum are noted together.

⁹ Gruterius, *Inscriptiones Antiquæ Totius Orbis Romanorum*, 175, 8.

houses and ships or boats for the society of freight boatmen located at Rome. He also gives one which Orelli quotes, taken on a stone slab in times as late as Justinian.[10] The word *epulantur* conveying the idea of entertainment, shows that these schools of the workingmen sometimes used their organization as a means of mutual enjoyment. Especially was this the case among the Greek fraternities which we describe in their place. After the great struggle with Spartacus, the right of organization was severely restricted by the Roman law; and it became necessary for the unions, in order to exist at all, to assume two forms of dissimulation by which to parry the attacks of enemies who had recourse to these conspiracy laws in order to gratify their whims of revenge, or to fortify their own schemes of making money through the cheap labor of the slave system which Rome in the later days had revived, and which such enemies of organized labor as Cicero or Crassus, were pushing with an almost fierce determination, on pretense of restoring the ancient purity of religion, family and vested rights. We have noted that certain kinds of organizations were permitted.[11] Among these were *collegia sancta*, or those unions and fraternities given to holy or pious purposes. So some of these were shrewd enough to combine business with holiness and thus shield themselves from their pursuers.[12] Mommsen speaks of them in clearest terms which leave no doubt whatever regarding the mysterious procedure [13] of those old Roman lawyers who were determined to suppress the trade unions, root and branch, in order to reinstitute slavery, the most ancient form of labor known to their religion, which had

[10] We quote the Latin as given by Orell., No. 4,088. "Ex S. C. Schola Aug. Collegii Fabrorum Tignariorum impendiis ipsorum ab inchoato exstructo, solo dato ab T. Furio primogenio qui et dedic. ejus HS. X. N. ded. ex cujus summ. redit, omnibus annis XII. K. August die natalis sui, epulantur." Gruter, 169, 6
[11] Dion. XXXVIII. 13, *Antiquitates*, says: "Τα ἐταιρικα . . . . . ὄντα μεν ἐκ τοῦ ἀρχαίου καταλυθέντα δὲ χρόνον τινά." Asconius 1. C. *Comment*, says: "Collegia sunt sublata præter pauca atque certa quæ utilitas civitatis desiderassit quæ sint fabrorum fictorumque." These saved were Pagan image makers who wrought the religious devices, q, v.
[12] Complures autem ob finei ejusmodi instituebantur collegia: religionis *ante omnia causa*, ut, qui idem vitae genus essent amplexi, iisdem quoque sacris uterunter," etc., etc. Orell. VII. p. 244· *Inscr. Latin Collectio*.
[13] Mommsen, *De Coll. et Sodal. Rom.*, pp. 87-88, says: "Ipsa illa simulata (referring to lex. 3, Digest, *de extr. crim*. XLVII, 11.) religio senatum promovit tu jus coeundi tolleret Explicanda sunt illa verba de coitionibus in templis ad rem divinam faciendam, quae etsi neutiquam contra SCtum erant, facile tamen in fraudem SCti usurpari poterant."

founded their patrimony, their law of entailment through primogeniture and their system of grandees and of slaves. Numa and Solon had been these fellows' enemies; Lycurgus their friend. Trade unionism the child of wills and manumissions, had first come among them, a spontaneous growth. It cradled and matured human sympathy. It had proved itself innocent, enterprising and good. It had succeeded in becoming legalized by those two powerful princes—a mighty stride. But it had, as the *gens* families fancied, usurped the ancient and holy system of slavery and thus interfered—by substituting communism—with their vested individual rights.[14] On account, probably, of their superstition, Cicero, Cæsar and the rest, after they had put down Clodius the intrepid orator and tribune who had restored the old and created new,[15] excepted such of the carpenters and joiners or cabinet-makers' unions as confined their labor to manufacturing all sorts of wooden idols, which in those days, were sometimes very large, and built for the temples, the fanes and the family altars. It it also quite likely that a few unions devoted to the carpenter work on the temples and the *aedes sanctae*, were saved. But we ascend from these cruel days of moribund Rome to an earlier and brighter age.

[14] We have repeatedly mentioned the impossibility, among the Indo-European Greeks and Italians, of there ever having existed in those peninsulas a communistic, or even patriarchal form of government. The bent of labor communes was towards it but they never succeeded in breaking down the power of the competitive system ; and it rules to this day. The oldest records of any kind shedding light, confirm the idea that originally the despotic form of government prevailed; the father *paterfamilies* as king, with his sons and daughters and others as slaves around his fixed abiding place, must have been the primitive government behind which there is neither record nor philosophy—no philosophy without overturning the theory of development. Man has grown into refinement through reason and experience and it is altogether inconsistent with reason to suppose that he ever tried so high a form of government as the communistic one, or that he ever had in those times other than selfish, cruel, beast-government in which all research into antiquity finds him. Mommsen, *History of Rome*, Vol I, p. 44, in corroboration says : " But there can be no doubt that, with the Graeco-Italians as with all other nations, agriculture became, and in the mind of the people remained the germ and core of their national and of their private life. The house and the fixed hearth, which the husbandman constructs instead of the light hut and shifting fireplace of the shepherd and represented in the spiritual domain and idealized in the goddess Vesta or 'Εστία, almost the only divinity not Indo-Germanic yet from the first common to both nations." So again (p. 48). " The Hellenic character, which sacrificed the whole to its individual elements, the nation to the township and the township to the citizen." This exactly expresses our idea, viz : that everything from the first, was subordinate to the unlimited, despotic control of the "father." For valuable information. See Funck Brentano *La Civilisation et ses Lois*, IV, I, p. 311, (quoting Plutarch Numa, VII) "Il en fut de même dans les cités de la Grèce ; ce fut une condition de leur progrès."

[15] Ascon, *Ad h. L.* "Diximus, L Pisone et A. Gabieno consulibus P. Clodium tribunum plebis—tulisse—de collegiis restituendis, novisque instituendis, quae ait ex servitiorum fæce constituta."

Fabretti gives us another union of carpenters and joiners whose inscription was found at Leprignani. It reads very plainly and shows that they had a federation of the trades.[16] Another *collegium fabrorum tignariorum* or carpenters' trade union is reported by Muratori.[17] The tablet was found at Ravelli in the province of Naples, showing that the unions of those days were not confined to Rome or any of the other large cities but were as frequent proportionately to population in any small town.

An inscription is reported by Gruter,[18] bearing evidence of another interesting school, *schola*, of the bona fide carpenters' unions, found in the Tolentine temple of Catharina—religious, of course, and of a later date. Orelli[19] quotes the learned Muratori of Modena as the authority if not the finder of an inscription which describes a *collegium* together with a *sodalicium*—another Roman name for trade union, in which the president or *Magister*, and the secretary are mentioned. It is a union of the skilled woodworkers. It was found in the town of Falaria, and appears to be very old. It is not unusual for the inscriptions engraved in the time of the emperors, to state an approximate of their date by noting the names of the consuls, or of the monarch who then occupied the throne. Unfortunately for the more ancient ones this is not so strictly done; probably owing more to the fact that, as the law at earlier dates fully protected them, they were not forced to inscribe the dates by little points or constructions such as characterized the laws after the restrictive acts were promulgated.

No less than eighteen of the genuine carpenters and joiners' unions are found in the work of Orelli.[20] As these working people used their unions as means whereby to parry off the many dangers that beset them on every hand, such as slavery, starvation, slurs of contempt and in later times conscription, we cannot too well understand how keenly alive they must have been to their welfare.

[16] Fabretti, C. IV, 529, of *Inscriptiones Antiquæ Explicatio*.
[17] Muratorius, *Thesaurus Veterum Incriptionum*, 521.
[18] Gruter, *Inscriptiones Antiquæ Totius Orbis Romanorum*, 169. 6.
[19] Orell., No. 4,056, Mur.tori, *Thesaur. Vet. Inscr.* 523. We give it with the abbreviations: " D. M. T. Sillio T. Lib. Prisco mag, colleg. Fabr. et q mag. et q. sodal fullonum Clavidiæ lib. uxori ejus matri sodali. C. Tullon, T Sillius Karus et Ti. Claudius Phillippus mag. e Q. Coleg. fabr. filii parentib. piissimis."
[20] *Scholæ Artificum et Opificum*, Vol. II pp. 227-240, and *Artes et Opificia*, idem, pp. 247-266, of Orelli's great work on the *Latin Inscriptions*.

On the other hand, the power of organization which kept them in a position to supply the orders given them by the state, was ever a great encouragement.

Among the many interesting monuments or schools of ancient trade unionism, where mutual love and care were taught and the noble element of sympathy was grafted upon the selfish, competitive body of irascible and acquisitive paganism which animated the Lycurgan rule at Sparta and the purely archaic slave code everywhere, are those to be found in the Order of masons, stonecutters and bricklayers. These with the painters, glaziers, roofers and plumbers, were indispensable to complete the building trades. They too, felt the necessity of organization, especially in the later time of Cæsar and the emperors, on account of the awful treatment of slaves by their ferocious masters. There existed no law by which the slave masters could be brought to account for savage acts of barbarity toward their slaves.

This distressing state of things was not [21] relieved until the emperor Adrian withdrew the slaves from the domestic tribunals and transferred them to the tribunal of the magistrates; in other words gave them government protection. But this was 200 years after the war of Spartacus. The fear of being relegated back to slavery was a constant urgent to ancient trade unionism; and this explains one reason at least, why they so tenaciously hugged their fraternities notwithstanding the conspiracy laws against trade and other organizations of the working people. It must not be forgotten that according to the law of B. C. 58,[22] all the new unions were suppressed. Consequently, we are to infer that those we find in the inscriptions are those belonging to the ancient plan of Numa and Solon which were spared on account of their veteran age and respectability.[23] Another thing requiring the nicest discrimination is the fact that it will not do to mention all the examples set down in the works of the archælogists. We only mention those where the labor organization is clearly defined. Many of these queer inscriptions appear

[21] See Granier, *Histoire des Classes Ouvrières*, pp. 491-487.
[22] See Mommsen, *De Collegiis et Sodaliciis Romanorum*, cap. **IV**, pp. **73-78**, *De Legibus Contra Collegia Latis*.
[23] Suetonius, *Cæs*. 42 "Cæsar cuncta collegia præter antiquitus constituta distraxit."

to us to be only private signs and have nothing to do with our theme. Slavery was everywhere prevalent and many of the slaves were as ingenious as the freedmen. We are told by Drumann and others that it was customary for masters to keep their slaves at work and obtain profit from their labor by letting it out to enterprising foreigners who contracted building repairs and other work on private houses and grounds. But the government was the true employer of the unions because they, possessing of themselves as it were, in a unit, all the men in organization, always ready, money, tools, raw material, skill and even the designs requisite to turning out a good job promptly, were dangerous competitors of slavery on large works.[24] From the time of Numa the government of Rome had always patronized the trade unions. Thus it would appear that some of the inscriptions may have been private signs used by slave employers who carried on private work upon a small scale, hiring their laboring force of the rich slave owning patricians; and it will not do to count the archæologists' lists of *artes et opificia;* while it is almost always safe to enumerate their specimens of the *Corpora, Sodalicia* or *Collegia*[25] in our list of trade unions and communes. Trade unionism in its highest form is the reverse of slavery. The true trade union of all ages takes care of its members who are co-owners of equal shares, on equal footing. Slavery then, is the exact antithesis of trade unionism in principle; but although it is certain that the principle on which slavery is based was, especially among the Spartans and Romans, carried out with all its repugnant and appalling brutalities,[26] yet it is, as a recognized system in the religio-social economy of the world, incomputably the oldest of the two. Trade unionism was a deadly rival to the slave system all through the antiquity of the Indo-European stock; and since slavery was a graft of the ancient religion—the natural child of its law of

[24] Granier, *Hist. des Classes Ouvrières,* p. 303, speaking of the insignificance of individuals when compared with the immense force of organized trades, says: "Ici les nombreux ouvrières de Caton (slaves), les 500 ouvriers (slaves) de Crassus n' auraient pu rien faire; il fallait des corporations, (trade unions) des collèges! de travailleurs."
[25] Cf. Orell. lib. II. pp. 227-246, *Collegia Corpora et Sodalicia. Scholæ Artificum et Opificum.* See also lib. III. Sup Henzen *Index to Collegia, init.*
[26] Granier, *Hist. des Classes Ouvrières,* chap. III and IV., also Plut. *Lycourgus and Numa compared.*

primogeniture and the fostered fruit of entailment in the social, political and economic development of those semi-barbarous families, phratries, curies and tribes which came to be nations and empires, it must not be wondered at that this hideous fledgling, before giving up the ghost, made a terrific struggle to regain what it had lost through the mild but determined enterprise of its great competitor trade unionism.

It was this that constituted the mighty struggle of the revolution in the social economy of the lowly and it so remains to this day; although in this comparatively gorgeous and brilliant hour the spirit of human slavery, resting upon absolute, merchantable ownership of man by man, seems to have forever fled. Nothing now remains of slavery but its skeleton—individual competism—hanging betwixt peace and war over the vortex of revolution and swinging to and fro at every fresh attack from the same trade unionism which, although of prehistoric longevity grows more youthful, enterprising and belligerent with every invention and discovery and every stride of literature, of science and of Christianity.

The unions of the masons at Rome do not appear so numerous as those of the framers among the building trades. Still we find tablets whose inscriptions show their existence.[27] We have already mentioned the fact that among the true workmen's organizations the slabs which appear to have been inscribed independently by themselves and without the correctional inspection of masters, often puzzle the experts on account of the sometimes ludicrously bad spelling and misplacement of words. Sometimes also there appear words belonging to the peculiar slang or *patois* monenclature, their trade's vernacular. But while this is somewhat troublesome to archæologists it is exceedingly interesting to students of ethnology and sociology; since it shows otherwise unrecorded proof that the freedmen, only one step above the slaves, were utterly neglected in all matters of education. The presumption must be that the reason they executed their inscriptions so well is that they had, in their mutual federation a trade

---

[27] Orell. *Artes et Opificia*, Vol. II, p. 258 of *Inscr. Lat. Select Collectio*, No. 4,289. It is a broken fragment. "Quadratariorum opus Augurius Catullinus Ursar." We read: "Quadratariorum Corpus." He thus ranks it as a union.

union of carvers and gravers *cælatores* whose business was to work in letters. It was consequently a part of their trade to study sufficiently the Roman and Greek literature to do their work well. Gruter mentions several of them.[28] Orelli tells us of the sculptor, *signarius artifex*, who worked in signs.[29] Any of these could make their signs or their monuments and tombstones by being called upon at any time; but we are reminded that then as now, economy was everything and that consequently they themselves might often have depended upon their own inexperienced self-confidence and thus have committed these literary faults which as amateurs they were too unlettered to rectify.

The *quadratarii* were the true stone cutters' unions and the probable reason why they are not numerous is that most of the work of the stone cutters was done by the *marmorarii*, marble cutters or marble masons. Of these we find inscriptions of genuine trade unions in considerable numbers. Now this paucity of hard stone-cutters and abundance of marble cutters is easily accounted for. The Geological formation of the Italian, Hellenic and Spanish peninsulas is largely of carbonates of lime. A great share of the Appenine range is composed of fine white marble. Many of the springs and even mountain rivers of Italy, Greece and the Archipelago deposit pure marble. Paros in the Ægian Sea was long a rival in pure white marbles of Pentelicus; and Mount Marpessa the seat of its quarries, may be considered an isolated spur of the Illyrian Alps, Mt. Olympus and the Cambunian range. All through these regions exist the characteristic marbles used in antiquity before the superior powers of duration of sandstone and granites were known. The splendid marble quarries of Luna in Etruria were near at hand and others as celebrated in history were always available to the marble cutters' unions who made the wonderful temples of Ceres at Eleusis, of the Parthenon at Athens and many of the great public structures at Rome. It is therefore, very natural that the marble cutters' unions predominated over the sandstone and granite-cutters in point of num-

---

[28] Grut. *Inscr. Ant. Tot. Orb. Rom.*, 583, 5. This, Gruter mentions as a sign of some emancipated slave— 'libertus qui post manumissionem vel argentarii ve. cælateris artem exercuerit.' But it often happened that a trade union was inscribed under the name of its *magister* or director.
[29] Orell. *Inscr. Lat. Select*, No. 4,282.

bers; and this explanation we accept for the fewness of trade unions found among the inscriptions under the name *quadratarii* or stone-cutters. At Rome, even though perhaps many worked in stone harder than marble, the name *quadratarius* was merged; because even the marble workers hewed and shaped large square blocks. We have, even as it is, enough evidence to assure us that the *quadratarii* existed and that they were organized into unions; for this is distinctly stated in the law of Constantine of the year 337. These, with the *structores* and other builders, were enumerated in the list of 35 trade unions recognized at that time. These 35 unions are permitted by this law to exist; although we have found inscriptions and other references giving evidence that at one time more than 50 trade unions existed in Italy, representing as many organized trades, and members innumerable. These will be exhibited as we proceed with the subject. The law of Constantine gives the 35 trade unions existing at one time as follows:

1. *Albarii*,[30] plasterers; 2. *Architecti*, architects; 3. *Aurifices*, goldsmiths; 4. *Blatiarii*, workers in mosaic; 5. *Carpentarii*, wagon-makers; 6. *Ærarii*, brass and coppersmiths; 7. *Argentarii*, silversmiths; 8. *Barbaricarii*, gold gilders; 9. *Diatritarii*, pearl and filigree-workers; 10. *Aquæ libratores*, waterers; 11. *Deauratores*, *auratores* or *bractearii*, gold gilders, beaters; 12. *Eburarii*, ivory workers; 13. *Figuli*, potters; 14. *Fullones*, fullers; 15. *Ferrarii*, blacksmiths; 16. *Fusores*, founders; 17. *Intestinarii*, joiners; 18. *Lapidarii*, lapidaries; 19. *Laquearii*, plasterers; 20. *Medici*, doctors; 21. *Mulo medici*, horse doctors, veternary surgeons; 22. *Musivarii*, decorators; 23. *Marmorarii*, marble-cutters; 24. *Pelliones*, furriers; 25. *Pictores*, painters; 26. *Plumbarii*, plumbers; 27. *Quadratarii*, stone-cutters; 28. *Specularii*, looking-glass makers; 29. *Statuarii*, staturies; 30. *Scasores* or *Pavimentarii*, pavers; 31. *Sculptores*, sculptors; 32. *Structores*, masons; 33. *Tessellarii*, pavers in mosaic; 34. *Tignarii*, carpenters; 35. *Vitriarii*, glaziers.[31]

Here we have the building trades represented in Con-

[30] *Codex Justiniani*, 10, 64. 1.
[31] Mentioned once in Orell *Inscr*, 4 277; whereas the more correctly Latin term is given by him as an organized union, *Idem* 4,112.

stantine's more human law for the post-Christian organization. It is well here to state that Constantine [32] became a Christian, being the first who threw off the yoke of paganism. He evidently did not understand its true ideas and was far from being a Christian at heart; but he was a politician, and Christian enough to be unbiased by the old Pagan belief in the divine aristocracy of the *gens* family, in which ratiocination Cicero had believingly fought the unions of working people on the ground of their unfitness to aspire to freedom and manhood. This stereotyped logic of the Pagan faith based on the divinity of the slave code, had been overthrown and completely annihilated by the new doctrine of Jesus, which did not war against slavery but subverted it by a new idea of equality —a plan which, at the time of Constantine, was already 300 years old.

Of the artizans in the building trades we find sufficient mention in history; but very little reference to their organization into trade unions. Plutarch [33] and others state most clearly that the builders were all ranked into a class by themselves under the wise distribution of King Numa and he applies for them the Greek term *technitai*. So in Latin, *artifices*. They held this organization uninterruptedly for 600 years at Rome and under the much praised laws of Solon, nearly as many years in Attica and other parts of Greece. In the year 58 before Christ the conspiracy laws struck them a hard blow, which like an earthquake severely shook them as far as the Greek provinces, their primitive cradle; but they became more secret and political, rallied and outlived their persecutors.

Among the other builders' unions were the architects. These interlinked with the masons, carpenters, joiners and others whenever a building was ordered by the government, and contracted to do the work at prices agreed upon. The *intestinarii*,[34] or as we call them, the joiners, or inside finishers of buildings, had also their trade or-

[32] See *De Excusationibus Artificum*, in *Codex Theodosii*, lib. 13, tit. 4, lex. 2.
[33] Plutarch *Life of Numa. Numa and Lycurgus Compared.*
[34] Muratori, *Thesaurus Veterum Inscriptionum.* 937, 7, mentions a fine incription found at Capua which is interesting, as it shows the plausibility of our conjecture, in the sketch of Spartacus, as to the causes of the immense multitude of freedmen who joined his army "Fabri intestinarii secundum Budæum, ex ligno opera confeciebant minutioris artificii, quibus tantum locus est intra ædes." S. pl. Mur. 929, 6.

UNIONS USED AS PEACE-MAKERS. 371

ganizations and appear to have been in the federation in undertaking contracts to erect and finish temples or other public edifices.

An organization of plasterers is also recognized in the law of Justianian and exempted from persecution, by the code of Theodosius. These unions are not mentioned in Plutarch's list of Numa's trades because the latter consolidated the building trades into one general fraternity with an object, as Plutarch explicitly recounts, of conciliating the jealousies of nationality well-known to have been a cause of contention and turmoil between the Albans and Sabines. By "breaking them up into powder," to use his own words, Numa taught them to mix and the contact of the particles produced a perfectly conciliatory effect. In other words, throw off the question of boundary lines which disturb workingmen and they instantly see that "an injury to one is the concern of all."

THE STONE CHEST CONTAINED THE URNS.
IT WAS LOWERED INTO THE SEPULCHRE.

SARCOPHAGUS OF THE FIRST CENTURY BEFORE CHRIST,
SHOWING HIGH ART OF THE MARBLE AND OTHER STONE CUTTERS.

BURIAL FIXTURE OF STONE-CUTTERS' UNION;
B.C. 100. See page 368.

CHAPTER XV.

THE ARMY SUPPLIES.

ORGANIZED ARMOR-MAKERS OF ANTIQUITY.

TRADE UNIONS TURNED to the Manufacture of Arms and Munitions of War—How it came about—The Iron and Metal Workers—Artists in the Alloys—How Belligerent Rome was Furnished with Weapons, Shoes and Other Necessaries for Her Warriors—The Shieldmakers, Arrowsmiths, Daggermakers, War-Gun and Slingmakers, Battering-Rammakers etc.—Bootmakers who Cobbled for the Roman Troops—Wine Men, Bakers and Sutlers—All Organized—Unions of Oil Grinders; of Pork Butchers; even of Cattle Fodderers—The Haymakers—Organized Fishermen—Ancient Labor brought charmingly near by Inscriptions.

OF the nine regular trade unions authorized by Numa Pompilius, one was that of the metal workers. They were all incorporated into a community, as workers of hard metals, before iron came to be much in use.[1] Writers who lived in ancient times often treat the subject of useful metals in the light that iron and steel did not come into use until after the foundation of Rome, or 758 years anterior to the Christian era. At that early time however, the *ærarii* or metal workers melted copper with the ores of zink and knew how to sprinkle the zink with powdered charcoal during the process of its fusion with copper to prevent it from escaping in fumes of the oxide. It may also be stated that little improvement has ever been made in the manufacture of brass; and even the ancient process of using zink ore instead of the refined article did not come into use until A. D. 1781. It would not be sur-

[1] Lucretius, speaking of brass, says: " Et prior erat æris quam ferri cognitus usus."

prising if further investigations should lead to the discovery that it was the enterprise of trade unions which led to this and other inventions and discoveries in the arts; for the purely slave system did little or nothing for art or science and the earliest forms of industry outside of slavery seems to have been those of workmen combined for mutual aid. Flavius Josephus in his history of the Jews makes elaborate mention of Solomon's temple, as having been built in a large degree by the trade unions under Hiram a man of extraordinary skill in the building crafts. Not willing to accept our own interpretation of Josephus, we refer the reader to the remarks of Granier upon this subject;[2] as he seems to have settled it that they were organized trades.

Little doubt can be entertained that iron, at the time of Numa, was also in use at Rome.[3] Yet there is no mention made in proof that Numa organized the *ferrarii* or iron workers of whom Orelli furnishes two inscriptions,[4] one of which represents a genuine trade union, which proves beyond any counter evidence that the iron workers were organized. But abundant evidence exists in the later laws restricting organization, and these clubs stand among the excused, in the list of 35 unions of the code of Theodosius. If any further doubt can possibly remain as to the use of iron by blacksmiths, forgers and finishers at the time of Numa, we have only to refer the critic to Homer, and the celebrated historic inscription called the Arundelian slab, also to the bible.[5]

[2] Josephus, *Antiquities of the Jews*, book VII, chap. II, noticed by Granier. *Histore des Classes Ouvrières*, p. 289, note: "Ce que Flavius Joseph raconte des travaux qui furent, à plusieurs reprises, exécutés à Jérusalem, soit pour bâtir le .emple, soit pour le relever ou le réparer, ne permet pas de douter que les ouvriers, tant juifs que sidoniens, qu'on y employa, ne fussent organisés en corporations. D'ailleurs toute espèce de doute est levé par le passage suivant, où il est clairement parlé de la hiérarchie qui régnait parmi ces ouvriers, et des trois mille deux cents MAITRES qu'avaient les quatre-vingt mille maçons occupés aux murailles du temple: Ἦσαν δ' ἐκ τῶν παροίκων οὓς Δαυίδης καταλελοίπ. . . . . . τῶν δὲ λατομούντων ὀκτάκις μύριοι· τούτων δ' ἐπιςάται τριχίλιοι καὶ τριακόσιοι."
[3] Pliny, *Nat. Hist.*, XXXIV, 39 says: "Proxime indicari debent metalla ferri, optimo pessimoque vitæ instrumento."
[4] Orell., *Inscriptionum Latinarum Selectarum*, Nos. 4,066 and 1,239. The first of these is a union of sling makers who constructed out of iron the formidable balistæ which threw with deadly effect stones and other missiles into the ranks of an enemy, it reads as follows: "Volcano sacr. T. Flavius Florus Sacerdos Dei Solis Statua Marmoris Collegii balistariorum et Collegii ferrariorum." It was found at Rome and catalogued by Donati, II, p. 225, §. We nil out the abbreviated words.
[5] Homer, *Iliad* XXIII, 261, ' Ἠδὲ γυναῖας εὐξάνους, πολιόν τ' σίδηρον.'' Sam Fettit's *Studies of the Arundelian Inscription;* Bible, *Genesis*, chap. IV Job, chap, XVII

The silver and gold workers did not confederate with these metal workers. We reserve mention of them for a place farther on. Orelli, among his inscriptions gives sufficient specimens carved upon marble and other slabs, some of which have stood the grim erosions of the ages of time that have seen all things else crumble into dust since they were fresh from the chisel of the *cælatores*.[6]

After the death of Numa the doors of the temple of Janus were again flung open, which meant that Rome was again ready for war. This king had closed them as was customary in time of peace. He desired peace with the world in order that the nation might develop upon its own resources, and by its own labor. The 43 years of his peaceful reign gave the artisans time to organize, forget their petty disagreements and settle down upon a basis of fraternity and thrift. And they not only developed their skill but organized it so that after the king's death, when war again broke out, the nation found these metal workers ready to turn their skilled labor to manufacturing swords, shields and all the arms and munitions of the contests which followed.

Thus labor at Rome did not suffer by war, because the Roman arms were successful through a long period of 600 years. During this time the Romans conquered the world with arms manufactured to some extent and we are inclined to think, to a very great extent, by the iron and metal workers organized by Numa. They loved their trade unions and remained organized, working in fraternal bond, in common enjoyment of the fruits of their united labor in spite of several attempts on the part of the senate to put them down. The system, as we have already shown, was to manufacture arms and other munitions of war directly for the government out of raw material which belonged to and was produced from, the mines of the government.

We have seen that the land belonged to the Roman state; that it was farmed by the proletaries on shares and that these shares were collected mostly " in kind," by an organization of unions. These customs-collectors distributed the products of the land each year among the citi-

---

[6] Orell. in his *Latin Inscriptions*, numbers the cælatores as follows: Nos. 4 133, 4,060. 4 066, 4,140, 4,061, 1,239. 361 and 946. Each of these numbers chronicles a genuine trade union.

zen class who virtually possessed and comprised the government. So also with regard to the mines which produced raw material for the iron and other metal workers to convert into lances, darts, swords and all sorts of armor for the Roman army. With the land, the mines also belonged to the government. There consequently had to be a trade union of miners whom the Romans called *ferrariarii*,[1] if miners of iron, and *ær fodinarii*, if miners of copper.

These miners of Copper and iron were naturally federated together. Neither the union of forgers and smiths nor of the copper and brass or bronze workers could buy and exploit their own mining works in order to supply the workmen and fulfill their contracts with the government, because they did not own the mines. Nor could the workmen at the mines accomplish such an end. The government possessed the mines and in many cases let them to contractors. It remained, therefore, for the workmen whose managers were often the contractors, to preserve a close federation of their trades, no matter how distant they were located apart. We are told[s] that at the winter quarters of the rebel army of Spartacus at Thuria, he established an armory of large proportions. It was near the mountains and probably near mines of iron and copper; and as his army was composed of workingmen, many of whom were skilful artisans they co-operated as by common consent, and practically used their federation at both the mines and the forge. The iron and metal workers, who were thus confederated or "distributed" by Numa into unions for the purpose of harmony in the arts of peace, were, after his death, thus kept in the same bond of union many hundred years, helping Rome to practice her arts of war. The plan of Government employment directly, without middlemen was a happy one and the long vista of time from the trade union laws of Numa to the conspiracy laws of Cicero and Cæsar was the true golden age of Rome.

Immediately after the death of Numa Pompillius, that wisest of monarchs, perhaps, of whom the world's history makes mention, the doors of the celebrated temple of Janus were thrown open and Mars, the bellicose myth

---

[1] Muratori *Thesaurus Veterum Inscriptionum*, 972, 10, also *idem*, 963, 2.
[s] Plutarch, *Crassus*, VIII, XII. See also Florus, III. 20, 6, speaking of improvising weapons. "E ferro egastulorum recocto gladios ac tela facerunt."

war-god rushed out with trumpets, javelins and the clangor of contention. We are going to recount one seemingly phenomenal instance in human history where labor and war existed harmoniously and thrived together. The king in instructing his people in the arts of peace had actually laid the foundation for the most gigantic successes ever before known in the arts of war! He had taught the state to employ the labor of trade unions direct. He had taught how to do this without the complications, individual emulations, avaricious ambitions and failures which, in wars often break up great schemes through the jealousy and incompetence of individual rule. He had simplified the labor of production, distribution, consumption by himself employing all the artisans of his realm and directing them to husband the resources of the state which was then the owner of the lands, mines and the waters. The workers being themselves exempt from serving in war by reason of their supposed ignoble origin and rank, had no fear of the tedious campaign nor dread of the carnage of battle. They knew how to make the steel that was to pierce the bodies of those they loved not, and whom when they were enslaved, their ancestors had hated as mortal foes. They were happy. Rome was turned into a vast armory. The members of the well organized unions were the first to receive employment from the government which was not theirs and for 500 years were the last to be maltreated or discharged.

Had it been possible for king Numa to live and reign with his peace measures during those 500 years we know not what would have been the consequence but it would have probably resulted in a far different destiny for the human race. His scheme was to cultivate the elements of peace and he was wise enough to understand that labor was a respectable factor. Under him it was indeed becoming a cult; and could he have lived long enough to engraft his peace system, with all its civilizing and soothing effects, until the people far and near had endorsed it as a second nature, the irascible and grasping as well as the concupiscent ingredients of our nature which dominate warlike tribes must have absorbed enough of the great refining gem of sympathy, to have started the Indo-Europeans in quite a different direction from the murderous warpath of conquest which they actually took, leading to ignorance and brutality. It might have been better for the trade unions to contine manufacturing the implements of peace as Numa ordered. But so long as the Roman arms prevailed, Roman trade organizations under the war system were safe; and the workmen doubtless cared little for the refinements of peace, although the neutral position they assumed as workingmen and their educational discussions among themselves certainly developed more of sympathy and far less of cupidity and irascibility than was possessed by the optimates who managed and fought out the brutal orgies of warfare.

From the foregoing we know that no great amount of work was done by the iron and metal workers in the line of armor manufacture during the lifetime of Numa. After his death, when the warring spirit of the patrician class was aroused to anticipations of the ancient scenes of valor and blood, it was found that Rome was without arms and munitions of war. The helmets and shields, the sabres and javelins had been forged into mattocks, spades and cutlery of domestic use. It was necessary to make a new beginning. That the *ferrarii* or iron workers possessed a federation with the sword cutlers is certain, although the exact date of that co-operation is difficult to ascertain. It must have been old, however. A number of inscriptions bearing evidence of this are recorded by Orelli;[9] and we have distinct mention in the digest[10]— showing that these unions or fraternities of workmen were fixed by law. The trade unions had then in their federation the *gladiarii* or sword cutlers, the *sagitarii* or arrowsmiths, the *scutarii* or elliptical shield makers who, however, made this armor of wood and sometimes covered it with thick rawhide, sometimes with plate metal; and the *clipearii* or round shield makers who made them of copper or bronze; the *telarii* or manufacturers of darts and javelins; the *scalperii*, knife makers, and the *hastarii* or spear makers. There was another trade union, the *collegium ballistariorum*,[11] mentioned also in the digest,[12] the special

[9] Orell., *Inscr. Lat. Select. Coll.* Nos. 4,197, 4,247, *Artes et Opificia.*
[10] Tarrunt 50, 6, 6, dig. "gladiarii, sagittarii, carpentarii, aquices, scandularii, etc."
[11] Orell., *idem,* No. 4,066, Donati, 2, p. 225.
[12] Tarrunt, *dig.* 50, 6, 6. This was a genuine trade union which had a con

business of whose numbers was to manufacture the celebrated *ballista*, a kind of *mitrailleuse*, or stone thrower, which with great force and deadly effect flung large pebbles or small stones and other projectiles into the ranks of an enemy. Much engineering skill was required to operate this engine of war. Doubtless the unions were obliged to send their own mechanics to adjust and manipulate these huge engines. But it is more probable [13] that they were federated with the great trade union now known by numerous very interesting and unmistakable inscriptions as the *collegium mensorum machinariorum* [14] or trade union of machine adjusters and setters, whose business was to oversee the work of transporting any finished machinery to the place of its destination and supervise or perform the work of setting it in operation. The body or union [15] which is referred to in the inscription given in the foot-note below evidently combined the two functions of trade union and burial society. Furius and Lollius were officers, being both members of the society of machinists; and were buried at the expense of the funeral branch and out of the funeral fund. The amount of 25 *denarii* [16] was mentioned for the funeral expenses. Roses costing 5 more were to be put upon the coffin. For the funeral expenses of their aged parents one-half this amount was to be appropriated. In case these requirements were not conformed to, there would be a forfeiture on the part of the trade union of double this sum annually, which forfeiture should be covered into the treasury of the funeral branch.

siderable membership, as the construction of these huge engines required much labor and skill.

[13] Mommsen constantly bemoans the silence of historians on these extremely interesting subjects We render for our readers some of his own lamentations: "The deep silence of the stones containing the inscribed constitutions and restrictions, prevents us from determining which (meaning the trade unions were under the law and which adverse to the privileges granted by the senate)." *De Coll. et Sodal. Romanorum*, p. 80.)

[14] Gruterius, *Inscriptiones Antiquæ Totius Orbis Romanorum*, 91, 1. Muratorius, *Thesaurus Veterum Inscriptionum*, 523, 3. Orellius *Inscriptionum Latinarum Collectio*, No. 4,107. The inscription reads: "D. M. C, Turius, C. T. Lollius quitquit ex corpore mensorum machinariorum funeraticii nomine sequetur, reliqum penes Rempublicam super scriptam remanere volo ex cujus usuris peto a vobis college uti suscipere dignemini VI diebus solemnibus sacrificium mihi faciatis. Id est IIII id. mart. die natalis mei usque ad XXV (denarios), Parentalis XII semis. Flos rosa V. Si facta non fuerint, tunc, fisco stacionis annonæ duplum funeraticinm dare debebetis."

[15] See Orell., *Inscr. Lat. Coll.*, Vol III, p. 170. Varia collegiorum nomina.

[16] A Roman denarius of the period of Cicero was worth 16½ cents. Böckh.

This strange, progressive co-operation of the lowly, industrious, ingenious but despised moiety of the ancient people may justly be regarded as a lost lesson. Until now it has rested in profoundest darkness. So utterly ignored was labor by the ancient historians [17] that even the nominal terminations affixed to nouns and particles in the Latin tongue, giving the technical forms that were in commonest use for artizans of every kind, do not appear, if we except a very few in Pliny and one or two other writers on art. On account of this extraordinary neglect our lexicographers are obliged to have constant recourse to modern archæologists in whose works appear inscriptions *verbatim*, from the time-crumbled stones! From no other source can they with classic authority complete the vocabularies of the language! But this authority is justly considered good. These stones tell tales which the prevaricating, mellifluous sycophants at the court of the Cæsars dared not smirch their parchment with.

The *arietarii* or battering ram makers do not appear as belonging to a union by themselves. If this was ever the case we have not been able to discover any inscription bearing record of the fact. But they existed. Livy repeatedly speaks of the *aries* or battering ram; and it is known to have been at first a simple device, consisting of a huge beam sometimes 150 feet long which a large force of men held on their shoulders and by repeated backward and forward runs, the bronze-plated ram or head, striking against the wall of an enemy's town, broke or rammed down the masonry so that the soldiers rushed through the breaches and sacked the place. It is quite probable that these ram makers were merged into the membership of the *catapultarii* or *balistarii* [18] who manufactured these huge machines, in connection with the catapults or stone slings. However this may have been, it was certainly due to the ingenuity and industry of the machinists that the battering ram developed from this simple form until, in its state of perfection, it was hung by chains to the boom of a tripod fastened by guys; and

---

[17] Drummann, *Arb. u. Comn.*, p. 155. "Befriedigende Nachrichten sucht man vergabens."
[18] Orel. No. 4,066, Balistariorum Collegium

thus swayed forward and backward by human or mule power so as to beat down the strongest walls.

Then among others of the armor makers were the *jaculatorii* or slingers. Darts, *jacula*, were in common use with the ancients. They were easily broken, were of short duration and consequently had to be manufactured in large quantities; and we are told they were manufactured along with other armaments in Rome and other industrial centers, by the unions who found in the government a reliable employer that paid well for the work.[19]

The *Collegium Caligariorum* (soldiers' boot makers or cobblers), was a trade union of shoemakers who manufactured and supplied shoes for the army.[20] During the warlike ages which intervened between the reign of Numa Pompilius and the first emperors, a large army was almost constantly employed by the Roman government. These had to be supplied with food, clothing, barracks, tents and *impedimenta* and all the paraphernalia of war. In those times, to be a soldier was a grace; to be a cobbler a disgrace; and as the membership of the *collegia* was always composed of freedmen or emancipated slaves, with their children and their children's children who constituted the great proletariat of Rome, the labor which their poor fathers performed as slaves, came down with them in disgrace. This is the real origin of the taint of labor—the social degradation of the poor who performed it. It is the blackened obloquy, flinging its attendant odium and fastening its stain alike on him who performs and on his performance. These corvine haters of those who fed them, painted social rank festooned in contumely which fastened upon and clung tight to the heart and soul of both rich and poor, cowing the workmen into the unmanly belief that both labor and the laborer were as mean as they were believed to be. Thus contempt for labor had descended from generation to generation with an ignoble belief in the lowliness of so-

[19] Granier, *Histoire des Classes Ouvrières*, chap. xii, pp. 302–304. "Dans son côté, le gouvernement avait besoin de trouver toujours un nombre et une variété d'ouvriers suffisants pour exécuter ses ouvrages; et quels ouvrages que ceux qu' a fait exécuter le gouvernement Romain ! Que de temples et quels temples! Que d' aqueducs et quels aqueducs ! Que de ponts et quels ponts !"

[20] Grüter, *Inscr. Ant. Rom.*, 649, 1. See also Drumann, *Arbeiter und Communisten in Rom*, who, quoting Ciciro, *Pro Flacc.* 7, says: "Eben so die Schuster *sutores*, welche Cicero mit den Gürtlern, *zonariis*, als verächtliche Volksklasse nennt, bildeten eine besondere Zunft nach Numas Einrichtung."

STATE EMPLOY OF TRADE UNIONS. 381

cial grade. But the work of the soldier was honorable. At first, only the patrician and his sons, the grandees of the realm, could enjoy the honor of a soldier's life. But times had changed. The slave who became a freedman had organized himself into the union of resistance against oppression and we find him now a member of the soldier's shoemaking union, by far the happier man of the two, purveying boots and shoes to the comparatively useless ranks of the Roman army whose trade, like that of the brigands, was to rob and destroy, not to produce. Especially must this great truth have gladdened him, since by reason of his organization which at that time there was no law to forbid, he realized easier times. There were then no organized, competing industries, monopolizing his business. In the certitude of employment and its remuneration, though there was little hope of affluance, he was content.[21] This was certainly the Golden era. The inscriptions bear witness that the society became the instrument of much social pleasure and probably instruction. Indeed, this could not have been otherwise as all the testimony of experience in the scale of social pleasures and means of advancement were similar to those of exactly similar unions of our own times. Working people were not honored by any of the noble or heroic professions; such as the pursuits of war, which were not considered ignoble, or of writing the history of war.[22]

[21] The whole truth is, government patronized, employed and protected the trade unions for more than 500 years. 'Granier in correctly denying that either the very rich or the indignant individuals upheld the unions, says: "Restait enfin le gouvernement. C' était lá le vrai client des jurandes, et les travaux entrepris par lui formait le seul atelier permanent où les ouvriers pussent gagner. chaque jour leur salaire." Granier, *Histore des Classes Ouvrièrs*, p. 303. Again, *idem*, pp. 303-4, Granier says: "De son coté, le gouvernement avait besoin de trouver toujours un nombre et une variété d'ouvriers suffisants pour exécuter ses ouvrages; et quels ouvrages que ceux qu'a fait exécuter le gouvernement romain! Que de temples et quels temples! Que d'aqueducs, et quels aqueducs! Que de ponts, et quels ponts! Ici les nombreaux ouvriers de Caton, les cinq cents ouvriers de Crassus n'auraient pu rien faire; il fallait des corporations, des colléges de travailleurs; et c'est parce qu'ils se firent perpétuellement leurs patrons et leurs commanditaires, que le sénat et les empereurs s'immiscèrent dans leurs statuts. La loi des Douze Tables, qui ordonne à toute corporation de se conformer aux lois générales de l'Etat, est donc en réalité le premier privilége établi en faveur des classes ouvrières déjà organisées régulièrement à cette époque." According to this, the Roman government was the employer of the trade unions to an enormous extent; and this explains the cause of the terrible conflicts reaching from the time of Viriathus to the suppression of the unions, B. C, 58.

[22] So proud was the *gens* family that even convicts, condemned to the Roman prisons for li'e, if of noble extraction, could not be put to hard labor because it would tarnish, not the man, but the family or *gens* name. This could not be sul-

Very few pursuits involving labor were looked upon as fitting a gentleman in ancient days; and any admixture however indifferent in these pursuits, sullied the proud claims to aristocracy and family prestige.

The trade union system therefore, which assumed the entire care and responsiblity of all labor both in production and distribution, except that performed by the slaves who always lingered upon the *gens* estates, was an economy to the ruling minority; for it relieved them from the real perplexities of toil, and it gratified their pride by absolving them from the stigma which attached to all manipulations of producing and distributing that, without which they must have starved.

We propose to devote a few pages to a consideration of the great trade union method of victualing not only this non-working minority and the army but the entire population of Rome. In the closely allied branch of this great system—that of the customs collectors—we have already approximately shown what may be called this system in outline; we shall soon give the system itself.

The use of wine was very common in those countries in ancient times and was an important article of food. There were two communes of wine dealers, one at Rome and one at the mouth of the Tiber. Maffeus cites an inscription, which was found at Verona.[23] Its date is that of the emperors, as it has the name of Augustus, and it portrays a genuine union of the wine men who furnished Rome with that beverage. These organizations were in communication with the productive interior of Italy and may have had wagons and boats, either of their own, or engaged and paid by them to bring the wine to their storehouses; if wagons, direct to the city; and if ships or boats, to the port of Ostia where it was stored and cured, often smoked as we shall describe, and at the proper time distributed to consumers. Not only the wine produced from the government lands and accruing to the citizens in form of rent payable in kind as noticed in the remarks on the *Vectigalarii* or customs collectors, but also all the remainder that the farmers did not need for

---

lied, even by crime until a later period. See Bombardini, *De Carcere et Antique Ejus Usu*, cap. VIII, p. 763 of *Thesaurus Grævii et Gronovii*.

[23] Maffeus. *Muscum Veronense*, 114, 2. "Quinquennalis corporum vinariorum urbanorum et Ostensium."

UNIONS OF WINE SMOKERS.

their own use was sent to market; and of course, in the absence of competing lines of transportation such as now exist, the wine was sent to Rome by the same watermen who took the rent. The most of it, however, went overland by wagons and we have reason to believe, in a crude state; for there existed at Rome more than one union of *fumatores*, or wine curers who matured their wines with smoke. This was done by an apparatus in shape of a hogshead containing wine, through which smoke was forced by means of force pipes. At Tarentum, was found an inscription which plainly mentions the *collegiem fumatorum*. It was sketched by Münter, and incorporated as a regular trade union into the great collection of Orelli.[24] The wines of the ancients were rich and excellent. The task of the unions was to finish the taste and color so that they constituted the richest and healthiest beverage to be found. To this day the wines of Italy are counted among the most delicious; but it is questionable whether they are as well cured as in ancient times or whether they are as plenty.

There was a union of cultivators and dealers in table or olive oils, *collegium oleariorum*,[25] whose business in part, was to grind and prepare the oils from the fruit of the olive tree which grows luxuriantly in southern Europe. The great *entrepot* of Rome,[26] was Ostia, at the mouth of the river Tiber 18 miles from Rome. The quantity of work carried on by the waterman between Ostia and Rome must have been enormous considering the slow, toilsome method

---

[24] Orell., *Analecta Nonnulla*, No. 5,044; " D. M. Fecit, Collegiam Fumatorum bene merente." It was found at Tarentum. Orelli adds: " Novam mihi accidit Collegium Fumatorum."

[25] Fabretti, *Inscriptionum Antiquarum Explicatio*, 731-750, citing the incription, originally found at Ostia, but now in Florence.

[26] Orell., *Inscr. Lat. Coll.*, vol. II, 238, remarks: " In magno Collegiorum et artium numero, notandum in primis, decurias, non corpora vel Collegia constituisse Ostiæ." In proof of this see Orell. *Inscr.*, No. 4,109, which enumerates 18 trade unions in one tablet, which we produce for the curious critic. The great epigraphist reminds us in a note that these are not mere corporations but trade unions, (see *ante*). The incription runs thus: "Cneo Sentio Cn. fil. ter. felici Dec. ædilicio adl. Decurionum decreto adlecto Quaestori Aedili ostiens II, vir. Q. juvenum.
Hic primus omnium quo anno decimo adlectus est et qui a facto est et in proximum duo vires designat. Est quinque curatorum navium marinariorum gratis adlect. inter *(sic)* novicular. Maris Hadriatici. Et ad quadrigam fori vinariorum. Patrono decuriæ scribar. præconum et—et argentariorum, et negotiatorum, vinariorum. Ab Urbe item mensorum, frumentariorum cereris. Aug. item collegia scaphariorum et lenunculariorum. Traject. Luculli et dendrophorum et lege Rogatorum. A faro et de sacomar; et libertorum et servorum publicorum. Oleariorum et juvenum cisianorum et veteranorum. Aug. item benificiariorum. Aug. et piscatorum. propolaricrum curatori lusus juvenalis.
Cneus Sentius Lucullus Gamala. Clodianus. F. Patri indulgentissemo."

of propelling little boats. In those days of crude method and meagre facility the functions of a trade union appear not to have been confined to this simple business. It appears from the inscriptions and other data that the manufacturers of an article were often the distributers of it. Thus in the case of the wine smokers, the same union that bought the crude grape juice which arrived through the labors of the unions of coasters, *lenuncularii*, plying between the Adriatic or Mediterranean landings and the chief depots as Ostia and Pisæ or Tarentum, or that which arrived on board the larger ships of the *navicularii* from greater distances, as Spain or from Gaul *via* Arles, assumed also the duty of curing these wines and of putting them into the hands of consumers. This explains the phenomenon as to there being comparatively few middlemen or petty shopkeepers among the Romans although there were many even of these.[27] It also leads to an explanation of the curious fact that merchants were considered nearly as low and unworthy the respect of the high-born class as the mechanics and laborers. In those early days, before the development of the vast commerce which belongs to the Christian era, business of any kind whether mechanical, mercantile or agricultural was held under ban and men did not espouse it except as a necessity. This contempt, an inculcation of the aristocratic religion, lived as long as that religion reigned; but when Christianity established itself upon its revolutionary basis of exact equality of all men, the contempt fell to the ground; and gradually the aristocracy of wealth rose in the place of the ancient aristocracy of birth. But as it was not inherent in manual labor to produce much more than the individual laborer consumes, and perfectly possible for the mercantile system to amass—sometimes enormously —the mechanic and laborer continue to be poor and considered with contempt while the speculators on their products rise to the loftiest respectability. But all this is because Christianity is only in its theoretical condition, having not yet, on account of the stupendous magnitude of the revolution it has undertaken, acquired and put in operation the mechanical instrumentalities for the practical realization of its scheme.

So also the oil grinders union was in the habit of buying

[27] See Orell., Nos. 4,139–4,300, *Artes et Opificia*.

crude oils or unpressed olives on board the ships and boats at Ostia, conveying them to their storehouses, running them through their presses or grinders, purifying, curing and bottling them in ollas, even placing them at the command of the *triclinarch* himself. To do this required a large number of members in the commune or union; but this furnished steady employ in which each member felt himself a co-operator or co-owner which not only secured him or her from the dangers of dismissal but must also have been a great comfort; since members felt the dignity of their position, lowly of course, compared with the rich non-workers who looked upon labor with disdain, yet independent in comparison with the dispropertied and maltreated slaves.

Bread was another commodity the supply of which became largely the task of the trade unions from very early times. The ancient method of baking differed little from that of the present day. The ancient bakers' unions, then, were in nearly all respects, identical with the bakers' unions in New York city to-day. We have abundance of testimony regarding the unions of bakers. A *corpus pastillariorum* mentioned by Muratori,[28] was one of the post-Christian communes. The *pastillarii* were manufacturers of dainty loaves, biscuits, cakes and bon-bons.

Then there were the regular bread bakers, *panfices* or *pistores* who also, as part of their task, ground or beat grain into flour or meal with a pestle.[29] One can at a glance conceive that the amount of this work was enormous. The method of making bread was the same as now; for very little has ever been added for facilitating its rapid manufacture; but the method of grinding has been so greatly improved as to admit of scarcely a comparison. It required a large force of workmen in those times to pound up and bake the three different kinds of bread consumed by the whole people rich and poor, of Rome.[30] But these men dur-

[28] Cf. Mur. *Thesaur. Veterum Inscriptionum*, 527, 5. Anno post Chr. 435.
[29] *Cod. Theod.*, lib. XIV, tit. 3. The bakers were among the unions which enjoyed the jus coeundi or right of organization. See *Codex Theodosii, de Excusationibus Artificum*, lib. XIII, tit. IV, leg. 2. The organized bakers and boatmen were among the most numerous and powerful in Italy.
[30] We have shown in our chapters on strikes and uprisings that the slave portion of the proletaries were fed on pease and nuts. See Granier *Histoire des Classes Ouvrières*, pp. 96-97. "Dès les premiers temps, avons-nous dit, les esclaves se trouvèrent séparés des hommes libres et firent race à part; ils allèrent nourris et vêtus d'une façon propre et spéciale. Les juifs leur perçaient l'oreille, les Grecs et les Romains les marquaient au front, d'où le nom de Stichus était resté commun et général parmi les esclaves. Dès le temps d'Homère, leur régime ali-

ing a cycle of 700 years were organized and they enjoyed a trade union in all probability from long before the time of Numa. Their scope was wide, their members large, their business steady, their work guaranteed; and they had the balmy satisfaction of knowing that they were safe.

Another great and very important organization of the laboring people was that of the butchers. A considerable branch of this business was performed by the *suarii* or pork butchers. It is stated that the wealthy repudiated pork and confined their diet of meat to fish, venison and mutton. But it must not be forgotten that there were organized unions of *suarii* or pork butchers, and we have evidence that they drove a heavy business. What did Rome want of pork butchers if her citizen population refused to use pork and her slave population was not allowed to use meat of any kind? This is a troublesome question, to be solved only by the student of history and archæology, from a standpoint of social science. By the student of social science it is seen, that there existed a very large class of the poor, but manly, better fed, self-sustaining, hard working element of the proletaries who were freedmen and always organized; and as we are assured by abundant evidence from their own inscriptions, always capable of living well. This is the class which consumed the products of the *suarii*. The animals were raised in southern parts of the peninsula, in great numbers and probably were of an excellent breed. According to Granier they were driven or conveyed in wagons to Rome alive. The work of the pork butchers was not confined to killing and dressing them. In the etymology of the word "confection" we have a history of a part of their business. The ancient confectioner was a slaughterer of swine; but in addition to this work he prepared his pork in a great number of ways. He made sausage meats of several varieties, corned pork, smoked bacon and ham, very much as we do now. From data which we have observed, there seems to be little difference between the ancient and

mentaire était réglé et ils ne mangeaient pas de pain fait de froment." So Guhl and Koner, *Life of the Greeks and Romans*, pp. 501-2, after describing the sumptuous dishes of the Romans of rank, conclude with the remark on the poor, that they "at all periods chiefly fed on porridge *(puls)*, made of a farinaceous substance *(far, ador)*, which served them as bread, besides vegetables, such as cabbage *(brassica)*, turnips and raddishes, leek *(porrum)*, garlic *(allium)*, onions *(cepa)* pulse *(legumina)*, cucumber *(cucumis)*, pumpkins, melons, etc." They had no meat except on occasions such as the entertainments of the *thiasos* and the *sodalicium*.

the modern methods of preserving and using the flesh of the swine. But there is one observation which cannot well be avoided here.

Pork, according to the ancient religions, both of the Indo-Europeans and Jews, was always repudiated. It was strictly a proletarian aliment. The reason why it became popular on the table of the Christians and lost its ancient stigma is, that the early Christians were themselves proletaries and did not belong to the nobles who fed on fish, fat venison and mutton. Christianity in boldly proclaiming the revolution on a basis of equality of all men, was not ashamed to live up to its professions. By far the largest number of its membership were poor. The poor freedmen were glad to get pork to eat. The Saviour himself was one of them, without an atom of aristocracy in his veins and consequently unhampered by old religious prejudices, restrictions or usages. This new sect, poor and persecuted, struggling for the existence of its tenets and its members, began life at Rome in earnest, although born in Judea. Its first members were the poor work people—freedmen and slaves—all of whom were not above a plate of ham and eggs; and to say the least, the new sect exhibited much sound sense in calmly adopting the usages of the diet and clothing of the commons.

Its tenets expressed and inculcated the new idea that by birth one was as good as another; and it also logically and by implication defended the dignity of pork and sausage as it did the makers of pork and sausage and every other food available which was found palatable and nutritious.

We do not find mention either in the inscriptions or elsewhere of butchers located at Ostia, the port of Rome. This, however, is accounted for by the supply of hogs, sheep and cattle being in an opposite direction from the emporium. There is an abundant mention of the *pecuarii*, or cattle breeders and their *greges* or herds. They took the government pasture lands on shares, and at the close of the year paid to the tax collectors the share agreed upon. What remained over this amount, which was paid in cattle, sheep and hogs more frequently than in money, was their own; and they sold it to the butchers at the market.

When the rich gentry made their encroachment upon the public land and drove these *pecuarii* from the pastures, thus usurped, as we have already shown,[31] the slaves were forced to do this work; and in many parts of Italy this ancient system was at an end. Very little mention is made of true trade unions of butchers in the inscriptions thus far discovered except those of the *suarii* or pork butchers. Granier suggests that these conducted the whole butcher business of Rome;[32] but this is a matter which we leave in abeyance, in the absence of more exact data.

There were unions of workmen whose task was to fodder cattle and other animals of the stock farms. One of these a *collegium pabulariorum* is given us by Donati.[33] They were allied to the haymakers; for hay is one kind of *pabulum* or fodder. It is an inscription of a genuine labor union, and is curious, showing how systematic they must have been in getting down to nice distinctions, something like the division of labor of the present day.

We have, however, an instance which comes near making up the missing link connecting the cattle breeders with the unions, in shape of a genuine *collegium faenariorum*,[34] or union of mowers who prepared the hay for the cattle and sheep. The inscriptions, of which there are several, are the result of the labors of Gruter, one of the most learned and reliable archæologists, who is constantly quoted and consulted by both Mommsen and Orelli. But the discovery of a union of mowers which once existed at a fashionable watering place like the Puteoli, where this was found, does not sufficiently attest. Orelli supplies the gap with several other unions of hay-makers.[35]

[31] See chapters on *Spartacus, Eunus, Athenion and Aristonicus.*
[32] See *Histoire des Classes Ouvrières*, chap. xii.
[33] Don. *Cl.* 9, n. 3 and 20.
[34] Gruter, *Inscriptiones Antiquæ Totius Orbis Romanorum*, 175, 9.
[35] Orell., *Inscriptionum Latinarum Co ectio*, Nos. 45, 4,187 which is Gruter's, and No. 4,194 which is Gruter's inscription 264.

CHAPTER XVI.

TRADE UNIONS.

THE GREAT TRADES VICTUALING SYSTEM.

How ROME WAS FED—Unions of Fishermen—Discovery of a Strange Inscription at Pompeii, Proving the Political Power and Organization of the Workingmen and Women's Unions—Female Suffrage in Italy—The Fish Salters—Wine Smokers—Union of Spicemen—The Game-Hunters' Organizations—Unions of Amphitheatre Sweepers—Unions of Wagoners, Ox-Drivers, Muleteers, Cooks, Weighers, Tasters and Milkmen—The Cooking Utensil-Makers—Unions of Stewards—Old Familiar Latin Names, with Familiar English Meanings Reproduced—Gaius and the Twelve Tables—Numerous Notes with References to Archæological Collections and to Histories Giving Pages and many Necessary Renderings, of the Obscure Curiosities Described.

UNIONS of fisherman, *piscatores*,[1] existed in numbers at Rome, Ostia, Pisæ and other points on the sea and the mouths of the Italian streams. Considering the fact that fish were in high regard with the wealthy people, the fishing business was extensive. An account of a union of the *piscicapii*, published in the *Wiener* Jahrbücher,[2] causes Orelli to remark that before elections for the ædiles and duumvirs in the municipal cities, the unions furnished

---

[1] Orell., *Scholæ Artificum et Opificum*, No. 4,115. The inscription of this pair of trade unions—the fishermen and divers—reads: "Ti. Claudio Esquil Severo decuriali licturi, patrono corporis piscatorum et urinator. QQ. III. eiusdem corporis ob merita eius quod hic primus statuas duas, unam Antonini Aug. domini N. aliam Iul Augustae dominae nostr. S. P. P. una cum Claudio Pontiano filio suo eq Rom. et hoc amplius eidem corpori donaverit HS. X. Milia N. ut ex usuris eorum quodannis natali suo xvi. kal, Febr. sportulae viritim dividantur praesertim cum navigatio scapharum diligentia eius adquisita et confirmata sit. ex decreto ordinis corporis piscatorum et urinatorum totius alv Tiber quibus ex SC. coire licet S. P. P.—Romae. Grut. 391, 1.

[2] XX. p. 12-15, *des Weiner Jahrbuchs*.

members to be voted for as candidates to the municipal offices; and what is more strange, women, if it happened that there were any thought proper for the places. The inscription which records this fact was found among the ruins of Pompeii.

The discovery of this ancient city has been of incalculable value to the students of sociology, in affording modern science an opportunity to compare ancient with modern life placed in juxtaposition. It brings to our vision in realistic form, such as no human being can for an instant doubt, the social and political life and habits of a great people concerning which the surface historiographers have been profoundly, painfully silent! Who can doubt the veracity of words inscribed on a tablet of marble, scrawled upon a wall and having been, perhaps, already a hundred years or more in use, and at last, in the awful eruption of Vesuvius, at whose foot it stood, overwhelmed, buried and lost to view under a thick stratum of lava for one thousand seven hundred years; then all at once dug out, delivered and held up to the gaze of men now living, fresh as though just from the chisel of the *artifex signorum* who graved it for his brother unionist? Yet there it stands, its own monument for our blazing enlightenment to decipher. In modern political English it reads like some very cranky caucus slate of a New York ward Tammany club. Freely translated the inscription reads as follows:

(*a*) "Phoebus, together with his buyers, asks the people to vote for Holcon, who was formerly president of the union and for C. G. Rufus—two men nominated by us." (Meaning two of *our* men.)

(*b*) "Licinius Roman nominates and calls for the ballots of constituents in favor of Julius Polybius for superintendent of public works."

(*c*) "The members of the fishermen's union (nominate) make choice of Popidius Rufus, for member of the board of public works."

(*d*) "The international gold workers association of the city of Pompeii demand for member of the board of pub-works, Cuspis Pansa."

(*e*) "Sema, with her boys, ask that you work with a will at the election and secure success, for the office of magistrate, to Julius Simple. He is a man in the fullest sense of the word; a faithful servant of the people of Pompeii; a good man; worthy of assuming public affairs."

(*f*) "Verna, the home-born, with her pupils in all right, and good faith, put Miss or Mrs. Capella³ to the front for a seat in the board of magistrates."

(*g*) "It is worthy of you that you work for P. Popid for member of the board of public works, with might and will."

(*h*) "Fortune (probably a female member) desires the election of Marcellus."

This is all very simple and homely. But it must be clear to every one that such talk was confined to those who were federated together and intimately acquainted with one another; not that we would arbitrarily construe the vernacular of a Roman municipal town, but there is a peculiarly quaint air of familiarity which savors so remarkably of what is taking place in the unions of our own cities and towns that it seems like a mirroring of the ancient upon modern brotherhoods.⁴

This remarkable find goes far toward clearing up points which otherwise might leave doubts upon our statements.

Orelli himself expresses surprise, especially upon the phases of woman's suffrage.⁵ Whatever may have been the actuating power at the bottom of general elections, it is certainly proved by this inscription that in the labor unions, women had not only accorded right but also a practical hand in securing the choice of their unions toward building up a democracy among the ancients.

³ We read this feminine because the context shows it to be so. Duumvir has no feminine termination and they could not alter the word as a political term.
⁴ The Latin of the inscription is as follows:
(*a*) "M. Holconium priscum, C. Gaium Rufum Q. Viros, Phœbus cum emptoribus suis rogat." (*i. e.* eis suffragium fert).
(*b*) "Iulium Polybium ædilem, Licinius Romans rogat et facit."
(*c*) "Popidium Rufum Ædilem Piscicapi faciunt"
(*d*) C. Cuspium Pansam æcilem, Aurifices universi rogant."
(*e*) Junium Simplicem ædilem, Virum amplissimum, servatorem Populi Pompeiani, virum bonum, dignum republica, omni voluntate faciatis, Sema cum pueris rogat."
(*f*) "Capellam duumvirum juri dicundo omni vel optima voluntate facit Verna cum discentibus."
(*g*) "P. Popidium Secundum Ædilum Omni Voluntate Facere dignus est.
(*h*) "Marcellum Fortunata Cupit."
⁵ Orell., *Inscriptionum Latinorum Collectio*, No. 3,700. "Ante comitia duumviralia et ædilicia in Municipiis Collegia, municipes, et, quod maxime mirum, feminas quoque, ut iis, quibus favebant, apud alios suffragarentur, hujuscemodi tabellas publice proposuisse, ex Pompejiorum parietinis nuper compertum est."

In this inscription we have not only a full verification of our conjecture that the trade unions were well organized about the time of the labors of Christ but that they were federated with similar communes all over the known world, *in universo* and also that they achieved so great a progress as to have actually been voting their own members into municipal offices at or probably long before the earthquake in A. D. 79. This does not, however, by any means show that they were in the majority. We have never claimed this. Far from it. The number of slaves was always far in excess of the freedmen; and then, there always were great numbers of freedmen who would not organize and who were two indolent to work either for themselves or for masters.[6]

In addition to the fish catchers there were numerous craftsmen who made it their business to dress, season and put up the fish in barrels, casks and packages. These were the ancient *salarii*,[7] of the Romans. It seems to be an established term. *Salarius* applies in the inscriptions to the fish salters; although it may apply to the salting of any flesh for food. Used much in early England it differentiated into the word "salary." The *salarii curatores* should be rendered fish curers,[8] instead of superintendents of the business of fish salting as Orelli imagines, in at least one case.[9] We have, in the inscriptions found in different places, evidence enough to settle the question about their being organized into unions. Sometimes they are called *corpores*, bodies; sometimes *collegia*,[10] unions. They were all engaged in the vast work of victualing the people.

There were societies of fruit-purveyors of several different sorts. We have already spoken of a queer inscription at Rome, noted by Oderic,[11] showing that one Julius Epophra, once a cabinet maker, changed this business to that of apple-man and with his wife Helen made a living near the Roman Circus. They seem to have kept an apple

---

[6] Dr. Bucher, *Aufstände der Unfreien Arbeiter*.
[7] Marini, *Atti*, 2, p. 294. Corpus salariorum. Orell., *Inscriptiones Latinarum Coll.*, No. 1092.
[8] This is the origin of the modern word "salary." In England, at other fisheries and salt works, workmen were paid in cakes of salt by the Romans. See Pliny, *Nat. Hist.*, XXXI. 7, and XLI. fin; Dion Cassius, lex. viii. 22, and lii, 23. *Digest*, 2 lex. 15, tit. 8.
[9] Orell., *Inscr.* No. 3,464, note, also No. 1,092.
[10] Supplement to Orelli's *Collectio*, by G. Henzen, Vol. III, p. 170 of *index* sub caption: "Varia collegiorum nomina. The several synonyms are here explained.
[11] Oderic, *Inscriptiones*, p. 74.

stand. So trivial a circumstance would scarcely have been worth the labor of graving upon a tablet of stone to be wondered at by their fellow men 20 centuries afterwards. The more probable solution is that he belonged to the cabinet makers' union, and from infirmity or other disability was pensioned off and allowed to pick up an occasional *denarius* by selling apples in the open air. In that case the union would naturally put his case on record.

The *vinarii*,[12] or vine dressers, and the *vinitores* often brought wagon loads of grapes to the city. We are not informed as to the exact manner of supplying the people with these grapes. They were fruit of a season and were probably disposed of somewhat as at present in any Italian city. Many of the houses of the rich had slaves of their own who went to the open market places and procured these fruits in their season. The fruit of the olive tree was sometimes used in the family.

Rome had its *mercatores*, wholesale and retail, who always kept a supply of every kind of fruit in season. There was a strong union of the wine dealers *vini susceptores* legalized in the code of Theodosius;[13] and they are evidently the same as the *vinarii* quoted above.

We may class the spice dealers' unions also among the purveyors of fruit; as these people had a strong organization called the *collegium aromatoriorum*.[14] An inscription proving this, has been discovered at Rome and cited by Muratori.

The lords of the land were often too dainty to eat the common products we have enumerated and were fond of indulging in what they considered the nobler fruits of the chase, *venatio*. Some 15 inscriptions have been discovered portraying different phases of this sport and its products. At least one genuine union of hunters has been found; the *collegium venatorum* brought out by Muratori, found in the vicinity of the fortified town of Corfinium of the Peligni and not far from Sulmo. Doubtless there was game in abundance at the time those hunters were there.

It would certainly be interesting to know more than an inscription on a slab of stone can tell, in regard to the

[12] Orell., *Inscr.* Nos. 3,921, 4,302, 6,430.
[13] *Cod. Theodosti*, lib. XVI., tit. IV, leg. 4.
[14] Muratori, *Thesauriis Veterum Inscriptionum*, 511, 4.

exact object of these hunters, away in the wilds of the Appenines; especially as they might have been runaway slaves who, under the protecting shield of some law regulating hunting fraternities, carried on business here.[14] Another inscription cited by Orelli[15] under his " critical observations of Hagenbuch, portrays a commune consisting of a number of persons, some of whose names are given, hunting, apparently for other than live game; perhaps for the ores of copper. It is credited to Cardinali and was found at Velitres. A still more singular one is that cited by Gruter and found at Naples. Orelli places it in his *Res Scenica*—scenes in nature. Were it not too long we would give its rendering, as it speaks of wild animals and scenes. Singularly enough its words *venatione passerum*, sparrow hunting, is insisted on by the great master[16] as meaning *struthionum*, of ostriches. We know that the *venator passerum* sometimes applies to turbot fishing; and we are inclined to think, notwithstanding the great respect we entertain for this expounder of abbreviations and hieroglyths in his practices in archæology, that he may be mistaken.

Another family or union of hunters; *collegium venatorum* is given by Gruter,[17] as coming from Monselice which is quoted by this author not as a business union but as a family because the words *familia venatoria* occur upon the stone. Orelli, however calls it a collegium in his index to *Artes et Opificia*.

A beautiful specimen of a genuine hunting club, *collegium venatorum*, was picked up at Beaufort in France[18] which verifies our suspicion, that some of the hunters' unions were escaped slaves who, without losing their organization or parting company, fled to the far distant forests and there established themselves in the new art of hunting, thus maintaining their existence in the wilderness. This is one theory. We shall presently speak of another. The inscription reads rather strangely.[19] There was a union of hunters who used to fight wild beasts in the amphitheatre, or the arena, but who broke away through

---

[15] Mur., *Thesau*., 531, 2.
[16] Orell., No. 4,895.
[17] Gruter, *Inscr. Totius Orbis Rom.*, 484. 6.
[18] Gruter *Inscr. Tot. Orb.* 331, 11.
[19] *Mémoires Présentés à l'Acad.*, d. b, livre II. p. 399.

conspiracy. It is well-known that gladiators most of whom were slaves were compelled to fight and kill each other or fight and be killed by wild beasts on the sands of the amphitheatre, enacting scenes of the most terrible and bloody character known either to the past or present history of the human race. They often had a horror and sometimes were repelled by their own conscientious scruples, against these ghastly scenes enacted in presence of thousands of spectators shouting, gloating and betting on their bloody exercise of muscle and wit. This seems to have been a union of them who, apparently in good faith, had formed a conspiracy to escape and remain together in the fraternal bond. At any rate this is the opinion of Orelli–Henzen.[20] This second theory, then, although somewhat in contradiction to the reading of the inscription quoted, suggests that the "*collegium venatorum qui ministerio arenario fungunt*," was no other than a union of servants of the ring, a part of whose duties, in addition to what we have mentioned, was to undertake long journeys officially in quest of the wild beasts that were used in the amphitheatres, during the emperors. These fierce beasts are known to have been sought, and highly prized by the spectators who delighted to witness a gladiator fighting an enraged lion, tiger, leopard, wolf or bear. Beaufort is at the foot of the mountains of Savoy where to this day, bears of a large size give the farmers and herdsmen trouble. Wolves also still linger among the great forests of the inaccessible mountain slopes; and although we are not aware of panthers or tigers or any of the largest feline animals being found in modern Italy or France, yet they might have existed there in ancient times. But there was game enough to have attracted the hunters for the great games of Rome.

The archæologists have found as many as five inscriptions of these unions of the arena. On one of them is written "*arenae gladiatorium purgandae*." A union of gladiators who clean the amphitheatre—giving incontestable evidence of a union of amphitheatre cleaners.[21] The unionists were not slaves. Slaves had no privileges.

[20] "Collegium Venatorum Deensium, qui ministerio arenario fungent. Ded. Ex. decreto soluto voto."
[21] Orell., *Collegia Corpora Sodalicia*, No. 7,209. *Inscr. Lat. Coll.*, Vol III, p 456. *Cf. Mémoires Présenté à l' Academic*, Vol. 2, p. 399, 1854.

They were freedmen, and those we mention were chartered and existed according to law.

But whatever might have been the special object of the hunters, their general object was, of course, to supply the table of those who could pay, with the delicacies of the chase. The unions had wagon transports to the stations in the forests, communicating with the cities. The difficulty of taking game must have been very great, considering that gunpowder was not in use. Bows and arrows were used and for the manufacture of such implements they had unions of workingmen making devices for trapping, for archery and harpooning. There being a great demand for them, not only for hunting purposes but for war, these weapons were of the best quality; and archery won a high station in ancient times as an accomplishment.

In the great system of victualing the people of ancient Rome and its almost innumerable provincial towns and cities, some of which were fully as aristocratical and fastidious as the Romans themselves, the teamsters' numerous associations played a no inconsiderable rôle. We find numerous evidences in the inscriptions, that they were at one time organized. There were the ox drivers *jumentarii*,[22] who worked at the port of Rome conveying grain, oil, wine and other commodities to the storehouses of the weighers' and measurers' association, *mensores portuenses*.[23]

These and the unions of muleteers, *coll. mulionum et asinariorum*[24] that existed everywhere in Rome and out of it, did most of the work of conveying provisions from producers to consumers. Perhaps, in making this remark we are exaggerating somewhat on the amount of work expected of them. Their system was such that they could have performed it all; but there seems never to have been a time when the trade unions obtained a complete control of this work. The large class of capitalists[25] were in constant competition with organized labor and always had a large force of mules or oxen at work. Nor must it be

---

[22] One was found or observed by Muratori, *Thesaur. Inscr.* 511, 3. The second by Connegietur, *Nom. Rat.* p. 219. A third by Cardinali, *Iscriz. Velêt*, p. 44, found at Veletri. A fourth, that at Beaufort and a fifth, prob. at Pisa by Marini, XIII. *Giorn. di Pisi*, p. 25.

[23] Orell., *Inscr. Lat. Collectio*, No. 4,093. Momm. *De Coll. et Sodal. Rom.* p. 97.

[24] Gran. de Cassagn., *Hist. des Classes Ouvrières.* p. 510, Grut, 462, 1. Orell., *Coll. Publica et Privata*, No. 7,194.

[25] Idem No. 7,206, coll. mulionum et asinariorum.

UNIONS CHAMPIONED BY CLODIUS. 397

understood that anything like all the work of any kind, was a great length of time, ever performed by the unions alone. The competition between the unions and the speculators must have raged with activity for at least 200 years, and finally the hatred of the speculating oligarchy went into legislation.

After endless turmoils, among which the unions, championed by Clodius, not only restored their old rights of organizations but gained many more, the struggle culminated in Cæsar suppressing nearly all of them. But the unionists were strong and influential and in course of time, after the death of Cicero, Cæsar and other enemies, they reassumed most of their fallen power. Nothing was able to grind them out entirely.

History gives us little in regard to the methods by which the armies of the ever victorious Romans were supplied with provisions. If there is any mention by historians of a union or association of sutlers who made it their business to supply the armies stationed upon Roman territory, we have failed to find it. There are inscriptions, however, which are beginning to reveal a subject pregnant of importance in solving misty queries regarding the phenomenal successes of Roman arms. We have already shown that from the end of Numa's reign the Roman armies were supplied with arms in a great degree by the unions of armorers.

It is here relevant to prove, if possible, that they were also supplied by them with provisions. For at least 500 years the armies used union made wagons, union made swords, union made javelins, bows and arrows, helmets and shields, wore union made shoes, trowsers, hats and coats, and tore down the walls and battlements of their enemies with union made catapults and battering rams. Did they not eat union made bread, union cured meat and drink the delicious wines and beverages prepared by the organized victualers? True, when far away in their foreign conquests the Roman soldiers depended much upon the pillage and plunder of their unfortunate victims; but at home, when the armies were at quarters this question sharply applies. The student of sociology is particularly interested in this subject, because this matter of union labor in supplying the legions goes far in settling the long mooted problem hanging over the decline and fall of Rome.

Rome prospered in peace and in arms, until the glut of conquest changed her statesmen from the wise tolerance of Numa and Servius Tullius to the rapacious slave-holding policy which sought to destroy the unions that made possible her unparalleled success. But when gorged with enormous wealth, she lost her manhood and swine-like fell upon and devoured her own nurslings and friends. The sin struck back upon herself like the fangs of the tortured crotalus and poisoned her own blood with a reacting plague of ingratitude and pollution.

The stones have already revealed to us that there existed unions of victualers who made a business of supplying the armies. They were called "collegia castrensiariorum,"[26] sutlers. We are not informed of the exact relation they had with the armies; whether like our sutlers they hung around the flanks and peddled with the soldiers, or whether they supplied the armies by contract with the senate or consular generals.

In addition to the unions already mentioned we find that the cooks and waiters also had their organization of self-help. They may all be classed as one family or commune, although in some cases at least, the cooks and the waiters were apart. In the inscriptions there are three unions of cooks; one a "collegium coctorum"[27] who took charge of the stately business of cookery in the palace of Augustus Cæsar, at Rome. Another is mentioned on the slab as "cocus,"[28] a cook which was found at Rome and is cited by Marini,[29] and the third also speaks of a man who was an Alban cook, evidently president of the society. It was found on the site of the ancient city of Alba.

Mommsen cites the "collegium praegustatorum"[30] mentioned by Gruter as a genuine trade union of waiters, who, as this designation implies, were foretasters as well as waiters. The rich in Rome were ever beset with fears of being poisoned. They were obliged to have their food tasted

---
[26] See Bücher, "Aufstände der Unfreien Arbeiter," pp. 3-16. Geldoligarkie, Pauperismus, Sklaventhum.
[27] Orell., Nos. 7,189, 6,344 and elsewhere. Also Gruter, "Inscriptiones Antiquæ Totius Orbis Romanorum," 649, 5, and several others.
[28] Cardinali, "Dipl." 410. [29] Marini, "Atti," 2, p. 610.
[29] Romanelli, "Topog." I, 3, p. 213. [31] Grut., "Inscr., Antiqu.," 581, 13
[30] Momm., "De Coll. et Sodal. Rom.," p. 78, note 25.

of by the waiter in their presence. If the waiter ate it with impunity they need have no fears. The waiters being in constant communication with the cooks were supposed to know all the dangerous designs that might originate among the kitchen people, to be consummated in the dining rooms; and were thus held responsible for the honesty of both themselves and the cooks. They were required to taste the milk they served to the gentry direct from the jugs or pots, *ampullae* of the milk men, or the *collegium lacticariorum* a milkman's union mentioned by Mommsen[31] as a corpus or labor union. This interlinking of many trades, whose sympathies and contact sometimes fitted them for carrying out cunningly concocted plots with the waiter thus became practically a sort of key to the treachery. Even the manufacturers of these milk jars had unions, one of which, in the collection of Gruter was found inscribed on a slab of slate or stone discovered at Narbonne.[32]

A stone has been dug up bearing the inscription *collegium vasulariorum*. It exhibits the relics of a union of manufacturers of cooking utensils. Most of their productions were of copper or bronze. The *vascula* were of various shapes; spits, ladles, cups, bowls, soup spoons and many other implements of cookery. Hammer work with the ancient artisans was a fine art. Sometimes the best workmen, if not slaves, had organizations, which were called the *malleatores*, hammerers and are mentioned by Orelli as inscribed on a stone.[33]

There also were the basket makers' unions the products of whom, *sportulæ*, figure in the decree of laws governing sacred unions as found in the Roman temple of Barberinis and given in full by Orelli in No. 2,417 of his great collection, which is in itself a curiosity. Other dishes used by the cooks were two-eared flagons or flasks for wine and other liquors, *amphoræ*, besides a number of others, for nearly all of which we have proof of unions having existed, who conducted their manufacture.

Finally the *tricliniarchs* or stewards who had the supreme charge of kitchen and dining room. Their name

[31] Gruter, *Inscriptiones Totius Orbis Romanorum*, 643. 10.
[32] Orell, *Inscriptionum Latinorum Collectio*, No. 3,229.
[33] Fabrett, p. 724. 443.

was derived from the celebrated *triclinium* or **dining-couch** of the ancients. It was a seat, generally cushioned, which extended around three sides of the table, upon which people did not sit, but reclined—a practice so demonstrative of exuberant luxury, if not of lasciviousness that it was abolished as one of the abominations by the Christians and seems to have completely disappeared from the earth. There is extant at least one monument giving clear evidence of a society of this kind, called in the inscription [34] *tricliniarum socii.* It is in the museum of Rome and bears a very queer, unpolished style of Latin.

[34] Fabett, 449, 59.

CHAPTER XVII.

INDUSTRIAL COMMUNES

AMUSEMENTS OF OLD. UNIONS OF PLAYERS.

THE COLLEGIA SCÆNICORUM—Unions of Mimics—Horrible Mimic Performances in Sicily—Bloody Origin of Wakes—Unions of Dancers, Trumpeters, Bagpipers, and Hornblowers—The Flute-Players—Roman Games—Unions of Circus Performers—Of Gladiators—Of Actors—Murdering Robust Wrestlers for Holiday Pastimes—Unions of Fortune-tellers—Proofs in the Inscriptions—Ferocious Gladiatorial Scenes between the Workingmen and Tigers, Lions, Bears, and Other Wild Beasts made compulsory by Roman Law.

THE Greeks and Romans are known to have given at an early period much attention to amusements, in which it appears there was a larger admixture of the lowly, with the noble class than occurred in other pursuits. The theatre with the Greeks, was quite a democratic affair. The earliest theatres were rude; but during the heroic ages immense buildings were constructed. That of Megapolis in Arcadia was of gigantic size. Their size was such that roofs were out of the question, and people sat on stone seats for from four to eight hours in daytime exposed to sun and rain, during the performances, listening to, and bound up in enthusiastic delight over the inimitable sallies of Aristophanes in the "Babylonians," satyring the tyrant Cleon, or thrilled by the sublime grandeur of tragedy and mimic of Sophocles and Euripides at Athens. Some of the great theatres were capable of holding 60,000 spectators. The great theatre at Ephesus was 660 feet in diameter and one in Syracuse 440 feet. An immense wooden theatre, built by Scaurus at Rome, 55

years before Christ, and at the moment when intolerance
to the labor unions and profligacy among the grandees
were beginning to crumble the proud Romans into demoralization and decay, was capable of accommodating
80,000 people.

We find no fewer than six genuine trade unions; called,
on the stones, *collegia scaenicorum*.[1] They are coeval with
the age of the Roman theatres. Their members of course,
fared better than the gladiators,[2] another class who contributed to the Roman pastimes; but they were hardworked people and all belonged to the proletaries.

We shall bring to view as illustrative of our object,
principally the Roman life in this section of the ancient
trade unions, not because we are wanting of archæological specimens; for there are very many profoundly interesting relics of the life of ancient labor now being discovered among the ruins of the Greeks. Renan, Wescher,
Foucart and Böckh have eloquently told the story and
the solemn silence of crumbling marbles, like skeletons
seem to be speaking in incoherent phrase of a day when
the whole Greek world was ablaze with labor communes,
whose secrecy was suggestive of a smouldering social
volcano. But if we gave them all it would make this
work tediously voluminous. Besides, the inscriptions in
the Latin tongue seem to bring the matter under investigation more conspicuously before us, not only because
they are topographically less remote but because the langauge in which they come to us is smoother and more intelligible to the readers of the western world.

In the Wiener Jahrbuch for 1829 there appeared a deciphering of an inscription on a plate of bronze containing
an epitaph of the president of a union of mimic actors.
It is written in the second person. He had lived to be
nearly a hundred years old; had never aspired above his
fellows and had died bidding them farewell. It is in the
Museum at Pesth. Several others have been found in
Austrian territory. Orelli[3] describes several anaglyphs

---

[1] One found at Wasserstadt, *Aquænicum*, a suburb of Buda, by Labus and published at Milan, 1827 reads: "Genio Collegio Scœniariorum Felan, Secundus Monitor Decreto Decurionum.
[2] Chapter xii., *Spartacus, init.*
[3] Orèlli, *Inscriptionum Latinorum Collectio*, in his *Collegia Corpora, Sodalicia* No. 7,183. Vol. III, Henzen.

in stone and metal composition, which have withstood the erosions of nature fully 2,000 years. In the *Res Scaenica* and *Ludi*, one is quoted from Muratori,[4] bearing uncertain evidence that it was a union of histrionic artists. It was from Præneste. Two remarkable tablets bearing record of the year 112 A. D. are noted by Gorius.[5] They were preserved in the museum at Florence, and unless recently removed, are there still. Upon these slabs are inscribed the names of soldiers of the seven Roman cohorts, of the prætorian force of Misenum ever on the alert conducting the scenic plays. Claudius Gnorimus is being made an *aedile* or superintendent of public works by the battalion; plays are going on by the acting comrades with their buffoons. Among all these are to be observed: 1st. The head mimic actor; 2d. The mimic Greek leaders; 3d. The clowns; 4th. The Greek clowns; 5th. The Greek actors; 6th. The jesting dandies; 7th. A workingman. All the names of the soldiers are given in the vocative case. Consequently the inscription is too long to be given entire in any work which we have seen. It portrays the kind of military theatrical scene which used to be enacted 200 years after the beginning of the Christian era, or about 1,700 years ago and of course, much earlier.[6] Another inscription appears among the *Res Scaenica* in Orelli's catalogue which still more clearly represents a mutually protective union of actors. It was found at the French city of Vienne, a few miles from Lyons, on the Rhone, by Millin.[7] It is also very ancient and shows that in that far off country of the Allobroges there was a great population long before Cæsar's invasion.

Although we are endeavoring to give the facts consec-

---

[4] Muratori, *Thesaur.*, 659, 1; Gruter, *Inscr. Tot. Orb. Rom.*, 330, 3.
[5] Cf. *Etruscan Inscr*. I. p. 125 and II, p. 447 and Mur., 886-887.
[6] Consult Orellius, *Inscriptionum Latinarum Collectio*, No. 2,608. Muratori, *Thesaur*, 886-7. Gorius *Etr.*, I. p, 128. "Memorabiles sunt tabulae anni p. Chr. 212, duae a Gorio *Etr*. 1. p. 125 (2,447). et Mur. 886 et 887 editae, Florentiae nunc adsertae, in quibus referuntur nomina militum ex Cohortibus VII. Vigilum et Classis praetoriae Misenatis, qui Ludos scenicos egerunt, quum Claudius Gnorimus aedilis factus esset a vexillatione, ludosque ederet, ' agentibus commilitonibus cum suis acroamatibus' In his notandi; 1. Archimimus. 2. Archimimi Graeci. 3. Stupidi. 4 Stupidi Graeci. 5. Scaenici Graeci. 6. Scurra. 7. Operarius. Omnia militum nomina vocativo efferuntur," For more on the *vexillum*, red flag, and *vexillatio*, consult our chapter on the ancient *red flag* of the workingman.
[7] *Voyage*, 2, p. 21.

utively, we shall here be compelled, for want of data, to mention in an anacoluthical manner, some of the most interesting of these unions known to have existed coeval with those times, or approximately so.

The *communiones mimorum,* one of which[8] was discovered in the ruins of the theatre *Bovillensis,* and others in great numbers in Greece[9] and elsewhere, were unions of mimic actors. They constituted an order by themselves. It appears that they marched around in the cities and took from their friends and the public whatever gifts were offered. We mention these data to exhibit to our readers the collossal scale on which amusements were conducted, that the mind may be prepared to comprehend the vast amount of labor of the lowly, which the evolutions of this business entailed.

Following up our scheme of inquiry into the dark chasms and gaps of history, from a standpoint of sociological investigation, our point of intensest interest is the question whether these purveyors of pastimes were organized. Of this there is abundance of evidence in the inscriptions. In the catalogue of the archæologist Orelli, there appear no less than 12 tolerably well preserved slabs which show not less than a hundred unions!

At Rome there is an inscription, much broken and defaced by time and neglect,[10] which bears positive proof that the theatre players were not only organized but that they, like the gladiators belonged to the plebeian stock. Caput VI., of Orelli's work, headed *Ludi, Res Scaenica et cet.,* has no less than 116 inscriptions, a large number of which are seen at a glance to be either genuine unions or corporate communes. But as some of these unions were those of gladiators, we reserve their description for that more tragical and brutal class of amusement.

A very remarkable mimic performance for enjoyment was once in vogue during the insurrection of the Sicilian slaves B. C. 143–134. It may not be generally known that in addition to accredited kings and tyrants of Sicily there once reigned a king of the slaves. The extraordi-

---

[8] Orell., *Inscr.,* No. 2,625, also Nos. 4,094, 4,101.
[9] Mommsen, *De Collegiis et Sodaliciis Romanorum,* p. 83. "Communia mimorum Romanorum, et in nomine et in institutis τὰ κοινὰ τῶν περὶ τὸν Διονύσοι τεχνιτῶν referent, quæ apud Græcos ampla et plurima fuerunt." *Idem,* note 6, "Communia Mimorum multa inveniuntur," etc., etc.
[10] Orell., No. 2,619; Marini, *Atti.* 2, p. 488.

nary history of king Eunus is so interesting and so replete with passages which enlighten the student of sociology on points that we have reserved for it a separate chapter as a special illustration of our theme.[11] It is enough here to bring forward the episode alluded to in evidence of the fact that in ancient times theatrical performances were sometimes conducted in presence of enemies whereby to tantalize and to wreak revenge. The Sicilian capitalists, landlords and slaveholders had for a long time been growing niggardly and cruel. It was a common thing for a slave master owning from 500 to 1,000 slaves, to call their poor little children together precisely as the herder calls his swine, and feed them nuts, pods and dried figs[12] because the helpless, enslaved and horribly cruelized beings were considered no better than hogs. One Polias, an enormously wealthy Agrigentine not only thus abused his slaves but often whipped large numbers of them at the post at night, to prepare them for obedience the following day. Damophilus, who owned 500 slaves at Enna in Sicily, was another extremely rich planter. He starved his human chattels, while at the same time driving them beyond their powers. One day several of them ventured to ask him for more clothing; for the place is many feet above the sea and chilly during some seasons of the year. Their supplication though given in a respectful manner was treated not only with refusal but with a severe castigation. His wife, Megallis, was, if possible, the most heartless and brutal of the two. She, with her own hand stabbed and whipped to death several of her female slaves, first torturing them with her knife and her stiletto or needle.[13] Unable to endure their inhuman tortures the infuriated slaves suddenly arose in rebellion and seizing their tormentors murdered them in great numbers. Damophilus was bludgeoned in the theatre of Enna in presence of his wife, Megallis. A council was held on her case, before her husband's dead body, in the theatre. Our authority does

[11] See Chap. VII. An account of the Mimic plays at the sieges, pp. 229-230.
[12] See Dr. Bücher, *Aufstände der Unfreien Arbeiter*, p. 63-64, quoting Stobæus on *Florilus*, LXII, 48. We have also in many places given quotations proving this by other authors. See index, *Food of the Slaves and Freedmen*.
[13] Consult chapter 'v On Eunus, and the first Sicilian war, where quotations explaining these brutalities, taken from the fragments of Diodorus, are given, together with excerpts from Bücher and others.

not establish that the mimic performance was gone through with during the wild gloatings of that bloody night; but no doubt the tables were turned upon the trembling millionaires who before were wont to shout with almost equal savagery at the mutual murder of their myrmidons acting as their slaves. The result of the trial of Megallis, was her condemnation and sentence to death. She was dragged to a rock and plunged headlong into the hideous abyss by the women themselves. Their daughter, a tender girl who had many times remonstrated against her mother's cruelty, was treated with respectful courtesy, guarded from danger and under escort sent to a place of safety. This uprising lasted 10 years; during which time many places were captured by siege. The slaves who, according to history,[14] at length arose to the number of 200,000 in Sicily, inaugurated the system of holding histrionic mimes composed in their own rude vehicles of thought and represented by performers who could best reproduce, in presence of their previous tormentors, scenes which they and their children had suffered when they were chattels. In this manner they doubtless wreaked a rude and gloating satisfaction too malignant for true humanity, but certainly not surprising, considering their former misery.[15]

Spartacus, the celebrated gladiator, after the battle of Picenum, when he held in his hands the officers and men of the Roman army as prisoners of war, although a humane and kind-hearted general, delighted his soldiers by compelling those proud and high-born gentiles to reenact upon the field of battle and in honor of the *manes* of Crixus their fallen hero, the same gladiatorial scenes which he and his comrades when slaves, were destined to perform on the arena. In the captive's hand was put the *gladium* and in the humiliating garb of an *ergastularius*, or convict, condemned to fight in the mock amphitheatre and for his audience the vast army of victorious rebel slaves and gladiators, many a haughty Roman knight with his unspeakable contempt for the very condition of

---

[14] For all known particulars of this great servile war, see Bücher, *Aufstände der Unfreien Arbeiter*.
[15] Bücher, *Aufst.*, S. 66-67. Diod. XXXIV., frag. 34. Lüders, *Die Dionysischen Künstler*, pp. 105-131, where are explained the numerous theatrical habits to which the Greek artisans were addicted.

slavery, was forced to make the runs and re-enact the bloody work it had been the now victorious rebels' own undignified misfortune to perform upon the Roman sands. Surely, the knights of Lentulus, Poplicola and the other captured soldiers could now have a practical insight into the causes of the great insurrection, when, under stinging urgents of their mock *scholae praeceptores*, they punched each other, to the music of jeer and of derision from 70,000 vengeance-wreaking infuriates!

Wakes [16] held over the deceased bodies of friends are not of Christian origin but of a much higher Pagan antiquity. Again, where history is silent, the inscriptions —those whispering chroniclers like grinning skeletons of the murdered—survive to lisp their testimony before our courts of science. This subject of the origin and practice of holding wakes, supposed by some to belong to the Christianized races, is really to be sought among the stones which tell the savage tales of haughty masters' funeral feasts whereat poor workingmen were forced to fight as gladiators; and when they fell by mutually inflicted gashes, were buried beside the great dead hero with the object of remaining guard to him as they had done in life. This is the true origin of wakes. They were originally, extremely bloody, and should be classed among other specimens of moribund or fading heathen customs, that are gradually disappearing from the earth.

Scholars reading the Latin classics, are sometimes puzzled to comprehend the reason why Cicero, Suetonius, Florus and the rest, so unexceptionally speak of the dancer, *saltator;* the female dancer, *saltatrix*, and the little girl dancer, *saltatricula*, with a species of contumely. Of everything not human, however humble, they could speak in praise. Their favorite horses, dogs, cats, even cows could earn a good word and a caress; and all things germane to their household were worthy of a feeling thought. But it is a seemingly strange fact that dancers who worked so hard to amuse the ancients, get only a reproachful mention.

Among amusements it may be best to class the various kinds of musical instrument players. There was a regular union of the trumpeters, *aenatores*.[17] Another sort of

[16] Friedländer, *Darstellungen aus der Sittengeschichte Roms.* II, 16.

trumpeter was the *buccinator*, who played the shepherd's horn which had a long range of sound.[18] These trumpeters also accompanied the army. Usually the horns were crooked. Mommsen who has worked out the evidences in regard to the Roman arrangement of centurians, in accordance with the military notions which distributed the trade unions into squads of tens and hundreds, thinks that another trumpeter, the *liticen*[19] also had his union, probably a mutually protective association like the musicians' unions of the present time. The *liticenes*, were clarion blowers and their music was shrill and exciting. Still another kind of trumpeters were the *tubicenes*[20] who are likewise known to have been an organized profession or trade. They played the tuba. It is difficult to understand how a separate society was necessary for each instrument. If there were a number of different instruments in each, corresponding to a band of music organized for self-support, as in our times, it would not appear remarkable.

The union of *scabillarii*[21] does not appear so inconsistent; since the ancient *scabellium* was an awkward instrument played upon by the feet, while very probably the hands were also employed thrumming another instrument whose harmonies combined, made a band of themselves. The bagpipe is known to be an ancient instrument—so old that its invention is ascribed to a god of the mythical antiquity. Whether the old *tibia utricularis* was the identical bagpipe of the Scotch Highlanders is a question; but judging from the derivation of the word there is a strong reason to suppose that no great change has taken place in its construction. The bagpipers had an association called the *collegium utricularium*[22] and there are several inscriptions to that effect. In addition to the one found by Donati, we have one described in Gruter's collection and catalogued by Orelli.[23] It was found at Lyons. It is something like an epitaph and the work bears the marks of having been dedicated to the name of the president, *mag-*

[17] Of this we have assurance in the work of Gruter, *Inscriptiones Totius Orbi Romanorum*, No. 261, 4; a marble slab giving unmistakable evidence.
[18] *Idem*, 1,116, 4. [19] Orell., *Inscr.*, No. 4,105.
[20] *Idem*, Nos. 2,448 and 1,803 both were collegia or unions.
[21] Orell. *Inscr.* 4,117; 2,643.
[22] Orell., Nos. 4,119, 4,120, 4,121, all were unions, also Donati, 2, p. 470, 3, cites a stone found at Cabelli, which has merited considerable comment. The inscription registers a genuine union.
[23] Orell., *Inscr. Lat. Coll.* No. 4,244. Nos. 9.208 and 5,803 are also unions.

ister, of the organization; although, in this case no mention is made of the usual word collegium or corpus.

The *cornicen* or horn player was another musician[24] who is found mentioned on the same marble with a *liticen* at Rome. But the music of the horn blowers and that of the clarion players was so similar that it may, in this case, be a confusion of the two in one.

The flute players deserve a more particular mention. Among the Romans they were called *tibicenes*, and among the Greeks *auletrides*. In very remote antiquity the latter existed at Athens and other cities of Attica. They were poor girls of lowly origin who went about playing their flutes and earning here and there a little coin, sufficient to keep them from suffering. Some of them were very beautiful; and as this natural accomplishment was sometimes more charming even than their music, there goes up a charge against their character.[25] It is now known that these flute players were organized in a trade union or some kind of a labor federation. In order to carry on their business they were required to pay a small tax to the government as a license, which tax was collected by the *vectigalarii* as stated in our chapter on the customs collectors. This was another union whose members were required by the state to collect the last *denarius*, even if they had to torture, imprison or sell the poor, impecunious creatures as slaves. It may therefore have happened that a beautiful auletrid, before surrendering her life as a slave and legalized concubine of the wealthy Roman or Athenian who bought her at the shambles, would sometimes procure the inveterate tax money by accepting the best available offers which promised life and liberty.

At Rome a genuine flute players' union, *collegium tibicenum Romanorum* existed[26] during the emperors which was shielded from the repressive laws against organization by being a sacred commune. Probably the girls played sacred music on occasions.[27] That there were male members in this commune is certain. The wording of the inscription shows this one name taking the masculine termination. There were also at Athens and the Pi-

[24] Idem, No. 4,105.
[25] Cf. Sanger's *History of Prostitution*, chap. iii, p. 46.
[26] Reines, pp. 184-167.
[27] " Qui sacris publicis præsto sunt. " Orell., *Inscr.* No. 1,803.

ræus many of the *aulitrides* or Greek flutists who lived under protection of their gallant unions. A study of the excellent work of Guhl and Koner [28] will afford the reader much additional knowledge upon the subject of ancient music.

The great *ludi cercenses* which, although in point of history, treatment of performers and other features, were very different from the gladiatorial style of amusement, so resemble these latter in many other respects that it seems consistent to treat of them as belonging to one variety. The Roman circus was not the only institution of its kind. There was evidently a circus at Lyons. An inscription mentioning a union of players, speaks of the right of organization at Lyons, for all who wish.[29]

Everything built to entertain amusement seekers among the Romans, whether at Rome, Pompeii or elsewhere, if public, took the amphitheatrical shape. There were numerous race-courses at Rome, some of which were of prodigious extent. The circus Maximus [30] was enormous. "According to the latest calculations, in late imperial times, it must have contained 480,000 seats. It is about 21,000 feet long by 400 wide."[31] It is very old, having been begun by Tarquinius Priscus. These figures are sufficient proof of themselves, that Rome once contained an immense population. Large numbers of slaves were necessary to supply the labor of these enormous public works. The many scenes of hippodromes, chariot-running, foot-racing, of archery, mock manœuvres, and sham battles were observable from a great distance. They thrilled vast audiences.

But the inner life of the poor who were to manage and carry out the innumerable features of those games is a subject which the reader of history learns little. They were all of the lowly class and eked out a living under many difficulties and humiliations; and many of those who were not slaves but existed in the capacity of freedmen, took refuge from abuse and overtoil under the meagre privilege left them to unite in mutual self-aid.

[28] Guhl and Koner, *Life of the Greeks and Romans*, Tr. F. Hueffer, (Lon. Chatto and Windus.)
[29] Grut., 431, 1. *Inscr. Tot. Orbis Rom.*
[30] Guhl and Koner, *Life of the Greeks and Romans*, Tr. pp. 422-428.
[31] Guhl and Koner, pp. 423-4 note. See fig. 431 note.

CARNAGE OF THE SANDS. 411

But the celebrated gladiatorial amusements are more generally known to us at this day, although the circus performance has outlived them, being yet common on a much smaller scale. There was no mockery about the amphitheatre. The combats were real. We have already spoken of the large traffic in lions, tigers, leopards and other wild animals for the combats. Not only did the Romans pit lion with tiger, panther with bear, lynxes and leopards with serpents, but they matched tigers, lions and serpents of terrible ferocity with men. When at the great games the stock of fierce wild animals was killed off they sent hunters in quest of more Romanelli [32] preserves an inscription which for clearness has been regarded by the archæologists as an object of much value. The inscription commemorates a family (probably a community) of hunters of Pompeii, who procured noble game from the forests, and mentions Popidius Rufus as the manager of the *familia gladiatorum*.

We have elsewhere seen that there were unions of sweepers of the amphitheatres, *collegia arenariorum*. They were not required to fight in the arena. They dragged the dead gladiators off the sands, shoveled up the blood, new-sprinkled the floor with sand, sharpened the *gladia* or swords as well as the javelins and other tools, stood ready to perform any service; even perhaps that of cutting off the heads of vanquished gladiators who heroically, when *hors de combat*, bleeding and dying with their gaping gashes, impatient of death, bent the head to receive the severing stroke of the broadsword.[33]

Marini found two queer inscriptions, graved on one stone, of gladiators who "fell fighting, steel in hand.[34]

---

[32] Romanelli, *Viaggio a Pompei*. tome I, p. 82; Marini, *Atti*, I, p. 165. It is clear that there must have been lions in the forests of Mt Olympus for Polydamus the wrestler (B. C. 404, see Plato, Bekk. Lond. chap. XII note) killed a huge lion there. Lions are known to have lived in Germany and hyenas in Eng. See Buckland, *Reliquæ Diluvianæ*, Lond., 1822 because their bones are now being found in the Pleistocene caves.

[33] Bulwer Lytton's, *Last Days of Pompeii*, where these awful scenes are graphically set forth.

[34] Marini, *Atti*, 1, p. 165. The modern ages are actively studying out the horrors of the gladiatorial combats. We refer the reader who may doubt as to whether those people fought under the most intense humiliations, to the cuts of Guhl and Koner, pp. 562-3, *trans.*, showing the distressing scenes of these fights with the wild animals, also to Carey, *Principles of Political Economy*, Part III, p. 123: "The great mass having sunk to barbarous rudeness, bloody gladiatorial games and combats of wild beasts took the place of dramatic representations while the few were becoming more refined and fastidious." To the *Iconographic Cyclopædia*, Division IV, New York, 1851, R. Garrigue. Tafel 15, magnificen

Inscription No. 2,552 of Orelli's *Res Scaenica* is designated by him as representing gladiatorial combats in the coliseum. It is a horrible thought for an age like this to endure; yet there was a time when killing men for sport was so popular that crowned heads were turned from meditation to convulsions of delight by the sight; and ladies dressed in the costliest attire of fashion could sit for hours bewitched with the whirl, the charge, the lunge of steel and shrieks of pain, the spurt of blood from the wounds of naked men, the roar of lions and screech and growl of tigers, bears and wolves, the murderous hand-to-hand fights of the *hoplomachi* with heavy swords and the whole swirling, mazy, gory labyrinth of the Roman arena! Surely, forced as we are to admit that such scenes of cruelty really once existed, as it were, among our forefathers, we feel almost constrained to admit that the many thousands of years which had flown before the present era, had produced little better than savages to people the world. Those awful brutalities were the product of the slave system. They could not have taken place where men were free.

The gladiators had several different names. Some were called gladiators, some mirmillions, some agitators, some *pugnatores*, some *ergastularii*, according to their social rank and the kind of weapons with which they were allowed to consummate their murderous tasks. But slaves though they were, they found means to accomplish fraternal unions. That there were unions of gladiators inscriptions exist so plentifully to prove, that the most skeptical can no longer doubt. There are several inscriptions, evidently signs of gladiator brokers,[35] showing that there were speculators in this species of human flesh. Being slaves and not freedmen, except in cases where they won freedom by killing their adversary, human or wild beast, thus achieving their manumission, they could only with difficulty organize for mutual help.

Orelli, in *Res Scaenica*, No. 2,066 reproduces the remarkable inscription of Donati, found in Rome, which is acknow-

steel engraving of the arena, where are seen fighting men, women, elephants, tigers, lions, panthers and serpents, for the amusements of myriads in the seats above! That they fought naked see *Idem* Hecht, Section IX, Tafel 7, Vol. II. Plates, showing men killing men.
[35] Orell., *Inscr.* 4,197 and 4,247 of *Artes et Opificia.*

ledged to have served a union. Of itself it is an object of surprise; and has not yet been studied enough to shed all the light that was latent in its curious palæograph. There are recorded in the *Res Scaenica* of Orelli not less than a dozen genuine trade unions of the gladiatorial art. This of itself makes it conjectural whether there was not some law relative to the organization of slaves.

Fortune-telling was so common that there is a law in the code of Theodosius providing for a union of fortune-tellers, *corpus nemesiacorum*.[36] They had a secret order whose members worshipped the goddess of fortune, called *Dea Nemesi*. They were something like our clairvoyants; some of them like our psycologists but more nearly resembling the *aruspices* and diviners of oracles. Such was the superstition among all classes that they were held in high esteem by rich and poor and probably patronized a good deal, thus affording an opportunity to combine profit with mysterious wisdom.

There are some great stories connected with superstition. Eunus the slave king of Enna in Sicily was a fortune-teller. The poor downtrodden slaves, crushed to the lowest condition which left breath and animation in their tortured frames, when they heard of his wise sayings—some of which, like those of our weather prophets, came true—and when they were informed by him that he was destined to quit the servile post of waiter in his master's family and assume the royal robes of a monarch, they believed him; and this superstitious credulity actually wrought the fact. He was fortune-teller, fire-eater, prestidigitator and stump speaker; and combined with all this a bluff managerial talent and a rollicking good nature and winsomeness which determined and cast the die to the greatest insurrection known in history unless we except that of Spartacus. If he had no organization at the start he soon effected one. He also showed much shrewd resignation of his prerogatives of kingship when he gave to the terrible Achaeos, and the impetuous Cleon the command of the armies. He showed a wisdom akin to revelation when he decided not to take arms personally but to stay in his palace and blow fire out of his mouth, dawdle with the trinkets of his throne and let these

[36] Nemesclaci, a dea Nemesi, quae eadem est cum bona Fortuna. Cod Theod. lib. XIV, Nat. ad leg. 2, tit V.1

generals fight his battles with a soldiery of slaves who believed that every word he uttered was dropped from the Almighty.

Witchcraft and fortune-telling have been twin trades from the earliest times and were well worth organizing for; and as they were intimately allied to the mysteries of early religions the membership had less difficulty in procuring laws exempting them from suppression. But they carried it to intrigue and machination, so that oftentimes it did not restrict itself to simple amusement. It gained a strong foothold upon the solemnity of religion and exercised so powerful a control of men's consciences that the hints and presages of the soothsayer sometime sdecided the fortunes of battle.

Great numbers of unions of mimic actors existed among the Greeks and Romans.[37] We have especially noticed that part of the ancient world inhabited by the Roman stock of the Indo-European race; but this was merely for the purpose of making the fact perspicuous that the ancient working people had a labor movement and that the freedmen were organized. In Greece, Syria Phœnicia, Gaul, Germany and the regions of the Danube are also found inscriptions and other evidences that once a great trade and labor movement existed covering most of the then Roman world.[38]

[37] Mommsen, *De Coll. et Sodal Romanorum*, p. 83, note 6. "Communia memorum multa inveniuntur."

[38] Wallace, *Numbers of Mankind*, p. 142, makes some remarks which, though written a century ago, are applicable to the study which engages these pages: He says: "As the riches and luxury of the great men in *Rome* increased so prodigiously, this must have occasioned a vast circulation, and a general plenty of gold and silver; nor was it possible to confine the money to a few hands; however, the necessaries of life continued at a moderate price, and did not rise in their value in proportion to the high rates which were set on the materials of luxury." This shows that yearning, at least, for the socialistic system largely prevailed among the ancient lowly.

CHAPTER XVIII.

TRADE UNIONS.

THE ANCIENT CLOTHING-CUTTERS.

How THE ANCIENTS WERE CLOTHED—The Unions of Fullers—Of Linen Weavers, Wool-carders, Cloth-combers—Inscriptions as Proof—Later Laws of Theodosius and Justinian Revised—Government Cloth Mills—What was Meant by Public Works—Who managed Manufactures—The Dyers—Old-fashioned Shoes of the Forefathers—How made—Origin of the Crispins—The Furriers' Union—Roman Ladies and Fineries of Fur—The great Ragamuffin Trade—Their Innumerable Unions—Ragpickers of Antiquity—Origin of the *Cenciajuole*—Organization of the Real Tatterdemalions—Origin of the Gypsies—Hypothesis.

IT is quite possible to establish the fact that the clothing trades were organized. Woollen goods in those times were not manufactured in large mills with costly machinery. Weaving was done on small hand looms, and the fulling of cloth was a trade by itself. Cotton was used for tents, theatres and also to some extent for clothing at an early date; yet our limited data will not permit us to state that cotton manufacturers were organized. But the workers in wool had societies, some of which were screened from the restrictions imposed on many other trades, on account of their innocent usefulness. There is a law of the Theodosian code [1] providing for the right or privilege of mutual organization to the fullers, *fullones*. We consequently have a fullers' union *fullonum sodalicium* [2] commemorated on a marble slab, found

---

[1] Cod. Theod., *De Excusationibus Artificum*, lib. XIII, tit. IV, lex. 2.
[2] Murator, *Thesaurus Veterum Inscriptionum*, 951, 9. Found at Spoleto among the Appenines. It is an inscription in marble. Cult of the union, Minerva.

at Spoleto; another, picked up at Falaria, inscribed with
lette s so well preserved that no hesitation is indulged in
by the critics in pronouncing it a genuine trade union of the
fullers, as the word "*collegium*" appears three times and
"*sodalicium*" twice;[3] both terms convey the meaning of
mutual union or organization; and as both these inscriptions
appear to be of the era of the republic, they are probably
very old. If, however, the two tablets above cited are not
sufficient as evidence of the union of fullers, we have a gem
from Pompeii in the from of an inscription of the fullers who
worked in some public establishment. These artisans, as
Mommsen observed in his disquisition on labor unions, evidently shielded themselves from the severity of the law suppressing the colleges, by having recourse to a certain amount
of piety[4] which they scarcely felt in their hearts. A society
of sacred fullers sounds ridiculous![5] Yet this inscription
commemorating a fraternity, or at any rate, a force of workmen fulling cloth for the use of the people, bears pious words
which would incline one to imagine that some of their wages
was devoted, like a collection at church, towards defraying
the expenses of the holy temples instead of providing for
the earners' hungry babes. This inscription is one of the
many contributions to ethnological science which the exhu-
mations from Pompeii have produced. Of course then no
one can question its greater antiquity than the earthquake
of Vesuvius, A. D. 79; and it might have existed many
hundreds of years anterior to that event.

The linen weavers during the emperors, enjoyed the free
right of organization, according to a provision in the *codex
Theodosii*,[6] and we accordingly have an inscription quoted
in Orelli,[7] of the linen weavers, *lintearii*, found at Nemausum,
by Muratori. But the stone is in a bad condition. It
might have been a private sign, in which case it proves
nothing to our purpose.[8]

The wool carders, *lanarii pectinarii*, used to card and

[3] Cf. Orellius, *Inscriptionum Latinarum Collectio*, Nos. 4,056, 4,091, 3,291 all of which were fullers.
[4] Mommsen, *De Collegiis et Sodaliciis Romanorum*, Cap. V. *passim*.
[5] Vide Orell, *Inscr. Lat. Coll.*, No. 3,291, Opera Publica. "Eumachiae filiii in-genui Sacred. pub. Fullones." *Pompeii*
[6] Cod. Theod., lib. XXX, 6. 8. 16.
[7] O ell., *Inscr Latinarum Collectio*, No. 4,215 also Cod. Theod., lib. X, 20, 16.
[8] For futher information on linen weavers, see Granier *Histoire des Classes Ouvrièrs*, p. 310: ' Les principalis corporations marchandes de l' empire étaient cel es des tisserands, *linteones* etc."

weave with similar cards and hand-looms as were used by the colonists of the United States. In all probability the teasel was used in dressing and combing the cloth the same as now; since no application of mechanical invention and science has ever superseded the use of the teasel in combing cloth, although new experiments of great ingenuity are constantly being made.

The weavers and carders were also organized. Of this we also have proof in the inscriptions. Gruter found at Brixia[9] a fragment of a slab on which were engraved a few words signifying that the *sodalicium* or union had added another emancipated slave to their numbers, either as apprentice or otherwise. The organization was one of wool carders. The same author records several others, one of them discovered in the village of Rummel *agri Silvaeducensis*.[10] At Rome there were several others discovered.[11]

Inscription No. 2,303 of Orelli is placed by him among *Opera publica*, public works, which is very strong evidence that the state farmed out the manufacture of wollen goods to the unions, who produced the goods for the government in its own mills. Did the Roman state own woollen mills? It would be well for political economists to consider this important question before proceeding to accuse the labor movement of this day of making demands which are "unprecedented" in the methods of manufacture and distribution of the means of human life and comfort. The evidences which are coming to light through the labors of archæologists, who dig up, interpret and record the tell-tale palæographs of an ancient civilization are accumulating proof of the conjecture that once in Rome, at Athens and elsewhere, the governments were owners of woollen factories; and that they were run for government by trade unions, watched, curtailed, hampered and restricted of course, by the jealous optimate politicians lest the immense advantages natural to such a method should conduce to the liberty and social emancipation of the proletaries. The student of sociology may dimly discern some obscure light from great writers to the effect that not only the woollen mills were counted as public works but also many other establishments of a nature to supply food, clothing and shelter to the population.

[9] Gruter, *Inscriptiones Totius Orbis Romanorum*, 648, 2, 957, 2.
[10] Idem, 957, 2.   [11] Idem, 648, 4.

When the linen or wool was carded, spun, woven into cloth and fulled, it was necessary to have it dyed. It is however probable that then, as now, the goods were dyed in the yarn. This required another trade—that of dyers.

There was a class of dyers, those who colored the celebrated purple hues, who were especially provided by law;[12] the *blattearii*. They enjoyed the free privilege of organizing their numbers and possessed trade unions, being exempt from the restrictions which so curtailed and embarassed some of the unions of other trades.

Another class of dyers were the *murileguli* who fished for shells and purple-fish that secreted an ink used for coloring silk and probably other materials. No inscriptions have been discovered that we are aware of which describe them, but frequent mention in the Roman law in connection with the franchise extended to some unions, corroborates the assurance that they possessed organizations. In fact their fraternity was mentioned and provided for in the codes both of Theodosus and of Justinian.[13] These workmen colored the exquisite red and purple of the ancient red banner.[14]

Thus we have the cloth ready for the tailor. The ancients wore a sort of loose cloak or flowing mantle called *sagum*. It was usually of long wool and colored. Tailors who made them were called *sagarii*[15] and they were organized; but as they were a branch of the tailors' profession there appear no special inscriptions of them except in the lists of epitaphs.[16] There was a union of tailors provided for by a law in the code of Theodosius, under the designation given them, of *gynaeciarii*[17] which is a warping of a Greek word and a Greek custom into the Roman tongue. At Athens the *gynaeceum* was that portion of any house where the women lived. They also worked there for their masters; and by this we know they were often slaves. But in Rome it served as a manufactory of clothing in addition to being the harem of the lord. Under the emperors there was a man to oversee this work.[18] As the emperor was the head of the

[12] Cod. Theod., *De Excusationibus Artificum*, lib. XIII, tit. IV, leg. 2.
[13] Cod. *Justiniani*, IX, 7. [14] See chapter on the *Ancient Red Flag, infra*.
[15] Cod. *Theodosii*, lib. X, tit. 5, leg. 12, also X, 20.
[16] Orellus, *Inscriptionum Latinarum Collectio*, Nos. 4,251 and 4,723. *Sepulcralia*. [17] Cod. *Theodosii*, lib. X, leg. 2, 3, 7 and X. 20, 2.
[18] Cod. *Justiniani*, lib. XI, 7, 3.

people he was considered the government and his palace like the residence of the president of the United States, was government property; so that it seems to be a fact easily proven that certain manufacturing establishments were carried on by the ancient governments; since it is well known that the spinners', weavers', dyers' and tailors' overseers who were called *gynaeciarii*, had shops in the emperors' palaces and conducted the manufacture of mantles, togas and other articles of clothing on quite an extensive scale for the household of his majesty, including family and retinue. These female clothiers worked in the same manner for others of the great *gentes* or lordly families. This prepares us for a distinct comprehension of the desire of ancient labor to be organized. It lifted the member one step higher than the slave and placed him or her in the co-operative supervision and care of the fraternity. The Roman *gynaeciarius* was generally a man who had charge of the workshop.

On account of a misapprehension of this word's true meaning, lexicographers define the *gynaeciarius* as an overseer of a harem! This is a cheap way of degrading the character of hundreds and even thousands of poor working women who plied the honest needle wherewith to eke out a wretched living. But it is the inscriptions—a late study—which bring out the original home-meaning, otherwise lost. Not only the code of Theodosius but that of Justinian contain well worded provisions for the organization of tailors into trade unions. This association was taken advantage of by the women as well as their chivalrous male companions in poverty and lowliness and they were only too glad to enjoy the patronage of their emperors, and work in their houses and those of the grandees, under a foreman, doubtless also a member of the union. The *gens* family thus furnished shop, tools and stock and the workers here performed the work. But family and state were identical terms.

We now come to the shoemakers. If the reader, in admiring the pictures of the ancients, will carefully observe the apparel in which their feet are shod he will notice that the shoe has the form of a sandal; and that it is laced to the foot like a modern half-slipper. That is to say, it is mostly sole; there being very little upper-leather, especially about the instep. This was the principal article of foot clothing manufactured by the ancients for popular use. Italy, Greece, Spain, Phœnicia, Northern Africa, are almost semi-tropical countries. It is the pinching cold of Central Europe that has forced differentiation in the shape of shoes and boots. The Roman sandal, *solea*, was manufactured in enormous quantities largely, no doubt, by slaves. But as we have positive evidence of unions of shoemakers, *solearii*, we know that they were also produced by free labor. The archæologist Marini, found at Rome a beautiful tablet [19] on which is engraved in unmistakable terms the name of the union and states that it was a *collegium saliarium baxearum*. This means that the members manufactured one particular kind of sandal or shoe—the *baxea* which was of a certain Greek pattern. In the Vatican is another mentioned by various authors,[20] which, however, does not so unmistakably represent a trade union. The Crispins, it is well-known, were a very powerful trade union of a later date, whose members carried with them a bigoted species of priestcraft. But as their existence is of so curious a character and their organization so secret, we have failed to find any genuine inscriptions. Their identity however has come down to us in history, and marks an era in the Christian religion, connecting it with labor and practically verifying its precepts by its commingling of the nobility with the proletariat, thus leveling all to one plane.

Diocletian was the tyrant who persecuted the early Christians. Under his reign two brothers—noblemen belonging to a *gens* family—were converted to religion. Their names, as the story goes, were Crispin and Crispinian. For a poor slave or freedman to embrace Christianity was not so much of an offense because he had no recognition, no family; but for a nobleman to forsake the worship of his ancestral *manes* and tutelary saints, abjure faith in the miraculous gods and goddesses who for unaccounted ages, by sea and land had presided over the destinies of men and had been believed in with an iron bound confidence and a terrorizing authority that left not a shimmering of option wherein to plant an independent

---

[19] Marini, *Atti*, I, p. 12
[20] See Orelli, *Inscriptionum Latinarum Collectio*, No. 4,213. Artes et opificia.

thought—such an offender was thought to deserve the punishment of death! These Crispins, therefore, having thus offended by embracing the new faith, were obliged to fly to Gaul, where, according to vague tradition, they settled at Soissons, preaching by day and shoemaking evenings, until in A. D. 287, they were executed by order of Maximian. They had first founded the order of Crispins which exists to this day. Many centuries afterwards, 1645, Crispins were chosen as the patron saints of a religio-industrial community at Paris—a secret order called the *freres cordonniers*—brother shoemakers. This secret order has had a varied experience. It was suppressed several times but grew again; and to-day the order of Crispins exists in the United States, and many other countries of the world, as a regular and genuine trade union of shoemakers.

There was also a union of soldiers' boot makers, *caligarii*, spoken of by Lampridius.[21] The archæologist Gruter[22] brought to light an inscription which may serve as proof. It commemorates the existence of a family of shoemakers who made such shoes, *sutores caligarii*, but is too brief, or at least the section of it which we have seen is too incomplete for a specimen to fix judgment upon. Another stone from Auximum is more elaborate but rendered vague by the endless abbreviations which the Latins seem to have been so fond of.[23]

Mommsen gives a long account of the Roman manner of dividing the unions into decurians, centurians[24] and other numbers, somewhat in the manner prescribed by king Numa, more than 600 years before Christ. This inscription alluded to refers to the centurians, and the division to which the union was allotted. Of the ordinary shoemakers, *sutores*, we do not find any inscriptions proving that they possessed trade organizations. Perhaps they were all slaves, as was the case with some trades. There are hopes, however, that more inscriptions may yet be discovered to prove that the *sutores* had their organization.

In Rome, as at the present time, it was fashionable to wear furs; and we also know that the furriers were organ-

[21] Lampridius, *Alexander Severus*, 33.
[22] Gruter, *Inscriptiones Totius Orbis Romanornm*, 649, 1.
[23] Orell., *Inscr. Lat. Coll.*, No. 3,868.
[24] Momm., *De Coll. et Sodal. Rom.*, Cap. II, p. 27–32.

ized into trade unions. The furriers were called *pelliones*. They were classed as innocent, and allowed the privilege of combination by a special clause in the code of Theodosius [25] and had numerous unions of the trade. Among other branches of the furriers were the fringe and border makers, *limbolarii*,[26] who trimmed ladies' dresses with furs or costly silk or laces. The *limbolarii* or fringers were connected with the ladies' head dressers on the one hand and *textores* and *textrices*, male and female weavers on the other. That they worked in the head dress or hat business is certain; but we are in the dark about the method and personnel of the hat manufacture for either sex.

A very remarkable and numerous trade union called *centonarii*, patchworkers and junkmen or ragpickers, crops out everywhere among the inscriptions. Near the ancient town of Como in Curia, Gruter[27] observed many queer inscriptions, among which are several which clearly indicate that at this *municipium* of Rome the rag pickers were numerous enough to get elected into the municipal offices. Indeed this is his own comment upon the matter. There is no ground for doubt about their being genuine trade unions, as the wording of the stone distinctly says: "*collegium centonariorum*." At Milan, the same great pioneer of the renaissance dragged forth another of these long forgotten witnesses of the ancient mode of living, to shed its light upon social science.[28] This led to further investigation, and Fabretti[29] from the same field brought out two other tablets of *centonarii* bearing equally good testimony. The centurian legion is mentioned upon one of them, and by this we are apprised of the fact that the law dividing the unions into tens, hundreds, etc., held good as far away as Milan in the extreme north of Italy.

Another, found at the ancient Mevaniola, is quoted by Orelli.[30] It is a slab of stone on which is inscribed the name of the president of the association. It is quite evident that these institutions had something to do with manufacture of rough articles of clothing if not also of any and everything they could pick up the makings for. If among all their col-

---
[25] Code *Theod.*, lib. XIII, tit. iv, leg. 2, *De Excusationibus Artificum*.
[26] Orell., *Inscr.*, No. 4,213.
[27] Gruter, *Inscr. Totius Orbis Romanorum*, Nos. 471, 5, 358, 6 and others
[28] Gruter, *Inscr. Totius Orbis Rom.*, 477, 1.
[29] Fabretti, *Explicatio*, p. 73, 72.
[30] Orell., *Inscr.*, No. 5,122, Collegium centonarirum Municipii Mevaniolae.

lections of rags picked up in the streets or obtained by beggary or otherwise in their wanderings by day, they found in their culling and sorting, material of mixed colors and qualities sufficient to make a coat, no matter how versicolored and *bizarre* it looked when finished, they set about cutting, patching and putting together the pieces, and of them creating a garment readily disposed of among the poor slaves and outcasts whose wretched lot it was often to work in sun and storm, heat and cold, without clothing, as naked as the gladiators who fought on the sands of the amphitheatres.

The immense number of inscriptions bearing record of these facts, affords proof of the formidable misery which poor despised humanity were obliged to suffer in ancient days. In proof of the position above stated, we have from Regium in Cisalpine Gaul a splendid stone containing over 100 words showing that the membership was allied to manufacturers, but of what sort is not given; that they had a temple of some kind of their own; and that they took an active part in public affairs by force of their organized numbers.[31]

We are inclined to the opinion that whoever investigates the subject of the ancient ragpickers from the numerous and unmistakable data already at command, will arrive at our conclusion that they were a sort of social jack-at-all-trades, undertaking in poverty, with limited means, and under many checks of social humiliation and contempt, any job that fell in their way by which they could make a living. Muratori exhibits in his enormous folio collection Nos. 563 2 and 564 1, of his *Thesaurus*,[32] two others, found at the town of Sentinum, a place in ancient Umbria, which, on the whole, adds little to the points already given.

In the Neapolitan museum is, or was a collection of bronze statues, statuettes, plaques and tablets, all conveying thoughts valuable to the study of ethnology—the Heraclian or Herculanean museum. Stored there is another interesting tablet of these *centonarii* or ragpickers. It was found by Fabretti, directly or indirectly, at Patavium.[33] According to Heineck it is very old.[34] Another from the *ager Co-*

[31] Orell., No. 4,133; Gruter, 1,101, 1 and Murator, 563, 1.
[32] Vide Orell., 4,134: "Similia decreta, nec minus verbosa, adulationisque plena."
[33] Fabretti. *Explicatio*, p. 485, 160.   [34] Heinec, *Antiqu.* p. 236.

mensis, classed by Orelli, among the societies of artisans is equally suggestive.[35] It is ascribed to Muratori, and is from Torcellum. Mommsen's great collection[36] contains another stone bearing an inscription of an Æsernian rag pickers' organization and Orelli gives a very fine specimen from Brixia, which he arranges with his *collegia, corpora et sodalicia*.[37] One that Orelli mixed up with his *Dii Immortales* seems to commemorate one of those unions, combining several kinds of labor under one set of rules.[38] When the monument was lettered the union had already existed 151 years. It is at Milan.

These things show how dear the union was to freedmen. We have already cited twelve of the evidences of a powerful organization of freedmen on Roman soil. There are over 40 more good specimens in the museums and other collections, and their record is made good for all time in the voluminous catalogues of Archæologists. The great number of inscriptions of the *centonarii*, or rag and old junk gatherers, in comparison with most other organized trades may be accounted for if we reflect that very many of the ancient lowly obtained their manumission late in life, after they had been worn out in toil, whose products had gone to their masters.

Manumissions were easily obtained at an advanced age because the owner of a man would be glad to free himself from the expense of maintaining him after he became old, decrepit and useless. Doubtless the owner often killed his ultra-aged slaves rather than accord them the boon called liberty to die in possession of. But we may be sure that such was ever the longing for freedom when offered the slave under whatsoever motive that he seldom refused to accept the gift, though its acceptance entailed all the anxieties and dangers of the precarious competitive struggle for existence. Assuming at an advanced age the responsibilities of life, he drifted into any labor, no matter how grovelling, and became the junk-man, rag-picker and patch-piecer; and with the mutual aid of his union succeeded in living happier in responsible independence than he was before in his irresponsible thraldom.

A second reason for their large numbers may be, that

[35] Orell., *Inscr*., No. 4070; Mur. *Theasaur*, 513, 3. See also Orell., No. 4071.
[36] Momm., *Inscr*., No. 5,060.   [37] Orell., *Inscr*., No. 7,201.
[38] Orell., *Inscr*., No. 1702.

many times no work could be found; consequently to obtain enough to live upon they took to picking what others threw away and found that by scouring the streets and alleys they could bring to their rag and junk markets sufficient to relieve the pinch of hunger, and with the otherwise unusable stuff, make fires to cook their food and warm themselves in winter.

The fact that these *centonarii* are found to have existed not only in Europe but throughout Asia, is a matter deeply suggestive to the student of ethnology. That they had already had their bands, and their bodies or *corpores* at the dawn of manumission from this primeval state of slavery there seems little doubt. The inscription that we cite from Orelli's catalogue[29] shows by its own words—the identical ones engraved in antiquity upon a piece of stone—that the union had existed *de facto* already 151 years. Further light is suggestively shed here, to the effect that the union had been able, traditionally or otherwise, to count the years of its age with precision.

These seemingly phenomenal things are cleared up when we come to discover that when the great wave of political antagonism to the growth and influence of organized labor struck backward and overwhelmed the unions which, as we have clearly shown by the inscription from the ruins of Pompeii, were able in some municipalities to elect their own superintendents of public works, a few were excepted with the proviso that they should keep themselves piously subject to the rules of the ancient religion, should fear and honor the *lares* of the gentile immortals and preserve their identity and their habitat by an inscription or register of each union in perfect accordance with the law. Provided with this inscription whereon was registered their habitat, the name of the deity they had chosen as their tutelary guardian, and the business which they professed as a means of existence, the law accorded them the right to organize, *jus coeundi*. But these regulations they must strictly observe; because they made it very convenient for the police whose duty it was to watch over them and report their behavior to senate and tribunes of the people.

Under the more ancient *jus coeundi* or right of combina-

---

[29] Orell., *Inscr.*, No. 1702, note 2 of explanation: "Collegii supra scripti anni 151, ex quo collegium isthoc constitutum fuerat."

tion into unions of trades and professions, it certainly, as proved by many inscriptions of the period of the emperors of Rome, could not have been obligatory that the unions should chisel out these lithoglyphs, so precious to us now. So when the law came, some of them searched back for their chronology and pedigree and had them inserted with the rest of the inscription. We know from abundant evidence that the oldest societies stood the best chance of escaping suppression. They were especially exempted by law. This exemption was based upon the respect for the laws and traditions of Numa, Solon and Tullius. The new societies, however, were looked upon with distrust; and it logically follows that if a *collegium, corpus* or *sodalicium* could prove its age by tracing its record back to a time anterior to the agrarian or servile troubles, it would have an almost certain chance of remaining unmolested.

We have enlarged upon this curious subject of the rag pickers with a view of preparing the mind of the reader with facts in regard to our theory—which we will admit to be original and unique—upon the origin of gypsies.

It is admitted that history has failed to record the origin, life and migrations of the gypsies. Of course everybody agrees both that they are a caste and that they are, so to speak, the pariah dogs of these later days; but everybody, upon reflection, also admits that they always were and still are organized. The fact is, their organization has always been exclusive and severe. Another fact always was and is, namely, that their language is Latin although mixed with Sanscrit and Greek; and this is the most incontrovertible stronghold to our suggestion that gypies are the still lingering, self-constituted, tribal relics of the archaic children of the great *gens* families of the Aryan race, both Asiatic and Indo-European.

We suggest that being outcasts of the *domus* or paternal home through the law of primogeniture, they served for unknown ages as slaves on the paternal estate; and at the dawn of the period of manumissions were among the first to form self-supporting, or mutually protective unions out of which the least qualified, most cunning and romantic never developed, but continued to pick up a living by petty theft, rag, junk and slop-gathering, horse-jockeying and piece-patching, warping their tongues to fit localities, and their ingenuity to all the cunning quibbles which characterize the competitive system. These we conjecture were the *centonarii* or rag pickers, whose compulsory inscriptions we study with wondering surprise. They are simply the fruit of the cruel condition of ancient society ; and the unique monument their name and shame have built must arrest the gaze of man, imparting to him a mournful lesson as he toils onward to the revolution.

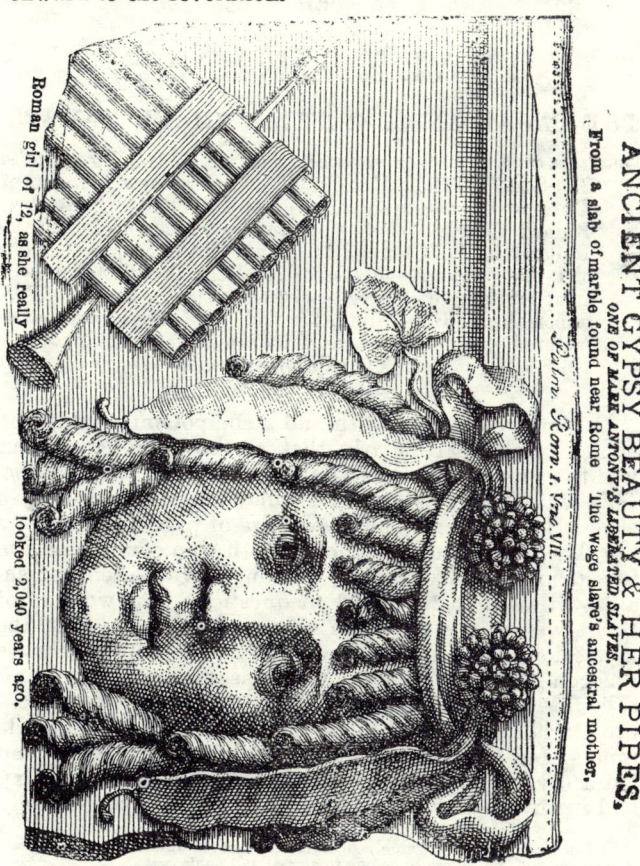

ANCIENT GYPSY BEAUTY & HER PIPES,
ONE OF MARK ANTONY'S LIBERATED SLAVES.
From a slab of marble found near Rome. The wage slave's ancestral mother.
Palm. Rom. I, Vae VII.

Roman girl of 12, as she really looked 2,040 years ago.

CHAPTER XIX.

TRADE UNIONS.

THE PAGAN AND CHRISTIAN IMAGE-MAKERS.

ORGANIZATIONS OF PEOPLE who worked for the Gods—Big and little God-Smiths—Their Unions object to the New Religion of Christianity because this, originally Repudiating Idolatry, Ruined their Business—Compromise which Originated the Idolatry in the Church of to-day—The *Cabatores*—Unions of Ivory Workers—Of *Bisellarii* or Deity-Sedan-Makers—Of Image-makers in Plaster—The *Unguentarii* or Unions of Perfumemakers—Holy Ointments and the Unions that manufactured them—Etruscan Trinketmakers—Bookbinders—No Proof yet found of their Organization.

DIRECTLY connected with and a component part of the ancient state, particularly that of the Indo-Europeans, was the great subject of the gods, *deorum immortalium*. This with them was no wild fancy but an institution so closely interwoven in all the affairs of public and private life that no person of patrician birth who could lay claim to a family[1] could possibly, without heresy often punishable with death, disregard or question. The worship of the *manes* at the domestic altar, and of the *penates*, the mysterious home of the *lares* and all the holy immortals was compulsory. All paganism was excessively, tyrannically, inexorably, cruelly, religious. It ignored the whole proletarian class; and most logically, according to its tenets; for they, possessing no family, no property, no paternity, could have no tutelary saint except by proxy and in an eleemosynary way, used by them superficially

---

[1] The proletaries or working people had no recognized family. To be born into an ancient family was to belong to a great and noble *gens.*

to flatter conscience,¹ and in all cases borrowed by them from the grandees, who sometimes permitted the loan of a family god² to act the sham of tutelary protector, and this sometimes out of mere contemptuous pity. But this archaic, aristocratic worship was in practice mechanical. Its temples, the work of the proletaries, were massive, often magnificent structures. Idols were numerous, some of them specimens of the finest sculptures the world ever produced. Its altars were solemn, massive and awful; its sepulchres, sarcophagi and mausoleums, striking in the solemnity of their incidents and surroundings; its little images and deities were visitants of every respectable household; its sacerdotal and sacrificial paraphernalia numerous and indispensable and the oracles and shrines of the aruspex and soothsayer had each to be adorned with furniture which best convenienced the cunning, flattery, superstition and makeshift of priestcraft.

All these things required tools to make them and were the product of skill and industry of the proletaries. Great numbers of these emblems of Pagan piety are preserved in the collections; and by them we know how to appreciate the methods of mechanics who produced them.

The *cabatores* had a union that made images of the greater gods. By this is probably to be understood, the most powerful immortals, Jupiter, Ceres, Vulcan and the like. They had their shops in Rome and Athens. If they were numerous we are without evidence of the fact; although their skill covered a considerable range. The *cabator* and the *imaginifex* made images of many kinds but the manner of their operations is obscure. We know more of their extent. The business of the former was to make the less elegant statues, reliefs, and perhaps pictures of the great deities; while the latter busied himself with the manufacture of the household and toy gods for which there was always a steady demand. In this manufacture of deities there was from the most ancient epoch of which we have data, enough demand to keep large

---

¹ Fustel, *Cité Antique*, livre II, *passim*.
² Mommsen, *De Collegiis et Sodalicits Romanorum*, p. 86: "Legibus collegii Dianæ et Antinoi et collegii Æsculapii et Hygiæ" Note 13, *Idem*, p. 78. "In familia Augustali multa collegia opificum fuisse." *Idem*, p. 10, *De Cultu Minervæ* "Nautes quidem accepit simulacrum, . . . Nautiorum familia sacra Minervæ retinebat."

numbers of mechanics employed. It grew with the numbers of the human race, and increased as human taste for luxury increased. Belief did not perceptibly change. Socrates, Plato, Aristotle, even Anaxagoras and Diogenes worshiped the immortal gods whose emblems, statuettes, and profiles adorned not only the temples but the residences of all respectable citizens. Such images, liable to accident and decay, had to be replenished or repaired, and the labor required to do this gave the incentive of organization.

We shall show in another chapter, that on the introduction of the Christian faith at Rome in after years, one of the objections most vigorously raised against the new doctrine was, not that it would interfere with them in point of conscience, but that it would interfere adversely to their means of earning bread! It threatened to sap the fountain of economic existence. The early Christians wanted no idols. The image-makers who wrought holy emblems out of wood, brass, gold, pearl and sometimes of amber and the precious gems, gained a living by their trade; and consequently, Christianity, however it might otherwise please their sense of mutual love, of equality, fraternity and freedom, yet so long as it threatened their means of livelihood in the slightest degree they opposed it with every effort within their reach; whereupon a share of the Pagan idolatry was bargained for, sufficient to restore the manufacture of images and idols. Then working people, always prone to accept, threw away their objections and embraced the new religion in such numbers and with such zeal that the old religion began to dissolve, and in course of a few centuries crumbled to the dust, while the workman's craft of image-making continues to this day.

Of the most celebrated idol manufacturers, Phidias, perhaps stands foremost. Like all proletaries his family is unknown. No blooded historian could taint the noble prestige with a line enlightening mankind upon his pedigree; and writers of his own class, there were none. His superlative genius, however, wrote his history in the exquisite images of Athena, in the great works on the Propylæa of the acropolis and the Parthenon, wrought by his combined imagination and chisel. Ivory and gold

GENIUS IN SHRINE MANUFACTURE. 431

entered into this last chryselephantine colossus; and his adornment of Olympia with the statue of Jupiter as a virgin goddess signalized his age by an exhibit of the mechanical in the most exquisite and costly details. Pericles the renowned optimate and politician, stood in astonishment and admiration before this workingman's genius and originality.

Myron, the cotemporary and celebrated rival of Phidias, could sculpture a quoit-player, a cow or a god with equal perfection. His Hercules, his Jupiter and his Minerva were so perfect that Roman warriors in capturing them were captured by them. When, afterwards, Lysippus, Praxiteles, Scopas and a great many others adorned this art with perfection it never had before or since, it became a trade at which many thousands earned a living,

Great schools of image-making flourished in Greece and Rome from times long anterior to Phidias. The Etruscans had schools of idol manufacture conducted, as in Greece, by the proletaries or working people. Once when the Romans beat them in battle and at the siege took Volsinii nearly 300 years before Christ, about 2,000 holy images and statues were a part of the trophies of victory. The Etruscans were hard working, faithful people who had trade unions in great numbers. Some of these were image-makers; and they well knew how to live and profit upon the superstitions which thus attached to the Pagan faith.

While Rome produced few image-makers of brilliancy she patronized enormously the manufacture of all sorts of holy trinkets. The household from the earliest times was the true patron, and ladies bought many little imitations of gods and goddesses together with an endless variety of sacerdotal paraphernalia, such as suited their fancy as to merit and price.

Orelli gives us an inscription of a genuine union of the *bisellarii*, who manufactured the great sacerdotal seat or chair; a splendidly finished and richly upholstered tête à tête for the gods.[4] There were also signs either of unions or private business of persons working ivory, *ebu-*

---
[4] *Inscriptionum Latinarum Collectio*, No. 4,137, note 1, also Gruter, *Inscriptionnm Totius Orbis Romanorum*, 12, 8, and Muratori, *Thesaurus Veterum Inscriptionum*, 544, 1.

rarii. The inscriptions are given by Orelli.[5] But we have more positive evidence of a trade union of ivory workers in a direct mention of them as such in the Justinian code which provided for them the right to organize and labor in the holy cause.[6]

The evidences indicate that the *tectoriolae* or little plaster images of which Cicero[7] and others have made mention, were the work of the *albarii*.[8] An inscription found at Rome and published by Gruter,[9] appears to signify by its reading that the business was managed by one C. Ateius Philadelphus but gives no clue to warrant that he was managing officer of a trade union of the plasterers' craft.

Besides the wonderful chryselphantine ivory workers belonging to the great school of Phidias, already mentioned, there were the *eburarii*, who, as we have already stated, were fortified by a law in the code of Justinian, and were excepted in the late statutes on trade unions.[10] These craftsmen made little statuettes, symbols, ivory chains, variously shaped charms and talismans propitiatory of the gods. They for this purpose carried on a considerable trade with the Africans and Phœnicians whereby to obtain pure and delicate ivory. Indeed, the superstition inculcated by the ancient religion led to a veritable industry which through many a long century furnished bread to these mechanics and their families.

Orelli,[11] gives an inscription of an association or genuine trade union of the gods' bed makers, or *pulvinarii*.[12] They were organized under the society name of *sodalicium* which Cicero characterized as low and mean; but we presume that as in this case their calling was to manufacture the elegantly upholstered couches and silk embroidered sleeping furniture of the mighty immortals, the piety and solemnity which enveloped their workshops rescued them from the rigors of the conspiracy laws which Cicero and

---

[5] Orell., *idem*, Nos. 4,180 and 4,302.
[6] Cod., *Justiniani*, x, 64, 1.
[7] Cic., *Fam.*, 9, 22, 3.
[8] Tertulian, *De Idololatria*, cap. viii. This author, however, admits that besides images placed in the walls, the *albarii* did several other kinds of plaster work.
[9] Gruter, *Inscr. Tot. Orb.*, 642, 11.
[10] Orell., Nos. 4,180, 4,302.
[11] *Inscriptionum Latinarum Collectio*, No. 4,061.
[12] We say "genuine" in cases where we find full approval as to their genuineness. Orelli, Fabretti, Muratorius, etc., are high authority.

Cæsar instituted for their extinction. Another inscription was registered by Oderic, of these couch makers.[13] It says that one Julius Epaphra was a fruit seller, formerly *pulvinarius* who worked at the couch makers' trade furnishing them for the great circus; and Orelli cites Suetonius to show that such seats or couches were common at the games although their usurpation by the grandees did not please.[14]

We close our section on the image-makers with the *unguentarii* or perfumers. The reader by this time begins to see that in reality all these fine things "fit for the gods," which were manufactured by the unions in such quantities, were appropriated and used by the rich who in thus usurping or assuming what was destined for immortals, substituted themselves therefor; and in that way threw a halo of glory around themselves and their great, inapproachable *gens* families. The whole of it was a sort of self-deification, using political priestcraft to puff their vanity, inflame their egoism, and widen the chasm which forbiddingly yawned between them and the proletarian classes.

These fine things, so pleasing to the sense of feeling and vision were not enough. They also required something to gratify the olfactory sense; and perfumes of the richest kind were manufactured for them. There were unions in considerable numbers who did this work. At Capua before and during the servile war of Spartacus, there were perfumery factories which were celebrated all over Italy. The perfumers can scarcely be called image-makers, but their art completed the category of delicacies and amplified the means of satisfying the voluptuous cravings of the enormously wealthy. Their perfumes were used in the temples, and at the sacrifices. They were esteemed at feasts and were used in dress. At the great circus, and afterwards the coliseum, the reserved seats of the grandees were known by their aroma.

The perfumers were not only workers but also merchants; and necessarily, because they had to carry on a considerable traffic with the east and south to obtain

---

[13] Oderic, *Inscriptiones*, p. 74.
[14] "Spectare cum circenses ex pulvinari non placet nobis." Suetonius, *Claudius*, 4.

IMAGE-MAKERS.

gums, spices, nuts, seeds and other raw material for their products. The perfumers or *unguentarii* also had similar unions in Athens and Corinth where they carried on a considerable business. There are found quite a number of inscriptions of different kinds of these workmen and their societies. One archæologist cites an inscription found in Rome, upon which there has been some comment made, arising from a disagreement about its exact meaning.[15] Publicius Nicanor, was a perfumer on the Via Sacra, and one Maximus Accensus, was one of the members of the union whose duty was to do up the goods. Most probably it was a union of perfumers chartered under the names of two foremen, or one foreman and one director as was customary in order to comply with the law. Marini[16] cites another inscription showing that these prominent officers were females, or at least one of them. The slab was found in Naples. Orelli[17] has an inscription found by Gruter at Venusia in Lucania, which celebrates the setting free of a bondsman and family, by the father, out of the money obtained as proceeds of the perfumery business. His name was Philargyrus, a perfumer. This was probably a private business of the Augustine period. The marble is broken here, leaving us with this conjecture.

All the image-makers and perfumers' trades were countenanced and provided for by King Numa who believed that religion was a thing most proper to cultivate. He further believed that it was impious to wage war; or at any rate, to risk the chances of war lest the sacred temples and altars be desecrated by its ravages. Thus from a high antiquity, and largely out of respect to the memory and works of this king, the image-makers were classed as the futherers of the holy cause and exempted from many of the restrictions and persecutions which in later times became the source of bloodshed.

There was a regular trade society of the pearl fishers, *margaritarii*,[18] who, it appears, communicated with the

---

[15] Donati, *Roma, Vetus et Recens*, p. 327, 51. It is also mentioned by Muratori, *Thesaurus, Veterum Inscriptionum*.
[16] *Atti*, 2, p. 516. *De Unguentariis*. [17] Orell., 2,988.
[18] Orell., *Inscriptionum Latinarum Collectio*, Nos. 1,602, 4,076 4,218. One of these, No. 4,076 is a genuine trade union. No. 4,218 comes under the title of *Artes et Opifica*, leaving it questionable as to its having been a private business.

workshops in the cities, which their labor supplied with pearls in the rough. Diving and scraping in the distant waters for pearls was, at the starting point of this precarious business, a trade which to render successful, nee led to be fortified by a federation with the inlayers and other pearl finishers working at home. Much of this pearl was used in decorating the images which the demands of an idolatrous faith places upon the market; and by thus furnishing labor, gave bread to the working people. On a superficial view, the fact that the great artists, such a Phidias, Myron, Polycletus, Alcamenes of the heroic school of Ageladas, or the still more versatile school of a few years later of which Lysippas, Praxiteles and Scopas were the heroes, we do not find the pearl industry to have extensively entered into the composition of the great sculptures. But we must remember first, that the descriptions are defective, and next, that the originals are lost.[19] We know that pearls were used in archaic times. If they entered into the composition of idols—and there seems to be no ground for doubt of this—it must probably have been by inla   g.

Great skill was required in the whole pearl business. Among the Etruscans and Romans the art turned rather toward the trinket manufacture. Many of the little gods of the household, emblems, talismans, mementos and charms were gemmed with pearls. Of course, these things, at this late period, if dug from the ruins, would fail to discover the perishable pearls; because the delicate carbonate crumbles with moisture, neglect and time.

We find a few dim accounts of book-gluers mixed up with the amanuenses or scribes. They acted the part, so to speak, of the modern printers. These, together with poets, teachers and persons engaged in medicine and surgery, were always, or nearly always, of lowly birth.[20]

[19] A more thorough ransacking of this subject may bring to light much of value regarding the unions of image-makers who inscribed their record in the Greek tongue.

[20] Guhl and Kohner, *Life of the Greeks and Romans*, p 526. "Three classes amongst the slaves and freedmen, held a distinguished position by their intellectual accomplishments, viz: the *medici. chirurgi* and *literati*," s to the literati, *idem*, p. 529 we quote as follows: "We have already mentioned the *literati*, cultivated slaves, generally of Greek origin, who had to copy books or write from dictation. By these slaves manuscripts were copied with astounding celerity, with the aid of abbreviations called, from their inventor, Ti , a freedman of Cicero, Tironian notes. These copies, sometimes full of mistakes went to the shops of the bookseller *(bibliopola)*, unless these kept copyists in their own

Gluers, *glutinatores*, are spoken of by Cicero.[21] That they were numerous is evident from the large amount of work required of this kind. The great histories of ancient writers were copied times without number and some of them were bound in boards or leather or cloth with much art and taste. It is, however, beyond our power, as yet to discover whether the book-binders possessed a trade organization. The fact that most of the other trades had unions renders it probable that they also were organized, and it is possible that inscriptions may yet be discovered revealing the fact.

shops. Numerous copies were thus produced in little time. The satirical writings of Ovidus, Propertius and Martialis were in everybody's hands, as were also the works of Homer and Virgil, the odes of Horace, and the speeches of Cicero; grammars, anthologies, etc., for schools, were reproduced in the same manner; indeed, the antique book-trade was carried on on a scale hardly surpassed by modern times." Much is taken from Pliny, *Natural History*, lib. XXIX, *init*.

[21] Cicero, *Ad Atticum*, liber, IV. c. iv. 1. See also Orell., *Inscriptionum Latinarum Collectio*, No. 2,925, 4,198. *Glutinarius*, the inscription is on an elegant tomb inside of a vault, according to Gruter, copied by Orell., *Artes et Opificia*, Vol. II. p. 293. See bookbinding, Ed. Bevan. **Series of British Manufactory Industries, (Article by Freeman Wood, pp. 70-94).**

ANCIENT SCULPTURED IMAGE FOUND ON A BROKEN STONE, AGE ABOUT B. C. ...... *Palm. Rom. viv IX.*

CHAPTER XX.

TRADE UNIONS CONCLUDED.

THE TAX-GATHERERS. FINAL REFLECTIONS.

UNIONS OF COLLECTORS—A Vast Organized System with a Uniform and Harmoniously Working Business—Trade Unions under Government Aid and Security—The *Ager Publicus* of Rome—True Golden Age of Organized Labor—Government Land—A prodigious Slave System their Enemy—Victims of the Slave System—Premonitions on the Coming of Jesus—Demand by His Teachings for Absolute Equality.

JUDGING from all the records within our reach, it was Numa who first recognized the necessity of regularly organized trades unions for express purposes of purveying goods of every kind, in a systematic manner. He was a strictly business man; and the most important business has ever been that of getting the means of life. In addition to the federated trades there had to be the tax collectors; otherwise the expenses of the government could not be defrayed. For this, there was a set of workmen, whose express business was to traverse city and country with their credentials from the regularly chartered union of the *Vectigalaria* or tax collectors. There were, at that early time, no such arrangements as now exist, by which the government did its own work of this kind. A labor guild or union did this work. We have evidence showing that the men going on their rounds collecting the taxes, were sometimes severe, even brutal to the poor farmers, forcing them to comply with the requirements of the law.

Of the branches into which king Numa distributed the

working people we have already spoken elsewhere, representing them as they appear to us from evidence, through a long vista covering what we, for our own scheme of reasoning, term the golden age because the workmen thrived. Meantime we are well aware that the so-called Golden Age of Rome, is reckoned between the years 250 and 14 before Christ; but this calculation is made by historians of the competitive system, and befits itself to conquest and literature, not to the progress of social prosperity. It actually begins about the time this social and economical prosperity had reached its zenith. We cannot admit the Golden Age of Rome to have begun at so late a date. From a well sought point of view of sociology this era began with the recognition, by the law of Numa, of the right of free organization; and the laborers' methodical assumption of the business of supplying the people with the means of life. This was the true golden age of Rome; and as it also covers the largest part of the era ordinarily admitted to have been the golden age, including the great period of Roman conquest and the splendid era of literature, it only varies in having commenced 670, instead of 250 years before Christ.

If it was necessary for the scheme of Numa to have the public lands formed by the guilds or societies of practical agriculture it was also as necessary for him to institute some reliable means of collecting the fruits of this labor and distributing them among those whom the law recognized as the true owners. We have had abundant evidence that among the ancient Indo-European Aryans, no persons except those born to an inheritance possessed the right of owning the public domain. Even the patricians who were the privileged class, and the makers of the laws, did not, until a comparatively late date, attempt to get personal possession of the *ager publicus* of Italy. The plebeians who were the only workers, never owned any land. The state owned the land and the proletaries worked it. The fruits of the lands had to be brought to the people. What is meant by the state ownership, in ancient law, is citizen ownership—the state holding it in common for the citizens. But who were the citizens? It certainly was not the working people, who were the outcasts, the descendants of the slaves, or the slaves themselves. They owned nothing and could own nothing. But their function was to do the work; and Numa permitted them to organize and do the work socially or in common.

After the harvest the grain had to be distributed among the citizens who, according to the law, were the owners of the land, the state holding it for them in trust. The workers were always obliged to recognize their lowly condition, and were always glad to get enough of what they produced to keep them alive.

The plan instituted whereby to collect these products and distribute them among the privileged citizens and others, was organization of the *vectigalarii* or collectors of incomes, who did this work through a system of societies. The society had a manager or principal overseer, *procurator*, and was also supplied with a *quaestor* or inspector, who was perhaps the chief clerk. Then came sometimes a secretary, a treasurer and foremen and the working hands, all of whom constituted the membership of the union or commune. The old name of the secretary was sometimes set down in the inscriptions found by the antiquaries, as *cornicularius*,[1] which signified that the secretary had risen to the place by promotion. It appears from the numerous inscriptions cut in stones, that these customs collectors had societies or unions all over the provinces under Roman domination.[2] At Lyons, after the conquest of Cæsar, there were several of them.[3] Their work was to collect the proceeds of the harvests. Others collected the products of the manufactories: others the proceeds of the fisheries. Even the proceeds of the brothels were collected and distributed in money.[4] All the multiform labor of collecting had to be done, and the state made it obligatory upon the customs-unions to do their work well. This accounts for Granier's[5] remark

---

[1] Later an assistant secretary, Cod. *Theodosii*, VII. 4, 32.
[2] See Orell., *Inscriptionum Collectio*, 6,642. *Vectigalia* and many others.
[3] Boissean, *Inscription de Lyon*, VII. 25, p. 272, found one which reads as follows: "Memoriæ Aurelii Ceciliani præpositus. Vectigalium posuit Epictatus Alumnus—Lugduni." Meaning that Epic the apprentice inscribed the slab to the honor of the director one Aurelius Cecil, in Lyons.
[4] Sänger. *History of Prostitution; Rome*, p. 68: "The *Prostibulæ* (strangers not organized) paid no tax to the state; while their registered rivals (organized *meretrices*, see p. 66 *idem*), contributed largely to the municipal treasury." *Greece*, 48. "Any speculator had a right to set up a *dicterion* by paying the tax to the state."
[5] *Histoire des Classes Ouvrières*, chap. xiv. *Ancient Trade Unions and Their Development*.

that these customs collectors were sometimes brutal to the poor farmers whose unions failed to garner as much as the law required.* It is evident that the collectors had to put themselves in direct business relation with the union of *vectuarii* or teamsters; as they more frequently took the produce itself than the money. Their practice was to supply the citizens, not so much with the money these proceeds of labor were worth, but with the proceeds themselves.†

The trade unions were recognized by the state and held responsible to the state for their work. If in conveying the grain from the farms to Rome, the wagon was attacked by mountaineer brigands and the goods lost, the citizens, who were the state, held, not the teamsters but the whole union responsible. In almost all cases, however, the produce of the *ager publicus* was transmitted to Rome by sea.

For instance; a certain quota of the province of Aquitania, or the neighboring province of Lugdunensis, where are found many relics of these societies, is claimed at Rome. Lugdunum or Lyons was connected by water every step of the way to Rome. The society at Lyons sent the grain down the river Rhone by barges to the Mediterranean. At Arles, a ship took it on board and consigned it to Ostia, the mouth of the Tiber and port of Rome. Now the barges of the Tiber had to belong to a union. So there were unions of bargers, *caudicarii*. The first society guaranteed the safe arrival of the grain as far as the mouths of the Rhone, *Ora Rhodani*. Here were the ships of another society to further convey it to the port of Rome, so hither it had to be conveyed on board a ship. Thus is seen why the seafaring men also must have an organization; otherwise, if the ship was lost, captain, crew and cargo, there would remain nobody responsible; and the citizens would be the sole sufferers. It became necessary therefore, since the government had jobbed out one part of this business to a commune, that it do the same thing in their case, because the rich citizens who were to be fed by labor, though, personifying government, could legislate or conduct war, could not *work;* because upon it there was a taint. So the order of the *navi-*

---

* Dionysius of Halicarnassus, book V. chap. 43, explains the power of the law permitting and furthering these organizations.
† Granier. *Histoire des Classes Ouvrières*, chap. xiv. Much additional information may be obtained by reading this valuable chapter of M. Granier's work.

cudarii existed; and being chartered by government, was made responsible for the loss of any cargo. When the cargo arrived at Ostia, the mouth of the Tiber, sixteen miles from Rome, it was conveyed to the granaries of the city by the societies of boatmen, known as *caudicarii*, bargemen, under guarantee, precisely in the same manner as in former cases. Thus for the least possible trouble and with utmost security, the government or non-laboring citizens got the greatest possible amount of produce from the *ager publicus*, or common land. Yet the people who labored were satisfied and thrived better than they were ever known to thrive under any system, because their industry produced enormously and their strong arms made labor easy, agreeable and safe.

Now the customs collectors or *vectigalarii* were interested in all these details of supply; because the government looked to them directly or indirectly for everything the citizen population had to live upon from year to year.

But the supply of grain, wine, oil and other agricultural products was not all these tax collectors had to attend to. There were many artisan societies. These we have treated separately and in regular order, according to their importance. They all had more or less to do with the tax or customs collectors, with whom they were interlinked in the great social bond. Sometimes, as in the case of the pork butchers union,* there were officers appointed whose business was to go personally, or send, into the stock farm country and collect the tax either in money or in kind. This would, of course, entail an immense amount more labor than that attached to butchery. It would entail the whole business of the drover. Weighing would require much attention and an inspection of all the various operations of several vocations.

Slabs have been found to the number of 262, bearing inscriptions of the *vectigalia*, of different dates, ranging mostly from the time of the first Cæsars to that of the emperor Constantine. These 262 include only those registered by Orelli in his work on the Roman Antiquities. Great numbers of those unions probably existed of which no record

---

* Granier, whose researches into these societies and the laws governing them reveal an astonishing versatility and accuracy, says that very many, if not all the commercial trades had officers, whose work was to oversee the customs collections. See *idem*, pp. 310–315. There was a Boatmen's insurance mentioned by Livy xxiii. cap. 44. Beckmann, *Hist. of Inventions*, (Bohn) I. p. 284. (Caudicarii).

was kept, and antiquaries of the future may yet reveal more. On the whole these facts regarding inner workings of the ancient human family present a picture of deep interest, revealing as they do a system of industry unique in its method of supplying the great population of Rome at that time containing probably about 2,000,000 inhabitants[9] and its numerous *municipia* or provincial cities and town with means of life. The *vectigalia* evidently covered more of the immense business of those times than the ordinary reader would ascribe to them. Orelli,[10] speaks of iron miners who sometimes interlinked with the mines situated at great distances from the city; yet it would appear by this mention that the miners far away in the mountains and perfectly organized, were in close and systematic, if not happy mutual communication with the forgers' association stationed at Rome.

The most remarkable part of the system was that it was government work; that the work was performed by trade unions instead of isolated individuals as in the competitive system; and that during many centuries through which this system existed, both in war and peace, the ancient working people were prosperous and happy. Of course, this organization does not apply in any form to slaves. This terrible scourge of the human race still existed; but there are strong proofs that the trade unions were at one time making inroads upon the slave system which required care by the masters and slave owners in order to conduct business; whereas the trade union system endorsed by king Numa lifted all the troublesome details and responsibilities from the shoulders of the patricians who regarded individual labor as a disgrace. Labor being a humiliation to the propertied class who managed the government land but did not perform the actual work, it was a matter of convenience for them to have trade unions. The state, then, was their great patron and protector. Rich individual slave owners like Crassus or Cicero or Nicias could job out their slaves' labor to persons of enterprise, but the very pride of their blood prevented them from undertaking any except the noble en-

---

[9] Consult Dr. Beloch. *Bulletin de Statisque de l'Institute International*, tome, I. année 1886, p. 62 sqq. *Roma.*

[10] Roman antiquities, No. 1,239 vectigalia ferrariorum also **ferrifodinarii.** See also Mur. 972, 10. The inscr. reads: "D. M. Primonis ferrariariorum vitalis contuber." Found at the mines of Nimea.

terprises of war and politics. There was nobody to compete with the unions and the state became their great employer. But we have seen in our account of strikes and uprisings that human cupidity, taking advantage of the slave system and by means of it, grasping, holding and tilling the *ager publicus*, finally destroyed the public trade unions.

That the trade union or social system was good there seems to be no ground for doubt; but the workman being stamped by the old religio-political jealousy of paganism which branded him as a wretch, preventing him from taking political action, whereby to secure and fortify his system, gave the grandees all the advantage because they made the laws. When, therefore, the unions found that they must exercise their political power, which they did in later times, it was too late. They were themselves too deeply tinged with the deadly, unmanly sense that their masters were superior to them by birth. There had been no Christ to boldly declare a new state of things based upon absolute equality by birth and natural rights of all men. Seeing the encroachments upon themselves as well as upon the public lands their sole source of raw material, the trade unions tardily fell into the struggle, learned to wrestle valiantly, suffered a more pronounced hatred of their masters, grew in self-dignity but gradually lost in vested rights, forced up a great social struggle but incurred the deep-rooted hatred of Cicero and Cæsar, grew poorer, more numerous, more secret, vindictive and conniving and wrought up a spirit all over Greece, Rome, Judea and the provinces, which rendered possible the kindling of that marvelous revolution that destroyed the identity of ancient paganism.

But there is one thing our researches fail to discover. We do not find clear and sufficient evidences of a system of agricultural communes. These may have existed. We are in doubt. Everything else was organized. Where is this missing link? Had it existed, would not the great trade union system have grown so complete as to gradually obtain the ascendency, political as well as industrial and thus been able to realize thousands of years ago, the revolution?

CHAPTER XXI.

ROMANS AND GREEKS.

THE COUNTLESS COMMUNES.

Unions Of Romans and Greeks compared—Miscellaneous Societies of Tradesmen—Shipcarpenters—Boatmen—Vesselmakers—Millers—Organization of the *Lupanarii*—Of the Ancient Firemen—Description of the Greek Fraternities—The *Eranoi* and *Thiasoi*—Strange Mixture of Piety and Business—Trade Unions of Syria and North Palestine—Their Officers—Membership and Influence of Women—Large Numbers of Communes in the Islands of the Eastern Mediterranean—Their Organizations Known and Described From their Inscriptions.

All antiquity was at one time a hive of trade unions. Nearly every species of business was organized. Especially was this the case in southern Italy, where Plato found a system of communism extensively prevailing, supposed by some to have been planted there by Pythagoras.[1] The early inhabitants of the Italian peninsula were well acquainted with trade unionism; and traces of it, if not mentioned are discernable in history and this fact stands as the fundamental solution to many of the otherwise incomprehensible things which have puzzled modern historians. Nevertheless the nobility and its laws of primogeniture reigned in circles of politics and power. Plato is known to have visited Italy several times in search of material for his ideal state. He was, however, so much of an aristocrat, or so enslaved by his environments that he signally failed to give

---

[1] Drumann, *Arbeiter und Communisten in Griechenland und Rom*, somewhere remarks that Pythagoras and Numa were not only contemporaries but personal friends. If so, we cannot wonder that Numa befriended the trade unions.

the world the benefit of his communistical lucubrations. The nearest he could possibly get to a decent government was to one of bosses, policemen and slaves, and the sociologist of our day is forced to drop Plato with a species of chagrin or disgust. Aristotle did better; but both were aristocrats, enslaved to great men of wealth. Both Solon and Numa, long before them had planted the real, practical government which the world is at this moment following. Though Aristotle could analyze the course the world should and does take, yet he was too Pagan-bound to see beyond the galling bands of slavery.

The *Fabri navalium*, ship carpenters and boat makers, of the Tiber had well regulated unions which were considered among the most respectable of the organizations. These Associations were found along the banks of the navigable rivers and the coasts of the sea on both sides of the peninsula and also in Sicily.

Of the boatmen's unions, *collegia naviculariorum*, the greater number, according to our evidence, were to be found in the country. There could not have been many boatmen at Rome; but we have a mention, among others, by the great jurist Gaius, who speaks of them in discriminating the right of organization in later times.[2] The unions of boatmen were naturally confined to the sea shores. We might speak of them as possibly connected directly or indirectly with the lawless boatmen who swarmed the sea from Naples to Syracuse, and whom Plutarch says Spartacus found to be treacherous, without principles and looking only for grain. Even to this day the Mediterranean is lined with them from Gibralter to Barcelona and thence to Toronto. At Genoa and Nice and on the Baltic, they are still well organized and take advantage of every opportunity to gain a lira by fair means and in all their methods to attain this end are thoroughly sustained by one another, as they enjoy all the mutually assisting quirks known to their union.

The *collegium vasculariorum*[3] (metal vessel makers), was, of course, a union of potters; but it appears their art was mostly, if not quite confined to manufacturing vessels in

---

[2] Gaius, *Digest*, 1, III. 4, "Item collegia Romæ certa sunt, quorum corpus sanctis coll. atque constitutionibus principalibus confirmatum est, veluti pistorum et quorundam aliorum et naviculariorum et in provinciis sunt."

[3] An old inscription mutilated by age and ill usage reads: "P. Monetius sociorum libert s Philogenes vasculari s Veturia C. l. salvia sibei et sueis." (See Fabretti, *Inscriptionum Antiquarum Explicatio*, 632, 276.)

metals. The *vascularii* were skilled workmen. They often wrought beautiful urns in bronze and other material. Some of the delicately chiseled *amphorae* having two handles were of their workmanship, although most *amphorae* were made of potters' clay. Many vessels in gold were the work of their hands. They are known to have realized well by virtue of their trade union; because their patrons were largely the proud *gens* who were not stingy about the amount of cost, if they could have their æsthetic tastes gratified.

The *collegium pistorum*, union of millers, who ground grain in mortars and afterwards in mills, was also a trade organization. This trade was a very important one, as it furnished the *farines* for the family use of all who could affored to eat wheat flour or any of the cereals, course or fine. When we further take into account that it required at least seventy men to grind as much grain in a given time as is now ground in a steam mill by a single man, we may realize that in Rome and vicinity there must have been several thousand workmen constantly employed at this handicraft in order to produce enough to supply the demand. It must not be forgotten, however, that there were many people at Rome and everywhere, and from the earliest times, too poor to enjoy bread and who were obliged to subsist on peas, roots and other cheap food.[4] Nevertheless the millers were numerous, and being organized, they succeeded in competing with slave labor and got considerable of the work to do as a free industry.

Originally or in the remotest antiquity, all such work was done by slaves on the paternal estate, under the eye of the *paterfamilies* or head of the family; but when those degraded slaves became numerous and began to think for themselves, as we have previously seen, they secured manu-

---

[4] Feeding the laboring class poor food is of early record. Herodotus (*Euterp* 125) expressly tells how cheap fed were laborers who built the great Egyptian monuments. They were glad to get onions, garlic and roots. The same paragraph explains the cost of their living: " Σεσήμανται δὲ διὰ γραμμάτων Αἰγυπτίων ἐν τῇ πυραμίδι, ὅσα ἔς τε συρμαίην καὶ κρόμμυα καὶ σκόροδα ἀναισιμώθη τοῖσι ἐργαζομένοισι· καὶ ὡς ἐμὲ εὖ μεμνῆσθαι τὰ ὁ ἑρμηνεύς μοι ἐπιλεγόμενος τὰ γράμματα ἔφη ἑξακόσια καὶ χίλια τάλαντα ἀργυρίου τετελέσθαι." Still earlier, Homer, (*Odyssy*, XIV. 414, 415, 416,) says:

"Ἄξεθ' ὑῶν τὸν ἄριστον, ἵενα ξείνῳ ἱερεύσω
Τηλεδαπῷ πρὸς δ' αὐτοὶ ὀνησόμεθ', οἵπερ ὄιζὺν
Δὴν ἔχομεν πάσχοντες ὑῶν ἕνεκ' ἀργισδόντων."

Shows that the poor fed on pork. See Guhl and Konor, *Life of the Greeks and Romans*, p. 501 for the later Roman food. Virgil, *Eclogue*, II. v. 9, 10. parsely smallage and onions; So Horace, *Ad Pisonem*; V. 249; " Nec si quid fricti cicari probat et nucis emptor." Pliny, XXVI. 3.

missions and thus the trade unionists were mostly freedmen who had the sagacity to organize. The advantages in those days, of a good, sound, business-like union for each trade must have been very great; especially so, as their unions were communistical, and used as means of convivial enjoyment, as well as for economic ends.

Of the *collegium incendarium*, or firemen's association mention is made by Mommsen, who wonders why they should be suppressed; since burial and firemen's societies were among those saved.[5]

The *collegium Vinariorum*, (wine dealers and wine vaulters) was an institution of later date than Numa, who did not encourage wine drinking. If there are data extant regarding them at so early a time, we have failed to find them. During the time of the emperors, however, they were the subject of discussion as to whether they should be suppressed or exempted.[6] The *collegium lupanariorum* (brothel keepers), as is seen in the passage here cited, was an institution well known in the later ages of the Roman empire and two centuries before Christ there were secret associations of the lupanarii,[7] of which an account has gone into[8] history. These were curious products of the mania for organization that must have existed at Rome. But it must be remembered that the whole plebeian class of inhabitants were out in the cold, competitive world, and depending each upon his or her trade or profession which he or she considered right, so long as it was patronized by the elegant people of the other class who had social as well as political institutions upon which they could base a guaranty of safety.

During a visit in Europe we became indebted to Mr. Henry Tompkins of the Friendly Societies' Registration at London, from whose hand was first received a copy of his pamphlet on the Friendly Societies of Antiquity. We also made the personal acquaintance of Professors Vogt, Errera, Huber, Vigano and many others who referred us to volumes

[5] "Ut enim senatus e. g. et funerum causa et incendiorum jus coeundi reliquerit, qua ratione vetiti sunt, ii qui funerariae cohortis intererant incendiorum causa societatem inire?" (Mommsen, *De Collegiis et Sodaliciis Romanorum*, p. 89).

[6] Corpora omnium constituit vinariorum lupanariorum caligariorum et omnio omnium artium bisque ex sese decensores dedit et jussit quid ad quos judices pertinerit. (Lamprid, Alex. Severus, c. 33).

[7] See Sanger's *Hist. of Prostitution*, p. 66.

[8] Livy, XXXIX. 8-19.

of Drumann, Foucart, Wescher, Lüders, Mommsen, De Broglie and others. It is through the great labors of such men that the modern students of the labor movements are made aware of what wonders in the social problem were wrought in antiquity. But their evidence is nearly all derived from the silent inscriptions upon slabs, urns and sarcophagi that survive the corroding vicissitudes of the sad centuries. In fact the industry of the archæologists may yet reveal as valuable contributions to the science of sociology as the fossil diggers have revealed to their branch of paleontology. It is now made certain from multitudes of inscriptions which have weathered the storms of more than two thousand years, that great numbers of social organizations of the laboring classes existed simultaneously in Asia Minor, Egypt, Greece and Italy.

The variety of names for them found on the relics are more attributable to epochs and languages than to differences in their character and tenets of association. Where the Greek was spoken they were called after the term *eranos*, meaning a meal of victuals in common, or food for which a common assessment was made upon members who enjoyed it by mutual consent. Thus it came to be a method of procuring or earning the meal—a trade union. Hence the eranoi were organizations or co-operations for the purposes of self-support; and partook more of the character of the community method, such as in our day exhibits itself at the Société de Conde sur Vesgre, than of the more prevalent co-operative associations,* like the Equitables.

This term Eranos is unmistakable in meaning. An obloquy attaches to it, pretty much the same as to our word communism, wherever it is used in the classics; because the societies existed during that period of the world's career in which the sovereignty of the individual was more fierce and intolerant toward the meeker spirit of mutual help than it is now; for the *eranoi* were the Greek guilds. Yet evidences are abundant that such communities existed in large numbers; that they obtained no little moral and pecuniary aid from outside; that they were persecuted by the politicians, hated by the optimates, and were obliged to assume

* Consult Lüders, *Die Dionysischen Künstler, Einleitende Uebersicht*, S. 1-49. Verschiedenheit und Ausbreitung der Organisationen.

a good deal of veneration for the gods, and play other social as well as political counter-tactics to exist.

Another name, that of *Thiasos*, was given to a similar, and it would appear cotemporaneous class of organization. In fact so far as we are able to determine, the *thiasoi* and the *eranoi* were pretty much one and the same thing. But as the term *thiasos* with the various forms of verb and substantive, refers to demonstrations of joy, such as marching, dancing, singing and the like, in the open streets, it appears they were one kind of organization with two names—that of *eranoi*, the secret union which met twice and sometimes four times a month; and of the more generally known *thiasoi* whose members sometimes paraded in large numbers in the open air.[10]

Mr. Tompkins, who has devoted his very useful life to statistical matters regarding the Friendly Societies of Great Britain, is prone to picture analogies between the ancient and the modern form. Studying the former from the light he and others have rendered, we are strongly suspicious, because they were distinct from the bacchanalia and the more ancient *erotiae*, that they were unions of trades whose tenets involved nearly all the elements of the socialists of to-day, rather than of the present standard of liberty and development to be found in the Friendly Societies of Great Britain. According to Mr. Tompkins' list, which was always official, the Friendly Societies in 1868 numbered 28,000, with an aggregate membership of 1,700,000, and a capital of nearly 50,000,000 dollars.[11] The comparison therefore is at least respectable. We quote from his pamphlet on Friendly Societies of Antiquity:

"Let us now consider what these companies were which are called by the names of *eranos* and *thiasos*, and of which the following and other inscriptions have revealed the number and importance. These companies were formed of members who met together to sacrifice to certain divinities and to celebrate their festivals in common; besides this they assisted those members who fell into necessitous circumstances, and provided for their funerals. They were at once religious associations and friendly societies.[12] Sometimes

---

[10] See further on these distinctions in subsequent chapters, also much respecting them and the Jewish and Egyptian cummunes.
[11] Report of the *Registrar of Friendly Societies of Great Britain*, for the year 1868.
[12] This author might have here said "trade unions;" for numbers of the

they daringly partook of a political and commercial character. These private corporations (recognized by the state), had their presiding and other officers, their priests, their funds supplied by the contributions of members and the liberality of benefactors. They assembled in their sanctuary and made decrees. They were found in great numbers in the important cities, and especially in the maritime ones. At Rhodes, for example, there were the Companions of the Sun, the Sons of Bacchus, of Minerva Lindienne, of Jupiter Atabyrius, of Jupiter the Savior. At Athens (or rather at the Piræus), there were the Heroistes, the Serapistes or company of the worshipers of the god Serapis, the Eranstes the Orgeons and lastly the thiasotes."[13]

Many of these were trade unions possessing a common fund, the amount of which depended upon the number of members who paid regular contributions, and the amount of the donations that were given from wealthier people who were in sympathy with them. There is plenty of evidence that women as well as men formed the membership of these societies. Woman took her stand with all the dignity and the honors of the man; and there are several slabs of stone and other relics on which are inscribed some of the particulars in regard to the kind and importance of the honors awarded her for faithfulness and ability in performing the duties of an executive officer. The monthly meetings or sociables held in enclosed gardens and groves were largely conducted by the women who gave the attractive convivial feature, which may account for their long existence and extraordinary status and power, that enabled them to do what no social society of our more enlightened age is doing —write their record as the dinotherium and the trilobite have done, in the irrefutable argument of their stone remains and inprints. There are at present very few societies of socialists of which we have any knowledge that are in the habit of chiseling out their archives with such a degree of minuteness and upon such imperishable material as was habitual with the ancient *eranoi* and *sodalicia*.

It is true, we are making so profound an impression that

friendly societies of Great Britain have become, since the repeal of the conspiracy laws in 1824, genuine trade unions of the best pattern. During the existence of the cruel law of Elizabeth they maintained the title of friendly and burial societies almost exactly like the colleges and eranes.
[18] Mr. H. Thompkins' pamphlet on the *Friendly Societies of Antiquity*. London, 1867.

the histories and printed records of our existence and of our important transactions are slowly becoming a possible thing; and such records may possibly save us from oblivion; but the true and thorough histriographer of the labor movements of the world has a broad and attractive field—not yet all laid open—in the study, and interpretation of the multitudes of reliefs, anaglyphs, and other queer paleographs upon slabs, urns, amphoræ and such objects of those by-gone ages; a work which falls to the lot of the archæologist to develop and complete. The truth is, the history of labor has been neglected; and there is reason to believe that very nearly all of that which in this more propitious age is attracting profound consideration by the wise and benevolent, has been gone over and tried, amid the vicissitudes of wars and other antagonisms of the outside competitive world, more than two thousand years ago.

But the fact that their non-competitive plan failed of general adoption need not be adduced as an argument against them. They seem to have been very successful so far as they were intended to apply. They were trade unions for the most part among the mechanics and laboring people; and so far as their societies concerned them, they succeeded. It had not become particularly a broad question. When, however, Christ took up the principle of community of interests involved in their tenets, and organized his system of advocacy, there immediately arose upon it a world-wide culture and an opposition; because this threatened the overthrow of the competism which has always been the basis of both social and political economy.

That the communes, called the *eranoi* in Greece, the Grecian Archipelago, Asia Minor and Egypt, in the Greek tongue, and the *collegia, sodalicia* or *coetus* in the Latin, were the chief cause and originators of Christendom, we can, after mature reflection, entertain little doubt.

Already faint glimpses of proof are extant that the principle or thesis of our modern community of interests, " no excellence without unity in labor," and that " endless toil in collecting good, both by experiment and observation," which is now giving preponderance to Aristotle's philosophy over that of Plato, is significantly crowding Christianity out from the impractical self-denying school of St. Jerome, back into its primeval socialism, or non-competism, in the defense of which Jesus, Nestor, and a thousand others have suffered.

Fortunately for us, the ancient trade unions were in the habit not only of writing their minutes and preserving them in their own archives, in each state where they existed but many of the great events were further inscribed either in alto, demi or basso-relievo; and many times this was done on marble or good blue or sand-stone, which has withstood all the erosions of time.

In some places, as at the Piræus the ancient seaport of Athens, in the Isle of Santorin, in Rhodes and in Asia Minor, the societies were very numerous. It is a well known fact that during the period of the existence of these nations, ranging about 58 years before Christ down to the destruction of the Alexandrian archives by Theophilus and St. Cyril, about A. D. 414, the laws against these poor people and their organizations where almost whimsically severe. M. Renan says of the Roman communes, that there was still less favor here given the disinherited classes than in other countries. During the Roman Republic, in the "affair of the Bacchanales," 186 years before Christ, the policy of Rome on the subject of these associations had first been proclaimed.[14]

It was the nature of the Roman people to cleave to fraternizing organizations, and especially to those of a religious character. This kind of association, however, was hateful to the patricians—the dispensers of the political power—who recognized the family and the state in actual force, as the correct social group. These patricians took the minutest precautions against allowing the plebians the scope of developing into a counter power. They had to be scrupulously authorized before they could become an association—probably by charter. They could not appoint a permanent president or *magister sacrorum*. The number of their members had to be limited. The meanest restrictions were enacted against their accumulating too large a fund for their commune. Similar peevishness continued against the disinherited classes during the existence of the Roman Empire. The archives of the law contained every imaginable provision for the repression of their growth.

[14] So we find the great social wars or the rebellions of slaves, assisted by the unemployed original inhabitants, to have raged from about this same period.

M. Renan further asserts that the Syrians gathered into these societies inoculating them with opinions which the patricians vainly sought to destroy. The Revue Archéologique says that there was a " contest of opinions between the communes and the patricians," which is very natural; since the whole gist of the former was to do away with competism and the system of intermediary commission men depended upon, by the patricians, as a principle for their very existence.

The Greek societies are known by inscriptions now in the Archæological Museum at Athens, to have had the following officers:

1. Three presiding officers—of both sexes : (*a*) the president (*prostates*), male ; and (*b*) the guardian in charge (*proeranistria*), female. They had also, (*c*) a president of finance (*archeranistes*).

2. A stewardess or housewife (*tamia*).

3. A manager or trustee; of whom, doubtless each *eranos* or union had more than one (*epimeletes*). There are evidences that the functions of this important office were divided among the men and women of the union.

4. The recording secretary or scribe who wrote the minutes for the archives (*grammateus*).

5. Lawyers (*sundikoi*), whose exclusive business was to watch and defend the society and its members, individually as well as collectively, against the persecution of the outside competitive world which was always too prone to enforce any one of the many repressive and intolerant laws and measures above referred to, against them.

6. The manager of religious rites (*hieropoios*).

7. Priest, one who attended to the religious ceremonies or rites (*hierokeryx*).

A glance at ancient mythology will show that a great many *isms*, creeds or denominations existed in hierarchical affairs ; and that the power of each was nearly coequal so far as political and social status or respectability was concerned. All seem to have been shielded by the law of the land. So the communes took refuge under the favors of religious discipline, and are known to have been obliged to do so to keep themselves reconciled to their persecutors. By these tactics and by the smartness of their own lawyers, who gave their time to the labor of love, they kept the hostile and restringent clauses of the law a "dead letter," in spite of the patricians and optimates. M. Renan and others declare that there were radical "differences of opinion" on the part of the unions all through those centuries. The truth is, that then, as now, their very existence was an organized socialistic state, though of a low order.

We find that some of the *eranoi* or Greek-speaking communities worshiped, and even dedicated themselves to one god with its peculiar litany, some to another. Here is a translation from the very slab or "stone tablet" referred to in the command of the decree, which strangely enough, has survived all the ages since the beginning of the third century before Christ. On looking it over, who shall doubt that this was a great and perhaps wealthy community, in every way respectable? It was dedicated to the mythical god, Jupiter, and chronicles the fact clearer than the recusant historian could have done upon papyrus, that it was an honorable and responsible body, and in nowise allied to the bawdy erotomania that inspired the orgies of earlier origin and that formed the subject matter of Anacreon's dithyrambics and the voluptuous bacchanalian ditties of Pindar. This translation is clipped *verbatim* from Mr. Henry Tompkin's pamphlet.[15] "It has been proposed: seeing that Menis, son of Mnistheus, of Heraclea, is full of good will toward the thiasotes, and of zeal for the temple, that at present, being treasurer, appointed under the archontate of ——— he has fulfilled that charge with zeal and honesty; that he has finished the portico and the front of the temple of Jupiter Lebraundos in a manner worthy of the god; that he has managed the common funds with honesty and justice, and that to all the thiasotes he has been irreproachable both before and after taking office as treasurer; that he has not hesitated to add his own money toward the expenses of the temple, showing thus, in an evident manner the good will that he has for the *thiasotes*, and that he has fulfilled the sacerdotal office in a manner worthy of the god. For all these things the thiasotes have decreed to award a vote of thanks (*eulogium*) to Menis, son of Mnistheus, of Heraclea; to crown him with a chaplet of foliage; to consecrate, in a part of the temple where it will be best seen, his likeness, painted on a

[15] For the original See *Rev Aerhéologique Paper* by M. Wescher.

piece of wood, according to law, in order to show to all those who wish to prove their zeal toward the temple what honors they may obtain, each one according to the good he may be able to do for the *thiasotes;* and to engrave this decree on a stone tablet, and to place it in the temple of the god."

We have proved in our own mind that the *thiasoi* whose members, the *thiasotes,* paraded in the open streets, "dancing in honor of the gods," were identical with the secret *eranoi* who met much oftener to enjoy their meals, convivials, discussions and social pleasures in common and to contrive for each other situations to work. The *eranoi* were much less known, though their purpose was far more significant.[16] They met from two to four times a month to transact business and to discuss their " difference of opinion." It was here that the above mentioned officers felt the responsibility of their functions. The treasurer was of so much importance that he was called president of finance. Doubtless the male president (*prostrates*) was considered to outrank the female president (*proeranistia*), if indeed the aristocratic idea of ranks was permitted to enter the commune. The number and importance of the offices seem to have resembled those of the Patrons of Husbandry, or Knights of Labor.

We are unable, as yet, to determine exactly what class of women it was who shared the communistic proletarian societies of Greece and the Greek-speaking inhabitants under trade union laws during the power of the Greek philosophies, but are of opinion that they were of the two most respectable classes recognized by law. It is quite certain that their movements at Athens were watched by the Areopagus or court of Mars, whose jurisdiction was over criminal cases and public order and decency. The two classes were the wives of mechanics, their daughters. and the *aulitrides* who made their living by playing the flute. It is almost certain that the wonderful, coexistant class of women known as the *hetairai* also participated in these *Eranoi* as members. But to prove that the *auletrides* frequented them we give a translation of a Greek

---

[16] Athenaeus, *Deipnosophistai,* VIII. "Ερανοί δέ εἰσιν αἱ ἀπὸ των συμβαλλομένων εἰσαγωγαί, ἀπὸ τοῦ συνερᾶν καὶ συμφέρειν ἕκαστον· καλεῖται δὲ ὁ αὐτὸς καὶ ἔρανος καὶ θίασος καὶ οἱ συνιόντες ἐρανισταὶ καὶ συνθιασῶται.

inscription cut in marble, edged with bas reliefs. It is of the Roman epoch and is from the Isle of Santorin in the Grecian Archipelago, not far from Nio. As Santorin was an agricultural country they might have been mostly cultivators. No matter how repressive and intolerant the laws, they could not disband. It is a slab first observed at Athens by the Archæologist M. Wescher, in which the *eranoi* fairly unveil their secrecy and come out in their own name. Before giving the rendering of the inscription, however, we beg to paint as we conceive it, a picture of ancient competitive life which formed the basis of Greek society. It ran to the extent of gambling; and the ethics of society may be said to have been fixed by law and public opinion at little higher than the gamblers' code. Society outside the *eranoi* and the *thiasoi* was a vast gambling hell; and the long existence of the associations, we can account for in no other way than that they in their secret recesses possessed a charmed circle. It was the infinite love that emanates from the infinite difference marked by the gulf yawning between competitive fraternal life.[17] The poor Greek working people must have felt all this difference.

Let anyone imagine himself obliged to contemplate the fashionable logic of a gambling den: A number of people sit round a table, each with his pile of gold, the sum of which is the stake involved. There is skill there. There is also genuine talent. Brilliant aptitudes in one, in the choice of cards or dice; intuition in another, to catch and forestall a niggling thought and checkmate a winning deal; shrewdness in a third at the study of features and in the reading of their inadvertent language; and in a fourth, tact to swoop in the sum of the aces against the competitors. There is no mutual adaptation of these natural gifts to a common good. These are the non-productive adornments in the "code's" diplomacy. In the usages of the gambler opinion has fixed a sort of reckless general law that acts as each gambler's guide; and to obey this law is to conform to the ethics of a code which is the competitor's idea of duty. The duty of each,

---

[17] Aristotle lived apparently in daily contact with these communes and seems to have been influenced by them . . . ἔνιοι δὲ κοινωνιῶν δι ἡδονισήν δοκοῦσι γίνε θαι, θιασωτῶν καὶ ερανιστῶν· αὗται γαρ θυσίας ἕνεκα καὶ συνουσίας. *Ethics*, VIII. II

whether in the exigency of the winning, or of the losing game, is to behave with decency. Such are the ethics at the gambling stakes and each must conform.

The excitement of the competitive game goes on. The lookers-on forget self, home and duty in their admiration of the contestants' skill. Their variety of method, their quivering versatility, their genius, bold of one, delicate of another, exhilarate as they amaze. But when the one more skilled in gaming or more favored in fortuity, sweeps the stakes and stalks off in triumph with the gold of his helpless neighbors, there must come a reaction of feeling, though the rules of the gambling table require resignation. The defeated need not try to hide discomfiture. A hungry wife and children, blighted hopes, baffled plans and chagrin, beget despair. They are the conjurers of distrust, jealousy, vengeance, hate, suicide. Even the winner dies in misery; for a little selfish ecstasy adds nothing to the sum of a life's possibilities and joys. He is often the next victim in the shifting vicissitudes of the trade.

Now this is a fair picture of that hell which constituted ancient society. The household, the shambles of voluptuous commerce and of deal, the judiciary and the war-spirit were so many sheols of licensed competism reeking with a virus of the gambler's code and intolerant of this socialism of the poor. Unfortunately it is too exact a picture of the maudlin present; but the present we are not dealing with.

Society was a vast concern in which fashions, means and fine things were huckstered and raffled from hand to hand; and then as now, the working classes or proletariat were the sensitive target which every club of misguided genius bruised and imbruted.

The discovery, then, of unquestionable proof that there existed comtemporaneously with this outside state of things an order of human association whose code of ethics, or whose accepted opinion of duty, one to another, was the antithesis of this; whose rule of home and labor was based deep in that love and mutual protection which afterwards became the doctrine of salvation as proclaimed by a greater teacher,[18] is a triumph glorius and incalcula-

[18] Plato, Aristotle and Socrates were all deeply touched by the brotherly love of the innumerable *eranists* whose works though humble were followed by them

ble to the struggling, disjointed love of the labor movement to-day. The fragment at Athens referred to is a piece of blue Hymettian marble with little border work. The inscription is in plain Attic Greek of the Aristotelian epoch, and its translation from the Revue Archéologique, is as follows:

"By a rulable and just administration of the common fund of money belonging to the community of eranistai, and having ever conducted himself with kindness and with honesty; and as he has righteously husbanded the funds successively paid by the *eranistai* themselves, as well as the annual subscription, according to the law of the eranos; and in view of the fact that in everything else he still continues to show integrity to the oath which he swore to the *eranistai*, therefore Hail Alcmeon!

"The community of the *eranistai* rejoice to praise Alcmeon, son of Theon, a stranger who has been naturalized—their president of finance (*archeranistes*); and do crown him with a chaplet of foliage because of his faithfulness and good will to them. They are moreover rejoiced and praise the trustees (*epimaletai*) and also the *hieropoioi* of Jupiter the Savior, and of Hercules, and of the Savior of the gods. And they crown each of them with the wreath of honor because of their virtue and their lively interest in the community of the *eranistai*."

The stone is here broken, leaving us in the dark as to the exact date of this interesting relic. The principle however, upon which this *eranos* was conducted, accepting the signification given this word by lexicographers and writers of the adverse school, was communism—means taxed from a common membership for mutual support. This settled, we next ask: did such an experiment thrive? The above inscription is full of praises and rejoicing over its success. Then if it did succeed, and if in conjunction with it, it is made clear that the less secret jubilees of the *thiasoi* furnished means out of the same well-husbanded fund, for the sweet convivials, and the dance, to the famous music of the female flute-players, did not this "community of the *eranistai*" greatly augment for the "disinherited classes," the means of happiness and virtue?

all. Lüders commenting, quotes Socrates from Xenophon, *Conversationes* VIII. "Wir sind ja alle Thiasoten deses gottes." This passage gives stong evidence that Socrates was a member of a commune.

SOCRATES A MEMBER OF A COMMUNE. 459

These are important conjectures coming from the unwritten mists of the finest of the world's ages of antiquity. Let the ethnologist and the paleontologist divest themselves of bias, and with these new skeletons of ancient history remodel and reproduce an ethologic anatomy of these two great rivals for power—individualism and communal love. For if the desired means of happiness was procured through this one experiment of whose relics we have given a rendering, then it is evident by the many other similar inscriptions that a thousand such microcosms embellished the morals and gladdened the hearts of slaves and outcasts.

These microcosms of a far future society must not, however, be supposed to have been as sweeping or as pure in their radicalism as some that are developing at the present time; for it must be remembered that though the ignorance of the present age is averse to the implanting of a system which means introversion and revolution of competitive disassociation, yet we possess at least the boon of tolerance which was almost utterly denied the struggling poor of those times.

According to the best information to be had regarding inscriptions that are resuscitating the history of the ancient proletaries, the societies called the *eranoi* and the *thiasoi* were by no means confined to the Hellenic Peninsula and the Ionian and Grecian Archipelagoes. Similar societies are known to have existed both on the continent of Asia and of Africa. Mommsen, Orelli, Böckh and other archæologists, in their Latin works of *Descriptiones Reliquarum*, have filled thousands of folio pages with sketches of all sorts of paleographs which are fac-similes of inscriptions, monograms, escutcheons and many kinds of hieroglyphic and anaglyphic gravery and embossing in stone and metal. These curious things are being dug up in different parts of Europe, Asia and Africa, wherever ancient history speaks of the doings of men.

Great numbers are described that have come from Dalmatia, the rivers and plains of Austria, Hungary and the Kranish provinces. They exist in countries once occupied by the Armenians, Phœnicians and Chaldeans; and as it is now becoming apparent that the most correct philosophies of the Alexandrians and Athenians were first inspired by Indians of the east, it is possible that great revelations are yet forthcoming from the Hindoo school, of which the Sankhya Kapila was the inspiring oracle. But however this may be—whether Buddhism was, or was not the idiosyncrasy that germinated the every-growing schism among dialecticians of all succeeding ages, it matters little.

One thing is certain in our mind: that the societies of self-help among the proletaries have uniformly followed the grouping, self-teaching, perpiatetic method of Aristotle and Kapila, while their competitive enemies and persecutors have followed the dreamy, non-practical Olympus-beclouded generalities of Plato. The communities always worked well under Numa, Solon, Jesus and Nestor, but always suffered under Lycurgus, Appius Claudius, Cæsar and Cyril. If the strange and newly unearthed library of Asshurbanipal, who was emperor of the Assyrians a thousand years before Christ, is ever scanned in a non-prejudicial spirit, its ideographs and its history of their systems of nomenclature, computation and collection may be found suggestive of similar doings.

We have already said something concerning the rules and by-laws of the societies, which by the marble tablet whereon their records are graven, are known to have existed. As a general thing these decrees and regulations are made on the stones that still honor some of the officers. Although the evident object of each of these organizations was to enlarge the means of happiness of the members by providing liberties for them through the associative sphere of the collectivity, and may be said on this account to have been temporal in their objects, yet they all partook strongly of some religious faith inculcated at the services of the gods in the temples.

Some writers upon the subject are convinced that they resembled the old semi-religious guilds of trade in England. They also intimate that like the continental guilds for a similar object, connected with the Roman Catholic Church, they seem to have been under the patronage of a tutelary saint, and that under this tutelage they sometimes founded industrial, commercial and maratime corporations. Sometimes they made it a specialty to aid each other in acquiring a profession. Our own opinion is, that they were a genuine type of the trade union.[19] The evidences of this are many; and it is no argument against the position if they are found to have been religious.

The objections will be, that they opened their sessions with prayer, and that they admitted women in large numbers. But some of our own trade unions undergo forms similar to prayer and Bible reading. As to their having had women as members it only proves that they were trade unions of a higher, more long-lived and a more successful development than these of the present day; and this brings us to the sad reflection that with all the boast of modern trade unionists and all the good they are doing, and with all their philosophy and practical forcing of the true political economy upon governments, they still fail to equal the judgment of the trade unionists of Greece, who based their associations upon co-operation for peaceful, rather than co-operation for aggressive self help. Another resemblance to the trade unions is seen in their extreme secrecy.

"The meetings of these pre-Christian societies opened with prayer; after which came the general business. The place at which they were held was called the synod, or sometimes the Synagogue, and the assembly was absolutely secret—no stranger could be admitted, and a severe code maintained order thereat. They were held, it appears, in enclosed gardens surrounded with porticos, or piazzas or little arbors, in the middle of which the altar of sacrifice was erected. The officers made the candidates for membership submit to a sort of examination, and they had to certify that they were 'holy, pious and good.' There was in these little confraternities, during the two or three centuries that preceded the Christian era, a movement which was almost as varied as that which produced in the middle ages so many religious orders and so many sub-divisions of these orders. Very many have been counted in the single island of Rhodes, of which several bear the names of their founders or of their reformers. Several of these confraternities, especially that of Bacchus, had sublime and elevated doctrines; and endeavored with a good will to give to mankind some con-

---

[19] The reasons for their being often religious and borrowing gods or tutelary deities are explained in our chapter on the Roman trade unions, q. v.

solation. If there still remained in the Greek world any love, any piety, any religious morality, it was owing to the liberty granted to such private religious doctrines. The doctrines competed in some measure with the official religion, the decline of which became more evident day by day."[20]

But it must not be inferred because the *eranoi*, or Greek-speaking unions took the name of the particular god they venerated, that they were exclusively religious.

The archæologist, Hamilton, has produced fac-similes of inscriptions on slabs that were found on the shores of the Gulf of Symi. The translation of one runs thus:

"Alexander, of Cephalonia, has been honored with the gift of a crown of gold, and also Nisa, his virtuous wife, of Cos. This honor is given by the Adoniastes, Aphrodiastes and the Asclepiastes. Epaphrodite and his wife, by wish of the Heroistes and of the Aeaciastes, have also been honored with a golden crown."

These Adoniastes, Aphrodiastes, Asclepiastes, etc., were *eranoi*, whose union was, on account of the peculiar religious notions of the members and of the country, dedicated respectively to the gods Adonis, Aphrodite, Esculapia, etc. Another inscription taken from Ross's *Inscriptiones Greques*,[21] is also very interesting as proof that these societies were usually dedicated to the popular gods of the mythic hierarchy of Mount Olympus.

It is valuable as a proof of the general position assumed, on account of its bold mention of union and confraternity thus showing that it belonged to the eranian and thiasian school of co-operation or trade unionism. It is from Rhodes, and is somewhat defaced. Here is the rendering as given in Mr. Tompkins' review: "* * * crowned with a crown of gold by the community of Jupiter Xenos, the Dionysiates Chæremoniens, as well as by the Panatheniastes and the * * * * * crowned with a crown of gold by the Soteriastes (worshipers of the Soter, or Messiah, the confraternity of Jupiter Xenos, and that of Minerva Lindienne, followers of Caius, crowned with a crown of foliage by the community of Jupiter Atabyrien and the Agathodaemoniastes Philoniens, as well as by the community of Dionysiastes Chæremoeiens and by that of Appollo."

[20] Tompkins, *Friendly Societies of Antiquity*. [21] *Researches in Asia Minor*

This date "in the year 178" is supposed to mean the 178th year of the existence of this union. Here we have, in the midst of the lady members of this old and probably rich and respectable *eranos*, or union and at the public feast or monthly sociable in the enclosed garden that always distinguished the open *thiasoi* from the secret business meeting of the *eranoi*, a flute-player; in all probability one of the famous *auletrides* whose charms are celebrated by Alciphron, Athenæus and Theopompus; and of whom a writer in his work on prostitution, unconsciously intimates that they were abandons [22] and would doubtless construe it so as to make this feast no nobler than the callipygian games, which though unfrequented by men must have been, of course, "scandalous." May not anything be scandalous when regarded in a censorious and uncharitable light. But this feast of the Communists described was nothing of the sort.

This invaluable memento is in good care and preservation in the museum at Athens. On the bas-relief are these suggestive figures: A god and a goddess in an enclosed garden. It is Cybile the Phrygian goddess who sits with her head crowned. In front of her crouches a lion? The god is Apollo in a flowing robe and in a standing attitude. He has a salver (*patera*) in one hand and a lyre in the other. There is a priestess or *proeanistria* standing, and a musician or *auletrid* is playing the flute.[23] A lamb for the feast is in the arms of a young man. Under this is the inscription of which the following is the translation.

"Stratonice, daughter of Menecrates, is crowned by the members, men and women, of this thiasos. In the year 178 she (Stratonice) was female president of the club (*proeranistria*), a crown of foliage is decreed her and a marble tablet ornamented with banderoles to honor her public proclamation in the assembly of Jupiter in honor of her virtue."

It is not only interesting but extremely useful as an example for the guidance of future society, that we be made acquainted with some of the inner and unrecorded life of antiquity. The same turbulent warlike millions swarmed the cities and thoroughfares then, as now. The same unorganized and inequitable methods of production and appor-

[22] Sängers, *History of Prostitution*, p. 46.
[23] See also Tafel II. Lüders, *Die Dionysischen Künster*. Explanation of the plates, S. 10–11.

tionment. The same egoism and sacrifice of neighbor for aggrandizement of self, and the same intolerance and bigotry in prevailing faiths that inspire the competing Muscovite Russians against the Rural Solidarities, the Mennonities and the Dutchobors to-day—the same selfishness that makes man hate man, and church hate church wherever we go. In this prodigious whirlpool of self-serving negativeness and ignorance—the painful, tiresome desert through which all proletarian humanity plods, it is gratifying to discover that a great counter element once existed with organizations based upon that community of equal interests which is fundamentally revolutionizing the policies of our own brilliant, but depraved and selfish century.

The specimen adduced was a festival of an *eranos*—it was the *thiasos* itself, and a glance at Liddell will satisfy the skeptic that it was a society of poor, persecuted people, who agreed to assess each other in common for their daily food and their monthly convivials; and the proof that these poor girls were sometimes members greatly intensifies the interest in them. Besides, it is a known fact that among these musical trades unionists were some of the most beautiful and intelligent people the world ever produced. It was not considered prostitution in those days to do what they did. The stern philosopher Zeno, hero of Stoicism, fell desperately in love with one; and if we are to believe Athenæus was ready to defend his love with the antics of a madman. This was after he had vainly insulted her because she came to him for protection.

CHAPTER XXII.

THE ANCIENT BANNER.

INCALCULABLY AGED FLAG OF LABOR.

The Old, Old Crimson Ensign—An Emblem of Peace and Good Will to Man—Strange Power of Human Habit—Descent of the Red Banner through Primitive Culture—White and Azure the Colors of Mythical Angels, Grandees and Aristocrats—Colors for the Lowly without Family, Souls or other Seraphic Attributes—How the Red Vexillum was Stolen from Labor—Tricks which Compromised Peace Tenets of the Flag—The Flag at the Dawn of Labor's Power—Testimony of Polybius—Of Livy—Of Plutarch—Causes of Working People's Affection for Red—The Emblem of Health and the Fruits of Toil—Ceres and Minerva their Protectresses and Mother-Goddesses Wore the Flaming Red—Emblem of Strength and Vitality—Archæology in Proof—Their Color First Borrowed from Crimson Sun-Beams—More Light and less Darkness—White and Pale Hues for the Priests—Origin of the Word "FLAG"—It is the Word-Root of "Flame" a Red Color—Proofs Quoted—Mediæval Banner in France and England—The Red of All Modern Flags Borrowed from that of the Ancient Unions—Disgraceful Ignorance of Modern Prejudice and Censure.

The typical color of the great non-laboring classes in ancient times was white and azure blue; while that of the strictly laboring element was red. This phenomenon has come down to us by the power of habit, from high antiquity.[1]

---

[1] Consult Tylor, *Primitive Culture*, (Vol. I pp. 70, sq, N. Y. 1888, *Survival*, for illustrations on the power of habit: "The saying that marriages in May are unlucky—believed so 18 centuries ago and more, see Ovid, *Fastus*, V.—survives to this day in England, a striking example how an idea, the meaning of which has perished for ages, may continue to exist simply because it has existed. There are thousands of cases of this kind which have become, so to speak, land-

White, in heathen mythology, was thought to be emblematical of degree. It was the color used by the *gens* families and by the priesthood. Very often a beautiful azure of various shades accompanied the pure white. Following this habit of the optimates and their hierarchy, we still imagine white to be the color of the robes of angels, and still make it a holy color.[1] All people, ancient or modern, having a history and a priesthood with concomitant crafts, have regarded white as the adumbration of holiness, of purity, of aristocracy. It is the color which befits itself to superstition and to property; therefore the *gens* or the gentle, who do not work, who are unsoiled, who eat up the products of labor, who robe themselves in white and ascend throne, see, chancel, pulpit or patriarchal seat, and who talk of their "subjects" whom they spurn and absorb, are of all others most certain to flaunt the robes of white and azure and shining purple. These colors date from a dim era of antiquity, and like the etymon they were self-suggestive as the antithesis of sweat and toil and grime. They embellished and decked the bodies of the "washed," and could not go hand in hand with creatures smoked and smeared at the furnace and the anvil. Hence a contempt of labor.[2] The idea of Plato which he copied from the Pagan religion and which Christianity unfortunately afterwards copied from him, under the name of Neo-Platonism was that of white robes, white wings, white banners—a mysterious power in the clouds, a home at Mount Olympus, and the vaulted dome of heaven—and myriads of slaves and menials in red, brown, dun and murk who were to plod without souls, liberties

---

marks in the course of culture." This author hereupon cites many instances showing the extreme age of our paltriest habits, some of which are really astonishing. One of the most striking instances which might have been enumerated by Mr. Tylor, along with the many that he here adduces, is the red banner, which for antiquity and pith of antecedent meaning has perhaps no rival in the tale of primitive culture. We have another remark illustrative of the power of habit and one which may be regarded as curious and far-fetched, made by Rogers, *Social Life in Scotland*, Vol. I. p. 6, in speaking of the giants and cave-dwellers of the stone period: "In popular superstition there still linger memories of the Neolithic age." This is really wonderful.

[2] *Revelations*, vii. 9, 14. So *idem*, xix. 8: "And to her was granted that she should be arrayed in fine linen, clean and white, for the fine linen is the righteousness of saints." So again xix. 14, "And the armies which were in heaven followed him upon white horses, clothed in fine linen, white and clean."

[3] Guhl and Koner, *Life of the Greeks and Romans*, tr. Hüffer, p. 485, speaking of the ancients says: "The usual color of the dress was originally white for the toga this was prescribed by law), only poor people, slaves and freedmen wore dress of the natural brown or black colors." Red, a "color," was always considered finer than brown or black, though all were labor colors.

honors or rewards, in the degrading service of keeping them white, clean-washed and fat. The idea of Aristotle, the practical, was, that labor itself was pure, worthy, and the only thing which could possibly lead men to knowledge and good; yet even his great mind could not at that early day discern a method of ridding the world of slaves, although Socrates, a member of a commune that waved the red banner, had told them that manual labor was a virtue.[4]

Again, white was the color of the ancient aristocratic flag or military banner, both of the Romans and Greeks. This is distinctly told to us in an elaborate description of all the phases of the subject, by Polybius,[5] who wrote just at the time when the greater slave rebellions were beginning fiercely to rage.

As long as the ancient military ranks remained undefiled by the presence of slaves and freedmen, or persons of lowly condition, the *semeion* or *vexillum*, that is, the flags and banners were white, azure and gray. But we find that curiously enough, the red *vexillum* comes temptingly into the Roman tent at the very time when the workingmen began to assume military and political importance. It was evidently introduced as a means for inspiring this class of soldiers to desperate acts of valor;[6] because the red banner of the communes was so sacred to them that they would recklessly cast their lives into the jaws of death in the act of recapturing it from an enemy. Multitudes of instances are on record proving that the Roman generals cunningly managed to toss the vexillum or red banner, in some surreptitious manner over into the enemy's camp at a moment of onset, thereby enthusing the soldiers with a reckless oblivion of danger, as they crushed into it in desperate haste and determination to seize from the polluted fingers of the barbarian their endeared and cherished flag.[7]

---

[4] For more on this great man's philosophy, see chapters iv. on the *Eleusinian Mysteries*, and xxiv. on the *Plans of the Ancient Benefactors*.
[5] Polybius Megal, *Historia*, VII. c. 39, pp. 676–677, ed. Gronovii, Amstelodami, 1670: 'Ὡς ἁπάντων ὡρισμένων καὶ συνήθων ὄντων διασημάτων μετα δε ταῦτα σημαίαν ἔπηξαν μείαν μὲν τὴν πρώτην ἐν ᾧ δεῖ τόπῳ τὴν τοῦ στρατηγοῦ σκηνὴν δουτεραν δὲ τὲ ἐπὶ τῆς πρεσθείσης πλουρὰς, τρίτον ἐπὶ μέσης τῆς γραμμῆς ἐφ' ἧς οἱ χιλίαρχοι τρέφουσιν τετράτην παρ' ποθεν τὰ στρατόπεδα. Καὶ ταυτας μὲν ποιοῦσσι φοινικὰς τε δὲ καὶ στρατηγοῦ λουκιον. Τα δε επι θάτερα ποτὲ μεν ψηλὰ δόρατα πηγνύουσι, πωτὲ δὲ σημαίας ἐκ των ἄλλων χρωμάτων."
[6] In earlier times the plebeian class were refused admission to armies as soldiers solely on the ground that military work is aristocratic. They finally overcame this prejudice to some extent
[7] Plutarch, Paulus Æmilius. "The Romans who engaged the phalanx, be-

The curiosity of the reader may by this time be aroused to understand what may have been the cause of this strange affection. We shall attempt to bring out, so far as authentic evidence can be had, the facts lying at the bottom of the ineffaceable love in the strictly proletarian class, for the beautiful and incomputably aged red banner; and in doing so, we may help the inquirer in the effort to discern the causes of this emblem having so successfully breasted the storms of adversity and time and come down to us embalmed in the same love and veneration that shrouded and shielded it in deep antiquity, when it knew and comforted men only as poor and lowly slaves.

In the heathen mythology two great and celebrated deities presided over labor—Minerva and Ceres. The Greek names of these celebrated and much adored mythic deities were Demeter for Ceres, goddess of agriculture and fruitfulness of the earth, and Athena for Minerva, goddess of manual labor and protectress of working women and workingmen. These two great deities wore flaming red.[8]

Bacchus of the Romans and Dionysus were the same myths with Ceres and Athena; that is, they seem to have personified in the male what these goddesses did in the female; and their vesture, like that of the goddesses, was flaming red. So Apollo, who was none other than the sun, was allied to them in functions. The reason of this is, that both genders of these imaginary beings represented the ancient sun-worship. The brilliant, flaming light of the sun is

---

ing unable to break it. Salius, a Pelignian officer snatched the ensign of the company, and threw it among the enemy. Hereupon the Pelignians, rushed forward to recover it, for the Italians look upon it as a great crime and disgrace to abandon their standard. A dreadful conflict and slaughter on both sides ensued." Cæsar, *De Bello Gallico*, often speaks of incidents of this kind.

8 The state robe of Athena was generally of a flaming red. Abundance of evidence also shows the colors of these two patrons of labor to have been red. Red was also the color of Proserpine, the daughter of Demeter or Ceres: This was not confined to Greece and Rome. The same myths wore red in Asia, Africa and even in Britain. See Hughes, *Horæ Britannicæ*, Vol. I. p. 294, Lond. 1818: "The British *Ked* or *Ceridwen*, is in many respects the same character as the Ceres of the Greek mythology and the Isis of the Egyptians. * * * * "She was arrayed in a vesture of flaming silk; a strong wreath of ruddy gold was about the neck, wherein was set a precious pearl, and rows of coral; yellower was her hair than the blossoms of the broom; her skin was whiter than the foam of the wave; her hands and fingers were fairer than the opening buds of the water-lily, amid the small ripplings of the fountain of waters; or the sight of the hawk after mewing, or the sight of the falcon of three mews; no brighter eyes than hers were seen; whiter was her bosom than the breast of the fair swan; redder her cheeks than the rose of the mountain; whoever saw her was filled with love; four white trefoils were seen to rise in her way wherever she came, and therefore was she named *Olwen* or the fair lady."

thought to have been the first object of awe and wonder before which primitive man bowed himself down in adoration. It was the great and magnificent orb of day that in spring warmed the first sprigs of vegetable life. To the grand monarch of the day, the ancient laboring man first gave homage for light and heat which caused the fruits of his planting to grow and ripen. As this wondrous being, always believed to be alive and rational, immense in bulk, exquisite in beauty, radiant with heat and life, rose out of the sea and skimmed over their heads, he shed forth his crimson flames upon their labor and his color was likened to the fluid that coursed in their veins. The Dionysus thus became the protective principle for the Greek-speaking and the Bacchus for the Latin-speaking world, on which the vast system of labor organizations we have described was founded, cultivated and perpetuated for thousands of years; and their natural color was red, or color refined.

This accounts for the high-born or optimate class represented in the priesthood, the military, the non-laboring element—in other words, the pretended pure, clean-washed and unsoiled—having a contempt for color and for labor that soiled; and it also accounts for all the low-born, represented in occupations of agriculture and mechanics like the laboring element, or the tainted, tarnished, sweat-begrimed, having a natural love of color, whose highest type is red.

It was a thing most natural that the emblems of Ceres should be of a red color. She was of herself a majesty of no inferior sort. The products of her care were wheat and other grain, the supply of which from the earth, furnished the red blood always known to be the animating and strength-giving fluid of life; although the exact action of blood from heart to lungs and thence through arteries, and its return through veins was a more recent discovery. It is thus very natural that we should find among the organizations which chose Ceres as their patron divinity, the strictest adherence to her coat of arms and her emblems and escutcheons, the same colors that she was known to prefer.

Accordingly the inscriptions contain representations of the ancient banner, so well known to have been carried at the innocent and legalized parades of the *thiasotes* and *orgiastes* in Greece, Palestine, Asia Minor and the islands, and by the *sodales* and *collegia* in almost every town, little or large, in Italy.⁹ Even at Carthage and all along the coast of North Africa remains of these organizations are being found.

A powerful natural reason for their preferring this color was probably its beauty. The color red is known in optics to be the first one on the list. Then come orange, yellow, green, blue, indigo and violet.[10] White is not a color. Azure is a hue. Red of a brilliant hue may be seen at a greater distance than any other color and it is of all gifts of nature one of the most beautiful and inspiring. Many have dubbed Ceres the tutelary patroness of the United States.[11] The flag adopted by the American Union is, scientifically considered, a very perfect one; the metaphorical meaning of the red which is placed in the stripes, being the same as that involved in the ancient, which has a wonderful history in the past of labor. If the modern republic has any divinity at all, it is Ceres, Rhea, Cybele, Isis, the protectress of the farmers, and Minerva the guardian of mechanics and inventions. The red means the stripes; not the revengeful, bloody red with the present meaning trumped up against it in some wilfully ignorant minds, covering with obloquy which present society, unable to disabuse itself of the ancient grudge and contempt of labor, still uses against the red flag, but the exact reverse—the stripes represent the blows which labor in her great conflict to free herself from enslavement, poverty and oppression, has received upon her back from the lash of aristocracy and brutal force. Unwittingly, perhaps, the United States adopted these stripes as a component part of its beautiful and suggestive national banner; and this act was a strictly scientific one; for it exactly conforms with the ancient symbol red, enormously used by Roman and Greek organizations expressive and significant of the scourge, the stripes and the lines of blood which

⁹ Consult chapter xxi, *supra*, also Lüders, *Die Dionysischen Künstler*; Encyclopédie Tech.

[10] The *Encyclopædia Brittannica*, in an exhaustive article on *Light*, (Vol. XIV. p. 582), reduces the primitive colors to three—red, green and violet. This makes red to be the monarch of colors, as the oak is the monarch of trees, the lion the monarch of quadrupeds, or man the monarch of mortals A respectable authority for modern colors, the *Encyclopédie Technologique*, Tome. I. Art. *Couleur*, init, says: "Ces couleurs fondamentales sont: Le rouge, l'orangé, le jaune, le bleu, l'indigo et le violet." Here also the red is the first mentioned of all colors. The *Encyclopædia Brittannica*, Vol· VII. p. 495, says; "the red holds the highest position among all dyed colors."

[11] Carnegie, *Triumphant Democracy*, p. 180. "Ceres the prime divinity of the United States."

streaked the naked backs of the poor and lowly of ancient labor.[12]

We now proceed to give a history of the red emblem as used against labor by the rich and strong, for the seeming purpose of making capital out of the reverence and affection always clinging in the organizations, which from more ancient times they had inherited as the chosen color of their divinities, Ceres, Minerva, Saturn and perhaps Apollo.

In the first place it is necessary to enter into an analysis of the word " flag." A glance at a Latin dictionary will explain that flag is the root of the word "*flamma*"—a circumstance altogether extraordinary. Andrews for instance, defines flamma as follows: " Flamma, æ. (archaic genitive singular flammai, used by Lucretius, I. 726 ; 899 ; V. 1088) feminine (flagma from FLAG ; whence flagro and flagito, Greek phlegma, from phlégo). A blazing fire, blaze, flame."

This is an aged word and has its real origin in the red beams of the sun which almost all men in primitive ages adored under the religion of the sun-worshipers. Without the slightest doubt this original flag was one of the names of the ancient banner which was red. Because it was red and carried by the secret organizations on which the ruling minority cast a taint, it never attained to enough popularity to be used by ancient writers, and consequently failed to come down to us in form of an emblem, or with the significance of a banner or flag, although it never lost its original meaning ; and its many variations of form appear in history times without number. The innocent original changed in time to a multitude of instruments of torture. It got to be *flagitium*, a shameful act, then *flagrum* a whip, and as such was stuck in bundles (*fasces*), along with an axe and carried in threatening pomp by the august prætors to scourge slaves with. How could the old red flag differentiate into a whip?

It was simply the work of hate and prejudice. The organizations would never give up their red banners ; they are carrying them still by the power of habit, although the be-

---

[12] Slaves and freedmen sometimes composed a part of the forces of armies in the time of Polybius. This author who wrote as early as B. C. 145, describes the arrangement in the camps, of both slaves and freedmen, as well as their duties; "Μετὰ δὲ τὴν στρατοπεδείαν συναθροιθέντες οἱ χιλίαρχοι, τοὺς ἐκ τοῦ στρατοπέδου πάντες ἐλουθέρους ὁμοῦ ἢ δούλους ὁρκίξουσι, καθ᾽ ἕνα ποιούμενοι τε ὁρκισμόν. Ὁ δὲ ὅρκος ἐστίν· μηδὲν ἐκ τῆς παρεμβολῆς κλέψειν· ἀλλὰ κἂν εὕρῃ τῆς τοῦτ᾽ ἀνοίσειν ἐπὶ τοὺς χιλιάρχοις." Polybius, *Historia*, VI. 31, init.

lief in the power of the once omnipotent Ceres and Minerva has long since faded from the earth.[13] The prejudice against their banner and the innumerable communes was based upon their supposed meanness, which is also fast being outgrown. This prejudice was also heightened [14] by the fact that the organizations grew powerful, sometimes rich and influential, always preaching a cult opposed to the despotism of capital and often and especially in Italy, as we have seen, becoming a potent factor in politics, which was a crime against the aristocracy of ownership and military and political power held by the great *gens* families and their slave-based religion.

It is thus plainly seen that in ancient days, the red banner was an emblem among the labor societies, of blood-*making*, not of blood-letting; while among the grandees it was emblematical of blood-*spilling* and torture; never indicative of building up, either the human body or the body politic. The system upon which the ancient aristocracy rested was cruelly and ferociously competitive and its product was slavery while its instruments of creating as well as perpetuating this thankless institution were legalized lasciviousness of its lords, and whips and scourges dyed red in the blood of laborers whose backs streaked with crimson which flowed from the furrows made by thongs, that their own greatness and their victims' littleness might be more widely contrasted.[15]

Let us now turn to the working people and their flag. In the first place the primitive mind of man conceives a fondness for flaming colors, and red, which is the champion of tints, attracted their delight by its beauty. One may stretch the imagination to conceive that this fact originated its adoption by his protecting divinities; for he would naturally incline to fix their favorite colors in harmony with his own tastes or fancies. We have as a result, of the natural and innocent fancy of primitive mind for this beautiful ground-color, all the lowly estate of antiquity, fixing their institutions in blazoned red, and nailing virtue, peace, social-

[13] See Bouillet, *Histoire des Communités des Arts et des Métiers de l'Auvergne*, passim. Text and plates, representing the "bannières" as were used in middle ages.
[14] Juvenal, *Satires*.
[15] Lycurgus, whose slave system in Lacedemon we have described, laid down a rule by which slaves were whipped at night without having committed an offense after having worked all day. This punishment was to humiliate them for submissiveness next day. They must also crouch lest should they stand erect they be compared with men. See Plutarch *Lycurgus*.

ism, poverty and resignation, to their unobtrusive banner—
a brilliant red. We find them, too, irrevocable in the belief
that God, dressed in the crimson glories of the sun and in
awful justice, threw light and warmth and glory upon the
crops of their sowing and the mechanical products of their
handicraft; while the power of habit—that second law of
perpetuation of being—has transmitted, even to this day,
an ineffaceable love in the poor, for those endeared and
cherished emblems.[16]

The celebrated red *himation*[17] and *chiton* were for a long
time the principal article of clothing. The dancing girls
and flute-players wore them during the voluptuous age of
Athens. They were worn at the feasts of Dionysus by the
communists of the thiasoi. Of this we have the positive
evidence of numerous inscriptions, some of which, although
engraved on stone, are very good pictures of the feasters returning from their march through the streets.

At Rome this love of the red banner among the plebeians
was often turned to profit by the rich. After the overthrow
of the Roman kings (B. C. 510), two officers little less in
power than the kings themselves, were installed as supreme
rulers in their place. These were the consuls. A great
growth of the power of the laboring element, as we have
shown in preceding chapters on Trade Unions, very gradually came into the world; and this new force immediately
began to make incursions upon and against the consular
authority. The red flag is involved in this quarrel. It had
been the kings who upheld the unions; the consuls, who

---

[16] **Examples** proving red to have been the primeval color among the servant class are being constantly discovered in the inscriptions. Dr. Schliemann, in *Tiryns*, pp. 303-307, gives Prof. Fabricius' descriptions of the "*mighty bull*," recently discovered in a wall-painting of that pre-Homeric city. The animal, mostly red, is leaping and bounding at the games, while an acrobat upon his back is girding him in the dangerous scene. These actors, always of the slave race (see chap. xvii. *Amusements of Antiquity*, pp. 401-414), were tugging and sweating without pay, for masters, a thousand years before Christ. This scene is represented in Plate XIII. while fig. 142 gives another proof of the remarka-ble proclivity in days before Homer, for red. "Whilst the lower broad stripe is red, the ground of the ornament shows a bright red colour; the two strokes of the scale-like ornament are black, the little circles and lines within the scales, white. Very noteworthy is the simultaneous occurrence of two different shades of the red color."

[17] Guhl and Koner, *Life of the Greeks and Romans*, p. 160, sqq. These gar-ments are here minutely described. "Men also appear in these pictures with the cherry coloured chlamys and the red *himation*." But we remark that the same authors assure us in both their descriptions of the Greeks, and of the Rom-ans, that colors were only for the common people. In course of time the hima-tion, originally white and worn by the rich, became **popular and took on the plebeian hue.**

from the very first, endeavored to suppress them. These magnates were the natural enemies of the working class; the kings their natural friends. This seeming phenomenon is a suggestive fact of history. The kings wanted and recognized their systematic, organized labor; the consuls, who where sure to be rich grandees of blood and family, were jealous as well as afraid of this new and growing power which the mild and favorable laws of the kings had made it possible for labor to develop under.

This was the origin of the greatest intestine contest Rome ever had. It was a death-grapple of lordship with labor, in which consular power aped the banner and color of communes,[18] and even bent all energy to involve Rome in Great wars of conquest for the express object of wriggling out of the terrible plebeian grip.[19]

The patrician consuls fought the hated workingmen, according to Livy, with such an unabating determination for about five years (B. C. 375–370), as to cause a *solitudo magistratuum*[20] or vacancy, in which there occurred what is now called an interregnum—neither the lords nor the people, holding the helm of power. This was under the plebeian, Licinus Stolo, author of the agrarian law, the most renowned statute of antiquity—a germ of the same contention which cost the Gracchi, Blossius and Clodius their lives, as champions for the poor in the memorable agrarian and labor turmoils, and finally brought Rome, with her Cicero and Cæsar to an ignominious end, because she purloined the ægis of laborers on whom she glutted herself while maintaining slavery as a fundament of her religion and government.

[18] See *Encyclopædia Brittanica*, 9th edition, Stoddart, Phil. Vol. VI. p. 279, describing the consuls: "A cloak with a scarlet border and an ivory staff were badges of their office." For more than 600 years thereafter the scarlet which darkened into purple became a state color. The consuls stole the red *vexillum* by a similar species of trick, from the communes—a blasphemy against the ancient peace-color of Ceres and Minerva the protecting divinities of laborers and the fruits of labor. The following modern criticism admits this: If the consuls "wished to subdue any outbreak of the plebeians, they feigned that some powerful enemy was marching against the city, and thus succeeded in obtaining extraordinary powers." *Encyclopædia Britannica*, Vol. VI. p. 280.

[19] Speaking of those patrician consuls, the same author in *idem*, column 2, says: "Having once begun the struggle (against the plebeians), however, they maintained it for the space of 80 years, with a spirit and resolution which made even a foreign war desirable as a relief from internal contests."

[20] Livy, VI. 35, *fin*. "Haud irritæ cecedere minæ: comitia, præter ædilium tribunorumque plebis, nulla sunt habita. Licinius Sextiusque, tribuni plebis refecti, nullos curules magistratus creari passi sunt: eaque *solitudō magistratum*, et plebe reficiente duos tribunos, et his comitia tribunorum militum tollentibus, per quinquennium urbem tenuit." Such was the tremendous power of the outcast element that Rome lost her aristocratic hold for 5 whole years.

PRÆTORS WITH WHIPS AND AXES.   475

In this aristocratic consular arrangement, next after the consuls themselves, were many prætors, lieutenants of the consuls and lord mayors of the provincial cities. These with the Romans were also generally the grandees who dispensed military force.[21] " The insignia of the prætor were those common to the higher Roman magistrates—the purple-edged robe (*toga praetexta*), and the ivory chair (*sella curulis*). In Rome he was attended by two lictors, in the provinces by six." The *curules* or ivory sedans, were from the state four and six horse chariots and represent extraordinary power.

An example of the power exercised by the prætor over the poor slave, is given by us in another page, where a brave man in Sicily, for killing a dangerous wild boar, so excited his lordship's jealousy, that, taking advantage of an ancient law prohibiting persons of lowly birth from the use of the javelin, he ordered the trembling man to be crucified upon the spot. These prætors made use of the red color of labor for the brutal purposes of war, and it looks seriously as though this was a sort of cunning ruse or dodge, played upon the credulous, whereby to curry favor with the already powerfully organized numbers of labor.

Next after the consuls and prætors in the military pageant came the lictors. They wore the blue and azure cloak when in the field, which was the *sagum caeruleum*, epithet of death, darkness, night. In this garb the lictor's fierce military characteristics were personified. The grand magistrate's attendant, he strutted at the pageant in line of march, with a bundle of rods in his hand and held on high the formidable axe of execution, that the people might understand the presence of a sublime power and bow their heads in respect. If a criminal or malefactor was caught, his duty was to whip him with the scourges and cleave his head from his body with the axe.[22]

[21] *Encyclopædia Brittanica*, Vol. XIX. p. 675
[22] Livy, I. 26. "Horatius cui soror virgo, quæ desponsa uni ex Curiatiis fuerat, obvia ante portam Capenam fuit: cognitoque super humeros paludamento sponsi, quod ipsa confecerat, solvit crines, et flebiliter nomine sponsum mortuum appellat. Movet feroci juveni animum comploratio sororis in victoria sua tantoque gaudio publico. Stricto itaque gladio, simul verbis increpans, transiguit puellum: 'Abi hinc cum immaturo amore ad sponsum, inquit * * * I lictor colliga manus quæ paullo ante armatæ imperium populo Romano pepererunt." The same ferocious order was given the lictor by the father of Manlius, Livy, X liber VIII. cap. 7(: "I. lictor deliga ad palum." A consul, prætor or other superior officers had the right to order a lictor to perform any execution.

But when there was peace and while they were in Rome, the lictors wore the toga, purple or purple-bordered, because the lictors must be of high-born stock; although the toga of the unions was red, brown or dark red. It corresponded in Italy to the *himation* in Greece; and was the color of the lowly class everywhere, representing peace, not war,[23] as seen in any Latin dictionary. This remarkable fact reveals itself more and more plainly as the arguments and material evidences upon which it is based, receive investigation. Full attention to the ancient communal inscriptions has not yet been given, partly on account of the fact that colors do not often survive even where they were painted on the tablets; but principally, because ensigns and emblems whose colors, being sacred were at all times universally conceded were never painted at all, but simply engraved on the stone or casting in the natural color of the material on which they were cut. But it must be borne in mind that the lictors who were required to be of the optimate class, wore only a purple-red, not the labor-red. This was a mixture of the genuine with the azure (cæruleus) or the white.

Thus color in ancient days, socially speaking, was a line of demarcation separating optimates from plebeians.[24] We have thus shown how in war the sagum and the vexil-

---

[23] See note —*supra*, on the *red himation*,
[24] See Guhl and Koner, *Life of the Greeks and Romans*, pp. 485-6 : "The usual colour of the dress was originally white (for the *toga* this was required by law): only poor people, slaves and freedmen wore dresses of the natural brown or black colour of the wool." "In imperial times, however, even men adopted dresses of scarlet etc." * * * "The bride wears a reddish violet *stola*, adorned with an embroidered *instita* of darker hue." These are the poorer class, as they seem to come under the general remark quoted, viz: *that only poor people, slaves and freedmen wore colors.* Then (page 486 , occurs this remark ; The outside of Perseus' dress is reddish brown, the inside white," as if to coax with the great rising element, while taking care to keep "pure" within, in difference to this fabulous royal potentate, son of the great cærulean Zeus. Speaking of the toga of Italy, or the *himation* of Greece, the same authors, p. 486 remark, that " Looked at straight, the blood-red dress thus prepared had a blackish tint: looked at from underneath, it showed a bright red color." Thus the *toga* no matter by whom worn, was red when it represented peace—a fact which remains good for all antiquity ; while the regular war-colors were azure and blue or white and azure-blue. So again *idem*, p- 168, speaking of the Greek robes and other articles of apparel, and the pictures whence the information is taken, says ; " Men also appear in these pictures, with the cherry-coloured *chlamys* and the red *himation;* and speaking of the Μίτρα or ancient turban, used also sometimes as a zone-belt, which was red, the same authors add: The Oriental turban is undoubtedly a remnant of this custom." Here again we have an example of the power of habit, to transmit itself through indefinite periods of time. In another phrase, *idem*, p. 168, speaking of the plebeian class, is the expression: "The original colors, although (particular the reds) slightly altered by the burning process, may still be distinctly recognized."

lum in its original tints, were white, cærulean or azure and blue, in the field of war,[25] while the peace *toga* which was red and the *vexillum* when seén among the communes, were of a brilliant crimson, So also we have explained somewhat the manner in which in later ages of the republic the phenomenal love and reverence of the lowly class, so soon as they exhibted a political and military weight was taken advantage of and even adopted in sham in the Roman camp, seemingly to curry favor with this rising class. It now remains to further proceed in explanation of the Roman military pageant.

The next officers in rank after the lictor were sometimes the equites or knights on horseback; and their military pomp, when preceded by consuls, prætors and their lictors, as the latter bore aloft their prætorian bundles of whips and their hatchets and axes when going out of the gates to war, or returning in triumph from it, was a spectacle anything but flattering to the poor, to whose backs and necks the scourges and the axes were too often applied.

Another powerful argument substantiating the prevalence of red as an adopted color of the gods of industry, where peace and not war was intended, is seen in the typical goddess Pomona, another name perhaps for Ceres or Demeter, Isis, Cybele and other guardians of agricultural labor. She presided over the orchard fruits and the gardens, and her emblem, symbol or sign was a flaming red. This old Roman divinity had charge of fruit-orchards. In the deep forests she was adored by satyrs and other sylvan fairies.[26]

Pomona stands out as an excellent corroboration to the argument that from the most ancient conceivable times red was the typical color for the symbols, emblems or banners of the strictly working people and shows furthermore, that to carry out the original idea of Pomona, a priest or priestess of a Pomona of to-day must be attired in a flaming red and must not represent strife; as her function is that of peace.[27] It was even forbidden on high penalty that her attendant servant or priest should look upon an

[25] Cicero. *In Pisonem*, 23: "Togulæ lictoribus ad portam præsto fuerunt, quibus illi acceptis, sagula rejecerunt et catervam imperatori suo novam præbuerunt."
[26] Ovid. *Metamorphoses*, XIV. 623 seqq
[27] Guhl and Konor, *Life of the Greeks and Romans*, p, 536

army; strife being to her a terrible sin. He must even turn his head from the sight of soldiers.

This divinity chose "from the plebs"[28] a priest called the *Flamen Pomonalis*. He was allowed to take a wife but could never be divorced from her; for that would be suggestive of strife. True to the typical color of the labor she represented, she was called *flaminica*, and she held in her hand a pruning knife, although this instrument is represented to have also been intended for sacrificing the lamb at the feasts of Pomona. She was robed in a *chiton* or *himation*, which in Rome was called a *toga*. It was made of wool, and was screened from the vulgar by a long veil, (*flammeum*), of a flaming red color or Phœnician glow,[29] typical of her plebeian estate. This *Flaminica* not only represented and presided over, but also performed, labor; for she busied herself in the toils of her husband, the flamen, in the work of the feasts and entertainments. The *collegia* were fond of celebrating by parading with flaming streamers and flags.

The worship of the sacred ibis has also something to do in this connection. It is mentioned in company with Pomona and was probably the sacred scarlet ibis, of the Egyptians, whose red colors have ever been unscientifically mixed or confounded with the flamingo. This bird, agreeably to its name, flamen, flaminica, flamingo was, especially all the wing part, of a fiery red (*phoenicopteros*). The imagination of the ancients pictured the red to be emblematic of love,[30] ardency and warmth; all of which were portrayed in the beams of the sun, and such impressions crystalized into a red color. But the aristocratic

[28] See Johnson's, *Universal Cyclopædia*, Vol. III. p. 1,328, Art. *Pomona*; Ovid. *Metamorphoses*, XIV. 623, says that she was courted by Puemunus another d vinity of the Italian forests and gained her by a trick. It is also stated that Pomona had a citadel or seat among sacred groves near Ostia called the *Pomonal* and that she had a vicegerent or *sacerdos*—a man or perhaps woman chosen from among the laboring element, who had to rank last and lowest of the 15 flames of Rome. From Varro, Lingua Latina, V. 15, 25: ". . . . flamines, quod in Latio, capite velato, erant semper ac caput cinctum habebant filo, flamines dicti."

[29] Consult *Flamineus*, sq. in any good Latin *Lexicon;* Guhl and Koner, p. 537

[30] So in Greek we have Ερωδιός for the heron presumably applied to both these birds the scarlet ibis and the flamingo sometimes adored for the scarlet or sacred ibis. But the 'ερωδιός was a form of 'ερως signifying the flame of love. So *Ardea*, the Latin for heron the self-same bird, has its etymology in *ardeo* to burn and blaze. It may therefore be strongly suspected that Pomona and the flamens had something to do with the temple at Ardea near Rome burned by Æneas, and from whose ashes, phœnix like, arose the wonderful red heron or phœnix. Nothing can gainsay this, for both *ardea* and φοίνξ are the flaming reds of Latin and Greek.

idea of the *ego* as known in the noble, opposed to the ignoble or plebeian, was always of an awe-striking or imposing hue, such as the white, azure, blue and gray.

Curiously enough the celebrated sacred scarlet ibis of the ancients is found more frequently in the Americas than on the Nile, which leads to a plausible conjecture that this heron was the flamingo, another red heron, migratory and common on the Nile. These well-known, gregarious red birds, "when feeding, or at rest, owing to their red plumage, have often been likened to a body of British soldiers.[31]

It is thus shown that red was the crystalization of all dark hues, while white, in primitive notions, was a state, purified altogether from color; and thus the true aristocratic symbol. Labor's warm, serum-reddened currents of love and life and manly vigor, together with its vast affixture of paraphernalia, which from the mythical ages clustered around this central color, was always based upon the opposite of those formidable, repellent hues residing in the awe-inspiring idea of nobility.

Persons inclined to doubt may here conceive an objection based in the fact that there was, common among the optimates, an aristocratic or imperial purple and that this purple was not only of a reddish hue but also an august color; so costly and grand that it could not be permitted by law to be worn, except by great dignitaries.

The answer to this objection is, however, easily met. In very ancient times owing to the popularity of the communal cult, an enormous trade and manufacture of the Tyrian red and purple was carried on. That nobody but the great masses dealt in this trade is evident from the fact that after the rise of the proletarian power, Rome began a conquest ending only in the massacre, subjugation and enslavement of these millions who had sustained the trade. Rome, probably to curry favor with her "dangerous class" at home, and after she had reduced the world by conquest, passed a law making it a crime for anybody to use the red except the nobles. After this law went into force in Phœnicia the workingmen engaged in the great and wide-spread trade of dyeing, so completely lost their business, that even the secret of their ancient

[31] *Encyclopædia Britannica*, Vol. IX, p. 250.

and beautiful hues was lost and it has never been recovered to this day." Now this all proves that, agreeably to our views previously expressed, the purple came in vogue with the power of the plebs, who had this beautiful color; since these great conquests abroad commenced less than 200 years before Christ. All agree with Polybius [33] who, himself one of the victims of these conquests, devotes pages to an account of the origin of Roman degeneracy. When Rome suppressed the manufacture of the hated red color of the organized communes she herself adroitly donned the purple of labor's goddess—" the brilliantly tinted garments " of the priests of Isis and Osiris, of Ceres and Demeter, of Pomona and her flaminica, for " a mantle of a Roman emperor." So that while it is easy to show that in later times, when Rome was tumbling into that great slave-holding period which brought degeneracy and death, she intriguingly filched the beautiful color, and after streaking it with the old aristocratic gray and adulterating it with blue or white or azure, she gave it to her lords and ladies; its makers with their aged secret, she gave to the wild beasts of the gladiatorial games to be " butchered for a Roman holiday." But it is not easy to prove that the purple containing the red was used by the *imperatores* before the conquests. True, it is so mentioned; but it was not the red-purple—only the azure-blue which received this name.

It is not in the scheme of these arguments to attempt a polemic for or against the primitive notions of mankind in regard to the choice of colors. We find species of innocent consistency all through. As white was the essence or crystal of *dis*color, symbolizing purity, aristocracy—*to agathoteron*, the better part, while its nuances of beautiful blue, its silvered gray and azure, all pointed to the etherial sky, lofty, forbidding and sublime, so red, among the divinities of a yielding or producing race, was the essence, or crystalization of all color, from the murky smut of earth to brown and dun, at last reaching the gorgeous

---

[32] Consult *Encyclopædia Britannica*, Vol. VII. p. 493.
[33] Polybius, in his *Histories*, distinctly states that the decline of the Roman honor and virtue began with these conquests. For modern opinion on the date of Roman decline see Bücher *Aufstände der Unfreien Arbeiter*, where numerous valuable quotations are made from Polybius, Athenæus and others will be found of much interest, shedding a new light upon the subject.

scarlet and the crimson coma of Apollo,[34] or the flaming *chiton, chlamys, himation* or *toga*, believed to be the trailing robes of Demeter and her red silk, flame-clad daughter Proserpine and all the other protecting goddesses of labor and its products. This consistency, in harmony with Plato on the one hand and Aristotle on the other, is borne out alike by science, and by trial of an immemorial duration.

The Christians when they afterwards came, adopted the red, wherever they planted among the communes; and in our next chapter we shall show this to have been the case at almost every instance, in their earlier career. So soon as priest-power showed itself the old white came back; and accordingly we find the white standard at Rome, while the red banner remains at Auvergne, Paris and London, with its *gules* in England and its *gueules* in France. Everything throwing light upon the subject, shows the same preference of mediæval guilds, for red among the poorer or working class who learned to adopt Christianity because unlike the old Paganism, it declared for the gradual emancipation of slaves. And they have never to this day, given up their pristime banner.

We have mentioned the extreme antiquity of the red color as applied to ensigns, symbols, signs and types of the plebeian classes. These curious facts came down to us through the industry-protecting priesthood when they appear in histories and geographies, and through inscriptions, when they appear as relics of the proletaries themselves. This priesthood which transmits the records of the red color is, so far as we have been able to ascertain, only that of Minerva, goddess of mechanical labor and laborers, and Ceres, goddess, or tutelary divinity who controlled agriculture.[35] These great mythical powers, implicitly believed in for so many ages, had different name in different countries; but preserved with a wonderful uniformity the same functions everywhere.

We carry the investigation to England, the ancient Britannia, now known through cumulative evidence of

[34] There has been found (see *Encyclopædia Britannica*, Vol. II. Art. *Apollo*), a fine round bronze head of Apollo stamped on the silver coin of Clazomenæ, preserved in the British Museum. This venerable midget is a curiosity.
[35] See Gerhard, *Antike Denkmaler* with *Tafel* CXX. 1, showing image of Cybele in her chariot with lions and two figures clad in the *toga*.

comparative history, to be as ancient as Greece or Egypt, and centuries older than Rome.

Exactly as in the case of Greece and Rome, the aristocratic and Druidical priests were clothed in white,[36] so likewise the Druids of the aristocratic religion, like the southern European, are found to have been the most cruel and bloodthirsty of the ancients, nurturing the practice of slavery and the sacrifice of human beings. In fact these abominable atrocities were found later by the Romans to so far surpass their own spirit of cruelty [37] that they sent Agricola to their fastness in the island of Mona with an army, who so completely destroyed them that they never again arose to become a great power. The account of the ferocity of this ancient aristocratic priest-power of the Druids, in their methods of human sacrifice is too shocking to be recounted.[38]

But notwithstanding the fact that priests of the state religion of ancient England were clad in white, the common or popular faith was that of sun-worship. Apollo, with all his relationship by similarity of functions, to Ceres, on the one hand, and Minerva on the other, was a protector and patron of industry by reason of his being the sun himself. He blazed forth with wondrous beams of crimson over old England as well as Europe and Asia, and was early the myth of that land and its people.[39] Perhaps there were two sets of opinions, one opposing the other among the Druids.

This blazing Phœbus, with his transcendental effulgence had to be imitated in the symbols of human labor; and how to make the crimson dyes of his train of deities was no small matter. But here the land of the Britons comes

---

[36] Hughes, *Horae Britannicae*, Vol. I. p. 158: "The Druid priest wore a white robe, and the bard sky-blue but the Ovati, green. These different colours, were, the first, the emblem of purity and peace; the other, of truth, and the last, the verdent dress of nature, in the meads and woods." They sacrificed human beings and white bulls

[37] Campbell, *Political Survey*, I. p. 525; III. p. 292; IV. pp. 475, 480. Wm. Camden, *Britannia, Druides;* Borlase, *Cornwall.*

[38] We refer the reader to Hughes, *Horæ Britannicæ*, Vol. I. pp. 232–250, who derives the facts contained in his dissertation, from Tacitus, *Annales*, XIV. cap. 29, for the Britons and Lucan, for the grove of sacrifice at Marseilles in Gaul.

[39] Consult *Idem*, p. 261. The Stonehenge Britons were sun-worshipers; that is, they deified the god of blaze. Minerva was their protectress of invention and manual labor. Stonehenge appears to have been an enormous temple, built of heavy rocks and fashioned in a simi-circle, having no roof. For a full description of Stonehenge, its structure and its surrounding influences, see *idem*, pp 258–26.

RED DYES MADE OF BRITISH TIN. 483

in for a share of our observation; for it furnished the tin of which the dye was made. After the Phœnicians found the tin mines of Cornwall and the Scilly Isles (the *cassiterides*), red colors were mostly produced in Sidon and Tyre, their southern home.

Now, without enlarging upon this matter as touching the earlier use of the red colors of England and the origin of the British *gules*, let us look at the phenomenal manner in which the habit of red colors has clung to these people. Every one familiar with the heraldic symbols has observed the frequent mention of the *gules*.[40] This, during the mediæval age, was a favorite color with the common people.

It would be well to show, in company with the English guilds, those also of the French, who are derived from the ancient Gauls. The reason of this is, that the trade union system of the Romans, elsewhere elaborately described, struck into England about the same time that it was popular in Gaul; and as the unions used the banner at Rome, the practice extended to Britain and Gaul.

The Crispins, who founded the order of shoemakers at Soissons, are the first unions we know of in the north of France. The story of the brothers Crispin and Crispinius belongs to the bloody days of Diocletian [41] whose terrible persecution of the early Christians added them as victims of martyrdom; and they have ever since been the tutelary divinities or patrons, guarding the shoemakers' art—another example of the power of superstition to perpetuate itself through the generations. So the shoemakers took the red flag; for we have a beautiful illustration of the color of the shoemakers' flag in the province of Auvergne, given us by Bouillet, in which are massed numbers of banners that were used by many trade organizations during the middle ages down to their suppression in 1780.[42]

---

[40] See *Encyclopædia Britannica*, Vol. XI p. 616, 9th edition, Art. *Heraldry;* Here, in a cut (fig. 3), in which 9 escutcheons are represented, 3 are of a red color, one being a genuine *gules*. The art of dyeing brilliant colors is very ancient. The chasuble or red mummy cloth found A. D. 1295 now in St. Paul's Cathedral, London, which is "*purpureo aliquantulum sanguineo,*" proves that the older Phœnix purple was blood red. Comp. *idem*, Vol. XVIII. p. 817. The celebrated tin dyes of the Phœnicians owed much to Britain. Consult Hughes, *Horæ Britannicæ*, Vol. 1 p. 47. It colored the finest textiles a pure red. This was going on long before Abraham or the Trojan war; and Britain yielded the tin for the scarlet dyes.

[41] Consult chapter xi. pp. 372-388, of our *History of the Ancient Trade Unions.*
[42] *Histoire des Communités des Arts et Métiers de l' Auvergne, Accompagnée des*

The *cordonniers* or shoemakers, of the middle ages and down to their suppression, were in all respects the same as in A. D. 280, when founded by St. Crispin and his brother, who are said to have stolen the leather or raw material in their zeal to make shoes for the poor. They even retain the same name. They held the same day of the same year (October 25th), for their feasts, parades and conventional jubilees, and carried the same red banner. This is the flag which the law of Theodosius excused on account of the men having been guilty of no wrong, and having always been "found peaceful, pious and upright."[43] The French called the flag or standard-bearer of these unions a *porte-banniere*, the Romans a *signifer*. These banner-bearers or more probably banner makers had a union by themselves; for a magistrate or president is found in an old inscription,[44] bearing words to that effect. Returning to the trustworthy member of the Legion of Honor and of the Institute, M. Bouillet, we find him presenting the red flag of the shoemakers of the middle ages and later, categorically somewhat as follows:

In Auvergne, city of Brioude with its antique social curiosities and its communal college, the shoemakers had their union amalgamated with the tanners, glove makers, furriers and cobblers.[45] Their banner, alike for these four trades, was all blood red, except a border of gold and a gilt fox's pelt hanging in the center. The staff was gilt and hung with beautiful tassels. An exquisite picture of this banner is given in plate 33, fig. 2.

In the old town of Ambert, department of Puy de Dôme, the shoemakers were amalgamated with the saddle

Bannières que portaient ces Communautés avant 1789. Par J. B. Bouillet, Paris, 1857.

[43] *Codex Theodosii*, Notul. Gothof. leg. 2, tit. vii. lib. XIV. *De Excusationibus Artificum.* "Signiferi, ... qui scilicet signa, et in his deorum, ferebant in pompis, festis, ludicris gentiliciis." etc.

[44] Muratorius, *Thesaurus Veterum Inscriptionum*, 25, 50; Granier. *Histoire des Classes Ouvrières*, p. 323: "Vénérable corps des maitres porte-bannières aux fêtes, et de leurs nonbreux variétés, depuis les *signiferi*, qui sont le genre jusqu' aux *cantabrarii* qui sont l' espèce." Comp. Orell, *Incriptionum Latinarum Collectio*, No. 4,282.

[45] Bouillet, *Communantés*, p. 109. describes the relations of the shoemakers with the cobblers as follows: "On comprendra facilement qu'il a du arriver de vives contestations entre les deux corps de métiers, de cordonniers et de savetiers; les uns achetaient des bottes ou des souliers vieux, les autres confectionnaient certains articles de leur état, hors des conditions prescrites par leur règlement, aussi les cours et tribunaux entendirent souvent leurs griefs pour ces faits ou pour les visites des uns chez les autres."

and bridle makers.[46] Their ensign, shown in plate 12, fig. 1, was of the same shape as that of Brioude; about one-half of the surface of the canvass within the border was of a brilliant red color. The whole banner was red, blue and gold.

An exquisite red banner was that of the shoemakers of Clermont. In the center of a similarly escutcheon-shaped canvass is a shoe-knife with gilt handle and steel colored blade of nearly the same shape that we see to-day in any shoeshop. A gold border shiningly fringed the whole, except the top and like the others, the standard and tassels were gilt. All the canvass is a flaming red. It presents, indeed a beautiful exhibit of the old French *oriflamme* and the older, pre-Christian FLAG and *flamma* which we have described as the ensign hues of the workmen's goddesses, so familiar and so endeared to the Latin lowly race.[47]

The ancient city of Nemetum and seat of the Cæsars, *Augustonemetum*, which was one of the early Christian centers (A. D. 250), became the Clermont-Ferrand of the present day. Here the *collegia* and communes of the early Christians long ago planted and always maintained themselves even through the persecutions of Diocletian and Maximian. No place seems to have more warmly cultivated the ancient, or rejected the innovations of modern life, than Clermont. The foregoing description of the shoemakers of Clermont is given by Bouillet.[48] Mommsen, in his history of Rome, makes this volcanic and ster-

[46] Idem, p. 110, and plate 12 fig 1. "Leur bannière portait: "Tiercé en pal: á bordure de *gueules*, à un conteau a pied d'argent, emmanché d' or etc., at a 3 d' or, á une bride de cheval de *gueules*."

[47] It may be well here to quote some of the definition of the English *gules*, French *gueules*, Latin, *gulae* because though somewhat rare, they appear in ancient and mediæval heraldry: Stormouth, *English Dictionary*: GULES, noun, pl. ral, pronounced *gulz*. [French gueules, red or sanguine in blazon—from gueule, mouth, the throat], In heraldry, a term denoting red, represented in engravings in upright lines."

Worcester, *English Dictionary*. (Unabridged), defines it thus: GULES, (gulz) n. Fr. *gueules*.—L, *gula* the throat: or the Ar. *gula*, a rose, Fairholt—" Corruption of *gueules*. red Fr, which is probably from the Pers. guhl, a rose."

Webster. *English Dictionary*, (Unabridged : "GULES, (*gulz*), n. [Fr. *gueules*, from Lat. *gula*, reddened skin]. (*Her.*) A red color--intended, perhaps, to represent courage, animation or manhood, and indicated in engraved figures of escutcheons and the like, by straight perpendicular lines."

[48] Bouillet, *Communautés d' Auvergne*, plate 11, fig. 3. On p. 110, is the description as follows : " A Clermont: De *gueules*, á un tranchet á lame d' argent emmanché d' or."

ile region of Auvergne an example in proof that the introduction of modern innovations would result in the place becoming uninhabitable,[49] although it has withstood many misfortunes, natural and ecclesiastical, and is yet a populous and thriving region. Here, where ancient customs have so tenaciously clung, we find them near the close of the last century, still with their flaming red banner; and no amount of prejudice could change the working people from its use at the feasts and parades, just as they were doing in the days of Socrates or Tiberius Gracchus.

One banner was a flaming red without a spot or blemish of any other color except in the center, where stood the Virgin Mary, dressed in silver gray, holding in her arms the naked infant. It symbolizes the peaceful handicraft of the shoemakers, carders, weavers and several others. This central picture of the Madonna or Notre Dame, holding the new-born child, as represented on the plate, is artistic; and standing upon a background of gorgeous red, presents with its gold fringes, its slender staff and its tassels, an admirable piece of art.[50] Among the various unions amalgamated under this banner were the masons; thus showing the red banner to have been an emblem of that trade.

We do not pretend to say that all the shoemakers of the mediæval ages used the red flag. Notable exceptions are given in plates 9, fig. 2, of the city of Maringues, and plate 11, fig. 4, of Riom, but nearly all of those given retain this color. Out of the eight shoemakers' unions represented on the plates no less than five sported the red color, some of them retaining the peace hues of the divinities unalloyed by anything except the device of the craft, generally placed in the center of the canvass.

In England we likewise find the *gules* upon thousands of escutcheons from as early as Constantine the Great. It is there yet. The habit of holding up the red as a

---

[49] *History of Rome,* (Eng. trans.), Vol I. p. 62, quotes Dureau de la Malle, *Economie Politique des Romains*, II. p. 226. In this passage it is mentioned that such sights as a woman yoked or harnessed by the side of a cow, are still of common occurrence.

[50] See plate 12, fig. 2, of Bouillet, *Histoire des Communautés des Arts et Métiers*. The description of the plate is on pages 110-111, as follows: "A Montferrand, les cordonniers, réunis aux cardeurs, aux tisserands, aux marchands revendeurs aux hôteliers, aux maçons, etc., portaient une bannière: De *gueules*, à Notre Dame d' argent, couronnée d' or."

symbol of some tutelary divinity—nobody knows what because everybody has forgotten—clings to the British Isles with a stubborn tenacity to this day. How comes it that the military coat is red? That French soldiers in parade look like a prairie on fire? That in blazonry the standards, and in shipping, the streamers, pennons, jacks and merchant-standards,[51] especially those representing peace, so many are of this color? The reasons for it are two-fold. First, they are the most conspicuous and beautiful and consequently the best. As proof of this we find in America and elsewhere the blood-red storm signals, in Switzerland the red arms, in Denmark, Great Britain, Norway, Turkey, Morocco, Peru, Chili, Bolivia and many other countries, the red merchants flags and ensigns; red occupying almost the entire surface of the canvass. So also, the British jack.

In the next place, these were the colors originally employed to represent the same object in ancient times when, in the imagination of men, red was believed to be holy like the gorgeous streams of light from the rising or setting sun, which shaped itself on the simple, primeval mind, into an omnipotent being with human form, like Apollo and Ceres, who were believed to be guardians of labor and its products. If then, it is the best, is still used because best, and if, after a trial of an æon of time it be found that the lowly class thus symbolized by it, judged rightly ten thousand years ago, and have preserved it in their unions and hearts through this long period, can there be any consistency in a paltry, time-serving-prejudice or its tricks and intolerant schemes against it? We leave this question to science.

We are told by antiquarians that when the Romans settled Kent, called by them *Cantiopolis*, large numbers of the trade unionists came from Italy and there established themselves; and engaging with the natives in the arts of brass and woodwork, taught them the use of the turning lathe and other machinery. So we find this section the chosen nucleus of several trade unions at this day; and right here and in London an hour's walk up the Thames

---

[51] See *Encyclopædia Britannica*, Vol. IX. pp. 241-245 Art. *Flag.* Let the reader open a late edition of Webster or Worcester's Unabridged *Dictionary* to the word flag, and his eye will meet as it were, a flame of fire.

is where the typical British *gules* is found in greatest abundance; for the same phenomenon of transmission makes London the bed-rock of modern socialism. Previously to the introduction of the mechanic arts this territory was a wilderness; and the people lived in tents, hovels, huts and caves, in the rudest state, almost without clothes or houses. Romans taught and helped them to construct habitations, married with them and mixed, as is now becoming known, planting among them all their home habits and customs.[52] Many of these Romans on their long journey through Gaul to Britain, lingered on the way; and those were the workingmen who planted the flag in such places as Auvergne; for Romans were in England 55 years before Christ. We will therefore suppose that if they planted it in Auvergne they did so in Kent, and having less positive evidence from the latter we allow ourselves to draw comparisons by what we positively know of the former, which was a way-station of the Italian emigrants.

As we have spoken of carpenters, let us take this trade in evidence. Drawing from Bouillet who has so faithfully worked this territory, we find the red banner to have been used by them as follows: Carpenters with patron Saint Joseph and with day of celebrations, the 19th of March, (March was the natal month of Ceres, Minerva and Apollo).[53]

Taking all the principal trades we might suppose to have been introduced into Kent and London at the same time that they existed in Auvergne, we find that in the latter place, the bakers' annual feast days were in the spring of the year, corresponding to the festival days of Ceres, goddess of grain-growing, and Dionysus and the other labor gods. Here we have in Bouillet's portrayal of the trades

---

[52] Comp. E. H. Rogers' correct and able statement in McNeill's *Labor Problem of to-day*, p. 335, drawing from Coote, *Romans of Britain*. "Rome held possession of the island more than 400 years, and it was never abandoned by those descended from the Romans." Mr. Rogers speaks of the mechanics who early emigrated to Massachusetts, as the "Men of Kent."

[53] *Histoire des Communautés des Arts et Métiers d' Auvergne*, pp. 80-83 : "On peut faire une étude très curieuse du rôle que joua la charpenterie militaire, dans la seconde expédition de Pépin-le-Bref, en 761. contre Gaifre, duc d'Aquitaine. Au siège qu'i fit subir à la ville de Clermont, profitant de l'expérience des Lombards, il fit dresser contre les murs de formidables béliers, des poutres énormes qui, mises en mouvement par des leviers et des cordages et roulant sur des cylindres, par l'impulsion que leur donnaient les charpentiers et leurs habiles ouvriers, heurtaient de leur front de fer les murailles et les mettaient en pièces. On peut le voir encore dans d'autres siéges que soutinrent Clermont et Montferrand en 1121 et 1126."

unions of Auvergne, six banners in red out of eleven mentioned for the bakers, and the six red flags were for the towns of Ambert, Brioude, Issoire and Thiers, where the flag was all red except the central device; and Riom and Saint-Flour, where they painted a part only of its surface in red.

Turning to Depping,[54] and Shepheard who wrote a curious statement on guild laws in 1650, at London, we find that there were unions in both London and Paris during the same period, or from the time of Constantine the Great; and if so, the habits of the people of Auvergne must have been about the same as those of the Parisians and Londoners because France was the territory of the overland emigration from Italy. The red banner appears to have been colored after the tutelary divinities or patron saints whose feast days still corresponded with those of the proto-divinities, tenaciously conserved through the ages, from the myths by the power of habit.

But we may follow this interesting subject farther, taking the various other trades together. Beginning with towns that adopted a banner as their device for arts and trades in general, we find at Langheac, the flag half red; Chaudesaigues, half red; Pont du Chateau, half red; Vic, Vic-le-Comte and Saint Germain, largely red; while many of the trades residing in these towns had all red for their banner.

In Mont-Ferrand, the carders, masons, weavers, small dealers and tavern keepers had blood red. In Aurillac and Riom, the saddle and bridle makers, confectioners, cheese handlers, locksmiths, shoemakers, cutlers and silk workers all had red and a number a bright fiery color all over except the device.

At Theirs, the marble cutters, glaziers and cutters had all red. At Ambert, besides the shoemakers, already mentioned, the saddle and bridle makers and weavers had a red banner, or one with more or less red on it.

Clermont de Cournières and Saint Germain-Lembron had total red except central device. So Saint Germain, the celebrated industrial suburb of Paris named, as it ap-

[54] G. B. Depping. *Règlement sur les Arts et Métiers de Paris*, this author quotes a state regulation covering the same period, which is curious as showing the honesty of freedmen from tricks such as characterize the present competitive system, causing much adulteration of manufactures.

pears from this more aged labor-hive of southwest France, still clings to, and fights for, its ideal red as a tutelary or patron color.

The tutelary banner of Pierrefort, had the top red far enough down to cover more than one third of its surface, the rest having several common colors but no white.

At Clermont-Ferrand the joiners had a red plane, and the marble-cutters other similar red objects for a device, while at Brioude, shoemakers, tavern keepers, tanners, glove makers, furriers and cobblers, had each all flaming red, and their parades, which used to be celebrated on the 11th of November, must have been a sightly spectacle indeed, all through the middle ages. They were devout Christians although their worship had differentiated in course of time from that of Minerva whose feast day was the same time of the year, whose colors were the same, and whose cult had only changed from that of a tulelary heathen divinty, to that of a Christian patron.

The banner of the painters of Montaigut was entirely of a blazing red. Hatters and glaziers of Saint Flour had their banner red at the top; and the hatters, saddlers, tinners, butchers and tavern keepers of Issoire had a great red ring like the sun's corona. Surgeons and apothecacaries, so well-known to have been classed among the plebs in former times, had all red banners in Aurillac. The tanners, glove makers and curriers of this place also flamed in the same color.[55]

Abundance of other evidence might be here brought forward; for the immense field of Europe is scarcely yet entered upon.

If any one should still contend that the red flag or the red color was warlike and antagonistical to life and its peaceful pursuits and labors, let him further observe the fact that in those lands where the communes left their traces most plentifully on their inscriptions, will be found the red banner to this day. Modern Turkey occupies one of these localities. And what is the merchant standard of modern Turkey? A blood red color tinges every shred of the canvass except an exiguous star and a tiny crescent

---

[55] See *Index* and *plates* of Bouillet, *Histoire des Communautés des Artes et Métiers de L'Auvergne*, where still more material may be found to confirm these statements.

moon, tne wife of the flaming Apollo! Certainly no warfare is symbolized in the peaceful standard of a merchant vessel.

Morocco, Algiers and Tunis, the north coast of Africa, once occupied by the Carthagenians and other colonies of Phœnicians, still have a flag which is totally red. When the origin of this habit is traced, it will be revealed that Baal, the great divinity of the Phœnicians, whose attributes were the same as Ceres, whose colors were red, whose home was that of the inventive and ingenius dyers, and who was the tutelary divinity or patron of labor, was the huge sun-god that inspired the color by his glowing beams.

The northern coast of Africa was colonized by the Punic race whose name both in Greek and Latin is the every day word for red. Both Turkey, which succeeded to Græco-Phænician domination in Asia, and Morocco, Tunis and Algiers, which succeeded to Carthagenian rule and influence, still retain for this peace-color the red in its altogether unadulterated state.

Spain, the ancient Iberia, a colony of Phœnicia which also planted the red banner in the land of Viriathus, conveyed this habit to Peru, where we still find the banner and merchant standard all red, except a white stripe through the middle. In Eygpt the peace-standard is blood red with the exception of a cresent of the moon.

Great Britain, likewise a colony of Phœnicia so ancient that the records descend to us only in the tin tincture furnished by her mines, of which the red dyes were made, preserves to this day an otherwise unaccountable habit of displaying the red *gules*, and her merchant standard is all red except a corner and even this is partly red. The Romans who later settled Britain only confirmed the same habit; since the labor communes of Rome had borrowed their tutelary divinities from Asia.

Thus Phœnicia whose æons of antiquity make her the proto-nursery of man along with central Asia, is alike, the home of Baal " the sun-god, conceived as the male principal of life and reproduction in nature," [56] and the mother of almost all the colonies where sunbeams paint the future flags and banners of the myriads of toil whose com-

[56] *Encyclopædia Britannica*, Vol. III. p. 152.

munal **culture was** one of peace, equality and good will to man.

Very much **more** evidence might be adduced in proof of the red banner having descended to the working family of man, as a legacy from ancient usages religions and beliefs; and showing that while memory and use have traditionally adhered, the superstitious reasons for much, have long been forgotten, though the economical reasons have remained. We submit these curious points to further study by antiquaries with the remark that the most striking feature of these phenomena is, that feast-days of the middle ages correspond for the peculiar crafts, very nearly with those of the same crafts and same divinities in the remotest antiquity of which we have been able to trace traditional and palæographic records.

We have constantly found the red banner to have predominated only in paths of peace; and never outside that domain except when the peculiar and well-known attachment of the lowly to it, was taken advantage of, do we find it in war. So it was used and so it careered in the early colonies of the United States. The early flag, true to the traditions of the past, was of a blazing red color in Massachusetts,[57] in New York, and probably in every one of the thirteen original states. It was the flag used by General Washington at the onset. When the war of the revolution broke out it was a beautiful red, with the old merchantman's ensign of the union jack—a peace-token—and men of peace suddenly found themselves compelled, in the absence of a war-flag, to float the red ensign amid the clank and din of cruel strife. It was the flag of Lexington, of Bunker Hill, of Ticonderoga; and in its center shone the patriotic motto "Liberty and union." A glance at the newspapers of those days best reveals these data But those men were struggling for the right of free laboı like the men of old. These facts rather stultify the prevailing notions against the old red banner.

[57] See *American Cyclopædia*, 1883, Vol. VII., pp. 250-251: "In the beginning of the revolution a variety of flags was displayed in the revolted colonies. The 'union flags' mentioned so frequently in the newspapers of 1774 were the ordinary English red ensigns bearing the union jack." The flag "displayed by Putnam on July 18th, following the battle of Bunker Hill), was red, with 'Qui transtullit sustinet' on one side and on the other: '*An appeal to Heaven.*'"

CHAPTER XXIII.

THE TRUE MESSIAH.

FOUNDERS OF GREAT INSTITUTIONS COMPARED

How THE REAL MESSIAH found Things at His Advent on Earth—Palestine—Syria—Rhodes and the Islands—Suffering Condition of Labor—Seeds of the Revolution already Sown—Further Analysis of the Conditions—The *Eranoi* and *Thiasoi*—*Orgeons* and *Essenes*—Falsehoods regarding the *Bacchantes*.

AFTER 417 years, from the strike of the 20,000 miners and artisans at the Laurian mines in Greece, and 70 years from the last strike-war—that of the gladiators under Spartacus in Italy—there arose an orator out of the laboring class, who in Judea in an open air meeting, probably before a great assemblage, told the world that resistance to evil by means of bloody uprisings, was fraught with failure. Undoubtedly having in mind those terrible scenes we have pictured in these chapters, this foremost of orators and teachers proclaimed at the mass meeting these words:

"Ye have heard that it hath been said (by them of old time), an eye for an eye and a tooth for a tooth; but I say unto you that ye resist not evil but whosoever shall smite thee on thy right cheek, turn him the other also."[1] Strange words! Inapplicable to this seething world. They were intended for some microcosm; some perfected state—the realized heaven on earth. In the competitive world to-day, Christian as it pretends to be, the old fighting eye for eye and tooth for tooth prevails, ever will pre-

[1] *Matthew*, V. 38-39.

vail; to talk otherwise is absurd except in the deep penetralia where that heaven is realized.

By taking these strange words in the light of true social science and reasoning upon their meaning from the point of view in which these pages are written, we may perhaps understand their import. Otherwise the task is difficult. Nations continue to demand an eye for an eye. Communities do the same. Even families, despite their consanguine ties, cannot but continue to enslave and often destroy each other. Individuals stand over-against each other in mocking and bitter competition. the shrewdest or most favored survive while the majorities languish and fail.

Jesus when he said these words was in the act of creating an association; and that association actually continued for 300 years practicing the precepts of its founder. It was no new thing. It had existed for centuries before; it existed then. What he did was to bring out into the open world that which had so long been secret.

It was at a moment when such doctrines were comprehensible to the masses. Notions of the Messiah existed everywhere and the deep religious tinge was indispensable. The irascible world had many a tilt with the terrible monster of competition whose religion had been deeply based upon human slavery and the grasp for acquisition was still so strong that although the principle of equality and hence of emancipation of labor from its degradation, has never even to this day been relinquished, it did not obtain for many ages. Through this great movement a ponderous, revolutionary blow certainly fell upon the old competitive system. But that blow though ultimately fatal, did not kill the monster on the spot. He still lingers and is to-day struggling in a temporary hope and exultation although nearly 2,000 years have elapsed since the word went forth against him.

It cannot be considered in any other light than that the revolutionary events treated in foregoing chapters, followed by the enormous wave of reform of the early Christians, produced a tremendous syncope or swoon; that an atrophy supervened; and that they benumbed the whole social organism of the great Indo-European race. The dark ages into which our race sank, after the adop-

tion of Christianity and its ratification and legalization
by Constantine must ever be considered a phenomenon
under any other reasoning than that this task it undertook was too prodigious for its powers. Æons of time
were necessary to accomplish so vast a revolution. To
overwhelm the great aristocratic Pagan religion with its
array of traditions; to engulf and annihilate its obstinate
cult; to emancipate the two-thirds majority on whose ill-
paid labor it had feasted, glutted itself and grown monstrous in bulk and arrogance, was a task so profound that
although actually undertaken, it caused a reaction, rolling
up moral and intellectual billows so high that the ages
and the nations were swept into a terrible jargon of dogmas tyrannies and bloody, inquisitorial intolerance which
destroyed the virility of the race for more than a thousand
years. And even now, after so many centuries, the end
of the convulsions is **far off**, though hopefully approaching.

All struggles **embracing deep principles are attended
by qualms, swoons and upheavals.** The numberless combatants who fell back in the swooning period that settled
upon the human race after the Council of Nice with its
mongrel Christianity, its idolatry, priestcraft and despotism, are emerging with higher hopes and broader views;
their armor, the mechanics of their own invention, redu-
plicated by their own labor, wielded by their own hands
and brain and their manhood cleared of doubts and superstitions—those deadly misgivings of the ancients. No
one to-day asks more than Jesus did; for equal liberty,
universal freedom and common ownership, with his sublime love and inter-care are quite enough. Squadrons
innumerable thus armed and outfitted are, in our bright,
regenerate century, returning to the conflict against the
aged, competitive and long successful enemy of equal advantages and equal care. The conflict in this second coming may be long, hopefully in our own land bloodless, because fought with arguments, organization, diplomacy and
law.

We have sketched several of the most renowned governments and ideal governments of the ancients. They all,
having their foundation upon competition and its natural
partiality, turned against the laboring people on whom

they fed. They failed and came to naught. What there was in them of good could not obtain because they insulted and disrespected labor and degraded the working people on whom they existed from day to day. Nature tolerated some of them for a fair trial but they have disappeared and are no more. Jesus came and advocated another form based upon equality and brotherhood.

But before further considering the form established by the lowly workingman let us look honestly and squarely at the condition in which he found things.

All Asia Minor was the scene of labor organizations, Canaan by no means excepted. The Phœnicians who boasted an antiquity of 30,000 years,[2] occupied the land of Canaan on the Mediterranean Sea, in which country Jesus lived and'passed the greater part of his life. These Canaanites appear before the researches of modern archæologists and historians to have been among the first who possessed labor organizations. In giving a sketch of several ancient forms of government, we have simply described the competitive system, ancient and modern. Even the plans of Lycurgus and Numa failed altogther of affecting the revolution by which we mean the complete change from the old Pagan central idea of slavery to one of social and economic equality. There was no socialism beyond that of the family, in the government instituted in the idea of common ownership, communal intercourse, common tables and impartial distribution of land, as arranged by Lycurgus and afterwards shadowed by Plato and Aristotle. Every idea of true socialism was utterly neutralized by their hostility to laborers. The gymnastics which took the place of physical energy supplied by well regulated labor, and no better for the bodily health and development, was less natural, more straining and far less satisfactory.

In point of true national economy, government and labor cannot remain separate. By the governments mentioned, labor was disgraced, the laborer denied instruction, enslaved. Who then, were the citizens? Who the people? An oligarchy consisting of one-third of the population. An imperious, oligarchy of landlords. The condition of Ireland or England, wherever worst overrun and

[2] Africanus, *In Syncellus*, p. 31.

monopolized by landlords to-day, is better. Again, so far as the family socialism is concerned it was still more pernicious; for it was hypocritically an acquiescence in the ancient aristocracy existing among the highest class, everywhere in the right of the first-born son. Lycurgus recognized this arch aristocracy in forbidding kings and a few select individuals from indulging in the voluptuous interchange of loves. As in the traditional Pagan family, the king like the *paterfamilias*, was the breeder of kings. The mass of the people were left without sacred or holy honors. By people we mean the citizens and favored owners, or rather the protected, recognized and favored of the state. What then, shall be said of the workers? Summing it all up, these governments were exactly what they turned out to be—the quintessence of competitive forms, breeding disunion and corruption, thus coaxing on their own dissolution.

But seeds of the true revolution were, from the earliest antiquity inherent in the labor organizations, which during these abortive efforts of aristocratic lawgivers and teachers, quietly existed in the midst of them. Had there existed only a few of these societies there would be no need here of pressing our subject. It would be allowed to slumber forever unmentioned. But they were innumerable. Comparative palæography indeed finds a new theme amongst them for the dignity of the labor problem; for it casts a fresh and charming color into the hitherto dry reading of annals.

But the fact that they were so numerous as to exist in thousands and perhaps millions and that their quiet existence covered unknown ages of time, is far less significant than the fact that they all seem to have possessed the kernel, not of the dishonest and hypocritical, but of the honest and real socialism, such as Jesus and the early Christians struggled to plant as the ultimate plan for all men to follow. They were all certainly alike in helping each other, in respecting and honoring labor and laborers, in co-operating for mutual aid, in a perfectly democratic form of religion though they were, in their credulous simplicity, constantly borrowing from the great grandees, their tutelary deities or patron saints. Whatever or wherever their tutelary god, one thing is universally observed—an uncompromising belief in, and a practical devotion to, the rougher forms of brotherhood. They had lived the revolution for unnumbered generations before Jesus came to sweep it, by one magnetic and amazingly omnipotent stroke, out of its modest secrecy into the open blaze of maddened, gnashing public opinion and fling it upon the warring tempests of the aged competitive system, the foundation rock of paganism.

It is a significant fact that Jesus should appear to the world in Phœnicia or Canaan which was at that time the wreck of the greatest nation of freebooters, buccaneers and kidnappers the world has ever known. From the earliest record these people were marauders and their world-wide successes legalized their daring and made them powerful pirates by sea and brigands by land.

But there was an inner history of these people which the pen of chroniclers has left unsketched. Great numbers of persons from all parts of the known world were kidnapped by their cruising corsairs, brought to the Phœnician shores and sold to the wealthy for slaves. These slaves, shortly before the advent of Christ, formed over two-thirds of the population. They were maltreated, made to do menial work, forced to till the lands, especially detailed to perform all the severe bodily toil in and out of the cities, their handsomest youths were made eunochs and apportioned to the service of the ladies of high estate, and their young girls, disallowed an education and brought up in slavery and dirt, yielded not only to labor but became susceptible to the offers of the unprincipled and voluptuous among the rich. The condition of the ancient Phœnician slaves was indeed a degraded one. In nearly all the towns of Canaan or Phœnicia, Syria and Asia Minor, as well as in the islands, slaves were the rule; the free working people [3] the exception. The cruel taint which blasted the toiler extended its devil-fingers beyond Greece over the Ægean sea and pointed at the Asiatic workman as a mark for its curse.[4]

In Egypt,[5] Greece,[6] Rome, Judea,[7] Syria,[8] Syracuse

[3] Drumann, *Arbeiter und Communisten*, p. 24. "In Epidamnos gab es keine Handwerker als die öffentlichen Sclaven. Das Handwerk is daher verrufen und verachtet u, in manchen Städten den Bürgern verboten."
[4] Plato, *Econ.*, 4 and 6.
[5] Josephus, *Antiquities of the Jews*, book II. Chap. v. 3.

and Spain the ignominious punishment of the cross was inflicted only on felons and working people, often for the most trivial, or merely imagined, or trumped up offences, while the arch criminals of "family" were allowed the noble *supplicium*. This state of things had come to such a pass since the conquest of the countries above mentioned that the utmost misery prevailed everywhere. The land was grasped by speculating Romans of court favor, who were at that time not only numerous but extremely enterprising. Being of the privileged or citizen stock they siezed the beautiful farms formerly worked by the industrious inhabitants, but now under the yoke of voracious conquerors, and assumed them to be their own. Instead of free labor, slaves performed the work.

But labor had been in sackcloth and ashes[9] for many ages, and it required no additional weight to make it bad enough.[10] Even Gellius who wrote laws to decide their fate, seems to speak with contempt of labor as though it were some noxious reptile to be hurled from his pen in disgust.[11] It is almost amusing to read over the queer whimsicalities of our ancestors whose *opera quae supersunt* often project expressions of petulency and of irritibility in view of some necessary but to them, ignominious mention of a class of people on whose toil they depended for their very existence from day to day. Cicero, sneeringly said, when describing his enemy Clodius, ranking him with those laboring men, that he was "without credit, without hope, without home, without goods."[12] This in

---

[6] Guhl and Koner, *Life of the Greeks and Romans*, p. 518. "In *crucem figere*."
[7] Cf. *Inscription*, recently found at Naples containing the death warrant of Jesus.
[8] Bücher, *Aufstände der Unfreien Arbeiter*, S. 69, and elsewhere.
[9] Vide Sallust, *Jugurtha*, 73. Also Dionysius, B. C. 476 made it lowly enough; Livy, X. 31. "Quinam sit ille, quem non pigeat longinquitatis bellorum scribendo legendoque, quae gerentes non fatigaverunt."
[10] Pliny, *Natural History*, IX. 25; II. 28.
[11] Quod genus Græcii αχϑοφορουϛ vocant, latine bajulos appellamus." *Gellius* 5, 3, §. 2.
[12] *Pro Marco Coelio*, 3. "Quare oro obtestorve vos, judices, ut qua in civitate paucis his diebus Sextus Clodius absolutus sit, quem vos per biennium aut ministrum seditionis, aut ducem vidistis: qui aedes sacras, qui censum populi Romani, qui memoriam publicam suis manibus incendit, hominem sine re, sine fide, sine spe, sine sede, sine fortunis, ore, lingua, manu, vita omni inquinatum: qui Catuli monumentum afflixit, meam domum diruit, mei fratris incendit." Cicero here had not the magnanimity to give Clodius credit for voluntarily casting aside his noble family and his wealth. Cicero, when he said that Clodius had no family, well knew that he was a brother of Appius Claudius, that he was one of the very most powerful representatives of the great *gens* "Claudia"—the same stock which afterwards produced emperors. We find little in the family to

his haughty mind was sufficient to damn them to oblivion. Occasionally there rose a character, so sympathetic and exalted, even in immoral Rome, as to be able to dispel this almost universal contempt and to give expression to the grandest and most truthful sentiments. Of such was the excellent Tiberius Gracchus, who a hundred and forty years before Christ was born, declared that "wild game have holes; and for eveything there is some shelter, some retreat; but the poor who struggle and die for Italy, though they have air and light, have nothing more. Houseless and homeless they wander with their wives and little ones. Those military gentlemen lie, who admonish soldiers against permitting workingmen's graves and sacred things to be desecrated by enemies; for not one has a family altar of his own; not one among all these Romans a burial place. The poor must struggle and die for the blustering drunkenness and the corrupted wealthy called nobility whom their labors create and sustain."[13] We have hitherto made reference to Mommsen who constantly bewails the paucity of mention by great authors, of the poor and lowly;[14] but Mommsen is not the only savant who in rummaging among the musty relics, after such rare gems in vain, sends up his moan of regret. Dr. Drumann repeats the same thing and in blunter and terser terms. "One searches in vain for satisfactory intelligence," regarding the producing class.[15]

Such are the difficulties the historian of the ancient lowly has to encounter; and were it not for the tell-tale inscriptions and the musty old rescripts of law, the task could never be performed. But while the most valuable records of bold writers have been left us in fragments and the more time-serving historians have shrugged themselves into silence fearing to face the storms of public opinion, the workers themselves were carving their own history in lines of amazing legibility for the far future students of ethnology and social science.

praise; for he was descended from the same *gens* with Appius Claudius; but if he turned into a friend of the unions, restored them, fought Cicero on these grounds, and if he comes down to us as their champion and martyr, then the whole labor movement must acknowledge it.

[13] Plutarch, *Tiberus Gracchus*.
[14] *De Collegiis et Sodaliciis Romanorum*, p. 41. "Quoniam exiguam tantum notitiam earum ad nos pervenisse admodum dolendum est."
[15] *Arbeiter und Communisten in Griechenland und Rom*, S. 15, 5, "Befriedigende Nachrichten sucht man vergebens."

We now turn to the labors of Jesus whom, in order to be consistent with our study of sociology, we must presume to have been what some of the great commentators and even some of the encyclopædists now consider him, an Essene or at any rate, a member of one of the great orders of secret associations so numerous in his day. Lest this announcement appear untenable in the minds of many, we present our proof in consistent detail; inviting further investigation on the part of critics, in rebuttal. Certainly, no harm can accrue from an honest comparison of facts as applied to lessons in anthropology. In proceeding to do this difficult task we must acquaint our readers with things as we find them and reason, like the physicist, from the premises.

We have already stated that there existed along the Mediterranean great numbers of palæographs mostly unearthed within the present century. There is still a dispute as to what they represented. That they are stone slabs, often handsomely graved in *relievo*, commemorating social societies, all archæologists are agreed. But until lately it has not occurred to their learned expounders that they were genuine *labor societies*. This however, is the fact.

But while these innumerable palæographs are really the work of labor organizations and economic advantages to manual toil being then, as now, the incentive, because labor then, as now, was the members' only capital or means of support, yet this labor, on account of the taint and disgrace as well as the ruffianly attacks it had in those days to submit to, was for many ages the cause of the societies and their inscriptions; and the thing that lies constantly concealed. But the more popular and trivial issues, like the paliatory flattery of idol worship, the vain-boasting of prophets, the popular flute music, dances, processions, and burial ceremonies, covered up the view of labor; a palliative which secured their permission by law, to exist in Palestine and elsewhere.

The common name of all the ancient societies of these regions, is *koinon*, and the most important of them, according to Lüders,[16] are the *synodoi* or synods. Then especially, among the Canaanites are found the traders, also known as

---

[16] Lüders, *Die Dionysischen Künstler*, p. 12.

synodoi plethoi and *symbiosis philia*. But of course in the widest sense the general name of phratry stood uppermost; since whatever applied to it means "union."

But the name under which the most of them are known in the inscriptions is *eranos* and *thiasos*, a description of which we have already given. The *eranos*, in the Greek was a labor or trade union. From the Greek, all the social societies of the Ægean sea, Syria, Phœnicia and Asia Minor borrowed this name. The same explanation applies to the *thiasos*. This was an association for common enjoyment, and is consequently considered by the modern archæologists as a branch of the *dionysia* or the *bacchantes*. But there is great misapprehension regarding the province and functions of the celebrated god Bacchus. While people of our day associate him with wine and drunkenness the great Numa Pompilius provided for the working people once a year at the Saturnalian festivals of the harvests,[11] and during his wise and much honored reign they were encouraged to indulge in festal recreations. The Saturnalia was a great harvest festival. Relaxation, merry-making and even wine conviviality were so far indulged in as to almost sink, pending its duration, the inequalities of rich and poor. Being in December, it was to the ancient Romans, what Christmas is to the Christians.

Now, considered as identified with the manners of the labor organizations, there is a similarity touching the *saturnalia* sanctioned by Numa. Tullus Hostilius and even the emperors, and the *bacchanalia* which were breathing moments of the secret labor societies. But the *bacchanalia* were common in all countries and the *bacchantes* had their feast at any time during the year. The true cause of their disreputable taint is not that the feasters drank wine All drank wine, when they were able to pay for it; it was a healthy beverage. The obloquy comes entirely from their being all lowly working people. They were attacked in a ferocious and brutal manner and threatened with extinction because they dared to have an evening dance once a month.

Unorganized, the ancient workingmen were powerless to enjoy even this; but the force of co-operation or confraternity bore its fruits; and by it they could enjoy their convivials.

[11] Plutarch, *Lycurgus and Numa Compared*.

The thiasos[18] was this community gathering, which in their marches and dances used to wear beautiful wreaths[19] and sport red flags and banners. Tracing these societies farther and clearing them of moral mud and slime with which vilifiers of the ancient quill have so bespattered them that the word bacchanal appears in our vocabularies like a synonym of sottishness, we have a decent, well ordered association or union of poor people who work for their living; such as existed all over the country about where Jesus lived. Böckh, cites an inscription of one found at Tyre about 20 miles from Nazareth and after deciphering its epigraph, arrives at the conclusion that although it was a *thiasos*, it was not a wine bibbing institution at all.[20]

From Phrygia among the celebrated Phrygian slaves there comes a stone slab which Lüders, in his excellent work, "The skilled mechanic of the bacchanal," has lucidly described. We translate one of his descriptions.[20]

"Above the lettering appears a general picture of the scene. On the right sits a goddess in a long *chiton* (flowing robe), holding a large shell in the right hand. In the left she holds a *tympanum*, the bottom resting upon her knee which, together with a *modius* upon her head, represents her as the goddess Cybele. Near here sits the lion which is known to be the favorite animal of the Phrygian goddess. Besides the goddess, also robed in a long flowing *chiton*, stands a man holding a cithara on the left arm. Over the altar erected on his right he holds also a shell. A tree shades the altar. A girl leads in a lamb for the sacrifice upon the altar, and another is playing the flute. An aged female figure is finally represented at the extremity of the room in the attitude of worship. Beneath this holy personification is represented another scene, presenting a symposium of 10 persons. With the left arm on the lap, they sit on their pillows eating and drinking, and in front of them

---

[18] "Θίασου, ὅσπερ εστιν ἡ ἀπὸ του πινειν συναγωγή." Phot. 82.
[19] "Polybius erzählt (XX. 6), dass diese Kränzchen in Böotien in grosser Blüthe gewesen seien." (Lüders, *Die Dionysischen Künstler*, S. 11). Cf. Droysen, *Hellenismus*, 11, 83, f.
[20] Böckh, *Corpus Inscriptionum Græcarum*. No. 2271. "Thiasos non bacchicus est."
[21] Lüders, *Die Dionysischen Künstler*, S. 9, Tafel II.
[22] The word "zechen" here used for drinking by the learned philologist, might have been well enough for the date at which it was written: but it is entirely unjust now; for it perpetuates the insults upon the poor. This word is evidently meant to convey to us the idea that they were eating and "tippling."

on one side, flute players while the time with music, and on the other side waiters are busy bringing the viands of the table and wine for the members. Two *batons* stand leaning against the wall on the right, on whose pointed ends, as we may safely surmise, the bread is toasted and the meat broiled. The inscription reads that the *thiasotes*, male and female, are in the act of honoring Stratonica their priestess with wreaths; and this for honest service she has rendered their saints or deities, Apollo and Cybele.

Such were the eranists and thiasotes. To our mind, reasoning from the now provable fact that these societies were numerous in the land of Canaan in the days of Christ, it is quite certain that he was a member of an *eranos*, or of some other secret association like an Eleusinian brotherhood; as by his time, these had assumed a cult [22] which was both practical and religious. His religion was monotheistic but he could not have been more devout.

But we have promised to thread the *eranoi* farther, that there may remain no doubt regarding their influence or their age and numbers. Having stripped the bacchic *thiasos* of its traditional terrors, we come to inquire, with Lüders,

whereas the solemnity of the particular occasion forbids any such rendering to the inscription. The real cause of the fling is the innocent lexicographer; not the faithful epigraphist. "Thiasotai" is made to mean *revellers* or *tipplers*. It means no such thing. The lexicographers are obliged to give definitions such as the sense implied in the historian's account, suggests. Where the fault, if any, resides, is at the door of the historian who throughout the literature of antiquity has signalized himself as the toadying accomplice of the aristocracy.

While therefore, we profoundly respect the careful philologist who, years ago gave us these treasured scraps, yet, from a standpoint of sociology, future archæologists must come to judge of the meaning of words from their self-evident premises. Indeed, the direct discovery of Böckh, whose authority stands pre-eminent, is that "*thiasos* is *not* bacchic," "*Thiasos non bacchicus est*." He makes this plain declaration, evidently not from the common definition at all; but because, on studying his inscription, he sees by its general appearance that though confessedly a *thiasos* it is far too serious to be a band of tipplers.

[22] Eusebius says boldly, quoting Philo (see chap. xviii.), that these Essenes or Therapeutæ were very numerous in all parts of the world. *Eccles.* lib. II. cap. 17. Much more may be learned from Philo Judæus, *De Vita Contemplativa* and *Quod Omnis Probus Liber*, 12; Lightfoot, *The Epistle of St. Paul; Collossians and Philemon*. This last author's stricture against the essenes being the order to which the early Christians belonged, brings even more proof of our theory that *Essene, Essenoi*, is only a phase of *eranoi*, suitably changed to fit the Judean dialects, of the Greek, and that also it took on phases to conform with the Mosaic code in Palestine and Egypt. A careful reading of Dr. Lightfoot's *Essenes, idem*, p. 347, sqq. may serve to convince many of this anology. "While the Pharasees were the sect, the Essanes were the order," (p. 354). We say however, that while the *thiasot* were the sect the *eranoi* were the order. Lightfoot (same pages), speaks of their tenets being "of foreign origin." This is still further proof. The grammatical structure, and how changed, is clearly seen on page 355. Εσσαιος, Εσσηνός resemble θίασος, θιασηνος. Again, they were baptists. This they got from the venerable custom among the unions, of the constant use of the baths.

more about the *Dionysischen Kuenstler*, or Bacchic skilled workmen. The Dionysia at Athens were of four sorts, but not necessarily connected with these social communes. In that country, in early times, the Dionysia were feasts, or autumnal jubilees at the vintage. They were amusements at which the boys and girls hopped and caroused. Sometimes they danced upon sacks or *ollas* filled with water, or climbed the greased pole, or jumped and climbed on bowlders smeared with oil which by their slipping and awkwardness caused great merriment. Undoubtedly the farmers at a bee of this kind sometimes drank wine to excess. The second Dionysia were feasts of the wine presses. It was almost exactly equivalent to our Thanksgiving; fully as religious but less sedate and reverential. It was a series of banquets and festivities at which the meats and dainties were paid for from the public purse. Then there were drinking festivities called *anthesteria* at which in the spring of the year the citizens gathered and indulged in enjoyments. But we are not quite certain whether the working part of the population were allowed to attend; since citizens in Athens, as elsewhere, in the Hellenic peninsula and, in fact, wherever Greek was spoken, were regarded as above labor. Lastly, the great *Dionysia* held mostly within the city. They consisted principally of theatrical entertainments at the cost of the state. These again were aristocratical and had little to do with workingmen's organizations.

The anthesteria in the month of February and the great *Dionysia* held in *Elaphebolion*, month of March, strikingly resembled the Eleusinian Mysteries, to the description of which we have devoted a chapter. They had secret sacrifices at which the wife of the *archon* was symbolically married to Bacchus, the celebrated god of plenty. It is quite probable that the poor working people and the slaves, in their longings to rise to enjoyment and esteem, aped these great aristocratic orgies of the citizens, which sometimes were performed—especially at Eleusis—with a display of magnificence only equalled by their mysterious secrecy and their religious pomp. Thus, the labor unions had nothing in common with those orgies and must not be mixed up with them.

In 1864, there appeared an article in the Revue Archéologique, on the *eranoi* and *thiasoi* of the inscriptions. The theme maintained that these unions tended towards a cult, and that the result of their humble existence for a period of many ages was an upward and civilizing tendency. The writer, M. Wescher, an archæologist who had devoted much time to deciphering the meaning of relics so curious, took the ground similar to that maintained in these chapters, although he does not pre-suppose that the unionists had anything to do with labor. This is the strongest of all the phenomena which beset the pen of scholars. Granier de Cassagnac wrote his history of the ancient laboring men from that point of view; and although his exceedingly scientific and rare penetration was for 30 years talked down by the savants of Germany and France, they are now maintained by greater ones who acknowledged that they were taught by him. Such was also the fate of M. Wescher, who ventured to suggest that the *eranoi*, very nearly identical with the Roman *collegia* or trade unions of which Granier had made his magnificent exposé, were something more than mere religious sects; for we find M. P. Foucart denying the truth of M. Wescher's remarks [24] and in his preface, expressing his sensation of pleasure at imagining himself able to disprove Wescher's hypothesis.[25] One would suppose that any discovery that they were labor societies would be hailed with pleasure by the most critical; but the contrary is hurled in his old friend's face with scorn.

We feel an interest lively enough in the little polemic of Foucart and Wescher to reproduce an example: Wescher examines the fraternal character of the Associations [26] in these words: "Now is it not natural that, at an epoch of inquietude and of religious agitation like that of the great Alexandrian school, the number of these societies should be considerable? Ought we to be astonished that many men and women abandoned the official religion which had long proved itself ineffectual to free culture, arid to the development of spontaneous, fraternal goodness such as responds to the innermost aspirations of the heart? The Greek soil must be considered the veritable cradle of this religious movement. It will redound to the inextinguishable honor of Greece for having planted such examples in

[24] *Associations Religieuses chez les Grecs*, pp. 139-153.
[25] *Idem*, Preface, p, 14. " Une certaine satisfaction et une certaine confiance.'
[26] *Revue Archéologique*, 1865, II. pp. 220 and 227.

the world, before the appearance of Christianity." M· Wescher continues: " The common fund of the societies was devoted to mutual assistance and assurance, destined to furnish advances to members in need,[27] to provide for them in cases of sickness and defray the expenses of a decent burial."[28] Farther along he says: "The members were a mutual community, one with another; the well-to-do paid, the indigent received, in rotatory form, as the case happened. Poverty was no motive of exclusion." This last declaration is stoutly met by M. Foucart who says it is based solely upon an expression of Rangabé. In point of fact this communistic mutuality is the only definition ever attached to either the Greek words *eranos* or Latin *collegium!* He further quotes from Theaphrastus,[29] a passage in rebuttal which substantially acknowledges not only, that the *eranoi* were mutual sharers, but also that the celebrated successor to Plato knew all about them. Not discomfited with this inconsistency he drags up the case of one Læocrates, an Athenian, who being about to move to Megara sells his house and his slaves, charging one of his friends with the task of paying and settling up with his creditors, money he owes and to straighten accounts with his *eranos*. It does not follow from this, that this rich man was even a member, any more than was Augustus Cæsar a member of the many *collegia* at Rome which he patronized under the well known name of *Collegia Domus Augustalis*.[30]

The whole of the matter is, that these were poor working people's societies for mutual aid. They corresponded very closely indeed to our trade unions. They had existed from immemorial times as trade and labor societies for mutual support and were almost indentical with the Roman colegia on which we have devoted a chapter, and regardinlg which evidences in inscriptions and otherwise, are overwhelming. Those poor people did not work all day at wearying drudgery and then labor at night in their unions merely for religion's sake as M. Foucart imagines.[31] They

---

[27] Here Wescher himself is unable to understand that the fund was for members out of employment, which places labor at the bottom of their organization.
[28] *Revue Archéologique, idem*, p. 226.
[29] Theophrastus, *Ethikoi Karakteres*, 17.
[30] Mommsen, *De Collegiis et Sodaliciis Romanorum*, Cap. V., *De Collegiis latis sub Imperitoribus*. The emperor Augustus was of course, not a member of the trade unions but he befriended, protected and patronized some of their labors while a great many of them he suppressed.

had to combine as the men are now combining, to take measures regarding the best advantage at which they might on the morrow, exchange the only goods they possessed—their labor—for their daily bread. Even slaves, when allowed, sometimes joined, to better their condition.

So much for the *eranoi*. The *thiasoi* were, as we have described them, simply clubs of the *eranoi* who arranged and conducted the little banquets and social amenities which throughout antiquity seem to have made life worth living. These *thiasoi* corresponded to the *sodalicia* of the Romans.

We have, however, in our description of the Roman trade unions, shown that owing to the severely restrictive and censorious laws, the unions, toward the commencement of the Christian era were compelled to assume a strongly religious and pious aspect in order to prevent being suppressed by these rigors, after the servile wars. Precisely the same in Greece, Asia Minor, Palestine and the Islands of the Ægean Sea; because all these provinces from about B. C. 200 had become Roman territory by conquest. Any law touching them at Rome in the Latin tongue was as rigorous against them in Greece, Asia Minor or Canaan in the Greek or Hebrew. These are the points which the learned Foucart seems to have forgotten. He is an expert as an epigraphist but lacks the aptitude of the comparative sociologist. The keen perception of Mommsen detected and cleared up the mystery in his laws on the Roman trade unions.[32]

These are things which seem strongly to support our argument that a spontaneous, genuine secret movement pervaded the Greek, Latin and Hebrew-speaking countries far and wide at this particular epoch of the advent of Christ. The unity and brotherhood shown to have existed among the secret societies is almost touching. The more the upper stratum of society was distracted by the consequences of the competitive system having failed, on a trial of thousands of generations, the more completely did the brotherly love system of the labor unions grow into usefulness, through accord and mutual support.

There is an example of this seen at the Piræus. The Phrygians were considered barbarians by Greeks and Romans. Their patron goddess was Cybele. Lüders reports

[31] *Assoc. Relig. Chez. Les. Grecs.*, passim. One comparison of them with the *collegia* of the Romans M. Foucart finds this error clearly proved.
[32] *De Collegiis et Sodaliciis Romanorum*. Passim.

that in the Piræus alone, such was the harmony among the orgeons and thiasoi, who represented, apparently without the least jealousy or dispute, many nationalities there, that the Phrygians had an especial temple standing close by the great temple of the goddess Metroon, where she was worshiped by the members of a society whose members called themselves *orgeones* and *thiasotes* on the inscription.

It reads that the decrees 15 and 19 provide that strangers be admitted to the society. One of the officers is himself a stranger. In the list of officers, one is a tutelary soter, or savior from Trœzen, and one, Cephalion, from Heraclia. So also women officiated in responsible functions in the same society.[13] At the Piræus was the *thiasos* embracing the cult of Serapis; of Zeus Labraundos, Metroon and Cybele; of Heroistes, Demos Collyte, Apollo, Nymph Lycia and others. Some of the inscriptions bear date of B. C. 324.[14] The fact of their having lived in their quiet fraternal way so many ages organizing, living in common, teaching as they went, and constantly inculcating the spirit of fraternity as it were, underground, while overhead in the great competitive world, kings, nobles, money-changers, and politicians were fighting and dashing each other against the competitory rocks of the Pagan aristocracy, is of itself, strong evidence that they were the real planters of a future state which could not obtain in the open world without a revolution.

Our maxim that the greater the organization of the laboring poor into a brotherhood for common help the higher will be the pitch of human enlightenment, certainly holds good so far as it was able to proceed in ancient times. Its corollary; the higher the enlightenment the more complete the extinction of social and economical grades, cannot be demonstrated until the associative energy expressed in the premises has been carried far enough against the competitive system to reach a majority. When this comes to pass the conclusion will be reached that the intensity of human enlightenment can be tested and measured by the *quantity* of social organization of this hitherto degraded stratum of society.

The whole story looks as if the offering of ignominy, of Bethlehem, foresaw these three great truths 20 centuries

[13] Lüders, *Die Dionysichen Küustler*. pp. 14, 15.
[14] *Idem.*, p. 16.

ahead, when he boldly took up the unionist's, culture of a dozen deities, their social methods, their fraternal, interacting love, their meek, silent humility and secret work, brought them grandly forth from their obscurity, proclaimed with an irresistible eloquence and pathos the obsolute equality of man and succeeded before the quarrelsome competitive system, its toadies and obsequious devotees, could bring him, like all the rest to the gibbet, in unifying all their gods into one god and forcing the vast movement upward into view and final adoption by the world. The failure of royalty and empire which at his time began to be seen in the states of Greece, Italy and western Asia, proved his words that " a house divided against itself cannot stand;"[35] and this celebrated apothegm from his lips is now being used, perhaps more than any other by the labor organizations of the 19th century. Mutual fraternity and arbitration of difficulties without resort to violence or other overt, unchristian acts is proved by unions of trades to be everywhere productive of the most satisfactory results.

The lines between the followers of the movement and its opponents were definitely and very distinctly drawn. He that is not for us is against us."[36] This again has become a common maxim among the trade and labor societies of modern times; so much so, that the investigation of the character of applicants for membership is found necessary before admission.

The law of Solon had provided for the free organization of burial societies among the Athenian poor. He called them *homotaphoi.* There were the communists who enjoyed their meals at a common table. The law and the language knew them as *sussitoi.* These also were numerous in Palestine and elsewhere along the coast of the Mediterranean. But it is certain that they were labor unions; for Lüders,"[37] speaking in general terms says that the brotherhood who partook with each other at the common table did this as a moral custom and that the custom was common throughout the ancient world; and in the larger societies received an especial character. There were even societies of privateers, of Phœnician or Canaan-

---
[35] *Luke,* XI. 17: *Mathew,* XII. 25; *Mark,* III. 25.
[36] *Mathew,* xii. 30; *Mark,* ix. 40.
[37] *Dionysch, Künstler,* S 4, 5. "Ausser diesen kleineren, ausschliesslich privaten Zwecken dienenden Genossenschaften gab es Schiffer—u Handelsvereine."

ite origin of course; for these were the most formidable of ancient brigands and freebooters. But Solon also permitted such secret organization at Athens.[38]

Lüders expressly states that there existed universally an organization called by the Greeks *deipna apo symboles*. It was an *eranos* or labor union; and "stretched from high antiquity into the second half of the 4th century of our era, when at the Council of Laodicea it was forbidden."[39] Our statement that the *eranoi* and *thiasoi* were in reality one and the same thing,[40] the *eranos* being the labor or business part of the administration, and the *thiasos* that part attending to the entertainments, is fully confirmed by Lüders,[41] who expressly says their identity as well as functions were mixed; and necessarily, since the *eranos* not only paid the expenses of its own business with the members, attending to the procurement of situations for members out of employment and to the burial and other expenses, but also helped pay the costs of the convivialities.

Thus, the self-evident fact that the *eranoi* and the *thiasoi* which were one and the same everywhere, being made apparent, we come to the further proof of their existence in great numbers in Asia Minor, Palestine and Syria. Lüders remarks that from the Hellenic peninsula the organizations there planted, spread into the islands and Asia Minor where their relics are found still more numerous than in Greece.[42] Still it is well known that at the Piræus or seaport of Athens, at Eleusis and many other places, including the Laurian silver mines in Attica they must also have flourished in large numbers; although their tendency to cultivate the principle of universal brotherhood was frowned upon by the outside world.

We must introduce here the quite singular but perfectly natural fact that wherever the unions were thoroughly established and, so to speak, nested together, the Christian church was sure to first plant itself. Thus Pergamus, the seat of the great uprising of workingmen under Aristoni-

---
[38] Vide Böckh, *Staatshaushalt*, I. 762. Lobeck, *Aglaoph*, p. 305.
[39] Lüders, *Dionysch. Künstler*, S. 7.
[40] Consult p. 455, chapter xxi.
[41] *Dionysch. Künst.*, S. 7. "Beide Arten von eranos scheinen schon in sehr früher Zeit mit den thiasoten Vereinen vermischt worden zu sein.
[42] *Die Dionysichen Künstsr*, S. 13.

cus in B. C. 133-129,⁴³ became the mellow ground wherein the early Christians planted and on which they reared one of their most celebrated churches. The laboring people were in trouble at the time of this uprising—one of the bloodiest on record. They possessed organizations throughout the country which they were enjoying in apparent peace, when they were startled by that paltroon act of Attalus IV. deeding at his death, the whole kingdom to the Romans. Fearing lest they be seized by the hated Romans and reduced to slavery, they unanimously joined the pretender. But there were inscriptions showing that the Pergamenian working people were enjoying a thrifty organization dating from high antiquity down to the coming of the Messiah.

Cappadocia which did not fall into Roman hands until A. D. 17, was also one of the early posts of the Christians. The first epistle of St. Peter bears this name. Here too the labor brotherhoods had a strong foothold. This is rendered certain by the recent discovery of several of their slabs and monuments bearing inscriptions. Laodicia was also a stronghold of both the unions and the early Christians. This place, together with Ephesus and Hieropolis, is where were founded the seven Apocalyptic churches.⁴⁴ The early church found mellow soil among the brotherhoods of the eranoi and thiasoi.

Apamea near Antioch, the birthplace of Eunus, instigator of the greatest of all the slave uprisings, was also the cradle of one of the early churches.⁴⁵ We have, in our account of this great strike shown that Eunus and his men seemed both to be deeply imbued with the everywhere present idea of the Messiah, who was to redeem the world, and also thoroughly acquainted with the methods of secret organization. His knowledge of the auspices, and plan of organization were really at the base of his success. These things, added to inscriptions found in the vicinity of labor unions of an antiquity coeval with this great servile war, show very plainly why Christianity took root so readily in those regions of Asia.

⁴³ See chap. x. p. 242. *Aristonicus*, giving a full sketch of the event.
⁴⁴ St. Paul, *Collossians*, IV. 15, alludes to it where he asks that his letter be shown to the brethren in the church of Laodicia.
⁴⁵ *Revelations*, 1. 11. John here also speaks of the church of Pergamus as one of the seven.

Rhodes was also one of the places where Christianity established itself, although its successes there have been sad. But of all spots in the world Rhodes seems to have been one of the most prolific in those queer inscriptions indicating a great labor organization in ancient times. They existed in great numbers on this island.[46] The abundance of these inscriptions found in Rhodes and at Piræus, have attracted much attention from the archæologists of late. The fact is, the societies being mostly eranoi or labor unions and enjoying in common brotherhood, the scanty proceeds of their toil, had for many ages, prepared the ground for the new plant; consequently it was found mellow and in readiness for the greater Messiah when at last he really arrived.

But one of the most interesting centers of the early church was Apamea, the birthplace of Eunus, the great slave-king of Sicily, Athenion, hero of the second Sicilian strike-war, and Saint Paul the most famous of the apostles of Jesus. This city, not far from Nazareth, was a hive of free labor organizations until stricken by the Roman conquest. It gave birth to three of the most wonderful characters of the history of the lowly and being warmed up in the old cult of the communes, easily became the seat of an early Christian church.

Another significant fact may here by mentioned that Plato takes Socrates down to the Piræus among the communal fraternities of the working people where he and his friends remained for days, as it were, in this socialistic atmosphere. They there discussed and drew up the whole of Plato's most celebrated work—the Republic. Socrates was himself a member and this may account for Plato's notion.[47]

Summing up the mass, we find five great revolutionary

[46] See Lüders, *Die Dionysischen Künstler*, S. 37*42 and elsewhere. Foucart, *Les Associations Religieuses chez les Grecs*, chap. xii. "Les associations religieuses n'étaient pas moins nombreuses qu' an Pirée." They were worshipers of numerous deities. M. Wescher in *he *Revue Archéologtqne*, 1864, tome II. p. 478, says he collected a list of 19 inscriptions representing as many organizations in the island of Rhodes.

[47] Plato, *Republic*, I. 1, Socrates says: "Yesterday I went down to the Piræus along with Glaukon, Ariston's son, to worship the divinity and attend the festival." This tutelary patroness was Artemis, sister to Apollo, central figure of the sun-worship (see chapter on *Red Banner*). She ranked with the group of labor protectresses, Cybele, Ceres, Minerva, under whom so many organizations were founded.

characters, aside from kings and men in absolute power, like Lycurgus, Numa and Solon. These five men represent the labor of five active lives devoted to the improvement of human conditions on a large scale. They are Socrates, Plato, Aristotle, Spartacus and Jesus.

Socrates and Jesus, the first and the last, seem like an incarnation of two great goodnesses in one. The analogy from beginning to end is wonderful. Both were sons of humble mechanics—one a marble-cutter, the other a carpenter. Both were surrounded by communes of the secret *eranoi*, and probably both were members. Both preached quietly to their disciples, occasionally addressing open-air mass meetings. Both were betrayed by the perfidy of their own pretended converts and suffered death on the plea of corrupting the morals which the ethics of the same Pagan faith had fostered and grown, out of the hideous philosophy of human slavery. The result to the human race, of these parallel lives and martyrdoms has been altogether incalculable.

Plato, the admirer of Socrates, dared not follow his master.

Aristotle, borrowing from Anaxagoras and Kapila, laid the foundation of human improvement, with great precision, upon the scientific ground-work of mechanics. His ideas, restored by Bacon, are those which the world is now following.

Spartacus, the greatest representative of the purely irascible, the most sublime character and type of the lower philosophy of resistance, who careered on the ground of "an eye for an eye and a tooth for a tooth," last, and just anterior to the great carpenter, was a shepherd, humble and without ambitions, but because implicated with an age of injustice wherein "opportunity makes the man," magnetized, split asunder, almost conquered the world, which in his day was Rome.

Jesus, who before coming to proper age, is said to have studied diligently, seems to have shaped his life-course from the results of lessons gained by these predecessors. He accepted the acceptable and sternly refused that which bore no promise of contributing to the establishment of a heaven on earth. He gained his great triumph over slavery by adjusting the three moral impulses of Plato and the dialecticians—irascibility, concupiscence, sympathy. He soothed the jarring bitterness of the first by coaxing concupiscence from its ancient realm and bringing it down to "*want;*" and married them together by the tie of sympathy, the impulse most matured by the social unions; and there formed the stronghold of his doctrine from beginning to end.

Plato, the ancient mouth-piece of them all, as he is resurrected in Neo-Platonism, after a test of 7,000 generations, must be placed, by those engaged in the labor problem of to-day, as an extraordinary tissue of harmony and absurdity. He wanted the better (or *individual*), to overcome the multitude (or *worse*).[48]

The experience of these 7,000 generations since Plato, forces the now living family of mankind to pronounce an opposite opinion. It is the masses who are "beautiful," (as Plato used that word); while the individual proves himself constantly to be the lying, bribe-taking, merchantable "*sell-out*" and under-dealer; ready as a rule, under the competitive system, for any trade, seditiously corrupt, planning schemes of jobbery; and he has actually to be watched by the honest masses.

Plato wanted slaves. His slave system, large already, during his life-time was small compared with its hugeness after his philosophy was promulgated and its influence extended to the Roman conquests. Before his time, slaves were the children of the citizens. Soon after him, Rome in her enormous conquests, turned the vast populations of that age into rebellious slaves, and the world became almost depopulated. This master not only wanted degraded slaves, but he laid down laws for them, consigning them to death by torture for unpremeditated homicide while the master was allowed, if he murdered a slave, to be tried by his friends, acquitted and no stigma inflicted upon his name; and Plato lays down a law to that effect.[49]

The entire enlightenment of our modern age repudiates

---

[48] Laws, I. 3, 4, Bekker, Lond. ed.
[49] *Laws*, IX. 9, More on Plato's views of Slavery will be found as follows: Breeding mean with mean and best with best, *Republic*, V. 8. Great fear of slave uprising in consequence of the system, acknowledged, IX. 5, *Id.*: "Abject race;" *Statesmen*, 46: Necessary to possess slaves *Laws*, VI. 19: Agricultural slaves, *Laws*, VII. 13; For homicide the slave must invariably die: preferably by torture, *Laws*, IX. 9; Such punishment must be "clean," *ie*, vengeance, *Laws*, XI. 2, 10, *fin.*

this as unfairness, **relegating the slave system to a** realm of low barbarity. On human slavery, the subsequent world has emphatically **pronounced** against Plato's views; and the little investigating mites of Aristotle, and the working elements of Jesus, are banishing it from the earth.

Plato wanted war.[50] He laid many plans and laws upon his theory of external strife, wishing only education and mutuality within. Neo-Platonism took it up, and in blasphemous contradiction to the teacher, endorsed it, and actually engrafted this **Pagan precept** into the mild and peaceful system of Jesus.

Things have not turned out to substantiate these counsels of the great philosopher. Wars the people had; and the wars killed a million slaves. Eunus, Athenion and Spartacus resented by warring back; and when the world, devastated by combined horrors of war and slavery, got time to breathe and recruit, another slave-war struck mankind even in our civil rebellion, with the final result to fix the conviction that the peace plan of Jesus was correct.

Plato wanted it understood and implicitly believed that all things spring from the most high, the mythical and invisible inhabitants of *Ouranos;* and that men derived existence, and were watched over from those heights in the vaulted dome of heaven, the Olympian abodes— whence an endless chain of priestcraft.

Neo-Platonism engrafted these absurdities into a Christian dogma.

Modern common sense, backed by science, with its innumerable tools proving the true laws of nature, finds the facts to be the exact reverse of the Platonic dogma, and is wheeling us back to the physicism of Aristotle, that it is the little things and the little men and women who perform all works, who produce all that is produced; that it is not the great, conjured to be so in the elastic imagination, who accomplish anything, but the infinitessimals that do it all.

---

[50] *Republic,* vii. viii. Polemarch is made to say that justice consists in doing good to friends and evil to enemies. Socrates however, in an ironical sally of moral reasoning demolishes Polemarch's logic, wheeling him unto the great thesis of Jesus which now proves to be the idea that alone can prevail: See *Matthew.* v. 43, 44, 24; *John,* xv. 17. *First Epistle* of John, ii. 10, 11. The anti-war teachings of Jesus are actively forcing these horrors from the earth just as chattel slavery has been forced out of existence and wages slavery is fast following.

Jesus, if we read him rightly, appears to have been less a Platonist than an Aristotelian and when he comes to be preached in our pulpits from labor points of view, there will be found hundreds of texts whose meanings, long smothered, will furnish substance enough to solve the problem.[51]

Emancipation came from Christianity.[52] The great principle of mutual love among all men was the really original idea and practical work of Jesus. He taught a new doctrine—a peaceful plan of salvation.

Spartacus, who represented the old method of alleviation from suffering, based upon the irascible principle with its wars and bloodshed, was, beyond all cavil, the highest type of that culture. He was evidently informed on the great wars of Viriathus, Eunus, Athenion and perhaps Drimakos. But in both opportunity and military aptitude Spartacus surpassed them all. He lost. But after the million crucifixions of his own and a few generations preceding him, and the enormous lessons which his own and his predecessors' blows had administered to cruel, concupiscent Rome, who shall have the temerity to say that these blows, crucifixions, bloody scenes and awful lessons did not go far, very far, toward shaping the convictions of Jesus, who but continued the great conflict with his milder leadership?

Modern progress, which has almost outgrown chattel slavery, still seems quite undecided in regard to the plan of Spartacus; and might even yet swing back upon it, were it not for the stern, inexorable hold which Jesus maintains in the wreck of his tortured, priest-ridden temples —and this hold is the hope of the future; for his plan applies with wonderful harmony to the investigations and experiments of Aristotle.

Plato wanted the unequivocal mingling of religion and politics.[53]

---

[51] There are many expressions recorded in the *New Testament* which are vague in meaning and must remain so until better understood. After this they may be used by ministers of the gospel, in the labor movement.

[52] Compare Canon Lightfoot, *On the Collossians*, p. 321: Böckh, *Die Laurischen Silberbergwerke*. Hundreds of the most candid authors acknowledge that it was the Christian cult which finally fought down this terrible institution. In going, paganism had also to go. But as we study the origin and course of events we must acknowledge that the blow against slavery had been struck before the advent of Christ. He it was, who killed slavery by tempering the spirit of human kindness.

Modern statesmen, notwithstanding the almost desperate struggles of priest-power to hold firm this Pagan grip, are now steadily disestablishing state and church; and the verdict of enlightenment both in the realm of science and sociology, is to cast overboard, as worthless and pernicious, this old idea of Plato and let religion and politics each take their course alone. Jesus not only separated church from state by admonishing the typical money-changers, but he said: "Render unto Cæsar" etc. The Cæsar here referred to, was the mild Augustus, whose reign was, in political respects, a model, and a glory to Rome.

Plato wanted an eye for an eye and a tooth for a tooth.[54] He encouraged hatreds even in his "city of the Blessed," and trained an army of both women and men to the science of fierce contention.

"Resist not evil," the law of the mechanic of Nazareth, has so far supplanted these savage doctrines, that already the trade unions and other social and labor organizations in many countries, are discussing and planning to resist against men of Plato's class, on grounds that they themselves are forced to become innocent victims of a hateful idea which pits them, like Spartacus and the gladiators, against their fellow men, who have given them no cause for offense.

Yet all things considered, the world cannot afford to belittle Plato, the father of idealism; even though many of his time-serving thoughts are passing away. His mind was too great for his age and his weaknesses were but subterfuges which saved him to a good old age while bolder men were martyred in comparative youth.

But Aristotle who began with microscopic things, whose mind, a consension of Kapila, of Anaxagoras, of Empedocles, of Parmenides, of Zeno, of Plato himself, is, as the world grows old and wise, and as light gleams in upon intelligence, beaming more brilliantly with each decade; and this great man's thoughts are laying bare the incrusted truth and leading to the final, perfected philosophy. Aristotle's is the mind which draws ever nearer as

---

[53] *Laws*, book VI. cap. 7, Bekk. It was always so in the ancient code. Neo-Platonism and the Nicine Decrees afterward succeeded in getting this old Pagan thing back into the Christian church where it still remains, in some countries.
[54] Plato, *Justice*, 5; *Republic*, passim; *Laws*, in many places.

the ages waft him farther away among the satellites of an awful forever.

Jesus, who planted among the communes and laborers all that was good and pure, but whose beautiful works have been almost banished by the proud old paganism still adhering in his temples, departed only to return; for these growing squadrons of the modern mites foretell that he is fleeting back to assume command of a great army of unreconciled but longing intelligences, which the ancient working people quickened, and which the suns of two thousand years have mellowed for the harvest.

CHAPTER XXIV.

THE FINAL REVIEW.

ANCIENT PLANS OF "BLESSED" GOVERNMENT.

WHY THE FACTS were Suppressed and the Books Mangled—Did our Era rise out of the Great Labor Struggles—An Astonishing Probability Unmasked—Plants and Plans of the Distant Past—Lycurgus—Reverential Criticism—His Fundamental Error—The Citizens were the Nobles—Public Lands, Meals, Schools and Games—The Grotto of Taygetus—"Hell Paved with Infants' Bones"—A Model Young Gentleman—His Introduction to the Ladies—An Earthquake believed to have been the Spartans' Punishment for Cruelty to the Working People—The Poor and Lowly were called "Slave Souls"—The Great Aristotle's Curse—Lucian's Choice of a Trade—Even Plutarch Lampoons Them—Kings Planting Poisons with which to Destroy Them—Prophets and Messiahs—Eunus the Prophet of Antioch—His Plan of Salvation—No Quarters—Wholesale Extinction of the Wealthy—What Succeeding Ages Learned from the Outcome of this Ordeal of Carnage—Plans of the Anarchists Taught Needful Lessons on Future Political Economy—Drimakos—His Home of Runaway Angels in the Skies—How his Plan Worked—Desperate Plan of Aristonicus in Asia Minor which offers the Toilers the Beatitude of being "Citizens of the Sun"—Sad Outcome—Innocent Plan of Spartacus—His Ideal "Salvation" was his Emancipation Proclamation and Armed Power to Enforce It—He Wanted to Go Home to the Green Hills of His Boyhood—All these Plan-Makers were Messiahs and Prophets—"The Kings Kill the Prophets"—The Great Messiah at Last—Long-Smothered Authors Dragged forth—Their own Utterances Quoted in the Living Tongue—Numerous Excerpts from their Books—Men Growing Wise in Their Understanding—The Vastness of the Revolution from the Pagan Cult which Denied the Majority Both Soul and Liberty, threw the Race into Bewilderment of Two Thousand Years of Trial

WHY THE FACTS WERE SUPPRESSED. 521

and Doubt—Plans of the Founders of Government Reviewed—Resemblance of Socrates and Jesus—Paralellisms Drawn—One Agitates by Simile the other, Allegory—Proof that they were Both Great Orators—Their Eloquence—Teaching Precepts that are just Becoming Applicable—The Intellectual Stagnation in after Ages a Natural Consequence upon a Revolution that Overturned the Great Pagan Cult—The Mohammedan Rescue—London's Socialism from Same Old Plant—What two Men Did in Twenty-five Centuries—Pagan Selfishness Exhibited in Prayers—Very Ancient Prayers of Our Germano-Aryan Mothers and Fathers—Specimens Quoted—Prayer of Alcestis—Of Other honest Pagans—All Based upon Self and Family—Prayer of Socrates to Pan for More Wisdom and Humility—Prayer of Juvenal for the Poor Slave's Deliverance—Finally, after many Centuries, the Dying Prayer Begged the Pan of Socrates or Universal Father for Universal Cancellation, to fit the World for a New Era—The Relation of the Jews to the Labor Movement—The Romans, Mad at the Spread of the Christian Doctrines of Universal Equality, Take Vengeance in the Slaughter of the Jews—Progress of Ancient Invention—The Labor-saving Reaper—Conclusion.

IN LOOKING thoughtfully over the evidences given in the preceding chapters, especially those detailing ancient plans of relief, through the irascible or war spirit which, though it wrought prodigious good, did not prevail, and those of the communal or co-sympathetic spirit which is the successful one, we cannot forbear an expression of our conviction that the phenomenal movement of which Judea afterwards became the theatre, rested upon and emerged from, the vast and altogether misunderstood and underrated communes; an underground civilization whose culture Socrates was not a stranger to, and whose influence, social, numerical and moral, has, until exposed in these pages, lain almost utterly unknown, buried as they were, amid the horrors which befel Christianity through the political trade of Constantine the Great. This man succeeded in turning the movement when it was three hundred years old into a Pagan faith hedged about with iron-bound creeds and enforced by the inexorable despotism which characterized the military and the priest-power of the ancient Pagan rule.

It will be asked why these important facts we have set forth have been so persistently kept concealed. The answer to this must be, that information was not the policy of priest-power. To acknowledge that the poor and humiliated laborers of the world had, through centuries of organization in secret, and centuries of resistance and persecution, at last overcome the proud old religion so far as to boldly martial a champion and bring their unique culture of human equality into recognition, so as to build up a new era, would destroy the aged prestige of the priesthood. This is the only theory furnishing a solution for the studied deception that has mutilated the books. Plato wanted distinction as to members of his communal state. He wanted priest-power and its concomitant, slavery. As the new era came with its practical putting into effect of the socialism of Plato, but applying it to everybody *without* distinction, thus emancipating Plato's slaves,[1] lifting up the freedmen and doing good to *all*, paganism was stabbed. Its aged priest-power then arose and, in revenge, killed Jesus, the last Messiah who in the philosophy and tradition of the poor and suffering, had been their hope and promise from immemorial antiquity. Having killed him it set to work to destroy his plan which he planted among the communes, " the vineyard of the Lord." The weapons used were assassination, dungeons, worse slavery than before—Neo-Platonism. But the great work of emancipation had made too much progress to be cut short by any power on earth.

We ask our readers to indulge us in this closing chapter, in a general review of the whole scene, covering the the various plans of great men, their trial and their consequences upon the subsequent human race.

---

[1] See Dr. Lightfoot, *Saint Paul's Epistle to Philemon*, pp. 321-2: "With this wide-spread institution" (meaning slavery,) "Christianity found itself in conflict. How was the evil to be met? Slavery was interwoven into the texture of society; and to prohibit slavery was to tear society into shreds. Nothing less than a servile war with its certain horrors and doubtful issues must have been the consequence. Such a mode of operations was altogether alien to the spirit of the Gospel. 'The New Testament,' it has been truly said, 'is not concerned with any political or social institutions; for political and social institutions belong to particular nations and particular phases of society.' 'Nothing marks the divine character of the Gospel more than its perfect freedom from any appeal to the spirit of political revolution.' It belongs to all time; and therefore instead of attacking special abuses **it lays down universal principles** which shall undermine the evil.

"Hence the Gospel never directly attacks slavery as an institution...... **In fact, he** (Paul) tells him to do very much more than emancipate his slave Similar also is his language elsewhere. Writing to the Corinthians, he declares the absolute equality of the freeman and the slave in the sight of God." *First Corinthians*, vii. 21.

Under a careful and thorough investigation of the evidence it will henceforth be found in order for students of sociology to place the origin of this wonderful era in which we are living, where it properly belongs. It is in order to come forth boldly with a new advocacy; an advocacy of the fact that the Christianity on which the present institutions rest and which, as we divest it of its mediæval excrescences century by century, is leading to the final and correct solution of the economic problem, is primevally that which emerged from the great, but little-known because throttled and unheard-of labor movements of the ancients—their numberless Messiahs, their persecutions and crucifixions, their plaintive "still small voice" groaning above the grime and din of lash-driven labor in sun and storm, in mines, dungeons, gladiatorial havoc, their sad but bravely-fought "eye-for-eye and tooth-for-tooth" policy, and finally their majestic, long-suffering, but all-conquering "father forgive them" policy wrought in the crucible of a thousand traditions, communes, blood-wringing rebellions, derascinating cyclones of retributive vengeance already explained, which had been previously experienced by the forefathers of this great era-making representative of the ancient lowly.

To those who are appalled by these sentiments, preferring to coax with a superstitious faith still lingering on the background of a struggling, on-coming fact-period, and still, like Arnobius, troubled with doubts and predilections regarding the sacredness of the conception and birth of this great founder, we must simply say that the labor movement, especially that phase of it dealing with the economic questions of the humble majorities, *is, and must come to be regarded, as the most sacred of all questions;* and its solution or non-solution involves a release of mankind from sin, or their compulsory and perpetual submergence under sin. The enormous sin of our era is its apostasy from the early economic plan laid down at its beginning and for three hundred and fourteen years carried out under persecutions, on the economic basis; and its substitution under emperors and prelate-politicians, by the very most unscientific plan conceivable—that of the ancient faith, which deceived and degraded the chattel and wretch of old, and still deceives and degrades the

PLANS AND MODELS.

victims of wage-vassalage the world over. This sin ruled, raged and devastated for over a thousand years through ignorance and dogma and cheat and inquisition, such as characterize the dreary annals of the dark ages and now looms up portentously in view; for we behold millions of men again organized, more determined, wiser by their experience, better equipped for the fray. And this huge sin, of apostasy we hope, will be discerned by the student of these pages to be freighted with a virus the more malignant as he observes that preacher and priest are still tenaciously hugging the slave-locked policy of Plato the immortal aristocrat, while backsliding farther and farther away from the sweet and loving brotherhood of the *thiasotes* and the *eranoi* of Socrates and of Jesus. They still cling to an old policy which was the meanest upon the Pagan schedule—that of the competitive system, with its economic slaves. Although in another form and blasphemously under another name it was a return to paganism, yet we shall attempt to show in this review that the apostasy from the original policy could never succeed in eliminating the bold ground-principles of equality which was ever the prodigious, the immovable, blood-bought rock-reef, on which those drifting strugglers founded and built this era. Despite the protracted spasms of the moribund beast[2] to wriggle back into its breathing element, these ground principles clung; they still cling; are now steadily developing a polity and men are, in some places, beginning to reap their fruits.

It must by no means be inferred, because the rebellions of the ancient working people failed in establishing the desired end that they were not a useful factor or that their efforts were lost. They failed because their military force was less than that of their enemies. They succeeded because through their defeat, furnishing necessary and indispensable experience, the world was taught that it must adopt another method—that of reason, diplomacy, arbitration, peace. Never was there a time when the world was drifting into these so rapidly as now. Two thousand years may seem a long time to impatient, fleeting man; but in the destinies of peoples and of nations, their slow

* *Revelations* XVII., 4, sqq.

development through creeping differentiation by trial and experiment, it is but a scroll.

The review, then, which we propose to make in this chapter, is that of man in the broadest sense; covering the entire stretch, from a time when he was but an animal—the weaker driven by the stronger—through the long period of family-breeding when the father, destitute of sympathy, enslaved, often killed his children in building up the established *gens* aristocracy of paganism; the rebellion of the children who multiplied, struck back, and built up counter organizations in self-defense, fought and resisted the paternal injustice based in the monarchical idea, and in their turn, after countless ages of trial by systems rebellious, systems patriarchal, systems predatory and systems communal, finally hit the system of inter-communal love, forgiveness, brotherhood, peace and ballot-democracy, which, though it has had an open trial of only 2,000 years—a short period compared with the duration of the others—has already brought him out upon the plane of acknowledged equality, in the supplanting of violence by arbitration, of aristocracy by democracy, of competition to some extent, by socialism. We shall show that all of these blessings were sought by the great and good men: Lycurgus, Numa, Solon, Socrates, Plato, Aristotle—even the contemned Eunus, Athenion, Spartacus—and finally Jesus, who is yet on trial. If we severely criticize Lycurgus, let it be done under an almost reverential respect; for he could not conceive of a state without slaves; if Plato, be it uppermost in our minds that he was unimpeachably pure; if we dare to reflect against Aristotle, let it be with homage, as if approaching the sepulchre of the mighty; for this great founder of technical science is the model from which the world still builds, and he even dared foretell a society in which there might be no slavery. Had these lawgivers been perfect their works would have been cut off by the same martyrdom that was suffered by the bolder Socrates and Jesus.

In making this review it is neither possible nor necessary to attempt any chronological system. This has been done strictly in the preceding chapters. We promise only a critical comparison of different systems and hope to deal fairly with all, giving the doings, sayings, prayers, struggles and models of each one, as his particular plan; and we likewise may find it to our profit to compare these with the plans and the men and their movements and demands of to-day, in order to amplify the comparison and honestly find out which of the ancient methods the modern age is following. One extremely important fact must be held uppermost to view: the leaders who form the subjects of these pages had each a very clearly defined plan. Even Spartacus was not without hope of emancipating the slaves of Italy and the rest of the world.

It is scarcely necessary, after our elaborate presentation of the history of the lowly and their ancient works, to premise in this review, that the whole array of deeds and plans of relief shows an undeniable harmony with, and corroboration of the modern theory of development upon the largest scale, and from a cold and secular, rather than an imaginative and religious or superstitious point of view.

Our history, true to its original scheme, covers only the great Aryan family and we shall let the Bible, the Zend and other Oriental records tell of its cruelties among the Semitic and other branches, referring to them only as collateral evidence.

Although many plans of law-making were tried during the great era covered by manumission, yet we have no history until we come to Lycurgus, and must consequently devote our first remarks to him and his wonderful and on the whole beneficent work.

Of the three classes of citizens in the system of Lycurgus the first was the governing, the second the police or military, and the third the burgher or business class[3]—that which Saint Simon denominates the *bourgeosie*. The mechanics and farmers were considered mean and unworthy. To the agricultural laborers, was given the task of producing, at what is now considered "starvation wages," that which the citizens used for their daily nourishment and comfort; yet so ungrateful were the arrangements deliberately established by this lawgiver, that to be a good farmer, a skilled mechanic, an inventor, a discoverer of the new in nature, was to be a most degraded and abject mortal, denied all citizenship and hopelessly doomed by "imperishable laws."[4]

No humane person of our age can peruse these accounts given by Zenophon, Plutarch and others, without feelings

[3] Plutarch, *Lycurgus*, 7, 17.   [4] Idem, *passim*.

of sorrow if not of anger. The progress and purity of human society may safely be said to have suffered a disaster in this inhuman feature of the otherwise generous Lycurgan law. It was self-defeating, contradictory and inconsistent with the principle intended by the lawgiver himself. Lycurgus the most ancient of the three great lawgivers of antiquity belonging to the Aryan stock, seeing the feuds and other inter-destructive effects of the competitive system at his time raging with great fierceness among the *gens* families, drew up a system of laws and got them adopted so as to go into practical operation. It was a system embracing the revolution from the competitive to the socialistic methods. It was based in the idea so quaintly and wonderfully developed nearly a thousand years afterwards by another inspired lawgiver—the workingman of Nazareth. Its very fundament was social love, forgiveness, tolerance, instruction. Lycurgus was attacked by the optimate party who rebelled against his equal distribution of nationalized lands, his nationalization of other property, his common table, his compulsory education of all alike, his athletic trainings, in fine, his extinction of property and of the competitive system so far as all internal policy of his people was concerned. One young man once pursued him and with a missile tore out one of his eyes. He turned about and faced his irate pursuer with the eye that had offended plucked out, and his face bleeding with the wound. The argument was eloquent and effective. The maddened mob of rich men were overcome and Lycurgus was allowed to go on with his work, unmolested.[5] His system of socialism was more detailed than has ever since been aspired to by any class except an occasional small community; for he added thereto a community of men and women which instead of being a complex method was a system of compulsory marriage, with a law permitting the finest and most beautiful to borrow and mutually inter-employ each other in cases of likings or of compatibility.[6] This was the Lycurgan law of mutual acquiescence, and it obtained to an enormous extent for over a thousand years and was made a strong and scathing point in favor of Christianity by Tertullian in defending the early Christians from attacks of the intolerant Pagans.[8] Tertul-

---

[5] Plutarch, *Lycurgus*.   [6] Idem, *Lycurgus and Numa compared*.

lian in this celebrated apology gives us invaluable proofs of the purity of the Christians, and shows that they had repudiated it.[1]

But these strange features were well intended by the great lawgiver. It was not to promote voluptuousness but to cultivate a principle—and scientifically enough—of human stock-breeding. At any rate, it was a feature greatly recommended among the ancients, and it lay at the base of the celebrated race-culture which made Spartans the most splendid men so far as stature, health and beauty are concerned, the world ever produced, and gave to the nation that mental and physical vigor which enabled it to overcome the mighty prowess of the Athenians and to finally transplant a branch of these curious features into the whole Hellenic peninsula, Phœnicia, Asia Minor and Sicily. The openly established object of this branch of the law Plutarch declares to have been the ownership of children by the state—not by the parents[8]—which is a step much in advance of anything ever advocated by any purely labor movement of modern days. But these enjoyments and privileges were only to be participated in by the citizens, the state police or military element and the burghers. The strictly working people were left out.

How Lycurgus, capable of coolly devoting a life-time, mostly in privations and hardships and without reward, to what he considered the redemption of the human race, could at the same time institute for those on whom he knowingly depended for his bread and every other element of existence as well as that of the people for whose happiness he lived, and consign the working people to the terrible fate left them by that law, is a problem that must startle puzzle-guessers amomg students of modern sociology. Only one method can possibly be pursued to unravel this mystery--the utterly demoralized and false estimate of the value of labor.

In this saddest feature of the law of Lycurgus we are brought back to our account of the Helots or slaves, in another chapter,[9] where figures the story of the assassination by a trained band of young Spartans, of 2,000 innocent prize winners of the Helot or laboring stock. It

[1] Tertullian, *Apology*, XXXIX.   [8] Plutarch, *Lycurgus*.
[9] Chapter iv., page 109 sq.; also pp. 97—102, of this work.

is not maintained that Lycurgus was the originator of the slave system. We find it spoken of in the books of Homer which are thought to cover a period commencing at least 300 years earlier; and we are entirely satisfied of the correctness of Granier's declaration that slavery existed even many thousand years previously to Homer.[10] Lycurgus only perpetuated the miseries of the working majority by fastening the odium already existing, upon slaves and legalizing their burdens.

No citizen, under Lycurgus, could be a laboring man so far as to personally perform the work of production or of distribution. By his "free citizen" he did not mean any person who was obliged to work for a living. To be a soldier was respectable. But the soldier produces nothing. He destroys. So also does the governing class. These the Spartan lawgiver made very numerous. The modern movement of labor all over civilization is struggling to diminish their numbers, not to increase them. Lycurgus also, among his favored class, allowed many of the trading or business men; although practically, if his communistic theory obtained, they could not have prospered because the state operated the evolutions of business with the labor of its slaves which was conducted or managed by the governing class. Nobody really owned anything in his theory, if perfected. All citizens were, however, rich in their "collective" wealth.

Coming to Lycurgus as a factor in the history of labor, we find his arrangement regarding working people to have been barbarous and horrible. The latter constituted two-thirds of the entire population. Yet so mean were they supposed to be that they could not be legally counted in the census as men, or in other words, human beings. The true population of the city of Sparta consisted of citizens. They were divided into three classes: the ruling class, the military or protecting class, and the business men. The whole three covered one-third of the existing population. All the others were working people, who, as slaves or artisan freedmen, were obliged to live in an abject condition, feeding on the poorest food;[11] go-

[10] Granier de Cassagnac, "Histoire des Classes Ouvrières," Chap. iii.
[11] For food of slaves, see Homer, "Odyssey," XIX., v., 414-416; Horace, "Ars Poetica" ("Ad Pisonem"), V., 249; Pliny, "Natural History," XVIII., XXIX. In addition to these consult "Index" of this volume.

ing almost, often quite, naked; living in caves, the meanest of huts, or in the open air, sometimes at the verge of starvation; if slaves, whipped every day to be reminded of their cringing humility; horribly brutalized with clubs whenever they dared stretch themselves at full height, lest they be taken to ape the human stature and the attitudes of manhood;[12] chained to the side of mules and oxen to draw loads like beasts of burden; waylaid by the trained assassins of state, equipped with daggers, and murdered for mere wanton sport, on a pretext that they were dangerous;[13] forced to work fourteen to eighteen hours preparing food and clothing for the citizens who expressed their gratitude by kicks and terms of lo... and contempt—such was the practical effect of the brated and of all others, most renowned law of Lycurgus. Such, through numberless ages have been the sufferings from that cruel competition that is based upon ownership by a privileged few.

The legislation of Lycurgus upon which Plato, making Socrates responsible, principally formed his ideal state, may be summed up about as follows: The whole kingdom was divided into 39,000 lots for the optimates, who were the heaven-born or the divine class, related to the gods[14]—nothing for the earth-born class who possessed neither family nor soul. A branch of education given the young gentlemen was the teaching them how to murder the earth-born or working people, with daggers, as we have already related, by slyly crawling upon them while they were at work.[15] Another branch was that of the gymnastic games, shared by both sexes and according to Plutarch, in a dirty and utterly nude condition, together; with an object, as that great biographer declares, of toning and moralizing the passions. The optimates were never allowed to work except in the aristocratic pursuit of war. Commerce with other nations was disallowed. No money

[12] Plutarch, "Lycurgus;" Granier, "Hist.," Chap. v.
[13] Thucydides, "De Bello Peloponnesiaco," IV., 80; V., 34.
[14] For the ancient idea of divine rights, see "Roman Law," in the "Encyclopædia Britannica," Vol. XX., pp. 688-692. It was the same in Greece.
[15] Consult Drumann, "Arbeiter und Communisten in Griechenland und Rom," S. 180-184. Whatever may have been Plato's own notions, his partiality to the plan of Lycurgus, which Dr. Drumann, author of the great history of Rome, admits, it is certain that he could not accept that lawgiver's plan as perfect. On the contrary he is believed by this author and many others to have borrowed considerably from the Pythagorean brotherhoods.

was permitted except that made of iron—a hundred and fifty dollars' worth of it being a cart-load. The people of citizen blood ate at the common table, waited upon by slaves. What became of it?

Sparta, in B. C. about 600, had 39,000 parcels or small holdings for all in the kingdom. In B. C. 360 there were only 2,000. In B. C. 290 the outside speculators and land grabbers had all but 1,000. At the time of Agis IV., B. C. 240, there were only 700 or really, but 100—as the holdings of 600 were annihilated by debts—and this great scheme of political economy of Lycurgus was gone.[16]

The historian, to flatter the vain theory of divine right is loud in bringing Lycurgus to us, as having descended from the gods to mortals, not only as a link in the royal lineage under Eurysteneid stock, but even as a distant relative of Hercules. Thus the Pagan religion is substantially pandered to and the monocratic idea established. A prince of almost unlimited powers by family prestige, he in youth became regent by inheritance, of the Spartans. But he was both a wise and good prince; and considering the age, much is to be overlooked. When the true heir was born Lycurgus named him Charilaus, and although he had an offer to take the crown himself he refused, preferring to be an adviser. Thus one of the first acts of Lycurgus was to establish a kingdom, after having himself reigned eight months. His next great edict created a powerful senate or council of the old and wise—a body seldom elected even to this day; and a recent expression to abolish them has gained popularity among labor organizations.[17]

These senators, twenty-eight in number, some representing the Spartans or Dorians, some the Laconians or Pericœci, formed another class and another institution, soon causing concomitant class enmities that fanned the final ruin. The senatorial government proved a failure. Afterwards they had to create the Ephori.[18] These tyrants were five in number and their function was to keep

[16] Drumann, "Arbeiter und Communisten in Griechenland und Rom," S. 130-134; Bücher, "Anfstände der unfreien Arbeiter," S. 86; Plutarch, "Lycurgus."
[17] The senate is thus seen to be an aged institution. Being seldom of the plebeian stock it has earned a bad record, as against itself; and is consequently still regarded by that element with distrust.
[18] Xenophon, "De Republica Lacedæmonia," says Lycurgus himself created the ephori.

peace between the two kings and twenty-eight senators. Thus Lycurgus fastened upon the Peloponnesus the two kings, twenty-eight senators, five peace-makers, but gave them no house of commons—three institutions.

His fourth celebrated measure was the apportionment of the 39,000 lots. The size of each lot was sufficiently large to yield eighty-two bushels of wheat as a yearly average, besides other produce sufficient for the families.

A fifth measure struck at common ownership of all movable goods and chattels. To do this it was found necessary to institute the famous iron money. It was wrought in the blacksmith's forge and stamped in the government dies. The result was, nobody would steal such a huge and ponderous thing. Foreign countries could not trade and commerce stopped. An ox cart-load of the Spartan money was equal only to a few dollars. The gewgaws of fashion were self-banished, luxury ceased and primitive simplicity revived. These innovations could obtain, so long as the overawing magnetism and command of Lycurgus was there to persuade by bland patriarchal smiles or austere commands, prevailing through suavity, intimidation and reverence. But before the majestic tread of human enlightenment already in Athens and knocking at the very portals of these haughty Spartans themselves, such simplicity was, in the terms of the shrewd Aristotle, simply "childish." It was ridiculous from within and without. It flourished for a time and perished, leaving a stigma which time has failed to efface and a denunciation so profound as to have forever prevented its resuscitation.

The sixth institution of Lycurgus was his public tables. It presents a sweet and touching reminiscence to us, still struggling in the awful vortex of competing interests. It seems indeed beautiful to look back and see our ancient fathers and mothers of whom we may feel justly proud, sitting on their rough stools around a great oaken or deal table loaded with good things from a common oven, every slice of the hot, steaming cutlets of veal or mutton and every savory morsel, recognized as the public property. The citizens were public property; the houses, tables and stools, the public property.

But who are those nude, suffering, half-starved, crouching forms noiselessly gliding to and fro, bringing these delicious fruits of labor to the happy partakers? They are the waiters, the cooks, the working people and their little ones—all under the curse of the Spartan law. This is what the magnanimous communistic rule of Lycurgus never provided for except to damn Plutarch informs us that at the public tables these people were all obliged by law to eat together, and in common. Although they had homes the law forbade them taking their meals there lest with the labor of the skilled butchers and cooks, they should fatten like voracious animals and become corrupt, sensual and dissolute."

This arrangement resembled the co-operative kitchens of our own times, only established upon a vast scale by government and universally enforced by the law and police of the land. Its principal object was to level the hitherto existing conditions of wealth and poverty in which Lycurgus had found his people; and according to the best account, the plan worked well, with the one exception that the healthful exercise of the citizens in labor was entirely left out, all work of every kind belonging to the economic class being performed by freedmen and slaves. Thus labor, so sacred to the prosperity of modern lands, was disgraceful in this "region of the blessed."

When a newly born babe on examination was found to be strong and without corporeal blemish, an order was published to have it educated by and at the cost of the state. It then received, if of the Dorian stock, one of the 9,000, or if of the Laconian, one of the 30,000 parcels of land. But should it prove weakly, malformed, marked or unseemly, the horrid death warrant was signed and the poor little innocent was pitched down a cavernous pit called "Apothetae," from a crag of the Mount Taygetus; and dashed to a jelly upon the rocks. So stern were mothers in their obedience to this law that they washed their little ones with wine instead of water; because this strong ablution best tested their innate powers. If the babe proved too weak to outgrow this treatment, it was ruthlessly thrown into the rock-lined maw of this Taygetan grotto. Surely, under the dispensation of Lycurgus "hell was paved with infants' bones."

[19] Plutarch, "Lycurgus."

A child when saved was educated. At seven years of age it was martialed into a species of military company and brought up under the rigors of obedience as under military discipline. The hair was cropped short, the body kept dirty, and all play was in a state of perfect nakedness. The children slept on beds made of reed tops which, without knives, they were obliged to gather for themselves. They were required to go barefoot at all seasons of the year. At the age of fifteen to twenty they had military manœuvres or sham battles. They were also required to perform such military duty as making soldiers' campaign outfits. The material for this they were required to steal. They were taught to crawl into the gardens and steal the melons and other fruits; if caught they were mercilessly flogged for the fault of being found out. The act itself was not a crime—logically too—for all things being common and there being no ownership, it followed that there was absolutely no incentive to steal, any more than a man has to steal his own property. Let the critic be cautious about reflecting against Lycurgus for this, as one is apt to do through the medium of a competitive or ownership system such as this in which he exists and from which stand-point he judges. The old lawgiver certainly had the best of us on this score. But one is still at a loss to analyze his motives for teaching youngsters to steal. This he did, however, and methodically.*

We now have the Spartan young gentleman before us, in perfect health, inured to excessive hardships, perfect of form, perfectly naked, unwashed, an adept at stealing —the glory of the great Lycurgus. In this most pefect condition he is intoduced to the ladies—those celebrated Spartan maidens.

This brings us to the next ordinance of Lycurgus—that of the calisthenics and games. It must not be forgotten that we are treating only of citizens, or the privileged class. They were a species of nobles and being born with the blood and lineage of aristocracy they disdained to work for their living. All ordinary labor was performed by helots or slaves. But Lycurgus, although he, like Plato and Aristotle, disdained labor, well knew its necessity as a bodily exercise. Thus in lieu of labor he instituted

* Plutarch, "Lycurgus."

his gymnasium. Good, hearty, honest labor in these modern days, with the ancient taint effaced and thus made respectable, is quite sufficient exercise; and consequently the gymnasium has fallen into disuse. But with Lycurgus labor was a disgrace; and the demand of nature for exercise was supplied by the calisthenic games.

Lycurgus, therefore, ordered that not only the young men but also the maidens should be vigorously exercised at the dances, games and races. Every girl was a professional tumbler; and the extent to which they carried their acrobatic sports may be judged from Plutarch's positive statement that the young maidens performed them in presence of the ephori (the judges of excellence in symmetrical beauty of body and of limb as well as of their winning powers), and before the admiring people in that innocent raiment, which we are told, decked the bodies of Adam and of Eve in the garden of Eden.[21]

"Lycurgus commanded the maidens to exercise their forms running, wrestling, quoit-pitching and hurling darts, with an object to make themselves vigorous so that their children might afterwards be strong. To assuage the natural tenderness of their sex, he taught them the habit of being seen in company with their young male companions and together dance and sing at the festivals. At these they practiced raillery and intellectual sparring, criticizing each other's propriety of behavior which in the young men excited useful emulations, while their sallies and satires often made them smart; since the kings, the senate and citizens were present. So far as the disrobed appearance of the virgins was concerned it was thought nothing of, because the utmost decorum prevailed . . . . . It even inculcates a simplicity in manners and an ambition to present the finest contour of the body."[22]

Marriage was compulsory in the Spartan state; but of its details we refrain from the particulars, with the remark that the closest critic, however much our modern habits have varied from those of our forefathers, certainly

[21] Dr. Drumann, as if unable to comprehend how this could be possible, cites a story told by Herodotus "Euterpe., viii. But on examination we find that there is no argument here presented rebutting Plutarch. Besides, this story refers to the habits of persons of royal degree, whereas our account treats only of common estate.
[22] Plutarch, "Lycurgus;" also "Lycurgus and Numa Compared."

cannot boast of any improved virtue, if purity of intention and strict obedience to law are the basis of virtue. But Lycurgus was probably the only practical stirpiculturist who ever enforced the scientific theory. The law of Moses may be honorably regarded as an exception from this remark.[23] The Spartan lawgiver had been a great traveler and there appears no conclusive evidence rebutting the possibility that he borrowed much of it from the law of Moses instituted four or five hundred years before. The law of Lycurgus like the ideal republic of Plato required marriage. But the connubial tie once fastened, the community idea struck all the married couples of the military classes and they were at perfect liberty to borrow and lend each other according to the passions and caprices of the married lovers. This system of hymeneal reciprocity which never gave offense, was sanctioned by law and was certainly recommended by physicians and judges who attended to the business of replenishing the state with excellent offspring. Indeed, though the law of Lycurgus was never written, it is very probable from the accounts of the ancient authors themselves, that this reciprocal interchange of marital passions was arbitrarily required.[24] If so, the apparent discrepancy in Plato's republic which Aristotle criticizes, is made clear and logical. But it certainly makes a sham of marriage; and presents about as great an apparent absurdity as teaching the young to steal when their goods had no value, being owned and enjoyed in common.

It has already been our sad duty to sketch the last finishing touch of this far-famed government of Lycurgus in our chapter on the Eleusinian Mysteries. We have there recorded the assassination of those 2,000 workingmen. Perhaps what we now say in description of the system of Spartan government may unriddle the subtle philosophy which lurked at the bottom of that and of innumerable other mysteries and shocking murders which blot the pages of Thucydides, Plato, Aristotle, Diodorus, Plutarch and all who have attempted to perpetuate a knowledge of the deeds of this extraordinary people.

[23] Bible, "Leviticus," xix., xx., xxi.
[24] Not only Plutarch, Plato and Aristotle, but also Tertullian, ("Apology" XXXIX.), confirm this statement.

The laboring class of that day were Greeks. Some of them were the sons and daughters of the Lacedæmonian citizens; some were Helots, descendants of a great tribe previously taken as prisoners of war and reduced to slavery. The remainder were slaves purchased from the Phœnicians. These poor creatures did all the drudgery, prepared their food and performed all those offices for them which they were too proud to do for themselves. Great strikes occurred, as related by Ælian,[25] and the inhumanity of these arrogant slaveholders when the reaction came, self-accused them; for taking advantage of a destructive earthquake in B. C. 467, the poor creatures revolted or engaged in a strike of great proportions; and probably, as in the strikes of Eunus of Enna[26] and of Spartacus at Rome, they wreaked redress through the fury of armed force first joining the Messenians. At any rate, amid the earthquake and the strike more than 20,000 Spartans perished, and the survivors for a long period of time held a self-accusing superstition that the calamity was their punishment for their cruelty to the working class.

Thus, for the plan of Lycurgus, we have the following synopsis: Planted, according to Herodotus, B. C. about 990; according to Thucydides, 830; equality recognized; communism of goods and children; kings maintained; labor disgraced; taint of labor, and the working population damned.

Results as follows: The secret Cryptia; constant fear of the dangerous outcasts; final downfall of the system after a trial of 500 years.

Of the plant of Numa Pompilius we have already sufficiently spoken.[27] This system began something like B. C. 690; a non-warfare kingdom; labor recognized; workmen highly esteemed; trade unionism established by law; nomenclature of their organizations made by Numa himself; the members of the unions employed by the state; peace, tranquility and great prosperity of Rome for 43 years, or until Numa's death and after that event, wars; but the unions now turn their energies to the manufacture of the implements of war greatly facilitating the Ro-

[25] Ælian, "Historia Varia," I.
[26] See supra, Chapter VI.
[27] Consult "Index" to this volume; points on Numa Pompilius.

man arms; so the state continues, and encourages the unions for over 500 years.

Among the ancient Indo-Europeans there were from the time of Aristotle, 331-322 B. C. two distinct lines of reasoning; those of Aristotle and those of Plato. We are not at all unaware that neither of these great men was the originator of the doctrine he taught; for both are known to have borrowed for their celebrated states, from others more ancient and less known. But for our purpose we must recognize them as they are recognized by the world.

Plato believed that all good came from a supernatural source. Every thing good was, as it were, handed down from on high. This pleased the manipulators of the priestcraft of his age; for it sanctioned their mysticism. It permitted and continued the lordly power of the gods whose abodes were high on the Olympian thrones. Power was seated in heaven, the vaulted firmament, the "ouranos." The manipulators of this power were the great immortals such as Jupiter and other celestials—all the great gods and goddesses whose names and fame have come down to us enshrined in classic majesty and mystified in a vesture of inimitable, captivating beauty. The marvels of that ancient political religion are made more awfully supernal by this great and good teacher having lived and labored. Nor must we spurn Plato's views because our age has outgrown them. In the bigotry and empiricism to which many ardent and honest persons cleave,[28] they are apt to treat with unforgiving frowns, his earnest belief in practices which we, in having tried, have found impracticable, sometimes abominable. We translate expressly for these pages from Plato's Gorgias, what he makes Socrates say about workingmen: "There exists a two-fold employment; it creates food, beverages, clothes and such other things as the body needs. We get such things from shop-keepers and from country folks and they have them prepared for them by the cook, baker, weaver, shoemaker and tanner. But the healing art and the knowledge of gymnastics necessarily preside over many of these trades because they foretell what the body wants. The working people, therefore, are slavish and unworthy to associate with free peo-

[28] Dr. Bucher, "Aufstande der unfrein Arbeiter," S. 132, pointedly puts it as: "Wust von Halbwisserei und Phrasenthum."

ple."²⁹ In another of Plato's writings is the remark that the laboring population, who produce what the body requires are, notwithstanding their servility "indispensable; and for this reason, they must be admitted into the republic."³⁰

Again, Plato acknowledges that workingmen and women who understand these mysteries of art "know what others do not know. They are educated so far as their peculiar art requires. They know how to build houses, ships, and to do other work and in consequence, must sometimes be admitted into the assembly meetings even though the Athenians laugh when ignorant people take the floor to explain.³¹ In matters of the state where such is needed, this right of explanation is given to every one. Now these workingmen, "demiourgoi," because they know the mysteries of their art, like the poets, imagine they know everything, being clever at their mechanic arts. But they are sadly wanting in manners, mostly, of course, from lack of leisure time without which a good education is impossible. All they learn is what their calling requires; for knowledge of its intrinsic self they have no appreciation, it having no charm for them."³² They busy themselves with mathematics only so far as it has practical contact with their business—not to enjoy a pleasure in the knowledge of the nature of numbers. In themselves they have not the power to strive for higher things, for mechanical craftsmanship brutifies them. The business man, "chrematistikos," declares that pleasure in honors and learning is valueless in comparison with money-getting.³³ Ambition for honors considers the pleasure of amassing lucre to be mean, and also ambition for learning if it fail to produce honors. Vapors and tricks bring the philosopher no such pleasure and joy as the knowledge of truth.³⁴ Be the smiths, carpenters, shoemakers ever so skilled in their work as artificers, the most of them are but slave-souls not able to comprehend what is good and just.³⁵ Lofty-heartedness and

[29] Plato, "Gorgias," 155, 517-518.
[30] Idem, "Republic," 369-372.
[31] "Apology of Socrates," 22.
[32] Plato, "Protagoras," 319. Consult Xenophon, "Memorabilia of Socrates," II., 7.
[33] Xenophon, Public Economics of Athens," IV., 6.
[34] Plato, "Republic," IX., 581.
[35] Compare Xenophon, "Memorabilia," IV., ii., 22.

heartedness and nobleness of impulse are in vain to be sought for among them. It is quite another thing, this learning a trade and educating an honest man.

We elsewhere show by producing his own words what Cicero thought of the poor working people. His contempt for them is still greater.

Aristotle in most respects is in perfect accord with Plato in this kind of talk against the working people. Here is what he thinks:

Humanity must be divided into several classes: citizen cultivators, and artisans, busied with the arts necessary to the welfare of the state. These two great classes are acknowledged to come first; not from the respect he entertains for them, but probably on account of the fact well known in Aristotle's time, that they were very numerous everywhere.

Then comes, as the third class, the dealers. These are designated to be the shop-keepers and merchants.

The day laborers or wage-earners constitute the fourth class. They have some slight independence, being no longer slaves, but freedmen.

Soldiers constitute the fifth class. They do the fighting; and agreeably to the nature of ancient civilization this fighting material that obtains nourishment without producing, is what modern enlightenment begins to recognize as plunderers and robbers.

The sixth class is that of the judges.

The seventh class undertakes the duties of the practical work of the state. It consists of rich men.

To the eighth belong the optimates or men of blood of still higher quality, such as hail from an exalted family or race, as a "gens"—gentlemen or aristocrats, born of God with that supernal gift, the immortal soul. These, according to this teacher of Alexander the Great, were fitted to be the advising statesmen. They are the finishing class, coming highest above all.

"Many times several of these different callings can be united into one; but occupations uniting poor and rich into one person cannot be allowed." [36]

The artisans and skilled mechanics whom Aristotle de-

[36] Aristotle, "Politics," IV., ii., 11-15.

nominates "technitai," or "banausoi technitai," are next to the slaves in lowliness and meanness. Aristotle makes their existence a sort of servitude. But some writers think that this philosopher places them a little more distant or farther from abject servitude than the slaves; for they are beyond the reach of the lash, except in aggravated cases. The difference is that the slave proper serves the collective individual or state, while the artisan serves the person who employs him; and thus the inference is that the ideal political state of Aristotle gets the labor of skilled workmen by contract, or in a second-hand fashion.[37]

Aristotle says that in former times the skilled artisans, or the class embracing all mechanics, were slaves; and even at his day (B. C. 330), there were skilled slaves in many of the Greek states.[38] This statement is valuable, as it shows the immense progress of abolition; and if we take notice of his other equally important hint, that all sorts of precautions had to be resorted to for preventing those dangerous revolts, and couple this with the fact that there were great anti-slave organizations, as shown by the numerous inscriptions still extant, and which have been described in our previous chapters, we may better understand the importance of history written from a social standpoint.

Aristotle teaches that inasmuch as the largest part of the working class must be allotted to attend to agriculture and the flocks, their life inuring them to out-of-door employments, they were for the ideal state best fitted for the muscular work of warfare. Their spiritual and bodily powers naturally develop more than those of persons engaged in business of the market or of the city who press among the crowds.[39]

Aristotle thinks that for his perfect government it is advisable to have slaves work as agricultural laborers; and especially those who have no yearnings for a home they have been deprived of, and so no foremost desires. Such laborers would be more useful, and would have no incentives to revolt.[40]

Aristotle makes the execution of work, for the artisans

[37] Aristotle, "Politics," III., iii., § 3.
[38] Idem, III., ii., § 9.   [39] Id., VI., ii., § 6-7.
[40] Idem, "Politics," VII., ix., § 9.   [41] Id., iv., § 8.

to be that which bruises the body worst; the task set for slaves, to be that which the body is in greatest need of; and for the most ignoble, that in which the least amount of intellectual force is required." This is exactly what would most effectively belittle a man and develop beastliness within him.

The farmers, mechanics and day laborers cannot be dispensed with; but the management of warfare and the giving advice and legal counsel belong strictly to the citizen class who do not work. The laboring class coming under the categories mentioned cannot become either office-holders or priests." They must not be admitted to hold office; for in well regulated communities they are not citizens as they have no duty of citizenship to fulfill and their incapable condition prevents it, the same as in children, slaves, free communers under protection, and strangers."

This philosopher further degrades the despised workers by his opinion that labor stupefies and deteriorates both mind and body. It creates roughness and makes people hoyden "phortikoi," or uncouth, depriving them of their dignity. Neither the good statesman nor the good citizen can tolerate labor."

Labor also leaves no time for public business. Only land-owners and well-to-do people who are citizens can rejoice in leisure time."

If the optimates or better people wish to remain faithful to their destiny and their dignity they learn nothing of skill for the sake of earning from it, neither do they learn music superabundantly, as sometimes is the case now where people engage in emulous contest in it for the profits accruing from out-doing one another; they only learn it so far as necessary to enjoy its delicious melody and rhythm." This most detestable clause in Aristotle's politics has long since crumbled away before christianity's well tried precept. "The laborer is worthy of his hire"" —one of our bulwarks of democratical government.

Aristotle's oligarchy emphatically forbids work people the right of citizenship, especially the day wage earners.

⁴² Id., "Pol.," VII., viii., § 6; III., iii., 2,   ⁴³ Id., III., iii., 2, 7.
⁴⁴ Id., "Pol.," III., iii., 9.   ⁴⁵ Id., VII., viii., 5, 8.
⁴⁶ Id., "Pol.," VIII., vi., 4.   ⁴⁷ New Testament, "Luke," x., 7.

Where a skilled artisan attains to wealth he may, in the ideal state, become a citizen.⁴⁸ Under the Pagan régime this narrow and contemptuous ruling is thought fit for an oligarchy based on optimates and slaves.

Theophrastus who, after Aristotle's withdrawal, succeeded to the Lyceum, described the wage-earning class as domestics or slaves at large—that of "people who shamelessly drive taverns and brothels. They are also known as mercenaries and hucksters who live on the gains of gambling, lottery-booths and cook-shops, gulping up the dishonorable winnings and letting their own mothers starve."⁴⁹

Demosthenes, still considered high authority in many things, is not much milder. He railed at Æschines because he was the son of a sausage man in very poor circumstances.⁵⁰

Demosthenes like Cicero despised the lowly. "He who carries on low and despisable business must not be expected to exhibit deeds of moral quality; for men are always in reality, in thought and in deed, what their calling in life designates. This is a logical necessity." ⁵¹

Lucian the satyrist of the second century of our era, who spoke and wrote the best classic Greek although of Samosata 350 miles to the north of Nazareth, was poor and undertook to learn sculpture. Breaking a partly finished slab of marble and getting soundly punished for it, he left his master and went home where he dreamed out his ideal of the relative merits of art and science. The dream was, that two young females, one called Art and the other Learning, were in love with a certain young man. Each sought to win him by the comparative merit of her trade. Art, as Lucian portrays it, appears before him clad in the dirty overalls of the workingman, specked with marble-dust, hands calloused with hard work. She promised him a good income, a strong healthy physique, and reminded him of the glory of Phidias, Polycletus and other great masters.

Science on the other hand, advanced the argument:

⁴⁸ Aristotle, "Politics," III., ii., 8; iii., 3.
⁴⁹ Theophrastus, "Ethical Characters," vi., B. C. about 290.
⁵⁰ Diogenes Laertes, II., 7; I.
Demosthenes, "Olynth., Orationes Atticæ," T., 4.

"As a sculptor thou art but an artisan, without celebrity, of mean low mental status; one only of a vast mass of humanity. Shouldst thou become a Phidias or a Polycletus and build for the world wonderful and admirable productions, then indeed would every one admire thy art; but no reasonable creature desires thy part; for however cunning thou mayest become, thou thyself art forever doomed to remain only a mere laborer."[52] This ancient taint received its death blow under the rules of Jesus; so much so that no such contempt attaches to Raphael, Leonardo da Vinci or Michael Angelo. Work, from the very first has been not only honorable, but correctly considered, a means of measuring honor and worth. Thus a complete revolution.

Plutarch, styled the honorable, just and fair critic of human character and its dealings with the ethics of men, is equally severe against the laboring class. He writes, about A.D. 75-80: "Virtuous dealings only allure imitations, morally considered; quite different with other, and often more material things, for these we may admire without desiring to ourselves do similarly. On the contrary we despise the authors of works we are delighted with. People love unguents and purple raiment but perfumers and dyers are considered to be mean handicraftsmen, nothing more. Antisthenes the cynic most wisely said, when they were applauding Ismenias for the delicious tones of his flute: 'very fine music' said the philosopher. 'He belongs to the meaner sort, otherwise he could not play so finely.'

"Philip of Macedon reproached his son Alexander who learned to play the cithara at a neighboring inn, with the words: "Art thou not ashamed to play so well? Honor enough for the muses when a king dignifies them by becoming their audience. But whoever degrades himself by making it a mean, low business betrays his indifference toward the beautiful and good. No young man with preferred natural gifts wishes, under the eye of Jupiter in Pisa, or of Heres in Argos, to become a Phidias or a Polycletus; nor an Anacreon, Philemon or Archilochus because delighted by their poetry. It follows not that we should treasure him whose works do excite our

[52] Lucian, "Somnium, 6-9.

admiration and joy"[53] We have here given our own rendering. The sense is so imperfectly brought out by any translation that we are unable to use it.[54] Though the labor product was admired, the creator of it was despised. To us moderns this is almost incomprehensible. Quite so, except we recognize the gradual inroads upon the ancient family blood, and its ultimate uprooting, through the resistance to the insult by labor itself, backed by the new régime.

Again, Plutarch, writing on education, cares nothing for any one but the rich; the remainder might as well be resigned to their fate which had not favored them.[55]

The brother-in-law of Phocion, that is, brother of his first wife, Cephisotodus by name, lived by his art as sculptor, and the family were not considered first citizens of the city. Phocion was one of the very few generals of ancient times who rose from the ranks. His own father was a pestle-maker by trade.[56] Yet he himself always had an openly expressed contempt for the working people.

Alexander was initiated into the study of natural history by Aristotle. He was of opinion that he could perform useful services at healing; and actually performed healing acts in his empire.[57] The news that the father of Eumenes had for a profession that of flute-playing at funerals in the Thracian Cheronesus by which to make a living for himself and family, was trumped up by the Macedonian dignitaries who were loth to permit Grecians in their territory, Eumenes being a stranger. The father was a respectable man; at any rate he was a table-mate of Philip the king.[58] But the whole affair shows the contempt that was universally felt against labor. Agathocles, Tyrant of Syracuse, began his career as a potter in the middle of the fourth century before Christ. In commemoration of his former calling he used to put earthen pots and jugs beside golden ones.[59] But the native pride of the Greeks seldom permitted them to humiliate them-

[53] Plutarch, *Pericles*, 1-3.
[54] For much that is valuable on the whimsical contempt felt by the ancient aristocrats against labor, see Drumann's magnificent researches, in *Arbeiter und Communisten in Griechenland und Rom*, passim.
[55] Plutarch, *De Puerum Educatione*, 11. [56] Id., *Phocion*, 4 and 19.
[57] Id. *Alexander*, 8.
[58] Cornelius Nepos, *Eumenes*, 1; Ælian, 1; Plutarch, *Eumenes*.
[59] Plutarch, *Apothegms, reg. et imp.*; Athenæus, *Deipnosophistæ* 11, 15 2 Polybius, *Histories*, 12, 15; 15, 35.

selves in this manner, or to pull men up out of the dark pits of disgrace, like that of labor, to a place of recognized honor.

But notwithstanding all the influence of the taint there were strong men who, knowing within their hearts that labor was honorable, dared to be brave. Thus in the third century before Christ it was not expected of Cleanthes the follower of Zeno in the Stoa, that he should seek to conceal the night-work on which, at his trade, he earned his living to strengthen him for delivering his lectures before the Areopagi or in the more private school-work connected with his useful life.[60]

Iphicrates was a low-born man; according to some the son of a shoemaker. When Harmodius whose kinsman Pisistratides the hipparch, treated Iphicrates with contumely on account of it, the latter replied: "My race begins with me, thine ceases with thee." [61] This is another scintillation giving light to the dark chasms of contempt into which honest industry was sunk.

Attalus III., whose crazy tricks caused a great deal of unnecessary persecution of the slaves and freedmen of Pergamos and vicinity over which he reigned, seems to have had the labor question uppermost in his brain. He was the last of the Pergamenian monarchs. There appears reason to conjecture that he feared an insurrection of the slaves, which caused him to bargain away to the Romans his inheritance; presumably to get their protection from his dreaded enemies at home. He was in the habit of putting to torture his suspects; and to perfect his art in cruelty became a practical gardener, taking lessons in the chemistry of gardening in order to produce his own poisons with which to kill numbers of imaginary foes. With these poisonous plants he practiced and toyed until his death. Immediately after that event a great insurrection broke out for the succession, in which the slaves and free organized workingmen sided with the pretender, a *banaus* or laborer and an illegitimate, against the legitimate successor. This was the Aristonicus whose great slave rebellion—one of the hugest of ancient times —we have already described in our chapter on ancient

[60] Diogenes Laertes, , 6.
[61] Aristotle, *Rhetoric*, l, 7; Pseudo-Plutarch, *De Nobilitate*, cap. 21.

slave rebellions.[62] Diocletian planted upon grounds of his private estate at Salona, poisonous and other noxious plants. For what exact purpose we are not properly informed. But he wrote a work on horticulture. We make these remarks to remind our readers of the rapidly onward marching strides of Christianity and the social revolution already in Diocletian's time beginning to be felt.

When a boy, Alexander who was swift at the races, was asked if he would match himself with the competitors. "Yes" he retorted : "I would had I kings to race with." Plutarch relates this story as an illustration of the conqueror's virtues.[63] The facts are that at the races the fleetest men were matched sometimes irrespective of birth or trade ; but the future conqueror of the world was too proud to humble himself by setting a democratic example. We may remark that little progress has since been made by way of extinguishing this foolish pride.

In the manufactories, *ergasteria*, most of the ancient workmen were slaves, and the states of Greece sometimes, especially in war in which the poor creatures had no patriotic interest, lost heavily by their running away to find work, more liberty and better fare. During the Peloponnesian war 20,000 slaves decamped from Attica where they were, as property of the state, at work making the machinery clothing and equipments of that celebrated and prolonged conflict. But whither? Directly over to the Spartan garrison at Decelea, the armories of the deadly and jealous enemies of Athenians who were hilt to hilt in the fierce fray for the hegemony of the Hellenic Peninsula! Here the 20,000 workmen wheeled their brawn and brain into arms and munitions which undoubtedly decided the great struggle against the Athenians.[64]

The orator Lysias owned a shield factory, *aspidopegeion*, in which he had 120 slaves, property of the estate, and probably in company with his brother Polemarch. Thirty of the slaves fell upon and murdered Polemarch for his money. Slaves were very dangerous in ancient days.[65]

If the student of sociology is at a loss to understand the causes of Demosthenes' slurs at Æschines, and the bitter-

[62] Bücher, *Aufstände der unfreten Arbeiter* S. 100–114.
[63] Plutarch, *Alexander*.
[64] Thucydides, *De Bello Peloponnesiaco*, VII., 27 ; chap. v., in this work.
[65] Eratosthenes, *Oratio, Lys.*

ness of his eloquence twitting him of mean birth, let him read Xenophen and others of his own period. Demosthenes was owner by inheritance of two manufactories; one, a butcherknife and the other a bedstead factory. The knife shop netted him a sum of 30 *minae*, $541.50 annually, and the mechanics, 32 in number who performed the labor, were slaves, and his own property. The bedstead factory turned out goods yielding 12 *minae* net, or $216.60 of earnings with the labor of 20 slaves. But the relative value of money was enormous compared with today. The total net income from the labor of these 52 slaves working for him in the two factories amounted to 42 *minae*, $758.10. After the death of his father and a settling of all indebtedness, an inventory disclosed the fact that the business was prosperous and a large stock of manufactured articles and also of raw material was left clear.[66]

Eunus the slave was a prophet. He foretold to his followers at Enna in Sicily, the fact that he, being a Syrian, a prophet of Antioch, was to become a king; and that his work should be the seed of an all-spreading revolution which should break the bondsmen's cords.

This is sufficient to show that Eunus had also his plan of salvation, like all the reformers of ancient days. His method, however, of realizing it varied from that of Lycurgus and Plato and Aristotle, about in proportion with his comparative condition. The aristocrats were educated and refined men; whereas, Eunus was a poor slave, without letters. And what was this plan? It was based on, and carried out, entirely from the central idea of *extinction*, by an almost complete extermination of the ruling and possessing class, and the rebuilding of an empire or government upon the same ground, but out of the purely laboring element—in other words, the exact equality of all men. It is perhaps the first purely anarchical idea ever put in full force and practically carried out upon a vast scale. Furthermore—and logically too—it struck the world just at the time when, according to Polybius, Rome commenced to decay. It succeeded, and logically enough, to the slave-crammed populations in Plato's ideal republic of the "Blessed;" for it is natural to suppose that through his immensely popular philosophy, he had indoc-

[66] Xenophon, *Memorabilia*, II., 7; Demosthenes, *Oratio*. V., 106, 9.

trinated all Rome—and her naturally savage military disposition—with the needful excuse for spreading this beastly institution of slavery. Eunus with his cataclysmal arms in Sicily, and Gracchus with his magnificent powers of family prestige, wealth and natural manhood, at Rome, fought a contest against Plato and the insolent lords for just 10 years, such as, search the records as we will, are not elsewhere to be found in the annals of history, ancient or modern. Eunus began by an extermination of his enemies, the slave-holding rich. He marched his first force into Enna, as related in our ninth chapter and began his work of blood and devastation the same hour, without giving either forewarning or quarter. As his masters had been merciless to the slave, so his plan of salvation was merciless to them. To stamp out the entire race of optimates was his bent and determination, leaving none even to tell the tale of woe.[67] It was the "eye-for-eye and tooth-for-tooth" referred to by a later Messiah in his great sermon on the Mount, after the unfortunate but indispensable experience of these "men of old time" had proved to him the futility of the plan of Eunus.

Plato had been dead but a couple of centuries. Rome had grasped his popular idea of government embracing an aristocracy grounded in human slavery. She had surged into the great waves of warfare with the exact advice of Plato in his "Republic of the Blessed!" and she was working to the master's lines. Slaves innumerable thronged into the marts as Rome's prisoners of war. Eunus, one of them, was a prophet and his beloved goddess, as he frankly believed, was directing him through this storm of vengeance and of blood. It was anarchy—a chaos of human life among a vast population; for Sicily at that time was populous. Dionysius the tyrant had built his yawning prison-workshops and these *ergastula* had been copied into every city and hamlet. Eunus set at liberty from these horrid slave-dens 60,000 workmen, who swelled his ranks to a vast army of 200,000 warriors, all of whom by his edict of emancipation, became destroyers of Sicilian and Roman life. Devastation!

[67] We find in Diodorus, *Histories*, the statement, quoted *supra*, p. 200, that Antigenes, one of the rich men, was exempted from his vengeance on account of a previous promise; as was also the case with the kind-hearted daughter of Damophilus (p. 206).

But who, when he calmly looks at the general conditions, after the brave words of Diodorus in his noble but tattered fragments of history of this terrible episode of retribution, will say that even the scourging, administered to those haughty millionaires, did not work an almost inestimable good? Were not these lessons necessary? Did not the world, in its tardy development out of barbarism, learn by the sorriest experience the deeper, more fundamental expression of reason, incrusted in the then, and for ages afterwards, unfathomable words of advice vouchsafed us by the last of the prophets and Messiah's to wit: that kindly treatment was as coals of fire upon their hard masters' heads?

Drimakos had his plan. It was a plan as fine in its details as it was strange in its conception. He set up an absolute monarchy in the lofty jungles of his mountain crag. He emancipated all slaves after their having passed examination as of a civil service. When once a runaway had passed this rigorous test he made him or her a member of his Blessed government upon an equality as severe as it was democratic. He forced the rich citizens of the green valleys below, to support him and his chosen angels of this aerial paradise; and for long decades of time had but to go down with his bands of warriors, armed to the teeth, and get from the barns, cellars and orchards the richest of nature's gifts. And the plan worked charmingly even to his tottering old age.

A very clearly designed plan was that of Aristonicus of Pergamus, whose anti-slavery rebellion followed that of Eunus. He promised the working people who were in great fear of being sold into slavery—a thing which actually came to pass after their defeat—that if they would take up arms with him, they should have a kingdom of the "Blessed;" that they should be made equal with all men, and become citizens of the sun, *heliopolitai*, which in their minds, since they worshiped the sun as their religion, was to be inhabitants of a heaven on earth, a democracy yearned for even to our day. With remarkable faith and energy they took up arms, fighting for their earthly paradise and when defeated, suffered like martyrs, many of them upon the cross.

Spartacus, the last of the ancient labor revolters, whose

enormous defeat went far toward convincing future philosophers and agitators that a halt must be called to the destructive havoc of reform, had a clearly traced plan. He wished to set the bondsmen free. For himself and his Thracians and Gauls he wanted freedom to return to his native hills, thinking, in his seemingly innocent simplicity, that this was the highest liberty—the enjoyment of his boyhood's home.

The mightiness of this man is seen in the two great facts: First, that his life was, as it were, a prodigious blast of unparalleled military power against the wrongs which despots, backed by military machinery, inflicted upon labor; and secondly, that through this awful and exterminatory blast, and by dint of its mightiness, the wondering, inquisitive and learning world was taught that the horrors of military despotism cannot be cured, but must ever be aggravated, by the application of military means. Through Spartacus, mankind awakened to realize that other means than that of "an eye for an eye and a tooth for a tooth" must be tried before the lowly millions of toil could be lifted to the dignity and equality of their calling.

Let these remarks suffice then, to introduce one who came next in the order of the prophets and messiahs; but this time with a statesmanship whose plan did not prove a failure. And what was this plan?

Jesus, a tradesman, messiah and prophet, coming just one hundred years after Spartacus, was obliged to labor and struggle during the greater part of his lifetime, to support himself, father, mother, brothers and sisters. Ministers of his Gospel, who preach it from any other standpoint, do so only because they have been imposed upon by the ruling of prelates who, since Constantine's political amalgamation with Neo-Platonism which upheld both chattel and wage-slavery and was no ingredient of the original precept, forsook the master and backslid into paganism.

He did not deny his lowly condition.[68] Right at the close of the Augustan or Golden Age, after the communes

---

[68] N. T. *Mark*, vi., 3: "Is not this the carpenter, the son of Mary, and are not his sisters here with us?" Aping the aristocracy of paganism which this workingman dethroned, the subsequent priesthood has vainly endeavored to trace his genealogy back to Abraham.

and **trade unions**, with Clodius at their head in Rome, had stormed lawyer Cicero out of his life, while that great tempest of agitations was yet surging on, shaping those memorable utterances of great jurists like Ulpian, to the effect that all men are born equal;[69] at that epoch-making period, himself born to the stigma of labor, Jesus was able to plant seed which has reared a system so democratical that it has already virtually overcome the terrible slave system and with it the contempt of labor; and his whole plan, though extremely revolutionary, is rapidly prevailing as people become wise in their understanding.

In the incipiency of his "state" of a perfect society which Tertullian calls a *coetus* (meaning a union),[70] Jesus considers working people regardless of trade or calling, to be the best element from which to choose his advisers. Among them were four fishermen,[71] one custom house clerk,[72] designated in Smith's Dictionary of the Bible as one of the publicans, who were at that time hated by the poor people as the meanest of men. The other seven were of various trades or professional callings. There is apparently no claim extant that any one of the twelve apostles whose names have become more renowned in the world than any others in the annals of our common race with the exception of the Master himself, of Paul, and a few others, were anything but poor workmen—a valuable assurance to any at the present day who languish in doubt lest the venture of their powers upon the labor movement may result in no glory to themselves and their names.

The organization of the early Christians, as we have constantly shown, was based purely upon the principle always advocated by *all* labor organizations, yearned for by the

---

[69] Ulpian, *Digest*, L., xvii., 32: "Quod attinet ad jus civile, servi pro nullis haberentur, non tamen et jure naturali: quia quod ad jus naturale attinet, omnes homines æquales sunt." Thus Ulpian who, some 160 years after Christ's labors closed, convinced of the justice of the already great liberating movement of the early Christian all around him, wrote these words, terrible to the Roman optimates. Justinian afterwards embodied them in his Pandects. Who shall say that Ulpian's brutal assassination by a mob of soldiers was not his punishment for righteous judgment? Again, Florentinus, not long after the time of Gaius, wrote: "Servitus est constitutio juris gentium qua quis dominio alieno contra naturam subicitur." *Digest*, I., v., 4; Böckh, *Laurische Silberbergwerke*, S. 123, declares that the Christians of these parts extinguished the slave system entirely.

[70] Tertullian, *Apology*, XXXIX., 1: "Coimus in coetum et congregationem ut ad deum quasi manu facta, precationibus ambiamus."

[71] *Matthew*, iv., 18, 21; *Mark*, i., 19, 20.

[72] *Matthew*: ix. 9; *Mark*, ii., 14.

myriad slaves, and emphatically demanded by Christ, its founder and his followers, to the effect that all men are created equal, whatever the social inequality unjustly imposed upon some by licensed managers of the products of their toil.[13] The original fathers struck out openly for all that promised equality and democratical ends.

Jesus forbids, in his ideal state, and even the approaches to it, that men should engage in war or conflict of any kind. "Whosoever smite thee on thy right cheek turn to him the other also."[14] He certainly modeled his plan from the organizations, the brotherhoods which discarded hatreds, and with them the competitive system entirely. Instead of hatred one for another, it was love one for another.[15] Socrates who says, "We are all *thiasotes* of this god,"[16] comes nearest to Christianity of all the more ancient advocates of reform; and this of course accounts for their killing him. Plato went through unscathed, and like him Aristotle. But both believed in slavery and were of *gens* blood; while Socrates was a born workingman. So likewise Jesus was killed for loving labor and laborers and denouncing hatreds together with the system on which they are based. He ruled that these working people were fully equal to any other class—a most pronounced advancement of matters in the ethics of the social, economic and political world.[17]

Socrates, if we believe his own words, was a member of an eranos, or a thiasos; for Xenophen quotes him as saying so, inasmuch as he declares to his friends and disciples gathered about him, that "under this god we are all thiasotes." He was not an Essene. His last words, as he lay dying, reminded his disciples that they (the thiasotai, or brethren), owed their cook for a chicken on which they

---

[13] Justin Martyr, *Dialogue*, xxxvi. 4; **Varro**, *De Re Rustica*, Proem.
[14] *Matthew*, v., 39. [15] *Idem*, v., 44.
[16] Xenophon, *Convivii*, viii., 2, speaking of Eros, the god of love, says that at the symposium, in all probability of a thiasos club, he made the following speech: "Ἆρ', ἔφη, ὦ ἄνδρες, εἰκὸς ἡμᾶς παρόντος δαίμονος μεγάλου καὶ τῷ μὲν χρόνῳ ἰσηλικος τοῖς ἀειγενέσι θεοῖς, τῇ δὲ μορφῇ νεωτάτου, καὶ μεγέθει μὲν πάντα ἐπέχοντος, ψυχῇ δὲ ἀνθρώπου ἰδρυμένου, Ἔρωτος, μὴ ἀμνημονῆσαι, ἄλλως τε καὶ ἐπειδὴ πάντες ἐσμὲν τοῦ θεοῦ τούτου θιασῶται . . . . ." Among the disciples of Socrates' was Xenophon himself. The subject of discussion was Love, and the duty of men to love one another, just as Jesus, at similar symposiums, used to teach the great philosophy of love nearly 500 years afterwards.
[17] *First Corinthians*, iv., 7. The church got an early foothold in Corinth. This great city was overrun with slaves. Of 680,000 inhabitants, 640,000 were slaves. Yet Paul, speaking against the distinctions which "puff" men up, one above another, asks them: "Who maketh thee to differ from another?"

had banqueted, and entreated them not to forget to pay it. These communes drank wine, sacrificed lambs, had fortune-tellers, messiahs, prophets, married and brought up children, and within their sacred pale had "all things common." This is what the early Christians organized their first communities upon; and it certainly seems, considering their lowliness and the fact that they were mostly workingmen and women, that Christianity was the organization invented to "PROCLAIM' the cult which the secret commune so long and so inveterately had in secret practised. In a word, the revolution of Jesus rose from a deep meaning, thoroughly digested, long tried and powerful culture, already inculcating, already impregnating the opinion and bias of that great working majority, the downtrodden lowly of mankind.

The idea—ignored by Plato, "the father of idealism," and hinted at in Aristotle's strange prediction[78]—of a society without slaves where all are equal, was original in the secret labor communes ; but so far as its open propagation was concerned, it was original with Jesus, totally and definitively. That idea could not mix with the old paganism. [79] Otherwise the ancient culture, philosophy and great-mindedness, had many magnificent virtues, which prevail to-day and which farther on, we shall show to have belonged not to paganism but to labor. The repudiation of paganism by the culture of Jesus, took on, in the ignorant, bigoted world, an enormous excrescence of supernumerary whims arising from infantile speculations of men, which were condensed through edicts, by the councils of different ages, into tyrannical faith-cures, inquisitions and superstitious "standard philosophies," and theological regulations which arbitrarily, building on such edicts, destroyed for a thousand years, the culture of inquiry founded by men like Aristotle and Socrates. But this very spirit of inquiry belongs to the plan of Jesus.[80]

They could not see the way clear to mix. The age we live in is that of mixture of the two great and immortal

---

[78] Aristotle, in *Œconomics*, predicted, foreshadowed that there might arrive a state of development in which there would be no slaves. Cf. id., Pol., I., 4.
[79] Draper, *Intellectual Development of Europe*, I., chap. xiii., *Passage of the Age of Reason*, has shown, by a cutting array of facts, that the inquisitive, or investigating spirit and its culture of the Greek Progressists school would both been extirpated altogether, but for Mohammed and the Arabians and Spanish Moors.
[80] *Thessalonians*, v., 21 : "Prove all things and hold fast that which is good."

plans.. It is the culture of inquisitive reason on the basis of equality of all mankind. This equality paganism did not allow.

The revolution accomplished by the efforts of the poor through their long succession of revolts, their messiahs, secret organizations, and at last their early Christianity, though it was perverted by Constantine and a long succession of prelates in the false garb of faith and priestcraft during the dark ages, never for a moment relinquished its hold on its real revolutionary idea. That idea was the equality of man, the teaching *by* the poor, *of* the poor; the building-up of a vast civilization without slaves, with one God, one father for all and salvation of all, economically.

When Christians concentrated priest-power into despotism there arose another vast and similar order—the Mohammedan—which resumed the same idea and in Spain went on for centuries with the plan based upon equality, carrying it out as well as could be done at that low age. This Mohammedanism appears to have saved mankind from sinking forever.

It took a thousand years for the world to learn and properly apply the new system. The relapses and swoons of the early centuries, when men were guided by ambitious demagogues, were, if we learn to reason upon them aright, most natural things. The world had, throughout all the previous ages, been cultivating a civilization based upon the system of masters and slaves. It was a civilization competitive in all respects. It had never known a moment of socialistic life. If its lowly millions had built up and tried a socialism, it was in the dense penumbra of secrecy. Whenever their socialism reached the light it had always been put down by the monster power of slavery and its military legions, as a loathsome and filthy thing; for it recognized equality.

Foolish then and short-sighted are the men who wonder at the vast tumble-down ages of demolition that supervened over the immortal revolution of Jesus and the working people, who, prying their socialistic civilization up through this despotism, at a choice moment when aristocracy was rotting by its own loathsome gangrene, sent their orators out, and with superhuman struggles urged it forth upon the broad plane of day where, for once and for all, the resplendant sun of unmasked intelligence shone upon it with beams so bright that, although since beclouded, it now rolls onward to a final day.

The new ages had to be built, but in their building their architects fell, times without number and nearly two thousand years rolled over the world before all things became adjusted to this civilization they have erected upon those great precepts which contain and set forth the economic equality of mankind.

This emergence of the culture of the great commune system of the ancient lowly out of the secret, into the open, out of the irascible, destructive, the bloody and warlike, into the peaceful world, which took place at Palestine after the great and last disaster under Spartacus, gave to humanity a set of immortal principles to accomplish their economic salvation. So inconceivably great was the change or revolution embodied in these principles that our race in applying them, sank into a swoon and well-nigh lost them forever. But after a struggle of nearly 1,900 years the world is at last re-emerging from its thrall and is now in the very act of applying them as a permanent principle to its political economy.

One of the greatest and fiercest struggles the Christians ever had was motived by the working people's demand for bread. The new sect, being largely of the labor element, its monks naturally were in their sympathy and allowed vast numbers of images, palladiums, amulets, talismans and incantations to be manufactured for the uses of every conceivable phase of priestcraft. There came, during the middle ages a protest against it, and for 120 years the war of the iconoclasts raged against the working people who in turn were savagely upheld by the monks. Thus, as ever before, the aristocracy were against labor, rightly, perhaps, for in course of ages, industry has, in the finer civilizations, given up its hold on image-making; but the truth is, the laboring classes would not accept Christianity at the cost of their means of life. That this does not apply to the early Christians is explained by the fact that they were co-operators who "had all things common."

"In the present world only evil reigns. Satan is the king of the earth, or prince of this world. All obey him." [82]

[81] Consult *Intellectual Development of Europe*, vol. II., for a full discussion.
[82] Renan, *Vie de Jésus*, p. 116; N. T. *John*, xii., 31, xiv., 30, xvi., 11; *Second Corinthians*, iv., 4.

Now working people, even those engaged in the great advocacy of labor, and the absolute equality of the rights of man, may possibly be misled by their honest belief that Jesus, in talking as he did meant only the world to come. He meant the present, just as he said: "The kings kill the prophets:"[83] "The just are persecuted:" "Thy will be done on *earth* as it is in heaven."[84]

But whoever thoroughly understands the ancients, well knows that among all the numerous turmoils of slaves, of gladiators, of agrarianism, of trade unionists, there have been prophets. The kings, according to this speech of Christ, killed them. We have sufficiently shown that the kings and rulers were not satisfied with their ordinary death; they hung them and their followers upon the ignominious cross.[85] "The world as it is, is the enemy of God."[86] The great master, speaking in his exquisitely perfect style of allegory, always represented God as the principle of goodness—nature.

Jesus preached openly a plan or system of absolute justice; and he, in establishing a foothold for it, also perished on the cross. The kings killed the prophets. They had just killed his friend and forerunner, the vigorous agitator and member of the order of free masons, John the Baptist, because his pure character and love of virtue forbade him from permitting unattacked, the voluptuousness and fornication going on in palaces and assignation houses of Herod and [87] intimates, over whom reigned the beautiful but silly Herodias by whose machinations Antipas had become the cunning ingrate whom Jesus denominated the "fox."[88] John and Jesus owe their death to this bloodthirsty female libertine. Very few know or even seek to know the real, human, home-viewed causes of these renowned events; they being mixed up in the mysticism of supernatural predilection and bigotry. When this labor movement comes to be regarded as a sort of "second coming," which it really is, we shall behold the amazing analogy of that mighty agitation of A. D. 31–33, in juxtaposition with ours of 1886–'96, our eyes opened,

[83] Renan, *Id.*, pp. 116, 117 [84] *Matthew*, vi., 10.
[85] See *supra*, the chapters on *Strikes* and *Uprisings*.
[86] Renan, *Vie de Jésus*, p. 117.
[87] Renan, *idem*, p. 111: " L' union presq' incestueuse d'Antipas et d' Hérodiale s'accomplit alors." *Leviticus*, viii.. 16; Josephus, *Wars of the Jews*, VII., 6. 7 and elsewhere: *Antiquities*, XVII., 13.
[88] See *Encyclopædia Britannica*, Article *Antipas*.

our hearts gladdened in an inexpressably glorious normal growth of 18 centuries which have shorn it of mysticism and theosophy.

Prophets and healers were everywhere. The wife of Spartacus was both. She foretold that the deeds of this gladiator should be great, by divining the causes of the serpent being found coiled around her husband's neck and face during his sleep. She was a sorceress; and her premonitory words all turned out too true to the cruel capitalists, for whose work of enslaving the people Spartacus punished them with some of the most disastrous military defeats and humiliating slaughters to be found in the annals of war.[89]

The Essenes had their prophets, some of whom turned off such excellent examples of foretelling that they became known far and near.[90] All antiquity was full of prophets; and they had the advantage of us modern mortals, in that they met an openly expressed belief in prognostication; whereas the people of modern times are on the alert for what they incredulously and correctly characterize as humbugs. When the true social history of the past shall have been written, and all its available phases presented from a point of view of the anti-slavery or anti-competitive movement, we shall come to a common sense understanding of this whole mesh, linked together, event with event.

Paganism by its law of entailment upon primogeniture logically made every child, except the first-born, or "anointed," a menial, a chattel, a slave.[91]

Jesus with a majestic swoop, hurled this cruelty from his state and turning to all the innocents, with an ineffable sweetness, uttered the irresistible command: "Suffer little children to come unto me for of such is the kingdom of heaven;"[92] and though Plato hove the consideration of the working class from him with a contempt that denied them even citizenship, the eloquence of Jesus rang out: "The laborer is worthy of his hire."[93]

Messiahships and prophetic lore, all through the sup-

[89] Consult *supra*, chapter ix.
[90] Smith's *Cyclopædia of Biblical Literature*, Article, *Essenes;* Bellermann, *Nachrichten aus dem Alterthum.*
[91] See *supra*, chapter on *Eleusinian Mysteries*, touching the cryptia, and secret wholesale murder of the laboring element.
[92] N. T. *Mark*, x., 14. *Matthew*, x., 10; *Luke*, x., 7.

erstitious ages have been strategical strongholds of economic philosophy. They have entered with immaculate conceptions, prophetic powers, voodooisms and fetichs. They have entered into all the efforts of the poor, struggling for economic emancipation. But they have acted a potent part in building and deeply rooting a philosophy whose slow and steady culture is terminating in the reasonable belief that such monstrous things are worthless and that the purified economic philosophy needs no masters, leaders or messiahs.

A thousand years after Lycurgus, Jesus denied that the estate of birth and family, as understood by the Pagans, was of any account whatever. He laid the axe at the root of this most egregious evil; and his doctrines have been quietly destroying it ever since.

From B. C. 55, the date of Julius Caesar's invasion of the British shores, the Roman organizations began. It is well known that the Romans mixed freely with the people whom they found living on these islands. Settling in Kent, Middlesex and other places, they taught the Britons as we have elsewhere explained, the mechanic arts. They also taught them the principle of combination against oppression which existed there in all its rigors. They planted the burial societies which to this day have never died out; communes, which smothered for thousands of years, still exist; trade unions, which, though often stifled into guilds and perhaps, in appearance, suppressed, smouldered through long generations until finally allowed to resume. Their burial associations were in Kent, Middlesex and London, the same as they were at Rome—practically more trade union than burial society.

We behold with astonishment, unable to comprehend because ignorant of the powers of transmission through habit, the tendency of the working people of London, to grasp the social problem. Yet here is the explanation. Their omnipresent burial societies are at heart both trade unions and socialist communes, just as were those of their ancestors. And now London crops out, the very leader of the great labor movement of the world. It has been so all along. A glance at the history of the social turmoils of Jack Cade, of Wickliff, will show that London and its vicinity have ever been as it were, the nucleus of a great

Anglo-Saxon cult of fraternity borrowed from the Greek and Roman Brotherhoods.

Our inference from evidence given in preceding chapters, that land was not primevally held as common property will be challenged. The opposite opinion is the popular one. But we have all through, insisted that we do not claim to prove it only in connection with the Indo-European stock, whatever may be hereafter ascertained as to others, the historic evidence shows more and more conclusively as we investigate, that the original settler was the paterfamilias, the low bully who took the land, and built about him like a sovereign, using his family as his slaves. The Aryan, we insist, was not a nomad. Nomads were the first runaway sons and daughters who, unable to endure the treatment they were subjected to, organized, revolted, took to the woods and built up sympathies and self-help coalitions which finally developed into the numerous social unions we have described, and gave origin to the nomadic life of the patriarchal system. In other words, the earliest of our forefathers were the monarchical stock, and the democratic stock followed. So we find also, true to the principle of development, that the older, or monarchical stock is gradually dying out while the democratic stock is growing little by little, century by century, all over the world alike. The first are the aristocracy the latter the working people.

We have stated before that there exists a similarity between Socrates and Jesus. The more this fact is studied the more beautiful the paralellisms appear. Both were workingmen by birth. Both preached the labor question. Both were guided throughout their lives by a dæmon; that is, by some invisible power for good; for the Greek dæmon was God. Both were betrayed by their own disciples. Both were orators of the most supernal eloquence, powers of magnetism and genius, the one with simile the other, allegory. Neither wrote, but both like the true workingman, were indefatigable in deeds and left their followers to do their writing. Both were prophets and messiahs and both died martyrs to their cause. To carry the similitude farther, both were surrounded to their dying hour, by friends who in after life, rose from their masters' seemingly inspired teachings, to the very pinnacle of fame—a fame which, in both cases, based clearly on the economic question, has been greater, more lasting and far more glorious than that of any other men.

But Socrates in less than 500 years, could only block out, and crudely present what Jesus, in 2,000 years, brings to perfection. From the great sayings of the reasoning Socrates arose the axiom of Aristotle, to be up and be doing, for nothing would come of itself, and Jesus in similar manner taught Paul to prove all things; hold fast that which is good — the basis since laid down by Descartes and Bacon, and spontaneously adopted as the ground-principle upon which our mechanico-progressive enlightenment thrives. No nation, no people that will not accept and pattern from it can proceed. They must languish like the Mongolian, in conservatism.

Let us first compare the prayers of these two masters with those of others. The prayer of Socrates ran as follows:

"O beloved God of nature, Guardian of many a clime! Let me become beautiful within; for whatever I have outward, I should be at peace within. Let me be wise enough to consider him rich who hath wisdom. May I be endowed with but enough of riches as no one except a prudent man can use and bear without pride."[94]

There was a dignified and honest humiliation about Socrates. He must have been a most heroic character. A poor workingman, born to a trade, and never owning more than a third class house to live in, he was able—though he went barefoot through the streets of Athens and some say, almost ragged and filthy—to attract and captivate, and actually convert into thinkers and philosophers, some of the wealthiest young aristocrats of that high-toned city. He constantly declared that he was guided by some unknown spirit. Jesus was also thus guided. Socrates was certain of nothing until he had reasoned the objection away and always thought that he himself knew little or nothing. The same unassuming sweetness and self-distrust is what makes the character of Jesus so lovely and captivating that all the ascerbity of his critics melts with the progress of their arguments

[94] Plato, *Phædrus, fin.*

The last scenes of Socrates as described by Plato in his Crito and his Phædo, are, for their wonderfully affecting simplicity, and their astonishing disclosure of the power of human resignation and of spirit over the flesh, unparalelled by anything that exists in story, unless we except the story of Jesus, his last supper and exquisite fortitude in the hour and agony of death.

The most celebrated and oft-repeated prayer of Jesus is that regarding his mission in favor of the poor—the Lord's prayer—in which, being one of them, he uses the second person: "Give *us* this day our daily bread."[95] It was a great problem among the poor of his time, how to get enough to eat. But for an example of his power to subjugate the hateful spirit of intimidation and vengeance, of conceit and shallow egoism which debased his age, nothing can equal the great prayer as he hung, dying in awful agony, upon the cross. This torture had been the invention of fiends of the prehistoric ages; by creatures who imagined that pain was the crystalized term embodying both vengeance and threat. They so framed both their law and their gibbet, foreknelling to the subjects, by cramming the imagination with the horror of pain. Yet even in this incomparable agony, with the spirit at the verge of departure, and the body writhing in qualms such as none can suffer so poignantly as a young man of his physical courage and vigor in the sensitive prime of life's hopes and joys, we see this person capable of casting up his eyes to heaven and meekly, touchingly, begging the Pan of Socrates; the Isis of the therapeut; the Pallas Athene of Phidias, the Cybele of the thiasote, the Ceres of Eunus, the God of Abraham and universal Father, to forgive them—the cruel mob—for they knew not what they did.[96]

Now let us look at some other celebrated prayers, study their exact meaning and ask ourselves how these two unselfish and self-sacrificing prayers of Socrates and of Jesus, differed in point of view of the plan of salvation for the poor and laboring lowly.

One of the oldest that we have is that of Alcestis, the faithful wife of Admetus, who was about to die that her husband might live. She invoked the altar of her

---

[95] *Matthew*, vi., 11.   [96] N. T., *Luke*, xxiii., 34.

SPECIMENS OF SELFISHNESS IN PRAYER. 563

family, the tomb of her fathers, the fire-eternal of her hearth: "O holy divinity, mistress of my *gens* and paternity! This is the last time that I bow myself before thee, and address thee my prayers; for I am about to descend into the regions of the dead. Watch I pray thee, over my children, who are to know no more a mother. Give to my son a tender wife, and to my daughter a noble husband. Permit that they may not die, like myself before their time, but let them, in the bosom of happiness and riches, find a protracted existence."[97]

All is selfishness. The family, the individual, the egoist, the concentrated wealth of slave labor, alone to be blessed, but not a word for the suffering world outside.

So again, another ancient aristocrat, approaching the tomb of a rich man believed to be happy in the abodes below, prays: "O thou who art an aristocrat under the sod."[98] Another prayer of a selfish son, concerned only in the welfare of his family and the wealth he has inherited, in the language of Euripides likewise invoking his dead father now a god in the beatitude of an underground paradise, reads: "O thou, who art a god under the ground, preserve me."

But Juvenal, the great satirist, a freedman's son and a low-born, had the kindness of Socrates. In one of his satires Juvenal prays. His prayes is for the poor slave, in bondage; and good old Juvenal died in exile, on the scorching plains of an African desert.

Xenophon who wrote the Œconomics, a treatise on the habits of life, makes Isomachus say to Socrates: "I open the day, each morning, by saying my prayers, like a gentleman well brought up."[99] The philosophers among the Greeks always said their prayers, and even at the symposiums of the thiasotes and other communes, prayers and pæans were regularly offered.[100] But all the prayers of the ancient rich, were for the rich and noble. Æchylus makes Orestes pray to the great God of the Greek theogony of his age, as follows: "O Zeus! If thou lettest the race of the eagle perish, who shall hereafter bear the auguries to mortal men?"[101] Nobody but the aristocrat, allied by blood to the God himself, could carry the messages from the high to the low, of mankind; and by this culture the aristocracy was maintained while the outcasts, the low-born who labored, were kept down, even by the prayers and entreaties of those in power.

An instance of the kind of prayer that was expected by a gathering of ancients before the beginning of our era, is told of Ptolemy Philadelphus, at a convention of guests called to examine the Septuagint at Alexandria, about B. C. 265. An old Pagan priest was called on to offer an extemporaneous prayer, and he made it with such show, and rhetorical eloquence that it caused a tumultuous outburst of applause.[102] How different from the command we have from the workingman.[103]

Far better than this have the simple aborigines of America done. The prayer of the Quiché race in their wanderings to find a fixed habitation was: "Hail! O Creator, O Former! thou that art in heaven and on the earth, O Heart of Heaven, O Heart of Earth! give us descendants and a posterity as long as the light endures. Give us to walk always in an open road, in a path without snares; to lead happy, quiet, peaceable lives, free of reproach."[104] The Aztec prayers preserved from the mouldering antiquities of Mexico, touch the heart as if they might be labor supplications; and they make us think of the wandering family outcasts of the ancient Aryan race.[105]

Socrates and Jesus pray with a similar humiliation, for improvement, liberty and modest emancipation from want while the others prayed for a continuation of the powers and riches already in their possession; and the farther we investigate these two characters the finer and more beautiful appears the paralellism between them, while their natures diverge more and more widely from the great class outside the social pale, buffeting, and vaunting in the competitive billows of pride and arrogance.

Not a few men of distinction of our age are awakening to a sense of the great modern truth, that it is noble to

[101] Æschilus, *Choephori,* 248-249; De Cassagnac *Histotre des Classes Nobles et des Classes Annoblies,* p 569.
[102] Draper, *Intellectual Development of Europe,* Vol. I., p. 89.
[103] *Matthew,* vi, 5, 6, 7.
[104] Bancroft, *Native Races,* vol. III., p. 49.
[105] *Encyclopædia Britannica,* vol. XVII., p. 220 (Stoddart).

acknowledge. When nations, or families, or individuals discover that they have been hugging an error, it is not disgraceful, it is noble, even grand, to come boldly out and acknowledge it.[106]

We premise this statement as a prologue to what we would say of the Jews who still despise, almost ignore the modern era. There is a solemn history in their case that ought to furnish a full excuse for this. But viewed from our standpoint of true sociology which treats man in his normal relation to the economic means of existence, there is no longer an excuse for schism, dissention and misunderstanding as to the acceptance by Jew or Gentile, of the present civilization, so far as it has been able to jostle into the plans of salvation laid down by Moses, Socrates, Aristotle and Jesus. When correctly understood by the Hebrew working man, he himself will acknowledge that no grounds for quarrel exists with these legislators—not even with the plan of Jesus. That he lived, is true beyond cavil;[107] and the Jew does not deny it; he only denies that he was the great aristocrat whom his own proud race expected. Here lies the trouble. Let it be remembered that those ancient Jews of whom we read, were at this time very proud people and that they had no sympathy whatever with persons who would stoop to an agitation in the cause of the slaves, or the working classes. This phase of the life and labors of Jesus, they were themselves the very first to condemn and reject. It was they who were maddened at his work, and they who betrayed and killed him. Had he come as a great prince, robed in

---

[106] Hewitt, Speech in the House of Representatives, on the *Emancipation of Labor*: "I have no apologies to make for having progressed out of the night of darkness into the open sunshine of truth. But I should have apologies to make if, having reached conclusions which contradict those that I held years ago, I should fail in this House and everywhere to announce them with that frankness which belongs to an honest man and a faithful representative." As the new era advances, we see more and more frequent exhibits of lofty acknowledgment like the specimen here quoted.

[107] The profane evidences that such a person actually lived are many and multiform; Consult Josephus, *Antiquities*, cap. xviii. As regards the authenticity of Josephus, we refer the reader to Tacitus, *Annales*, XV., 44; Origen, *Commentatio in Matth.*; Eusebius, *Evangeliorum Demonstratio*, III.; Idem, *Ecclesiasticus*, I., cap. xi.; Hieronymus, *De Viris Illustribus, In Josepho*; Sozomen, *Historia Ecclesiastica*, I., 1; Justin Martyr, *Dial. cum Tryphone*; Georgius Syncellus, *Chronica*; Scaliger, *Prolegomena, De Emendatione Temporum* and many others. A curious book, purporting to be a copy of an ancient MS. of the Secret Order of *Essenes*, now in the possession of Mr. G. L. Wild, the piano merchant of Washington, D. C., and which we have carefully perused, bears the following suggestive title: "*Wie ist Jesus wirklich gestorben?—Beantwortet.*" Baltimore, 1850.

gorgeous and shining attire, with lofty tread and lordly mein, and had he preached the philosophy of property, the sanctity of priesthood and the vengeance of Jehovah, things to-day would have been different. The Jews would have acknowledged him.

But his work launched incomparably above that level, in that, while it in no sense, attacked the Pagan science or any of its powerful steps in development, it resulted completely in breaking up the hideous system of slavery. It built up what had ever before been a stranger even among the Jews, the free family; legalizing that institution on a completely democratic basis, such as makes every one, no matter how poor, a noble. In this it has excelled everything hitherto known among either Pagans or Hebrews; for Moses provided the ghastly institution of slavery.

This aged stamp of slavery removed, nothing remains to hinder Hebrew working people from rising in science and the scientific adjustment or application of the inventions, manufactures and all other products of their hands and working harmoniously with all others of the industrial class.

The Jews are easily convinced of any truth when it is reasonably explained; for they are logically and scientifically disposed. It is well known that while they were living peacefully in Spain, during the Middle ages, under the then excellent Mohammedan rule which cultivated the sciences and arts, great numbers of Jews embraced the Mohammedan faith. Among others was the great Maimonides.[108]

But Jerusalem at that time being a grand, beautiful and proud city, ruled over by an aristocratic stock who numbered many priests among them, the Hebrews naturally wanted and expected a man of noble extraction, as their Messiah.

Another point must here connectedly be borne in mind— the destruction of Jerusalem. Early christians are known to have looked unconcerned upon this awful scene under Titus, A. D. 70. This again maddened the Hebrews; for they found themselves if possible, worse persecuted than the new brotherhood.

Josephus gives the number of Jews, men, women and

[108] See Draper, Intellectual Development of Europe, II., pp. 122-12

children destroyed, at 1,100,000, and Tacitus gives it at 600,000. Considering the almost unparalelled massacres to which they were subjected, after the new brotherhood began to take root, and that they naturally thought these brotherhoods were the real cause of it, we cannot wonder that they consider them and their organizer and champion as at the bottom of many of their disasters.

It is only when they begin to look upon this Jesus from the point of view of social science, that the brilliant Hebrew race can ever see and persuade themselves to admit that there was no imposture; for the labor movement is at this moment without a tincture of class hatred or of national prejudice. It is slowly working for the improvement of all mankind; and any one plan that succeeds must logically be the one accepted by both Jew and Gentile.

The knowledge of these facts leads to the review of ancient plans, in a light that contrasts them with the modern. In extreme brevity it is as follows:

The plan of Lycurgus was this of our modern socialists who desire that society or government possess, operate, distribute with mathematical accuracy, the product of labor. The state of Lycurgus did as much for a period of 500 years.

The plan of the moderns is, that the state shall own all land and all implements of labor. But the Spartans did exactly this, under a test of 1,500 generations. What, then, is this political economy that has *not* been tried?

The answer to this gives a mirror in which is reflected the vast progress under the new era. It is simply that the *tools of labor* were originally the *slaves*; the human, animate, quickened *things*, that thought, resented, rebelled, fought organized, wrote their record upon the slabs and finally brought out their great culture and master; these were the tools of the ancient Pagan state! And in Sparta, in Crete and in Plato's Republic, they had them in common.

The laborer then, as the subjugated tool of the ancients did right, we claim, no matter how destructive his methods or how disastrous for the moment, their outcome; he did right under the circumstances, terrible and irrepressible in his slavery-cursed ages; he did right to rebel and teach those cruel optimates who owned and whipped and strangled him, the first stern lessons in democracy.

Men and women then, were the tools, the implements of labor. owned in common by the state; and they were worked and whipped for the "blessed" of "God's chosen people." The change from the human tools to the labor-saving tools; from the servile state to the democratic; from the groans of ignorance to the joys of equality in enlightenment, is the revolution in which the advocates of modern labor reform desire to have "all things common," as Jesus arranged through his followers. It was the economic part to be accomplished, which he presaged and ordered for adoption on the vast scale, at his "second coming"—the Labor Movement of to-day.

We have now arrived at our closing remarks on these implements of labor. We have already shown that the economic problem of the ancients was never Pagan. It was then, just what it is now—Christian, or that which afterwards became Christian. Paganism never could endure any mechanical progress. It was conservative. When mechanical genius of the industrial earth-borns wrought at Athens, and in Asia Minor and the islands of the Archipelago, wonderful works, they were aggressive against paganism and its sullen culture.

What was the mechanical progress of the ancient low-borns, then, despite the contempt of a system based on slavery that has always, even to this day, made them as slaves and poor wage-earners, the tools of an aristocracy?

We reply, basing each word carefully upon history, that it was *labor*—labor degraded, but labor. Nothing else. No nation ever made an iota of progress without it. The bully in a spirit of brigandage could seize the product of labor and use it; but not without first forcing a laborer to perform the task.

But a curious fact is here opened to view. Not only is labor the origin of all things among mankind which make life and enlightenment, but it is the poor little infinitesimal creature, the laborer, that makes language. No power can withstand or overcome that of the proletarian inroads. A desperate effort was once made in England to introduce and perpetuate the Latin tongue. High-priests and prelates, university doctors, kings robed in majesty, and governmental powers, were almost unanimous in the upper atmosphere of rule, in pressing the subjection of the tongue of the proletarian million. For centuries their power imperfectly succeeded. But a Chaucer, and a Shakespeare rose from the ranks to the rescue and backed by the rough and heedless populace, teeming in the by-ways already the proud old classic is dead. It is this little, insignificant mite, so long in the swaddlings and sackcloth of contempt, who adds almost every new word, as he adds every new thing, by the unrecognized toil of his invention, contrivance, discovery, in industry; and the multitude of mechanical as well as literary plagiarisms, ancient and modern, practiced at his expense to aggrandize others, will be the subject of some future treasure-hunter, for an invaluable book.

The ancient world before the Roman conquests, was not only full of inhabitants, but full of inventions. They had a reaper among the Gauls, the operations of which are traceable for hundreds of years. It was a real reaping machine or harvester. Pliny tells us that it was pushed by an ox harnessed in thills behind it and that it had some sort of reel which threw the heads of the grain over so that somehow they were severed—or as he erroneously states, torn, —from the stalks.[109] The reaper mentioned by Pliny is again found much more perfectly described by Palladius, 400 years afterwards. It is perfectly obvious to any mechanic or farmer who has tried a reaping machine that no grain, however ripe or brittle, will admit for a moment, of having its ears "torn off" and dropped into a trough. On the contrary, the greatest precaution in the construction of cutters that sever the heads from the stalks must be observed. Here was the secret of the recent inventions.

---

[109] Pliny, *Nat. Hist.*, 18, 30, describing the *messor*, or harvester, speaks as follows: "Messis ipsius ratio varia. Galliarum latifundiis valli praegrandes dentibus in margine infestis, duabus rotis per segetem impelluntur, jumento in contrarium juncto; ita direptae in vallum cadunt spicae. Stipulae alibi mediae falce precidunt, atque inter duas mergites spica distringitur." This same machine is more fully described by Palladius, in his *De Re Rustica*, for *June*, lib. VII., cap. ii., as follows: "Pars Galliarum planior hoc compendio utitur ad metendum, et praeter hominum labores, unius bovis opera spatium totius messis absumit. Fit itaque vehiculum quod duabus rotis brevibus fertur. Hujus quadrata superficies tabulis munitur, quae forinsecus reclines in summo reddant spatio largiora. Ab ejus fronte carpenti brevior est altitudo tabularum. Ibi denticuli plurimi ac rari ad spicarum mensuram constituuntur in ordinem, ad superiorem partem recurvi. A tergo vero ejusdem vehiculi duo brevissimi temones figurantur, velut amites basternarum. Ibi bos capite in vehiculum verso jugo aptatur et vinculis mansuetus sane, qui non modum compulsoris excedat. Hic ubi vehiculum per messes coepit impellere, omnis spica in carpentem denticulis comprehensa cumulatur, abruptis ac relictis paleis: altitudinem vel humilitatem pterumque bubuculo moderante, qui sequitur. Et ita per paucos itus ac reditus brevi horarum spatio tota messis impletur. Hoc campestribus locis vel aequalibus utile est, et iis, quibus necessaria paica non habetur."

Pliny was a superficial observer and knew little about mechanical niceties. But he could correctly inform us that this labor-saving machine worked so well that it was universally employed by the farmers of the great valleys of what is now France; and the fact that it worked, shows that the ancients used the reciprocating shears. No doubt this machine had been in use hundreds of years before Pliny saw it. Palladius tells us that it economized labor so greatly that one man with a strong, gentle ox could reap an entire canton in a day.

Thus, while Caesar, a military noble of aristocratic stock was attacking the defenseless people of Gaul, and killing his million[110]—the harvest of his brutal invasions—the working people were quietly inventing the invaluable implements of labor, which afterwards were to be exchanged for the animate tools of labor in form of slaves and wage-bondmen of the ancient oligarchy.

So long as the enslavement of man remained at so low a level that man himself was the tool or implement of labor, there appears to be no fierce exhibits of the competitive system, such as prevails to-day. When slaves, as tools of labor, were emancipated, the true competitive business era appeared, and nourished by its corollary, the wage-slave system, will continue, until the inanimate tools or implements of labor—the inventions or labor-saving machines, have become nationalized just as the animate tools, the human machines were nationalized, in the plans of Lycurgus and Plato. This difference between the kind of tools to be nationalized, from those of Lycurgus to those which make our wonderful civilization, is in reality, exactly what workingmen of to-day are organizing and struggling to create. Labor wants Lycurgus' nationalization of the implements of production and distribution on a basis in which all may enjoy their product equally.

But reasoning from the point of view of social science, it is worth while to recur to the actual mechanical advancement attained to, in spite of the hatred borne by the ancient cult, for any kind of laboring machines except the slave.

[110] Something on the destruction of the Gauls may be found in Cæsar, *De Bello Gallico*, VI., cap. 24. Wallace. *Numbers of Mankind*, p. 70-75, shows that there were 39,000,000 people in Gaul. Cæsar killed 1,000,000, and took as many more prisoners, many of whom were consigned to slavery. See Plutarch, *Pompey*, showing that he siezed a thousand cities; Id., *Cæsar*.

Long before Christ the Alatri had used the inverted siphon[111] and Pliny informs us of enormous hydraulic mining plants.[112] Wallace has collected a great number of references to authors showing the height of perfection to which art had arrived before the opening of the present era.[113] Fine porcelain was manufactured in high antiquity.[114] The building art outstripped all others, even those of destruction in the military line. The cause of this, is that more solemnity and reverence existed among the Pagan temples than in any other realm, and consequently more time, energy, genius and money were expended in this sphere, than elsewhere; consequently the building trade and the manufacture of images excelled all other industries for exquisite workmanship.[115]

Long before the Roman invasion of Britain. there existed considerable art among the mechanics; but it is well established that the friendly Roman Brotherhoods brought and taught the art of lathe-work in pottery into a town which has since become the great London.[116]

The whole subject sums up in the grave conclusion that the plants and the plans of the ancient brotherhoods however ancient—even thousands of years before the coming of the last Messiah—were really the plant and plan which, under the Christian civilization, the modern world is following.

Pure paganism was that of the idea of an aristocratic religion whose priesthood was a part of the state government. It denied the equality of men. It strenuously upheld and stubbornly contended for the divinity of rights—a divinity that was based upon the august power of the paternal despot, and still adheres in form of the aged law of inheritance and the rule of entailments upon primogeniture, or a species of godhead for the first-born son, and in the inheritance of living monarchs. Pure paganism exalted this first-born, who was believed to have relationship by blood and family, with the immortals. It was a despotism of masters over slaves, which despised the laborers, originally its own children, while it feasted upon their works.

---

[111] Bowie, *Hydraulic Mining*, pp. 158–9.
[112] Pliny, *Natural History*, XXXIII., cap. 4.
[113] Wallace, *Numbers of Mankind*, p. 141; Guhl and Koner, *Life of the Greeks and Romans*, p. 490, sqq.
[114] Pliny, *Natural History*, XXXVI., cap. 26.
[115] A fine specimen of building art was the temple of Jerusalem; Campbell, *Political Survey*, I., p. 23, note; Diodorus Siculus, *Bibliotheca Historica*, XVI.; Dionysius, *Periegesis*, v. 109; Pliny, *Natural History*, VII., 56.
[116] Hughes, *Horæ Britannicæ*.

The *laborers and the products of labor were therefore never Pagan.* The beautiful chiselings of Phidias belonged, not to the ancient, but to the modern civilization; for pure paganism despised these makers. They were before their age.

All the great industrial triumphs therefore, were, by anticipation, though unrealized, germane to the modern era. As they were a source of contention, and were innovations against paganism in ancient days, so they are crystals of the pure, in philosophy and political economy of modern days; since by the dissolution of the old order of things the economic problem slowly triumphs over the old warring cult of the competitive system, and is already showing signs of a tendency to reconsider, and upon a vast scale, re-adopt the ancient germ—long suppressed—of having "all things in common."

Judging from the evidence, we could almost infer that the modern labor movement is not only a genuine revival of the ancient one, but the surprising appearance presents itself that with all its vastly greater advantages, on account of mechanical developments and the filling of the world with inventions and implements of progress which the ancients lacked, yet it has not become much purer in the true method of realizing needful equality than the Italian trade unions had grown to, before the Christian era; for we find their organizations in the use of the ballot shown on the inscriptions at Pompeii,[117] and many other such evidences, that they actually used their ballot; whereas modern trade unions still refuse this mighty instrument of power. The remarkable fact is seen uppermost, that the ancients have discussed every sort of socialism now being forced to the front by the returning labor associations, such as lay at the bottom, inspiring these world-renowned plans. Every one of the great schemes, from that of the Cretans, borrowed by Lycurgus, to those of Numa, Solon, then Socrates—spoiled by aristocratic Plato—then Aristotle and the others, down to, and including Jesus, was a plant of socialism. Every one that treated or even tried to treat working people as equal with the rest of mankind, like the plans of Numa, Solon, afterwards of Jesus, proved successful; and we challenge the critical world to prove it otherwise. But every one, like those of Crete, borrowed by Lycurgus, and those of Plato, Aristotle, Agis, the Roman *gens* and all succeeding ones

---

[117] See *supra*, p. 390-391, quoting the *Pompeian Inscription.*

that have been based upon the competitive, or slave, and wage-slave systems, failed.

MORAL.

Let all men take warning from the past, that the plans of those great aristocrats based on the social idea, failed because they left the laborer out; denied him liberty, soul and an enumeration in the census, as a man. He rebelled; and in his crude numeric might, broke them up and killed them. He destroyed their governments at last, and is building a new era upon their ruins. Let then, the world accept this new era, expunge every lingering heathenism, recognize and acknowledge that equality means justice meted out to all—not a "divine" few who use the outcast as a mere implement of labor; himself, his toils, his products nationalized, only for their minority. Let now, this rallying hero's inventions be nationalized instead; his products nationalized; his body freed. Then *all*—not a presumptuous few—become divine, and all enjoy the plentitude which the ancient plan of nationalization is well known to have brought forth.

What shall the gilded pulpit say when arraigned for dereliction, in Pagan-like, forgetting the millions whose toil still supplies its luxuries?

Many years since, the earliest step of the writer of these pages—on determining to devote his life to the advocacy of labor's rights—was to visit the monarchs of the pulpit, in his simple, mistaken supposition that the Church was Christian; with ready welcome, ready-made halls; with ready-made orators, precepts, directions and a ready-made system of practical benevolence—in fine, the natural place to appeal for a solution of the problem.

Like one *in mentis gratissimo errore,* he eagerly presented himself before the learned doctors, pleading that theirs was the task to study such turmoils and uneasiness as exhibit themselves awry. To his surprise his cause was spurned. He was driven from the temples to lower zones; to truer Christianity; places of human sympathy; into dingy beer halls—and it was here, not in the churches, that open hearts, and hands of welcome gave reception and incipiency to a great movement. The "low" beer hall still proves a welcome, mellow garden for the first sowings; and if the fruits of the harvests be crude and bitter, let the Pagan temple that spurns its mission, accuse itself.

APPENDIX.

A TRANSLATION

OF THE

NOTES.

CHAPTER I.

PAGE 38, NOTE 1: "So long as there exists among the rich and the poor an intermediate class of considerable proportions, the moral influence which that class exercises will be sufficient to prevent any collision."

CHAPTER II.

Page 49, Note 4: "It is thus we may now announce that we have discovered the first slaves that existed—they were the children." The Iliad says: "I had fifty sons born to me of the Achæans—nineteen through wedlock, and the rest were brought into the world for me by the women of Megara."

Page 49, Note 5: "The best (ancient) state excluded working people from the right of citizenship; and whenever they succeeded in obtaining it, they still remained a class, under contempt and devoid of influence."

Page 53, Note 16: "He lives on pods and second-rate bread.'

Page 53, Note 20: "They used to believe that the remains of the dead were still alive and doing active duty."

CHAPTER III.

Page 70, Note 12: "The original belief among the generations of antiquity was, that human beings still lived in the tomb; that the soul did not separate from the body, and that it remained fixed to that part of the ground in which the remains were buried."

Page 75, Note 19: "'The dead person,' says the law of the Twelve Tables, 'shall be neither buried nor burned within the city of Rome.' How could that be? The fact is, all who now are buried within the city are of noble stock."

Page 75, Note 23, Dr. Fustel says: "These beliefs are certainly not borrowed either by the Greeks from the Hindoos nor by the Hindoos from the Greeks; but they belong to both races, far apart and are derived from Central Asia."

Page 76, Note 25: "The lawgiver of the Romans" (meaning Romulus) "is reputed to have given great power to the father to exercise over his son; and for all causes whatsoever he could kill him. He even possessed the choice of murdering him himself." The Code of Justinian has it, that "the right of life and death was once permitted to fathers over their children."

Page 79, Note 32: "I declare myself much better than the earth-born multitude—mere porridge-eating mortals."

Page 79, Note 33: "This distemper did not trouble the well-to-do among our forefathers."

CHAPTER IV.

Page 92, Note 18: "They played the rape of Proserpine in a sort of hieratic or religious drama. They went through the veritable rencounter of the nuptials."

Page 98, Note 27, Lüders says: "One thing indicating the character of the unions, especially of later date is, that slaves too, could not only take part in an *eranos* but were even permitted to share in a religious mutual aid fund. As proof of the fact that the eranos was thus used there have been found in the vicinity of Delphos, very many specimens. There was a union of slaves at Rhodes who worshiped under the protection of Jupiter Atabyrius." Again Lüders says: "Naturally enough, there were societies that had slaves in their service. Kraton, who organized an eranos and was its priest, under the arrangement made by the will of Attila had among other things belonging to the temple and parsonage, also some slaves." And farther on: "Kraton, who was in the favor of Attila, and who was a member and a priest in high standing, of the great synod of the Dionysian mechanics of Taos, had organized an association of *thiasotes*, composed of mechanics, and had consecrated it to the honor of the Pergamenian king, Attila, as he possessed some brilliancy at the court. The members were called 'Attalists.'" Still farther on: "In his will at last, according to evidence that is preserved for us in a fragment, he gives to the union a respectable sum of money that they may be able to indulge in proper festivities out of its interest, according to a clause in their rules and by-laws. He left them, among other things necessary to this purpose—such as furniture of the meetinghouse, tools used in the lamb-sacrifice and pomp of their festivities—also a number of slaves."

Page 99, Note 29: "In Epidamnus there were no mechanics other than the public slaves. The mechanic arts were for this reason, forbidden and despised."

Page 107, Note 46: "Among the Helots who had a claim and desire to be sent home, there appeared at the town of Pylos a multitude who had served the Lacedæmonians as faithful soldiers and guards. On an investigation a large number of these men had been adjudged worthy, by their conduct, of being set free. A process of honorable discharge in which they were to be crowned with wreaths, was to be gone through with as soon as the number deemed worthy were chosen. Some two thousand of them were accordingly selected from the multitude to be adorned with wreaths of honor and led to the altar for sacred consecration. Not long afterwards they mysteriously disappeared, every one of them, from the place; and nobody ever could conjecture whither they had vanished."

Page 110, Note 50: "There came to my father's mansion a very wise man having a golden chain, or collar studded with amber beads. In the hall the female servant and my noble mother were toying with, and admiring it while in the act of bartering for its possession. Secretly he nodded to the woman and disappeared to his ship."

Page 112, Note 58: "Communes of Roman mimic actors are referred to, both by name and institution, as the Greek communists (mutual aid associations) of the Dionysian mechanics that were very numerous among the Greeks."

Page 113, Note 62: "Ti. Claudius, consul, and Severus his lictor in the divisions,....presents are distributed among the members, man by man; especially where the manning of the boats shows by his actual work that he has been diligent. Done by degree of the order of fishermen and divers of the whole valley of the Tiber, who are granted permission to keep an organization by a law of the Roman senate."

Page 113, Note 63: "It is here worthy of observation that the law of Solon so constitutes that the sacred and civil communes possessed no other legal right than as associations organized for purposes of business or plunder."

Page 118, Note 72: "And Plato, when a babe sleeping in his cradle, the honey-bees used to come and alight upon his lips. The interpretation of this was, that it foretold the remarkable sweetness of the future eloquence with which nature had gifted the infant."

Page 119, Note 74: "Seeing that certain landed estates under mortgage, being provinces of the Roman people, are, so to speak, our revenues (vectigalia)."

Page 121, Note 75: "It being not in the province of man to curtail the unlimited power which it is necessary that masters should have over their slaves."

Page 123, Note 76: "Cæsar broke up all the unions except those which were very ancient."

Page 127, Note 87: "The sodales are those who are of the same union as that which the Greek call hetairæ." Again: "'The Law of the Twelve Tables,' says Gaius, 'gives to the sodales unlimited right to combine for any business they require for themselves, so long as they do not rupture the law of the land. But this law appears to be a translation of the law of Solon; which is as follows (speaking of societies understood): 'whether they be the people, or brotherhoods, or priests and priestesses, or boatmen, or communists who eat at the common table, or burial societies (including those who prepare the feasts and holiday festivities of the members), or those occupying houses in common, or engaged in traffic at sea; in fine all those living for one another, hereby are publicly proclaimed in writing, free to unite themselves.'"

Page 127, Note 88: "The words of Gaius it is clear, do not admit of being construed as those of the Twelve Tables, so as exactly to make them include all of the unions; nor does there appear any reason why the unions of handicraftsmen should be deprived of the right of making rules, which was granted to those organized for religion's sake."

Page 130, Note 95: "Out of a kind of hard marble found in the vicinity of Eleusis."

Page 130, Note 96: "Near an olive tree was a well—the Erecthian spring—which, when the south wind blew, gave an indistinct murmur like the terrible roar of waves—so the Athenians used to relate. This was believed to be Neptune when he opened the abysses with his trident; and his track is impressed in the living rock even to this day. No man desires to question the story of this briny fountain; for in the citadel there was another whose waters were bitter when the dog-day winds were blowing, at the time that Sirius rose; and its floods would rise and afterwards fall, giving to the well the name of Clepsydra."

CHAPTER V.

Page 134, Note 1: "From Thrace there arrived, during the same summer, one thousand three hundred light-armed soldiers with shields, being related to Jupiter, who came to Athens, and who had been with Demosthenes, the Athenian general, in his naval expedition against Sicily. The Athenians, as it afterwards became known (after the disaster of Demosthenes), had been sent to Thrace from Syracuse. The war at Decelea had become expensive, as each one received a full drachm or seventeen and a half cents a day for his services. Decelea, during this summer, was the first place fortified by the forces of the Lacedæmonians. Afterwards guards were placed about the towns with relays, as relief guards; so that a man occupied a station as watcher, constantly and without intermission and thus the Athenians suffered severe losses by seizures of many things, and also by the ruin of their means of producing money, thus spoiling their sinews of war. At first these tactics were mild, but grew with time, and the Lacedæmonians were unhindered from enjoying their position on the land. Following the example of their king Agis they placed guards everywhere to further the advantages of war, thus badly perplexing and entangling the Athenians. Every place was lost. Even the force of hands in the silver mines, consisting of more than half of the laborers and skilled mechanics, amounting to upwards of twenty thousand men, together with the flocks and the draft oxen and horses, ran away and escaped over to Decelea by aid of the guards, doing much damage day by day to the Athenians by this conduct, but freeing themselves from many of their hardships."

Page 137, Note 16: "Cimon was not so generous as rich; for he had amassed a large fortune in the mines."

Page 139, Note 28, Drumann says: "Also in the workshops called ergasteria, slaves only were to be seen."

Page 140, Note 32, Bücher remarks that: "In the year B. C. 413, some twenty thousand Athenian mechanics struck work and went over to the Lacedæmonians—a severe blow to the silver mining business at Laurium."

Page 141, Note 34, Drumann says: "The greatest part of the twenty thousand who, during the Peloponnesean war ran away and went over to the Spartan garrison in the town of Decelea in Attica, were from the workshops. Among other things it was stipulated that each would have the advantage of working for himself, giving a certain part to the master. By this arrangement industrious and frugal workmen could lay up something over and above expenses and thus buy themselves free. Many lived more sumptuously than those who were free." Same note, quoting Bücher: "'Where many slaves of the same nationality lived together in the same city' (so says Plato, Laws, vi., 777), 'great misfortunes will occur; and this is something to be attributed as the true cause of insurrections with all their cruelties.'"

Again; same note, quoting Macrobius: "I have heard of the great indignation of heaven caused by the punishment of slaves. Once, in the 474th year from the foundation of Rome one Autranius Maximus fastened his slave to a forked gibbet and in this condition whipped him around the ring in the circus before the spectators. On account of this cruelty Jupiter was so incensed that he ordered a certain Annius to inform the senate that he should withdraw his heavenly protection if such cruelties were not put an end to."

Page 142, Note 38: "Tens of thousands of the slaves of Attica worked in the mines. Poseidon the philosopher declares that they rebelled, formed themselves into a compact body with a guard and marched to the acropolis of Sunion where for a long time they held themselves, sending out forces to ransack the country. This was at the very point when the second slave insurrection began in Sicily."

Page 143, Note 39: "I, Xanthos, the Lycian slave belonging to Gaius Orbius, working to the glory of the God who, as tutelary protector of men and women, is our star of fortune, have consecrated this temple of Men Tyrannus, as God desired." In same note Foucart proceeds: "The person who, towards the second century of our era introduced the cult of Men, was a slave from Lycia and was employed by a Roman property owner in the mines. The god himself, either in a day-dream or by apparition had signaled to him to construct the temple. Thus the founder took care to repeat in two inscriptions that he had executed the behest of Men."

Page 143, Note 40: "In the six hundred and twentieth year of Rome, or before Christ 134, the slaves working in the silver mines of Laurium arose, killed their guards, took the citadel of Sunion and laid Attica waste for a long time."

Page 144, Note 41: "In the mines of the Athenians, also, there occurred a tumult of slaves which was subdued by Heraclitus the prætor."

Page 144, Note 42: "In a similar manner the Greek world was subjected to a visitation, although of less proportions. According to Augustin (De Civ., III, 26), insurgent slave bands just prior to the first Sicilian insurrection, laid waste Macedonia and the neighboring districts."

CHAPTER VI.

Page 147, Note 8: "Romulus gave to married men the right to take the life of, and the right of intimate indulgence with, their female slaves."

Page 149, Note 12: "The award given out of the public treasury to the informants who were slaves, was a wealth of ten thousand standard coins each, besides their liberty."

Page 151, Note 18: "At this time, when Gaul was quiet excepting in her hopes, there arose an insurrection of the slaves near the city of Rome. There were some Carthagenian hostages held in custody at Setia. In addition to these who were free men, there was also a great host of slaves. The number of these was increased from different nationalities by the recent African war in which they had been taken prisoners and sold to masters in and about the city of Setia, as captive bondsmen. Forming a conspiracy, they sent men of their number, first into the farm country of Setia itself, and afterwards to Norba and Circijus to stir up auxiliaries. It happened that there was soon to take place a pastime (the games); and they arranged to have all preparations ready on the event of those games; so that at an auspicious moment when the people were engrossed in the enjoyment and excitement, they should rise in sudden insurrection, seize the cities of Setia, afterwards Norba and then Circeji, and take possession. Intelligence of this terrible thing was transmitted to M. Cornelius Merula at Rome. Two slaves, before daybreak approached Merula and exposed all the plans and intentions of the insurgents. When the prætor had ordered these slaves to stay and guard his house he called the senate together and told them what the informants had said and how they had come to ask that he should hasten to suppress the conspiracy. The result was that he was set on the march with but five lieutenants (and their divisions), giving orders along the road for reinforcements to follow. With these troops, hurriedly collected as they marched, amounting in all to about 2,000 armed men, he fell upon the unsuspecting mutineers. The ringleaders of the conspiracy being seized, the slaves took to flight from the town, the soldiers following on their track........ The two informers were rewarded on an enormous scale and their freedom given them. The fathers ordered that each should receive 25,000 standard coins and his liberty; while one—Merula perhaps—received 100,000 coins. The masters received also the price of their slaves lost in the affray."

"Not long after the quelling of this insurrection it was announced that the remainder of the conspirators were stirring up the same tumults afresh and were preparing to take the town of Præneste in the same manner. Thither Cornelius (Merula) marched with a force of about 500 men; and as a result, those who were engaged in the trouble were punished. The country being plunged into fears, it was necessary to remove the Carthagenian hostages and prisoners. At Rome and among the towns and villages, guards were ordered to be stationed and a more vigilant watch was established over the great prison and the prison quarries, which work was consummated by the triumvirs. The prætor caused a written circular to be published throughout Latium saying that henceforth the prisoners were to labor in solitude and that they should be deprived of the privilege of appearing in public and those not Carthagenian hostages should wear shackles of no less than ten pounds weight, and be confined in any, except the public prison."

Page 152, Note 20, From Livy's Epitome: "A conspiracy of slaves attempted for liberating the Carthagenian hostages is suppressed."

Page 153, Note 22: "On the whole, it was conjectured that the blame rested with some secret doings of the Punic hostages and prisoners."

Page 154, Note 27, Pliny says: "L. Piso is the author who first gave an account of it and says that Tullus Hostilius the king who succeeded Numa, constructed at the same place many and great changes in the city. While excavating the earth under the Tarpeian rock the workmen unearthed a human head. Tullus sent ambassadors to Olenus Calenus, a celebrated Etruscan soothsayer, or prophet and fortune-teller to know what he and his tribe thought about it."

Page 155, Note 30: "In spite of this he did not succeed without the greatest difficulty."

Page 157, Note 31: "Of these (the insurgents), many were killed and many taken prisoners; others were scourged and hung upon the cross."

Page 160, Note 38: "L. Postumius, to whom the care as propraetor of the province of Tarentum fell, made resistance against a conspiracy of farmers and shepherds and the rest of those bacchanalian creatures."

Page 160, Note 42: "Those seized were sent to the Roman senate which ordered P. Cornelius to cast them into prison."

CHAPTER VII.

Page 164, Note 2, Macrobius says: "Would you call to mind those who come of the same seed? who live under the same skies and who, like you, must live and die? Slaves though they be, they are nevertheless human; though only poor slaves, yet they all have some rights if you would but reflect. Even if you could see that the slave were free, he would still serve you just as well. Do you not know that Hecuba was once during her lifetime a slave? that Crœsus, that the mother of Darius, that Diogenes, even Plato were all of them slaves? And why, in the light of all these examples should we hold in horror the name of servitude? Slave he is, indeed, but because forced to it; only a slave, but perhaps he wears the soul of a freeman. What will he not do for you even though it be wrong? This one administers to lusts, that one to avarice, another to your ambitions? All are objects of your hopes and all are causes of your fear." Continuing: "It is impossible to mix love and fear together. Whence, think you, emanates the proverb: 'just as many enemies as there are slaves?' We may not think we have those enemies, but it is true; we make them when with our superb, contemptuous cruelty we force them to submit to our voluptuous frenzy, is it otherwise possible than that it should evoke their anger and fury?"

Page 164, Note 3: "So also, the wealthy island of Chios was at the same time (B. C. 134), the theatre of a wild slave uprising which was not put down until many years afterwards."

Page 166, Note 4: "In the middle of the third century of the Christian era."

Pages 168-169, Note 7: "Hermotius who was of the Pedasian race, was a man who meted out the severest vengeance for any injury. When taken by an enemy and sold in slavery, he was bought by a man named Panionius, a Chian —a person who got his living by the practice of the most iniquitous vices. Boys of remarkable beauty whenever purchased by him, he caused to be castrated, and he was in the habit of selling them in Ephesus and Sardis at a high price; since those barbarians valued eunuchs more than other servants on account of their being more reliable. So Panionius among many others, had this Hermotius emasculated, as he made his living by that business. The man, however, was not in all respects, unfortunate. He was given to the king at Sardis, as a present. In the course of time he became the most highly regarded by Xerxes, of any of his numerous eunuchs. As the king was making preparations to march with his expedition upon Athens, and while at Sardis—having gone to the Mysian country with the Chians—Panionius was met at Atarneus. Hermotius became acquainted with Panionius by recognition, and induced him to come over to Asia with his family and settle there, offering him many advantages. He accepted the plan with cheer and brought his family. Hermotius thus succeeding in getting him into his power together with his whole family, uttered to him the following words: 'You, who, meanest of mankind by trade and deeds of infamy! To your face I demand to know what I have ever done, or what harm any of my race have done to you that from a man I should be made into nothing? You thought, perhaps, that your tricks should be passed over by the Almighty, unheeded, unavenged. But you have been allured into my grasp by your dastardly deeds. You cannot, therefore, complain of the retribution I am going to inflict upon you.' After upbraiding him in this strain his sons were also brought into the place and Panionius was forced to commit the act of castration upon his own sons, four in number. He did it; and then in reverse order, these very sons were driven to emasculate their father on the spot. Such was the vengeance of Hermotius, the Chian."

Page 169, Note 10: "It was quite the reverse with the thiasotes and eranists. Not only were their doors open to women but also to strangers. Persons who were well-to-do or even slaves had access. This last point is very important; and fortunately the witnesses of their epigraphic monuments are sufficiently explicit and precise in language to establish the evidence completely. It would be useless to cite all the inscriptions in proof; and I have chosen a few only, and of those which show this to have been the cause in the different countries. The specimens are numerous enough to warrant the conclusions; for where one fails, another makes the point good, that the admission of women, of strangers, of freedmen and of slaves was a universal characteristic of all these associations." Same note, page 170, Foucart further explains: "One inscription in the island of Rhodes mentions a religious society composed of slaves belonging to the state or public. Part of its value is diminished by a mutilation which detracts from its testimony. But an examination of the proper names to be found in other inscriptions proves that these Rhodian associations were in the common habit of admitting freedmen and probably, also slaves." Farther on: "A fragment of an inscription restored by Keil, by great perseverance and to all appearance, with correctness, shows the composition of the society in the particular membership which placed it there that it was under the patronage of Jupiter Atabyrius (or the Jove that dwelt in the tallest mountain of Rhodes). It appears to have been composed of the public slaves of the city of Rhodes, and is one of those which exercised the priesthood. It reads: 'Under the god of Atabyrius is the union of the slaves of the city. Inscribed in letters, by order of the holy priest of Zeus, and governed by the ruling authorities of the Rhodians, in obedience to Jupiter Atabyrius.'"

Page 170, Note 11: "These things wrote Nymphodorus in his voyage to Asia. He described how the slaves of the Chians ran away from their masters and how they escaped to the mountains and the highest summits, and how these masters were devastated by their combined forces."

Page 171, Note 12: "A little before our own time—so the Chians tell us—there was a certain slave, who having escaped, lived in the mountains; and being endowed with a warlike spirit, was declared the commander and king of the fugitive slaves, and following the habits of other kings, gathered an army, against whom the Chians afterwards sent military expeditions. But they could make no headway against him. Drimakos (Primacus), as this slave was called, when he saw his masters overcome, made a speech in their presence as follows:"

Page 177, Note 19: "Should any of the features of this story appear doubtful and fictitious it may be said that there exists not the least ground for uncertainty as to its genuineness; and even if the shrewd Chian merchants put up the temple for the object of awing down their slaves, the lesson still remains as a true mirror, showing the condition of things at that time."

CHAPTER VIII.

Page 180, Note 2: "Viriathus, who took the command. and many times broke the Romans to pieces, was himself, one of the Spanish (Lusitanian) workpeople who lived in the place. From boyhood he had worked and passed his life in the mountains and came up with energy, strength and spirit. He excelled in bodily forces, swiftness and agility all the rest of his associates and was much thought of in Spain. He used to abstain from luxuries, even getting along with just enough food to barely answer his necessities. He had with him many strong-hearted friends, and became widely known among lawless mountaineers, settling their quarrels; and at length assuming their leadership he established a sharp discipline about him and thrived with the success of his combats with the brigands. He was looked upon as a superior; not only in personal strength but also for his tactics."

Page 180, Note 3: "Viriathus, the commander of the guilleras, was a Lusitanian Spaniard who was just in his distribution and sharing of the spoils, and had sufficient honor and humanity to make a just choice in distributing presents; for he gave them simply a division in common, and was the right person to be regarded by them as a common benefactor and savior."

Page 180, Note 4: "Viriathus in Spain, who was originally a shepherd, turned from a shepherd to a hunter, and from a hunter to a robber, and from that, was even created general of the army and took possession of all Lusitania."

Page 181, Note 5, Livy says: "When L. Scribonius the tribune of the people, brought in a bill, taking back into the confidence of the Romans, all the Lusitanians whom Galba had brought as slaves with him into Gaul, restoring them to liberty, M. Cato made a strong speech in its favor. His oration is still extant in the histories. Q. Fulvius Noble, who had often been excoriated by Cato, defended Galba. When Galba saw that he was going to be condemned, or that the case was going against him, he threw his arms around his two sons already young men, and also embraced the young son of Sulpicius Gallus, of whom he was the guardian; and in this miserable and pitiable condition so pleaded that the decree was not sustained."

Page 182, Note 6, Appian says: "This man fought the Romans for about eight years; and it appears to me that Viriathus made it exceedingly uncomfortable for them; for things became so entangled in that time that even the loss of Spain was threatened." Livy says: "Viriathus broke up the army of Vetillius and seized also that general himself; after him C. Plautius the prætor, continued the struggle with no better success. So great was the terror caused by this enemy that it was necessary to send both a consul and a consular army." Eutrope says: "Instigated by terror, Viriathus was killed by his own men, after having waged war for a period of fourteen years against the Romans. He was first a shepherd, afterwards a robber and then a general and roused all the population of the land against the Romans, being regarded as the emancipator of Spain."

Page 183, Note 7: "Viriathus, after performing a three-days' march, took sure possession of Segobria and there devoted a day to religious sacrifices,"

Page 183, Note 8: "It seemed advisable to get away to the others; and in the night he escaped through pathless ways with fleet horses and arrived at Tribola, the Romans following; but they had not the power to overtake him on account of the weight of their armor, their ignorance of the roads and the inexperience of the horses."

Page 183, Note 9, Frontin remarks: "Viriathus, placing some of his soldiers in secret localities, sent a few of them out foraging for the cattle of the Segobrians. These retaliated by frequent sorties against the pickets, pretending to escape, drew them into an ambush where they were cut to pieces by the army."

Page 184, Note 10; This remark of Diodorus is but a cutting from his more complete sentences given in note 2, page 180, of which see translation.

Page 186, Note 13: "At the request of the allied army, another general arrived with a force of 15,000 foot soldiers and 2,000 horse. They marched into Orsena, a city of Spain."

Page 186, Note 14: "In all, about 18,000 foot and 1,600 horse. He sent letters to Mikipse, the Numidian king, ordering him to send the strongest and swiftest elephants from Africa, into Itycca, to augment the army in those parts of the Spanish peninsula."

CHAPTER IX.

Page 192, Note 1: "During the power and under the command of Sempronius Gracchus, the army of Rome subdued

TRANSLATION OF NOTES. 587

the Sardinians. In this province the number of the enemy taken prisoners or killed, amounted to upwards of 80,000."

Page 193, Note 3: "We are informed that 30,000 were captured and reduced to slavery."

Page 195, Note 13: "In Epidamnus there were no mechanics except the public slaves."

Page 196, Note 17: "They were all branded. Only the field workers were fettered."

Page 199, Note 27: "He was a great magician and performer of miracles and stood in close communion with the gods, receiving inspirations from them not only by dreams, but actually seeing them in open day, as in life."

Page 201, Note 32: "It should be understood that in Sicily there was a daughter of Damophilus,........Hermias took her to Catana and left her in the care of some relatives."

Page 208, Note 42: "More than ordinary capability." Siefert also says: "They elected him their king because he had originated the outbreak."

Page 209, Note 43: "This was the first strange thing done; he gathered 2,000 as he moved along, and then breaking open the prisons made soldiers of more than 60,000 inmates."

Page 211, Note 49: "And he sent those who were bound in chains and fettered, into the prison workshops."

Page 212, Note 54: "One Gorgos with the surname of Cambalos, who on account of his wealth was a well-known citizen of Morgantion in the upper districts of Symæthus, was out on a hunting excursion and fell in with a band of the slaves belonging to the insurrection. He fled back homeward, following the main road to the city, but soon met his father on horseback riding along the same road. The father immediately dismounted and begged his son to save himself by the use of his own horse. Father and son thus in tender solicitude for each other's safety squandered the precious moments and whilst in the strife of filial love and parental tenderness they were exhausting their time, the insurgents arrived and killed them both."

Page 214, Note 57: "Regarding the chronology of the Sicilian slave war and other matters thereto related, consult the Excurz."

Page 215, Note 64: "'Out of those places situated about Taurus.' According to paragraph 20, his brother was named Comanus (Coma in Valerius Maximus); and it is tolerably safe to conclude from this that Comana was the birthplace of the two brothers. But whether this was the Coma of Pamphylia or that of Cappadocia, whence this name is derived is a question impossible to answer. The

Cappadocian Comana was situated among the Anti-Taurian hills, upon the river Saros, and was a capital city of Syria, where the cult of Ma (Artemis Taurica), according to Strabo, XII., p. 535, was encouraged. If this be so, it serves as a cause for the bold turn of Cleon when he came in juxtaposition with the religious superstition of Eunus."

Page 216, Note 66: "At the time C. Fulvius was consul, this war of Eunus began. Eunus was a slave who was by race a Syrian and who gathered a force of agricultural slaves. Breaking open the workhouse prisons, he raised his army to 70,000 strong and massing them, fought many battles with the Roman people."

Page 217, Note 67: "A certain Syrian named Eunus, pretending like a fanatic, to be in the good graces of the goddess by throwing forth fiery scintillations resembling her hair, aroused a multitude of slaves as great as an imperial army, and these he emancipated and supplied with arms. To prove that he was divine, he would place a nut in his mouth, in which was hidden sulphur and fire, and drawing the breath gently, would blow forth flames."

Page 218, Note 70: "The army amounted to about 200,000 men." Again: "Not long afterwards the number of the insurgents is found to rise to 200,000 men including in all, the soldiers, sythe-armed militia and raw troops; and they fight successfully, seldom suffering defeats."

Page 219, Note 72: "Whenever the slightest victory was won the strike towered with redoubled fierceness and pressed onward without cessation in all the cruelty of social wars."

Page 220, Note 78: "Never was there such a condition or such an assembling of the slaves in Sicily. There were many powerful cities which came to grief; and innumerable were the men, the women and the works of art that were hurled into direst misfortune; in fact the whole island fell into the power of the runaway slaves."

Page 221, Note 81, quoting Bücher: "Eunus at length became master of almost the entire island of Sicily **** probably even of Syracuse. Diodorus (fragment 9), says: 'To these gluttons even the sanctity of the Holy Fish did not cause a pause to the evils which the gods used, making an example of everybody to show their desperate condition; for the gods used these dreadful methods to teach against the blasphemy of the people of the age and to show men better ways. This fragment of Diodorus is found in close proximity to the Vatican excerpt which is entirely on the slave uprising. It is impossible to consider this 'Holy Fish' as any other than the Arethusa of which Diodorus speaks in book V., 3, as follows: 'This Arethusa was not only regarded from very ancient times as having many and large fishes but even the same reverence is handed down to this day, ascribing to these fishes a sacredness to men; since men eating of them are strong in war and are endowed with the faculty of combined physical force and vigor of understanding great things. So also in our time these virtues we seek in our youth.'"

Page 222, Note 84, "Tiberius Gracchus was a famous man, brilliant in his love of honor and it may be said, exceedingly powerful in his gift of language; and was everywhere known by all the officers of the government. He told in solemn words to the Italians, how the want of means for the people and the depopulation of the country were caused by destruction perpetrated by the military powers, and how hopeless was the condition of the inhabitants. With this servile element, never having any confidence with their masters, the feeling rose high against despotism and made them comrades. The evil augmented among the agricultural districts and the war of the Romans against them was not slight nor easily quelled. Things assumed a venturesome phase both many colored and huge. Gracchus declared his intention to re-establish the old law of Licinius Stolo, according to which no person could possess more than 500 acres of land—a law which though many years old, remained unchanged."

Page 224, Note 89, The reading of these words is: "Ritchl, P. L. M. VIII, 1, Body of Latin Inscriptions, by Theodore Mommsen, no. 642 and others. Compare Nitsch. in another place, p. 249. Evidence regarding the second Sicilian insurrection is to be had in Dr. Böckh's Body of Greek Inscriptions, nos. 5,570, 5,687, 5748, z. Th., where occurs the name of Athenion. No. 5,748 is a stone slab coming from Leontini on which is inscribed the word APAMEO, and it is probable that this refers to Eunus of Apamea. In the Body of Latin Inscriptions, no. 646 and others following, are certainly inscriptions which were designed to represent the wars of Eunus."

Page 224, Note 94, Siefert in his First Sicilian Servile War, Says: "Pseudo Asconius comments on Cicero's Verres, II, p. 212: 'A certain Rupilius, one of the aristocratic tax-gatherers, was made consul.' Again, Valerius Maximus, vi., 9, 8, narrates that he was even an employé at an earlier date, of the government service as follows: 'P. Rupilius did not collect the taxes in Sicily but gave out the work to the equestrian taxgatherers. In fact he upheld the frauds committed in cheating the government out of the revenues, by the authority of office, colluding with his associates.' He was a friend of Scipio the Younger, according to Cicero (Lælius, 19,). When consul he conducted, during the first part of his consulate year, an investigation of the so-reputed misdeeds of Tiberius Gracchus and was aided by his colleague, Popilius Lænas (Cicero, Lælius, 11; Valerius Maximus, iv., 7, 1). According to Vellejus Paterculus, (II., vii.), he was, on account of the pressure with which this investigation was urged, driven, like Popilius, before the tribunal; and other writers on the subject only mention Popilius as the object of the persecution. Compare Pauly, R. E., V., 1900. Later, Rupilius in indignation and horror, came to his end for fraudulently intriguing to get his brother elected consul."

Page 226, Note 97: "Throughout Sicily misfortune prevailed. Cities, together with their inhabitants, indiscriminately fell into the hands of their conquerors and many were the armies that were hacked to pieces, until Rupilius, the general of the Romans, saved Tauromanion to Rome in the stanch blockade and siege which he conducted against this city. He starved the rebels into indescribable want and famine to such extent, that in their enclosure they fell to killing children and then their helpless women, and even devoured one another to gratify the cravings of hunger."

Page 229, Note 101: "The slaves were delivered to torment and butchery, most of them being thrown from steep precipices of rocks. So also here at Enna, thousands were chopped down. The total number of the slaves killed at Enna and Tauromanion exceeded 20,000."

Page 230, Note 105, Diodorus says: "Secured and under guard, his body devoured by lice, he passed a life of wretched indolence at Morgantion." Livy says: "He was caught, and was devoured by lice in prison." Farther on (same note), Siefert: "With four of his servants, one of whom was the cook, the others the bath attendant, the baker and the king's fool, he was caught in a hole. He died in prison of the lousy sickness, either in Morgantion or in Rome."

CHAPTER X.

Page 234, Note 3: "Eumenes, for whom they pompously exhibited their friendship, advancing the idea of peace for Antioch, by means of bribes, was held in check. After the death of Eumenes, a guard was kept at the cost of the state, and the agricultural captives were held in pitiable slavery and contempt by Attalus, the king. He made, under deception, an impious will by which his son Aristonicus was ignored because he had asked for the succession. This being a triumph for the latter's enemies, the combined power of the slaves laid Asia under siege. All Bithynia soon fell and Nicomides dying, this son of Nusa whom they called the queen, created havoc."

Page 236, Note 8: "The term 'Heliopolitan' calls to mind that it was the same that Eunus used in fanaticizing his Syrians."

Page 236, Note 9: "Likewise the Syrians celebrate and worship the sun in the name of Jupiter whom they call a 'Sun-God' in their greatest ceremonies, and the country where it is done is termed 'Heliopolis.'"

Page 238, Note 12: "P. Crassus who came as consul to Asia for the purpose of waging war against Aristonicus, had acquired such perfection in the Greek language that he could speak five different dialects of it so as to be thoroughly ready in all parts. This was a thing necessary in obtaining the love of the allies through the persuasive force of conciliation; as it gave him the advantage of making known and demanding the enforcement of the decrees."

Page 241, Note 18: "When the senate called the consuls, Rupilia and Lænatus, to demand of them what Gracchus really wished to do, and they referred the matter to Lælius whose prayers and counsels they were in the habit of consulting, an accusation was found against Blossius who had been familiar with Gracchus. Blossius was brought before them and the following question put: 'What would you have done if Gracchus had ordered you to destroy the temple of the great Jupiter? Would you not have executed the wish of that man?' 'Gracchus would have never given me such an order,' said Blossius, 'because he was too wise a man to do that; but he was not afraid of demanding the right, even in the teeth of the whole Roman senate.' But what followed was much more daring and dangerous; for on being pressed further by the question of Lælius who persevered in obtaining the answer, Blossius acknowledged that if Gracchus had given him the order he would have obeyed.'"

Page 241, Note 19: "The brothers Tiberius and Caius Gracchus had been adjudged guilty of grave seditions by the senate in forcing their laws against the Roman people and both had been killed by the nobles—one by Nasicus and the other by Opimius. When Tiberius Gracchus fell, Blossius escaped to king Aristonicus. The affairs of Aristonicus having gone wrong, Blossius committed suicide.

Page 242, Note 20, Speaking of the strength and fortitude of the soldier's soul when in a great misfortune, I will tell the story of a Roman consul: P. Crassus, when directing the war against Aristonicus in Asia was, after his defeat, in custody of Thracians at a prison between Elea and Smyrna. But he would not surrender, and resented indecent actions against him to obtain a coveted death. One day he thrust his horsewhip which he used when riding, into the eye of his barbarian guard. So great was the pain inflicted that this guard drew his sword and plunged it into his side. But in taking vengeance upon a Roman soldier he liberated a consul from disgrace. This shows that Crassus in a broil with an unworthy man, wished the good fortune of escaping graver humiliations· since by the act he prudently, valiantly, courageously, broke away from the miserable condition he was held in by mean persons, and was free. Aristonicus had reduced him but he had gained his own liberty."

Page 243, Note 21: "Not slight was the shamelessness of M. Paperna in his disgrace of the consulship which he held after he got to be consul before becoming a Roman citizen; though he was more serviceable in war than Varro. He conquered king Aristonicus, becoming the punisher and avenger of the disaster of Crassus. While he was triumphing, he was condemned to death under a clause of the Papian law; since as his father was not a Roman, the people demanded his return to his original estate because he had no right to rise according to decision of the Sabelline judgment. In this manner the good name of Paperna fell because he had obtained his consulship under false pretences. The glory of his victory fell away and he wandered about for the rest of his life in exile."

Page 244, Note 22, From Bücher: "The latter consisted in celebrations on the part of those enjoying their holidays, in fasting and expiation, also in luxurious dances amid the music of flute and drum and the wild tumult which they imagined would call up and propitiate their divinities, and bring to pass wondrous things. If at that time, this cult was in practice in Greece by great numbers of secret societies and upright brotherhoods (see pp. 34, 92), then it becomes obvious how they spread their advocacy, not so much through the smoother waters of mere turbulent thought in which they expressed the dizzy dissatisfaction of their race, as through the more suggestive suasion of their peculiar communist fraternization and the natural social system of propaganda of the Greeks whose organizations admitted and accepted all members from foreign parts whether Greek or barbarian, male or female, free or enslaved. Thence comes the designation 'citizens of the sun.' This term drew the line between the followers of Aristonicus who were the anointed of the congregation of Adad, and the unbelievers; thus separating the poor and wretched from enemies who persecuted them, as already shown in the case of Eunus, who was called a Syrian to distinguish him in religious matters—he being a representative follower of Atargatis."

TRANSLATION OF NOTES. 593

CHAPTER XI.

Page 247, Note 1: "Sources of our knowledge regarding the second Sicilian slave-war are as follows: Florus, Condensed Roman History, book III, chapter 19; Dion Cassius, Excerpts by Piresc, nos. 101, 104; Diodorus the Sicilian, book XXXVI; Livy, book XLIX. The length of the time that it lasted, according to the following paragraph, was about four years: 'The slave-insurgents' war, as I say, therefore lasted nearly four years and was a stately and majestic upheaval.' M. Aquillius brought it to an end iin the year B. C. 99, after having taken supreme command which was at the beginning of his term as consul, B. C. 101. The war broke out at the time Licinius Nerva was propraetor. L. Lucullus succeeded him in the command, and after him came C. Servilius. Thus the rebellion rose during the year B. C. 104. Eusebius erroneously makes the end to have occurred four years later, or at the 171st Olympiad, that is, B. C. 95."

Page 247, Note 2: "The pool of the twins."

Page 248, Note 3: "Speaking of all the divinities it is not worth while to leave unmentioned, notwithstanding the want of faith which we remember, on the whole, attaches to the very ancient temple of peculiar surroundings, called the pool or crater. The tradition is, that this temple and place of refuge is of awe-inspiring origin and in the minds of many it is strange and marvelous. To begin with, there are craters out of which spout monstrous sparks from the unspeakable depths. Along side these is the cauldron heated by great fires which throw red-hot flames and waters high into the air above. This seething fluid tossed up into the sky, presents a whitish appearance, and nobody has the force of determination to venture to touch it; for the moments of quell are succeeded by other spoutings of the foaming and boiling waters. This water which has escaped from the abyss has the smell of brimstone; and the yawning hole roars with loud, frequent and frightful bellowings. But the most marvelous of all these things is, that the waters neither overflow nor vary in volume though there is a motion as of life in the water that floods and sinks and rises again in a manner wonderful to relate. So strong is the sacred essence surrounding this temple that the greatest of the earth assemble there to have the gods bear solemn witness to their deal; for they administer condign punishment upon those who have used falsehood and perjury. Some who have been deprived of sight receive it back by visiting this temple. Regarding the superstition as to these great properties, there are men who dispute the exceeding merits of the temple, and doubt its superhuman attributes as a witness between right and wrong. This holy place is sometimes an asylum for watching over and preserving the unfortunates and slaves, from their unreasonable masters, affording them refuge in which to conceal themselves, and furnishing them aid to deliverance. The despots are here without power to exercise against fugitives, so that they can remain unhurt until, through the holy witnesses and mediation of the sacred power, an arbitration can be adjusted between them by means of reason and persuasion. Here all are on an equal footing, masters and slaves alike; and the poor and faithful are no more pursued under this awe-inspiring fiat of the divinities. This temple stands in august magnificence in an open, neglected spot, and is furnished with porches and other befitting places for repose."

Page 248, Note 4: "The weird legend is abroad that this temple is among the most awe-inspiring and ancient of all the wonders of the world."

Page 249, Note 5: "Marius gave orders that an allied army should be summoned from the outstanding nations bordering on the sea. Following these orders they were sent for. He also sent to Nicomides, king of Bithynia for aid. Nicomides however, sent back word that most of the people of his realm were slaves reduced to that condition by conquest. But as nobody of such as would answer the summons could be made soldiers while slaves, it would be necessary to enact emancipation decrees touching their case. So in consequence of this law, Licinius Nerva would have to set the slaves free before they could become recruits. Thus in a few days, more than 800 of the strongest slaves were assembled to receive their liberty. All the slaves on the island held hopes of deliverance."

Page 249, Note 7: "Flower of the Roman cavalry, ornament of the state, the very fundament of government."

Page 250, Note 10: "Drove the war in every possible manner, in blasphemy against gods and law and order, with allied armies, made up of freedmen and freemen whether of domestic or of foreign birth."

Page 251, Note 11: "Here abounded prisons where the agricultural hands were chained."

Page 251, Note 12: "What marvelous work! First 2,000, gathered from the wayside and then, as by the customs and rights of war, after breaking open the prisons, he constructed an army from over 60,000 prisoners."

Page 251, Note 13: "When called together to be made soldiers of the army and they beheld their danger, they revolted; but Nerva, incited to it either through desire of gain, or in compassion for the masters, accommodated himself to the situation, and breaking faith in his haste, with the forms of law before a tribunal, advised the slaves to go back to their masters again, as the circumstances did not at present admit of their emancipation. Hereupon the slaves, after holding a conference, got away from Syracuse and escaped to the temple of the Twins at the brimstone lake and resolved with each other, upon rebellion."

Page 251, Note 14: "The city is to be sought for among the hills of Nebrode, in the neighborhood of Engyon."

Page 252, Note 15 "The soldiers butchered the insurgent rebels, and those who had been captured and proved to have acted as leaders, were hanged (crucified)."

Page 253, Note 16: "Among the soldiers who had quit their huts and liberated themselves were some belonging to a man named Poplius Clonius, a Roman cavalier or knight. The slaves murdered him and collected a force of 80 men."

Page 253, Note 17: "The rebellion rose to not less than 2,000 persons."

Page 254, Note 20: "And the many insurgents who, augmenting day by day in secret, amounted in a short time to more than 6,000, who acted a scene truly wonderful. When they had called a general council, their first step was to elect a king named Salvius, believed by them to be in the good graces of the gods and sacred things—a fluteplayer, skilled in sleight of hand, fond of women, and held choice by the goddesses, Ceres and Proserpine."

Page 255, Note 22: "Nevertheless Salvius showed greater ability in his command than might have been expected, judging by the station he rose out of."

Page 256, Note 25 "The insurgents suddenly made an attack and having the advantage of position to aid them violently burst upon their enemy quickly gaining a victory, taking the place and driving some of the army to flight. The proclamation of the general that he would hurt none of the rebelling slaves who should throw down their arms had its effect; for most of them did so and fled. Salvius by this turn of things, gained a strategical point over his enemy, took the citadel, turned the battle into a victory and seized a large quantity of arms. The number killed outright in this battle was not above 600. These were Italians and Sicilians. They had felt sympathy with the strikers and used the general's proclamation favorably. The number taken prisoners amounted to about 4,000."

Page 257, Note 26: "But he did not at first succeed in taking Morgantion. Whether he ever took the city in consequence of this victory is not fully apparent from the information that has come down to us."

Page 257, Note 27: "Salvius laid siege to Morgantion over-

APPENDIX.

running the country, to the base of the Leontine range, and gathering a large army of select men not less than 30,000 in number. With these he gave sacrifice and offerings to the hero Twins, allotting one of the choicest purple robes as an offering of gratitude for the victory. He proclaimed himself king. His name among the insurgent soldiers was henceforth Tryphon." The language is unmistakable. Still Dr. Siefert muses: "However, these words of Diodorus may have reference to the victory over Licinius Nerva; and indeed, it must be so, for 'poliorkesas' (laying siege to a city), cannot be construed to comprehend as much as 'ekpoliorkesas' (taking a city by siege."

Page 257, Note 28: "In some incomprehensible manner the prætor proved treacherous to these promises, and by the means, drove the larger part of these valiant men into the camp of the insurgents."

Page 258, Note 29: "Athenion, a shepherd, having murdered his owner, and set his family at liberty from the work prison, put himself in martial order. This man dressed himself in purple, assumed a silver cane and adorned his head with regal trappings in no less sumptuous taste than did that fanatical fellow (Eunus) before him, bugled his army together and even much more bitterly than Eunus for whom he seems to have fought in vindication, overthrew towns, castles and cities, raving and raging against masters and slaves more and more violently as deserters (from the slave owners) swelled the ranks."

Page 259, Note 33: "This man, clothed in purple, sporting a silver cane."

Page 260, Note 35: "Being conversant with the star-gazers' art he had read in the heavens that he was to become king over all Sicily; and to this end he looked about him for a place that would seem most suitable on the island —which he considered his own property—whereat to locate himself. He made an attack upon the fortified town of Lilybæum which did not succeed. This was with a force of 10,000 men. It however, served to strengthen his powers of foresight; for he resolved, with great wisdom, to abandon the siege, actuated by the impression that the gods were against the enterprise and consequently a disaster could be avoided only with a miracle. This foreknowledge soon verified itself. A body of Moorish troops auxiliary to the Romans, sent by Bocchus of Mauritania under the new treaty, and commanded by Gomon, for the relief of the besieged city of Lilybæum, immediately on their arrival made in the night, an attack on Athenion and before he could withdraw to a place of safety, succeeded in inflicting upon him a considerable damage."

Page 260, Note 36: "One can scarcely estimate the difficulties which were to be expected by the leaders of an insurrection of slaves."

Page 261, Note 37, Diodorus says regarding tramps: "An immense confusion of things took place and we are told that all worked badly. Vast multitudes got possession of Sicily entire. Not only slaves but also freedmen in a state of great poverty were committing every sort of rapine and flagitious deed. And whoever interfered, whether bond or free, or spoke against their wrong-doing, they shamelessly murdered. Scarcely could people venture into the open spaces in cities which belonged to them; and as for matters outside, these freedmen and emancipated slaves judged themselves unrestrained by any law from committing acts of violence. More than this, many others, forgetting their natural instincts of humanity and right, audaciously wandered throughout Sicily on their course of destruction." Continuing, Diodorus says in fragment 11: "Not alone were the rebels who devastated Sicily, slaves, but often free people; and all persons who possessed neither home nor lands were converted into robbers and bandits who ranged up and down the country, impelled alike by their poverty and their evil-mindedness, carrying off horses and cattle, tearing into the granaries of the towns and indiscriminately beheading slaves or free men, or whomsoever they met, so that none should remain alive to inform on their deeds of deviltry. And when all sources of justice in Sicily had been uprooted—not even a Roman prætor left to demand law and order—they all fell into an unrestrained debauchery and with impunity carried on a horrible licentiousness. There was no place free from the hordes who ravaged and robbed, particularly where the wealthier ones had premises to invade. And those who, a little before, were surrounded by fortune and fame as being the richest among the citizens, suddenly found themselves not only reduced to misery and poverty, but cudgeled and hacked in the most contemptuous manner by slaves, and subjected to all sorts of insolence. Everywhere were the robbers stationed, ready to commit outrage in the free places of cities, outside their walls or wherever they thought they could do violence. Great was the confusion in each one of the large towns and cities; for no law of justice remained. The insurgents, when they had beleaguered all with their army, and the land of their masters whom they hated with ungovernable rage, marched up and down the highways with fire and sword, motived by some inexplicable cupidity. Whoever remained in the cities, such as slaves, the sick, and those sympathizing with the rebellion became a terror to their masters."

Page 261, Note 38: "These free people often practiced more henious acts of power than the slaves. A reign of confusion

—an enormity of troubles, as Diodorus calls it—fell upon them."

Page 261, Note 39: "Athenion, who did not take a city." Siefert however, remarks: "Cicero must here be interpreted with circumspection as having had an object in making this mention."

Page 262, Note 40: "'*Athenio pastor,*' the shepherd...... laid waste the country. By this man the prætorian army also, was cut to pieces and the camps of Servilius as well as Lucullus were seized." Note h. of Fisher: "The camps of Servilius and of Lucullus were seized.' Florus had other histories which we do not possess; for in these that we still have, it appears that not only was Servilius not captured but that Lucullus also, was not driven by the slaves." Duker's comments read: "From this too, Diodorus in his 36th book, charges these things to a certain Salvius, to whom Athenion was like a commander to a king."

Page 264, Note 42, "What were the motives inspiring him to this conduct is not clear; it is nevertheless apparent that Tryphon suspected him as a secret rival; for so soon as favorable opportunity presented itself he had him arrested and put where he could do no harm."

Page 264, Note 43: "Having by the exercise of judgment gotten rid of certain powerful persons and established his councils around him, he put on the Greek robes of rank and donned the mantle of purple with the broad-bordered tunic and chiton to denote great name and style, he surrounded himself with a guard of lictors having their whips and sacrificial axe, and all other such things as seem to befit themselves to the kingly estate."

Page 266, Note 45: "After some skirmishing, they closed in upon each other in regular conflict, which swayed to and fro for a long time ere its results were decided." Same note quoting Diodorus: "They closed together, but not until they had been drawn in by the skirmishing."

Page 266, Note 46: "Athenion with 200 picked cavalrymen undertook an assault and struck down every one in his way; but unfortunately he received three wounds as a result which rendered him helpless. The slaves seeing this, lost courage and ran."

Page 267, Note 49: "When at last, after nine days from the date of the battle, Lucullus arrived before the fortifications to commence a siege, the wavering courage of the insurgents had again been restored."

Page 267, Note 50: "The camps of Lucullus having been taken, Athenion overturned villages, cities and castles." Siefert, same note: "Certainly, the camps of Lucullus must have been stormed."

Page 268, Note 51: "Tryphon dying, the command of the army fell to Athenion who laid siege to cities."

Page 269, Note 55: "M. Aquillius the proconsul, contended vigorously."

Page 269, Note 56: "Athenion who, after the death of Tryphon which had occurred in the meantime, had become king of the slaves, met Servilius with great boldness and drove him from the field. After his camps were taken, Servilius dared not again venture into battle, and the slave-king was able to ransack the country unhindered and got into his grasp the castles and small cities."

Page 269, Note 57: "The revolted cities followed, among which were Hybla and Macella and some others of less importance."

Page 270, Note 58: "By force he seized Macella, a city situated in the neighborhood of Ægesta,"

Page 270, Note 59: "Athenion threw himself against him in open conflict and drove him from the field."

Page 271, Note 61: "Athenion threw himself against him etc., but fell while thus engaged, at the hands of the consul, who himself received wounds upon the head and breast."

Page 271, Note 62: "Athenion the king of the rebelling slaves, throwing together his forces, fought heroically. Rupillius killed him, although he himself received a wound in his head."

Page 271, Note 63: "Whilst prætor in Sicily, I pursued and captured runaway Italian slaves and restored 817 of them to to their masters."

Page 272, Note 66, Same as note 55.

Page 273, Note 68: "Many thought that the glory of the fallen ones was greater than that of the surviving victors."

Page 273, Note 69: "When M. Aqnillius, accused of malfeasance in office, was defending himself, he was unwilling to question the umpires (witnesses) and M. Antonius acted as his lawyer. While making a powerful speech in his defense Antonius tore the garment from his client's breast, revealing the honest scars. The judges no longer remaining in doubt, Aquillius was adjudged innocent."

Page 274, Note 70, Granier says: "A very characteristic trait existed, which was the same in Eunus and in Athenion; and this was, that in revolting, neither one of them had any idea of abolishing slavery and of establishing conditions of equality. Hardly did they see themselves in command of force than they forthwith forgot that they ever had their own necks skinned with chains. They tasted with delicate relish the prerogatives of masters. It is thus easy to understand how castles, villages and cities were delivered over to pillage."

APPENDIX.

CHAPTER XII.

Page 277, Note 1: "In the great work of Nicholas of Damascus the slave war was recounted in the 110th book, from which we have a fragment that appears in Athenæus, IV., 153, F. This fragment is given by Müller, in a Latin translation which I here give, on account of the Latin being generally more easy to read than the Greek. It is as follows: 'Nicholas of Damascus, a philosopher of the peripatetic sect, writes in his 110th book of histories these words, describing how they used to pair gladiators at their dinners: The Romans not only hold gladiatorial spectacles in the assemblages and amphitheatres, such as were borrowed from the Etruscan customs, but they also do it while at their banquets of guests. The way they do it is this: They invite their friends to a dinner; and between the courses they introduce, sometimes one, sometimes two, or sometimes three pairs of gladiators whom they exhibit to the guests in battle. In this manner after they have been gorged with wine and are full of sumptuous hilarity, the gladiators are ordered on the scene; and when one of them falls with his throat cut, the whole company of feasters fall to applauding, exhilarated by the spectacle. Indeed, there is proof that sometimes beautiful women whom the master has bought for the occasion, fight each other with steel. There are others also who say that even little boys below the age of puberty, contribute to the gratification of this delicious passion. But the public who held such atrocities in detestation, ordered a law to stop it.' The whole looks as if these dreadful things might have given a motive to the revolt of Spartacus."

Page 277, Note 2: "The first gladiatorial function ever performed at Rome was in the Forum Boarium at the time Appius Claudius and M. Fulvius were consuls. It was given by M. and D. Brutus, in honor of their deceased father who was incinerated. A battle of athletes was arranged through the munificence of M. Scaurus."

Page 278, Note 3: "'Function of gladiators.' The origin of the gladiatorial combats is in the funeral and comes from the Etruscans, although the Etruscans may possibly have derived it from the Greeks. But from whatsoever the source, the cause was the funeral, or burial. For inasmuch as it was formerly believed that the souls of dead men were propitiated by human blood, they used to immolate their captives of war and even slaves of their own hearth and nourishment, to the funeral rites. After having been customary in placating the avengers of impiety, it differentiated into a source of voluptuousness; and thus the practice operated in two ways to propitiate the wise and great, and afterwards for funeral solemnities where feasts or banquets were given. Such is the gladiatorial function. So from this the fighters are called funereal or sepulchral gladiators. The gladiators, or, as Livy and others have it, 'gladiatorial function,' did not necessessarily mean the function in this sense, but was the common or popular term in use when speaking of the amphitheatre."

Page 279, Note 5, No. 2,551 reads: "Poetelius, a Syrian who teaches a gladiatorial school at Forina where you can buy or sell a lot for the ring." No. 2,555 is: "Inscriptions representing gladiators, that have been preserved in the museum at Rome and catalogued by Marini in his Records, vol. I., p. 165." The inscription itself reads: "Astianax came out victorious on the first day of the ninth month of the Roman year; although he lost his own life. One antagonist was Symmachus Maternus (or perhaps, a relative of Astianax on his mother's side), who was skillful in the use of weapons." Schambach, studying the probable age of Spartacus from data given in various inscriptions, says: "Regarding his age, we have no historical reports from the ancients; yet in spite of this fact the age of Spartacus is by no means hard to get at. It is natural that people should have chosen young men; at any rate those not above middle age. The tombstones for gladiators that have come to our knowledge showing ages at the time they fell in battle, establish this fact. We find in Hegenbuch's edition of Orell's Inscriptions the following data of deaths of gladiators: No. 2,572 gives the age of the gladiator, at 22 years. No. 2,592 shows one who fell at 27 years. No. 2,571, one who fell at 30. No 2,590 gives the age at 46. Very rarely does the age of the gladiator rise above this latter figure. We shall consequently not miss far from the mark by setting the age of gladiators at something between 30 and 40 years."

Page 281 Note 10: "For although slaves are low in estate of manhood and fortune, and liable to punishment, yet they are a species of mankind."

Page 281, Note 11: "The true meaning of family is property. It comprehends the land, the house, the money, the slaves, etc."

Page 282, Note 13: "The war that was instigated by Spartacus the general, I am at a loss to find a name for." Schambach, same note, says: "That Spartacus was a Thracian by birth is a matter on which all information agrees. Plutarch even adds that he was of a nomadic tribe. Steven of Byzantium mentions a Thracian city of the same name. From Thucydides, II., 101, we learn that there was a royal dynasty of the Thracian house of Odrysæ, bearing the name Spardokos. We are shown by the inscriptions and coins that the name Spartokos was common among the rulers along the

APPENDIX.

Bosphorus. Compare Böckh, Body of Greek Inscriptions, vol. II., 91. It is possible, therefore, that our Spartacus, in his own country, might have been clothed with the rank of nobility.

Page 283, Note 15: "On the laws that were enacted against the unions: 'Frequently they organized communistic societies without authority of the public statutes, out of the quarrelsome elements of the people, who thus became a public nuisance...... and on this account many of the unions were afterwards suppressed by law.'"

Page 284, Note 21: "Speech of Spartacus: A group sculptured in marble by Barrias, 1872; Spartacus the father of the hero, appears chained and nailed to the trunk of a tree, about to expire, etc."

Page 285, Note 22: "That Spartacus was a Thracian by birth, is agreed to by all accounts of him."

Page 286, Note 27: "From this reflex of humanity as one views it in the light of a fresh power overwhelming the world, the regular demand of business enterprise was satisfied. All the time there were multitudes of slaves imported to Italy from the north, from the regions of the Black Sea, from Syria and Lybia through slave merchants. For a long time Delos was the head-quarters of this business. At the time of its highest success, which was about B. C. 100, no less than 10,000 slaves are said to have been landed here in a single day. It is self-evident that Rome was an important center of the slave trade. How the slave dealers came in possession of their wares was never questioned. Kidnaping by land and sea constituted the man-hunt such as is to-day being carried on in Africa. It was no uncommon thing to see a great multitude brought in who had been victimized through secret machinations and private feuds as well as those coming into possession of traders by exchange and barter."

Page 287, Note 28: "Pyrrhus, who had been called by the people of Tarentum as an aid against the Romans, in order to help the effeminate citizens, forbade the communistic table or Greek system of taking their meals in common, as one of his first regulations."

Page 287, Note 32: "And they built the prison which is said to have been called the 'home of the Roman proletaries.' Thus, in order that he might call out at any time, and often, that is, in order that he might frequently, and again and again be her judge and lest she should resist him, and vindicate herself through the law, he took away her liberty and reduced her to a slave. If she did not succumb, he could in this case, order her to prison and in chains. Seldom was there ever such a commotion of human feelings, or such a power of the people, determined to bring him to punishment; for they saw by this, how easily their own liberty might be taken away. So Appius Claudius was thrown into prison."

Page 289, Note 35: "He had served in the legions as an auxiliary; but being too proud to accept a species of servitude disguised in the name of the 'alliance,' he had deserted at the head of a company of his fellow citizens. But being caught and sold, his courage and physical powers were forced into play as a gladiator."

Page 289, Note 36: "He met with some gladiators belonging to a certain Lentulus Batiatus at Capua, many of whom were Gauls and Thracians." Remark of Florus: "Since they had already done menial work in the army, they were ordered to act as gladiators—a sort of infamous human creature of the meanest quality and a butt of derision; yet they brought on a calamity." Schambach's remark: "They now elected the Thracian, Spartacus, general-in-chief, and the two Gauls, Crixus and Œnomaus, as generals of the second degree. It is with extreme probability, judging from the vote which decided this result, that we can set down the proportion of the Thracians as one-third, and that of the Gauls as two-thirds—a proportion which does not materially vary in the coming course of events."

Page 290, Note 37, Schambach's remark: "So far as the previous vicissitudes in the life of Spartacus are concerned, this holds good: that he had for a time been a soldier in the Roman militia, with pay; probably in the force of the proconsul P. Claudius, who had been assigned to the work of breaking down what remained of the free ranks of the Macedonian Thracians. He had in this service probably acquired that exact knowledge of Roman military tactics which was an indispensable condition to his future victories. According to Florus, he then deserted and became a marauding guerrilla. He was taken prisoner while in this capacity. Appian does not coincide with this view where (book I., 116), he says: 'Being sold as a prisoner of war to be one of the gladiators.' Neither does Varro's fragment (Charis, I., 108), where he says: 'Spartacus, who was innocent, was thrown as a gladiator, to be killed with steel;' since they speak against the testimony of Florus. We are informed by Plutarch (Crassus. 8), that 'he first came into Rome on sale;' that he had many a time changed owners before he came to the Capuan fighting school of Lentulus Batiatus. Plutarch also relates an anecdote of him after his arrival in Rome, to the effect that a snake once coiled itself about him in his sleep and that a female Thracian fortune-teller interpreted the circumstance to mean that 'he was to become great and feared, and even to his unhappy end, happy.'—a prophecy which, especially in its last part, leaves nothing more to wish for."

Page 291, Note 39: "Nor did he decline his pay, as a soldier of Thrace. From a soldier, he became a deserter; from that, a robber and then a gladiator, doing duty to the amusement of gentlemen."

Page 291, Note 40, The inscription reads: "M. Aquillius and M. F. Gailus were proconsuls at the time I was marching from South Italy to Capua. Along the highway of Pontis I put registers showing the number captured, as follows: 2 at Nuceria; 123 at Capua; 73 at Murianum; 123 at Cosanum; 180 at Valencia. On the strait were put 231, and at Rhegium 237. In the stretch from Capua to Rhegium, 1,321. And also at the time I was prætor in Sicily, I captured 917 Italian slaves and returned them (to their owners), to cultivate the land."

Page 292, Note 41: "About this time gladiators were brought to Italy and lodged at Capua to be trained for the show. Spartacus a Thracian by race, who had been a soldier in the Roman army, and who, as a prisoner of war, was sold for a gladiator, being one of them, persuaded some 70 of the most daring to make an escape, pleading that a forceable attempt at liberty was better than to be butchered at the amphitheatrical spectacle; and arming his fellow adventurers with cudgels of wood and knives, they forced the guards and escaped to Mt. Vesuvius."

Page 292, Note 42: "With scarcely more than 30 men of his own fortune they forced themselves out of Capua."

Page 293, Note 43: "They first compelled their best comrades to leave Capua and seizing weapons suitable for fighting, safely got away; and luckily, as they got hold of more, they threw away their old weapons as barbarous, unworthy the dignity of gladiators." Cicero says, speaking of Sicily: "In the insurrection of Spartacus there were very few at first. But what evil would those fellows not have done in so small an island!" Florus, speaking of their numbers, says ' Spartacus, Crixus and Œnomaus broke out of the ring school of Lentulus and with scarcely more than 30 men of their own sort, escaped from Capua."

Page 294, Note 46, Same as note 43 at the close.

Page 294, Note 47: "Plutarch says: 'People generally call it the Spartacan war' and Florus, who designates the Sicilian labor war the war of the slaves, sets the caption 'Spartacan war,' which brings this Italian insurrection likewise among the great wars of Rome, like the Hannibalic, the Sertorian and the Mithridatic wars, in which a single pesron exhibits such superior qualities as to constitute the soul of the conflict, that it takes its name from him. In fact, we find other weighty references to this, among the Roman authors. Augustin, in De Civitate Dei, III., 26; Ampelius,

TRANSLATION OF NOTES.

Book of Memory, chapters 41 & 45, calling it the servile war: Cæsar, Gallic Wars, book I., 40, calling it the slave insurrectionary war; Frontin; Orosius: 'This war of the runaways or as I may more correctly call it, war of the gladiators.' But in all these appellations the main idea is expressed, that the glory of the strikers, or insurrectionists, must not come down to posterity except as the hated and despised leaders."

Page 294, Note 48: "Slaves are held subject to the power of their masters, and this is in fact the power recognized by the *jus gentium* (law common to nations); for we are to understand that with all citizen and respectable classes, owners of slaves have the power either to kill them or permit their existence."

Page 295, Note 51: "Seventy-four companies were killed by the gladiators." Florus remarks that: "The general thought nothing of what was going to happen, when all at once his camp was burst into by a sudden onset." Schambach remarks: "All information agrees that the fighters were immensely inferior in numbers. Frontin even bears witness (I., v., 21), that there were only 74 in the battle. He says: 'But he also from the other side, so terrified Clodius that his gladators killed some 74 companies of his soldiers.' The attack succeeded perfectly. The Roman soldiers who had been hastily gathered, fled from the battle ground leaving their camp with all their baggage, which became the booty of the insurgents."

Page 297, Note 53, Florus says: "His force gathering in numbers every day until it assumed the proportion of a real army; and he made shields from the vines and the skins of the cattle, and forged swords and javelins out of the iron of workhouse prisons." Appian adds: "Spartacus gathered very many soldiers and soon had an army of 70,000. He forged arms and collected the implements of war. On the other hand, the inhabitants of the cities sent against him two consuls with an army of two complete legions."

Page 297, Note 54: "As he shared the spoils of battle equally, his army became numerous; and the first commander sent against him was Varinius Glabros, and with him one Publius Valerius. They did not carry out the tactics of a regular army but thought only to proceed with all haste possible, the Romans not looking upon it as a war but thought they were merely dealing with a robber and his unorganized hordes. They were allured into a weak spot and defeated. The horse of Varinius was seized by Spartacus himself, Varinius escaping, although the Roman general was well-nigh taken prisoner by the gladiator."

Page 297, Note 55: "And I may drop a thought upon that Mars-like warrior, Spartacus; though every scrap plies its deceptive art in making him a vagrant." Tacitus says: "Never contumely toward the Roman people brought Cæsar greater pain than did this deserter and robber—not even Spartacus, after so many disasters of Rome's consular armies, who raged and burned up Italy with impunity."

Page 399, Note 57, Remarks of Schambach: "We have most of all to regret the loss of the greatest work—that of Sallust—bearing the title of 'Books of History of the Roman People.' Sallust was not only the person nearest in date to the events, among Roman authors who wrote a history of this war, but he was also the most trustworthy in his historical tracings. On account of his position in the state and his far-reaching communications he was in condition to give the best information; and he combined a characteristic for description, with method and criticism. His histories were very thorough."

Page 299, Note 58: "In a disastrous conflict Varinius lost his troops, his baggage and his horse, even his prætorian bundles with the rods and battle-axe."

Page 300, Note 59: "He not only seized the mountains around Thuria but the city of Thuria itself; and forbade merchants bringing gold and silver into camp, using only iron and bronze and discountenencing other things. Piles of wood were brought and worked up for the coming expedition and large quantities of plunder were accumulated. By exchange among the outstanding Romans, and with the booty which came into their hands, they became a power."

Page 300, Note 60: "After Spartacus had drawn to himself all the elements of revolt offered by Campania, he turned toward other regions. We are unforunately, not instructed with exactness regarding the route he took; nevertheless by employing the Vatican fragments of Sallust which agree with Orosius, we may conclude that he first marched toward the peninsula, on the coast of the Adriatic, whence he turned in southerly direction and came to Lucania. At any rate the fragments show that Varinius of whom we shall speak more as we proceed, confronted the revolters at Picenum. On this march he took Annii Forum and perhaps Avella, whose inhabitants displayed a feeling against his offer of protection. It is perfectly certain that the slaves pursued their course with fire and murder."

Page 301, Note 64: "Not only are unions restored which the senate suppressed, but others, new and innumerable, are trumped up out of all the dregs of the city."

Page 301, Note 65: "During the consulate of L. Julius and M. Marius, noted by Cicero, the unions were suppressed by a law of the senate."

Page 301, Note 66: "That not only the ancient unions, but others, innumerable, and entirely new ones, should be created by a gladiator."

Page 302, Note 67: "Concerning the restoration of the old and the institution of new unions, which he (Cicero) says, are created out of the dregs of the city."

Page 302, Note 69: "For which cause the conscription may be instituted; and I have already explained as to which unions this law applied. In this matter I ought to observe two points: first that when slaves belonged to the unions they should not be considered as being in the unions of mechanics; since I do not think that these admitted slaves. But it was those devoted to religion. Therefore, the law of Clodius must be regarded as having effect only in the city of Rome, as Cicero says: 'Also unions created out of the dregs of the city'— those which Clodius conscribed and organized into companies in the forum."

Page 302, Note 70, "Golden and gilded things are luxuries which we know Spartacus prohibited from his camps; for no soldier was allowed either gold or silver. This shows how much nobler than ours were the souls of our runaway slaves."

Page 303, Note 72: "Certain feeble glances are brought to mind upon the constancy of women, the intercession of their prayers and the fine sentiment of the breast in cases of imprisonment. Sometimes the tedium of long and impatient confinement is thus assuaged; and it comes to great use in binding together the souls of states, as in cases where girls, even of noble parentage are wanted to comfort those held as hostages. Nor do men put aside their counsel or neglect their answers. We have as examples, Veleda, who was held high for her predictions and her method of worship among the Germans. But there were also Aurinia and very many others who long ago were venerated. They did not fawn or descend to superficial adulation before the goddesses."

Page 304, Note 77: "Spartacus made an avenging sacrifice of 400 of the Roman prisoners, to the ghost of the dead Crixus. Having 120,000 foot soldiers he thought to march on Rome. Making a bonfire of all unserviceable things of the expedition, tying all of the prisoners and slaughtering the beasts of draft in order to render the army light and easy to manage, and many deserters from the Romans offering themselves, he took them in. The consuls straightway coming to the rescue against him in the country of Picenum, he fought and beat them in great battles at every hand." Julius Obsequens says: "From Capua, they tell us, comes a horrifying clamor—a hundred thousand men destroyed in the Italian civil war!"

Page 305, Note 78. Granier's remarks: "**Spartacus who**

was a man whose heart was above his condition had only one idea: he wanted to get to Gaul, on the other side of the Alps, and once there, his wish was to have every one return to his own country. The military manœuvres of the consuls and the insubordination of his comrades prevented the realization of his desire." Schambach says: "Florus however, can be excused, as giving a useful tinge to the subject, where he says, speaking of the leaders of one of the Sicilian wars: 'We should hold in mind that the disasters were great.' But people were not content with simply making silence cast oblivion over Spartacus; they even smeared public opinion of him by means of invented misdeeds, and brought his name down as a term of contempt and abuse. And even men like Cicero and the elder Pliny are not entitled to remain free from this opinion regarding them. But we, who have no cause to regard Spartacus as a terrible enemy to be held in dismay, have a duty to perform in exhibiting his personality in its correct light and thus redeem it from an undeserved blame. Drumann says: "Nature had created him to be a hero and a ruler by endowing him with wisdom, courage, love of liberty and moderation. These caused him to stride in advance of his companions. He brought unconquerable Rome to fear and trembling when he broke his chains; though all he desired was freedom. The cruelty of his unbridled hordes is not to be attributed to him, nor charged to his reckoning, so far as it was not directed against their oppressors; it was only to the Romans who played their part against his manhood, those whom he prevented from nailing him to the cross, that he knew no mercy. He also remained in the resolve to act as for himself, for those who fell victims of Rome. He did not wish to destroy Rome, because he desired nothing that was impossible. The prophecy of his Thracian wife regarding his forthcoming greatness did not dazzle him. But the slaves confused, frustrated and baffled his plan."

Page 306, Note 79: "Œnomaus had already fallen in battle." Schambach says: "This Œnomaus must have been killed early. Crixus, who appears as the next in command after Spartacus, played his part for a longer time."

Page 306, Note 80: "Q. Arrius, the prætor, killed Crixus the general, together with 20,000 of his troops." Appian says: "Crixus who was the other commander, having under him 30,000 men, was met (by Arrius), at the foot of Mt. Garganus and defeated; himself and two-thirds of his army being destroyed. Spartacus, the other commander, was in consequence hindered from carrying out his intention of crossing the Appenine mountains, and so moved toward the Alps in the direction of Gaul, pursued by the Roman consul." Sallust so far as can be made out of the broken scrap, says:

"The rage of the conflict was powerful. Forgetting the body lacerated with gashes, and half-alive, some of them fought wickedly while others on the house tops hurled down fire upon the enemy. Many slaves of the place who had enrolled themselves in the love of liberty as allies, secretly stole things from their masters as they set themselves at liberty and nobody, holy or wicked, was spared the anger and servile revengefulness of the barbarians; deeds were these which Spartacus was unable to hinder though he sent messengers in haste and with many entreaties." Again Sallust says: "In a few days the faith of our troops began to augment and the force to increase unexpectedly. Varinius moved incautiously on his prey which was in view, and fell into a new ambush like the others, and his soldiers suffered a shock. He however, led them up to the camps of the revolters. With quick step they silently advanced but not in such self-conscious splendor as they had hitherto assumed. Again on the other hand, the slaves, it was perceived, were quarreling among themselves and were at the point of sedition; for Crixus and his Gauls, together with the Germans were anxious to offer battle while Spartacus opposed it."

Page 307, Note 81: "He also tore to shreds the consular forces under Lentulus, in the Appenines; and under Caius Cassius at Mutina."

Page 307, Note 82: "Their numbers rose so that at last he brought to bear against the Romans as many as 40,000 men." Note of translator: This absurd remark attributed to Vellejus Paterculus is a false statement of an early amanuensis; for the real, and undeniably correct figure actually given by Paterculus was 300,000; see pp. 324-5,-and notes 122, 124.

Page 308, Note 83: "Being driven by him and dispersed in flight—be it said to our shame—the enemy retired to the farther side of Italy."

Page 308, Note 84: "On the route he met and crushed two consular, and two prætorian armies and arrived, fighting and always victorious, at the Po, whose waters overflowing its banks, debarred his progress." Sallust remarks: "M. Trequius, having scarcely enough troops, could hardly escape being injured. But Varinius, so long as his force was pressed upon by the insurgents and rendered weak-spirited by the odds against him, ordered his men with a severe threat, not to fall back and encouraged them to rally by means of signals; and those who lagged he lowered to the rank of militia with anathemas of disgrace. His commissary C. Thoranius" (Here the scrap is so broken as to be no further intelligible).

Page 308, Note 85: "He ordered the prisoners (Roman) to fight each other as gladiators with weapons, in celebration of the funeral and to the honor of the immortal spirits of the dead leaders; plainly as if to resuscitate a gone-by abomination and revive the old funereal function of the gladiatorial wake."

Page 309,   Note 89: "C. Cassius the proconsul, and the prætor Cneus Manlius, continued the war against Spartacus but were defeated."

Page 310   Note 92: "Therefore the two consuls joined their forces on the plains of Piceno, and attacked him both together. But here again Spartacus raged against them and defeated them with great loss."

Page 310,   Note 95: "He did not dare to march to the city."

Page 311,   Note 96: "At last with all the forces at his command he marched against the Thracian gladiator." Translator's note. According to law, Crassus, being the consul was commander-in-chief of all the forces recently returned from Spain and Asia.

Page 311,   Note 97: "There happened an affair on a gigantic scale. Steadily they found allies of their own class, besides many farmers—men of a tough and pernicious sort."

Page 311,   Note 98: "Spartacus the leader of the runaway slaves, was able with his 500 robbers to perpetrate enough of evil."

Page 312,   Note 101: "The war had already been raging three years and was becoming more fearful and the gladiators more disdainful in power and spirit. When the vote for new consuls was about to be taken candidates were tardy in coming to hand, as they would have to be commanders. At length Licinius Crassus, well known by family and wealth among the Romans, manifested a willingness to assume command and with six fresh legions bore away against Spartacus."

Page 313,   Note 104: "The Roman general only intended to invade Latium, not daring to risk a battle with the terrible gladiator, and was content to harass and render him miserable, with his lieutenants, who were invariably beaten whenever they ventured to come to battle."

Page 315,   Note 108: "Immediately choosing one out of every ten from the whole lot of those who had been defeated they were condemned to death and destroyed. This was regardless as to which one the lot fell upon; for every soldier in the army who was beaten was called up and the tenth of the whole number chosen. The total number enrolled was about 4,000, no one escaping. No matter how this was considered, the thought of defeat became one of terror and straightway Crassus fell upon the myriads under Spartacus and his disdainful gladiators, with these newly invigorated men, and drove them." Remarks of the commentator Thirsius: "'He kills those who were chosen by lot, with clubs. I think it should read: 'He kills those led out.' Concerning the severe military discipline of Crassus, we must reflect that it was in the case of the two legions of Mummius who, contrary to the orders of the consul, had dared to attack the enemy under Spartacus and who had been defeated. Four hundred of those who had been the first to take to their heels were led forth, after being drawn by lot. This ancient manner of punishment by making them kill each other, and which had long since fallen into disuse, was resuscitated by Crassus."

Page 315, Note 109: "Defeating him, he smartly followed him to the sea, where he (Spartacus) was to cross over into Sicily. Here Crassus set to work and threw up a breastwork and an intrenchment."

Page 316 Note 111: "About the same time the gladiators forced themselves into the town of Præneste and endeavored to break into the garrison of the army which here held the munitions of war, and spread terror among the people; for it started amidst these a desire to reënact the old scenes of Spartacus; and not much later a naval defeat was sustained. It was not a war, for all this was in a time of profound peace but Nero had ordered the fleet to return to Campania on a certain day, taking no notice of the nets of the sea. The governors therefore, inasmuch as the sea thronged with pirates who had their head-quarters in Formiæ (Mola de Gæta), and were strong in Africa as well as in Miseni, which they had taken, sent war boats with three pairs of oars and a large number of smaller vessels everywhere along the Cumanian shores."

Page 317, Note 113: "L. Metallus the prætor, prosperously carried on a warfare in Sicily."

Page 318, Note 115: "So great was the terror which he (Spartacus) had inspired, that Crassus undertook to shut him up in the peninsula of Rhegium by a breastwork and ditch some 45 miles long! The chief of the slaves manifested profound contempt for this immense work, as well as for his enemies, who did not dare to attack him in the front. Therefore, when the provisions began to fail, he broke down a part of the breastwork during a stormy night, forced the lines of the Romans and manœuvred freely in Lucania where he exterminated the troops of the two lieutenants of Crassus who had the temerity to molest him in his retreat."

Page 318, Note 116: "Spartacus, relinquishing his intention to give battle with his entire command, ordered his cavalry to harass and teaze the besiegers as much as possible, by continually attacking them of a sudden. He broke into the defenses of Crassus and burned them, accomplishing the destruction of much difficult work. He hung a Roman prisoner

612   *APPENDIX.*

in the open space between the two armies, showing his own men by plain view that they were not to disobey orders. He threw fagots and wood bundles into the ditch and escaped."

Page 319,   Note 117: "The people in the city of Rome, on inquiry, learning the escape of Spartacus from the blockade and reflecting upon the length of this war with the gladiator, sent word to Pompey to return with his army, from Spain, writing him that the affair had become a great and difficult work. Since the election which created Crassus consul, he had kept back the rumors of the war with Spartacus from the knowledge of Pompey and made every possible turn to get Spartacus into his hands. Spartacus knew that negotiations were going on for the assistance of Pompey." The French Dictionary says: "Crassus wrote to the senate asking that Pompey, then about to return from Spain, be sent to his assistance; likewise for the aid of Lucullus, who was about to return from Asia. He however, soon regretted this step, and sought every measure possible to terminate the war himself, so that he might enjoy all the honor."

Page 319,   Note 118, Remarks of Frontin, quoting Livy: "'Thirty-five thousand armed soldiers of the insurgent slaves who were defeated by Crassus were killed in this battle, together with their generals, Castus and Gannicus,' so says Livy and the Romans recaptured 5 eagles, 26 ensigns and much plunder, among which were the prætorian fasces."

Page 320,   Note 119: "Crassus had in the war of the gladiators, at Catana, built a couple of palisade-like intrenchments that walled the camps of Spartacus from his own army. In the night, Spartacus set his army in motion while the prætorian guards remained on high ground in their camps, in order to deceive the Romans. He thus led out all his force and going to the foot of the mountains they all met at a place indicated in advance. The cavalry was attacked by L. Quinctio and the part under Spartacus was drawn off so as to frustrate a battle with him. The other part consisting of Gauls and Germans who had been in a faction against their head leader and who were commanded by Castus and Gannicus, were allured into an attack (upon Quinctio), by his pretending to escape. In this way the Roman drew up his forces against them and when the barbarians came up he formed his cavalry in squares and suddenly throwing off the mask, fell upon them with a clamor. Thirty-five thousand armed men, Livy tells us, fell in this battle, together with both the leaders, Castus and Gannicus." See also last words of Frontin, above.

Page 323,   Note 121: "Pompey was bending his energies to reach and seize Spartacus; and the latter believed him to be bearing down upon him—even then, summoned to a consultation with Crassus. Disdaining to find out by inquiries what was going on, he had the cavalry brought up, forced his entire army through the barriers of the intrenchment and escaped to Brundusium, followed by Crassus. Spartacus however, learned that Lucullus had arrived in Brundusium, having finished his defeat of Mithridates. He now became desperate; for he knew that he was about to fall into the hands of Crassus, with all of his great army of so many times ten thousand in number. Spartacus received a wound in the thigh by a dart, in the great battle that took place. Bending the knee to the fight and throwing away his shield, he stood out upon the approaching enemy and in single, hand-to hand conflict, fell, covered with wounds, leaving many, in a circle around him, dead."

Page 325, Note 123, Schambach says: "Vellejus is of little value to us. We get nothing through him that is not already known, except this statement regarding the numbers, that 'of the 300,000 slaves engaged in the last battle, only 40,000 were left.'"

Page 325, Note 124, What Vellejus, interpolated by somebody, is wrongfully made to say: "Runaways from the training school for gladiators, at Capua with a leader named Spartacus, escaped, and having seized swords in the city, grew in numbers day by day until they became a multitude. With traps and tricks they inflicted great damage to Italy and their numbers rose so that at the last battle there were 40,000 in line" (the original MSS. written by Vellejus himself, had it 300,000, the number 40,000 surviving) "who arrayed themselves against the Roman army." John Campbell's note is as follows: "Although I do not think that I ought to alter anything myself, I will say that there is a great dispute here, among writers. Among those known to hold a diversity of opinion is Vossius, the exceedingly learned author of a dissertation on translations, in his edition of Florus, book III., chapter 20." Again: "Forty; Some others augment this number by a great deal. Eutrope is among those who make it smallest of all. He writes it down as 60,000 men who were collected by Spartacus. But Appian extends the number to 120,000. Orosius who continued the histories of Livy is observed to hold a medium between these. Thus I shall scarcely go wide of the truth by stating it, with Vossius, at 90,000. This is but a paltry pivotal number from which the writers vary one way or the other; since the real edition of Vellejus gives it at 300,000 men." Signed by Heinsius. Remarks from the Hudson edition, note 5: "Vossius does not dispute that the number should be read 90,000 or 100,000, because the original edition of Vellejus reads 300,000 men."

Page 327, Note 128: "The battle became great and obstinate as so many times ten thousand men grew desperate. Spartacus was wounded in the thigh by a javelin (dart) and bending his knee, threw off his shield and plunged in upon the approaching columns of the enemy until he himself and many more, fighting in a circle around him, fell."

Page 328, Note 132, Words of Heinsius on the number of men under Spartacus who fell in the last battle: "Since the main edition (of Vellejus) says '40,000 out of the 300,000 men.'" Words of Schambach, the best modern critic, see note 123; Words of Appian: "The rest of the army fell into disorder and the men were cut down in great numbers while the loss on the part of the Romans was not very great, reaching only to a few thousand men. The dead body of Spartacus could not be found."

Page 330, Note 136: "The number of killed, according to Athenæus, in this and other less important slave uprisings which peradventure have, or have not come down to us, rose to something like a million. He probably got his figures out of the exaggerated calculations of Cæcilius Calactenus."

CHAPTER XIII.

Page 334, Note 1: "We search for the place and the nature of the skilled workmen in trade unions engaged in public affairs and government work, who were tolerated by law —and this is being examined into so far as may be—although among authors this thing is kept very dark."

Page 335, Note 6: "Declares that Numa the king, created the third union, that of the bronze-workers, in the city of Rome......Numa the king, instituted the seventh union— that of the potters."

Page 335, Note 7: "The Roman state originally granted the trade organizations, such as did service to its religious functions and its military, complete privileges and its immediate protection, together with a code of self-sustaining rules on the communal plan."

Page 335, Note 8: "In very ancient times the right of combining into organized form was allowed to everybody."

Page 336, Note 10: "In the divisions of the trades and professions there were included along with the skilled arts, the flute-players, gold-workers, dyers, shoemakers, tanners curriers, braziers, potters and all the others instructed to operate under the same system."

Page 337: Note 13: "It is worthy of remark here that this is the law of Solon, as it relates to the sacred and civil communes."

Page 338, Note 14: "Amasis made a law for the Egyptians which made it compulsory upon all to inform the governors of their districts as to how they maintained themselves, on pain of death. Solon brought this law to Athens and established it there."

Page 340, Note 17: "Although much was destroyed in the civil war, yet there were in his possesssson, 4,116 slaves."

Page 340, Note 19: "Not only those ancient unions were restored in spite of the senate, but new ones, too numerous to count were enrolled by a gladiator."

Page 342, Note 21: "To his most virtuous wife Numisia, with her incomparable love, with whom he lived 17 years, 11 months and 17 days."

Page 343, Note 26: "We are nevertheless surprised to see in Livy who knew the old traditions, that the optimate class denied the admission of plebeians as citizens, not because they were from conquered countries, but because they were without religion and without family. Now this reproach, unmerited at the time of Licinius Stolo and which those living contemporaneously to Livy, could scarcely understand, coming down from a high antiquity, reminds us of the ancient organization of cities."

Page 344, Note 27: "Men of the inferior class formed a body or union among themselves. What was meant by the people was the patrician class and their clients. The plebeians were outside of this."

Page 344, Note 28: "This was a renunciation of religion. Let us again remark that a son born without the regular ceremonies and rites, was recognized an illegitimate, the same as one born of an adultery; and the domestic, or home religion was not for him at all."

Page 344, Note 29: "But such, and of such a sort was the religion of the unions called the sodality that they were prohibited by the public laws in order to be rid of annoyances."

Page 344 Note 30: "The sodalis (union of a pretended religious nature), is a species of wild thing, evidently derived from the stock farms and farms of the Germans, and addicted to their lupercalian orgies, whose meetings in the forest were instituted before the laws that govern mankind."

Page 345, Note 33: "In a great many places Cicero inveighs against P. Clodius who by his law, restored the unions, 58 years before Christ, and even caused the creation of new "

Page 346, Note 35: "Be it known that whoever commits suicide for whatsoever cause, shall for that offense, be denied a burial."

Page 346, Note 36: "This deceit which used religion as a cloak caused the senate to withdraw the right of combinaion." Again: "Under pretext of religion, those forming illicit combinations for purposes of political power by vote

APPENDIX.

(the ballot), are not to be included among ancient organizations."

Page 347, Note 38: "We have elsewhere shown that the Roman law of the Twelve Tables touching the corporations, continued the same dispensations as the Greek law, to such an extent that they appeared to Gaius to be a translation from the Greek to the Latin."

Page 347, Note 40: "Combinations also of quarrelsome people without legal authority, often commit mischief,......on account of which the religious unions were suppressed by various laws."

Page 350, Note 44: "It did not ameliorate the low estimation in which the laboring people were held; even though quite a number of celebrated men belonged by birth or business to this class."

Page 357, INSCRIPTION AT LANUVIUM Completed.

"Be it ordained that whoever shall be created a five-years' magistrate in this union, shall, from the date at which he so became, as appears stamped on the records, be free and exempt from the duties of the other members; and double as much shall be given him out of all the resources, as to the others. So also to the scribe or amanuensis as well as to the traveling agent, once and a half as much is to be paid, out of the revenues, from the time he takes the office."

"Be it ordered that whoever conducts the office of the quinquennal or five-years' magistrate faithfully and honorably, shall receive one and a half times that of an ordinary member, out of every revenue; that those behind may be imbued with an emulation and a hope, by following in his footsteps."

"Be it ordered that if any one wishes to bring complaint or to make any demands, let the same be done in a session of the union, that it may be done quietly and in the good feeling that prevails when we are enjoying our banquet on stated occasions."

"Be it ordered, that if any one go from his place over to another, for the purpose of sedition (disturbance), let him be fined the sum of 4 sesterces (17 cents U. S. money). But if any one speak against another, using opprobrious language, or become tumultuous, let him be fined and disgraced. If any person during his term of the five-years' magistracy behave indecently, using contumelious language during the festivities, let him be fined 20 sesterces (about 82 cents), and be disgraced."

"Be it ordered that the five-years' magistrate of the union shall, during his term, behave himself with holiness on the solemn days of the feasts, by offerings of frankincense and wine and through other offices, himself performing the function of lord-priest, robed in white; and on the birth-day of the goddess Antinœ, he shall put oil before the union and in the public bath, before the banqueting begins."

CHAPTER XIV.

Page 360,   Note 3: "The Order of Wood-workers, divided into bodies of 100 to each union, was put between the first and second categories; or if we follow Dionysius of Halicarnassus (VII., 59), we shall have: 'two bodies of 100 mechanics each, who are wood and brass workers, engaged in making the armaments of war."

Page 361,   Note 8: "The union of ship carpenters,....and in the same manner there were the mechanics in wood, of the city of Pisaurum."

Page 362,   Note 10: "By the law (senatus consult), there was the school of the unions of wood-workers under Augusta which was maintained at their own expense, founded by T. Furius, the first son who, at its dedication, gave 10 sesterces (about 42 cents) out of his own purse, so that they might enjoy a banquet every year in honor of his birth-day which occurred on the 12th of August."

Page 362,   Note 11: "All the unions were suppressed, except a few particular ones, such as he considered useful; and these were the wood-workers and the image-makers." Note of Dion Cassius: "The ancient brotherhoods....being regularly recorded and known to have existed for a long time."

Page 362,   Note 12: "But a great many unions had been created before. The first cause for this was religion; some thinking this a matter essential to their lives and they used these associations for sacred purposes."

Page 362,   Note 13: "Feigning religion and making a false show is what caused the senate to suppress their privilege of combination. These words must be explained as touching their meetings in the temples on pious pretenses, which, however, was in no wise against the law; though they could fraudulently use this clause of the law."

Page 363,   Note 14, at bottom, Funck Brentano says: "It was the same in the cities of Greece; this was a condition of their progress."

Page 363,   Note 15: "We have said that during the time L. Piso and A. Gabienus were consuls, P. Clodius who was a tribune of the people, strove to restore the unions and to create new ones which Cicero says were organized out of the dregs of the city of Rome."

Page 364,   Note 19: "Sacred to the holy ashes of T. Sillius & T. Liberius Priscus, president of the union of wood-workers and five-years' magistrate with the brotherhood of cloth-fullers; and also sacred to the memory of Clavidia his free wife, who was matron of the brotherhood. Signed by C. Tullanis, T. Sillius Caris and Tiberius Claudius Phillippus, who were presidents and five-years' magistrates (quinquennals), sons of these most pious parents."

Page 365, Note 23: "Cæsar suppressed all the unions except those of ancient origin.

Page 366, Note 24: "In this case the many workmen belonging to Cato, or the 500 belonging to Crassus, would not have been able to do anything; it was necessary for government to have corporations of trade unions of the workmen."

Page 367, Note 27: "The union of stonecutters, organized by (or perhaps presided over by) Augurius Catalinus Usar."

Page 368, Note 28: "An emancipated slave who, after his manumission, became either a silversmith or an engraver and die-sinker."

Page 370, Note 34: "According to Budæus, the joiners or inside finishers (house finishers etc.), worked in wood of a smaller sort, and consequently they used to work finishing dwellings, temples, etc."

CHAPTER XV.

Page 373, Note 2: "What Flavius Josephus tells us about those works which were several times executed at Jerusalem, either in building the temple or repairing it, does not leave a chance for doubt, that the workingmen, whether Jew or Sidonian, were organized into trade unions. Furthermore every particle of doubt is removed by the following passage where he clearly speaks of the hierarchy which prevailed among the workmen and their 3,200 foremen who had 80,000 masons at work on the walls of the temple, to wit: "Of the neighbor workingmen employed by David, there were eight times ten thousand hewing stone, whose work was directed by three thousand and two hundred foremen."

Page 373, Note 3: "It should be stated at the start that the mines of iron come first; although it is both the best and the basest commodity in human use."

Page 373, Note 4: "Statue to the honor of the most pious Volcanus, erected by (or at the instance of) T. Flavius Florus, who was priest of the Sun-god. It is of marble, for the union of sling-makers and the union of iron-workers."

Page 373, Note 5. The Arundelian slab is not so old as Numa but it embraces time remotely anterior to him. Its authenticity is subscribed to by Böckh. The passage quoted seems to speak of women who combed their hair with toothed instruments made of iron.

TRANSLATION OF NOTES. 619

Page 375, Note 8: "They forged swords and javelins out of the iron of their prisons."

Page 377, Note 10: "The sword-makers, arrow-makers, wagon-makers, water-wheel-makers and shinglers."

Page 378, Note 14: "To the honor of my remains! C. Furius and C. F. Lollius, chief officers of the union of machine-makers; let this be enregistered that I desire and ask of you a sacrifice; and that the union consider me worthy of a six-days' solemnity—this to take place from the Ides of March, the fourth and on my birth-day; and that as much as four dollars and thirty-five cents be expended for that purpose. Let the finest flowers be used, at a cost of eighty-seven and a half cents. If this request be not punctually fulfilled, then you shall forfeit double that sum for funeral uses, collected by subscription" (not from the treasury of the union).

Page 379, Note 17: "One searches in vain for satisfactory information."

Page 380, Note 19: "The government on its own part, had need, all the time, of a number and variety of workmen sufficiently large to execute its works. And what mighty works were those performed by the Romans! What temples, and such splendid temples! What aqueducts and such mighty aqueducts! What bridges and they were magnificent!

Page 380, Note 20: "Just so the shoemakers, whom Cicero calls the girdlers, to express his contempt, as being no better than common people, formed, under Numa's categories, an especial trade organization."

Page 381, Note 21: "There was, in fact, the government. It was the true supporter of the trade unions. And the enterprises undertaken by it formed the only permanent manufacture in which the laboring people could obtain their living, or wages day by day." Again, Granier says: "On the part of the government" etc. (see note 19 above), "it was indispensable to have unions of workingmen; and this is because they were constantly under the service and pay of government that the senate and the emperors had them provided for by laws. The law of the Twelve Tables which ordained that the unions should conform to the general statutes of the state, is therefore, in reality the first established privilege in favor of the working class already organized at the time."

Page 382, Note 23: "A five-years' magistrate of the unions of wine-curers of the city of Rome and the port of Ostia."

Page 383, Note 24: "The union of wine-smokers put the epitaph: 'sacred to the memory of'"..and Orelli adds: "I have found another union of wine-smokers."

Page 383, Note 26: "It must be observed that among the great numbers of unions and organizations of the arts at the port of Rome, the decurians (those of the category of 10, by law) were not simply corporations, but real trade unions." Text of the inscription: "Sacred to the memory of Cneus Sentius, son of Cneus senior, three times the successful candidate for superintendent of works and buildings, and twice elected captain and secretary-treasurer of the company at Ostia the port of Rome; a man who died while yet a youth." "This person is the first who is known to have been received as a member of a union at ten years of age; and he in fact, designates two men. He appears five times admitted during his youth, through the good nature of managers of the order of boatmen, and he belonged to the good-fellowship in the order of wine-men. He was secretary's accounting clerk under the patronage of the company and herald or crier to the unions of silversmiths, traders and wine-men. So also, he officiates in the bread supplies for the city of Rome, for unions of measurers and fruiterers, and also for the unions of light and heavy boatmen, split and corn-grits unions for furnishing food to freedmen as well as the slaves belonging to the city, for the cabriolet-drivers young and old, the oil-drivers' unions, and was youth of the plays for the fish-hucksters. Cneus Sentius Lucullus Gamala, a Clodian, beloved of his father."

Page 385, Note 30, Granier says: "From the earliest times the slaves are found to be apart from free people, forming a race by themselves. They were fed and clothed in a manner special and appropriate. The Jews used to pierce their ears while the Greeks and Romans branded them on the forehead whence the name 'Stichus' which became common and general among the slaves. From Homer's time their mode of living was regulated and they never ate bread made of wheat flour."

CHAPTER XVI.

Page 389, Note 1: "To Titus Claudius Esquilius Severus, lictor to the company of ten, under the patronage of the union of fishermen and divers and who was three times a five years' magistrate of the same. On account of his meritorious actions two statues are placed to his honor—one through the gift of money made by Aug. Antonius at Rome and the other costing more, donated by the union itself, in the sum of 10-000 sesterces, which is placed at interest, the earnings to be expended every year on the 15th calends of Feb., his birthday, in a banquet at which each member shall have a flagon of wine apportioned to him accordingly as he shall have diligently behaved in the work of the society's business with the boats under the rules of the order of fishermen and divers of the whole length of the Tiber, to whom the right of organization has been decreed by a law of Rome."

Page 391, Note 5: "At the elections of duumvirs and the board of public works of provincial cities, the trade unions, the public, and what is wonderful, women also, when they favored the candidates, voted for them. For this purpose they placarded the place as seen on the walls of Pompeii through a recent discovery."

Page 395, Note 20: "Union of hunters of Deëns who furnished the amphitheatres with wild beasts."

Page 398, Note 26: "Oligarchy of money, with its concomitants of pauperism and slavery."

CHAPTER XVII.

Page 402, Note 1: "In mirth and jollity to the union of play actors at Felan; second prompter of the companies of 10."

Page 403, Note 6: "The two inscriptions are remarkable which Gorius (Etruscans, I., p. 125, which is the same as Orelli's no. 2,447, and Muratorius' nos. 886 and 887), thinks dates from A. D. 212. In these they hold that by the wording, it is to be understood that the names of the soldiers are taken from 7 cohorts (or from the 7th cohort). They are now in the collection at Florence. An inhabitant of the seaport of Misenum arranged theatrical plays, making actors of the guards in the prætorian fleet. When Claudius Gnorimus was made a superintendent of the board of works he organized a division under one flag, and had entertainments and diversions performed by the military companions themselves. Among them are to be mentioned these names and epithets: archimimus (first mimic); archimimi Græci (Greek mimics); the clowns, the Greek clowns, the Greek performers, the jesting dandies and the machinist or scene-adjuster. All the names of the soldiers appear."

Page 404, Note 9: "The unions of mimics, both in name and kind of association are the same in arrangement as the Greek communes of skilled workmen of the Dionysian order, which were exceedingly numerous among the Greeks."

Page 413, Note 36: "The fortune-tellers whose tutelary divinity is the goddess of justice Nemesis (sun-worship), the same as good fortune."

Page 414, Note 37: "Very many unions of comic actors are being discovered."

CHAPTER XVIII.

Page 416, Note 5: "The freeborn sons of Eumachia, of the sacred union of cloth-fullers, who worked for the state (or public)."

Page 416, Note 8: "The principal corporations of the empire of Rome were those of the weavers and drapers."

Page 422, Note 30: "Union of the rag-pickers and patch-piecers of the provincial city of Mevaniola."

Page 423, Note 32: "Similar laws which were neither less wordy nor less stuffed with fawning language."

Page 425, Note 39: "The date, 251 years of the union, was written above, showing that it must have been founded at that time."

CHAPTER XIX.

Page 429, Note 3: "In the rules of Diana and Antinœ and of Esculapius and Hygæa." Also: "In the domestic establishments of the Cæsars (from Cæsar Augustus), there were many unions of skilled mechanics." Again: "The appearance is that there were also sailors. They dedicated the 'family' of sailors as sacred to Minerva."

Page 433, Note 14: ' We do not like to look at the circus performance from cushioned seats."

CHAPTER XX.

Page 439, Note 3: "Placed to the memory of Aurelius Cecilius. Epictatus the student or apprentice, placed it to his honor at Lyons." This is an inscription commemorating the union of collectors.

Page 442, Note 10: "Tax collection of the iron forgers and iron ore miners." Also: " Sacred to the memory of Primon the tent associate, comrade of the forgers in the iron mines."

CHAPTER XXI.

Page 445, Note 2: "Again, there are certain unions at Rome defined under the law as sacred, with regular rules and by-laws; such as the millers and bakers; and certain others, as the boatmen in the provinces."

Page 445, Note 3: "P. Monetius a freedman member, and Philogenes, a worker in metals.

Page 446, Note 4: "There is shown on the pyramid, by letters engraved in the Egyptian style, the statistics of living for the workmen. If I remember the interpreter rightly, the expense for eatables for them alone was, for radishes, onions, and garlic, no less than $1,690,000.

Page 447, Note 5: "For both on account of the necessity of burials and their usefulness in putting out fires, the senate continued their right to organize. For this reason, those only were prohibited who had ostensibly gone into a burial association with the real purpose of forming one of incendiaries."

Page 447, Note 6: "He (or the senate) gave permission to organize, to all the wine-men, brothel keepers, shoemakers and the artisans generally; and ordered that the magistrates should keep an eye upon them, seeing to it that they maintained their proper relations one to another."

Page 448, Note 9: "The variety, extent and propagation of the organizations."

Page 455, Note 16: "There are unions of brotherhoods of eranoi, allowed to combine by the consent of the magistrates of Athens, with their help, good will and indulgence toward those that were called, sometimes the eranos, sometimes the thiasos, and by others, the commune or union of the brotherhood, and the union of the thiasotes."

Page 456, Note 17: "Some of the communistic societies are thought to be for pleasures or enjoyment, among which are the thiasotes and eranists. Some are combined for the purpose of performing sacrifice to the gods."

Page 458, Note 18: "We are all a brotherhood (thiasotes) under this divinity" (meaning the god of love).

CHAPTER XXII.

Page 467, Note 5: "Of late, in order to make the arrangments easy, all the between-distances are designated, and so well learned as to be in familiar use. So the custom is to drive down the staff of the banners (vexilla). One of them, and in fact the first one, must be put at the place where the general's tent stands; another is fixed at one side and the third at a central point between the lines toward which the tribunes march. A fourth is put in a position at which the legions are to be stationed. Then certain other flags which are red, although the consul's banner is white, are placed as follows: Among these red flags some are placed on the side opposite the prætorian guards. Sometimes they are fixed to naked spears or lances driven into the ground, the banners being frequently of more than one color."

Page 470, Note 10 "These rudimental colors are the red, the orange, the yellow, the blue, the indigo and the violet."

Page 471, Note 12: "To finish the arrangements of the camp, tribunes find it necessary to exact an oath from all, whether freedmen or slaves, and this is done in the following manner: 'You solemnly swear that you will not steal anything from the camp; and moreover, if any one finds anything, that he will bring the same to the general."

Page 474, Note 20: "Nor could the angry and threatening aspect of things be assuaged. There was no election except for members of the board of public works and for tribunes of the common people. Licinius and Sextius were re-elected tribunes and it was impossible to fill the aristocratic chair of consul; so that there was an interregnum during a period of five years; for as the plebeian party succeeded in restoring the two tribunes, these broke up the election of military tribunes or commanders, and thus held the city for five years."

Page 475, Note 22: "Horatius had an unmarried sister, in love with, and engaged to, one of the three Curiatii (antagonists whom he killed). When he observed her in front of the gate of Capua, in tears and rending her hair knowing by the military cloak over his shoulder that it was her dead lover he became aroused by her weeping, being worse aggravated by the congratulation of the public at his moment of victory. These awakened the ferocity of the young man's soul. Drawing his sword and at the same time shouting, he stabbed the girl through the body, crying: 'Hence with your love! Get you gone to your lover! Go down with the dead men into oblivion! Be done with life and fogret the land of your fathers! Hello, hangman! bind together the hands which but now were in arms against the power of the Roman people!'" The words of the father of Manlius were: "Heigh there, executioner, tie him to the post!"

Page 477, Note 25: "The little toga was put on the lictor near the city gate and when he took it he cast off his saga and went again into the service of the consul."

Page 484, Note 43: "Flag-bearers who carried banners and colors in honor of the gods, at the pageants, the festivities and the games."

Page 484, Note 44: "Ancient and revered union of master flag-bearers at the banquets and their numerous varieties extending from the image and ensign-bearers who are the genus to the standard-bearers who are the species."

Page 484, Note 45: "One will easily understand that there might have been lively quarrels or differences among these unions of shoemakers and cobblers—the one selling old boots and shoes, the other bartering certain articles of its trade but in doing so, trenching upon the conditions prescribed by the rules and regulations. Indeed, oftentimes the courts and tribunals of justice heard their grievances and interfered against acts which they often committed, or prevented their combats."

Page 485, Note 46: "Their banner was in three colors divided from each other by a pale blue strip, the first division being red, with a gilt-handled knife; the third part was gold with a horse bit in red."

Page 485. Note 48: "At Clermont, blood-red with a blade of silver and a gilt handle."

Page 486, Note 50: "At Montferrand the shoemakers, in union with the carders, weavers, dealers in old junk, tavern-keepers and masons carried a banner the color of which was red and in the center was the virgin in silver, with the infant. It was margined with gold."

Page 488, Note 53: "One may make a very curiosity-gratifying study of the part which the military carpentry played in the second expedition of Pepin-le Bref in the year 761 against Gaifre, duke of Aquitania. At the siege in which he took the city of Clermont he profited by the experience of the Lombards, and caused formidable battering-rams to be slung against the walls. These consisted of beams of enormous size set swinging by levers, and rolling upon cylinders made to oscillate backwards and forwards by ropes, the impulse being given by carpenters and skilled men who hurled iron-headed ends against the walls and stove them to pieces. To this day one may observe the marks of damage thus sustained at other sieges of Clermont and Montferrand, A. D. 1121 and 1126."

CHAPTER XXIII.

Page 498, Note 3 "In Epidamnus there were no artisans except public slaves. Manual skilled labor was in consequence condemned and despised, and in many cities even forbidden the citizens."

Page 499, Note 9: "Who is he that is not tired and disgusted with reading and writing of long and irksome wars and the motives that propel them."

Page 499, Note 11: "That sort which the Greeks call burden-bearers, but which we in Latin denominate drudges."

Page 499, Note 12: "Wherefore I plead and beseech, O judges, that you see in the true light this work which Sextus Clodius has, within these few days accomplished. I demand that you look after this man whom you for two years, have seen as the minister or leader of sedition—the man who is burning the holy altars and the wealth of the Roman people, blotting them from public memory by his own hand; a man without condition, without a faith, without hope, without a home, without fortune, mouth, tongue, hand or even life that be not smirched and polluted; the man who brought to disgrace the name of Catulus, who consummated the ruin of my house and burned the home of my brother."

Page 500, Note 14: "It is very much to be regretted that so slender details of them have come down to us."

Page 500, Note 15: "One seeks in vain for satisfactory information."

Page 503, Note 18: "Relating to a thiasos which is an assemblage of people for purposes of drinking."

APPENDIX.

Page 503, Note 19: "Polybius recounts in his Histories, (book 20, chapter 6), that these garlands and wreaths were in their finest stage of effusion in Bœtia."

Page 503, Note 20: "The thiasos is not an association for wine and drunkenness."

Page 506, Note 25: "A certain degree of satisfaction and of confidence."

Page 510, Note 37: "Besides these smaller unions devoted exclusively to private objects, there were also boatmen and dealers who had their unions."

Page 511, Note 41: "Both sorts of eranos appear to have been mixed with the thiasotes at a very early time."

Page 513, Note 46: "Nowhere were the religious societies more numerous than at the Piræus."

CHAPTER XXIV.

Page 552 Note 69: "So far as the civil right is concerned, slaves are not considered anything; not so however, the natural right, for in the natural right, all men are equal." Again, Florentine says: "The condition of slavery is provided for by a code of rights for high-born citizens, by which a man may be subjected to an outside owner or master contrary to nature."

Page 553, Note 70: "We come together in our brotherhood and our congregation in order that we may walk and work together as it were in prayers and deeds."

Page 552, Note 76: "So it seems, said he (Socrates), O comrades; in all likelihood we ourselves resemble the great spirit; and in the realm of time, the mortal probation, our life is the same in stature and shape as the immortal divinities, but when once fixed in our seats in the newer form and shape, forget not that then, we are all thiasotes and members of the brotherhood, under Eros, the God of Love."

Page 557, Note 87 "The well-nigh incestuous liason of Antipas and Herodias was then and there accomplished."

Page 569, Note 109: "The harvesting was accomplished in the following manner: In the great estates occupying the larger valleys and level tracts of land, a machine is used having its outer margin full of teeth and this they force through by means of two wheels, and the power of an ox harnessed in thills behind (and pushing the machine). In this way the heads of the grain are torn off and fall into a trough attached to the vehicle. The stalks which are left below the heads thus harvested, they afterwards cut with a sickle." Palladius says: "In the more level parts of Gaul the following apparatus is in use for harvesting, which does away with the labor of man to such an extent that an ox performs the entire task of harvesting. A cart or carriage is constructed furnished with two small wheels. On this carriage is mounted a square box made of planks, with the top larger in size than the bottom. The height of this cart-box is less in front than in rear. Here are fixed many small teeth, curved backwards, not so thickly set but that the grain can get between them, and arranged in such an order that the heads may enter above. Behind this cart are two small tongues or thills, as if the animal were harnessed in a chair. Here the ox is fastened, his head towards the machine, by means of a yoke and chains; and when all is ready, he begins to push the cart forward, into the grain. Thus every head is caught between these teeth and torn from its stalk—which is left standing—and falls into the box. The machine is generally about the height of an ordinary small ox that propels it from behind. Thus by a few bouts and in a very short space of time, the entire harvest is accomplished. This machine is useful in valleys and level fields, and in those places where straw and chaff are necessary for manure."

GREEK INSCRIPTION

CORONATION AT SYMPOSIUM OF A THIASOS,

(FACING AND INCLUDING PAGE 463).

The male and female members of this thiasos crown Sratonice, daughter of Menecrates, who was presiding officer for prophecy and predictions of the eranos, in the one hundred and and seventy-eighth year of its existence; since she was loyal to the great mother Ceres, and to the sun-god, Apollo. An upright tablet of stone is engraved to her honor and ornamented with wreaths and ribbons, and she is further honored by a public proclamation at the meeting in the temple of Jupiter."

INDEX

A

Abolition, Aristotle's day, 541.
Abomination, a certain practice, 538.
Abraham, tried low form of patriarchism, 72; the God of, 562.
Abyss, or crater of the brimstone lake, 248, note 3.
Achæus, compared, 167; chosen by Eunus as his adviser, 209; his character, 210; organizes an army of slaves, 210; beats the Romans often, 214; lieutenant general to Eunus, 217; with Cleon, defeats Hypsæus, 217; mysterous death of, 228.
Achaia, Roman conquest of, 210.
Acknowledgment honorable, 565 and note 106.
Acragus, a state in Sicily 214.
Acrobatic sports (Spartan), 535.
Acropolis, of Athens, 126; of Sunion, 142, note 38.
Actors, unions of comic, 112; at seaport, Misenum, 403, note 6.
Adad, Syrian sun-god, 236.
Adam and Eve, 535.
Admission, of women, freedmen, strangers and slaves to the thiasos and eranos, 169, note 10.
Adrian, withdrew slaves from the old domestic tribunal, 365.
Adoniastes, a divinity, 462.
Adultery, what its equivalents were, 344, and note 28.
Advent, of Jesus, 493.
Ædile, superintendent of public works, 403.
Ægesta or Segesta, a city, 258.
Ægis, protector of labor, 474.
Ælian, what he says of the inhuman slave-holders, 537.
Ænator, buccinator, played the shepherd's horn, 407, 408.
Æon, great period of time 495.
Æschines, orator of low birth, 101; railed at by Demosthenes in consequence, 543.
Affection, strange tenacity of, for the red flag, 468.
Africa, modern slavery of, 68; fame of the ancient mysteries in, 88; comparative numbers in northern parts, 195.
African, slave trade, 286, note 27.
Africans enslaved by the ancient Roman and Greek traders, 195.
Agathodæmoniastes, 462.
Age, of gladiators, 279, note 5:

INDEX.

of ragpickers inscription, 425.
Aged word, "red," 471.
Ager Comensis, 423, 424.
Ager publicus, explained, 285-8; how tilled, 287, 443; inimical inroads upon, 288; usurpation of, 285; further explained, 360 note 4; cultivated by the proletaries, 349; products of, carried to Rome by sea, 440; when seized by the landlords, 438.
Ages, the new, 556.
Agis, an ancient king of Sparta, 115; labor insurrection in the time of, 115; vast murder of Helots by, 116.
Agis, the Fourth, 531.
Agitation, ancient, against the slave institution, 141, note 33.
Agitator, a gladiator, 412; John the Baptist, 557.
Agony, of the crucifixion, 562.
Agriculture, Ceres, its protecting divinity, 469, see Ceres.
Agrarianism, 557; see Gracchus.
Agrarian, trouble, 213; law, 474.
Agricultural, organizations rare, 443; laborers, how treated 526.
Agriculturists, found organized in the isle of Santorin, 456.
Agrigentum, state of, in Sicily, 214; slave owners of, 405.
Agyrium, number of its property owners, 194.
Alaba, river, 253; the battle of, 255; Tryphon's camps, 263.
Alatri, invented the siphon, 571.
Albarius, one who made plaster images, 432.
Alcestis, prayer of, 562, 563.
Alcibiades, 140.
Aleuts, an American tribe, 92.
Alexander, the Great, 117.
Alexandrian, school, the many communes, 506.
All things common, 572.
Alliance, with Crassus in Asia Minor, 241, 242.
Allobroges, an inscription at Vienne, in the country of, 403.
Allegory—agitation by, 557.
Altars, the domestic, 428; massive and awful, 429.
Altruistic system, see co-operative system.
Amalgamated societies for victualing the Roman people, 286.
Amalgamation, the political, of Constantine, 551.
Amanuensis, 435.
Amasis, king of Egypt, 115; his Solon's labor law, 338, note 14.
Amazons, 87, note 12; Theseus and his battle with, 130.
Amber, beads of, 110, note 50.
Ambert, town in Auvergne, 484.
Ambition, of Spartacus, 305; Plato's idea of, 539.
Ambuscade, of Lycurgus, 102; the Spartan, 104; Crixus allured into, 306.
Americans, the aboriginal, 92; working classes, 57; republic, slaves of, 77.
Amphictyonic council, 80; exterminating wars, 81; article of agreement of the brotherhood, 82.
Amphipolis, battle of, 107.
Amphitheatre, butchered at the, 292 note 41, 332; cleaners of, 395; wild beast hunters for, 395 and note 20.
Amphoræ, showing fine workmanship, 446
Amusers, the whole of chapter xvii.; of gentlemen, 291, and note 39.
Anacreon, Plutarch's comparison, 544; dithyrambics of, 454
Anaglyphs that have survived for 2,000 years, 403.
Analogy, of experience between Socrates and Jesus, 553, 560.
Anaxagoras, Aristotle followed the ideas of, 117; wisdom of, 156; laid the foundation, 514.
Ancient competitive system, the

INDEX. 631

ideas of, being dispersed, vii.;
unions spared, 123, note 76;
lowly, their longings to cross
over to the beautiful river, 353.
Ancyle, a city of ancient Sicily,
251 and note 14.
Anecdote, of wild boar, 475.
Anglo-Saxon cult, London the
nucleus, 560.
Anii Forum, 300, note 60.
Animal, form of primitive man,
72; man but a high type, 525,
voracious and cruel, 533.
Animate vs. inanimate tools, 567.
Annihilation, 495.
Anthesteria, spring sports, 505.
Anthropologist, suggestion to, 80.
Antigenes and Python, 219; a
dealer in slaves, 199; owner
of Eunus, 200.
Antioch, prophet of, 199; Eunus assumes the name of, 208;
cradle of the brotherhoods, 512.
Anti-slave organization, 541.
Antipas and Herodias, 557; the
machinations of, 557, note 87.
Antiquaries, question of the red
color submitted to, 492.
Antiquities of the Phœnicians,
496; of Mexico, 564.
Antisthenes the cynic, 544.
Antonius defends Aquillius, 273.
Apamea, birthplace of Eunus,
199; cradle of many brotherhoods, 224, note 89; 512.
Aped the pomp of circumstances,
274 and note 70.
Aphrodiastes, 462.
Apocalyptic church, 512.
Apollo, community of, 462; with
other deities, 468; chosen color of, 471; human form, 487;
Apollo, Ceres, Minerva, 481.
Apology, of Tertullian, 527.
Apollonis is taken by Aristonicus, 237.
Apostasy, the sin of, 524.
Apothetæ, cavernous pit of, 533.

Appian Way, lined with the crucified men of Spartacus, 299.
Appius Claudius got a license to
butcher the plebeians, 277; is
cast into prison, 287, note 32;
mention of, 339, 500, note 12.
Apportionment of land by Lycurgus, 532.
Apprenticeships, 439, note 3.
Apulia, bandits of, 158, revolts
of slaves in, 159,
Aqueducts, constructed under a
plan of socialism, 380, note 19.
Aquillius, kills Athenion, 271,
and notes 61, 62; inscription
of, showing records, 271.
Arabs or Ishmaelites of the Semitic family, 48.
Arbitration, 510, 525; supplanting violence by, 525.
Arcadia, 401.
Archæologist, future work that
awaits him, 451, 501; what
he is accomplishing 496.
Archæology telling of the deeds
of human society, 48.
Archaic children of the *gens* families, 426; genitive of, 471.
Archery, trapping, spearing, 396.
Archilochus and Philemon, 544.
Archipelago, the Greek, 81; the
communes of the, 451, 459.
Architecture among Egyptians,
74; great era of Grecian, 128.
Archives chiseled out, 450; Alexandrian, destroyed, 452.
Archons, 114.
Ardency, from ardea, the red
bird, 478, note 30.
Arenariorum collegia, 411.
Areopagus, the Greek, 129; Cleanthus and his lectures, 546.
Arethusa, Holy Fish, 221, n. 81.
Aristonicus, his rebellion, 100;
uprising at Pergamus, 140, 31,
150; huge mutiny of slaves,
546; Natural son of Eumenes
234; comparison, 351; chap. x.

Aristotle, on immortality, 62; acknowlegment regarding slavery, 71, 96; recognized labor brotherhoods, 74; his philosophy, 116; his idea of the work people, 117; remarkable movement of, 132; his wisdom, 156; classifies the workers, 540; too pagan-bound to see beyond the chains of slavery, 445; one of five remarkable men, 514; described, 518-19; criticism, 525.
Armory, of Spartacus, 375.
Army, of Athenion, how organized, 259; of Spartacus, numbers of, 310, 313; of Spartacus and Crassus campared, 324-5; strength of, at Silarus, 324 sq.
Arno, its fine landscapes, 155.
Arnobius, his doubts regarding immortality, 62, 129, 523.
Aroma for reserved seats of the grandees, 433.
Armoratorium collegium, 393.
Arrangement, of Roman camp, 467, note 5; 471, note 12.
Arrius, Q., in a battle at Mount Garganus beats Crixus, 306-7.
Arrow-makers, 377, note 10.
Art, architechtural, in Egypt 73.
Art and Learning, two females in Lucian's dream, 543.
Artemis Taurica, 215, note 63.
Artes et opificia, 366.
Art and industry not pagan, 572.
Article of agreement, in the amphictyonic league, 82.
Artisans, organization of, 119; all slaves in remote times, according to Aristotle, 541.
Artificers, Plato's opinion, 539.
Arundelian slab, 373, note 5.
Aruspices, divined oracles, 413.
Aryan race, aggressiveness of, 40; struggles with the Semitic, 41; always competitive, 41; original home of, 48, 55; their slave system, 68; religion, 69; they settle permanently in one place, 73; strange beliefs of, 75; not nomadic, 84; two classes of society, 108; an ancient stock, 526-7.
Asconius, testifies that the religious union secretly continued the trade union tactics, 347.
Ashes, the holy, 364, note 19.
Asia Minor, free labor driven out of, by slavery, 156; effect of third Punic war in, 178; the field of labor organization, 496; more relics found there than in Greece, 511.
Asiatic races, 70; workmen, 489.
Aspasia, a beautiful Greek, 125.
Aspidopegeion, a shield factory, 547.
Assassination, in ancient Greece 98; later, of 2,000 men, 107, note 46; of Viriathus, 187; of Clonius by Salvius, 254; by Horatius, of a sister, 475, note 22; of Polemarch by his own slaves, 547.
Assassins, of the Gracchi, 241, note 19.
Assignation houses, 557.
Asshurbanipal, library of, newly unearthed, 460.
Associations, protective, formed by freedmen, 85; for protection and pleasure, 111.
Asylum, of the *Palikoi* Twins, 247, 257; of the castle of Sunion, 143-4 and note 34.
Atabyrius (Jupiter), 450.
Atargatis, the sun-goddess, 236.
Athena, statues of, 101; her image, 430; Greek Minerva, 468.
Athenæus, the Egyptian author, 166; quotes Nymphodorus, Zeno, 168.
Athenian, marine force, 107; defeated by a strike, 138; compared with the Spartans, 139; census, 193; slaves desert, 140.

INDEX.

Athenio Pastor, the farmer-slave who revolted, 262 and note 40.

Athenion, terribly punished in his rebellion, xii.; the under current of news, 140; a poor man, 181; born in Syria, 199; was a Cilician, 258; described, 258, note 29, also 263; in chains, 264; wounded, 266; recovers, 267; still victorious, 269; at last killed, 271, note 61; Saint Paul, 513; influence of, as well as of Drimakos, 517.

Athens, two classes at, 108; toleration of the brotherhoods at, 113; the jugglers, 112; census of, 193; dangerous slaves, 211; numerous communes at, 452; magistrates encouraged the brotherhoods, 455, note 16.

Atrocities, that caused Gracchus to revolt, 193.

Atrophy, benumbing the social organism, 494.

Attalists, members of an eranos, 98, note 27.

Attalus III., deeded his kingdom to the Romans, 232, 233, 512; his crazy tricks, 222, 546.

Attica, rebellion of miners, 100; Ceres worshiped in, 198.

Augury, foreshadowing death of Gracchus, 240; how conveyed and understood, 564.

Augustalis, *domus collegia*, 507.

Augustan unions, 429, note 3.

Augustonemetum, 485.

Augustus, emperor of Rome, 80; mild reign of, 518.

Auletrid, female flute-player, 463.

Auletrides—they were members of the brotherhoods, 455.

Auvergne, red banner at, 481.

Autranius Maximus, cruelty of, to his slave, 141, note 34.

Aurinia, wife of Spartacus, 290 and note 37; what Tacitus says regarding her, 303, note 73;

her prophecy, 305, note 78.

Avella, 300, note 60.

Avenger, of the disaster of Crassus, 243, note 21.

Avenging sacrifice, of Spartacus, 304, note 77.

Awe-inspiring divinities of the Thalian temple, 248, note 3; reverence necessary to ancient leaders of revolts, 274, note 70; striking hues, 479.

Axe, sacrificial, of Triphon, 264, note 43; lictor's instrument of execution, 475.

Axiom, of Aristotle, 561; a conclusion from this research, 509.

Aztecs, gladiatorial feast of the Mexican Xipe, 276; a specimen prayer of the, 564.

Azure, 466.

B

Baal, attributes of, 491.

Babe, Plato when a, 118, note 72.

Babylonians, 401.

Bacchanalia, ill-founded prejudice against, 502; ditties, 454; slander of the, 161; affair of the, 452,

Bacchantes, societies of the, 158, 493.

Bacchic, not the characteristics of the thiasos, 503 note 20.

Bacchus, sons of, 450; protective principle, 469.

Backsliding, 524, 551.·

Bagpipe, age of the, 408.

Bagpipers' union, 408.

Baker, bath attendant and king's fool, of Eunus, 230.

Bakers, 349; six out of eleven of their banners red, 489.

Ballista, or stone-thrower, 378.

Ballot, democracy of the, 525; the ancient, as shown in the inscriptions of Pompeii, 572.

Banausoi technitai, of Aristotle,

INDEX.

541; uncouth and hoyden, 542.
Bancroft, on monumental archæology, xi.; quotation from, 278.
Banderoles (ribbons), 463 & cut.
Banner, makers of the ancient
red, 418, 471; bearer or signifer, 484; color of, note 46.
Banquets, gladiatorial spectacles
at, 277 and note 1.
Baptism, day of, at Eleusis, 91;
it was the form of the bathing
custom of thiasotes, 504, n. 23.
Bastardy, of what it was constituted, 344 note 28.
Batons, with ends pointed for
cooking, 504.
Battering down the walls of Tauromanion, 227.
Battering-ram, 379; described p.
378 & note 12; makers' unions
demolished walls, 488, note 53.
Battle, of Zama, 152; between
slaves and Romans, 157; the
Hill of Venus, 183, sq.; of Drimakos, 171; of Pydna, 186;
of Erisane, 187; of Cleon and
Achæus with Hypsæus, 217;
of Alaba, 254; before Morgantion, 256; of Triocala, 262, 266;
of Scirthæa, 265-6; of Messana, 269; of Macella, 270; of
Silarus, 327, note 128; of Lu-
cæ, 242; of Morgantion, Salvius, 256, note 25; of Scirthæa,
265-6, note 45, of Macella—
Athenion killed, 271, note 61;
first, of Spartacus, 293; Vesuvius, 295, note 51; victories
of Spartacus, 308, note 84; of
Mt. Garganus, 306-7, note 80;
of Picenum, 310, note 92; of
Silarus, 323 sqq. and note 121;
in Epirus, 340, note 17.
Battle-axe, and prætorian bundles, 299, note 58.
Baxea, ancient shoe, 420.
Beasts, wild, for the amphitheatres. 395, note 20.

Beaufort, a hunters' union found
there, 394.
Beautiful, under Plato's meaning
or as he interpreted it, 515.
Beatitudes of the underground
paradise, 563.
Beauty, of the boys emasculated
by slave merchants, 168–69,
note 7; of the red color, mak-
ing it prefered, 470.
Bedstead factory, owned by De-
mosthenes, 548.
Beer halls, rather than churches
welcomed the agitators, 573.
Beggary, ragpickers' unions, 422.
Behavior, criticism of, 535.
Beleaguered, by tramps, 261 and
note 37.
Belles-lettres, of Greece, 128.
Bellowings, the frightful, of the
brimstone lake, 248, note 3.
Berberinis, temple of, 399.
Bethlehem, offering of ignominy
of, 509.
Betrayal, both of Socrates and
Jesus, 514.
Bible, in Greek, 87; Zend and
other oriental records, 526.
Bigotry, and empiricism, 538.
Bird, a new analysis of the red
bird, 478 and note 30.
Birth and standing of Spartacus,
282, note 13, 285, note 22.
Birthday, of the goddess Antinœ,
357; of the patron saint Jo-
seph, 488.
Birthplace, of Athenion, 258; of
Eunus, 512; it was a cradle of
the brotherhoods, 512; of sev-
eral wonderful characters, 513.
Bisellarii, union of the, 431.
Bismarck, 71.
Bithynia, 249, note 5.
Bitter waters, 130, note 96.
Black sea slave traffic, 286,
note 27.
Blasphemy, 250, note 10.
Blattearii, or dyers, 418.

INDEX.   635

Blaze, analysis of, 471.
Blazoned in red, 472.
Blemish, infants with a, 533.
Blessed, kingdom, government of the, 550; the, of Plato's ideal republic, 548.
Blind, cured by visiting the temple of the Twins, 248, note 3.
Blockade, and siege of Tauromanion, 226, note 97.
Blood-making, not blood-letting 472; spilling, what was emblematic of, 472; red banners, 484; red storm signals, 487; blood and lineage, 534.
Bloody uprisings, 493.
Blossius, the labor agitator, 173; in Asia Minor, 239; friend of Gracchus, 222, 240; story of Cicero, 241, note 18; commits suicide, 243.
Blotting the page of history, 536.
Blue and azure, 479.
Board of public works, election of, by plebeians, 474, note 20.
Boatmen's unions, an inscription, 113, note 62; trade union of, 119, 383, note 26, 384; in the provinces, 445, note 2; collegium naviculariorum, 445.
Bocchus, the Moor, 260, note 35.
Boeckh, 112, 161; his analytical works, 343.
Bodies, of mechanics, 360, note 3.
Bodily powers, of Viriathus, 180.
Body, or union, 378.
Boedromion, Greek month embracing September, 87, 130.
Boetia, a state in Greece, 79, n. 32.
Bombardini, Italian jurist, 154.
Bonfire, of Spartacus, 304, note 77.
Book-gluers, 435.
Boot-makers' unions (caligariorum), 380, 421.
Booty, of Spartacus, 300, note 59; of Crassus by recapture, 319 note 118,

Borrowed, and lent, sexual loves in Spartan state 527; Lycurgus, from the Cretans, 572.
Bouillet cited, on red colors, 483.
Bounty, given informants, on slave strikes, 151, note 18.
Bourgeoisie, so called by Saint Simon, 526.
Bows, javelins, arrows, helmets, shields, 397.
Boys, forced to fight at gladiatorial spectacles, 277, note 1.
Boyhood of Viriathus, 180, n. 2.
Branded, all slaves, 196, note 17; and ears pierced, 385, note 30.
Brasidas, a Spartan general, 107.
Brass-workers, 360, note 3.
Bravery, grand exhibits of, 321.
Bread, slaves not allowed to eat the white kind, 135.
Breastwork, of Crassus, 315, the note 109.
Bribe, offered Nerva, 249; bribe taking, 515.
Bridle-makers, 485, note 46.
Brigandage, common in early times, 119; was no crime in ancient days, 121; the origin of Italian, 161; existed in extremely early ages, 280; once very formidable, 511.
Bridges, constructed under the state control, 380, note 19.
Brilliant red hue, 470.
Brimstone lake, 248, note 3, 251, and note 13.
Brioude, unions of, 484.
British soldiers, likened to a flock of red-birds, 479; the signal jack, 487.
Brixia, weavers' and carders' union found at, 417.
Broadsword, 411.
Broil, of Crassus, with the Thracian soldier, 242, note 20.
Broker—gladiator, 412.
Bronterre O'Bryan, on the slave-wars, 274, note 70.

INDEX

Bronze workers, 335. n. 6, 375.
Brothels, a comparison made by Theophrastus, 543.
Brotherhoods, 127, note 87; the ancient, 362, note 11; of the eranoi, 455, note 16, and 458, note 18; they had already lived the revolution, 498, ; the great Eleusinian, 504; frowned upon, 511; of the thiasotes, 524; Christianity modeled, 553.
Brundusium, Spartacus marches to, 320; he again attempts to cross over to Sicily from, 321-2; arrival of Lucullus prevents it, 323, note 121.
Brutal conduct, of the customs collectors, 440.
Brutus, the brothers, 135.
Buccinator, who played the shepherd's horn, 408.
Budæus, 370, note 34.
Buddhism, 460.
Buecher, 136, 138, 157, 177.
Buffoons, 403.
Building, performed by slaves, without pay, 39;–trades under two names, 360, 369, 370, 380.
Bunker Hill, flag of, 492.
Bully, society began with the, 84; the first slaves were his children, 84; the low original bully, 560.
Bulwark, of democratic rule, the reverse of slavery, 542.
Bundles, fasces and axe, 471.
Burden-bearers, 499, note 11.
Burial, the rite refused the slave, 75; this stamped his disgrace, 75, 85; society for, 97; societies for, in Greece, 115, 127; in Rome, 278, 342, 347, 353, gladiatorial, 278, note 3; of Lanuvium, with entire inscription, 353-8; associations, 559.
Business tenets, of the Greek sacred and civil communes, 113, note 63; chrematistikos or business man of Plato and Aristotel, 539.
Butchered, at the amphitheatre, 292, note 41.
Butcher-knife policy, of Eunus, 228.
Butchers—where their unions were located, 388, 490; for a Roman holiday, 307.
Butchery, of rebel slaves, 252, note 15.
By-laws, of the millers and bakers, 445, note 2.
Byzantium, unions at, 113.

C

Cab-drivers, unions of, 383 and note 26.
Cade, Jack, 559.
Cecilius, Calectenus, words of, 165; on the statistics of crucifiixions, 330.
Caepio, causes Viriathus to be murdered, 187; fifth general sent against Viriathus, 187.
Cæruleum, (sagum), 475; the cærulean Zeus, 476, note 24.
Cæsar, 123; suppressed all the unions, 365, note 23, 397; conquest, 439; kills a million, 570.
Caius, confraternities that followed, 462.
Caligarii, soldiers' boot-makers' union, 421.
Caligula, despotism of, xiii.; his cruelty, 280.
Calisthenic games, 535.
Calliades, they were nobles, 95.
Callias, manager of the mines of Laurium, 136, 137.
Callicrates, one of the architects of the Parthenon, 125.
Calumniators, of Diodorus, 220.
Cambalus, a wealthy citizen of Morgantion, 212; death, 212; the story told, 212, note 54
Camps of Servilius and Lucullus

INDEX. 637

262, note 40; 267, note 50.
Canada, organized labor in, 128.
Canaan, 496, 498; numerous communes in, 504; rigorous law against the brotherhoods, 508.
Canaanites, the first among the brotherhoods, 496.
Candidate, for membership, 461.
Cannibalism, 226, note 97.
Cantiopolis, or our Kent, and its trade unions, 487.
Capitalists, 54, wealth.
Capitoline Hill, prison under, 154
Capitolinus, a Roman consul, 145,
Cappadocia, 239; Comana of, 215, note 63; an early post of the brotherhoods, 512.
Captos, mines near, 138.
Capture, of Syracuse, 221.
Capua, description of, 285, 288, 289; amphitheatre at, 289.
Carcer Tullianus, 230.
Carders, their flag, 486.
Caroused, the Spartan boys and girls, 530.
Carpenters, wages paid to, 137, 361 n. 8; unions of, 364; patron saint Joseph, 488; their battering-rams, 488, note 53.
Cart-load of iron money, 531.
Carthage, destruction of, 178; horrible bloodshed, 179.
Carthagenian hostages, join the slave uprising, 152-4; these, and the other Phœnician colonies still have red, 491.
Carvers organized at Athens, 127.
Cassiterides, or tin islands, 483.
Cassius, at Mutina, 307, note 81; defeated by Sparteaus, 313, 314.
Castle, of Sunion, 100.
Castrensiariorùm collegia, 398.
Castus and Gannicus, 319, note 118.
Catacombs, of Paris, 155; those of Rome, 155.
Catana, daughter of Damophilus taken by Hermias, to, 206.
Catastrophe, of Tauromanion, 229; being hemmed in caused the dire disaster, 269.
Categories, of Numa, 335, note 6; of Dionysius of Halicarnassus, 360; of the federations, 368-9; Numa's shoemakers, 380, note 20; of Aristotle, 541.
Cato the Elder, a slave driver, 141, 159, 178; tried to punish Galba, 181.
Catulus, deplored by Cicero, 499, note 12.
Caucasian, an Aryan race, 48.
Caudicarii, (bargers) on the Tiber, belonged to the unions, 440.
Cauldron, of the brimstone lake, 248, note 3.
Cave-dwellers, 42.
Caves, relics found in, 67; men living in, 530.
Celeus, king, 130.
Census, of Corinth, 193; of Athens, 193; of antiquity, slaves, freedmen and children were not counted, 340, note 17; the workers and non-workers so distinct that the former were not counted as human, 348.
Centers, of the early church, 513.
Centonarii, or ragpickers, 422.
Central America, the inscriptions found in, 112, note 57.
Centralization of wealth, upon individuals, at highest stage, 283, note 17.
Cephalion—a savior from, 509,
Cephalonia, Alexander of, 462.
Cephistodus, a brother-in-law to Phocion, 545.
Cercenses (Ludi), 410.
Cerberus, watch-dog of the infernal regions, 90.
Ceres, or Demeter, 77, 87; story of her daughter, Proserpine, 88, 89; represented the cereal

products of farm labor, 90; ridiculed by a slave, 130; temple of, at Enna, 198; she shielded Sicily from famine, 198; was believed to be the mother of the world, 198; revealed herself in dreams to Eunus, 200; temple to her honor, 208; goddess of Sicily, 223; she was related to their great sun-god, Apollo, 463 and plate; goddess of agriculture, 469; she is identical with many other divinities of farms and gardens, 470-1; see Minerva and Apollo, and 488; for further details of, consult chapter iv., Eleusinian Mysteries.

Chained, the father of Spartacus, to a log of wood, 284 and note 20; to mules, 530.

Chair, see bisella, sacerdotal seat, 431; honorary, 360; ivory, 575.

Chaldeans, 459.

Champion colors, 472; boldly marshaling a, 522.

Change, of systems, what was meant by, 496; from human tools to labor-saving machanical tools, 568.

Character, of Spartacus, 305, and note 78.

Characteristics, competitive, not derived from Hebrews, 40; of the Aryan and Semitic families, 48.

Charilaus, Spartan king 531.

Charon, 90.

Chasuble, or the red mummy, 483, note 40.

Chattel slavery extinct, 68; contempt of masters for, 72.

Chaucer and Shakespeare, rescued a language, 569.

Chaudesaigues, its half-red banner, 489.

Cheap deal, of Eunus, 219.

Cheek, smite, 553.

Chemists fortify the arguments, of the new philosophy, 62.

Chians, superstition of the, 169; their vices, 168-9 and note 7; Drimakos, see chapter viii., pp. 163-177; horrible story told by Herodotus, of the vengeance of Hermotius, 168 note 7.

Chicken, entrails of the, for the aruspex, 240; the, which Socrates and his companions owed for, 553.

Children, numbers of, by Pallas Gideon, Apson, Jair, 49; killing of, among the ancients, 53; the first-born son, 69; cannibalism which devoured them at Tauromanion, 226; forced to fight each other with knives, 277; not reckoned, in the census, 340, note 17; enslaved and killed, 525; communism of, 537.

Chiton, and toga, or himation, 478; chlamys, himation, toga, 481; at the feast, 503.

Chlamys, was red, 476, note 24; chiton, toga, 481.

Choice of a trade, Lucian's, 543.

Christianity, its introduction, resisted by the image-makers, vii.; account of, 41, 42, 46; strifes about idol worship, viii.; present movement is building upon it, xi.; modern greed not, xii. 68, 74, 78, 97; first planted among the communes, 341-9; exclusion of the brotherhood from Eleusinian mysteries, 86; era of, based upon absolute equality of all mankind, 337; took up the community principle, 451; why it so readily took root, 512; by whom perverted, 555; true functions of, yet hopefully returning, 519, and 573.

Christmas compared to the Sat

INDEX. 639

urnalia, for relaxation, 502.
Chroniclers, what they left unwritten, 498.
Chronology, of the Sicilian slave war, of Eunus, 214, note 57.
Church, celebrated plant, upon grounds mellowed by the communes, 512; based upon the ancient brotherhoods, 509 and the whole argument contained in chapter xxiv., pp. 520-573.
Cicero, an admirer of Paganism, 87; on the vectigalia, 119; his contempt for the workingmen, 102; spurned and cast obloquy upon the bacchanals, 159; enemy of the plebeians, 284; as a valuable historian, 301, 302; an aristocrat, 345; the mortal foe to the ancient brotherhoods, 345; his tirades against Clodius who befriended them, 499, note 12; his opinions as he expressed them, 540; the lowly despised, 543.
Cimon, riches of, 137, note 16; a mine contractor, 136-7, 140; and Nicias, 146.
Circumvallation, line of, at Rhegium, 318.
Circus, 332, 411.
Citadel, of Sunion taken by slaves, 143, & note 40; of Morgantion in which Comana was besieged, 257, note 27; of Macella, 270.
Cithara, Alexander played, 544.
Cities, did not exist in the earlier ages, 82-85, note 4.
Citizens, of the sun, 244, note 22; what constituted a, 344, note 27; who he was, 496; stock, and what they seized, 498; the three classes of Lycurgus, 526; those of Sparta, 529; in collective goods they were rich, 529; citizens of the sun, 550.
Civilization, outgrew slavery, 71.
Clairvoyant, 413.

Classes, two among the ancients, 96; the distinction defined, 344, note 27; of the working people, 540.
Classic, the old Latin, dead, 569.
Claudius, Appius, 277, 287, see Appius; Marcellus, a Roman consul, 157; another consul at the time of the first gladiatorial spectacle, 277, note 2; Pulcher, who curried favor with the plebeians, 344.
Clazomenæ, silver coin from, 481, note 34.
Clean-washed, and fat, 467, 469,
Cleaners, of the blood in the amphitheatres—a union of, 395.
Cleft, hiding place of the mountain, 230.
Cleon, 62, 167, 196, 413; a Silician brigand, 215; his rebellion in southern Sicily, 216; he defeats, assisted by Achæus, the Roman, Hypsæus, 217; his death, 228.
Clepsydra, 130, note 96.
Cleptius, the bold, 264.
Clerk, to unions, 383, note 26.
Clermont, exquisite red banner of, 485; color of its flag, 485, note 48.
Clients, their relation to the citizen class, 344, note 27.
Cloak, religion as a, 346 note 36; of blue and azure, 475.
Clodian Gamala, the precocious youth, 383, note 26.
Clodius, 161; Glaber, defeat of, by the gladiators, 295; his terror, 295, note 51; law of, 302, note 69; brother-in-law to Lucullus, 322; prevents the enactment of conspiracy laws to suppress the unions, 344; Cicero inveighs against, 345, note 33; intrepid orator and tribune, 363; compared with Blossius and Gracchus, 474; speech

of Cicero against, 499, note 12; in favor with the trade unions, 552.

Clonius, murder of, 253, note 16.

Cloth-fullers' brotherhoods, who worked for the state, 416, n. 5.

Clothes, manner of ancient, 415; of the slaves, 385, note 30.

Clowns, 403, and note 6.

Clubs, soldiers of the defeated Mummius killed with, 315 and note 108; of the eranoi, 508; brutalized with, 530.

Cneus Sentius', inscription, 383, note 26.

Coarse bread, for slaves, 385 and note 30.

Coat of arms, 469.

Coctorum collegium—union of the cooks, 398.

Code, of Lycurgus, 69; of Solon, 127; communal, of self-sustaining rules, 335, note 7; of Theodosius, 373; of the gamblers with methods, 456.

Collective, wealth, 529.

Collectors, of tax, 382; the vectigalia, 437; unions of, at Lyons, 439 and note 3.

College-Gymnasium, of Altona, 247; of ancient collegium of working people in the guise of piety, 357; of Italy, 77; the sancta and their tactics, 362; naviculariorum, 445; they were fond of parading in red, 477; the collegium was a veritable trade union, 341; of the ragpickers (centonariorum), 422; identical with eranos, 506.

Coliseum, reserved seats of the grandees known by the aroma at the, 433.

Colophon, in the labor war, 235.

Colors, what were the true rudimental ones, 470, note 10; tutelary patron of, 490; a charm to season the dry annals, 497; their enumeration, 470.

Colossus, the cryselephantine, of Athena, 431.

Coma, of Pamphylia, 215, note 64; a brother of Cleon, an escaped slave, 215.

Comana, what Valerius Maximus says, 215, note 64; a town in Asia Minor, 215.

Comanus, extraordinary suicide of, 227.

Combats, at wakes, 135 : gladiatorial, 278, note 3; no mockery in the arena, 411.

Combine, for economic purposes, 508.

Come, in Italy, 422.

Comic actors' unions and inscriptions of, very many found, 414 and note 37.

Commerce, under Lycurgus, 69, disallowed, 530.

Common table, abolished by Pyrrhus, 287, note 28; robber, a cognomen for Spartacus, 297; fund, how distributed, 507, and note 27; eating in, 510; table of Sparta, 533.

Commotions, caused by attempts at reform, 69.

Communal, institutions, 68; proprietorship, 69;. government, not mentioned by inscriptions, 73; organizations, at Rome, 335, note 7; culture, what it was, 492; state of Plato, 522.

Communes, formed by freedmen and slaves, 85; the civil and the sacred, 113; the countless, chapter xxi., pp. 444–464; the Greek world ablaze with, 402, of the early christians, at Ferrand in Auvergne 485.

Communism, slavery earlier than, 67; in Sparta, 109; of Piso, 223; of the Roman trade union system, 335, note 7; see also 363; what it was, 458; that of

INDEX. 641

the isle of Crete and Sparta, 567.
Communistic form, the highest attempted, 72; of a social government, 80.
Communists, in Greece, 115; contemplated in an uncharitable light, 463; under what auspices they did or did not work well, 460; ancient tribal kind, 68; their ancient system, 70; participation of both the sexes, 527.
Companies, unions organized in, 302, note 69; arranged in categories of ten, 389, note 1; the companions of the sun, 450.
Comparative palæology, 497.
Comparison of the last battles of Athenion and Spartacus, 271; of commentary on numbers in the army of Spartacus, 325, n. 124; of various plans tried by the great men, 526.
Competition, no conscience in the world of, 64; of capitalists, 396; none among the unions, 442.
Competitive, system, 38, 40; defined, 40-42; struggles to be extricated from the, 41; oldest system known, 42; the idea among the Greeks and Romans 48; prevalent with all the animals, 55-6; world still struggling in it, 61; competitive labor, 68; slavery, 71;—system based in concupiscence, 206; a description, 494; ancient and modern, 496; comparison, 510; more about it, 524; system has nearly always proved itself a failure, 573.
Compulsory, the law of Amasis, 338, note 14; inscriptions, 427; education, 527; marriage, 527, 535.
Concatenation, linking the labor wars, 237.

Conceptions, immaculate, 559.
Conclusions—axioms reached by investigation, 122, 509, 561.
Concupiscence, 74; under Lycurgus, 109; Paganism rested on it, 206; moral impulses, 515; of Rome, 517.
Conde sur Vesgre, (society of), 448.
Condition, of working people in ancient times, lowliness of, 49.
Conference, of slaves about to revolt, 251, note 13.
Conflict, of Triocala, 267.
Confraternities, 461, 502.
Confusion, Diodorus on tramps, 261 and note 37.
Congregation, of the Hebrews, 40; Tertullian on the, 552, and note 70.
Connubial, tie opened free intercourse, 536.
Conquest, the Roman, 480, 499.
Conscience, annihilation of, 59; the origin of ghosts, 61; animals have little, 64; it may be based in cunning, 62; a powerful agent in bringing about good, 66; the foundation of religion, 62; ethical customs and habits built upon it, 61.
Conscription, 302, note 69.
Conspiracy, against Plato's life, 119; laws to curtail liberties, 120; those of Roman Cæsars, 123 and note 76; law of Elizabeth, 126; of slaves to burn Rome, 148; laws to suppress, 283, note 15; laws passed B. C. 58, 346; crucifixion the penalty and punishment, 152.
Constancy, of woman, 303, note 72.
Constantine, customs and habits at the time of, 486, 489; the Great, 521.
Consternation, at Rome, after the victories of Spartacus, 311.

642   INDEX.

Contempt, for the workers fell with the establishment of the new era, 384; of the low-born people, 407; of labor, 544; a specimen shown, 545, also the note 54.
Contour, fine, of the body, 535.
Contractors, at Laurium, 135.
Convent, Pagan temple of the Twins, 247.
Convicts, working in the mines, 138.
Convivialities, ancient, 502.
Convulsion, in nature, 276; that caused by introduction of the new principles, 495.
Cooks, of Eunus, 230 and note 105; unions of, 398; shops—ideas of Theophrastus, 543.
Co-operation, aim of the ancient labor movement, 38; it undermines the incentives to crime, 61; reasons why slaves were partial toward it, 86; its good works, 379; peaceful rather than aggressive, 461; co-operative system defined, 40; its struggles to bring about much wanted changes, 41; used by the Semitic races, 48; the harmonious system, 56, 57; associations of the lords to obtain the benefits which it offers, in protection, 81.
Copied (writings of the ancients), times without number, 436.
Copyists, wages paid to, 137.
Cordonniers, of the Middle Ages, 484.
Corfinium, the union of hunters found at, 393.
Corinth, census of, 193; gulf of, 210; population in B. C. 300, 193; its slavery, 522, note 1.
Corn grits, for slaves and freedmen, 383, note 26.
Cornicularius, an old term for a secretary, 439.

Corporations, of trade unions, 366, note 24; of the Roman empire, 416, note 8.
Corpores, sodalicia and collegia, implied the same meaning as unions, 366 and note 10.
Corsair, for kidnaping, 498.
Cos, inscription at, 462.
Cosseir, mines near, 138.
Cossinus, a man of uncommon judgment, his defeat, 297-8.
Cost, of living, engraved on the Egyptian pyramid, 446, note 4.
Cotton, how used, 415.
Couch, celebrated dining couch, 400; makers, registered by the archæologist Oderic, 433.
Countless myriads of women in the island of Crete, 340 vide note 17.
Cournières, had a nearly totally red banner, 489.
Court, of appeals, 94.
Coward, Spartacus given that epithet by his insubordinate soldiers, 319.
Cradle, of Plato, 118, note 72.
Crafts, of workmen, 430; divinities, of remote antiquity, 492; —manship brutifies the individual, 539.
Crassus, xii.; spoke Greek and its Asiatic dialects, 238, note 12; Publius, his character, 241; L., made consul, 312; loses the battle of Mutina, 313; his tactics, 313; adheres to the Fabian mode of warfare, 321; he becomes the legal commander of the combined armies of Lucullus and Pompey, 323.
Crater, of the brimstone pool of the Twins, 248, note 3.
Credentials, of regular chartered unions, 437.
Cremation, 75, note 19; in ancient times, 71; was the usual form of interment among the

INDEX. 643

freedmen, 75; the working people were too poor to bury, they were obliged to burn their dead, 345.
Crescent moon, wife of the flaming Apollo, 491.
Crete, great schemes, 572; countless myriads of women, 340, note 17.
Crier, for traders and winemen's unions, 383, note 26.
Criminals or malefactors' punishment, 475.
Crispin, the unions first organized by, 483; account of him and of his brother Crispinian, 420, 421.
Criticism, of Lycurgus, 525; of Aristotle, 536.
Crito, scenes of Socrates, 562.
Crixus, actions of, 62; his compatriot, Œnomaus, 289, note 36; elected lieutenants, under Spartacus, 294; death of, 307; retaliation of Spartacus for the fallen hero, 308-9, 332, 406.
Cross, see crucifixion.
Croton, battle of, 320.
Crouching, nude and suffering, 532-3.
Crown, of foliage, 462; of Stratonice, 463 and plate.
Crucible, of a thousand traditions, 523.
Crucifixion, of 8,000 slaves, 222; of the kitchen mates of Eunus, 230; at Enna, 229; of slaves, 252; of the devoted farmers of Aristonicus, 243; after the defeat of Athenion, 271; estimated total number of the laboring people who so perished, 330; in what countries this ignominious punishment was inflicted, 499; a million crucified, 517; invention of, and its origin described, 562.
Crude grape juice, 384.

Cruelty, of the forked gibbet, 141, note 33; of Damophilus, Polias, Megallis, 201, 405; of the Pagan religion, 428; of religion, 482.
Crusades, origin of, 87; the Eleusinian, 87; conflict of classes at the, 95; march to Eleusis, 130.
Cryptia, secret, of Sparta, 537.
Crystalization, of all dark hues, 478.
Cudgeled, by tramps, 261, n. 37.
Cudgels, 292, note 41.
Cult, of Men-Tyrannus, 143, note 39; of Ma, (Artemis Taurica), 215, note 63; a world-wide, 451, secret, in Canaan, 501; of Zeus Labraundos, 509; of Serapis, 509; of the great commune system, emerging, 556.
Cumæ, home of Blossius, 239; a city near Rome, 186.
Cumanian shores, pirates of the, 316, note 111.
Cunning, the weapon of primitive man, 60.
Cup, of bitterness, 233.
Curias, 94.
Curiatii, story of Horatius, 475, note 22.
Curies, the outcasts converted into, 86.
Curiosity-gratifying study of military carpentry, 488, note 53.
Curry, to obtain favors, 475.
Cushioned seats, 433, note 14.
Customs unions, or collectors, 439.
Cutting each others' throats, 277, note 1.
Cybele, the Phrygian goddess, 463; also, 470, 471; image of, 481, note 35; goddess of farming, in Palestine, 503; tenets of, 562.
Cyclones, of retributive justice, 523.
Cyme, in the labor war, 235.

644 INDEX.

Cyril, St., burnt the archives, 452.

D

Dadouchos, the priest and torch-bearer at the Mysteries, 92.
Dæmons, governors during Saturn's reign, 47; afterwards the lares or ghosts, 48; of the wailing wood 248; of Socrates, 560.
Dagger-duels, 291.
Damophilus, his treatment of his slaves, 65; a rich slave owner of Sicily, 196; cruelties of, 197, 200; his wife, Megallis, and their tender-hearted daughter, 204-6, 221; owned 500 slaves, 405; murdered by them, 203-4.
Dances, of the members, 503, note 22; under a species of contumely, 407; among wreaths, red flags and banners, 503; the races and tumbling, 535.
Dandies, the jesting, 403, note 6.
Dangerous slave element, 331.
Dared not march to the city of Rome, 310, note 95,
Dark Ages, by what caused, 494.
Darwin, views man as an animal destitute of an immortal principle, 59; on immortality, 62.
Data, of ages of gladiators given in the inscriptions, 279, note 5.
Date, of the wars of Eunus, 214, note 57.
Daughter, of Damophilus, 201, note 32.
Da Vinci, 544.
Dawn, of manumission, 425.
Day, of the feasts, 484.
Dea Nemesi, 413.
Dead letter, the Licinian law, 222 and note 84; that of the conspiracy laws, 454.
Deal tables of Spartan state, 532.
Death, ancient opinions on, 70; of Viriathus, 187; of Cleon, 228, of Eunus, 230; of Eumenes, 234, note 3; of Attalus III.,
234; of Blossius, 241, note 19, of Gracchus, 241; of Crassus 242; of Aristonicus, 243; of Athenion, 271; of Tryphon—Athenion made king—269 and note 56; of Athenion, note 61 of page 271; of Aquillius, 273; of Spartacus, 327, note 128; death grapple, 374; warrant, 533; of Socrates, 553, 562; of Jesus, 562; of Juvenal, 563.
Debts, of Sparta, 531.
Decay of Rome, date of beginning, according to Polybius, 548.
Deceit, which used religion as a cloak, 346, note 36.
Decelea, strike of silver miners, 134, note 1, and 146; a town in Bœtia, 139; Spartan garrison at, 140.
Declaration, regarding slavery, made by Granier, 529.
Decline, of the Roman honor and virtue, 480 note 33.
Deeded his kingdom to the Romans, 512.
Deeds, of the Spartans, 536.
Deëns, unions of hunters, 395, note 20.
Deep-rooted hatred, 443.
Defeat, of Aristonicus, 242; of Lentulus, 308, note 81; Spartacus, 327-30.
Defense, of Aquillius, 273.
Deification (self), by using political priestcraft, 433.
Deipna apo symboles, old eranos forbidden by council of Laodicia, 511.
Deities, fed by slaves, 75; worshiped through sacrifices, 75; their sacred cult, 510.
Deliverance, of slaves, 249, and note 5.
Delos, the great slave mart, 286, note 27.
Demand, emphatical, of Christ, 553.

INDEX.   645

Dameter, and Eunus, 168; herself, Cybele, Isis and others, for Ceres, 477.
Demiourgoi, workingmen, 539.
Democracy, laws of the, 38; in worship, 51; a Christian basis, 165; the Spartan, 104.
Demon, see dæmon.
Demophon, nursed by Ceres, 88.
Demos Collyte, 509.
Demosthenes, the great orator, 101; oration against Pantætus the mine contractor, 143; he despised men of humble birth, 543; knife factory of, 548.
Den, description of the gambling of competitive life, 456-8.
Dendrophori, 360, 361.
Deorum immortalium, 428.
Depping, 489 and note 54.
Depths unspeakable, 248, note 3.
De Quincey, quoted, 280.
Descent, of the red color as a legacy of the ancient usages, 492.
Descriptiones reliquarum, books of the archæologists, 459.
Deserters, how treated, 70; escaped from slave owners, 258, note 29.
Desperadoes, the maratime, 330.
Desperation, of the slave soldiers of Tryphon and of Athenion, 265; of the fight of Athenion, 266; of the slaves, 306 and note 80; of Spartacus, at the last battle, 326-7 and the notes 128, 131, 132.
Despised humanity, in formidable misery, 423.
Despotism, military, of Nero and of the Cæsars, xiii.
Destinies, of peoples, 524.
Destroyed by lice, 230 and note 105.
Destruction, work of the soldiers, 229; was the basis of the plan of Eunus, 549; of Jerusalem,

1,100,000 persons massacred, according to Josephus, 566.
Deterioration, of mind by labor, 542.
Devastation, of Sicily by tramps, 261 and note 37.
an element of the plan of Eunus, 549.
Development, theory of, 55; of the growth of the soul, 59; theory, of believers in an immortal life, 59, 63, 64, 72.
Devices invented and constructed by the unionists, for weapons, 396; of banners, 489.
Deviltry, deeds of, by tramps as reported by Diodorus, 261, in note 37.
Dialecticians, moral impulses of three, 514, 515.
Dictionnaire Universel, quoting Maury, 92 and note 18; used further on Spartacus, 326.
Differentiation, of gladiatorial functions, 278, note 3; which made nations out of isolated families, 281; of worship, from Minerva to Jesus, 490; the creeping, 525.
Difficulties, in the way of the historian of labor, 500.
Dinner, gladiatorial combats at, 277, and note 1.
Dining room, 399.
Dinotherium and trilobite, 450.
Diocletian, empires of, 79; his persecution of the early Christians, 483; planted poisons in his garden, 547.
Diodorus, 138, 180; lost chapters of, 165; quotation from, 206; mutilated scraps of, 211; veracity of, 220; on the temple of the Twins, 248, note 3.
Dion, his conquest of Syracuse, 77; a friend of Plato, 119; Cassius, lost books of, 165.
Dionysia, what they were, 502;

of four sorts, at Athens, 505.
Dionysiates Chæremoniens, a sacred divinity, 462.
Dionysian skilled workmen, 503, and the notes.
Dionysius, of Halicarnassus, 47, 114, the tyrant of Syracuse, 77; spurned Plato, 118; he engaged the caudicarii to put him out of the way, 119; dug the cavern prisons of Syracuse, 208; built the prison workshops, 549.
Dionysoi, societies of the, 158.
Dionysus, a god—protective essence presiding over skilled labor, 468; god of the mechanics, 488.
Dirksen, on the hetairæ and sodalicia, 115; on the Twelve Tables—says the Roman trade unions were communists, 335, note 7.
Disaster, of Demosthenes (the Athenian general), 134, note 1; unchronicled, of Piso, 225; entailed in the law of Lycurgus, 527; under Spartacus, 556.
Disbelief, good cause for, 565.
Disciples, of Socrates and Jesus, 514.
Discipline, of Crassus, 315, note 108.
Discovery, of the first slaves, 49, note 4.
Discrepancy, in Plato's republic, 536.
Discussion, among the lowly, 129; caused the formation of a public opinion, 236.
Disdain, of Spartacus, 312, note 101, and 323, note 121.
Disgusted with wars, 499, note 9.
Disinherited classes, 458.
Dismal, the fear, regarding Eunus, 218.
Dispensation, of Lycurgus, 533
Distaste, of Florus, 268.

Distemper, spoken of, by Pliny, 79, note 33.
Distinction, the basis of Plato's slave state, 522.
Divers, a fishermen's union of the Tiber, 389, note 1; searching for pearls, 435.
Divine right, theory of, 531.
Divinities, of the brimstone pool, 248, note 3; of love, of Socrates, 458, note 18; of a yielding race, 480.
Divisions, of the trades and professions, 336 and note 10.
Dog-day winds, 130, note 96.
Dodge, for the credulous, 475.
Dogmas, and inquisitorial intolerance, 495.
Dome, the vaulted, of heaven, 236.
Domestic establishment, of the Cæsars, 429, note 3.
Domus Augustalis, 507.
Doom, of liberty, 233; of Spartacus, 324; as a consequence of the law of Lycurgus, 526.
Dorians, killed their imperfect children, 53 and note 18; they were the Spartan stock, 531.
Downfall, of Rome begun by Eunus and Gracchus, 222; of the Spartan system, 537.
Drama, religious, of the mysteries, 92, note 18.
Drawn by lot, 315 and n. 108.
Dream of Lucian, 543.
Dregs, of the city, 302, notes 67, 69; of the city of Rome, quoting from Asconius, 363, note 15.
Drimakos, strike of, did not turn out disastrous to his cause, xii.; his prolonged resistance, 164, note 3; bloody wars of, 166; regarded as a savior, by his friends, 168; his speech, 172; the young friend of, 174; reward offered for his head, 175,

INDEX. 647

his death, 176; Chians render homage to his ghost, 177; influence felt, after his decease, 517.
Drinking festivals, called anthesteria, 505; beer halls wherein was first planted the modern movement of labor, 573.
Droysen, Hellenismus, 503 and note 19.
Drudgery of the Helots, 537.
Drudges, 499, note 11.
Druids, their colors, 482 sqq.
Drumann, the author, 141 and elsewhere much referred to.
Drunkenness, not a habit of the thiasos, 503, note 20.
Duel, fought between Athenion and Aquillius, 270, 271.
Dungeons, of the Sicilian quarry prisons, 231; opened by Eunus, 219; more about, 523.
Duration, of wars of Viriathus, 182, note 6; of the great slave war, 195; comparison of time with progress, 525.
Dutchobers, 464.
Dyers, of the woollen and linen cloth, 418, note 40.
Dyes, how made, 483.

E

Eagle, the race of the, 563, 564.
Early Christians, what they were struggling for, 497; their organization, 552, 553.
Earth-born multitudes, 79, and note 32, 530.
Earthquake, at Sparta, 107, n. 49 & 164, note 2; of Vesuvius, 416.
Ebb and flow, of the brimstone lake, 248, note 3.
Eburarii, ivory workers, inscription of, 431, 432.
Economic unions, proof of, 511.
Eden, garden of, 535.
Edict, of Lycurgus, 531.

Editio princeps of Vellejus Paterculus, 325, note 124.
Education, under Lycurgus, 69, note 8; Plato's view of, 539; Plutarch on, 545.
Egoism, 479; originated sainthood and notions of religion and of immortality, 85.
Egyptians, superstition of, 45; their gold mines, 138-40; enslavement of the Hebrews, 39, 40; form of their government, 73; food of their slaves, 79.
Elaphebolion, 505.
Election, of Aquilius and Marius, 270; of Licinius Crassus, 312; of officers hindered five years, 474, note 20.
Elephants, used by the Romans against Viriathus, 186, note 14.
Eleusinian mysteries, 86; their too absurd exclusiveness, 88; origin of, 88, 89, 90; grievance against, 94; a popular resentment, 97; the sting of insult, 99; peculiar games, 93; access to membership, 114 the; cause of dissatisfaction, 121; interwoven with the ancient labor troubles, 198; humiliating exclusion from, 351; a brotherhood 504.
Eleusis, a town in Attica, near Athens, 87; scenes at, 89; the crusade to, 95; ancient city of the Pelasgians, 130; its orgies not those of proletaries, 505.
Elizabeth, queen, 126.
Eloquence, of Plato, 118, note 72; of Gracchus, 239.
Elves, and urchins at the brimstone lake, 247.
Emancipation, the movement of, 68; by running away, 70; the cause of Christianity a proclamation of, 78; no mention of, in the Iliad, 80; movement of, 164; note 2; the agitation for,

raging over the world, 241; of labor, 494.
Emancipator, of Spain, 182.
Emblems, of the mysteries, 87, 88; talismans, mementos and charms, 435; of Ceres were red; 469; of Pomona, a flaming red, 477.
Emergence, of the culture of the great commune system, 556.
Empedocles, 518.
Emperor, considered as the government, 419.
Employment, of the unions by the state direct, 376; through Plato's two-fold method, 538.
Emulation, Aristotle's plan based upon, 542; useful, 535.
Enfranchisement, the treachery in, 107, note 46.
Engine of war, 378.
Engineering skill, 378.
England, oligarchy of landlords, in, 496.
Engravers and carvers' federation (cælatores), 367-8; a union of die-sinkers, 368, note 28.
Engyon, slaves broke chains at, 251.
Enjoyment, system of, 455 with note 16.
Enlightenment, it repudiates unfairness, 515, 516.
Enna, number of the laboring class massacred at, xii.; a city built upon a height, in Sicily, 88; the plateau of, 149, 195; labor organized at, 198; temple in honor of Ceres at, 198; the scene of a horribly bloody murder, 202; captured by the slaves of the resident owners, 203-4; attempted recapture by Piso, 224; his protracted siege of, 224; at last taken by Rupillius. Crucifixion and extermination of the inhabitants, 228-30.

Ensign, of the saddle and bridle makers, 485; the popular one was red, 492.
Entail, law of, 69; entailment upon primogeniture, 558.
Enumeration, see census; of the unions allowed to combine, 127 note 87; of the unions of Numa, 336, note 10; of trade unions of Constantine, 369.
Environments, Plato entangled in his, 444.
Epaphrodite, 462.
Ephesus and inhabitants in the labor war, 235; theatre at, 401; it, and Hieropolis were strongholds of the brotherhoods, 512.
Ephori, the despots of Sparta, 103; their trained assassins, 104; under-dealing tyrants of the state, 531-2.
Epidamnus, no workmen except slaves, 99, note 29, 498, note 3.
Epidemics, among the ancient slaves, 79, of strikes, 146.
Epigraph, one near Nazareth deciphered, 503.
Epimelites, a manager or trustee in a Greek brotherhood, 453.
Epirus, destruction of life and property in, 179; Paulus Æmilius by order of Rome, enslaved 150,000 of the inhabitants, 186.
Epistle, of Saint Peter dated at Cappadocia 512.
Epitaph, of wine-smokers, 383, note 24; of the president of a bagpipers' union, 408-9; of the man who died while yet a youth, 383, note 26; of gladiators killed in combat showing their ages, 279, note 5.
Epitomies, of Livy, 269.
Epoch-making period, 552.
Equality, social, a law of Moses, 40; Christian temple of, 66;

how indoctrinated, 68; perfect at the temple of the Twins, 248, note 3; of birth, 443; of the rights of man, 552, with note 69.
Equites, or knights on horseback, 477.
Era-making period, 523.
Eranos, of Greece, 77; together with its thiasos existed in great numbers in Asia Minor, 236; a term unmistakable in meaning, 448; took the name and inspiration of particular divinities, 462; festivals of thiasos and, 464; analysis of both of them, 502, 3, 4 and notes; of it, and essene, the same word, 504, note 23; eranos and thiasos one and the same association, 511, note 41.
Erebus, descends to Hades, 89; and the dark river, 90.
Erechtheis, priestess-assistant to Orpheus in the initiations, 92.
Erecthian spring, 130, note 96.
Ergastula, the Greek ergasteria, prisons, mostly underground, 139, note 28; how used in Sicily, 209; further account, 219 the Greek and Latin distinctions in Sicily, 251; how applied in Italy to gladiators, see prisons, also cf. chapter xii., on Spartacus; copied from Dionysius into every city, 549; a serious thing, 274, note 70.
Ergastularius, convict condemned to fight in the amphitheatres, 406; a kind of gladiator, 412; something like the ergastulus, ergastuli, gladiators changed to freemen, 297.
Erisane, siege of the town of, 187.
Eros, Socrates on the god of love, 253 and note 76.
Escape, of Spartacus, 290, note 37; of the people from Morgantion, 256, of Athenion, 259.
Esculapia, 462.
Escutcheons, monograms etc., 459; in red, 483, note 40; on some of them are found gules in Great Britain, 486.
Essence, the sacred, of the brimstone lake, 248, note 3.
Essenes, and the Orgeons, 493; conjectures regarding the, 501; proved to be identical with the thiasotes, 504, note 23, their prophecies, 558.
Estate, the paternal, it was made criminal for the slave to leave it, 69.
Ethics, based upon conscience, 61; a history of, 97.
Ethnologist, and paleontologist, future duties of, 459; student of ethnology, 500.
Etruria, strike of the laborers in, 155; in the hands of the masters, 156; Roman standing armies in, 211.
Etruscan, soothsayer, Olenus Calenus, 154, note 27; people the first who introduced gladiatorial fights, 278 n. 3; a hard-working and faithful race, 431; trinket manufacture, 435.
Etruscum Fretum, 268.
Etymology, of red flag, 485.
Etymon, of essenes, is eranos, 504, note 23.
Eumenes, and Nusa, 234, note 3.
Eunuch, revenge of, 168-9, and note 7.
Eunus, ten years war of, viii; punishment for the rebellions, xii.; deeds of, 62; enormous servile war, 89, note 13; an account given, 140-166; Syrian slave-king, 195; how elected, 208; the cause of the insurrection related, 198; was both a magician and messiah, also a prophet, 199; meeting of him-

self and his followers, 202; a popular choice for leader, 207; turns 60,000 prisoners loose, 209; great victories enlarge his territory, 214; joins with the revolter Cleon, 216; their union creates an immense army of slaves, 217; his supernatural powers, 219; various successes and eventual reverses, 220-31; hope lost, 229; perishes in the filth of a Roman prison, of the lousy sickness, 230 and note 105; interesting history, 405; his plan that of extermination, 548-9; plan of followed by Aristonicus, 550; Ceres as his goddess, see entire chapter ix. and 562.

Euripides, language of, in prayer, 563.

Europe, working classes of 57.

Euristheneid line of the Spartan kings, 101; Lycurgus of that stock, 531.

Eusebius, on dates, 247, note 1.

Eve, the temptation of 89.

Evolution, phenomena of, 69; law of, 73.

Examination, of infants, 533.

Excerpts, Peiresc quoted, 247, note 1.

Executioner, same as the Roman lictor, 475, and note 22.

Exercise, the gymnastic, 534-5.

Exiguous star, 490.

Exile, Paperna dies in, 243, and note 41; of Juvenal, 563.

Experiment, trial by, 525.

Extermination, plan of Eunus, 219; of 20,000 workingmen, 271; it was the plan of slaves, 549,; extinction and, the central idea of the great slave-king, 548.

Eye for eye and tooth for tooth, 514; what Plato wanted, 518; sermon on the mount, 549.

F

Fabius, Q. deprived of command, 226.

Fabretti, 364.

Fagots, used in escaping blockade of Crassus, 318.

Failure, of ancient governments, 496; of the Spartans, 531; of the great plans, 573.

Faith, importance of a, 499 and note 12.

False translation, of Vellejus Paterculus, 325, note 124.

Falsehoods regarding bacchantes and bacchanals, 493.

Family, great numbers of them, 49; size of a patrician's 69; a term substituted for "union" from the time of Augusta, 429, note 3; the word property conveys the true meaning of, 281, note 11; under the competitive system its members will sometimes destroy each other, 494; the Pagan, 497.

Fanatic, Eunus, 217, note 67.

Fanaticizing his Syrians, 236, note 8.

Farmer, sons of a rich, 49; and shepherd, called by Livy the bacchanalian creature, 160 note 38; sufferings of the, 179; or shepherd, Viriathus, 180, note 4; of Asia Minor as a people, 233; chained in prisons, 251, note 11; as a slave, 240; Athenion, first mentioned, 258; organized to cultivate the ager publicus, 286; lupercalian orgies, a vile comparison made by Cicero, 344, note 30; an inscription of a farmers' organization translated, 453, 454; at the Dionysian sports, 505; how looked upon by Lycurgus, 526; he is Aristotle's soldier, 541, 542; inventor of the an-

cient reaper, 569, note 109; as a free and organized agriculturist in Etruria, 156.
Fasces, bundles, 471.
Father, worshiped as a god after death, 49.
Fatherland, of Eunus, 220.
Fawning language of the unions, 423, note 32.
Fear, of slave insurrections, 141, note 33; all-prevailing, of being murdered, 164, note 2; superstitions, of the victorious slaves, 224; of Romans, 355.
Feasters, applause of the, at the gladiatorial spectacles, 277, note 1.
Federations of trades, 375, 377; in politics at Pompeii, 391; all over the land at the time of Christ, 392.
Fenestella, lost works of, 165.
Ferocious necessity, 219.
Festival, in honor of Ceres, 87; days of the, 488.
Fetichs, 659.
Fighting school, 289 and notes 36 and 37.
Fines, 356, 357, 358.
Fire, the sacred, 51; and murder 300, note 60; spitting, of Eunus described, 217 and note 67; brands of torture, 229.
Firemen, unions of, 447, note 5.
First, Sicilian servile war, 224, note 94; born son, right of the, 497; born—his allotments by paganism, 571.
Fish, the Holy, of Diodorus, the Arethusa, 221, note 81; fish, venison and mutton, the aristocratic food, 386.
Fishermen's unions, inscription of, 113, note 62; their organization, 119; combined with a divers' union, 389, note 1.
Fittest, survival of the, 56; this theory of the survival creates a new philosophy in reason, 57.
Five years' magistrate, 389, note 1; years' interregnum at Rome 474, note 20; men, who they were, 514.
Flag, of theatrical company, 403, note 6; the ancient red, 418; origin of the word, 465; it was excused by a law of Theodosius, 484; bearers, 484, notes 43 and 44.
Flagitium, a derivitive from flag, 471.
Flame, flamma, 471; of fire, 487 and note 51.
Flamen Pomonalis, 478.
Flaming red canvass, 485.
Flamingo, 478.
Flaminica, 478.
Flogged once a day, 103.
Florentine, on the natural rights of man, 552, note 69.
Florus, quotation from as to the battle of Silarus, 324; also elsewhere much quoted.
Flower of the Roman army, 249 and note 7; use of, at funeral ceremony, 378, note 14.
Flute, drum and wild tumult, 244 and note 23; player, Salvius the slave-king, 254, note 20, 255; players, the famous, 458; another mentioned, 463; inscription showing ancient playing, 503, 504; player at court of Eumenes, 545; players of the Romans and Greeks, 409, 410.
Foaming, waters of the brimstone lake, 248, note 3.
Focus, part of Roman and Greek dwelling, 54, note 21.
Food, poor quality of, for slaves, 78; corn-grits union for feeding freedmen and slaves, 383, note 26; 385, note 30; of slave 386; of working people, 529, 530; and clothing, 530.

652   INDEX.

Foothold, of the brotherhoods, 512.
Forbidden, warfare, by the plan of Numa, 335; later, by the plan of Jesus, 553.
Forefathers, our genuine, 101, 525.
Foremen, of the masons, at Jerusalem, 373, note 2; of the ancient government cloth factories, called gynæciarii, 419.
Forests Pomona in the, 477.
Forfeiture, case of a union, 378, note 14.
Forger of the armor for slaves in rebellion, 297, note 53; union of, 442, note 10; of swords and javelins, 375, note 8.
Forgiveness, 525.
Forked gibbet, 141, note 31.
Form of government advocated by the Messiah, 496,
Fortifications, of Triocala, 264; of Rhegium, 318.
Fortitude, story by Valerius Maximus, of Crassus, 242, note 20, of Christ in the hour of trial, 562.
Fortune, teller, Olenus Calenus, 154, note 27; tellers in Rome, 208; teller, Athenion as a, 259; teller, Aurinia as a, 290, note 37; telling and witchcraft, 414; Nemesis, the goddess of, 413.
Forum Boarium, where was enacted the first gladiatorial tragedy, 277 and note 1.
Foucart, denies the statements of Wescher, 506; erroneously imagines the communes to have had no other object than religion, 507; expert epigraphist, 508.
Foundation, of paganism was the competitive systems 497.
Fragments, of 1st books in illegible form, 271, note 64; of Sallust quoted, 306, 308, note 84.

France, organized labor in, 128.
Frankincense, offerings of, 357.
Fratry, consolidated into a state, 100. See phratry.
Fratricide, the mutual, 273.
Free masons, antiquity of the order, 124; John the Baptist one of them, 557.
Freebooter, Gaddæus of the Nebrode, 252; negotiated with, by Spartacus to land his army in Sicily, 317.
Freedmen, 39, 47, 70; of Aristotle's time, 71; cremated, 75; not mentioned in the Iliad, 80; a class at Athens, 113; arose out of slavery, 173; numbers of, in Athens, 193 organizations of, in Greece, Syria etc., 197; compelled to beg in Sicily, 213; raved in great and murderous revolt, 261, note 37; of Asia Minor, 233; Thracian, in Pergamenian labor war 235. as tramps in rebellion, 261; in Rome, as members of the unions generally, 333; their enfranchisement a blow to paganism, 522; working without clothing, 530; ring cleaners, 396
Freedom, desire of Spartacus, 551
Freres cordonniers, 421.
Friendly societies of antiquity, 447.
Fringe-makers, (the limbolarii), 422; in gold, 486.
Fruit purveyors, 392.
Fruiterers' union, 383, note 26, also 393.
Fullers, unions of, 415; worked for the state, 416, note 5.
Fulvius Flaccus, second general sent against Eunus, 218.
Funck Brentano, 363, note 14.
Funeral, ancient, 75; origin of gladiatorial combats, and why, 278, note 3; 378.
Furius and Cossinus, defeat of.

by the forces of Spartacus, 297.
Furniture, of a thiasos, 98, note 27; of the mighty immortals, 432.
Furrows made with thongs, 472.
Fustel, de Coulanges, 68, 75, 82; proves the statement of Granier, 83; other proof by, 111, on origin of the plebs, 343.

G

Gaddæus, treachery of, 252.
Gades, the strait of, 183.
Gaius, who wrote the original of the Justinian law, 100; was of opinion that the Roman xii Tables were a translation from the Greek, 127, 346; Digest from, 112; Orbius, the owner of Xanthos, 143 and note 39; Plautius, sent to Spain, 185; the jurist, discriminates on the rights of organization, 445.
Galba, his treachery in Spain, 180; accused by Cato, 181 and note 5; the trial and cause of acquital, 181; greedy objects, in Spain, 181; departure for Rome, 182.
Galerius, emperor of Rome, 79.
Gallantry, of Athenion, 266.
Gambling, the ancient system described, 456-7.
Games, the Eleusinian, 93; of the Spartans, both sexes were engaged in, 530.
Gannicus and Castus, 319, n. 118.
Garganus, Mount, battle of, 306, 307.
Garlands and wreaths—where they flourished, 503, note 19.
Gauls their ancient reaper, 569.
Gellius, beats the lieutenant Œnomaus, in battle, 306.
Gens, ancient lands belonged to, 348; aristocracy of paganism, 525; families, their fierceness, 527; Aristotle's eighth class, 540.
Gentiles, and proletaries, a civil duel between the, 345.
Germany, 43, 71, 303; organizations of labor in, 128.
Ghosts, origin of, and beliefs in, 53; conscience the originator of, 61; ghost of the dead lieutenant, Crixus, 304, note 77.
Giant, Spartacus, the prophetic, 294.
Gibbet, the forked, on which to crucify slaves, 141, note 33; of Stratonicæ, 244; and thongs of Lucullius, 264; a description of its invention as a means of torture, 562.
Girdlers, Cicero's term of contempt for shoemakers, 380, note 20.
Gladiatorial, scene with Satyros, 272; games, their cruelty, 276; origin in the funeral, 577, note 3; ad gladium and ad ludum, explanation made, 291; business, its growth, 332.
Gladiators, bloody pairing of, 277, note 1; ascertained age of, 279, note 5; fighting wild beasts in the amphitheatres, 395; enumeration of the different kinds, 412; Spartacus, as a, pitted against his fellow men, 518.
Gladium, ad, kind of fight, 406.
Gluers (glutinatores), 435, 436; bookbinders, not found organized, 435.
Gluttons, that devoured the Holy Fish, 221, note 81.
Goblins, that haunted the asylum of the Twins, 248.
God, that slept under the hearth of the heir, 69; of nature, 85; of love, 457, note 18; of Abraham, and universal Father, 560;
Gold, mines of Egypt, 138-142.

654　*INDEX.*

melters poured gold down the throat of Aquillius, 273; and silver forbidden by Spartacus, 300 and note 59; border, 485; golden chain, 110, note 50; "Age" 122; Age, of prosperity; and happiness, 376; era, of a high stage of plentitude, purveying for the Roman state, 381; age, at Rome covering a long vista, 438.

Gorgias, quoted, 538.

Government, social, it did not exist, 38; a legendary but extremely improbable social form during the reign of Saturn, 47 and note 1; animal form of, 73; earliest known plan of, 82; public servants, or slaves belonging to the state did the work of, 113; the ancients employed and patronized unions of labor, 381 and note; slaves shown in note 26 by inscriptions; employ, by law of the Twelve Tables, 381, note 21; state workshops, the fullers, 416, notes 5, 8; ownership of mills, 417; system that of government, 442; ideals of, cursorily sketched, 495; form of, adopted by Lycurgus, 536.

Gracchus, as described by Appian, 222, note 84; struggles of, 222; desperate resistance against, 333; his proposal to distribute the will of Attalus among the needy of Rome, 233-4; furious dissentions at his time, to break up the unions, 283; his friend Blossius, 239, 474; his noble speech, 500.

Greased pole, merriment at the Dionysian sports, 505.

Great Spirit—speech of Socrates, 553, note 76.

Granary, of the world, 258; torn into by tramps, 261, note 37; of Italy, Spartacus in the, 304.

Granier, 79, 83, 111; quotation from, 115; for thirty years is talked down, 506.

Granite-cutters, 368.

Greece, ancient, prevailing scene in, 54; incidental mention, 69, 73; slaves of, multiplied within their own rank, 77; manner of food for the slaves of, 79; the twelve tribes of the Amphictyonic council, 81; prehistoric assassination of slaves, 97; a majority of the people were of the laboring class, 108; the true golden Age of prosperity of, lasted about four hundred years, 123; disastrous strikes of, varied in character from these of modern days, 133; oppressive conditions in, 138; fear of slave rebellions, 141, note 33, 164, note 2, 224.

Greeks, were of Aryan stock and used the competitive idea, but Hebrews and other Semitic races used the co-operative, 48; early recognized private property, and no patriarchism found—de Laveleye refuted, 68 and note 5; and their organized trades, 98, 99, 106; their clerks enjoyed protective unions but they also had their grievance, 111; language was spoken in Sicily, Lower Italy the Archipelago and Asia Minor, 198; great and mighty men before the Roman conquest, 210; much in chapters xxiii. and xxiv.

Grievances, of working people at Athens, 131; of the strikers or revolters, 134.

Grinders, with morters, 446.

Groves, meetings held at, 450; see Pomona.

Gruter, an archæologist of great

INDEX. 655

patience and erudition, 342.
Guardian, of mechanics, 470; of labor, 487.
Guests, invited to banquets with gladiatorial spectacles, 277 and note 1.
Gueules, in France, was the red color, 481.
Guicus, river of Pergamus, 149;
Guilds, the mediæval, 481.
Gules, in England and gueules in France, 481, 483; on English escutcheons, 486.
Gulf, of Symi—the inscriptions around it, 462.
Gulping up dishonorable winnings, 543.
Gunpowder, not in use, 396.
Gymnastics, took the place of industrial exercise, 496, 535.
Gynæciarii, overseers of the government cloth factories, 419.
Gypsies, theory on the origin of, 426, 427.

H

Habit, tenacity and phenomena of, 483 ; power of, 489.
Had all things common, 556.
Hagi Constantios, slab discovered there by Vlastos, 91.
Hair cropped and body dirty, 534.
Hamilton, archæologist, 462.
Hammerers, their organizations, 399.
Hand-looms, 417.
Handicraftsmen, Greek unions of, 127, note 88.
Hangman, same thing as lictor, 475, note 22.
Hannibal & Napoleon compared with Spartacus, viii.; & Scipio, 152, 178.
Harmodius and Iphicrates, 546.
Harvester, of the ancient Gauls, 569, note 109.
Hatters and glaziers of Montaigut and St. Flour, 490.
Head-quarters of ancient slave traffic, 286, note 27.
Headlong, down the rocks, 252.
Healers, 558.
Heaven on earth, 493 ; born, 530.
Hebrew, different from other nationalities, 39; slavery partly abolished, 39 ; originator of socialism, 39 ; fights only when attacked, 40 ; the only ancient with but one deity, 45 ; fixed customs of, 46; his excellent qualities not appreciated, 73; secret association always characterized the race, 508; willing to accept any truth of sociology, even a recognition of his celebrated kinsman, 566–7;
Heer, Prof; Oswald, 72.
Heights, of Enna stormed by Piso, 224; of Engyon, 251 ; of the Mount Taygetus, 533.
Heinesius, quoted 325, note 124.
Heliopolis, why so called, 236, note 9.
Heliopolitai, the workmen-Sun-worshipers, 236; farmer warriors of Aristonicus, 550.
Heliotry, the ancient, 45, note 11.
Hell, paved with infants' bones, 533.
Hellenic peninsula, organizations of, 511.
Helots, war with, 98; great and first known massacre of, 97; as to their numbers, 102 ; how murdered by nobles' sons, 105; their systematic assassination, 107, note 46; laboring stock of Lacedæmon, 106, 528 ; a pen picture of their hideous misery, 107–8 and notes; their descent, 587.
Heracleia, Minoa, slave rebellion at, 254 ; and Trœzen, —soters or saviors from, 509; museum named from, 423.

INDEX.

Heraclitus, who subdued Greek slave strike, 144, note 41.
Heraldic symbols, 483.
Herbita, numbers of property owners in, 194.
Herculaneum, museum, 423.
Hermes, the Pelasgic, 87.
Hermias, a slave of Enna—kills Damophilus, 204; escorts the kind-hearted daughter to place of safety, 201, note 32, 206.
Heres in Argos, 544.
Hermotius the eunuch, the revenge of, 168-9, note 7.
Herodias the beautiful but silly, 557; and Antipas, id., note 87.
Heroic professions, not belonging to workers, 381.
Herodotus, 79, 101; his rank as a historian, 168.
Heroism, mutual suicide of Satyros and companions, 273; of Spartacus and his men at their trying hour, 326.
Heroistes, 462, 509.
Heron, the ancient sacred redbird, 478, notes and 479.
Heroön (temple), to Drimakos, built by the Chians, 176-7.
Hesiod, Greek poet, 79; quoted, 82; was the first known labor agitator and writer, 161.
Hetairæ or hetæræ, same as the sodales, 127, note 87.
Hideous forest, of the brimstone lake, 247.
Hierarchy, of masons, 373, and note 2.
Hieroglyphics, 67, 73.
Hierokeryx, a priest, 453.
Hieropoios, manager of religious rites, 453.
Highlanders' bagpipe, 408.
Hill of Venus, the battle of, 183.
Himation and chiton, 473, 476; with chlamys, toga, 481.
Hipparch, Pisistratides the, 546.
Hippodrome, chariot-running, foot-racing etc. 408.
Hiram, architect of Solomon's temple, 123-5; chief of trade union, 124; another, king of Tyre, 125, note 81; the architect, skilled in building crafts, 373.
Historian, seldom mentions the efforts at reform, 69, 71; his praise of royal lineage, 531.
History, students of, divided into three classes, 37; of labor begins with manumissions, 67; the great ones copied, times without number, 436; from a sociologic standpoint, 541,
Histrionic entertainments, 220; tablet found at Præneste, 403; unions, 402, 403, notes 1, 6.
Hive, of trade unions—all antiquity, 444; of labor, 490; of free labor organizations, Nazareth, 513.
Holdings, of the Spartan lands, a summary, 531.
Holy Wars, the, 81; Fish, Arethusa, 221, note 81.
Homotaphoi, common table communes, 510.
Homer, quotation from, 110; the slave system of his time, 529.
Hondurus aborigines of, 93 n. 18.
Honey-bees, Cicero on Plato, 118, note 72.
Honorable, discharge of soldiers, 107, note 46; to acknowledge an error, 564-5 and note 106.
Hoplomachi, 412.
Horse, of Spartacus, 327.
Hors de combat, 268, 411.
Horticulture, Diocletian's work on, 547.
Hostages, Carthagenian, and the slaves, revolt of, 151, note 18.
Hours, of labor, 530.
Houses, of the ancient Greeks and Romans, 54; house finishers' union, 370, note 34; house

INDEX.   657

of Cicero burned 499, note 12; of Socrates, 561; -hold and toy-gods, 429.
Hudson edition, of Vellejus, on Spartacus, quoted, 325, note 124.
Hues, 486.
Human equality, doctrine of 57; beings, as tools, 567.
Hunger, and cannibalism at Tauromanion, 226.
Hunter, Viriathus styled a, 180, note 4; of ostriches, sparrows etc., 393, 294; of Pompeii, 411, of wild animals, 411.
Hurled down the precipice, 227.
Huts, hovels and tents of the Britons, 488
Hybla and Macella, 269, and the notes 57, 58.
Hydra, 519.
Hymeneal reciprocity, 536.
Hyponicus, slave owner, 137.
Hypothesis of Wescher, 506.
Hypsæus, defeated by Achæus and Cleon, 217; was a Roman general, destroyed by Eunus in the slave war, 218.

I

Iambe, slave of Ceres, 130 n. 93.
Iconoclasm, traced back to organized resistance, x.
Ideal, 518; state of Plato, 530; of Jesus, 553; Plato the father of the ideal state, 554.
Idol worship, introduction into Christianity, viii.; origin of, x; the idols, 44, and 428-36.
Ignominious cross, 265; punishment-in what countries, 498-9.
Incas, massacres of the, 102.
Iliad, antiquity of the, 80.
Ilias. or period of calamity, 261, note 37.
Illegitimacy, what constituted, 344, note 28.

Image worship, viii.; making by trade unions, 123; makers, unions of, in Athens, 127; making elsewhere, 362 and n. 11; makers, their business and organization, 429; 2,000 images and statues taken at siege of Volsini, 431; makers, chapter xix., pp. 428-36; sculptured, of a female, 436; palladiums, amulets, talismans incantations etc., 556.
Imaginifex, 429.
Immaculate conception, 147, 559.
Immolation, of gladiators, 278, note 3.
Immortality, theory concerning, 59, 60, 90; opinions of Aristotle, Lucretius, Darwin on, 62; of the soul denied by a philosophy, 62; crowning problem, 66; originated by egoism, 85; further opinions, 90, 91; the working classes too mean to possess a soul, 95.
Immortals, the most powerful of whom were Jupiter, Ceres, Vulcan etc., 429.
Imperishable laws, 526.
Imprints, as best arguments, 450.
Incantations, 556.
Incendiorum collegium or firemen's union, 447, note 5.
Incentive to steal does not exist in communism, 534.
Incestuous liason of Antipas and Herodias, 557, note 87.
Indo-Europeans, original home of, 48, 55; their laboring class organized, 68, 73, 82; strange beliefs of, 75; communism of property among, 80; a democratic people, 122; an atrophy that benumbed the race, 494.
Indulgence, masters' accorded right of, with female slaves, 147, note 8; in voluptuousness and interchange of loves, 497.

INDEX.

Initiation, into the Mysteries, 92, of Alexander, 545.
Innocence of Spartacus, 290 and note 37.
Innovation, of Lycurgus etc., 69; introduction of, would make Clermont uninhabitable, 485-6.
Innumerable new unions created, 301, note 66.
Inscriptions, the genuine, mentioned in book, xi.; evidence of the, 73; of the Eleusinians, 87; an interesting one, 98; evidence of, 112, 205; specimen by Aquillius, 271; the same, with inscription verbatim, 291, note 39; true history revealed by, 342; one found at Lanuvium, showing rules, 353-58; at Pompeii, 390-2; law compelling their registration, 426; they prove the red color not to have been warlike, 490; one found twenty miles from Nazareth, 503.
Inspection of candidates, 510.
Insubordination of the soldiers of Spartacus, 306, note 80, 315; malignant spirit of, 321.
Insurrection, 86; of slaves which frightened the masters, 94; a great cause of fear, 141, note 33; of Carthagenian hostages and the slaves, 151, note 18; at Præneste, 153; in the interior of Asia Minor, 235; greatest known in history, 413; of Sicilian slaves, 404, see chapters ix. and xi.; of slaves, that was feared by Attalus, 546.
Intrenchment, of Crassus, 315, note 109.
Intrigues that filched the beautiful color, 480.
Inventions, 372; the ærarii understood alloys, 372; the carpenters made the battering-ram, 379, 488, note 53; Minerva, the protecting divinity of, 470; discovery of the new in nature, 526; implements of torture, 562; other doings, 569; of the ancient farmers, their reaper, 569 and note 109; let them be nationalized, 573.
Inventory, of Demosthenes, 548.
Invincible, force of Eunus, 219.
Iphicrates, a low-born, 546.
Irascible world, 494; a war spirit, 521; destructive and bloody, 556.
Irascibility, 74; and vengeance, 269; coupled with concupiscence and sympathy, 515.
Iron workers, 373; miners federated with the forgers, at far distant Rome, 442; the famous money made of, 532.
Ishmaelites, belonging to the Semitic family, 48.
Isis, of the therapeut, 562.
Ismenias, and Antisthenes the cynic, 544.
Isomachus, on prayer, 563.
Italian, schools of painting, 101; insurrection, 294, note 47.
Italy, ancient, prevailing scenes in, 54; slaves of, 77; Greek was spoken in lower part, 197.
Ivory, and gold in the chryselephantine colossus, 431; the ivory-workers, 431, 432.

J

Jack-at-all-trades, the ragpicker of Italy, 423.
Jack Cade 559.
Janus, temple of, closed by king Numa, 335; same thrown open after his death, 375.
Jagatnatha, 90.
Jargon, of dogmas and inquisitorial intolerance, 495.
Javelin, only allowed to nobles, 475.

INDEX. 659

Jealousies, among the revolters, 229; of Tryphon, 264, note 42; and revenge, 268; of Crixus, against Spartacus, 304; see insubordination.

Jerusalem, temple of, 123; trade unions at, 373, note 2; its destruction, 566-7.

Jesting dandies, 403, note 6.

Jesus, his plan a basis of hope, 57, 122; a workingman, 152-3; openly preached against slavery though indirectly, 173; revolution of, 237; in the act of creating an association, 494; nobody asks more than he did, 495; the labors of, 501; one of five remarkable personages, 514; not a Platonist, 517; his rules, 544; yet on trial, 525; planted the successful seed, 552.

Jews, easily grasp socialism, 43; their purity, 44, 45; without a land of their own, 46; a race of the Semitic family, 48; the mechanics, 373, Sidonian, 373 and note 2; pierced the ears of their slaves, 385, note 30; must eventually become proud of Christ, 566-7.

John the Baptist, 557.

Joiners, (intestinarii), 370.

Josephus, and his account of the tradesmen, 373 and note 2.

Journey through Gaul to Britain, 488.

Jove, see Zeus and Jupiter.

Jubilee, a coronation, 463 and plate; parades, feasts and red flags at, 484.

Judea (Judæa), a farming country in ancient times, 46; orator of, sprung from the laboring class, 493.

Jugglers organized, 111.

Jugs, or pots of milk, 399; made by the tyrant Agathocles, 545.

Julius, Obsequens quoted, 304, Epaphra, 433; see Cæsar.

Junkmen, 422, 425.

Jupiter, the father of Proserpine. 88; exposed a conspiracy o rebels, 148; Atabyrius, who he was, 169, note 10, 462; see Zeus.

Jus coeundi, or law permitting free organization, 283, 425; jus gentium, 294, note 48.

Justinian, emperor, 100; see also Digest.

K

Kapila, plagiarized by Aristotle, 117; laid the foundation, 514.

Karpetania, redeemed by Viriathus, 185.

Kent, (Cantiopolis), 487; Middlesex, and London, 559.

Key, to the success of Athenion, Eunus, Tryphon and others, 274, note 70.

Kind, taxes collected in, 441.

King's fool, of Eunus, 230 and 403, note 6.

Kitchen, presided over by the triclinarch, 399; co-operative, 533.

Knives and cudgels, 292, note 41.

Knights, on horseback, 477.

Koinon, and other names for the communes, 501.

Kicks, as an expression of thanks, 530.

Kidnapers, 286, note 27; were the buccaneer freebooters of Canaan, 498.

Kraton, inscription by, 98, n. 27 priest of a labor commune, 98.

L

Labor, movement, its aims, 38; no manual, among patricians of early days, 39; party, founders of, 43; inculcations degrading, 52; problem, counsel to those studying the, 60; swelling legions of, 62; its products are in the hands of monopolies, 62; ancient, generally interlinked with religion, 64; history of, begins with manumissions, 67; Semitic classes of, organized, 68; unions of, their laws recorded on slabs of stone, 71; scarcity of records of ancient, 71; taint upon, 72, 101, 110; unions recognized by Socrates and Aristotle, 74; movement, unions and agitations, 77, 79, 80, 96; Ceres protected its products, 89; socially degraded, 95; unions of great antiquity, 111; how debased, 112; laws of Solon, 113; the Greek brotherhoods, 114, 130; source of a thinking success, 117; leading the world, 118; a reputed disgrace, 120; efforts to suppress the organizations of, 157; societies of, in Hesiod's time, 162, the first war of, 142; bureau of labor of the U. S. and its report, 146; brotherhoods, not strictly religious societies, 170; had prophets and messiahs, 173; organization in Spain shown by her antiquities, 179; connected with the mysteries, 198; as a problem in the time of the Gracchi, 222; unions, did the work of collecting the taxes for the state, 437; worthy of pay—the laborer worthy of his hire—558.

Laborer, wages paid the ancient, 137; all the products were not Pagan, 572; left out 340, note 17, 348; and he rebelled and killed them, 573.

Lacedæmon, or Sparta, 79, 103; slaves of, 98.

Laconians, or Pericœci, 102, 531, the Spartan branch, 533.

Ladies, the youths introduced to the, 534.

Lænatus, story of Cicero, 241, note 18.

Lænus and Rupilius, who persecuted the Gracchi, 225.

Læocrates, his interest in a commune, 507.

Lake, of brimstone, 248, note 3; near Croton, whose waters are sometimes pure and sometimes salt, 320.

Lamb, of sacrifice for the thiasos, 98, note 27; 463, 503.

Lanatus, a Roman tribune, 145.

Land, equally divided by Lycurgus, 69; tenure, ancient systems, 80; division of, by Lycurgus, 101, 532; belonged to the state in Greece, 109; owners, the number of, in Rome, 192; in Athens, 193; Sparta, 101, 532; the Land of Canaan, 496; speculation, after the Roman conquests, 499; –lords, an imperious oligarchy of, 496; still holding the monopoly of, 497.

Language, of Hebrews, 39; the product of the low-borns, 568.

Lanuvium, the inscription of, 357.

Laodicia, stronghold of the brotherhoods, 511-12.

Lapicidinæ, 221.

Lares, or dæmons, 48; superstition, 51; remains of the dead still alive and active, 53, note 20, and 70, note 12; lar familiaris, 61; fear and honor of the, 425.

Lassalle, 43.

Last supper, 562.

Latifundia, of Clonius, 253.

Latium, in Italy, 149.

Laurium, in Attica, strike not unsuccessful, xii.; strike at

the silver mines, 134; contractors at, 136; Athenian silver works, 134, 138, 493.
Laveleye, M. de, 55, 68.
Laws, of Moses, 39, 40, 43, 44; the Jewish, recorded in the Pentateuch, 40; ancient laws of usurpation, 50; the laws of marriage among freedmen, 77; of entail, 69, 102; those recorded on slabs of stone, 71; of heredity, 96; of the Twelve Tables, 100; of Solon, 100, 113, 127 and note 87; of Lycurgus, 101, 104, 109, 525 and full account, 530, sqq., of primogeniture, 102; of Numa Pompilius, 109, 126; of Amasis 115; the conspiracy, 120, see conspiracy; of organization generally, 127; Roman enforcement of the slave laws, 178; of Solon borrowed from Egypt 245, note 23; of suppression, 283, note 15; law of lust, 147; compelling inscriptions, 425-6.
Lawgiver, 497, 529.
Learning and Art, two young females of Lucian's dream, 543.
Lebanon, mountains of, 236.
Legality, of will of Attalus, 234.
Legend, weird, of the brimstone lake, 248, note 4.
Legerdemain, of Eunus, 217 and note 67.
Leges populi, 340.
Legion, number of soldiers in a, 312; of Honor, 484.
Leisure, the necessity of, according to Aristotle, 542.
Leleges, Chios a primeval home of the 163.
Lentulus, C. Cornelius, prætor in Setia, 151; Piso, Rupillius, 218; third man sent against Eunus, 218; Batiatus, teacher of the games, 285; proprietor of, incomes to, 289 and note 36; the consul, dogging Spartacus, 307; disaster of, 311; mystery as to fate of, 311; and Poplicola, 407.
Leo X., Pope, 125.
Leonardo da Vinci, 544.
Leontini, number of land owners at, 194.
Le Play, 70.
Leslie, Dr. Cliffe, his opinion, 111.
Lexicographers, obliged to consult the inscriptions, 379.
Lexington, flag of, 492
Liason, of Antipas and Herodias in Judea, 557, note 87.
Lice, Eunus devoured by, 230, note 105.
Licinian law, 156, 222, note 84; Stolo, 474.
Lictor, of Tryphon, 264, note 43; same as executioner, 475, note 22; fierce military pageant of, 475; his functions, 475.
Lightfoot, quoting Digest on the power of life and death, 294, note 48; on the Essenes, 504, note 23.
Lilybæum, where situated, 258; attacked by Athenion, 260 and note 35.
Line of circumvallation, against Spartacus, 318.
Linen weavers' union, 416.
Lions, tigers, leopards, wolves, bears in the ring, 188-90 and plate, 395; and other wild animals, 411; crouching in front of Cybele, 463.
List, of trade unions 369.
Liticen, or clarion, 408.
Livy, account of Spartacus by, but lost, 211; other mention, 79, 146, 148, 152; he spurned the bacchanals, 159.
L. Domitius, horrible cruelty of, 136; Furius, a Roman consul, 157; Postumius, a prætor in charge of Apulia, 159.

Lokrians, did not tolerate slavery, 169; were the communists of Italy, 194.
London, the bed-rock of modern socialism, 488; leader of the labor movement, 559.
Long-lived unions, 461.
Lord's prayer, 562.
Lords, forced to fight as gladiators, 308, note 85.
Lordship, and slavery, first established condition of society, 54.
Loss, of the books, 262, 268, 269; of Livy, 298; of Sallust, 299; how the art of dyeing was lost, 479-80,
Lots, the Spartan division of, 101, 102, 530.
Lottery, booths, taverns etc., of Theophrastus, 543.
Lousy sickness, 230, note 105.
Love, incomparable, inscription, 342, note 21; Eros the god of, whom Socrates worshiped, 553 note 76.
Low-born, inferior to a dog, 244, note 22, see slave, slavery.
Lowly, ancient, 60; nature of discussion among the, 129; socialistic atmosphere of, 513.
Lucanians, under Cleptius, 264.
Lucanus, 79.
Lucian, dream of, 543.
Lucretius, compared with Vogt, Spencer and Darwin, 59; his celebrated apothegm, 60; his belief regarding the soul, 62; the doctrine of, 129; a Roman tribune, 145; an etymological reference, 471.
Lucullus, object of, in Spain, 181; leaves Spain, 182; L. Licinius, sent to Sicily, 264; routed by Athenion, 267; a third, of the same name, in war with the gladiator, 319, note 117; approaches Spartacus from one side and Pompey from another, 321; drives Spartacus from the port of Brundusium, 323.
Lueders' Skilled Mechanics of the Bacchanals, 503.
Ludi, and the incorporated communes, 404; cercenses, 410.
Lugdunum, (Lyons), shipping produce from, 440.
Luna, marble, 368.
Lupanariorum collegium, 447.
Lupercalia, 344, note 30.
Lusitania, prosperity of, before the Roman conquests, 179 see chapter viii., pp. 178-190, Viriathus.
Luxuries, prohibited by Spartacus, 302, note 70.
Lybian, slave traffic, 286, note 27.
Lycurgus, law of, 62, 69, 94, 101, 103, 139; a model and a monster, 102; recognized aristocracy, 497; a review of him, 526, sqq.; was attacked and blinded, 527; what he accomplished, 532; his doctrines detailed, 559.
Lyons, unions of collectors, 439, note 3; connected with Rome by water, 440.
Lysias, his shield factory, 547.
Lytton, Sir Edward Bulwer, his opinion as to gladiators, 289.

M

M. Acilius Glabro, Roman prætor, 157.
Ma, a divinity, the cult of, 215, note 63.
Macedonia, mines in, 137; an uprising in, 142.
Macella, a great battle between Athenion and Rupillius, 270 its castle, conjectures as to its geographical situation, 270.
Machinists, union of, shown by an inscription, 378, note 14;

INDEX. 663

machine adjusters, 378; others, of the plays, 403, note 6; at the theatres, 570.
Mackenzie, and the Twelve Tables, 337, 339.
Macrobius, his arguments against slavery, 141, note 34; quotation from, 146, 164, note 2.
Madonna, or Notre dame, 486.
Magician, Eunus the, 199, and note 27.
Magister sacrorum, 452.
Magnetism, of Lycurgus, 532.
Maidens, the celebrated Spartan, 530, 534; before the ephori, 535.
Malfeasance, 225, note 94; of Nerva, in office, 250-51, note 13; of Lucullus, 274.
Mamelukes, massacre of the, 102.
Mamertine caves, 230.
Man, original division of, into classes, 39.
Manes, jealous, omniscient and on guard 53, of Crixus-Spartacus' revenge by forcing his victims to fight as gladiators, 308, 309, 406; as tutelary saints, 420.
Man-hunt, after Silarus, 286, note 27; for remnants of routed army of the gladiators, also for the pirates, 330.
Mania, for organization, 447.
Manlius (Oneus), defeat of, by Spartacus, 314.
Mantle, the purple, of Tryphon, 264, note 43.
Manufactories, their wares and the collectors, 439; of arms of war operated by the brotherhoods, 123; by the freedmen, 218; establishments in the emperors' palaces, 419; of colors in red, how suppressed, 480; others, of the armaments of warfare, 537.
Manumissions, the dawn of, 48;
era of, 51; idea of, 56, 67-9, 74, 112, 526; history of labor begins with, 67-8; movement and progress of, 541.
Manure, straw for, 569, note 109.
Manuscript, the original of Vellejus Paterculus, 325, note 124.
Maringues, 486.
Marauder, of the Nebrode, Gaddæus, 252.
Marble, cutters' organizations, 127; quarries, 368; of Brioude had red devices, 490.
Marius, C. election of, consul at outbreak of second Sicilian labor war, 248; and Julius, unions suppressed, 301, note 65.
Markets, of the slave traffic, 286 and note 27.
Marriage, under the Lycurgan law, 527; form of, in Sparta, 535.
Mars-like warrior Spartacus, 297, note 55.
Martyrdom, at Tauromanion, 227; and incalculable results, 514, 525.
Marx, 43.
Masons, of the organized building trades at Rome, 367; stone masons of Rome, 368, 369; at Jerusalem, 373, note 2.
Massachusetts, its early flag was red, 492.
Massacre, of Stone Henge, and others, 102; of the Helots, 115; at Ancyle, 251; and crucifixion of the slaves, 299; of the Hebrews at Jerusalem, 567.
Materfamilias, conduct of the, 52, her virtue beyond suspicion, 74; kept herself secluded at home, 78 note 30; worked at the spinning wheel, 108.
Mauritania, sends a force to fight Athenion, 260, note 35.
Maury, critic on Eleusinian mysteries, 92.

INDEX.

Mausoleums and sarcophagi, 429.
Maw, the rock-lined, of Taygetus, 533.
Maxim, theorem, axiom, 509–10; saying, eye for eye etc., 493.
Maximian, kills Crispin aad Crispinian, 421; persecutions, 485.
Meals, in common at Tarentum, 287, note 28; see table.
Measures, of Lycurgus, 532.
Mechanics, 39; progress in, was unendurable to the pagan system, 568; skilled, of the bacchanals, see Lueders' Minerva.
Megallis, wife of Damophilus and the cruel slaveholder, 201; her fearful death, 204–5; plunged headlong over a precipice, 405 and 406.
Megapolis, theatre of, 401.
Megaron, temple of, 91; 95; 130.
Mellow garden for the first sowings, 573.
Membership, granted the slaves, 98; note 27, 169, 355.
Memento, talisman, incantation, charms, palladiums, 463; 556 ;
Memphis, Egypt, 112, note 56.
Men-Tyrannus, a god, 143; note 39; men great and good, 525; and women the tools of labor, 568.
Menecrates, 463.
Menestheus, the demagogue of Athens, 99, note 28.
Menial work, 498.
Menis, son of Menistheus of Heraclitus, 454.
Mercenaries, slaves used as, 77; a trade union of, 119; Thracian freedmen as, 235; and hucksters, of Theophrastus, 542,
Merchants, unions of, 98; 393; flags, 487.
Mercury, his visit to Erebus, 89.
Merula, prætor and tribune, 151; suppressed the slave revolt id. and note 18; defeats a second and similar insurrection, 153.
Messana, spared by slaves, 221.
Messenian war with Sparta, 98; 103.
Messiah, slaves believed in a, 173; Eunus a, 199; also Athenion, 259; and Salvius or Tryphon, 263; soters, worshipers of the, 462; the greater one, how He found things, 493; mellowed and in readiness for the, 513; Eunus the, acquainted with secret organization, 512.
Messiahships, 558.
Metagenes, Greek sculptor, 131.
Metal, vessel-makers, 445; proscribed by Lycurgus, 69, n. 8.
Metanira, mother of Demophon, 89.
Metaurus, battle of, 193.
Metroon, temple of Cybele, also goddess of the Piræus, 509.
Mevaniola, where a ragpickers' union was found, 422.
Mexico, ancient people of, 93.
Microcosms, of a far-future state, 459; inapplicable except for the, 493.
Middle, men, the first of Rome, 340; ages, 461.
Milk, and milk-tasters, 399; the ancient milkmen, 399.
Millers, wages paid the, 137: they were called pistores, 349; and bakers' union (sacred), 445; other brotherhoods of, 446.
Mills, did the Roman state own woolen mills? 417.
Milo, the pugilist, 323; note 120.
Mimics, communes of Roman, 112, note 58; the unions of, see chapter 18; pp. 401; sqq., 220; inscription of, 403; n. 6.
Miners, insurrection of, 100; of copper, 375; their unions, 442, note 10.
Minerva, goddess of the thiasote, 114; temple of, 137 ; statue

431; the Lindienne, 450, 462;
the Athena, goddess of manual labor, 468; with Apollo,
etc., 488; feast-days and colors of, and when, 490.
Mines, belonged to the state, 136; sufferings of the workers in, 138; rebellious slaves sent to the, 158; of iron, 373, note 3.
Mirmillion, a kind of gladiator, 311, note 96, 412.
Missing link, connecting the cattle-breeders with the unions, 388.
Mithridates, tyrant of Cappadocia, 169; his punishment of Aquillius, 273; his defeat by Lucullus, 323, note 121.
Mixing, Numa taught them to mix, 371.
Mnason, a great slave owner, 135.
Mnistheus, 454.
Mob, of Roman lords, 234; of nobles who assassinated Gracchus, 241; of gladiators, 323; of young men set upon Lycurgus, 527; cruel, that murdered Jesus, 562.
Mock, theatricals, 220; manœuvres and sham battles, 410; combats in the arena, 411.
Mohammedan rescue, 555.
Mola de Gæta, 316, note 111.
Moloch, 44.
Mommsen, 112, 127, 187; on the law of Solon, 113; always reliable, clears up the doubt, 508.
Mona, Isle of, and the Druids, 482.
Monarchism, earliest European, 112; that of Numa a wise, 375.
Money, changers, 509, 518; the iron, of the Spartans, 531.
Monks, what upheld by, 556.
Monotheism, Jewish, 40, 504.
Monselice, union of hunters discovered at, 394.
Mont Ferrand, carders, masons, weavers of, had blood-red, 489
Moors, in Sicily against Athenion, 262.
Morgantion, 255 sq.
Morocco, Peru, Bolivia, red, 487.
Mortars, for grinding, 446.
Mortgages, on landed estates, 119, note 74, 531.
Mosaic law, 43-5.
Moses, 39-45; Pentateuch containing the law of, 40; other 59, 72; divine authorship of his law, 46; provided for slavery, 566.
Mount Garganus, battle of, 306-8; Taygetus, 533; see Olympus.
Muenter, who sketched a wine-smokers' society, 383.
Muleteers, a union of, 396.
Mummius, disastrous defeat of, 314; frightful punishment of his men for cowardice, 315 and note 108.
Munitions, the manufacture of, by trade unions, 443.
Murder, of the Gracchi, 233; of Clonius, 253, many shocking, 536.
Murileguli, who fished for shells and purple fish, 418.
Murillo, 84.
Muscovite, 464.
Musical instruments, 408; see chapter on organized amusers,
Museum, 400; at Pesth, 402; of Athens, 453.
Mutice, number of property owners at, 194.
Mutina, battle of, 313.
Mutilation, of the books, 268-9; also 299, note 57; of slaves, 385, note 30; of Hermotius, 168-9 note 7; of the valuable literature, 522.
Mutiny, of the soldiers of Spartacus, 320.
Mutton, fish and venison, the aristocratic food, 386.

INDEX.

Mycænæ, servant in the league at, 110, note 50.
Myndum, in the labor war, 235.
Myron, rival of Phidias, 431.
Mysteries, the little, 87; their religious rites, 94; Eleusinian, see chaper iv. pp. 83–132, 536; of skilled art, 539.
Mythology, Saturn and Janus chained the god of war, 47; the ancient, 88, sq.

N

Nahuas, gladiatorial sacrifices of, 278.
Naked, both sexes worked so together in the mines, 138–9; sweat-begrimed slaves, 248; maidens practiced gymnastics with the young men, 534, 535; lowly and living in caves, 530, 532.
Naples, divers' unions at, 113 n. 61.
Napoleon, compared with Sparcus, viii.
Narbonne, inscription of milk-jar makers at, 399.
Narcissus, stupefying influence of the, at the mysteries, 92.
Nassicus, assassin of Gracchus, 241, note 19.
Natal months, of Ceres, Minerva, Apollo, 488.
Nationalization, of implements of labor, 570.
Native Races, Bancroft's 278, n. 4.
Naturalists, and the new philosophy, 62.
Nautii, family of the, 114.
Nazareth, the unions around, see chapter xxiii.; 503.
Nemesis, goddess of justice, 413, note 36.
Nemetum and Augustonemetum, 485.
Neo-Platonism, 466; engrafted as a Christian dogma, 516, 551; amalgamation, 522, 551.
Neptune, the reign of, 47; and his trident at the Clepsydræ, 130, note 96.
Nero, despot, xiii.
Nerva, 247, note 1.
Nestor, 452.
Nets of the seas, 316, note 111.
New England states and their colors, 492.
Nicanor, a perfumer, 434.
Nicaragua, 92, note 18.
Nice, unions of divers at, 113.
Nicias, a slave owner, 135; had also convicts working for him in the mines, 138, note 25; and Cimon, 146.
Nicholas, of Damascus, 165, 168, 277, note 1.
Nicomides, king of Bithynia, 249, note 5.
Niebuhr, 299.
Nile, 112, red-birds of the, 479.
Nio, 456.
Nomads, 70; see gypsy; Spartacus a, 282, note 13; not Aryan, 560; the first runaways, 560.
Nomenclature, of the Greek communes, 455, note 16.
Non-laboring class preferred the white color, 466; non-warfare of Numa's system, 537,
Norba, Circijus, Præneste, 151,
North American Indians, analogy between *gens* and, 86, n. 6.
Nuisance, communes declared a 283, note 16.
Numa Pompilius, 146; laws of, 109, 119; encouraged trades unions, 123, 146, 156. 161; his celebrated provision, 285; upheld the labor societies, 303; promoted trade and labor unions and the brotherhoods 700 years before Christ, 335; the first king that recognized, befriended & legalized labor, 336;

538; reigned 43 years 338; his greatness, 339; death of, 375; compared with Solon and Tullius, 426; sanctions the bacchanals, 502.

Numantia in Spain, bad condition of slaves, 179.

Numbers, of children of the rich, 49, note 5; of slaves at Greek mines, 143, note 38; of captive slaves in the conquests, 193, note 1; in the armies of Eunus, viii., 218, note 70; of Piso's army, 223; crucified at Enna, 229; slaves in rebellion, 254, note 20; of the army of Salvius, 255, 363; of army of Lucullus, 264; combined force of slaves at battle of Scirthæa, of imported slaves for cheap labor, 286, note 27; killed in battle with Spartacus at Vesuvius, 297, note 93; of army of Spartacus after Garganus, 304, note 77; Appian's estimate in Thuria, 306, note 82; killed, according to statement of Frontin, 319, note 118; total force of Spartacus at Silarus according to Vellejus Paterculus, 324-8, notes 123-4, 132; also of combined Roman armies at same battle, 424, note 122; of slaves estimated killed in all uprisings, 330, note 136, of slaves owned by Claudius, 340, note 17; of the Dionysian communes, 404, note 9; of warriors of Eunus, 549; of Jews murdered by the Romans, 567; comparative, of mankind, 570.

Nymph, Thalia, 247; Lycia, 569.

Nymphodorus, little known of, 165; a Sicilian geographer and historian, 163-4; his lost book, 165, note 10; his remarkable story of Drimakos preserved by Athenæus, chapter vii,

O

Oaken tables, of our forefathers, the communal, 532.

Oath, exacted from freedmen & slaves in camp, 471, note 12.

Obligatory rule, compelling the unions to chisel out their lithographs, 426.

Obloquy, falsely attaching to the ancient bacchantes, 502.

O'Bryan, on slave leaders, 274, note 70.

Oderic, 392.

Odium, attaching to slave rebellions, 294, note 47; attaching to labor, 502, 529.

Odyssey, shown to be younger than the Iliad, 80.

Œnomaus, 289, note 36; elected a lieutenant under Spartacus, 294; his defeat and death, 306 and note 77.

Offerings of frankincense, 357.

Officers of the brotherhoods enumerated, 357, translation 617 Greek, 453.

Offspring, replenishing the Spartan state with good, 536.

Oil-grinders, 364.

Olenus Calenus, soothsayer, 154, note 27.

Oligarchy, of money, 398, note 26; of one-third of the population, 496; Aristotle's 542, 543.

Ollas, jumping and tumbling on, 505.

Olympiad, 247, note 1.

Olympian Zeus, statue of, 101; heights, 236; abodes, 516; & thrones, 548; mount, home of the gods in charge of the welfare of mortals, 351.

Opimius, the murderer of Gracchus, 241, note 19.

Oppression, ancient resistance to, 68; of the dominant class. 79; of ancient slaves, 96.

INDEX.

Optimate class, 469; lictors required to be of the, 476; did not work, 530 of Aristotle's state, 542.

Ora Rhodana (the mouths of the Rhone), and modes of ancient commerce, 440.

Oracles, diviners of, 413.

Oration, of Cato against Galba, 181, note 5.

Order of the wood-workers, 360, note 3; of the masons, stone and bricklayers, 365; tax-men, 440, 441; see trade unions.

Organization, ancient secret, 69, 71; of freedmen, 74; of mercenaries, 78; the Eleusinian, 87; secret, 90, see communes; antiquity of labor, 94; of families and fratries, 101, of the Helots, 108; people driven to, 110; of fish-mongers at Syracuse, 119; encouraged by Numa, 123; grievances discussed by, 129; of slaves in Sicily, 197; of the laboring class, 333; see chapters on organization p. 333, sqq.; of trade unions, index of them; of farmers, see farmers.

Orgeons and Essenes, 450, 493; and the orgiastes, 469.

Orgies lupercalian, of the German farmers, 344, note 30; of Eleusis not belonging to the labor question, 505.

Oriflamme, 485.

Origin of the gladiatorial games, 278, note 3; of conscience, see chapter ii.; of life, 59; of cunning, 60; of ghosts, 61; of the word flag, 485; of Christianity, Wescher quoted, 506.

Orpheus, the priest, 92.

Orsona, Æmilius' camp at, 186.

Ostia, port of Rome, unions at, 382, note 23; inscription showing the political action at, 383, note 26; its business, 440.

Ouranos, the vaulted dome, 236; its invisible inhabitants, 516, 352.

Outcasts and descendants of the slaves, 438; the plebeian population, 344; the dangerous, 437; victimized by prayer, 464.

Ovation, to the Palakoi, 263; to Aquillius, 272.

Overseer, of collectors' union, 439.

Overturned villages, cities and castles, 267, note 50.

Ownership, by the government, of mills, 417.

Ox, harnessed to Pliny's reaper, 569, note 109; car-load of Lycurgus' iron money, 532.

P

Pæans and prayers of thiasotes, 536.

Pagan, religion, 69; was overturned by the labor unions, its true basis, 76; religio-slavery the outcome of it, 83, 495; its temple, 114; traditional family, 497; Pagan law of entailment upon primogeniture, 558; prayers, specimens brought forward, 561-64; institutions and adherents, and what became of them, see the chapter xxiv, and pp. 513-520; final, 315.

Painting, a master of, 101; era of Grecian, 128.

Palæozoic era, 276.

Palæstra, of suffering, 249.

Palaeographic and tradional records, 492; anaglyphs etc., 451; unearthed during the 19th century, 501; showing a microcosm of a far future state, 459.

Palenque, inscriptions at, 112.

Palestine, 41, 46, 88, 444; secret communes of, 501, the

entire chapter xxiii., pp. 493-519.
Palkoi, 247; asylum of the 252; twins of Thalia and Jupiter, 247.
Palisade-like intrenchments or fortifications against Spartacus 320 and note 119; 318.
Palladiums, etc., 556.
Palladius and his account of the ancient reaper, 569, note 109.
Pallas, children of, 49; Athene 562.
Panatheniastes, 462.
Pangaetus, strikes in the mines of gold at, 144.
Pangaeus, mines in Thrace, 137.
Panifices, or bakers, 349.
Panionius, revenge of Hermotius, 168-9, note 7.
Pantaetus, 143.
Paperna, campaign against Aristonicus, 242, 243.
Paphlagonia, 239.
Papian law, 243, note 21.
Parallelisms, of Socrates and Jesus, 514, 560.
Paraphrase, Dindorf's, on tramps, 261, note 37; Dio Cassius, and Diodorus, 261.
Paris, vast catacombs at, 155.
Parmenides, 518.
Paros, the slab of, 87, note 10.
Parrhasius, great painter, 101.
Parthenon, 101, 124, 126, built under Pericles, 124, its marbles and material, 368; made by the genius and chisel of the sculptor Phidias, 125.
Passions, toning and moralizing, 530.
Patavium, inscription of the ragpickers found at, 423.
Patch-workers, 422; piecers, 424, how they drifted into the business, 425.
Paterfamilias, 69, 74, 497; his power over brothers and sisters, 50, 51; worships his dead father as a god, 51; becomes saint and god after death, 85.
Patriarchal, government unmentioned by inscriptions, 73.
Patrician, 39, 72; Plato a, 39; disposal of property of, 49-50; contest of opinion between the, and the communes, 493; consuls fought the workingmen, 474; smiles of the, 532.
Patron, saint or divinity, 469.
Paul, Paulus, Aemilius in Epirus, another, defeated by Viriathus, 186; Aemilius, havoc of, 340, note 17; Saint, 552.
Peace, hues were red, 486; standard of Egypt is still red, 491; banner, of American colonies, red, 492; makers, of Lycurgus, 532.
Pearl, brass, gold and amber entered into manufacture of images, 430; fishers (margaritarii), 434; used in decorating images, 435.
Pelasgians, Chios, primeval home of the, 163.
Peligni, union of hunters found at, 393, 394.
Peloponnesian war, 105, 134; decided by a strike, 138; breaking out of, 139.
Penates, the home of the lares, 52.
Penetralia, 52, 494.
Pennons, jacks, and merchants' standards, 487.
Pentateuch, 40.
Pentelicus marble quarries, 368.
Pepiles, an aboriginal American tribe, 92, note 18.
Pepin le Bref, 488, note 53.
Perfidy, of the workingmen to each other, 228; of Nerva, 250; of Aquillius, 272; & betrayal, 514.

INDEX.

Perfumers' society at Capua, 291; unguentarii, who made things "fit for the gods," 433; had unions in Athens and Corinth, 434.
Pergamus, see all of chapter x., pp. 232-45, Aristonicus; inscription from, 98; insurrection at, 150; seat of the uprising of Aristonicus and the farmers, 511; become mellow ground for Christianity, 512.
Pericles, archon of Athens, 124; wages in the time of, 137; an admirer of Phidias, 431.
Perioeci, a favored class of Lacedaemon, 101, 106.
Permian age, 276.
Persecutions, of Diocletian, 483; of the centuries, 523.
Perseus, the siege of, 193.
Petinax, emperor of Rome, 79.
Petelia, battle of, and victory of Spartacus, 321.
Phidias, a descendant of slaves, 160; great sculptor, 100; a friend of Pericles, 125; transcendent genius of, 128; magnificent works, 101; with Myron, Polycletus, Alcamines, 435; in Lucian' dream, 543.
Philemon and Archilochus, 544.
Philip of Macedon, 544.
Philo Judaeus quoted, 504, n. 23.
Philosopher, Aristotle's prediction, 71; is discovering wonderful things, 84; Nicholas of Damascus, quoted, 277, note 1; what his greatest pleasure 539, 542.
Philosophy, 39; one that denies the immortality of the soul, 52; effect of such, on a workingman, 63-4; the Aristotelian, 116, 118; great era of Greek, 128; of annihilation, 129, n. 90; see Plato and Aristotle.

Phocaea, favors Aristonicus, 239.
Phoebus, 390; in Britian, 482.
Phocion, 545.
Phoenicia, 110; Greek spoken, 197, its lost art of red dyes, 479, 480; see Palestine.
Phoenicians, see Palestine, chapter xxiii., pp. 493-519; were not an aggressive race, 40 and notes; belonged to the Semitic family, 48, 120; enterprise of the, 124; were slave traders, 164; and their trade with the Africans, 432; dyes, 483; kidnapers, 498.
Phœnicepteros, 478.
Phœnix, Greek and ardea Latin were the flaming reds, 478, note 30, fin.
Phratries, 86, 94, 99, 367; outcasts formed into, 86; name uppermost for Greek organizations, 502.
Phrygia, stone slabs from 503.
Physicism, of Aristotle, 516.
Picenum, 311.
battle Mummius at, 312.
Piræus, the unions at the, 113; trade unions at the, 125; organizations of workers in great numbers, 361; unions of Greek flute players at, 410; at the unions of the Heroistes, Serapistes, etc., 450; exampl. at, 508; a thiasos mentioned, 505.
Pirates, in Chios after the death of Drimakos, 176; supposed to have assisted Spartacus, 316; account given by Tacitus, 316, note 111; more about, 498.
Pisaurum, wood-workers of, 361 and note 8.
Piscicapii, 389.
Pisistratidæ, an Athenian family of high estate, 125.
Piso, fourth general against Eunus, 218.

Plans, of salvation, of working-people, 46 and note 14; of Eunus, extermination, 219; of slaves in rebellion are exposed, 151, note 18; a peaceful, of salvation, 517; of the various leaders, 525; of Lycurgus, a summary, 537; of Eunus, 548; of Aristonicus, 550; of Drimakos, 550; of Spartacus, 551; of Salvius, 255; the two immortal, now mixing. 555; of salvation, of Moses, etc., 565; of the moderns, 567.

Plant, the new, how prepared, 513; of Lycurgus, 537; of the great men who figured for the cause of humanity, see chapter xxiv., pp. 520-573.

Planted, the red, all along, between Auvergne and Kent, 488.

Plaster images (tectoriolæ), mentioned by Cicero. 432.

Plato, 39, 53, 59, 107, 109; was willing to take gifts from the wealthy, but refused pay, 39; on the soul, 60; reference to his Phædrus, 93, note 19; was an advocate of slavery, 102; the two moral elements of, 109; Aristotle against, 117; his episode at Syracuse, 118; sold as a slave in Italy, 119; general movement of, 132; hardheartedness in some things, 136; on immortality, 193; his visit to Italy, 444; ideas copied from the Pagan religion, 466; takes Socrates down to the Piræus, 513; one of the five remarkable men, 514.

Plautius, defeated by Viriathus, 185; Hypsæus, his arrival, to fight Eunus, 217.

Plebiscita, 340.

Plebeians, 39; not citizens, 344, note 27; were the theatre actors, 404; their love of the red color, 473; Licinius a, 474; the power of, 474, note 20.

Pliny, his natural history, 79, 154; celebrated naturalist, 129; on ancient reaper, 569, note 109.

Plumage, of the red-bird, 479.

Plutarch, 98, 103; evidence of concerning the murder of the slaves, 86; quoted, 105; battle of the Po, 311; q .oted as to, 311; as to Silarus, 327; lampoons the workers, 544.

Pluto and Proserpine, story of, 88, 198.

Poison, for the working classes, 546, 547.

Polemarch and Lysias, shield-makers, 547.

Polemic, Wescher-Foucart, 506;

Polias, architect of the temple of Minerva, his wages, 137, cruel slave owner, 215, 405.

Policy, of priest-power to curtail information, 522; a, which is the meanest on the pagan schedule, 524.

Political economy, 43; economy, prevalence of priest-power in, 45; institutions and the work people, 94; actio . of unions at Ostia, 383, note 26; of federated trade unions of Pompeii, 390-91 and notes 3, 4, 5.

Politics, a noble calling, 113; forbidden the ancient unions, 113; Politics, title of Aristotle's celebrated book, see Aristotle; politicians, or the upper class were wrangling while the communes were harmonious, 509.

Polution, the touch of a workingman supposed to polute, 349.

672   INDEX.

Polybius, on the red flag, 467 & note 5.
Polycletus, in Lucian's dream, 543.
Polyglot, P. Crassus, who spoke many Greek dialects, 238, and note 12.
Pomona, presided over the orchards, 477; herself, Isis, Osiris and her flaminica, 480.
Pompey, xii., 317; in war of the gladiators, 319 sqq., note 117; arrives from Spain, 323; bears down upon Spartacus, 323 and note 121.
Pompeii, an important inscription found at, 128; volunteers to Spartacus from, 297; women in the labor politics of, 390, 391 and note 5; inscription of cloth-fullers who were employed by the state, 416, note 5.
Pomptine swamps, the, 149.
Pont du Chateau, half-red banners, 489.
Po, Spartacus marches to the, 307, 309; his arrival at, 308, note 84.
Pool of the Twins, 247, note 2.
Pooling, of sums to bribe Nerva, 249,, 250 and note 8.
Poor food, for the slaves, 43, note 16; there were unions for furnishing its supply, 383, note 26.
Popidius (Rufus), manager of the family of gladiators, 411.
Poplicola, tactics of, 308; great battle with and defeat of, 308.
Poplius Clonius, murder of, 253, note 16.
Population, of Corinth, 193; in the slave era, enormous, 340, note 17; of Sparta, 529; see census.
Porcelain, ancient invention, 571.
Pork butchers' unions, 386, 441; see food

Port, of Ostia, unions of, 382, note 23; of the Rhone (Ora Rhodani), 440; of Athens, or the Piræus, 361; see Piræus.
Porte bannières, 484, note 44.
Poseidonius, the stoic, 169.
Postumius, defeats the strikers at Apulia, 160.
Potters, Numa's union of, 335, note 6; ampulæ or jugs, of the milkmens'· union, 399; another union of, 445; the tyrant Agathocles a, 545.
Powderly, stand taken by him, disclosing the power of organization, 334.
Power, of the ancient father over his children, 76, note 25; of masters over slaves, 121, note 75; of married man over his female slaves, 49 and note 4, 147 and note 8; of Eunus, 221, note 81; of life and death, 294, note 48; of habit, 465-6, 483, 489; of the plebians in Roman elections, 474, note 20.
Prægustatorum collegium, union of tasters, 398.
Præneste, 150; slave insurrection at, 151, note 18; inscription at, 403.
Prairie on fire, 487.
Praxiteles, Lysippus, Scopas, 435.
Prayer of woman, 303, note 73; the unions opened their sessions with, 461; sayings and doings compared, 525, sqq.; and deeds, of Tertullian, 552, note 70; of Socrates, 561; of Jesus, 562; of Alcestis, 562-3; of a selfish son, 563; of Orestes, 563; pæans and, of the thiasotes, 563; of the Queché, tribe, 564; of ancient Pagan priest, 564.
Pre-Christian societies, 461.
Precipices, hurled down the, by Rupillus, 227; cast headlong,

from the Nebrode, 252.
Precocious trade unionist, 383, note 26.
Prediction, of the wife of Spartacus, 558.
Presses, 386.
Prestigiation, 45, 274, note 70.
Pretex of religion, 346, note 36.
Priest, power in political economy, 45; was a public officer, 114; the Druid, 482;—craft, origin of, 53, superstitious belief in, 352; his sacerdotal and sacrificial paraphernalia, 429; of Aristotle's age, 538; priesthood, bound in the secret mysteries, 90.
Primeval, men, 72; race, 73; colors, 473, note 16; mind, 472, 487.
Primogeniture, law of, 50; entailment upon, 558; laws of inheritance and rules of entail upon, 571.
Prince of this world, 556.
Prison, description of the Roman, 154; the public, 151 and note 18; description, by Bombardini, 154; the strikers cast into, 160, note 42; broken open and 60,000 prisoners set free; 251, note 12, 254; was called the home of the proletaries, 287, note 32.
Private union, 510, note 37.
Privateers, societies of, 510.
Probus, emperor of Rome, 79.
Proclaim the cult, 554.
Procurators with their quæstors, 439.
Proeranistria, female guardian, 453, 455, 463.
Proletarian class, ignored by paganism, 428; origin of the, 85; the army of, 320.
Prompter, at the theatre, 402, note 1.
Propaganda, system of, 244, and note 23; of organization, 448, note 9.

Property, see family; common, under Lycurgus, 69; owners of, organized for protection, property and family originally one and the same thing, 281, note 11; comprehends money, land, house, slaves, 281, n. 11.
Prophecy, of Aurinia, 290, note 37, 305, note 78.
Prophet, Athenion a, 259; also Eunus, 548; were in all turmoils, 557; they existed thro all antiquity, 558.
Propitiation of the divinities by wild tumult, 244, note 23.
Proportion of Gauls to Thracians of Spartacus, 289, note 36.
Proprietorship, system of communal, 69.
Propylæ, of the Parthenon, 101.
Propylæa, 430.
Proserpine, or Persephone, the story of, 88-9, 92; rape of, 90; carried to Enna, 198.
Prostates, a president, 453.
Prostitution, 463, 464.
Proto-divinities, 489.
Protoplasm, 59.
Proudhon, 60.
Provisions, and who furnished them, 396; see chapters xv. & xvi., Rome's army supplies, & victualing system.
Prytaneum, the, 126.
Pseudo-Asconius, 225; note 94.
Psomokolophos, or runaway, boy friend of Drimakos, 174.
Ptolemy Philadelphus, 564.
Public works, 403.
Publicans, Cicero's praise of the, 249, note 7.
Publishing, how done, 436.
Publius Varinius, defeat of, 207.
Pulvinaria, inscription by an association of, 432.
Punic hostages, 153, note 22; war, the third, 178, 215.

674 INDEX.

Punishment, of slaves, 244, note 22; for falsehood and perjury, 248, note 3; inflicted upon the Romans, 266; by Crassus, of cowards, 315. note 108; of the soldiers of Mummius by Spartacus, 315.
Putnam, red flag displayed by, at battle of Bunker Hill, 492.
Purple, clothed in, 258, note 29; why a mixed color, 476.
Purveying, systematic method of, 437.
Puy de Dôme, 484, note 46.
Puzzle-guessing, 528, 558.
Pydna, the battle of, in Epirus, 179, 186.
Pyrrhus, in Tarentum abolished common tables, 287, note 28.
Pythagoras, thought to have known Numa, who through him was a communist, 359. note 1; plants communism in Italy, 444; and the sect, **194**.

Q

Qualms, swoons and upheavals. 494, 495.
Quarrels, between Crixus, Ænomaus and Spartacus, 305. 306; involved in the red flag, 473; of the mediæval shoemakers and cobblers. 484. note 45.
Quarries, 368.
Question, of Lælius to Blossius, 241, note 10.
Quinquennial, five years' magistrate, 357.
Quinquennium, city of Rome held 5 years from electing an aristocrat, 474, note 20.
Quinctio L. in battle with Castus, 320, note 119.
Quinctius, defeated by Viriathus, 186; and Tremellius Scrofa defeated by Spartacus, at Petelia, 321.

R

Race, Asiatic, 70; culture, 528; of the Spartans, 535; of the Eagle, or aristocracy, in the prayer of Orestes 563; the Hebrew, 567;
Rag-pickers and patch-piecers unions, 422, note 30; see gypsy.
Rangabé, quoted 507.
Rape of Proserpine, performed as a drama at Elausis, 91, 92, note 18; of Virginia, 287 and note 32.
Raphael's intimacy with Pope Leo, 125; taint of labor, 544.
Ravelli, a place where inscriptions are found, 364.
Reaper, of ancient Gaul, 569, note 109; of Pliny and Palladius, 569.
Reason, guided by social laws, 60; dawn of, 72; the world to adopt, 524; used on two distinct lines, 538.
Rebellion, slaves in prodigious, 86; in the United States, 140; other, 405; see insurrections, strikes, turmoils, xii.; of the children, 525; of the animate tools of labor, 567, 573.
Reciprocating shears, in ancient reaper, 570.
Records, scarcity of, on ancient labor, 71; tracing back to prove their age, 426.
Red, flames, 248, note 3; banner, see chapter 22, pp. 465-92; flag, an account given by Polybius, 467, note 5; the champion of tints, 472; prevalence of, in industry, 477; prohibition law killed out the invention of red dyeing, 479-80; red and white the essences of color, 480; adopted by the Christians, 481; the early flag in the United States, 492.
Redemption, 528.

INDEX. 675

Regent, Lycurgus a, by inheritance, 531.
Registration, of friendly societies, 447.
Rehabilitation, of ancient labor, and the harvest, 519, 572.
Religion, bringing of, into this history, a necessity, x.; was arranged by an Intercessor, 42; the original or first, 43; its omission impossible, 45; it governed political habits, 48; was based upon conscience, 62; the handmaid of, 63; the working people were religious, 64; of the slaves of antiquity, 53; of Jesus, was planted by a laborer, 57; ancient, 60, 68; Pagan, 69; Aryan, 69; a part of an ancient workingman's life, 70; ancient forms exist in modern, 70; belief of slaves, 75; basis of Pagan, 76; slavery the outcome of the Pagan, 83; origin of the Pagan, 85; slaves organized under pretenses of, 86; of Jesus, 88; slaves debarred from the glories of, 95; denying the equality of men, 97; Pagan, 109; belonged to the state, 121; in this history, 143; of Sicilian slaves, 197; used as a cloak. 346; note 36; working people had none, 345; communes numerous in the Piræus. 513, note 46.
Remains, honored, 378, note 14.
Renaissance, a new, 194.
Renan, Wescher. Foucart, 402; asserts the power of the societies, 453; on the ancient discussions, 454.
Rencountre, of the nuptials, 92, note 18.
Render unto Cæsar, 518.
Rent, 382, 383.
Republic, of Plato drawn among the communes of the Piræus, 513; of the blessed, 549.
Rerum Natura, greatest of didactic poems, 60.
Rescue, of Lilybæum, 260.
Res Seænica, 403; 412.
Rescue, the Mohammedan, 555; events of the, 494; of rank, 264, note 43.
Resemblance, of Socrates and Jesus, 553.
Resignation, power of, 562.
Resistance, unions of, 381; 522.
Restoration, of old unions, 303, note 67.
Restrictive laws, compelled unions to appear religious, 508.
Resuscitation, of harsh old law 315, note 108; prevented, 532.
Retaliation, 332; of Spartacus, by forcing the Romans to fight as gladiators, 308, 309; and cut showing the scene, 332; of Eunus, 549.
Retribution, to Aquillius, Lucullus & Servilius, 273-4; terrible, of Spartacus, 308; of Eunus, 550; of Mithridates, 273.
Revenge, of Hermotius, 168-69, note 7; of Spartacus, 332.
Revival, of the old funereal wake, 308, note 85; the present labor movement a. 510, 572.
Revolt, prevented b. superstition 76; always feared by the masters, 79; was common in Chios 170; at Syracuse, of slaves, 251, note 13; of prodigious extent against Spartacus, 319; and vengeance, 331.
Revolution, not involved in any change from competitive to co-operative systems, 38; great social; 57; description of the, 63; begun by Christ, 122; the magnitude of, 384; that destroyed the identity

of paganism, 443; the war, the red flag at the outbreak, 492; events of the, 494.
Revue Archéologique, 453; article quoted from, 505, 506, 567.
Reward, given to slave informants, 149; note 12.
Rhadamanthus, 95, note 24.
Rhea, Ceres, Isis, Cybele, one and the same, 470, 471.
Rhegium in Cisalpine Gaul, 423.
Rhodes, 461; communes at 493; one of the early Christian seats, 513; the inscriptions of, 169, note 10.
Ricardo, Jewish speculator, 43.
Rich men, Cimon, 137, note 16.
Rights, equal. 40; Spartacus, 297, note 54. ,
Robes, Greek, of rank, 264, note 43.
Rock, lined maw of Taygetus, 533.
Rodbertus, 71.
Rogers, Social Life of Scotland, 466, note 1.
Romans, were Aryans, 48; used competitive idea, 48; private property early recognized, 68; downfall of their empire, 84; literary era of the, 123; for social and servile wars see chapters under those heads; conspiracy, 148; treachery of, 181; attempt to enslave all Spain, 188; conquestion of Achia by the, 210; depended on the militia to crush Eunus, 211; armies of organized to quell rebellions, 211; slow to realize t e power of Eunus, 213; armies of. defeated by Eunus and his generals, 218; cities of the, built of wood, 360.
Romanelli's inscription of gladiatorial fight with wild beasts, 411.
Romulus, gives to married men power over female slaves, 147, note 8.
Roscher, 38.
Rose, learned Greek scholar, 343.
Ross' Inscriptions Greques, 462.
Rotatory form of mutual community, 507.
Rudimental colors, 470, note 10.
Runaways etc., cremated, 75; slaves called psomokolaphoi among the Chians, 169, 174; slaves, inscription, 291, note 40; slaves, 094.
Runs, forced to make the runs of gladiators, 407.
Rupillius, . fth man sent against Eunus, 218; malfeasance, 225, note 94; consul attacks Eunus, 228.
Rhythm, of Aristotle, 542.

S

Sabelline judgment, 342, note 21.
Sacerdotal seat or chair, 431.
Sackcloth and ashes, 499.
Sacred, hearth, 69; and civil communes, 113, note 63; associations, 362, note 12; which unions, 445, note 2; unions so defined under the law 445, note 2; questions, 523.
Sacrifice, Pagan mode of, 51; rites of, 92; given by Viriathus, 183, note 7; of Salvius to the Twins, 257 263 n. 8; at Messana, 269; human, 278; avenging of Spartacus, 304, n 77, asked by Lollius, 378, note 14; Archon, 505.
Saddle and bridle-makers, 484-5
Saga and toga, when used, 477, note 25.
Sagum and vexillum, 476, 477.
Sailors, a trade union of, 119, 127.
Sailors' union, sacred to Minerva, 429, note 3.
Saint, Bartholomew massacre

INDEX. 677

of, 102; originated by egoism, 85; Cyril, 452; Flour, 489; Germain-Lembion, industrial suburb of Paris, 489; Simon, the originator of the term "bourgeoisie" 526.
Salarius, 392; origin of the word "salary," 392, note 8.
Sallust, 165; mutilated works of, 211; regretable loss, 299, note 57; describes the battle of Mt. Garganus, 306, note 80.
Salona, estate of Dioletian at, 547.
Salt works, 392.
Saltatrix, saltatricula, 407.
Salvation, doctrine of, taught by Christ, 517; in the plan of Eunus and others 548, sqq.
Salvius, first mention of, 254; elected slave-king, 254, note 20; a flute player, messiah and prophet, 263; his history finished, 263, sq.
Samos, in the labor war, 235.
Sandal, (solea), how made, 420.
Sagum cæruleum, 475.
Sankhaya Kapila, 460.
Sanscrit language, mixed by the gypsies with Latin, 426.
Santorin, isle of, where the societies were very numerous, 452.
Sardinia, vast numbers of slaves from, 193.
Satan, 89; king of the earth, 556.
Satirical writings of Ovid, Propertius, Martialis, were in everybody's hands, 436, note 20.
Satrapy of Rome, 240.
Saturn, his government, spoken of by Plato, 47, note 1; Jupiter's escape from, 89.
Saturnalia, 123; the feats during which all mankind were equal, 338; a great harvest festival, 502.

Satyrs, 248; Ceres adored by, 477.
Satyros, and the mutual fratricide, 273.
Sauromatides, countless women of ancient Crete, 340, note 17.
Sausage-maker, Æschines son of a, 543.
Sayings, doings, prayers, compared, 525; sayings of Socrates, 561.
Scamander, scene of great battle, 270.
Scars, of Aquillius, 273, note 68.
Scaurus, built theatre at Rome, 401, 402,
Scene, of vengeance, 227; adjuster, 403, note 6.
Scenicorum collegium, 402.
Schambach, quotations from, 277 to 330 notes.
Schliemann, 110.
School, of gladiators, 289 and notes 36, 37; of mutual love and care, 365; scholæ præceptores, 407; of idol manufacture, 431 of Ageladas, 435.
Science, evidence accumulated by diggers in, 59; heeds not the tablets and inscriptions, 84; a young female seen by Lucian in a dream, 543.
Scillato, ancient Ancyle, 251.
Scilly Isles, 483.
Scio or Chios, strike in the island of, 163.
Scipio and Hannibal, 153; Africanus, 218; Africanus, Gracchus his grandson, 241.
Scirtheæa, a drawn battle, 267.
Scopas and other great artists, 435.
Scourges, scourged & hung upon the cross, 154, note 27, 475; for lictors, 477.
Scroll, 2,000 years are but a, 525.
Sculptor, (signarius artifex), p. 368; Lucian's dream, 544.
Sculpture, a great era of Gre-

cian, 128; of Spartacus, 284, note 21; the great master of, 101.
Seaport of Athens, see Piræus.
Seats, cushioned seats of the gods, 360.
Second coming, the labor movement, 557.
Secret and secrecy of the unions, 461; recognition, 110, note 50; societies in Homer's time, 111; intense secrecy of the unions, 346; organizations carried red banners, 471; of red dyes lost, how, 479, 480; cult secret in Canaan, 501; communes, and great men who knew of them, 514; commune, and its ancient cult, 554.
Sedition, of soldiers of Spartacus, 306, note 80.
Seething, fluid, 248, note 3.
Self-command, superhuman of Comanus, 227; aid, 410; defense, counter organizations in, 525; defeating, 527.
Selfishness, of prayers, 563.
Semeion, or vexillum, 467.
Semetic family, Hebrew branch, 40; race-struggles with the Aryans, 41; race characteristics, 48; laboring classes organized, 68; enterprise, 124; used in collateral evidence. 526.
Senatus consulti, 340.
Sentinum, inscription of the rag-pickers found at, 423.
Sentius (Cneus), the man who died while yet a youth, 383, note 26.
Septuagint convention, 564.
Sepulcralia, or Roman burial societies, 343.
Sepulchres, sarcophagi and mausoleums. 429.
Sepulture, right of, 70; dread of being deprived of, 75.
Sermon on the Mount, 549.

Servile wars, 54; of Sicily, 77; of Spartacus, what caused by, 284; revolt, considered a national degradation, 294; also 433, 508, and see chapters on the war-strikes of the ancient workingmen.
Servilianus, defeated by Viriathus at Erisane, 187.
Servilius, reduced to disgrace, 274.
Servius Tullius, king of Rome, 146, 156, 161; Sulpicius Galba, a Roman commander, 179; Tullius and Numa, succeeded by a rapacious slaveholding policy, 398.
Setia, a city in Italy, 149; the revolt of slaves at, 150, 151, note 18; traitors, 228.
Seven Apocalyptic churches, 512.
Sexes, relation between, among the ancient slaves, 77; working together naked in the various mines, 138; both likewise in same condition at the games, 530.
Sharpeners, of swords and javelins, 411.
Shepherd, see Athenion, Aristonicus, Cleon and the word, farmer; and farmer, nicknamed bacchanal, 160, note 38; humble and without ambitions, 514.
Shinglers, 377, note 10.
Shoemakers, Cicero's contempt, and nickname of, 380, note 20; quarrels of, 484, note 45; Order of Crispins took the red flag, 483.
Shop-keepers, of Aristotle, 540.
Sicilian Olympus, the, 88; servile war, 513.
Sicily, disastrous strike in, 133, 142; effects of third Punic war, 178; shocking condition of slaves, 194; Eunus made king of, 196; Greek language spoken, 197; the granary of

INDEX.

the world, 258, 304; tramps of, torn open by tramps, 261 and note 37.
Sickle, 569, note 109.
Sidon and Tyre, home of all the Phœnicians, 488.
Siege, of Enna by Piso, 224; second of Enna, 228; of Leucæ, 242; of Lilybæum, 260; by Lucullus of Triocala, 267, note 49.
Signs (private) not inscriptions of the societies, 366, 368.
Silarus, and Macella, great battles, 271; head waters of, 324; battle of 324-5, 327 note 128.
Silver, mines of Attica, 100; the Laurian, 134; cane of Athenion, 259 and note 33; and gold workers, 374; smiths, 383 note 26, and see strike.
Similarity between Socrates and Jesus, 560.
Sin, a terrible, 478, 523, 524.
Sinus Sejestanus, 258.
Siphon, in use before Christ, 571.
Sister of Horatius murdered by him, 475, note 22.
Situations, procured by the unions, 511; see co-operation.
Size of army of Eunus, 218; of Spartacus, 324-5; see army.
Skinned, human beings, 278.
Slabs, the ancient, lying unobserved, in their original places or in museums, xi; are being constantly unearthed, 110; the law record d on, 71.
Slave, relics of the ancient, 67; equals of their masters, 68; system among Aryans, 68; African, 68; a rich man's children became, 69; runaway, 70, 175 to 177; not mentioned by the very ancient writers, 71; the contempt of masters for, 72; poor outlook in ancient times for the, 74; slaveholders used to kill their children, 74; the fear of, 75; superstition at first prevented his revolt, 76; he multiplied within his own estate, 77; branded and marked on face and elsewhere, 79, 196, note 17, 385, note 30; poorly fed, 46, note 16, 79, 385, note 30; emancipation of, 80; system, 81; differentiation in his favor, 83; self-enfranchised, 85; denied the right of burial, 85; but his body burned, 86; or hung up to rot, 299; murdered by his masters, 86; was admitted into the brotherhood, 98, note 27, 169, 355; social condition in Greece, 99; of war, 103; trade, 103, 266, note 27; prices paid for his hire, 137; of Athens deserts, 140; one man sometimes owned a great many, 135, see numbers; his attempt to burn Rome, 146; assisted by king Servius Tullius, 147; insurrection of Scio, 163, see Drimakos; fear of his rebellions, 141, 164; citizens of Enna massacred by, 202; system, Eunus attempts to destroy the, 207; vengeance of the, at Enna, 209; often became brigands, 215; many a Roman general in Sicily was defeated by the, 218; slaves of Eunus were socialists, 223; Piso defeated and driven by a, 225; in the majority, 249; set free by Spartacus, 302; numbers that were crucified, 330; system, inroads upon by the trade unions, 442; had a religion, 472; his condition in Phœnicia, 498; crammed populations of Plato, 548-9; dens of Sicily, 549.

Slavery, partly abolished among the Hebrews, 39; origin of, 49; a second condition in the establishment of society, 54; earlier than communism, 68; resistance of slaves to, 68; at present, that of chattels is extinct, 68; unwritten age of, 71; society outgrowing, 71; long night of, 78; phenomena of, 93; degradation of Spartan, 102; the curse of, 111; Plato believed it just, 119; hideous conditions, 156; superstitions against, 168, 169; Viriathus' fight against, 188; immense growth of, just before Christ's time, 192; in Asia Minor, 233; reviewed, 286, note 27, 141, note 37, 146, 164, note 2; the antithesis of trade unionism, 366; Romans grasped Plato's fashionable idea of, and calamities which resulted, 549.

Saveholders, wealth and numbers, 314-5; see numbers.

Sleight of hand, 254, note 20.

Slings, 378, 379, 380.

Slipper, half-slipper, 419.

Smart, in sallies and satire, 535.

Smokers of wine, 382.

Smyrna, burial place of Crassus, 242.

Snakes, superstition of Gracchus, 240.

Social wars, nearly all turn out disastrously for cause, xii.; ages of past, marked by a want of feeling, 65; organizations, ancient, 69; habits of poor, 77; wars, 84, 97; life of working people, 88; condition of slaves in Greece, 99; wars, 99, 110; organizations that helped Spartacus, to almost achieve a remarkable conquest, 301.

Socialism, 38; not easily seen through competitive system, 43; the perfect, 101; employment by the state, 380, note 19; 381, n. 21; none beyond the family, 496; of Jesus, 497; in the festivities, state paid the bills, 505; the radical of Lycurgus, 527.

Socialistic system, 59; organizations, 97; a state, 121; Germany stifled the efforts of, 71; enjoying their booty in common, 223.

Society, present condition of, toned by Mosaic law, 45; its deeds of, transmitted by history and archæology, 48; first form of, 48; conditions in the establishment of, 54; ancient, 113; middle condition of, 55; developed by ethics, 63; history of ancient, 67; outcasts of, 69; will outgrow slavery, 71; began with the bully, 84; two ancient classes of, 96; two great classes of Lacedæmonian, 101.

Sociology, students of, 71, 80, 97; students of, are forced to drop Plato, 445; consistency with the study of, 501.

Socrates, recognized the labor unions, 74; Plato, Aristotle, Anaxagoras and Diogenes, worshiped immortal gods, 430, 486, at the Piræus, 513; one of 5 remarkable characters, 514; on the God of love, 553, note 76; Crito & Phædo, 562; a member of the brotherhood, 553.

Sodales, what they were, 127, n. 87; of Italy, 77, 364; fullonum, 415; corresponded to the thiasotes, 508; unions of the, suppressed, 344, note, 29.

Soissons, Crispins settled at, 421; seat of the Crispins, 483.

INDEX. 681

Soldier of high stock, 381.
Solemnities of labor unions, 378, note 14.
Solidarities, rural, 464.
Solitudo Magistratuum, 474, and note 20.
Solomon, trade unions as early as, 115; King of the Jews, 123; the temple, 373.
Solon, laws of, 100, 113; regulations of, 119, 123; trade unions under laws of, 126; Solon and Numa's law the same, 337, n. 13; law of Solon and of the Twelve Tables identical, 347; Solon of Athens, followed Numa's trade union scheme, 359; his homotaphoi or common tables, 510.
Solution, the natural of the problems, 573.
Sons born to the gods, 49, note 4.
Soothsayers, Etruscan, 154, note 27.
Sophists, 39, 132.
Sophocles and Euripides, 401.
Sorties, of Cleon, 225.
Sosias, a Thracian contractor, 137.
Soter, or Messiah, 462.
Sottishness, false opinion, 503.
Soul, see immortality; consult chapter iv., Eleusinian Mysteries; apothegm of Lucretius, 60; a philosophy which denies the immortality of the, 62; origin of and belief in, 47-66; fed the disengaged, 75 and note 22; of states, 303, note 73; who plod without, 466; slave-souls of Plato, 539; of Aristotle's theory, 540.
Soup spoons, spits, ladles, bowls, cups, 399.
Southern states, slavery of, 77.
Spain, slavery drove free labor from, 156; see wars of Viriathus in, pp. 178-90.

Sparta, massacres of, 97; its war with Messenia, 98, 103; brutal spirit and unfeelingness, 132; jealous of Athens, 141; slaves dangerous, 211.
Spartacus, great general; is compared with Hannibal and Napoleon, viii.; punishment for rebellion, xii.; allusions to, 62, 120, 148, 149; uprising of, 140, note 3; well received in Apulia and Metapontem, 158-9; his fortune-telling wife, 168; was a poor man, 181; the prodigious conflict, 187; in winter quarters he disallowed gold and silver, 202; was called a robber, 215; a Thracian, but family unknown, 282, note 13; in all respects a workingman, 282; legends of, 284; a man of giant frame, further description of, 285, 288, 290; a serpent coils about his head, 290, note 37; escape of, 292; elected commander-in-chief, 294; line of march and tactics, 300; humane qualities and character, 302-3, 305, 311; required to march through Campania to Rome, 321; after the death of Crixus, he marches to the Po, 507; and his army hemmed in, 323; his death, 324-332; 70 years after him, Christ came, 493; one of the 5 remarkable men, 514; his mightiness, 551.
Spartans, under Lycurgus, 69; a favored class, 101; compared to the Athenians, 139; an unsympathetic people, 103; believed slavery was right, 119, division of land, 530; senators, 531.
Species, preservation of, 42.
Spectacles, gladiatorial, 277, and note 1.

682   INDEX.

Speculators in human flesh, 412.
Speech, of Drimakos, 169, note, 172; of Christ, 557.
Spencer, 59.
Spice unions, 393; gums, nuts, seeds and other raw materials of the perfumers, 434.
Spinners', weavers', dyers' and tailors' overseers had charge of the state work shops, 419.
Spirit-worship, command against in Mosaic law, 54.
Split-corn grits for slaves, 383, note 26.
Spoleto, inscription of fullers' union found at, 416.
Spooks and goblins, 248, note 3; see asylum, also goblin.
Sportula, figures in the laws governing sacred unions, 399.
Spouting monstrous sparks, 248, note 3.
Spurius Rutilus, a Roman tribune, 145.
Squares, of the Roman army, 320, note 119.
Standard, white at Rome, 481.
Star-gazer, Athenion, 259, 260, note 35.
Starvation of human chattels, 405; of Morgantion, 227; of Cleon, 260; wages, 526.
State, ancient social, 123; slaves owned by the, 383, note 26; factories, 416, note 5; control of works, 417-19; without distinction is without slaves, 522; paid the festive bills, at Anthesteria, 505; the celebrated, 538;- ownership, 567.
Statesman, a work by Plato, 118; of Aristotle, 540.
Statistics, of gladiators, 279, note 5; of slaves' living, inscribed on the Egyptian pyramid, 446, note 4; of crucifixions, 330, 517.
Statue, of Augustus, 80; of the Greek Athena, 101,, 125.

Statute, the most renowned of antiquity, 474.
Stealing, authorized by Lycurgus, 69, note 8; even taught the children, 532.
Stichus, on the faces of slaves, 79; their brands, 385, n. 30.
Still small voice, 523.
Stoa, of Zeno, 546.
Stock-farms, the German, 344, note 30; breeding, 528.
Stoicism, 464.
Stolo (Licinius), law of, 222, note 84; see Gracchus.
Stonehenge, massacre of, 102.
Stone masons, of Athens, 127; cutters, 369, 369, remains, 450.
Strabo, 112, 205.
Strangers, admitted to the membership, 509.
Stratonice, crowning of, 463, and plate; honored jubilee, 463, 504.
Strikes, ancient, unknown to the living age, viii.; turned out to be disastrous in most cases, xii.; evidence regarding them, 67. 3; the ancient and modern, 133; in Greece, Rome and Sicily, 133; of the 20,000, at Declea, 134, note 1, 140, 473; one that decided the Peloponnesian war, 138; the servile wars, 140, note 32. 155; one at Sunion, 142, 144, of slaves in Macedonian mines, 144, note 42; of slaves at Rome, 146; of Setia, 149, note 12; in Etruria, 155, 157; in Apulia, 159; at Enna in Sicily, 195; causes of rupture of Eunus, 198, see Eunus; in Asia Minor outlined, 237; a match for, 270; strife-war, hero of the, 513; see Eunus, Spartacus and Drimakos.
Strongoli or Næthus, 326.
Struggle, going on, 43; humanity's ancient, 68; an early,

INDEX.

between rich and poor, 99; did our era rise from labor struggles? 523, sq.
Styx, flowing between Hades and Elysium, 90.
Suffrage, woman, 391, and notes.
Suicide, of Comanus, 227; of Blossius, 241 and note 19; the mutual, of Satyros and braves, 273; forbidden by a rule and penalty of burial society, 355.
Sun-god, Syrian, 236; worship, in Asia Minor, 236 and note 9, 373, note 4; worship of Nemesis, 413, note 36, 450, 471; god Apollo, 463, 491; brilliant and flaming color of, 469, 69; worship, the common, or popular faith, in England, 482; heliopolitai or farmer-warriors of Aristonicus, 550.
Sundays, none for workers, 135.
Sundikoi, lawyers, 453.
Sunion, castle of, 100, 143; the miners' strike at, 142, note 38; an Athenian mining city, 145; bloody mutiny of slaves, 143.
Superintendent, of public works, inscription showing political action of unions, 383, n. 26.
Superstition, of Egyptians, 45; of slaves checked their revolt, 76; was the masters' bulwark of protection, 81; among the Greeks, 107, note 49; of the Chians about Drimakos, 177; in favor of Eunus, 216; and of Gracchus, 240.
Supplicium, the noble, 499.
Suppression of the unions, 301, note 65; of religious unions, 347, note 40; of all unions, 362, note 11; union of cranists, by council of Laodicia, 511.
Survival, man fighting for, 61;

of Tryphon and Athenion, 266.
Sussitoi, common table communes, 510.
Sutlers, union of, 397.
Sutores, or shoemakers, 421.
Sweeping extermination, 219.
Switzerland, fossils of, 72.
Swoon that fell over mankind, 494, 495.
Sword-makers, 377, not 10.
Symbiosis philia, name of Greek commune, 502.
Symbols of the ancient farm, 66; of human labor, 482; heraldic, 483.
Symethus, river, 212, 255.
Sympathy, see irascibility, concupiscence; growth of, 206; there arose an occasional character, 500; irascibility, concupiscence, 515; how formed, 560.
Symposiums, see cuts and illustrations representing various ancient; customs and manners at a, 111, note 55; prayers and pæans of, 363, 461.
Syncope, that fell upon mankind, 494.
Synod, or sometimes called the synagogue, 461.
Synodoi, Greek, the synods, 501.
Syracuse, unions at, 113; Plato's experience at, 118; and the great strike, 146, 213; proof that it was taken by Eunus, 221; slaves straggling from, 248; theatre at, 401.
Syria, great numbers brought from, as slaves, to Rome, 195; slaves organized in, 197; Greek Spoken in, 197; Ceres worshiped in, 198; Greek speaking unions of, 502.
System, slave, 87; of common proprietorship, 69; patriarchship, 73.

T

Tabernacle, 40.
Table, the common, 115, note 67, see Roscher; meals in common suppressed by Pyrrhus, 287, note 28; mate of Philip the king, 545; see communism or triclinium; the Twelve, see the Twelve Tables.
Tablets, unheeded by science, 84, 367; see inscription.
Tactics of Eunus, extermination, 219; of Athenion, 259, 260 and 274, note 70; against enclosure in sieges, 269, 274, note 70; military, of Rome adopted by Spartacus, 290, note 37; of Crassus to teaze, 313.
Taint, upon labor, 72, 78, 466, 533 and 537; some strong men dared be brave, 546.
Talismans, emblems, mementos and charms, 435, 556.
Tamia, a stewardess or housewife, 453.
Tarentine gulf, 158, 211; city, the slaves captured at, 192, and 300.
Tarpeian rock, 154, note 27.
Tarquin, king of Rome, 147.
Tartarus, 93, 123.
Tartessus, Romans fortify themselves at, 185.
Tassels, of banners, 484, 486.
Tasters, union of, 398.
Tauromanion, number of workingmen massacred at, xii.; taken by Eunus, but recaptured 226.
Tax gatherers, unions of, 119, 349, 382; slabs showing great numbers of such, 440, 441, & 442; gatherers, chap. xx., pp. 437, 443; of forgers and miners, 442, note 10.
Taygetus, dashed to jelly on the rocks of, 533.

Teamsters (vectuarii, and the collectors, 440.
Technitai, of Aristotle, 541.
Tectoriolæ, little plaster images, 432.
Temple, of Demeter, 81; Apollo, 81; of Megaron, 91, 95; built by the outcasts, 108; of Jerusalem, how built, 123; of Solomon and Hiram, 124; Eleusis 125; of Minerva, 137; of the horoön, dedicated by the Chians to the *manes* o. Drimakos, 176-177, note 19; of Ceres at Enna, 198; of Thalia, 248 and note 3; great, erected through government employ, 380, note 19; of Jupiter, 463.
Tenets, business of sacred communes, 113, note 63; of Syrian theogony, 236-7; of the thiasos, 503, note 18.
Tents, of Roman military system, 467, note 5.
Tertullian, in defense of the early Christians, 527.
Testament, of Attalus, 233.
Textores, and textrices, 422.
Thalia, nymph, 247; the temple to her Twins, 248 note 3.
Thames river, 487.
Thætetus, of Plato, 118.
Theatres, their size, 401; see circus, amphitheatre.
Theophanes, 165.
Theophilus, 452.
Theophrastus, knew of the communities, 507.
Theseus, battle with the Amazons, 87, note 12, 130; unions as early as, '15.
Theta, Greek letter, meaning on the inscription, "death," 279.
Thiasos, of the Greeks, 114; the prophets of the, 203; translation from stone tablets, 454; defined, 449, 493, and shown in plate facing page 451; also 463, 493; "non bacchicus-

INDEX.   685

est," 504, note 22; became mellow soil, 511.
Theirs, 489.
Thrace, mines in, 137; Spartacus' home, 285, note 22; wife of Spartacus also from, 290.
Thucydides, 105, 139, 536; wrote while in exile, 107; he owned mines in Macedonia, 137.
Thuria seized by Spartacus, 300, note 59; where he established a large armory, 375.
Thyratira, taken by Aristonicus, 237.
Tiber river, 112, '55; valley, unions of, 133, note 62, 389, note 1.
Tibicenes, Roman and Auletrids, Greek flute-players, 409.
Tigers, panthers, bears, etc., 411.
Tin islands, or Cassiterides, 483.
Titinus Gaddæus' treachery, 252.
Toga, peace garment, 476; peace garment, red, 477; and saga, when used, 477, note 25; chiton, chlamys, himation, 481.
Tombstones, of gladiators, 279, note 5.
Tompkins, Mr. Henry, 447, 449, 454, 462.
Tools, for sacrifice, 98, note 57; of labor, a difference between ancient and modern, 567; men and women, the ancient, 568, 570; as tools men were nationalized, 570; and they rebelled and killed their masters, 573.
Torcellum, slab of, inscribed by the ragpickers union, 424.
Toy-gods, manufacture of, 429.
Trades, organized in ancient days, vii.; multitude of ancient secret, 69; unions, formed by freed slaves, 85; existed early, 86; are courts of appeal, 94, 96, 100, 113; organizations of freedmen, 112; as early as Solomon and Theseus, 115; unions in Sicily, 119; unions, a state institution, 121; during the Golden Age, 122; at the Piræus, 125; organization, upheld by king Servius, 147; unions, crowded out, in Rome, 192; unions, search for, 334, note 1; union genuine of shoemakers, 421; unions under aid and guaranty of government, 437; unions the most powerful ancient proletarian societies, 348; unions recognized and employed by the state, 440; unions of Greece, 461; unions the same as the eranoi, 507; Lucian's choice of a, 543; of Jesus, 521.
Traders, of Canaan, 501, 502.
Training school of gladiators, 292, note 41; 325, note 124.
Traitor, perfidy and treachery of the workingmen to each other, 151, note 18, pp. 187, 228, 272, 304.
Tramps, and freedmen, 213; between masters and slaves were ground to powder, 261, note 37.
Transition, period, 71.
Translation, of Solon's law for the Twelve Tables, 127, notes 87, 88.
Trans-substantiation, 89.
Traps and tricks of Spartacus, 325, note 124.
Treachery, of workmen against themselves, 227; of Nerva, 251, note 13; and 257, note 28; of Tryphon, 264; of Aquilius, 273; against Spartacus, 304.
Tribal community, ancient, 68, note 5.

INDEX.

Tribunal, slaves withdrawn by Adrian from the domestic tribunal, 365.
Tribunes, elected by the plebeians, 474, and note 20; Clodius, 363, note 15.
Triclinarchs or stewards, 399, 400.
Triclinium, abolished by Christians as an abomination, 400.
Trident, of Neptune, 130, note 96.
Trinkets, of the throne, 413; the holy, as enormously manufauctured, 431.
Trœzen, tutelary soter or savior from, 509.
Trojans, 114.
Trumpeter, 408.
Tryphon, assumed name of Salvius, 263; sends for Athenion, 264; his fear, 265; death of, 269, note 56.
Tubicen, 408.
Tullus Hostilius, 154 and note 27.
Tumbler, every girl was a professional, 535.
Turkey and its red, 490.
Turning-lathe, use of, taught the Britons, by the Romans, 485.
Tutelary, divinity of the fortune tellers, 413, note 36; saints, 420; which controlled labor, 481, 487; banner of Pierrefort, 490; soters, 509.
Twelve Tables, law of, 100, 283, 285; Dirksen, on hetæræ and sodales, 115; Gaius on right to combine, 127, notes 87, 88; they permitted labor organization, 303; celebrated ancient code, 337; engraved on eleven slabs, 339; same laws as the Greek, 347, note 38.
Twins, pool of the, 248, note 3; of Jupiter and Thalia, 247, 263.
Tyrannus, Men, 143, note 39.

Tyrant, of Sicily, king of slaves, 404; the ephori, 531, 532, see ephori; Agathocles, a potter, 545.
Tyre, Phœnician city, 123.
Tyrian red, 479.

U

Ulpian, on natural rights, 552, note 69.
Unions, of mercenaries, 77, 78; of slaves, 98, see slave; of laborers (Greek), 99; of clerks, 114; of workingmen for resistance, 117; turned into banditti, 120; discussion in secret, 126; dangerous competitors of slavery, 366; of farmers rare, 443; synonyms, for different countries, 502; see organization.
United States, growth of labor movements in the, 126; the great civil war, 140, note 31; bureau of labor, 146; note 3; appropriately adopted the stars and stripes, 470.
Unwashed, the Spartan youth, 534.
Uprisings, the ancient, almost unknown to the living age, vii.; vague evidence of their antiquity, 67, note 2; ancient strugles and strikes, 78; in Attica, 141; contagious, 146, and note 3; of Eunus, immediate cause, 201; at Pergamus, 232-245; see slave, wars of the.
Urinatores (divers), 112, 389, note 1, 435.
Utica, near Carthage, furnished elephants against Viriathus, 186 and plate.
Utopia, 47, note 1, 55.
Utricularis (bagpipe), 408.

V

Vacancy, 474 and note 20.

Vale of tears, 352.
Varinius, defeat of, 297, note 54; great battle, 299; and of Picenum, 300, note 60.
Varro (Charis) quoted, 291 and note 37.
Vascula, spits, ladles, cups, soup-spoons, and bowls, 399.
Vascularii (metal vessel makers), were skilled workmen, 399, and 446.
Vatican, the ancient works lost in, 201, 207; fragments, 300, note 60; where is a baxea or ancient shoe, 420.
Vaulted dome, 466; firmament, 538.
Vectigalia, means, revenues, 119 and note 74; system of the, 156, 409; see tax collection.
V leda, 303, note 73.
Vellejus Paterculus, his account of the wars of Viriathus and Spartacus, 187; Paterculus on numbers of army of gladiators, 325, note 123.
Vengeance, of Hermotius, 168-9, note 7; of Rupillius, 227; intimidation and, of Plato, 244, note 22; irascibility and, once more vindicated, 269; wreaking infuriates, 407; 549, note 67; of Jehovah, 566.
Venison, fish and mutton the aristocratic food, 386.
Ventidius Bassus, consul, 79.
Venus, battle of the hill of, 183.
Venusia in Lucania, inscription of perfumers found at, 434.
Verna or home-born, 391.
Verona, inscription of wine commune, 382.
Verres, a prætor or governor of Sicily, 119, note 74, 195, 284; had no respect for humanity, 179-80.
Vesuvius, the then peak of, 293; height of, before the eruption, 293.
Vessel-makers (Vascularii), 445.
Vetilus, overthrown and killed by Viriathus, 182, note 6, 184.
Vexillum or semeion, 467; was a her flag, 467, note 5, 476-7.
Via, the Appian, or Appian Way, 293; Way, scene of the crucifixion of six thousand working people, 329; Aquillia, join the Appian Way, was taken by Spartacus, 293; Sacra, P. Nicanor the perfumer, on the, 434.
Vic, Vic-le Comte, its half-red banner, 489.
Victualing system, 389, 400.
Vigano, Prof. Francesco, 447.
Vineyard of the Lord, 522.
Vini Susceptores, 393.
Virgin Mary shown on red flag, 486.
Virginia, rape of, 287, note 32.
Viriathus, chapter viii.; story of, commenced, 179; personal appearance of, 180, and notes 2, 3, 4; was a poor man, 180; collects his band, 181; speech of, 182; governor of Spain, 182; successful retreat to Tribola, 183; defeats a Roman auxiliary force and Vetilius killed, 184; made king, 185; destroys the forces of Quinctius and Æmilius, 186; and defeats Plautius, 186; defeats Servilianus at at Eresane, 187; makes a treaty of peace with Rome, 187; held Rome in check, 188; murdered by his own men, 187; great gladiatorial wake, 188-9; red banner planted in the land of, 491; influence of; 517.
Vitellius, emperor of Rome, 79.

Vlastos, recent discovery by, 91.
Vogt, Professor, mentioned, 59, 447.
Voice, plaintive, still small 523.
Volsinii, siege of, where 2,000 statues and images were taken, 431.
Voodooism, 559.

W

Wages, early aversion to, 39; slavery, 71; in time of Pericles, 124, 137; slavery fast going, 516, note 50; earners, as Aristotle's 4th class, 540.
Wagon-makers, 377, note 10.
Waiters were also tasters, 399; and cooks of Sparta, 533.
Wakes, antiquity of, 135; origin of, 277; gladiatorial in honor of Crixius' ghost, 308, note 85.
Wallace, numbers of mankind, 283, note 17; on the ancient census, 340, note 17.
Wanderers, what Gracchus said, 500.
Want, tie that married irascibility with sympathy, 515.
Wars, slaves used as mercenaries in, 77, and note 29; the Holy, 81; causes of the social or servile, 77, 84, 99; between Messenia and Sparta, 103; Peloponnesian, 105; discouraged by Numa, 123; strike during the Peloponnesian, 134, 138, 142; third Punic, 178; of Eunus—evidence of the stones, 224, note 89; brutal purposes of, 475; forbidden in the plan of Jesus, 553; farmers best fitted for, 541, 542.
Warning, 573.
Warwick and Spartacus compared, 327.
Watermen, 383.

Wealth, of Crassus, 340, note 17; of Cælius Claudius, 340, note 17; number of slaves owned by different persons, 350; of Damophilus, 196, sqq.; of Demosthenes, 548; see slave.
Weavers and drapers, 416, note 8; carders, etc., and their red flag, 486.
Wescher, archæologist, 506; his theory now maintained, 506.
Whips, and sacrificial axe, of Salvius, 264, and note 43; horsewhip of P. Crassus, 242, note 20; original derivations, 471.
Whipped every night, 472, note 15; and strangled, 567; men and women, for the "blessed" of a chosen people, 568.
White, in heathen mythology, emblematic of degree, 466; essence of non-color, 480; and red were essences of color, 480; see chapter on red flag.
Wickliffe, 559.
Wiener Jahrbücher, article on union of piscicapii, 389.
Wife, the favorite, often buried alive with head of tne house, 82, note 40; of Spartacus, 558.
Wild, Mr. G. L., piano merchant of Washington, possessor of a curious book on Jesus and the Essenes, 565, note 107; slave insurrection in Chios, 164, note 3; beasts, men thrown into dens of, 280; beasts in the amphitheatres, 394, 395; beasts, lions, tigers, leopards, etc., for the combats, 411; boar, story of L. Domitius and the slave who killed a, 136. 475.
Will, of Kraton, 98, note 27; of Attalus III. 232, 333, see testament.

Wine-curers, unions of, 382, note 23; smokers' unions, 383, note 24, 384; vaulters, 447; drinking, false notions regarding, 502; presses, feasts, 505.
Winter quarters of Spartacus, 300, 375.
Witchcraft, among Egyptians, 45; and fortune telling, 414.
Women, paired as gladiators, 277, note 1; constancy of, 303, note 73; in politics at Pompeii, 390-91, and notes 3, 4, 5; were prominent officers in the unions, 434; took their stand in the unions with dignity, 450; as members, 461; in the thiasos, 463.
Wonder world, primitive man in the, 85; of the ancient world, 248, note 4; and awe caused adoration of the sun, 469.
Woodworkers under two names, 360; workers under Augusta, 362, note 10.
Work, procured by the unions, 511.
Workhouse, 274, note 70; prisons, iron of, for armor, 297, note 53.
Workingmen, number massacred at Enna and Tauromanian, xii.; number crucified by Crassus, and Pompey, xii.; not originally citizens, 49; condition, lowliness of, in ancient times, 49; of America and Europe combine against brute force, 57; as a slave, 78; figures little in history, 86; societies of, 87; political institutions, no court of appeals, 94; assassinated, 98; had the right to organize, 100; excluded by Lycurgus, 101; condition of, in Sparta, 103; fought for Sparta, 106; murder of 2,000, 107, note 46; worked directly for the government, 114; littleness of the ancient, 117; Plato against the, 118; driven from the crusade, 131; hated Plato, 132; protected by gods, 142, note 34; terrible condition of, in Rome, 179; cruel treatment of, causing great wars, 192; had no souls, 193; as a class, how formed, 528; Jesus in all respects one, 153, 514, 551, 552, and 560.
Works and Days, a book by Hesiod, on labor question, 161.
Workshops in the emperor's palaces, 419.
Worship, in laws of Lycurgus, 69; right of, 70; by sacrifice, 75; of gods, 81; of the Lord by his children; character of, at Eleusis, 88; important right of, 115.
Wreaths and ribbons, 463.
Wyoming, massacre at, 102.

X

Xanthos, a slave, builds a temple, 143, note 39.
Xenocles, a master mason, 131.
Xenophon, 92, 135, note 9; and the "imperishable laws," 526; quotes Socrates, 553, note 76; on prayer, 563.
Xipe, gladiatorial feasts of, 278.

Z

Zama, battle, of, 152.
Zend, 526.
Zenoa, in love with the girl trade unionist, 464; Aristotle borrowed from, 518; the stoic, 546.
Zeus, man-god, 48, note 2; great statue of the Olympian, 101.
Zeuxes, and Hermias, slayers of Damophilus, 204.